W9-BNP-169

DUKE ELLINGTON

and his world

A BIOGRAPHY

DUKE ELLINGTON
and his world

A. H. LAWRENCE

ROUTLEDGE
NEW YORK · LONDON

Published in 2001 by

Routledge
29 West 35th Street
New York, NY 10001

Published in Great Britain by
Routledge
11 New Fetter Lane
London EC4 4EE

Routledge is an imprint of the Taylor and Francis Group.

10   9   8   7   6   5   4   3   2   1

Library of Congress Cataloging-in-Publication Data

Lawrence, A. H.
    Duke Ellington and his world: a biography / A.H. Lawrence.
      p. cm.
    Includes list of compositions (p.), bibliographical references (p.) and index.
    ISBN 0-415-93012-X (alk. paper)
      1. Ellington, Duke, 1899-1974. 2. Jazz musicians—United States—Biography. I. Title.

ML410.E44 L39 2001
781.65'092—dc21
[B]   00-051711

To Natalie

Contents

Acknowledgments ix

Introduction xi

Prelude xv

Chapters One through Forty-five 1

Epilogue 403

Chronology 405

Biographies 423

Band Members 437

Compositions by Duke Ellington 451

Bibliography 465

Source Notes 467

Index 477

Acknowledgments

This book never would have been written had Luis Russell not hired a seventeen-year-old high school graduate who was bound and determined to earn a living playing in a dance band. A decade later when our paths crossed again, he encouraged me to do the study of Harlem musicians that ultimately turned into this book. It was Russell who made the critical telephone call to Sonny Greer that gained me entree to members of the Ellington band and the Harlem musicians whom I subsequently interviewed.

I owe a debt to the Ellington musicians, friends, and family members all of whom were most generous with their time: MacHenry Boatwright, Ruth Ellington Boatwright, Lawrence Brown, Harry Carney, Benny Carter, Willie Cook, Mercer Ellington, Frank Galbreath, Fred Guy, Lionel Hampton, Coleman Hawkins, Charlie Holmes, Manzie Johnson, Walter Johnson, Sy Oliver, Wilbur DeParis, Russell Procope, Billy Strayhorn, Fredi Washington, Bernice Wiggins, Cootie Williams, and Joe Williams.

This book is also, in part, a product of my professional training and education at the Massachusetts Mental Health Center, Department of Psychiatry, Harvard Medical School, from September 1967 to January 1974. I acknowledge my great debt to Dr. Lester Grinspoon, who supported and encouraged my application for a staff position at that institution; to the late Dr. Julius Silberger, who along with his colleague Dr. Jose Barchilon, introduced me to the concept of a psychobiography; and Dr. John Mack, who gave me a model of how to write one.

I must thank my close friends and professional colleagues, Dr. Clifford Briggin, Dr. Sara Cooke, Ms. Joanna Donovan, Dr. Stuart Feder, Dr. Kendra Schecter, and Dr. Richard Sens who read this manuscript in whole or in part and offered valuable comments and feedback. Also, many thanks to Jim Smith and the staff of the Cambridge Center for Adult Education who graciously provided a space to finish this book; to my son Daniel W. Lawrence, whose laser printer churned out the many revisions of this manuscript; to the gang at Giannono's, especially John Nesbitt, for whose support at a critical point during the production of this book, I shall forever be grateful. Thanks to my agent, Dick McDonough, who stuck with this project for close to fifteen years. And last but not least, to my editor Richard Carlin, who took a mountain of data and organized it into a book that I am proud to have my name on.

Introduction

"WHERE YOU GOING?"

I was standing at the corner of Seventh Avenue and 50th Street in New York City when I heard a familiar voice call out. *Where you going?* It was a question I had been asking myself all day. I turned and found myself face to face with my new boss, the Harlem band leader Luis Russell, and the current woman in his life. It was August 1944, and earlier that day I had become a member of his orchestra.

I told him I was meeting some old high school pals who were waiting to hear the results of that morning's audition. Taking me firmly by the arm, Russell said, "They can wait. Come on with me and Evelyn. We're going over to the Roxy. I'll introduce you to Duke Ellington."

I tried hard to stifle my anxiety about meeting the man who had been my musical hero since 1940. That was when I first heard his 1926 recording of the "Black & Tan Fantasy," complete with the tuba underpinning of "Bass" Edwards. From that day on, I was a fervid Ellingtonian. "Black & Tan Fantasy" is still one of my favorite recordings.

As we walked, I thought about the events that were bringing me to meet Duke Ellington. Two months earlier, I had graduated from a suburban high school and moved to the city, firmly expecting to find work as a musician in a dance band. Soon after arriving, I called Russell and told him I was looking for a job. It was the hubris of adolescence and the fact that I had gone to school with his son that impelled me to approach him.

Russell mentioned that he was thinking about adding a third trombone to his band, but he was leaving town the next day for engagements in Chicago, Philadelphia, Baltimore, and Washington. He told me to look him up when he got back. I later learned that in Chicago, his son had put in a good word for me. And when Russell returned to New York, I was invited to audition for a chair in his band.

And here I was, backstage at the theater where Duke Ellington was playing. I saw faces that I had known only from newspapers, magazines, and films. The elegant, light-skinned man sitting with a white towel on his left leg and oiling the slide on his trombone was Lawrence Brown.

Short, portly Joe "Tricky Sam" Nanton was talking vigorously about the allied invasion of France to bald-headed saxophonist Otto Hardwick. Fellow saxophonist Johnny Hodges sauntered by, saw Russell, and asked about his close friend and fellow Bostonian, Charlie Holmes, who held down a saxophone chair in Russell's band. "Sonny" Greer, pipe-stem thin, his trousers sporting a knife-edge crease, was holding a deck of cards. Greer suggested that Russell join in a game of cards so that Greer could win back the money he had lost to Russell in Chicago.

As I stood there absorbing the scene, I heard a voice behind us exclaim, "Ah, Luis—and the beautiful Evelyn, how *nice* of you to come by." I turned around and there stood Ellington, clad in a white silk shirt, gold cuff links, fawn-colored slacks, and brown suede shoes. Because of the heat, he was tieless.

There was a bandage on his right hand. On opening day he'd been in the backstage elevator when it dropped a short distance into the cellar. The globe on the light burst and one of the shards sliced his hand. Ellington's aide-de-camp, composer Billy Strayhorn, played the piano for him during the three-week engagement. It was Russell who introduced me to the great musician, telling Duke he had just hired me and that I was only seventeen years old. Ellington's only response was to smile at me, squeeze my shoulder, and say, "I hired Harry Carney when he was your age."

Thirty-five years later, when I first put pen to paper to begin this book, I realized that this was my first introduction to a narcissistic character, a man who could not allow himself to be one-upped. As his son Mercer told me, "My father always had to be on top."

My next significant conversation with Ellington was two years later. I was working with Milton Larkin's band at Don Robey's nightclub in Houston, Texas. Ellington was in town to give a concert at the Municipal Auditorium, and on the way to work, several band members and I went backstage to say hello. Ellington waved us into his dressing room and greeted the musicians he knew.

Spying me, he asked what was under my arm. "A French horn," I said. I had bought it in Vancouver.

"Play something," he said, handling the instrument, "I'd like to hear how it sounds." I was about to do so when the business manager came in and told Ellington it was time to go onstage. Patting me on the shoulder, Ellington said, "If I have time after the show, I'll come out to the club; maybe you can play something for me then."

He didn't get to the club that night. In fact, our paths would not cross for the next four years. When they did, I was in college and had come back to New York for Christmas vacation. The Ellington orchestra was booked for a dance at the Rockland Palace Ballroom. During intermission, my date and I went backstage to see him.

The room was packed with musicians, friends, and family, but Ellington was nowhere to be seen. Suddenly, the door behind us opened and Ellington and his manager entered the room. Seizing the advantage, I extended my hand and said, "Happy New Year, Duke. I don't know if you remember me."

Cutting me off, he replied, "Of course I do. You're 'Junior,' the French horn player." As I was about to introduce my date, he took her hand and said, "I always gravitate to the most beautiful woman in the room."

She blushed and stammered something in reply. By now we were in the center of a crowd. I told him I wanted to wish him a happy New Year, and we began to move away. He grabbed my arm and said, "You never did play that French horn for me, you know." Before I could reply, he had turned away and was embracing a very attractive woman in a sable coat.

I never did get to play for him. I had given up the instrument professionally and gone to college with the idea of pursuing a more stable and intellectually stimulating career. But whenever I saw Ellington, in Boston or anywhere else, his greeting to me was always the same: "Junior, the French horn player."

During the fall of 1960 I received a telephone call from my mother, who was a teacher at the Roosevelt School, a private school in Stamford, Connecticut. She had called to tell me she had seen Luis Russell. He was now working days as the chauffeur for the president of New York's Yeshiva University, and one of his tasks was to drive his employer's son to school. He and my mother had run into each other in the administration building that morning and recognized each other immediately.

Russell had asked her about me, and my mother told him I was living in Boston. He gave her his phone number and suggested I call him the next time I was in New York. I visited him a few weeks later and was happy to learn that he still had a six-piece band that played on weekends.

When I joined Russell's band in 1944, one of the thrills was being in the presence of a man who had been there at the beginning of American jazz. He had played with King Oliver, Louis Armstrong, Kid Ory, and Johnny Dodds. He considered Fletcher Henderson, Benny Carter, Duke Ellington, and Count Basie his close friends.

Many nights while we were on the road, I'd ask about his early days in New Orleans, Chicago, and New York. On more than one occasion, he suggested I write a history of that era. I pointed out that others had already done that.

As we shared a drink that Saturday afternoon more than a decade later and talked about our past, Russell said he was 58 years old. Remembering my curiosity about the early days of jazz, he began reminiscing about his contemporaries, many now dead.

He looked at me and said that someone should get to the old jazz musicians who were still alive and chronicle their experiences. He offered to be as much help as possible. Taking him at his word, I asked him to call Duke Ellington's drummer, Sonny Greer, as well as many other musicians, whom I later interviewed for this book. At that point, I had the idea of doing a series of socio-biographical interviews of Harlem musicians.

For the next few years, I spent many weekends in New York talking to musicians. Unfortunately, around the time I was finishing my meetings, I learned that Nat Hentoff had already published *Hear Me Talking To Ya*, a book covering the same ground as my proposed study.

One of the things that struck me during the interviews was the absolute awe in which Duke Ellington was held by the average Harlem musician. When Ellington died, I happened to be in Washington D.C., on business. On my way back to Boston, I stopped at Cooke's funeral home in New York to pay my respects. The next day I was lucky enough to get into the Cathedral of St. John the Divine for the service. As I drove home to Boston that night, I began thinking about writing an Ellington biography.

Prelude

EDWARD KENNEDY ELLINGTON, "Duke." As a musician, there was no one quite like him, a man whose name became synonymous with personal elegance and musical excellence. The music he created had a profound impact on the twentieth century. Igor Stravinsky, Darius Milhaud, Aram Khachaturian, Percy Grainger, and Leonard Bernstein all proclaimed his genius. The eminent conductor Arturo Toscanini commissioned Ellington to write a work, "Harlem," to be played by Toscanini's NBC Symphony Orchestra. Fellow conductors Andre Previn, Leopold Stokowski, Arthur Fiedler, Sir Thomas Beecham, and Paul Whiteman lauded his music.

As early as 1932, European critics were comparing Ellington's compositions with Bach, Debussy, and Delius. Two years later, the English composer and conductor Constant Lambert compared Ellington's works with those of Franz Liszt. Lambert said that for him, the real beauty of Ellington's music lay not so much in the color—brilliant though it may be—as in the skillful proportions in which the color was used. Lambert did not mean "skillful" only as compared with other jazz composers, but as compared with modern classical composers. Hearing Ellington's recording of the ebullient "Hot and Bothered," Lambert said, "I know of nothing in Ravel so dexterous in treatment as in the varied solos . . . and nothing in Stravinsky more dynamic than the final section. The combination of the themes at this moment is one of the most ingenious pieces of writing in modern music." Lambert said that Ellington gave the same distinctiveness to jazz as Strauss did to the waltz or Sousa did to the march.

The 1936 edition of the *Gramophone Record Shop Encyclopedia of Recorded Music* praised Ellington's "incomparable powers of rhapsodic invention, instinct for tonal nuance, and orchestral ingenuities equal to the most brilliant flights of Rimsky-Korsakov's or Richard Strauss' imagination." The encyclopedia's editor, Robert Donaldson Darrell, wrote that jazz usually did not fall within the book's purview. However, he felt it would be stupid to arbitrarily rule out music that soared far above the level of Tin Pan Alley. He wrote that Ellington's compositions were uniquely significant "for their poly-timbres, their complex textures, the spontaneous and rhapsodic flow of the melodies, the homogeneity of style, and—above all—for their sensitive and poignant revelation of pure feeling in tone."

Aaron Copland, the dean of American composers, reviewed Ellington's recordings of "Diminuendo in Blue" and "Crescendo in Blue" for the journal *Modern Music* in 1938. Comparing him with other jazz composers, Copeland said, "The master of them all is Duke Ellington." In 1965, the jury of the Pulitzer Prize committee on music unanimously recommended Ellington for the prize. Unfortunately, Columbia University's advisory board rejected the nomination, at which point the committee resigned. (Ellington finally received a special Pulitzer Prize in 1999, on the 100th anniversary of his birth.)

Over a period of sixty years, the extraordinarily talented Ellington produced more than three thousand musical compositions, beginning with "Soda Fountain Rag" and "What You Gonna Do When the Bed Breaks Down," both written in 1915 for solo piano. "Mood Indigo," "Sophisticated Lady," "Solitude," "I Let a Song Go Out of My Heart," and "Satin Doll," among others, later earned him a well-deserved reputation as a composer of popular songs.

Not content to rest on his laurels, Ellington continued to expand his musical horizons, composing for films, ballet, musical comedy, stage productions, and symphony orchestras. Three major sacred works were the culmination of the last decade of his life. On his deathbed, Ellington was still attempting to finish an opera, as well as edit the recording of his last sacred composition. No composer of note in any field was able to write as much music while simultaneously putting a great dance orchestra through a nonstop schedule of working in nightclubs, theaters, concert halls, and dance palaces in virtually every country in the Western world. This orchestra, a collection of temperamental virtuosi, had within its ranks men whose preeminence on their instruments was a direct result of their relationship with Ellington. When Ellington died in 1974, there were men whose entire musical lives were spent in collaboration with him, from twenty years, in the case of Russell Procope, to forty-seven for Harry Carney.

Much of Ellington's inspiration came from the world around him. The human comedy of the black experience was an unending source of musical inspiration, from "Black & Tan Fantasy" in 1927 to "The Three Black Kings" in 1973. As black America's unofficial music laureate, his compositions eloquently portrayed the beauty, sorrow, anger, cynicism, joy, affection, and sadness of that experience.

Ellington began his career in the 1920s, one of the most fertile periods in the history of American popular music. Jazz was in its infancy, but was soon to reach dazzling artistic levels powered by the genius of such musicians as Sidney Bechet, Louis Armstrong, Fletcher Henderson, and Jelly Roll Morton, as well as Ellington. His music was influenced by his contemporaries, but as I will show, it was also developed in the matrix of the social, cultural, political, and economic realities of the times.

Ellington, the grandson of slaves, was a black man born in white America. At the time of his birth, the Wright brothers were developing their aircraft; at his death, man had walked on the moon and begun to explore outer space. In 1899, blacks in this country were subject to systematic policies of discrimination and segregation and had virtually no enforceable civil rights. Ellington lived to see African-Americans serving in the highest echelons of government, elected to the House of Representatives and the United States Senate. In 1969, he was awarded the Presidential Medal of Freedom, the highest honor his country could bestow on a civilian.

Over his lifetime, the music created by Ellington and his fellow black artists was to emerge from brothels, pool halls, and segregated nightclubs to be performed on radio, on television, in concert halls and cathedrals of all denominations, and before the leaders of Europe and Asia.

1

ELLINGTON OPENS HIS autobiography, *Music Is My Mistress* with the
story of his own creation in the form of a fairy tale. "Once upon a time,"
he begins, a beautiful woman marries a handsome gentleman and soon
they are blessed with a bouncing baby boy. The woman is his mother,
Daisy Kennedy, and the man is his father, James Edward Ellington. The
blessed boy, of course, is their son Edward, later known as Duke, who
was born on April 29, 1899. Ellington's only son, Mercer, said that his
grandmother Daisy had such a strong influence that all the Ellington
men felt a strong urge to preserve her family name. Thus, Duke
Ellington was Edward Kennedy Ellington, his son was Mercer Kennedy
Ellington, and his grandson was Edward Kennedy Ellington II.

Born on January 4, 1879, Daisy was the oldest of nine children. In
his autobiography, Ellington described Daisy's father, James William
Kennedy, as a captain in the District of Columbia police force, and the
book includes a picture of him in uniform. However, there were no
black senior officers in the D.C. police until Franklin D. Roosevelt's
administration, and there is no evidence in the census reports that
James Kennedy held that occupation. Some African-Americans were
deputized police officers for special events in the black community, and
it may be under those circumstances that Daisy's father held the title.

According to the family, James William Kennedy was born a slave
on a plantation in King and Queen's County, Virginia, the illegitimate
son of the owner and a slave woman. As a young man, James fell in love
with a fellow slave, herself of mixed blood, part African and part
Cherokee. This relationship was interrupted when James's master freed
him, as slave owners often did with their mixed-race sons, and he emigrated to the District of Columbia. After Emancipation, James
returned to Virginia and brought his love back to Washington. Their
first child, Daisy, born on January 4, 1879, was described as light-
skinned, very pretty, and cultivated.

James Edward Ellington was born in Lincolnton, North Carolina, on April 15, 1879, and moved with his parents to Washington D.C. in 1886. They were among thousands of blacks who had moved north, away from the rural and semirural towns of the South, between the Civil War and World War I. His mother found employment as house-keeper and receptionist to Dr. Middleton F. Cuthbert, a prominent white physician listed in the District Social Register. At age seventeen, J. E., as he was known, was hired as a coachman for Cuthbert, and over time he progressed to driver, butler, and, by 1919, caretaker and general handyman.

Given the status of his employer, J. E. carried a great deal of weight in the black community. And it appears that he was also a charmer who swept Daisy off her feet. "You think Duke was charming?" I was told by a woman who had been a chorus girl at the Cotton Club in the 1930s. "He couldn't hold a candle to his daddy. That man could charm the birds out of the trees."

William "Sonny" Greer, a charter member of the Ellington orches-tra, offered this portrait of J. E. The band had arrived at the King Edward Hotel in Toronto just as it had begun to snow. A young woman was walking out the front door and exclaimed with surprise about the change of weather. J. E. took off his hat, made a sweeping bow, and declared to the startled, but pleased, young lady, "Those millions of snowflakes are in celebration of your great beauty."

J. E. and Daisy were married on January 3, 1898. Their first child was stillborn, or died shortly after birth. Daisy's second pregnancy became emotionally complicated toward its end. According to Mercer Ellington, she went on an excursion on the Potomac River and the boat sank. It was a frightening experience. According to her sister Florence, she became phobic and refused to leave the house. Daisy's mother dis-patched one of her sisters to live with her until the child was born.

This prenatal trauma, combined with the loss of Daisy's first child, carried over into Ellington's early years. One of Ellington's early mem-ories is of being ill with pneumonia. He remembers his mother "kneel-ing, sitting, standing to lean over his bed praying and crying."

There is also contemporary evidence that, following her marriage, Daisy became depressed and remained intermittently so throughout her life. Her youngest sister Florence told an interviewer, "Daisy was the

'Belle of the Ball' until she got married. Then she changed. But once Edward was born, she was alive again, but she was never the girl she was before she married J. E."

Shortly after their son was born, they moved into J. E.'s parents' house at 2129 Ward Place in Northwest Washington (now 1217 22d Street N.W.). Greer told the author that after he met Duke in 1919, Daisy would occasionally invite him for Sunday dinner. She was always a gracious hostess, inquiring about Greer's family, even though she didn't know them personally. Taking note of his slight stature, she would always ask if he was getting enough to eat. He said she always looked sad, "[b]ut when Duke walked in, she'd light up!"

Daisy was the oldest in a family of five girls and four boys, two of whom died at an early age. Ellington said that all of the girls, even after they were married, spent a great deal of time at his mother's house. He felt some of them even preferred it to their own homes. "It was a wonderful, warm family," he wrote. "And whatever one owned they all felt they owned a part of it, and that included me."

He was right. All the women in the family felt he was special. Ellington was the first grandchild on his mother's side, and, according to Ellington, he was "pampered and spoiled by aunts and female cousins alike." One of his cousins recounted, "I never seen nothin' like it . . . . We were so happy to see him we thought he was the grandest thing in the world." Sonny Greer told the author that a close relative described the family interaction as "Daisy, the Queen, and Edward, the Crown Prince."

While perceiving him as someone special, his family introduced him to the world of elegance at an early age, with assistance from Dr. Cuthbert, J. E.'s employer. His medical practice included the socially prominent, as well as the politically well-connected. The Morgenthaus and DuPonts were known to be his patients. When Ellington had to have a hernia repaired at age eighteen, the physician recommended by Dr. Cuthbert was later appointed surgeon general.

As the butler, J. E. made the decisions around the Cuthbert house and oversaw the activities of the cook and maid. He also catered many of the parties Cuthbert threw for his well-placed friends and associates. Mercer Ellington remembers both his grandparents helping prepare food for these occasions. They also worked with other family members for different caterers, including on one occasion, a reception at the White House.

Being in service to Washington society had another (albeit minor) benefit for the Ellingtons. Their employer would pass on to them used household articles, generally of good quality. Over time the family owned fine secondhand sets of silverware and china. "Maybe we never had a complete genuine set," Mercer stated, "but all the silver was first class." He said that both his father and grandfather had an extensive knowledge of glassware, china, and silver.

There were excellent cooks in the family, and dinners at home tended to be quite grand. Mercer noted that the table was always set like one of the many elegant functions his grandfather had butlered. "This you might say is where the 'Dukedom' began," Mercer recalled, "his experience of being around when his father was working for splendid people." Ellington himself remembers being pressed into duty as a page at one of these functions, when the boy who usually performed this task was unavailable.

Being the pampered son in this elegant household had its disadvantages too. Ellington's mother, besides being depressed and fearful, had ambivalent feelings about Duke's growing up. For example, when he was five years old, she listed his age as six so she could send him off to the Garnet Elementary School. But having sent him off early, she would secretly follow him to school every day and often wait for him outside the building at the end of the day.

Her anxieties about him were further exacerbated the following year when Ellington was hit on the head with a baseball bat during a game. She rushed out in the street and took him to Dr. Cuthbert, who closed the wound with stitches. Ellington said, "The mark is still there, but I soon got over it. With that, however, my mother decided I should take piano lessons."

Most middle-class black families of that era had a piano in their home; the Ellingtons had two. Daisy Ellington played the instrument quite well, mainly popular and semiclassical pieces. Ellington said that when he was a young child, one day his mother played the "Rosary" with such affect, he "busted out crying." She also played hymns and ragtime but, like most middle-class black women of her era, she disapproved of the blues.

Duke's father played the piano by ear and could sing excerpts from several operas and operettas. During card games at the Ellington house, J. E. would lead a group of his friends in songs like "Sweet Adeline." According to Mercer, his grandfather made up the arrangements, hummed the individual parts, and conducted from the piano. Many years later, Ellington composed *The Girl's Suite*, a work incorporating four songs his father and friends had rendered in barbershop fashion: "Sweet Adeline," "Peg O' My Heart," "Juanita," and "Sylvia."

After deciding on piano lessons, his family placed him under the tutelage of the aptly named Mrs. Clinkscales. According to Ellington, the lessons did not go too well. He missed more lessons than he took. At this point in his life, at age ten or eleven, he didn't feel the piano was his recognized talent, and he didn't take it seriously. He said, "After all, baseball, football, track, and athletics were what real he-men were identified with."

Fortunately, Duke did have a real he-man to identify with, his cousin William "Sonny" Ellington, the child of his father's older brother, John. In his autobiography, *Music Is My Mistress*, Duke never mentions his father's family, with the exception of Sonny. Yet, there is evidence of a large extended family on J. E.'s side: Estimates vary from fourteen to twenty members. Perhaps his mother did not approve of them, because Ellington stated that Sonny was the only person she would allow to take him "out of her sight."

Sonny was a combination older brother, mentor, confidant, and role model for the young Ellington. He would arrive at the Ellington household on Saturday morning, and they would stay out until dinner, roaming the city. Together they would explore Rock Creek Park, the National Zoo, or the Chesapeake and Ohio Canal. Sonny was also an excellent athlete, renowned for his prowess in baseball and track. He taught Duke how to swim, and a year later, Ellington saved a boy from drowning. That child, Rex Stewart, would later play in Ellington's orchestra.

Duke was also influenced by his strong identification with his father. J. E. was an elegant man, an excellent ballroom dancer, and a connoisseur of wines. According to Mercer, J. E.'s presence was guaranteed to light up any party. Late in his life, Ellington wrote a song inspired by a statement he heard his father say to women, "Gee, you make that hat look pretty."

Daisy Ellington was a very religious woman and an avid churchgoer. Every Sunday she took her son to two churches, the 19th Street Baptist Church, where her family worshiped, and the John Wesley AME Zion of her husband's family. As a young child, Ellington was not aware of the difference in denominations. The important thing to him was sharing the religious experience with his mother. It gave him an extraordinary feeling of security. He said, "Believing gave me that, as though I was some special child. My mother would always say, 'Edward you are blessed, you don't have anything to worry about, Edward you are blessed.'"

Ellington always maintained that he was guided by some mysterious light to help him make crucial decisions. He felt that whenever he reached a critical point in his life, "he ran into someone who told him what and which way to go to get what or where he wanted to go or do."

Duke's cousin recounted to an interviewer an incident that took place when Duke was in his teens:

> He used to come to get his dinner and he would say, "You know Mother, I'm going to be one of the greatest men in the world." And she used to say, "Oh, Boy, hush your mouth." He'd say "Yes, I am." Then he would kiss her when she would be scolding him. And he would say, "Everybody in the world is going to call me Duke Ellington. I'm ze Duke, ze grand and ze glorious Duke." We used to laugh, it was so funny. He predicted his future. Everybody in the whole world did call him Duke. He said, "I'm going to bow before kings and queens." *And he did that, too.*

Freud said, "He who knows his mother's love and is secure in that knowledge will never know failure." Daisy Ellington seemed to have provided her son with just such secure love, so that Edward lived a truly blessed life.

2

As a young teenager, Ellington's main interests were those of many adolescent males, mostly sports and pulp magazines. His cousin Sonny helped develop this latter taste by passing on to him his old copies of Sherlock Holmes stories, mysteries, westerns, and the *Police Gazette.*

By age fourteen, Duke had begun going downtown with his friends, where they would lie about their ages and buy tickets to the local burlesque house, the Gayety. Even here, Ellington was putting his experience to good use. "I made a lot of observations, on show business techniques, on the great craftsmanship involved," he wrote.

During this time, Ellington's creative interests focused on the visual arts. When he was in eighth grade, his teachers suggested he enter the vocationally oriented Armstrong High School, rather than the local M Street High School, so he could major in graphic arts. He was clearly a talented painter, so much that he was later awarded a scholarship to Pratt Institute in Brooklyn.

Armstrong High School was an all-black segregated school. But more important in Ellington's case was that the consultant to the black school system—and, later, Armstrong's principal—was the noted African-American historian, Carter G. Woodson. In 1915, he founded *The Journal of Negro Life and History.*

As consultant, Woodson insisted that black history become an integral part of the curriculum. He reminded the faculty that, despite President Woodrow Wilson's recent segregation of the District of Columbia schools, their race partook of a rich historic past. While the basic curriculum for black students was established by the white superintendent and the Board of Education, Woodson saw to it that black history was incorporated into the curriculum at all levels in the black schools.

Roscoe Conklin Bruce, a politician and contemporary of Woodson, observed, "Woodson's work gives our children and youth a sense of pride in the black stock from which they sprang, an honorable self confidence, a faith in the future and its possibilities, to know what men and women of Negro blood have actually done."

"They had a pride there, the greatest race pride," Ellington remembered. Beginning with "Black Beauty," written in 1927, the theme of race pride was to be a salient feature of many of Ellington's finest works. Over his lifetime, he acquired a substantial library of black historical literature.

Ellington's interest in the piano was reawakened in 1914, when he was fifteen. Every summer, his father sent him and his mother for a vacation to Wildwood, on the New Jersey seashore. Lying about his age, Ellington got a job as a dishwasher at the Plaza Hotel. His supervisor, a man named Bowser, learned of his interest in the piano and suggested that Ellington stop off in Philadelphia and listen to an up-and-coming pianist named Harvey Brooks. Bowser mentioned they were both about the same age.

The young Duke went, listened, and was impressed by Brooks's "swinging" rhythm and his "tremendous left hand." For some reason, hearing a musician his own age playing the piano inspired Ellington. He was encouraged by Brooks, who taught him some of the shortcuts he used when playing. Duke wrote in his autobiography, "When I got home, I had a real yearning to play. I hadn't been able to get off the ground before, but after hearing him I said to myself, 'Man you are just going to have to do it.'"

That fall, Ellington sought out a few teachers but felt that none of them could teach him what he needed to know. Finally, he tried a novel experiment. His family had an upright player piano. One afternoon he went to a local music store and bought a piano roll of James P. Johnson's "Carolina Shout." Ellington wrote, "I learned the work by slowing down the action of the keys, until I could play it at the regular tempo."

This story is open to conjecture, because Johnson did not record piano rolls until three years later. By then, Ellington was a working musician in Washington. However, Ellington may have used a piano roll to teach himself.

"I had two educations, the Bible and the poolroom," Ellington often noted. In fact, his musical education had begun in Frank Holliday's poolroom during the fall of 1914. Situated in the heart of the black community, across an alley from the Howard Theater, it was a place where one could pass the time of day playing cards, pool, or billiards. It was less than a mile down the hill from Howard University, and people from all strata of black society could be found there, including the university's students and its graduates, with degrees in law, medicine, and the liberal arts.

The area was not without its seamy side; gamblers, pimps, card sharks, and pool hustlers could be found plying their trades. It was here that Duke began to spend a lot of his spare time. "You do a lot of listening in a poolroom, and all of this sounded very big," he wrote. The most important thing in the poolroom for the young Ellington, however, was not the ambience, but the piano.

"I used to spend nights listening to Doc Perry, Louis Brown, Louis Thomas—they were the schooled musicians, they'd been to the conservatory. And I listened to the unschooled, to Lester Dishman, Sticky Mack. There was a fusion of the two right where I was standing, leaning over the piano with both my ears 20 feet high."

Throughout his entire career, listening would be fundamental to Ellington's creative process. He referred to himself as "the world's greatest listener." Tom Whaley, later his copyist and musical aide-de-camp, considered Ellington's capacity to listen his greatest asset. At this point in his life, it seems he began developing his retentive memory, the capacity to hear musical phrases from other musicians, store them in his consciousness, and retrieve them when needed.

It took Ellington only a few weeks at the piano to synthesize his early piano memories to create his first composition, "Soda Fountain Rag." The title derived from Ellington's part-time job at the Poodle Dog Cafe, where he had been hired as a soda jerk.

It is impossible to know what the original version of "Soda Fountain Rag" sounded like in 1914–15, when Ellington ostensibly composed the piece. A recording exists, but it is an amalgam of versions played over the years. Ellington used the composition in various forms over five decades. In 1929, he used it as part of an arrangement for his band under the title "Oklahoma Stomp." In 1937, it became a solo vehicle for a radio broadcast. In Paris, for a concert in 1965, it served as an introduction to his composition "Rockin' in Rhythm." And in 1972, during a concert at Carnegie Hall, as his former drummer Sonny Greer walked on stage, Ellington played it to conjure up old memories and feelings of their early days together.

"Soda Fountain Rag" consists of a series of musical ideas strung together as a basis for improvisation. When Ellington first performed the work in public, it was the only piece he knew. He solved this problem by changing the rag's tempo and rhythm to come up with a one-step, two-step, waltz, tango, and fox trot.

It was Ellington's close friend Edgar McEntree who dubbed him "Duke" around this time. They had just met at a party where Ellington was playing his first musical composition, and McEntree was taken with Ellington's sartorial elegance and his flashy piano playing. McEntree named him Duke on the spot.

A few days later, at McEntree's instigation, the two friends crashed a party given by members of Armstrong's senior class. McEntree announced that his friend the Duke was a pianist who would not object if asked to perform. Ellington played his only composition. When it was over, the audience requested an encore. On the spot, he improvised another composition, which he called "What You Gonna Do When the Bed Breaks Down?" He later described the work as a pretty good "huggin' and rubbin'" crawl. The song was very popular with his high school contemporaries, probably because of its titillating lyrics:

> Tried it on the sofa, tried it on the chair.
> Tried it on the window, didn't get anywhere.
> What you gonna do when the bed breaks down?
> You've got to work out on the floor.

By the time he had composed this ribald ditty, Ellington had been "working out" sexually for the past six years. He told an interviewer, "I was trying to fuck ever since I was six years old. I wasn't doing very much of it, but I was tryin' and it felt pretty good, whatever it was. I finally got it in when I was around twelve years old, I guess, out in a field someplace, I don't know where it was; I don't know who it was." Very early Ellington learned that sex, like music, was a competitive sport:

> We'd get girls, all the same social clique, and go down to the reservoir.
> . . . They would line up there, everybody had his own girl of course . . .
> and we'd be in hearing distance, you couldn't look. . . . The object was
> to see who did the greater job as a man. If the girl's reaction was greater,
> then he was a great fucker, because this chick was hollering and

screaming, "Hello Daddy!"; "Oh, baby, I'm coming!," and all that shit, and we found out some of those cats were cheating. Some of them were pinching the chicks to make them holler, and we found one cat whose old man had a taxi cab company was slipping the chick quarters! It's always been competitive, all the way along the line!

In August 1915, a new addition came to the Ellington household with the birth of Ruth Dorothea Ellington. At about this time, Ellington was using music mainly to enhance his social life. Gifted with a raw pianistic ability, he had not yet been schooled in technique. It was his contact with Oliver H. "Doc" Perry, a professional musician trained at the Washington Conservatory, that took him to the next level. One afternoon Perry heard Ellington playing at the poolroom. Impressed with what he heard, Perry invited him to his Ninth Street home for refreshments. Soon Ellington was studying regularly with Perry, and the effect on the young musician was profound.

Sixty years later, Ellington described his mentor in glowing terms: "He was intelligent, had a beautiful posture at all times—sitting, walking in a poolroom or playing the piano—and talked with a semi-continental finesse. He was extremely dignified, clean, neat, and had impeccably manicured nails and hands. When playing the piano he had the form that athletes have. . . . 'Doc' Perry was an impressive sight no matter what he was doing."

It was not long before Ellington was at Perry's house almost every day listening, in his words, "with a glow of enchantment" and learning. Sometimes in the middle of a passage, the musician would stop and explain to his pupil the theoretical basis for what he was doing. Perry's excellent musical ear made it possible for him to switch from his own precise, clean style to that of any pianist he had heard. For young Ellington, "He was the most perfect combination of assets I could have encountered at that time. . . . He was my piano parent."

Duke's description of his teacher resembles that of his father. He experienced them both as men of elegance, culture, bearing, and sensitivity. As the leading musician in the District, Perry had the pick of the better jobs. In February 1917, the *Washington Bee*, a black weekly newspaper, described a formal reception at which his band played: "The main hall was draped in evergreens and decorated at intervals with colored lights and fine art paintings. Doc Perry's Society Band played all the latest dance music and a local artist sang popular songs through a megaphone while beautifully gowned women tangoed with their well-groomed partners."

Perry served as more than just a teacher to Ellington. He would allow him to sit in with the band and take his place at the piano. Ellington said, "He broke me in to a sort of apprenticeship. It didn't cost him much and it was an advantage to me." Ellington would also fill in for Perry occasionally at Wednesday afternoon dances when the latter played at the Ebbitt House, an elegant downtown hotel. In addition, Duke played with a group of fellow students at Armstrong High School. After class they would rehearse at the True Reformers Hall, at Twelfth and U streets.

By 1916, this student group had grown to include the children of one of the music teachers at the school, William Miller. His three sons, Felix, on saxophone, Brother, on drums, and Bill, on saxophone and guitar, along with Ellington, formed the nucleus of the band. Other members included Lloyd Stewart on drums, Ted Nickerson on trombone, Sterling Conaway on banjo, and William Escoffey on guitar. The following year, they were joined by Arthur Whetsol on trumpet and Otto Hardwick on saxophone.

Duke dropped out of high school in the spring of 1917, and the art scholarship to Pratt was awarded to someone else. On some level he felt that he would not succeed as a painter. Many years later, he told the *Christian Science Monitor* that he knew he could not make a career as a visual artist, even though he had thoroughly studied illustration, wood-carving, and modeling. "It was something you put away in your knowledge," he said.

The most important thing Ellington "put away" from his flirtation with graphic design was his fascination with color and visual imagery. It was to emerge in the titles of the works Ellington composed from the mid-1920s on. The following are just a sample: "Azalea," "Azure," "Bird of Paradise," *Black, Brown and Beige,* "Black & Tan Fantasy," "Black Butterfly," "Black Swan," "Blue Bubbles," "Blue Light," "Cafe Au Lait," "Golden Cress," "Lady of the Lavender Mist," "Magenta Haze," "Mood Indigo," "On a Turquoise Cloud," and "Sepia Panorama."

Perry introduced Ellington to another mentor, Henry Grant. He was a supervisor of music in the school system, and, at Perry's behest, taught Ellington elementary harmony. Once a week, the young Duke would stop by and Grant would give him eight, twelve, or sixteen bars of music for which to provide harmony. Each time Ellington picked up his lesson, the previous one was there with Grant's corrections, suggestions, and encouragement.

When interviewed by the *Christian Science Monitor* in 1930, Ellington noted his debt to both Perry and Grant: "From both these men I received freely and generously more than I could have ever paid for. I repaid them as I could, by playing for Mr. Perry and learning all I could from Mr. Grant."

In 1919, Ellington went into the music business full-time, unwittingly aided by Louis Thomas, one of Washington's premiere booking agents, who had arranged for Ellington to play a solo engagement at a country club in Virginia. At the end of the evening, the employer, by mistake, gave Ellington the entire fee of one hundred dollars. Ellington's rate was ten dollars, and the remainder was to go to the booking agent. The next day, after turning over the money, Ellington went downtown and arranged for a "Music for All Occasions" ad in the telephone book. Recruiting musicians from the True Reformers Hall, he went into business with his first band, Duke's Serenaders.

World War I was being fought at the time. The city was inundated with out-of-towners. As Ellington said, "There were a lot of people who didn't know Meyer Davis and Louis Thomas from Duke Ellington. My ad looked like theirs." By late 1917, besides working himself, he was booking four or five other bands a week. The business also allowed him to exercise his artistic talent. Along with banjoist Sterling Conaway's brother, Ewell, Duke was a partner in a sign painting business. The shop was down the block from Holliday's poolroom. When customers came for posters to advertise a dance, Ellington would ask who was doing the music. When they came to book a band, he would ask who was painting their signs. By any standard, he was doing well. He was in the music business full-time, earning anywhere between $150 to $200 a week when a glass of beer cost five cents and a glass of whiskey ten cents.

Although Ellington achieved professional and financial success at this point in his life, he continued to be plagued by his ambivalent feelings toward women, particularly his mother. He tried to handle his discomfort by using the psychological defense Freud and others have described as "splitting." In other words, while Ellington venerated his mother almost to the point of saintliness, he regarded all other women (with the exception of those in religious work) essentially as whores. Mercer felt his father had a "basic contempt for women."

Ellington's unconscious feelings of affection, contempt, love, hatred, sexuality, and rage would be played out with every woman who shared his bed. In a set of unfinished lyrics titled "Shame on You, Suffer," written at the Ritz-Carlton Hotel in Montreal, Duke made a graphic statement about the way he viewed and treated women other than his mother. The piece repeatedly admonishes an unnamed "beautiful witch" to suffer, and ends with the wish "And let me hear you crying out loud."

As we will see later, the first woman to suffer was Edna Thompson, who lived across the street from Ellington. They attended grammar school together and then their paths diverged. Ellington went off to Armstrong High, and Edna enrolled in the M Street High School, later known as the prestigious Dunbar High School. Some time in 1917, they became lovers, and she became pregnant. The couple was married on July 2, 1918, and in early 1919 their son Mercer was born. A second child, a boy, was born the following year. He died in infancy. Many years later Edna told an interviewer, "It was too close to the first; we were very young, kids then, we thought Mercer was a toy."

While Mercer's mother may have experienced her son as a toy, his father was furious that he was not a girl, because he feared male competition. It made Mercer's infancy difficult. He told an interviewer that his mother kept his hair in braids for months after the time most boys his age would have had their hair cut. Finally, his grandmother Daisy put her foot down and insisted that Mercer be taken to a barber.

By age twenty-one, Ellington had seriously begun his life's work in music. But as he entered young manhood, two themes emerged that would develop over his lifetime. His personal life would be spent celebrating women, wooing them, and writing music about and for them, but he would remain ambivalent about them. His creative life, however, would be different. For the next fifty-five years, it would be centered on an extended second family. This family would be known as the Duke Ellington Orchestra.

3

"FROM THE MOMENT I was introduced to Duke I loved him. It was just something about him. He didn't know it, but he had it then. I've never seen another man like him. He walks into a strange room and the whole place lights up."

Forty years later, drummer William "Sonny" Greer could still remember vividly his first reaction to meeting Ellington. Greer was a slim, dapper, highly engaging young man. Born in Long Branch, New Jersey, Greer dropped out of high school to follow a career playing drums. He first studied with Eugene Holland, a member of composer J. Rosamond Johnson's musical revue, while the show was playing in Greer's hometown.

"He fascinated me," Greer said of Holland. "He could sing, dance, play, and had great finesse." They had met in the local pool hall, where Greer was the reigning champion. Anyone who came into the pool room could play Greer for ten cents a game.

The company was in town for two weeks, and every time Holland came to the poolroom, Greer would beat him. During one of the games Greer told Holland how much he liked the way Holland played the drums. Holland offered to teach him if Greer would give him pool lessons in exchange. Greer went out and bought a box of cigars, "just to put an edge on it," he said. Holland gave Greer six or seven lessons, and Greer's career as a professional drummer was on its way.

By age twenty, Greer had already toured with Wilbur Gardner, Mabel Ross, and one of Harry Yerek's many orchestras. He had also spent time in New York City rehearsing with the Clef Club Orchestra. In the summer of 1919, he took a job at the Plaza Hotel in Asbury Park, New Jersey, as part of a trio along with Ralph "Shrimp" Jones on violin and Thomas "Fats" Waller on piano.

The hotel also employed a string ensemble called the Conaway Boys, led by Sterling Conaway, an alumnus of the True Reformers Hall. Over the summer, Greer and the Conaways developed a close friendship. At the end of the season, the Conaways invited Greer to Washington for a weekend. He liked the city and immediately found work at Louis Thomas's Dreamland Cafe. He was part of a trio with Sterling Conaway on guitar and banjo, and Claude Hopkins, a sixteen-year-old pianist, who would become a famous bandleader in his own right ten years later.

Within days of his arrival, Greer found his way to Holliday's poolroom, and soon became a regular at the tables. One afternoon as Greer was chalking his cue stick, the manager of the Howard Theater, E. C. Brown, burst in. The drummer with the house band—the Marie Lucas Orchestra—had fled town after being served with a subpoena in a paternity suit. Brown needed a replacement immediately. Greer stepped forward and offered his services. He played the show and was hired for the rest of the season.

The Howard Theater was the focal point for black musicians in the District. The house band played in the orchestra pit and was responsible for the music during the show. Local musicians got a chance to be heard at the evening supper show, when they would battle it out for the title of most popular, based on audience applause.

The day Greer was hired, Snowden's Jazz Aces, led by banjoist Elmer Snowden, was one of the groups in residence. Snowden was assisted by Ellington's teacher, Doc Perry, on piano, Black Diamond on drums, and Otto "Toby" Hardwick on saxophone and violin.

Hardwick was one of Ellington's teenage friends. He lived a block away on T Street, and he had played on the baseball team managed by Ellington's cousin, Sonny. His first instrument was the violin, and he subsequently learned the bass. It was the bass that got Hardwick his first job at the age of fourteen, playing with Carroll's Columbia Orchestra. But he soon found the instrument too cumbersome. Many nights his father would accompany him to work just to help him carry it home.

Hardwick switched back to the violin, but at Ellington's suggestion, he also took up the C melody saxophone, which allowed him to read from a violin part without transposing. Toby subsequently joined the group at True Reformers Hall and often played with Duke's Serenaders. Hardwick then became a charter member of the Washingtonians, the major musical group then working through Ellington's booking agency.

Along with Hardwick, Ellington, and Elmer Snowden (when available), the group included Arthur Whetsol on trumpet. Unlike other members of the band, though, Whetsol was in music mainly to earn money for his college education.

Greer's debut in the orchestra pit was impressive. "I knew all about showmanship," he said. "The audiences ate it up. It ain't what you do but the way you do it. Things like hitting three rim shots and opening and closing one side [of] my jacket in time." Hardwick, quite taken with Greer's style and musical personality, invited his two friends to the theater to see him in action. They were impressed and decided to check him out after the show.

"Everybody used to stand on the street corners then, trying to look bigtime," Ellington remembered. "So along comes Sonny. I'm sure that I'm a killer with my Shepherd plaid suit, bought on time. I take the lead in the conversation. Sonny comes back with a line of jive that lays us low."

Within days Greer, Hardwick, and Ellington became inseparable companions. They considered themselves something special, wearing flashy, expensive suits, drinking corn whiskey, and smoking overpriced cigars. It is quite possible, of course, that psychologically they did not feel too secure, and were trying to shore up their image with these symbols of high living.

They spent a good deal of their spare time driving around the countryside in Hardwick's car, a two-door Pullman sedan, which could be counted on to break down at least once a month. Greer continued working at the Dreamland Cafe, while playing at the theater. His main contribution to the group was to serve as an unofficial cheerleader whenever Ellington played at jam sessions around town.

Besides being the group's resident sophisticate, Greer was also its main connection to the music world of Harlem. He had rehearsed with the Clef Club Orchestra and had two aunts in the city. Describing the place in glowing terms, Greer offered to take them there.

On March 10, 1921, according to Greer, he went to New York with Toby, Duke, Artie Whetsol, and Elmer Snowden. "I introduced them around to James P. Johnson, Lucky Roberts, and so forth." Ellington was totally captivated by the city. During the taxi ride uptown he remarked to Greer, "It's just like the Arabian Nights!"

However, the lights of the city would ultimately be of secondary importance to Ellington that evening. He was about to meet his next musical mentor, Willie "the Lion" Smith. The D.C. musicians were off to the Capitol Palace, a large, boisterous nightspot on Lenox Avenue between 139th and 140th Streets, where Smith served as resident pianist.

"My first impression of the Lion, even before I saw him . . . was the thing I felt as I walked down the steps," Ellington recounted. "A strange thing. A square-type fellow might say, 'This joint is jumping,' but to those who had been acclimatized . . . the tempo was the lope. . . . Actually everybody and everything seemed to be doing whatever they were doing in the tempo the Lion's group was laying down. The walls and the furniture seemed to lean understandingly . . . one of the strangest and greatest sensations I ever had. The waiters served in that tempo; everybody who had walked in, out, or around the place walked with a beat."

As they walked in, Greer took the lead, waving to people Ellington was certain he didn't even know. When they reached Smith at the piano, Greer proceeded to rattle off the names of a few hustlers and pimps from Long Branch that he said he and Smith both knew. Greer introduced Duke, they shook hands, and Smith got up from the piano and asked Duke to sit in for a few numbers. Smith went to the back of the room and began talking to some of the musicians.

Soon after Ellington began playing, another pianist asked him to surrender the seat. Ellington got up, and the musician sat down at the piano. Within minutes, the Lion himself was standing over the other pianist. According to Ellington, he was yelling, "Get up! I'll show you how it's supposed to go." The Lion had used Duke to set the pianist up for a confrontation. Such was Ellington's introduction to the musical life of the city.

Willie "the Lion" Smith was a strapping, swaggering man, who invariably had a cigar in his mouth while playing piano. An aggressive self-promoter, full of fast talk and coiled energy, Smith was born William Henry Joseph Bonapart Bertholoff-Smith in Goshen, New York, on November 25, 1897. Following the death of his father in 1901, his mother remarried and the family moved to Newark, New Jersey. Initially self-taught on the piano, by age fourteen Smith could be found at the town's red light district, "the Coast," refining his musical skills in brothels and saloons.

Arriving in New York City the following year, he immediately caught the eye of many legendary piano regulars around town, including Willie "Egg Head" Sewell, "One Leg" Willie Joseph, "Jack the Bear," and Richard "Abba Dabba" McLean, whom Smith considered his mentors. He claimed that French officers gave him his leonine nickname during World War I, while observing his prowess in handling their 75-millimeter cannon under fire. His unit, Battery A, the all-black 153d Brigade of the 350th Field Infantry, was attached to a French division.

By the time Ellington first heard him, Smith was considered one of Harlem's best. He was also strongly opinionated, conversant in several languages, and enamored of astrology; his breadth of knowledge and musicianship impressed the young Ellington. Smith's delicate touch and taste for impressionistic, diaphanous composition was reminiscent of Debussy and Ravel. But if need be, he was able to pound the piano with the best of them.

When Ellington, Greer, and Hardwick got home to D.C., they were dying to return to work—but on their own terms. They made a pact that they would not accept a job unless there was work for the other two. This agreement was put to the test in early 1923, when clarinetist Wilbur Sweatman and his band came to the Howard Theater on a tour that would finish in New York. Unhappy with his drummer, and taking note of Greer's playing in the Howard pit orchestra band, Sweatman offered Greer a job.

Greer made it plain that he would take the job only if Ellington and Hardwick were hired too. Sweatman needed a drummer with Greer's skill and finally agreed to hire all three musicians. But now that Ellington had the opportunity to go to New York, he had second thoughts about leaving his family and business in D.C. He ultimately decided to stay, and Greer and Hardwick left with his blessings.

According to Greer, he and Hardwick would drop Duke a note once or twice a week, telling him what a wonderful time they were having and imploring him to join them. Ellington finally capitulated and joined them in New York the week of March 5, 1923, during their engagement at the Lafayette Theater. Ellington said he learned a lot from Sweatman. The bandleader was a good musician, but worked in vaudeville because that was where the money was. The D.C. trio played a series of split-week engagements before the tour was over. When the money from Sweatman ran out, the trio survived on occasional jobs, along with Greer's ability to earn a few dollars at the pool table. Greer and Ellington roomed with one of Greer's aunts in Harlem, and Hardwick stayed across the street from them with his own aunt.

Ellington used some of this time in Harlem to renew his friendship with James P. Johnson, the renowned piano player. Greer claimed to have introduced them in 1921, but Ellington and Johnson had met before that. When Johnson came to Washington, D.C., to play a concert at Convention Hall, he stopped at the Dreamland Cafe. While there he was told that there was a young man in the house who was known for his rendition of Johnson's masterpiece, "Carolina Shout." Ellington played for him and he was impressed. They spent the next day together, and when he left, Johnson suggested Ellington look him up if he ever got to New York.

James P. Johnson, considered one of the great Harlem pianists, was born in New Brunswick, New Jersey, in 1894, the youngest of five children. His first teacher was his mother. The family moved to New York in 1911, and as a teenager, Johnson began playing at rent parties, but his main interest was always composition. By 1914, he had arranged several blues compositions for publication and familiarized himself with the music of Beethoven and Bach. At age twenty, his talent and reputation were such that he was awarded a contract as a recorder of rolls for player pianos. In some respects this was the highest honor a popular pianist of the day could be accorded. "I was considered one of the best in New York, if not the best," he said.

Altogether, Johnson produced twenty piano rolls, seventeen of them original ragtime-based compositions. Included among them was the landmark "Carolina Shout," the composition Ellington and other young jazz pianists used to test their mettle. While cutting piano rolls, Johnson was also in demand as a soloist and accompanist to singers, including Bessie Smith and Ethel Waters. In 1922, he traveled to Europe as pianist with the all-black revue *Plantation Days*. The following year Johnson wrote the score to the successful Broadway show *Runnin' Wild*, which included his famous piece, "Charleston."

For the rest of his life, Johnson devoted his time to composition. He premiered his first extended work, "Yamecraw," at Carnegie Hall in July 1928. The following year, he conducted the orchestra for Bessie Smith's film *St. Louis Blues* In the early 1930s, he wrote his symphony *Harlem* and a one-act opera, *De Organizer*, with the poet Langston Hughes. As a composer, conductor, and accompanist, this lumbering, shy, self-effacing man was considered the dean of Harlem pianists.

Luis Russell always maintained that Ellington's piano style was an amalgam of Johnson's and Smith's. "Whenever I listen to Duke I hear the Lion in his left hand and James P. in the right."

Ellington considered Smith "the greatest influence on most of the great piano players who were exposed to the luxury of his fire, his harmonic lavishness, his stride." The Lion noted, "I took a liking to him and he took a liking to me." Smith encouraged the trio to stay in the city and try to make it as musicians. He was earning good money and helped them out financially in addition to using his influence with club owners to try to get them work. Nothing developed, however, and finally when Duke found fifteen dollars on the street, the trio used the money for train fare home.

Duke never forgot Smith's support during that time. "Portrait of a Lion," Ellington's 1939 composition (rewritten in 1955) gave Smith musical immortality. In later years, Ellington supported Smith financially and included him as one of his guests at his seventieth birthday party at the White House.

Returning home, Ellington, Sonny Greer, and Toby Hardwick received a warm family welcome. Duke said, "We got to Washington on a Sunday morning. I still remember the smell of hot biscuits. . . . My mother broiled six mackerel and there was lots of coffee." Ellington went back to booking bands. Occasionally he, Hardwick, and Greer teamed up with trumpeter Artie Whetsol to do one- or two-night engagements, usually on weekends. According to Greer, they didn't want steady work, because they were looking to get back to New York. Their chance came a month-and-a-half later, with help from Elmer Snowden.

In June 1923, Snowden was leading the band at Murray's Casino in Washington. The first week of that month, the vaudeville act, "Liza and her Shuffling Six," appeared as part of the show downtown at the

Gayety Theater. The show was managed by the dancer and producer Clarence Robinson and starred dancer and singer Katie Crippin. Lou Henry, Crippin's husband, played trombone in the sextet that accompanied her. The multi-reed instrumentalist Garvin Bushell led the band, which included Fats Waller on piano.

According to Bushell, one night after the show, he and Robinson dropped in at the casino. Later that evening, they had a fight and Bushell told Robinson that he and the musicians were leaving the show when it got to New York the following week. There were six-and-a-half weeks left on the tour. Robinson, needing a band in a hurry, went back to the club the following night and offered Snowden the job.

Greer heard about this turn of events and volunteered his services along with those of Hardwick, Whetsol, and Ellington. Robinson accepted the offer, and everyone except Ellington left for New York. Duke planned to join them the following week.

But when the quartet arrived in New York, there was no job. Prior to their arrival, Bushell had gone to the booking agency and told them he and his musicians had left the show, and that Robinson was bringing in an unknown band. At that point, the agency canceled the remainder of the tour. Feeling lost, angry, and upset, the group (instigated by Greer) sent Ellington an ambiguously worded telegram, suggesting he come to the city as soon as possible.

Assuming things were going well, Duke left Washington, traveling in grand style. After purchasing a seat in the parlor car, Duke ate a lavish dinner and left an excellent tip for the waiter. On arriving, Ellington took a taxi uptown to the apartment on 129th Street, where Snowden and Whetsol were staying. As he stepped out of the cab, he was met by Greer, who said, "Duke, give us something. We are all busted and waiting for you to relieve the situation." By "something" he meant money, but it was too late; Ellington had spent everything on the trip up from Washington.

As Greer recounted, "Duke didn't have a penny, but we felt better just having him around. The first thing he said to us was 'Don't worry, things are going to work out.' He was so confident, we just had to believe him. And damned if it didn't."

At this point, Ellington was not the leader. Snowden led the band and was also its business manager. With his flashy personality, Greer was the vocalist and the *perceived* leader. Yet when the group was in a critical situation, its members turned to Ellington for leadership and support. He moved into the apartment, sharing a room with Whetsol. Greer and Hardwick were living with their relatives. The quintet then set out looking for work.

Their first attempt was a disaster. They auditioned for the Everglades, a club in a basement on Broadway and 48th Street. According to Greer, Robinson had set up the audition. The quintet assumed he did this to make up for their losing the job with Katie Crippin. The manager said they were hired and, to their surprise, began to negotiate their salary with Robinson. Snowden, who was responsible for the group's business dealings, objected. Soon it become clear to the musicians that Robinson was negotiating as a dancer and bandleader and that the musicians' task was to accompany him. The group picked up their instruments and left.

Fortunately, within a few days, they were able to pick up some spending money, thanks to Fats Waller. Waller had been working at the Orient Cafe in a trio that included banjoist Fred Guy. He persuaded Guy to let the Snowden group play during intermission and keep whatever tips they made.

The owner of the Orient, Earl Dancer, had many irons in the fire and left much of the management of the club to Guy. Dancer was part owner of the Golden Gate Inn on 133rd Street, and he aspired to become a theatrical producer. To further this goal, he was spending a lot of time with blues singer Ethel Waters, whose career was in limbo.

Needless to say, the Orient was not high on Dancer's list of priorities, so he put Guy in charge of the room and allowed him to keep whatever money came in, until the band's salary and his expenses were met. Anything beyond that went to the owner. According to Ellington, "[Guy] practically owned the place."

The Orient Cafe was upstairs over a poolroom on Eighth Avenue, between 133rd and 134th Streets. One block away, at the corner of Seventh Avenue and 134th Street, was a club, owned and operated by Barron D. Wilkins, a black racketeer. He had operated a series of nightspots throughout the city since 1909. With the advent of Prohibition, he bought the old Exclusive Club and renamed it the Club Barron.

For entertainment he hired singer Ada Smith, who as "Bricktop" was to captivate Paris for the next three decades. As she recollected, "Men had to wear jackets and ties and women, long dresses. It was *the* Harlem spot. Frank Fay the actor, Al Jolson . . . a chorus girl named Lucille LeSeur, who would be later known as Joan Crawford, came there. Every night the limousines pulled up to the corner of Seventh Avenue and 134th Street, and the rich whites would get out all dolled up in their furs and jewels."

The quintet had been playing and hanging around at the Orient for less than a week when Smith dropped in to see her old friend Waller on her way to work. Much to her surprise, she found the Washingtonians playing for tips. She had worked with them back home, at the Oriental Gardens. "I knew a good outfit when I heard one," she said. "The Washingtonians were something." She was not very happy with the band that was accompanying her, and that night she convinced Wilkins to fire that band and hire the quintet.

Barron's, and other clubs in Harlem that featured black entertainment primarily for a white clientele, were known in the vernacular of the 1920s as "Black and Tan" clubs. Konrad Bercovoci, a novelist and journalist, described the club as being for members only, frequented by whites and some blacks, mainly entertainers: "*Bons viveurs* from all the strata of society, financiers, lawyers, and the theatrical people, with their women or in search of them, were dancing to the black jazz band, while being served at the tables. . . . Between the dances they were entertained by a professional dancer or singer."

The band earned about $30 apiece a night in tips, plus salary. The manner of tipping at the club was unusual. On entering, big spenders would ask Wilkins to change a hundred-dollar bill into fifty-cent pieces. If they appreciated the entertainers' offerings, they would toss the two hundred coins on the dance floor. Ellington said that "this action would go jingling deep into the night. At the end of the evening, at 4 A.M. or maybe 6, when our bountiful patron thought we had had enough setting-up exercises picking up halves, he would graciously thank us and wish us good luck."

"You have no idea what it sounds like when those half dollars hit the floor," Greer said. "At the end of the night, we'd split the take [Bricktop, four dancers, and the band]. Wilkins would change them to bills, and the same thing would happen the next night." For the band, it was heaven. "We'd got our feet on the first rung of the ladder," Hardwick recollected. "It seemed they liked us. Our music was different; even then we had arrangements on everything."

The arrangements Greer spoke of were nothing more than ordinary stock compositions. However, the music was given a different sound by Hardwick's and Snowden's switching from one to another of the many reed instruments they could play. Besides the C melody, Hardwick had mastered the soprano, alto, baritone, and bass saxophones, as well as the violin and string bass. Snowden, besides the banjo, played the C melody, alto, and baritone saxophones. This combination of instruments, along with Whetsol's muted trumpet, created a quiet, subdued sound described by Ellington as "conversion" music. Solos by the musicians added more variety.

One of the regular customers at Barron's was the songwriter Maceo Pinkard. The previous year, in collaboration with Irvin C. Miller, he had written the score for the show *Liza*, which he patterned after the very successful all-black musical *Shuffle Along. Liza* was the first of the "speed shows," as they were often called, relying on their frantic dancing for success. This show, although it was a failure, was responsible for introducing the Charleston to Broadway on November 27, 1922. The Charleston became a trademark of the 1920s, and even today is probably the first visual image that comes to mind when that decade is referred to.

Pinkard had a slight connection with the Victor Recording Company. The company was always auditioning black performers, but rarely signed any of them. On July 26, Pinkard arranged for the band listed as "Snowden's Novelty Orchestra" to record one of his songs, titled "Home." The company did nothing with the pressing but had enough interest in the band to ask it to return in the fall. Snowden felt that their quiet, understated style was not what the company was looking for in a black band. "Our music wasn't the kind of *Negro* they were interested in," he said.

He was partly right. The kind of music the band was playing at that time was of no interest to any of the white recording companies or music publishers. Victor had little interest in any black musicians, while the rest of the white recording companies were caught up in "Blues Fever."

4

"WHEN WE WERE in Washington," Sonny Greer said, "our little band played quiet, tasty music. It got us gigs at white country clubs, weddings, college dances in Maryland and Virginia, Hunt Club balls and cotillions. We played the same kind of music for Wilkins, and he liked it. Until we got to New York we didn't know nothin' about 'Blues Fever.'"

"Blues Fever" had its beginnings on July 14, 1920. The OKeh Recording Company released two songs by the black singer Mamie Smith. She was accompanied by a white band under the directorship of Fred Hagar. Luis Russell described her as a short, plump, buxom, light-skinned woman with a better-than-average contralto voice. At the time, she was starring at Harlem's Lincoln Theater in Perry Bradford's revue, *Maid of Harlem.*

With little or no advertising, the recordings "That Thing Called Love" and "You Can't Keep a Good Man Down" sold briskly and made a small profit. The company used some of it to record Mamie Smith again. "As I remember it," her accompanist Willie "the Lion" Smith recollected, "the . . . day we went to make the sides there was only Mamie, [producer] Ralph Preer, myself, and the band in the studio. We waxed two tunes, 'Crazy Blues' and 'It's Right Here for You.'"

In record shops in Harlem and Chicago's South Side, as well as in urban black communities in Philadelphia, Baltimore, and Washington, D.C., "Crazy Blues" sold more than 175,000 copies within months. At first, the OKeh executives thought there had been an arithmetical error. After confirming the figures, the recording company called Smith to return to the studio and record more blues. "Crazy Blues" was also the first authentic black blues performance many white record buyers heard. By December, it had sold more than 1.5 million records.

The song had a strong impact on the music business. It began the era of "race" records: music published and recorded specifically for the growing urban black population. Migrants from the South were buying what they heard as "down home" music in great numbers. Soon OKeh saw that there was another audience. F. Scott Fitzgerald's "Jazz Age" contemporaries were also drawn to the naughty, raunchy double entendres of the blues. If they didn't find black blues in local record stores, they could always find it in the black section of town.

Booking agents, talent scouts, and record producers were soon out in the field looking for black singers and entertainers to compete with Mamie Smith. By the mid-1920s, there were at least five singers named Smith—none of them related—among the classic female blues singers.

Prior to "Crazy Blues," Paramount, OKeh, and Columbia had recorded black artists along with their white counterparts, marketing these records as part of what was known as the "popular" series. As the companies began to sign more black musicians and singers, these artists were now consigned to a new category called "race" recordings.

OKeh had originally recorded Mamie Smith and the Norfolk Jubilee Singers as part of its popular series. But the recordings of new OKeh artists Victoria Spivey, Sara Martin, and Sippie Wallace were segregated and issued under the "race" series (catalogued beginning with a new number, 8000). Paramount had recorded Lucille Hegamin as a popular artist in 1922. When the company signed Alberta Hunter, Ida Cox, and Ma Rainey, their recordings were issued on the 12000 "race" series. Columbia, too, had initially issued its recordings of Bessie Smith, Clara Smith, and Edith Wilson in the same series as their white counterparts. As Columbia's stable of black performers increased, their recordings were issued in its 14000-D "race" series. Other companies followed suit: Vocalion with its 1000 series (1925); Perfect with its 100 series (1925); Brunswick with its 7000 series (1926); and Victor with its V38500 series (1927).

Recording companies' rush to find black women singers was not the only indication of the growing popularity of the blues. The 15th Infantry held a blues singing contest in New York's Manhattan Casino along with its first band concert and dance. Appearing at the event on February 20, 1921, the future mayor of New York, Fiorello LaGuardia, announced the four finalists: Lucille Hegamin, a favorite in Harlem; Alice Leslie Carter; Daisy Martin; and Trixie Smith, who won the contest with her rendition of "Trixie's Blues."

Before "Crazy Blues," white music publishing firms had no interest in the blues or black music in general. This was the exclusive province of black firms, notably Clarence Williams, Pace & Handy, and Perry Bradford. In late 1920, Harry Pace left his partner, the great blues composer W. C. Handy, to set up his own publishing and recording company, Black Swan, which he advertised as "The Only Genuine Colored Record—Others Are Passing for Colored."

Black Swan's board of directors, which included the noted black educator and writer W. E. B. Du Bois, had high aspirations for the company. Black Swan was to have class and reflect positively on the race. With that in mind, the company began an ambitious program of recording black "cultural" artists. Every type of music, from grand opera to sacred and popular, was recorded. But these lofty ambitions were not reflected in the monthly balance sheet, which at the end of January 1921 totaled a paltry $674.64.

With that in mind, Black Swan's music director, William Grant Still, auditioned a young singer named Ethel Waters. She was accompanied at the piano by the company's director of recordings, Fletcher Henderson. There was considerable discussion among board members as to whether Waters should sing popular or "cultural" numbers. They did not want the company to appear "too black." They considered the blues to be black music for black audiences, shabby and second-rate. The fact that Pace had the blues singers Alberta Hunter, Josie Miles, and Trixie Smith under contract did not help matters.

The board had previously rejected Bessie Smith after she made the mistake of showing up for her audition with a bottle of liquor in her purse, from which she drank liberally and spat on the floor. Bessie Smith further compounded her sins by use of sexually explicit four-letter words in ordinary conversation, shocking the middle-class sensibilities of DuBois and the other board members.

The demure presence and behavior of Ethel Waters was more to Black Swan's liking. Board members agreed that she should sing popular numbers—that is, the blues—but had some qualms about continuing to paying her one hundred dollars for each recording session. As it turned out, she was worth every penny. Waters's recordings of "Oh Daddy" and "Down Home Blues," followed by "There'll Be Some

Changes Made" and "One Man Nan," plus several others, pushed the company's income to an average of $20,000 per month. At the end of the year, Black Swan's profits from record sales totaled $105,000.

Attempting to capitalize on the success of the recordings, Black Swan organized a tour, featuring Waters and a band led by Fletcher Henderson. They were booked for Philadelphia, Chicago, and the South. Waters left the tour in New Orleans after a dispute with the board, and her contract was terminated.

A few years later, Orient club owner Earl Dancer convinced Waters to switch from singing blues to popular songs in front of white audiences. He secured her a series of successful break-in dates, and soon she was on her way to fame and fortune. Columbia Records signed her, and she became one of its biggest stars. Waters's versions of "Dinah" and "Sweet Georgia Brown" were two of the best-selling recordings of the mid-1920s. Dancer's personal dream of a theatrical career would be realized in 1927, when he produced and directed the show *Africana*, featuring Waters. Years later, Waters said Dancer was "intelligent, a good showman, and he knew the theater."

Waters had been Black Swan's prime moneymaker. The remaining roster of blues singers contributed to the company's income, but could not offset the losses incurred by "cultural" artists. With expenses mounting—and the board adamant against continued development of the blues repertoire—Pace threw in the towel. He sold the company's catalog to Paramount in March 1924 for $50,000. One of the terms of the contract included his being hired as director of recordings for Paramount's 12000 "race" series.

Pace hoped to use his position to record black musicians and singers, as well as to develop the catalog of black music he brought with him from Black Swan. He was unable to do so. The $50,000 capital outlay left Paramount with a thin operating margin, making it difficult for Pace to sign up and record the many artists he had in mind. Even if he could, it was too late. A white firm, Jack Mills, Inc., which three years later would have a major impact on Ellington's life, had gotten into the act a year earlier and beaten Pace to the punch.

In July 1923, Harlem's *Amsterdam News* and the *Pittsburgh Courier* reported that Jack Mills, Inc., was attempting to "corner the blues business" by making exclusive contracts with black composers and buying their works outright. In exchange for immediate money, the musicians gave up any claim for royalties. The list of Mills's artists read like a "Who's Who" of black musicians: Will Vodery, Will Marion Cook, Henry Creamer, Spencer Williams, Lieutenant Tim Brymn, Shelton Brooks, and James P. Johnson, among others.

The company was founded in 1919 by Jack Mills and his younger brother, Irving. Jack had been a song plugger (that is, a company salesperson promoting new sheet music to music stores) for Waterson, Berlin, and Snyder, a Philadelphia music firm, as well as office manager for McCarthy and Fischer in New York. Waterson hit the jackpot with "Dardanella," which sold a million copies of sheet music. Jack Mills took his $500 bonus and set up his own company, Mills Music, Inc. He gave his brother Irving a 39 percent interest in the firm and he gave 10 percent to the lawyer who set up the corporation. With a catalog of three newly copyrighted songs, the brothers found some Philadelphia garment manufacturers to put up the remaining $4,500 needed to form the company.

Two years later Mills Music got its first break when the tenor Enrico Caruso died. The Millses had heard an unknown songwriter's composition, "They Needed a Songbird in Heaven, so God Took Caruso Away," which they bought outright in order to publish the sheet music. Music stores in those days employed a singer and piano accompanist to demonstrate songs, so customers would buy the sheet music. The song was a hit, and Mills Music was on its way. This was followed by a huge success, "Mr. Gallagher and Mr. Shean," which sold a million copies. By the early 1920s, besides publishing music, the company managed performers, as well as supervising and arranging recording sessions.

The brothers were shrewd businessmen. They always tried to buy a song outright. If the author refused to sell, they would offer "suggestions" that would supposedly improve it and then claim coauthorship. It was well-known in the business that any enterprising songwriter who wanted his or her song published by Mills Music had to endure this policy.

In the spring of 1923, the *Clipper*, a weekly publication for the entertainment business, took notice of what Mills Music was doing. The *Clipper* reported that composers placing songs with Mills were complaining of the indiscriminate "cutting in" of house men like Irving Mills, an officer of the corporation, and Jimmie McHugh, a stockholder. Sometimes the house men were declared coauthors for making minor suggestions, as one sarcastic songwriter said, "for dotting I's and crossing T's."

But as it turned out, "Mr. Gallagher" and "Dardanella" were the last of the million sellers in sheet music. Phonographs were replacing pianos in American parlors, and the success of Mamie Smith's recording of "Crazy Blues" was not lost on the Mills brothers. They were determined to find another smash seller. They began looking for similar music and bought it wholesale. In July, *Phonograph and Talking Machine Weekly* reported that the firm had bought "Down Hearted Blues" and "Bleeding Heart Blues" from a prominent Midwestern publisher.

According to this journal, Mills Music bought these songs to help achieve its plan to establish a catalog of black music that would include popular songs and blues. It would be published by a newly formed subsidiary, Down South Music, Inc., whose director was Fletcher Henderson, Black Swan's former director of recordings. In October 1923, *Billboard* wrote that Mills's blues catalog was "second to none." In November, the *Pittsburgh Courier* announced that the firm had rented offices in the Roseland Building on Broadway and 50th Street.

The following year, Mills moved to 148-150 West 46th Street. Andrew Sissle, brother of the bandleader Noble Sissle, was installed as business manager and W. C. Handy's daughter Katherine and Henderson's cousin Myles Norman were members of the office staff. Taking note of this, the *Amsterdam News* observed, "Add to this the picture presented by a view of the [Mills] home office with its big percentage of Negro visitors, the race members of our group obtained an interview with the executives, and one begins to believe that . . . one liberal minded concern has opened wide the gateway for Negroes into a field that very properly belongs to us, yet under whose fence we have heretofore been obliged to crawl, if we would enter."

The Mills brothers were no social revolutionaries. They realized that if they were in the business of black music, then black faces in their offices would make their musicians feel more comfortable and probably help ease the firm's business dealings. Also, black musicians undoubtedly would know the better young composers, and could bring them to the firm.

The addition of Henderson to Mills Music's stable of musicians led other firms to follow its lead. E. B. Marks Music Company announced its "African Opera Series of Blues." Shapiro, Bernstein & Co. set up Skidmore Music Co., and Irving Berlin, Inc., financed Rainbow Music Company, directed by Bob Ricketts and Porter Grainger. In September of that year, Fred Fischer announced that Jo Trent, a black songwriter, had been hired as supervisor of its blues and recording division. (In 1929, Trent would write the lyrics for the hit song "My Kind'a Love.")

One of the major reasons these companies began to develop blues catalogs was their realization that they did not have to print a song in order to make it popular. This meant a company's only capital outlay was for the recording session. The companies now expected to make their profit not from the sale of the sheet music, but from the recording.

Duke Ellington's introduction to the music industry began with Maceo Pinkard. Shortly after they met at Barron's nightclub, Pinkard took Ellington downtown and introduced him to the music publishing district. This area of Broadway, from 40th to 55th Streets, was known as Tin Pan Alley because of the cacophony of so many pianists playing different pieces of music in different keys. It was there that Ellington had his first meeting at Mills Music with younger brother Irving, who would later become his manager. Pinkard also introduced Ellington to Jo Trent. Ellington and Trent decided to form a songwriting team and join the list of musicians who would show up at Mills Music with songs they had written, hoping the firm would buy them. The company was usually the last stop for writers who had been peddling songs all day without success. Although Jack Mills ran the office, Irving Mills was the one who negotiated with the songwriters.

If a casting director had been looking for someone to play the part of an impresario, Irving Mills would have won it hands down. He was a short, burly, fast-talking, cigar-chomping promoter. He was born on New York's Lower East Side in 1894, to Russian-Jewish parents. Along with his contemporary Irving Berlin, he began his musical career as a "song demonstrator," singing popular songs of the day in music stores. He also sang in dance halls, with a megaphone in the style of Rudy

Vallee. In addition to his better-than-average singing ability, Irving Mills was also a lyricist. His first published song, in 1922, was "Lovesick Blues."

Irving Mills was the firm's outside man, always scouting Broadway and Harlem for new talent. He assembled the musicians for several of the budget recording labels in New York (such as Ajax, Harmony, and Cameo). For a few dollars, he would buy outright lead sheets (the music, written out with chords and lyrics) by out-of-work songwriters, as well as uncopyrighted new material written by musicians at recording sessions. He would also buy work from people walking in off the street.

Luis Russell told me, "When I came to New York in '27, the first thing I learned was, you could take songs downtown and sell them to the publishers. If nobody was buying there was always Mills; he was good for fifteen or twenty dollars most of the time." Sammy Fain, the songwriter, once said, "If a guy put his elbows on the piano, Mills said, 'We'll take it.'"

Ten years later, a member of the Ellington orchestra approached Mills with a lead sheet of a tune he had written. When asked what it was, he replied, "Just a blues." "Oh no!" the publisher screamed possessively, "I own *all* the blues!"

Ellington and Trent didn't sell any music to the firm, but they did begin to spend time on the Mills company's "professional floor." There Ellington met the songwriter Mitchell Parish, who later observed, "composers, lyricists, bandleaders, singers [and] vaudevillians would come and sit around and talk. . . . That's how writers got to meet each other. And songs happened to be written that way."

In August 1923, Ellington and the band appeared on the New York City radio station WDT. They were part of a blues program, sharing the bill with singers Trixie Smith (accompanied by Fats Waller) and Rosa Henderson (accompanied by Fletcher Henderson [no relation]). The advertisement in the *Pittsburgh Courier* listed the band as "Bruce Ellington [sic] and his Serenaders Orchestra."

Besides acquainting Ellington with the New York musical scene, Maceo Pinkard also introduced him to the next person to give him a boost up the ladder, the dancer and choreographer Leonard Harper. Harper was born the same year and month as Ellington. With nineteen years of theatrical experience under his belt, Harper was no show business neophyte.

Harper began dancing when he was four or five years old, in his hometown, Birmingham, Alabama. His excellent voice brought him to the attention of the Baptist church choir director, and he was soon a featured soloist. Harper, his brother Jean, and a contemporary, Dave Schaffe, were such a clever trio of child dancers that they were hired to perform in traveling revues.

In his teens, Harper toured in the family vaudeville houses of the East and Midwest as the male member and solo dancer of a trio billed as Venable, Harper, and Owens. Following this, Harper became a partner of the legendary black producer Bob Russell in a traveling stock company. He also served as juvenile lead.

In 1918, Harper moved to Chicago, where he met his future wife, Oceola Blanks, of the Blanks Sisters vaudeville team. The couple became famous locally as the dancing team of Harper & Blanks, and soon eastern booking agents discovered their act. Engagements for the Loew's Keith and Shubert theater circuits had the duo on the road for most of the year. Tiring of the constant travel, the couple returned to Chicago. It was then that Harper's career as a producer began. He started teaching dancing and training choruses for nightclub revues such as *Lucky Sambo*, *4-11-14*, and *Jimmy Cooper's Revue*.

Harper created *Plantation Days* (unrelated to the *Plantation Revue*) to make use of the chorus girls from his first show at the elegant Green Mills Gardens on Chicago's Gold Coast. The production had a very successful tour of the major theaters in the Midwest and the East, climaxed by a record-breaking run at the Empire Theater in London.

According to Greer, Ellington met Harper during their first week at Barron's nightclub. Harper had recently returned from Europe and was commissioned to stage the revue that was to open Connie's Inn. The brothers George and Connie Immerman, two white men born and raised in Harlem, had decided to parlay their success in the delicatessen business into a nightclub located in the basement of the Lafayette Theater.

The show was going into production, and Harper needed a daytime rehearsal pianist. He offered Ellington the job. The show opened on July 21, 1923, and was a great success. Oceola was the lead dancer, and Wilbur Sweatman's Acme Syncopators played the score and music for dancing.

Harper's name would become synonymous with Connie's Inn productions. He became the preeminent creator of floor shows for nearly every black nightclub in New York City, including the Cotton Club uptown, the Club Lido, the Club Richman, and the Plantation Cafe downtown. Such was his demand as a producer and choreographer that at one point in his career, he had four shows running simultaneously: Connie's Inn; the Carleton Terrace in Brooklyn; Ciro's; and the Plantation.

Harper's greatest triumph was Connie's *Hot Chocolates*, staged at the Hudson Theater during the summer and fall of 1929. The hit songs from the show, "Ain't Misbehavin'" and "Black and Blue," were written by Fats Waller and Andy Razaf. Louis Armstrong, Cab Calloway, and Edith Wilson were featured artists.

In 1934, Harper was in Chicago staging the *Grand Terrace Revue*, the *Royal Frolics*, and the show at Club Mid-Night. The following year, Frank Schiffman took over the Apollo Theater and brought Harper back to New York as staff producer. Geraldine Lockhart, who worked in several of Harper's New York productions, told the author that Harper was an excellent teacher and choreographer. Like most producers, he preferred to hire tall women with long legs. His routines were fast-paced, stately, with just a hint of sex. "He could teach an elephant to dance," she said.

Despite his brilliance as a creator of floor shows throughout the twenties and thirties, his frequent "spot productions" of set pieces for white Broadway revues (such as *The Passing Show*), as well as his coaching of many white performers, Leonard Harper never got the call from Hollywood. Lockhart recalled that when Busby Berkeley movies were shown in Harlem theaters, she would attend with many of the dancers Harper had trained. "We used to laugh out loud at what he was doing. We knew Leonard could do it a lot better. Had he been white, he'd been in Hollywood by then." But Harper would remain a nightclub choreographer until he dropped dead on a Harlem street in 1943.

Working as Harper's rehearsal pianist had several benefits for Ellington. As soon as Ellington's wife, Edna, heard he was working, she began pressuring him to bring her to New York. Harper and Oceola had recently rented a six-room flat at 2067 Seventh Avenue. Hardwick rented one of the rooms, and the couple offered to sublet one to Ellington and his wife. Edna was tall, good-looking, and an excellent dancer, and when she arrived, the producer took one look at her and put her to work as a showgirl in one of his productions.

Mercer remained in Washington with his grandparents. When he came to visit his parents, the three of them lived in one room. There was a couch for him and a bed for his parents. If he awoke before his parents and wanted to go anywhere, he had to go down to the street. There was no place in the house for him to play.

Ellington's salary at Barron's was quite respectable for the times, and he already owned a house in Washington. But he and Edna were living at Harper's place not for financial reasons, but because Harlem had become de facto segregated. From 1900 to 1923, the population increased from 60,000 to 150,000. This meant that the inhabitants, 60 percent of them black, found themselves crammed into an area of seven square miles.

The cramped living was of little consequence to the musicians, because Harlem's night life was their reality. Ellington said bars were open around the clock at that time, because there were no regulations about closing times. At three or four in the morning, musicians would be out with their horns, making the rounds, looking for a place to play. "The average musician in Harlem hated to go home those days," Greer said. "Someplace, somewhere 'cats' were jamming, and nobody wanted to miss anything."

The drummer Manzie Johnson lived and worked in Harlem during those years. He said that most of the time they would jam from four to six or seven o'clock in the morning. During the warm weather, the corner of Lenox Avenue and 135th Street became a regular musicians' hangout. They would stand around for hours talking about music and musicmakers. "That was our entire world," Johnson said.

The last week in July 1923, Snowden's quintet left Barron's because Wilkins closed the place for renovations. During the first two weeks in August, the band was at the Music Box in Atlantic City. In a way, the job was a short vacation for them. Thanks to Leonard Harper, they would be working downtown on Broadway in September. The success of the Connie's Inn show led to Harper's being hired to produce a revue for the Hollywood Cafe, located at Broadway and 49th Street.

The management was looking for a band with a quiet, intimate style of playing. With Harper's glowing recommendation, they were hired on the spot. Snowden booked them as the "Washington Black Sox Orchestra," with a six-month contract, beginning the first of September.

However, before the engagement began, a historic change was made in the band. After the last night at Barron's, trumpeter Arthur Whetsol went home to Washington to enter Howard University, and a replacement had to be found. The man chosen was James Wesley "Bubber" Miley, Ellington's first great musical influence and collaborator.

5

"BUBBER MILEY WAS a skinny guy, with a lot of gold in his mouth," was the way Luis Russell remembered him. "He spent his money as fast as he made it, and acted as though he didn't have a care in the world. But when he put that horn in his mouth and played the blues, nobody, I mean nobody could touch him."

Miley was born in Aiken, South Carolina, in 1903. In 1909, his family moved to New York City and settled on West 63rd Street. The area, known as San Juan Hill, antedated Harlem as a black community. It was the spawning ground for many famous black musicians. Benny Carter, a bandleader and arranger, was born there. He remembered being thrilled as a teenager when Miley allowed him to carry his trumpet to the Broadway subway station.

Bobby Stark, who would later grace the trumpet sections of McKinney's Cotton Pickers, the Fletcher Henderson Orchestra, and Chick Webb's band, was a resident. James P. Johnson lived there after moving to New York. Three future Ellingtonians, Joe Nanton, Freddie Jenkins, and Russell Procope, grew up there, as did the pianist Thelonius Monk. In the early 1960s, however, the area was razed to make way for the Lincoln Center for the Performing Arts.

Miley's father, Valentine, a carpenter by trade, was also an amateur guitarist. His mother, as well as his three sisters—Connie, Rose, and Murdis—were singers. In the 1930s the sisters formed a singing group called the South Carolina Trio and performed on radio as "Six Hundred Pounds of Rhythm."

As a young child, Miley began singing in backyards for pennies, and later with a friend, Arthur Sanford, ventured to Broadway to sing and dance for coins. He was caught by a truant officer and enrolled in P.S. 141, on West 58th Street. Miley began studying the trombone, but soon switched to cornet and joined the school band. At age fifteen, he joined the Navy as a band boy, serving for eighteen months. Following his discharge, he joined the Carolina Five, working on 53rd Street at

Purdy's and later at Dupre's cabaret. In early 1921, Miley joined Willie Gant's band and remained with it until the fall, when blues singer Mamie Smith signed him on as a member of her band, the Jazz Hounds.

Although Mamie Smith was famous for her rendition of "Crazy Blues," compared with Bessie Smith, Ma Rainey, or Victoria Spivey, she was not a true blues singer. However, she surrounded herself with excellent musicians. Willie "the Lion" Smith (piano), Coleman Hawkins (tenor saxophone) Garvin Bushell (clarinet, saxophone, and flute), Charlie Irvis (trombone), and the premiere trumpet player of the day, Johnny Dunn, were a major part of Smith's musical retinue. On several of her recordings, she was accompanied by the pianist Harvey Brooks, whose playing had once inspired the teenaged Ellington to return to studying the instrument.

When he joined the Jazz Hounds, Miley was strongly influenced by Johnnie Dunn. Later that year, the band worked in Chicago, where they heard cornetist Joe "King" Oliver's Creole Jazz Band at the Dreamland Ballroom. Garvin Bushell accompanied Miley that evening. He recounted the impact the New Orleans musicians had on the two of them. The trumpet and clarinet players in the East had a more "legitimate" sound on their instruments. But the sound of the Oliver men, while less cultivated, was more expressive of how people *felt*, especially when they played blues. "Bubber and I stood there with our mouths open," Bushell said.

What impressed Miley the most was Oliver's use of "blue" notes and mutes to alter the sound of his horn. According to Buster Bailey, with an ordinary tin mute, "the King could make the horn talk." Mutt Carey remembered him on occasion using a cup, glass, or bucket as a mute. Hearing Oliver had a profound effect on Miley. Bushell said that after that night, Miley changed his style and began using his hand over the tin mute that came with all the cornets.

Miley left Mamie Smith's Jazz Hounds in the fall of 1922 and worked very hard developing a style based on what he had heard in Chicago. That winter, Miley and his close friend Charlie Irvis could be found at O'Connor's Royal Cafe experimenting with mutes, plungers, and anything else that would alter the sound of their horns. Irvis once even used an old tomato can.

Other Harlem musicians began to emulate Oliver. By the late 1920s, a mute and plunger were part of many trumpet players' armamentarium. Miley was not alone. At various times, Sidney DeParis, Ward Pinkett, and Cladys "Jabbo" Smith played in Charlie Johnson's band. Chick Webb's band had Bobby Stark, and Cecil Scott had Frankie Newton. What set Miley apart from his contemporaries was that he used a cornet mute in the bell of his trumpet, as well as a plunger; he also growled from his throat as he played, a technique he picked up from Johnny Dunn. The fusion of these effects gave him a unique style.

Miley continued to refine his craft while a member of the house band at Reisenweber's on Columbus Circle. A tour with the *Sunny South* revue followed. When he was not working, he could be found sitting in with Willie "the Lion" Smith's band at the Capitol Palace. It was here that the Washingtonians first heard him play.

Another tour with Mamie Smith followed before Miley joined her entourage in Atlantic City. By this time, Miley had superseded Oliver in the ability to produce a variety of sounds on his instrument. A gifted melodist, his use of the growl, mute, and plunger—within the context of a solo in any tempo—gave his music a melancholy, introspective quality that would not be heard again until thirty years later with the advent of Miles Davis, another master of musical understatement.

Miley's style never changed over his lifetime. The low-key, muted sense of nuance, sound, and rhythm withstood the pyrotechnics of Louis Armstrong, who exploded on the musical scene a year later. Miley's style made him an ideal instrumentalist to back up singers. In 1921, he began accompanying Mamie Smith. Two years later, Clarence Williams brought Miley, Charlie Irvis, Sidney Bechet, and Buddy Christian into the studio to accompany Bessie Smith on her first recording date. They worked on "I Wish I Could Shimmy Like My Sister Kate," which was never issued.

By the end of 1926, Miley had been in recording studios at least twenty times, to accompany such singers as Alberta Hunter, Kitty Brown, Ida Cox, Lillian Goodner, Helen Gross, Rosa Henderson, Mary Jackson, Margaret Johnson, Sara Martin, Viola McCoy, Josie Miles, Julia Moody, Hazel Myers, Alberta Perkins, Nellie Potter, Clementine Smith, Eva Taylor, and Louise Vant. As late as 1928, Miley and James P. Johnson accompanied Martha Copeland on a recording date.

When not playing for singers, Miley recorded with a group known as the Six Black Diamonds. In June 1923, he played second trumpet to Johnny Dunn with Bradford's "Jazz Phools," on their recording "Daybreak Blues," while Perry Bradford and Clarence Williams used him on several band recordings from 1923 to 1926. Miley and the organist Arthur Ray joined forces in October 1924 and recorded "Lenox Avenue Shuffle" and "Down in the Mouth Blues" as the Texas Blues Destroyers.

When Miley returned from touring with Mamie Smith at the end of July 1923, the Capitol Palace was closed, and he happily accepted the Washingtonians' invitation to join them in Atlantic City. From opening night, Miley's down-and-dirty trumpet playing stood in stark relief to Whetsol's gentle lyricism. That, coupled with his first-rate jazz solos, immediately changed the character of the band. As Ellington recollected, "Bubber used to growl and play gutbucket on his horn all night. That was when we decided to forget about sweet music." When the job was over, the musicians decided they wanted Miley in the band permanently. According to Hardwick, a few nights later they went up to the Capitol Palace and "got Bubber stiff [drunk], and when he came to he was in a tuxedo growling at the Hollywood on Broadway."

The club was located in the basement of 1157 Broadway, in a space that was formerly the Palais de Dance. The room did not live up to its glamorous name; it seated no more than 100, and the bandstand was very small, with room for only six musicians, but not for the piano, which stood on the floor. When a visiting musician sat in with them, he would take a chair from one of the front tables, turn it to face the audience, and play from there. According to Greer, the place was always thick with smoke and dank from the rain. When seated at the drums, his head was within inches of the ceiling.

Nevertheless, it was downtown, on Broadway, where the action was. The Winter Garden was up the street, and above it, the Plantation Cafe. The Strand Theater, its Roof Garden, and the Columbia and Capitol theaters were across the street. Paul Whiteman was holding forth one block south at the Palais Royale. Greer said that by the time they got to work, the place was always packed with customers, along with prostitutes, musicians, and entertainers. It was also one of the few downtown places that made black musicians and entertainers feel welcome.

The band's engagement at the Hollywood began on September 1, 1923. They played until midnight, when Harper's *Dixie Revue* went on; then the show repeated at 2 A.M. Following the band's debut, every Wednesday at 3:45 A.M. members would broadcast from radio station WHN in the nearby Loew's State Theater building. The *Clipper* reported that several Broadway cabarets were sending bands to the radio station to plug their nightly entertainment. Besides the Washingtonians, "a colored band from the Hollywood Cafe," the California Ramblers, and orchestras from the Strand Roof and the Clover Gardens made the trip.

Reviewer Abel Green at the *Clipper* was particularly impressed by Miley, calling him "a trumpet player who never need doff his chapeau to any cornetist in the business. He extracts the eeriest sort of modulations and 'singing' notes heard."

John Anderson, who doubled on trombone and trumpet, and Roland Smith, who played saxophone and bassoon, joined the band. Snowden was the leader, playing banjo and doubling on soprano saxophone; Hardwick played alto saxophone and violin; Greer played drums and sang; Miley, besides playing cornet, doubled on mellophone; and Ellington was listed as pianist and arranger. On October 18, they returned to the Victor studios. Besides re-recording "Home," they also recorded another Pinkard tune, "M. T. Pocket Blues." The personnel on that date included the original Washingtonians, including Miley and his close friend Charlie Irvis on trombone.

In December, Greer told the Hollywood Club's management that the band expected a raise when the contract came up for renegotiation. Management told him that the band had already received two salary increases since the engagement began. According to Mercer Ellington, Snowden, who was in charge of business matters, immediately resigned. Greer then took over the band and passed it on to Ellington. Notwithstanding Snowden's decision to leave the group, Ellington was quietly being drawn into the leadership of the band. Because the group had turned to him in times of stress, it was only a matter of time before the mantle of leadership would be passed to him. Hardwick remembered, "Even then we were pulling for Duke. He had everyone on his side. He was that kind of guy." The following week Hardwick, Ellington, and Greer took out an ad in the *Clipper*.

WASHINGTONIANS
Combination of Symphonic Jazz
Plus Versatility

Now Playing At The Hollywood
Cafe, New York City

Where The Professional Musician
Makes His Rendezvous

Roland Smith and John Anderson went uptown with Snowden to work at the Bamville Club on Lenox Avenue and 129th Street. George Francis replaced Snowden on banjo. Miley's close friend Charlie Irvis replaced Anderson; they had played in the same school band.

Born in Harlem, Irvis had joined blues singer Lucille Hegamin's Blue Flame Syncopators in 1920. The following year Willie "the Lion" Smith brought Irvis into his band at the Capitol Palace. When Smith left to join the *Holiday in Dixieland* revue, Irvis remained behind as a member of the house band. He joined the Washingtonians in the first week of January 1924.

Ellington felt that Irvis was vastly underrated. He played in a different register of his horn, using a unique device to produce his signature sound. At the time there was a mute available that would make a trombone sound like a saxophone. One night Irvin accidentally dropped it, and it broke into several pieces. He picked up the biggest piece and began using it. Ellington said it sounded better than the original. Irvis was able to produce an elegant sound at the bottom of the trombone—melodic, masculine, and full of authority. Ellington often said he wished he could find a musician to make that sound again.

The band's contract was renewed for four months. However, several weeks into the run, the first of a series of accidental fires closed the club for a few weeks, and the band found itself out of work. Ordinarily, this would be considered a bit of hard luck for a band, especially at that time of the year. For Ellington, it was the reverse. Because of the hiatus, he met the man who would give him his next boost up the ladder, the impresario Charlie Shribman.

Shribman owned the Charleshurst Ballroom in Salem, Massachusetts. Along with his brother, Sy, he ran an active band-booking agency that began bringing New York bands to New England in 1921. In 1924, the Shribmans joined with other ballroom managers in Massachusetts, Connecticut, Rhode Island, and Maine to form a "circuit" that planned to feature the best bands available. On this circuit, a band would have its headquarters in one town and would drive to play one-nighters in other dance halls in nearby towns. While the musicians were constantly on the move, the changing music menu kept up the interest of the customers, who now had a different band to dance to every night.

It is unclear how Ellington and his men were brought to Shribman's attention, but on Easter Monday 1924, the Washingtonians were playing a dance for the Salem, Massachusetts, Young Men's Christian Temperance Society. The band appeared in Boston and Lynn, Massachusetts, on a vaudeville bill at the Waldorf Theater. As the *Salem Evening News* reported, the Washingtonians' appearance was "the biggest sensation in the history of the theater."

On April 25, 1924, the band appeared at the College Inn in Salem, sharing the bill with Frank Ward's Boston Orchestra. The following day, the group returned to New York. Throughout his life, Ellington always acknowledged his debt to Shribman. Ellington said that Shribman turned up "at a crossroad in his life to tell him which way to go."

The Hollywood reopened in May 1924, and the band became part of a revue that featured the noted black mime Johnny Hudgins. At this point, Ellington's ambition to be a songwriter finally paid off. He and songwriting partner Jo Trent were still going downtown several times a week to demonstrate their wares to music publishers. Trent would sing and Ellington would accompany him. One afternoon, Trent's employer, Fred Fischer, heard their song "Pretty Soft For You," offered them $50 for it, and told them to leave the lead sheet with his secretary.

This posed a problem for Ellington. Because he had never sold a song before, he had never needed to write out the music. It was late afternoon and he knew the music publisher would close at five, but he did what he had to do. He explained, "In spite of ten pianos banging away in ten different booths, I sat down and made a lead sheet. It was satisfactory, we took the money, split it and split the scene." The ability to write music in the middle of chaos and under pressure was a talent Ellington would develop into a fine art over his lifetime. He would often say he needed the urgency of a deadline to motivate him.

One night in June, pioneering saxophonist Sidney Bechet dropped by the club and sat in with the band. He was a friend of Leo Bernstein, one of the owners of the Hollywood. Miley, Bechet, and Irvis began jamming. They created a stir and Bernstein insisted that Ellington hire him. Bechet joined the band playing clarinet and soprano saxophone, and accompanied the band on a trip to New England in July. According to Greer, "He fitted out the band like a glove."

Bechet did more than that; ultimately, he became the dominant personality of the group. A few days after his arrival, the band went to the Palais Royale down the street from the Hollywood to play a benefit. Ross Gorman led the house band there, and when the Washingtonians came on, they stopped the show. Greer said, "Bechet, Charlie, and Bubber came down front. [Bechet] cut [outplayed] everybody, Ross Gorman's band, everybody. When he had finished, the manager of the place came up to Gorman and said, 'Play waltzes. Don't play any more jazz.'"

Bechet's florid, exuberant style of playing completely overshadowed that of the group, so much that it was only a matter of time before his musical personality would clash with those of the rest of the band. Miley and Irvis, whose style of playing was more low-key, began to resent him. They felt that his New Orleans style was taking the band in a different direction with less emphasis on the ensemble. His suggestion to management that the band be billed as the "Washingtonians, featuring Sidney Bechet" did not sit well with the other band members, either.

Many years later, Bechet told an interviewer that he got along well with Ellington, but was at loggerheads with Irvis and Miley. He was particularly angry at Miley. Shortly after the band returned from New England, the trumpet player didn't show up for work. He sent word that he was being held at Toombs prison on a paternity charge and needed someone to put up cash for his bail. Greer said, "Sidney reached into his pocket, pulled out two hundred-dollar bills, gave them to one of the busboys, and told him take a cab downtown and bail Bubber out. He felt that after that, Bubber owed him some respect. Bubber was grateful for what he did, but that didn't mean he was going to let him take over the band."

Strife among the band members was compounded by Bechet's insistence on bringing Goola, his full-grown German shepherd, to the job every night. Ultimately, though, it was Bechet's unreliability that cost him the job. He missed work three days in a row. When Bechet finally showed up at the club, Ellington, who already had his hands full with Miley's occasional disappearances, demanded to know where he had been. "I jumped in a cab, we got lost, and I just now found out where I was," Bechet responded. They parted amicably.

During Bechet's tenure with the band, the group had given up rearranging stock compositions, and the communal spirit typical of the later Ellington works was evolving. Bechet observed:

> At that time Otto, Duke and myself used to go over to the piano, talk [about] how we were going to build this thing with all the band. Duke, he'd be making arrangements for the band—not this kind of hit-parade arrangements I had been saying about, but a kind of dividing of the piece, placing its parts. What we were after, it was to get the *feeling* for the band playing it together. That way the music was working for itself.

Ellington's collaboration and friendship with Jo Trent began to pay off during three recording dates beginning in November 1924 for the Blu-Disk Company. For the first session, Ellington and Greer accompanied Alberta Prime, a cabaret singer who performed in her own clubs. She was to record two of Trent's songs, "It's Gonna Be a Cold, Cold Winter" and a novelty, "Parlor Social Deluxe." On the former, Ellington's voice can be heard as he murmurs "poor thing" during the patter section, in mock sympathy with the singer's tale of woe. On the latter, Prime and Greer share the vocal. The drummer banters with the singer as they do a studio recreation of a Harlem Saturday night rent party, complete with police whistles and gunshots.

A week later, Ellington, Hardwick, Francis, and Greer were in the studio to accompany Trent. Billed as "Jo Trent and the Deacons," they recorded his song "Deacon Jazz." On this recording, Trent sings with enthusiasm, but little technique. He sounds just like what he was: a songwriter singing his own material. On the reverse side, Greer steps front and center to sing a popular song of the day, "Oh How I Love My Darling." It had been recorded earlier by the Phil Napoleon and Adrian Rollini bands. The drummer sings in a tenor voice, with enthusiastic backing from the band.

The third session had Ellington and Hardwick back in the studio, accompanying Florence Bristol singing another popular song of the day, "How Come You Do Me Like You Do." Not much is known about her. The recording appeared to be an audition for her and the deep-voiced young man singing on the reverse side, Paul Robeson. Accompanied by William Jones, he sang a simple ballad by J. Rosamund Johnson titled "Since You Went Away."

The management then offered the band a session on their own. They chose to record two popular tunes, Ellington's composition "Choo-Choo" and "Rainy Nights." "Choo-Choo," a novelty song, was gaining popularity. The Ambassadors had recorded it the previous month, and several companies were in the process of issuing versions by the Original Memphis Five, Earl Randolph's Orchestra, and the Goofus Five.

During this period, all recording companies used the acoustic method to capture sound on disc. The musicians played into a megaphone coming out of the control room. The piano had a megaphone of its own, and if drums were used, they were muffled by a blanket or quilt. Needless to say, this method of recording was hardly adequate to capture the true sound of any band.

Listening to the recordings sixty-five years later, it is clear that Ellington took "Choo-Choo" seriously. This was probably the beginning of his use of his orchestra to musically recreate train travel. He begins with Irvis's simulation of a train leaving the station. George Francis provides the bell with tremolo chords on his banjo, and at the recording's end, Irvis, Miley, and Hardwick play a minor chord that is answered by Greer tooting an actual train whistle.

Trent was listed as one of the composers of "Rainy Nights." On the recording, Hardwick, Irvis, and Miley stay fairly close to the melody, rather than improvising around it during their solos. These recordings make it clear how Miley was the dominant personality in the band. His musicianship surpassed the contributions of Ellington and Hardwick. Charlie Irvis was the only one who could hold his own with him.

During this month, Fletcher Henderson recorded "Naughty Man." The composition, credited to Don Redman and Charlie Dixon was, in fact, Redman's arrangement of "Rainy Night." Henderson played the work with a faster tempo, and Redman's arrangement is superior to Ellington's. But when it comes to the trumpet solos, Miley more than holds his own with the twenty-four-year-old Louis Armstrong. Armstrong's solo is a predecessor for what would come two years later in his "Hot Five" and "Hot Seven" recordings, namely, rhythmic exuberance and use of the entire range of his horn. Miley's solo is understated as usual, and he makes his musical points using the growl and mute.

Despite a prime location on Broadway, the Hollywood was still not doing well. The managers took steps to recoup their losses. Another "accidental" fire closed the club in January 1925. As Greer recounted, "Right after New Year's, one of the owners told me to take my drums home that night. I said, 'Boss you don't think there's gonna be another fire, do you!' He just looked at me. I called a cab and got my drums out of there real fast."

When the dust had settled, the band was promised its job back. The club was scheduled to reopen in April. Once again, what appeared to be bad luck worked to the band's advantage. Charlie Shribman was looking for a group to replace the popular Mal Hallett, who was then working in Haverhill, Massachusetts. Hallett had been booked for an engagement at New York's Arcadia Ballroom. When Shribman heard that the Washingtonians were available, he brought them to Haverhill to fill in for a month.

The engagement went well. The *Haverhill Evening Gazette* wrote that the band played a dance at City Hall on February 4, 1925, and were seen "as the equal to Mal Hallett." Shribman also brought them back for one-night stands several times during the year. According to *Variety,* the band subsequently played in Haverhill on March 4 and 11, April 8 and 29, May 27, and July 8.

The band returned to New York in the first week in March 1925 and was booked for its first Harlem theater engagement. The group shared the bill at the Lincoln Theater with the singer Gertrude Sanders; the Brown and McGraw Fast Steppers; the Three Danubes; Riggo and Dorothy; and Wilson, Wiles, and their Midget. The following week, Ellington suddenly found himself in the position of having to compose the music for a show overnight.

"Jo Trent came running up to me on Broadway," he remembered. "He had an urgency to his voice. Tonight we have to write the music for a show, *tonight!* Being dumb and not knowing better, I sat down that evening and wrote a show." The songs, "Jig Walk," "Jim Dandy," "With You," "Love is Just a Wish (for You)," and "Yam Brown" were written for the revue *Chocolate Kiddies.*

The next day, they played the music for the publisher Jack Robbins, who bought it. Another song was needed, so they tossed in "Deacon Jazz." Later in his life, Ellington said, "How was I to know composers had to go up to the mountain or the seashore or commune with the muses to write a show?" His self-deprecation should not blind us to the fact that the tension of a deadline had already become an integral part of his creative life.

Chocolate Kiddies opened in May 1925 at the Admiral's Palace in Berlin, Germany. The young Brooklyn-born singer Adelaide Hall was one of the featured performers, along with singers Lottie Gee and Margaret Simms, and the dancers Arthur "Strut" Payne, the Three Eddies, Arthur Bryson, and George Staton. The revue also featured an acrobatic team, Bobby and Baby Goins; a chorus of eleven; and Sam Wooding's eleven-piece band, which played in the pit. *Chocolate Kiddies* presented European audiences with a variety of African-American music, dance, and comedy. Following an overture, Act I opened with "Night Life in a Negro Cafe in Harlem in New York." "Deacon Jazz" was the first song the audience heard, describing the irresistible force of the music. It was sung by Adelaide Hall and the *Chocolate Kiddies* chorus. Wooding's band gave a "symphonic jazz" concert in Act II, and three more Ellington tunes turned up in Act III: "Jim Dandy (A Strut Dance)," "With You," and "Jig Walk," to which the ensemble danced the current craze, the Charleston. These four songs were only a small part of the show as it was presented in Europe, but they clearly had an impact on the audience.

Garvin Bushell, who played with the band, remembered how Ellington's music was received. "They were calling for encores. 'With You,' sung by Lottie Gee, took about three, and 'Jig Walk,' they just couldn't get over that. . . . It was the hit of the show."

The audience liked Ellington's music, but Wooding chose not to record any of it because he was more interested in recording already-popular songs. While in Berlin, on July 20, the band did a session for the Vox recording company. Wooding chose "O Katherina" (a favorite in Germany), "Alabamy Bound," "Shanghai Shuffle," and "By the Waters of Minnetonka" (in both 10-inch and 12-inch 78-rpm versions).

Several Ellington songs were recorded by Europeans as well. In August, Bernard Ette's dance orchestra recorded "Love Is Just a Wish (for You)" in Berlin for Vox. The song was also recorded by Andreozzi's South American Orchestra in Berlin later that year and released by the German Schallplatte Gramophone Company. In October, Odeon released "Jim Dandy" by the Hungarian bandleader Dajos Bela. Although Europeans had begun to take an interest in Ellington's music, there is no indication that Ellington knew of the European recordings.

Besides playing to sold-out performances at the Thalia in Hamburg and the Cirkus in Copenhagen, the show toured many other cities on the Continent, as well as England, Russia, and South America. While the show was in Stockholm, Bushell and Wooding went to the royal palace to play some of the music for the crown prince. In Spain, the king and queen saw the show several times. When the troupe finally returned home in 1927, Jack Robbins was a wealthy man. Trent and Ellington had split $500 between them, having sold the music outright. But as a result of the show, there were greater dividends than money in store for the young musician. By the end of summer, news of the success of *Chocolate Kiddies* and Ellington's songs began drifting back to New York, bringing Ellington to the attention of two of the country's best-trained black musicians, Will Marion Cook and Will Vodery. They would teach the unschooled young musician the art and craft of musical composition.

6

ELLINGTON DESCRIBED HIM as "Will Marion Cook, His Majesty the King of Consonance." Cook was born in Washington, D.C., in 1869, to graduates of Oberlin College. His father was a professor at, and later dean of, Howard University Law School. As a child, Cook's talent on the violin was soon obvious to anyone who heard him play. When he was thirteen, his parents sent him to live with an aunt in Ohio while he studied at the Oberlin Conservatory. After his second year, he was urged by his teacher to continue his training at the Berlin *Hochshule für Musik*. On returning home, he gave a concert at the First Congregational Church. Frederick Douglass sponsored the event and raised enough money from Washington's leading blacks to allow the young Cook to study abroad for three more years.

In Berlin, Cook studied with the celebrated teacher Josef Joachim, a close friend of the composer Johannes Brahms. Cook remained in Berlin for nine years, mastering the fundamentals of the violin and music theory. He returned home in 1893, intending to become a concert virtuoso. He brought with him a letter of introduction from Joachim to the Czech composer Anton Dvořák, who was directing the National Conservatory in New York City. Joachim's letter gained Cook entree into Dvořák's class on musical composition. Cook's fellow students included the future composers Rubin Goldmark and Harvey Worthington Loomis.

Two years later, at the age of twenty-six, Cook made his solo debut at Carnegie Hall. The reviewers hailed him as the "the greatest *colored* [italics added] violinist in the world." Deeply stung by the racist limitation on his achievement, Cook vowed never to play the instrument publicly again, and he never did. At the same time, he found himself drawn more and more to the exciting possibility of the genius of purely "black expression" in American music.

Cook received encouragement from Dvořák, who could not understand why American composers did not embrace their native folk music, especially that of blacks. "In the Negro melodies of America, I discover all that is needed for a great and noble school of music," Dvořák wrote. "They are pathetic, tender, passionate, melancholy, solemn, religious, bold, merry, gay or what you will. . . . There is nothing in the whole range of composition that cannot be supplied with themes from this source."

The composer knew of what he spoke. He and his countryman Bedrich Smetana had incorporated Czech folk music into their works, and the Russian nationalist composers—including Borodin, Rimsky-Korsakov, his friend Tchaikovsky, and others—were writing music reflecting their nation's ethnic roots.

Taking Dvořák's counsel to heart, Cook collaborated with the black poet Paul Laurence Dunbar in 1898 to write the first successful ragtime operetta, *Clorindy, or the Origin of the Cakewalk*. The show, featuring the well-known Ernest Hogan and forty performers, had a successful engagement at Broadway's Casino Roof Garden, and established Cook's reputation as a composer and music director. Two years later, he formed an association with the George Walker-Bert Williams theatrical company, where he served as music director and composer until the company folded in 1908. In a period of five years, Cook was involved in the productions of *The Sons of Ham* (1900), *In Dahomey* (1902), *The Southerners* (with a white cast and black chorus) (1904), and *In Abyssinia* (1905).

In Dahomey, which also featured a libretto by Dunbar, was the most noteworthy production of that collaboration. It opened at the New York Theater on February 18, 1903, for a run of fifty-three performances. On May 16 of that year, the show opened at the Shaftesbury Theatre in London to critical acclaim. The cast gave 250 performances in London over a period of seven months, capped with a command performance for King Edward VII on the lawn at Buckingham Palace. The show toured the provinces before returning to the United States in 1904.

The following year, Cook became involved with the Memphis Students, a singing and dancing troupe (organized by Ernest Hogan) that was making history with its "syncopated" music concerts at Hammerstein's Victoria Theater on Broadway. In October, he took the group abroad.

His classical training and superior musicianship made Cook the leading proponent of black music. He assumed the musical leadership of the rapidly developing Harlem community, organizing black choral societies and lecturing and writing about black music. Among his many accomplishments, Cook conducted "all black composers'" concerts, and collaborated with others to write musicals, including *The Traitors* (1912), *In Darkeydom* (1914), and *The Cannibal King* (1914).

In 1918, Cook organized the Southern Syncopated Orchestra, which toured throughout the country. The following year, the orchestra toured England, where it was asked to play a command performance for King George V at Buckingham Palace. During its engagement at Royal Philharmonic Hall, the band and one of its musicians became the subject of the first serious jazz review by a most unlikely person, Ernest Ansermet. The thirty-six-year-old mathematician-turned-conductor had made his reputation by championing the works of modern composers Debussy, Ravel, and especially Stravinsky.

"The first thing that strikes one about the Southern Syncopated Orchestra," wrote Ansermet in the Swiss music journal *Revue Romande*, "is the astonishing perfection, the superb taste, and the fervor of its playing. . . . Their form was gripping, abrupt and harsh with a brusque and pitiless ending like that of Bach's Second Brandenburg Concerto. . . . There is in the orchestra an extraordinary clarinet virtuoso who, it seems, is the first of his race to have composed perfectly formed blues on the clarinet. I wish to set down the name of this artist of genius, as I shall never forget it, Sidney Bechet."

Returning to the United States in 1922, Cook toured with the Clef Club Orchestra and continued to promote black music. One of his concerts featured a young black lawyer-turned-singer named Paul Robeson. Two years later, Cook's Negro Folk Music and Drama Society sponsored the concert series "Negro Nuances" at the Times Square Theater in New York, and the next year, "Virginia Nights," billed as "all Negro-music" programs, at a Greenwich Village theater.

Five years later, Cook served as musical advisor and chorus director for the Vincent Youmans production *Great Day*, and collaborated with Will Vodery to write and produce the musical *Swing Along* at the Lafayette Theater. Until Cook's death in 1944, he was the chief music advisor, teacher, and patron of many of New York's young black musicians.

When Ellington got to know Cook in the summer of 1925, Cook was a tall, handsome man with a shock of white hair. He was a familiar figure on Tin Pan Alley and was treated with great deference by all the music publishers, especially Mills Music. Ellington had a nodding acquaintance with Cook since their introduction by Maceo Pinkard the previous summer, but the success of *Chocolate Kiddies* gained Ellington entree into the inner circle of young musicians mentored by Cook.

Ellington's lessons with Cook took an unorthodox form. Ellington would plan to "accidentally" run into Cook downtown on Tin Pan Alley in the late afternoon. Ellington would then hail a cab and ask Cook to join him for the trip back to Harlem. "He and I would get in a taxi and ride around Central Park and he'd give me lectures in music," Ellington recounted. "I'd sing a melody in its simplest form and he'd stop me and say reverse your figures." Cook taught Ellington two things. The first was how to get the maximum effect from the music he chose to work with. This included such techniques as playing a melody backwards or upside down, repeating it lower or higher, or turning it inside out.

The other lesson Cook taught Ellington was far more important. It was to follow his *feelings*. Many times while Ellington was struggling with a composition, he would ask the older man for direction. Cook's response on one critical occasion was, "You know you should go to the conservatory, but since you won't, I'll tell you. First you find the logical way, and when you find it, avoid it and let your inner self break through and guide you. Don't try to be anybody but yourself." In other words, Cook directed Ellington to develop musical ideas in the context of traditional black folk music and blues, something Ellington was beginning to absorb from the thousands of hours he would spend playing with Miley and the rest of his Harlem contemporaries.

Cook had a strong influence on Ellington despite the relatively brief period they spent together. "[S]ome of the things he used to tell me I never got a chance to use until years later when I wrote the tone poem *Black, Brown and Beige*," Ellington wrote.

While Cook taught Ellington how to organize a musical canvas, it was Will Vodery, one of Cook's pupils and collaborators, who educated

Ellington in the art of mixing the various musical colors available from the instrumentalists in his orchestra.

Vodery, born in Philadelphia in 1885, was a gifted musician whose talents were apparent at an early age. He played organ at his family church when he was eight and then studied music with Henry Clark at the University of Pennsylvania. Following graduation, Vodery accepted a job as the librarian for the Chicago Symphony Orchestra and its conductor, Frederick Stock. He studied orchestration with Stock, and over time developed a reputation as a first-class arranger of musical scores.

Vodery moved to New York City in 1907. His first job was to orchestrate the music for the show *The Time, the Place, and the Girl*, starring Joe Howard, the white singer-composer who would write the sentimental favorite "I Wonder Who's Kissing Her Now" two years later. Vodery spent the next few years working as an arranger and conductor for a series of black musical revues, which culminated in a collaboration with J. Leubrie Hill on the musical *My Friend from Dixie* (1910).

During World War I, Vodery directed the 807th Pioneer Infantry Band. This sixty-seven-piece unit was widely known to have been a favorite of General Pershing. The band performed before the crowned heads of Belgium and Monaco, as well as the president of France. At the end of the war, Vodery returned to New York.

In 1922, Vodery orchestrated George Gershwin's first opera, *Blue Monday*. The one-act work was set in Harlem and staged as part of *George White's Scandals of 1922*. It was withdrawn after the first performance, but Gershwin would finally realize an opera based on the black experience thirteen years later in *Porgy and Bess*.

In 1923, Vodery led the Will Vodery Plantation Orchestra in the London productions of *Plantation Revue* and *Dover Street to Dixie*, the former choreographed by Leonard Harper. The following year Vodery led the orchestra in Lew Leslie's *Dixie to Broadway*. And in 1927, he prepared the chorus for Jerome Kern's *Showboat*.

With a show or two on Broadway every year, Vodery had developed a cadre of "audience boys," young musicians and orchestration students he would invite to watch rehearsals. He brought Ellington into this group in the fall of 1925.

In late 1929, Vodery went to California to become the first black musician to be staff arranger for the Fox studios. Ziegfeld died a year later, but Vodery remained in Hollywood, where he scored the music for the film *Virginia City*. He returned to New York in 1933, and that March his Will Vodery Singers appeared in the Broadway musical *Strike Me Pink*, featuring Eddie Cantor. Vodery then resumed his career as an orchestrator and musical consultant to Broadway producers until his death in 1951.

Ellington remembered that "Will Vodery was a strict and very precise musician. He would stand up and write an orchestration without a score." Vodery's musicianship was such that during a rehearsal for one show when a difficult change of key had to be made, he went through the orchestra from musician to musician, changing their parts individually. When he finished, he offered to pay five dollars for any wrong note. He had no takers.

"Sometimes he would bring one of his very legit arrangements and make the cats in our band play as though they, too, were legit," Ellington wrote. "He used to give me valuable lectures in orchestration. . . . His chromatic tendencies penetrated my ear and are largely responsible for the way I think music even today."

Ellington's ability to create rich, complex scores for his own orchestra can be traced directly to his lessons with Vodery. Vodery's orchestrations for the Broadway stage reflected his musical acquaintance with the giants of orchestral writing: Berlioz, Wagner, Rimsky-Korsakov, Strauss, Debussy, and Ravel. And Ellington absorbed something of Vodery's breadth of reference by listening to his work. Later in his career, Ellington built on this basic knowledge of classical music that he had distilled from Vodery.

Vodery also served as a role model for Ellington's developing sense of personal elegance. Vodery was a close friend of the great black comedian Bert Williams, one of the featured performers in the Ziegfeld *Follies*. Ellington wrote:

They were regularly seen together during the Ziegfeld period. Handsome, debonair, and always in gentlemanly attire, they were respected by everyone as they walked through the downtown streets. They patronized any place they chose in the Glitter Belt, even sometimes in the company of those gorgeous Ziegfeld beauties, and there was no sweat, no color compromise.

From the time of Ellington's birth, and for nearly sixty years, Washington, D.C., was considered a southern town. It was officially segregated by Woodrow Wilson in 1912. Vodery—whose acquaintances included white producers, musicians, singers, and dancers—may have given Ellington the message that it was possible to rise above segregation.

In 1943, Ellington was asked by *Metronome* magazine to name the best arrangers. He put Vodery first, in a short list that included Benny Carter, and it is very possible that *Metronome*'s editors had no idea who Ellington was talking about. Vodery and Cook, along with J. Rosamund Johnson, were outstanding musicians who were able to integrate classical training, black music, and black show business with white popular music and productions. Their musicianship won them influence in both black and white circles. They used this authority to infuse spirituals, plantation songs, ragtime, and blues into Broadway shows and concert music.

Alain Locke, the philosopher and chronicler of the Harlem Renaissance, wrote that these men "organized Negro music out of a broken, musically-illiterate dialect and made it a national and international music." In 1936, he observed that even the black artists who performed this music did not realize its "revolutionary musical significance."

7

When the band returned to the Hollywood Club in mid-April 1925, the group discovered that the club had been enlarged and renamed. The owners chose the Club Kentucky (although everyone called it the Kentucky Club) to conjure up images of the Old South. Anxious to increase business, the owners wanted to emphasize the club's most distinctive feature: the black musicians who played there.

There were also important changes in the band. Prince Robinson joined the band on saxophone and Henry "Bass" Edwards on tuba. George Francis left and was replaced by the man who helped them when they needed it the most: banjoist Freddie Guy.

Virginia-born Prince Robinson was a mainly self-taught musician who had been playing since he was fourteen. His professional career began in 1919 with Lillian Jones's Jazz Hounds and continued in 1922 with Quentin Redd's band in Atlantic City. The following year, he went to New York City to join Lionel Howard's Musical Aces before joining Ellington in the spring of 1925. Luis Russell remembered him as an excellent section man who soloed well on either the clarinet or the saxophone.

Henry "Bass" Edwards began playing tuba in his native Atlanta at age fourteen in a band sponsored by the local Odd Fellows Hall. He went on to major in music at Atlanta University and played in the 305th Artillery Band during World War I. Moving to Philadelphia after the war, he played in several concert orchestras, as well as in Madame I. O. Keene's Dance orchestra. He joined the Charlie Taylor band in 1921, and remained with it until 1923, when he was summoned to Atlantic City by Sam Wooding.

While in Atlantic City, Edwards caught the eye of Charlie Johnson, who brought him to Harlem that fall, when his band opened at Smalls Paradise. When Edwards joined Ellington, he was the best-trained musician in the band. He switched to string bass in 1933 and, two years later, left the band to play with light and classical orchestras.

According to Walter Johnson, Fletcher Henderson's drummer, Edwards was a superior musician. If Edwards had been white, Johnson believed, he could have held down a chair in a major symphony orchestra.

During Edwards's tenure with Ellington, he was considered an excellent jazz soloist. Greer remembered Edwards as "a big guy with blinker lights in his sousaphone, and he'd call for four or five choruses, just like a trumpet player and play them all different. As a soloist, he could hold his own with Bubber anytime."

Freddie Guy explained that when Ellington approached him, he was "working with a fellow called John Smith who was getting a lot of work. I told Duke that he'd have to wait for a while. I finally went with the band in time for their opening at the Kentucky Club. I even took a cut in pay to join."

Greer said, "Freddie had a right arm like a metronome. Of all the banjo and guitar players I ever worked with, he could keep that beat rock-steady, and Duke used to say when he hit a chord you heard every note."

In a band that had its collection of heavy drinkers and general cutups, Guy stood out for an unlikely reason: his sense of responsibility. He was always on time for work and didn't drink or gamble. "Out of the whole aggregation, whole band, Freddie was the sensible one," Barney Bigard said.

Luis Russell said that Guy and Ellington were two of the better dressers among the Harlem musicians: "In those days if you wanted to look sharp all you had to do was check what Duke and Freddie were wearing and buy something like it."

Guy remained with the band for twenty-five years and was Ellington's closest friend until he left. "For a while they lived in the same building," Greer said. "The were always in and out of each other's apartments, when they weren't out on the town together. Freddie got a lot of women just by hanging around with Duke."

During one of Ellington's visits to Mills Music in June, he found himself in a recording studio. Irving Mills and Jimmy McHugh had recently written a song titled "Everything Is Hotsy Totsy Now." The California Ramblers had recorded it in April, and the Original Indiana Five and Herb Weidoft issued versions the following month, when

Billboard noted that the song was "taking first place as the number one plug song of Jack Mills."

For some reason, the company decided to make a test recording of the song at the Gennett Studios on June 8, 1925. This collection of wordplay and infectious repetition was typical of the many inane lyrics of the 1920s. Accompanied by Ellington, Irving Mills played the kazoo with some aplomb and exuberantly sang the lyrics. In August, Mills took out a full-page ad in *Billboard* touting the song, and by September, *Variety* was referring to it as a "current dance favorite."

The Kentucky Club remained open through the summer, and Ellington and the band were part of a lavish revue featuring Bobby Burns Berman, singer and master of ceremonies; the popular singer Julia Gerrity; the dancer Hazel Goodrow; and Jean Gaynor, Billy Stout, and Gladys Sloan. The band was billed as the "Washingtonians, the hottest band this side of the equator."

A review in *Variety* described the band as one of the "best 'hot' colored combinations in town." And three weeks later, the publication was even more ecstatic, calling the band a "wow" and "Trojans for hard work."

George D. Lottman's review of the show in *Billboard* seemed to be responding to *Variety* when he wrote that the band was *not* just another "'hot' colored combination" but a professional ensemble that ranked with the best he knew. "Possessing a sense of rhythm that is almost uncanny, the boys in this dusky organization dispense a type of melody that stamps the outfit as the most torrid in town," Lottman said.

Perhaps as a result of the reviews in *Billboard* and *Variety*, the band left the club a few weeks later to go uptown to Harlem, where a new restaurant, the Cameo Club, had opened. However, the very music that had been considered "hot" downtown was seen as far too tepid for Harlem, and after the first night, the band was fired.

Greer said that everyone in the band but Ellington took the Cameo Club debacle badly. Somehow, Ellington remained stoic and his quiet self-assurance served as a beacon around which his seven musicians could rally. As Greer recounted, "He never let us lose confidence in ourselves; he kept telling us not to worry, something would turn up, and sure enough it did. Earl Dancer got us a gig with Ethel Waters, and a few weeks later the owners of the Kentucky Club called and offered us our old job back!"

The band returned to the Kentucky Club in late November 1925 to find that Bert Lewis had replaced Berman as the master of ceremonies. Entertaining during intermission was their old friend, pianist Fats Waller. Wearing a bejeweled turban and Eastern finery, he was billed as "Ali Baba, the Egyptian Wonder." It was because of Waller that Ellington's band played its first show at a major Broadway theater.

Waller's Kentucky Club booking flowed from his friendship with George H. "Captain" Maines, an influential downtown press agent. The room was one of Maines's clients, and Maines wanted to further the twenty-year-old Waller's career. To give Waller more exposure, Maines arranged a one-night stand for the Kentucky Club revue, including the Ellington band, at the New Amsterdam Theater on the night that the Ziegfeld *Follies* was dark. According to Waller's son, the show actually ran at the New Amsterdam one night a week for two months. *Billboard* said that Waller often sat in with the band when Ellington took a break.

Since its days as the Hollywood Club, the Kentucky Club had always advertised itself as the place "Where the Professional Musician Makes His Rendezvous." Only recently had it become the place for Broadway entertainers and musicians to go. "That was the first time I used to look forward to going to work," Greer said. "You never knew who would turn up. One night [George] Gershwin came in with the cast of his show [*Tip-Toes*] that opened that night, for a party."

Al Jolson, Oscar Shaw, Bobby Clark, Fanny Brice, Ruth Etting, and other Broadway stars frequented the house. One night the movie star Tom Mix, in full cowboy regalia, sat in on drums. The bandleader Vincent Lopez and the son of the financier Otto Kahn, Roger Wolfe Kahn, who was leading his own band at the Knickerbocker Grill, were considered regular customers. Irving Berlin would drop in from time to time.

One block away, down Broadway, Paul Whiteman and his orchestra were holding forth at the Palais Royale. Henry Busse, Mike Pingatore, and other musicians associated with Whiteman would visit the Kentucky Club regularly to sit in with the band. On occasion they were joined by two brothers from Shenandoah, Pennsylvania, who had come to town with Jean Goldkette's orchestra: Tommy and Jimmy Dorsey. Whiteman was a big fan of the band's, and as Ellington said, "He always showed his appreciation by laying a big fifty-dollar bill on us."

1926 brought with it another change in the band, when Harry Cooper joined on second trumpet. However, Ellington insisted that Cooper learn the "growl" so he could fill in for Miley. Cooper said that Miley often got so drunk that he passed out and rolled under the piano. Then Irvis would comment on Miley's condition by making appropriate noises on his trombone. Despite this situation, Cooper was delighted to play in the band. Cooper's was the first contemporary account of the band's life at the club.

Harry Cooper was born in Lake Charles, Louisiana, in 1903, and his family moved to Kansas City, Missouri, during his childhood. He learned the trumpet while in high school, and when he went to Virginia to study architecture at the Hampton Institute, Cooper supported himself by working with local bands. Ultimately, the lure of music was too compelling and Cooper soon forgot architecture. The following year he moved to Baltimore, Maryland, and joined a band accompanying the singer Virginia Liston. A recording date with OKeh brought this band to New York City.

Following this, Virginia Liston's band added several more musicians and called themselves the Seminole Syncopators. They were offered a three-month engagement at the "81" Theater in Atlanta, led by the pianist Graham Jackson. Cooper returned to New York in late 1924 and worked with Elmer Snowden and Billy Fowler's bands before joining the Cotton Club Orchestra led by Andrew Preer during the 1925 season. He joined the Washingtonians in February 1925, playing second trumpet.

Cooper said that the band members played their own arrangements. Ellington would indicate on the piano what he expected of each instrument, including the introduction and the supporting riffs for the solos, just as his father had done with the vocal choirs at home. For most of the compositions there were no written parts. Cooper admired the timbre of the instrumentalists, as well as their extraordinary memory.

The band was back in the recording studio the following month when Pathé offered it another session, but Miley missed the date. Ellington added Leroy Rutledge on trumpet and Don Redman on saxophone to the basic core of the Washingtonians. The addition of Redman gave the band a three-man saxophone section for the first time on a recording date. This new combination recorded Spencer

Williams's "Georgia Grind" and an Ellington original, "Parlor Social Stomp."

Redman was responsible for the arrangement of the Williams composition. At the time, he was writing for Fletcher Henderson's ten-piece band, and he often pitted the three-man saxophone section against the three-man brass section in call-and-response fashion. Henderson would later use this device himself when arranging for Benny Goodman. Redman's arrangement for this recording is good, but the band sounds stiff and uncomfortable, probably because the arrangement was new to them.

On the other hand, "Parlor Social Stomp" came off quite well. The work, a multistrain, ragtime-derived composition, sounds as though Ellington had been listening to Jelly Roll Morton for inspiration. The band sounds much more relaxed, even though three members were playing for the first time.

On April 1, 1926, the Gennett Recording Company brought the band into the studio for the first of two sessions. The band recorded two pop tunes, "(You've Got Those) Wanna Go Back Again Blues" and "If You Can't Hold the Man You Love." Greer was the vocalist on the former, and trombonist Jimmy Harrison on the latter.

On "Wanna Go Back Again Blues," the band plays a heavily edited stock arrangement originally done by Bob Haring. It is unclear who did the editing, Ellington or Don Redman. Either way, Greer's singing leaves a lot to be desired. He delivers the first two lines of the song incorrectly, and it is clear that he is uncomfortable with the entire project, which was doctored with an eye to Broadway rather than Harlem. The usual train whistle sounds the introduction, the reeds produce little tweets that are expanded into a Bronx cheer by the brass, and the work ends with a *whee!* on the slide whistle.

"If You Can't Hold the Man You Love" was written by Sammy Fain and Irving Kahal. It had been recorded earlier that year by Ethel Waters, accompanied by Fain on the piano. Again, the band plays a heavily edited stock arrangement, which is clearly the work of Redman, even though he was not playing on the date. In the first chorus, the brass plays a call and response, with the reeds using the same kind of separation heard on Redman's arrangements for Fletcher Henderson. Jimmy Harrison does an excellent rendition of the vocal.

The Kentucky Club was closed by the government in May 1926 for violating the Volstead (Prohibition) Act, but there was plenty of work in sight. The first week in June, "Happy" Rhone, a Harlem nightclub owner, booked the band for a series of one-night stands in Connecticut. And Charlie Shribman, the band's old friend, signed the group for another tour of New England beginning in July. In the interim, Leonard Harper arranged for the band to be part of the show *Messin' Around* at the Plantation Cafe.

With a score by Maceo Pinkard and James P. Johnson, *Messin' Around* was typical of the Plantation's elaborate productions. Ellington led the band during its featured spot in the show, but the overall musical direction was left in the capable hands of the violinist-conductor, Ellsworth Reynolds.

Because the tour of New England was arranged for a ten-piece band, Ellington added Freddie Skerrit as third saxophone (he would be replaced by Percy Glascoe when they got to New England) and LeRoy Rutlege as second trumpet. However, Ellington still had a personnel problem. Charlie Irvis had given notice to join Charlie Johnson's band at Smalls Paradise. The trombone player suggested his close friend and drinking companion Joe Nanton as a replacement, and Ellington went to hear him at the Nest Club, where he was playing. Ellington liked what he heard and offered the chair to the man whose career would be in Ellington's service until he died on the job twenty years later.

Born in New York City of West Indian parents in 1904, Joe "Tricky Sam" Nanton spent his early professional life working in Harlem cabarets, all within a few blocks of each other. When he was nineteen, he began working at Edmonds, at Fifth Avenue and 132nd Street, and then moved to the Green Parrot on 135th Street. Two years later, he joined Cliff Jackson at Leroy's Club one block away, and moved with Jackson to the Nest Club on 133rd Street. Nanton's engagement in *Messin' Around* was his introduction to the Ellington band.

Some years after the Plantation Cafe show, Nanton recollected, "The first week I had to wait two days for my pay, the second week there wasn't any pay. So the place closed and we went to New England."

Before the band left, it was back in the Gennett recording studios on June 21. Miley had returned, and Ellington added Charlie Johnson (not the bandleader) on second trumpet to the core group that included himself, Nanton, Hardwick, Robinson, Greer, Guy, and Shaw. This unit recorded "Animal Crackers" and "Li'l Farina." It was during this session that the creative seeds were planted that would begin the evolution of Ellington's style.

Ellington's trips to the Gayety Theater as a teenager had whetted his appetite for dramatic presentation. His visits to Frank Holliday's poolroom allowed him to develop his skill as a great listener. While at the Kentucky Club, he would often go across the street to see the productions at the Capitol Theater and listen to the symphony orchestra under the direction of the future conductor of the Philadelphia Orchestra, Eugene Ormandy. He could also be found one block away at the Palais Royale listening to the Paul Whiteman orchestra, or being an a "audience boy," sitting in one of the Broadway theaters listening to Will Vodery rehearsing the pit band for whatever show he was currently involved with.

Many years later, during an interview with the British Broadcasting Company, Ellington said, "I am a man of the theater." What he meant involved more than the love of appearing on stage. In 1965 he told the theater critic Kenneth Tynan that his hobby was writing plays, but ones he would not let anyone see. Throughout his career, Ellington's music had a theatrical dimension. Soloists were deployed like characters in a play, their comings and goings planned and orchestrated often with dramatic introductions. He began to work out some of these concepts during the June 21, 1926, recording session.

"(I'm Just Wild about) Animal Crackers" was a novelty song written by Sam Coslow and Harry Link and the bandleader Freddie Rich. The tune had already been recorded by the California Ramblers and a group out of Harry Resor's band, called the Seven Wild Men. It appears that the Gennett studios were using Ellington's band to capitalize on what was already a hit song. As it had done on its previous date for the company, the band played a stock arrangement, this one by Paul Van Loan, but as Mark Tucker has noted, Ellington edited it and substituted some ideas of his own.

The piece begins with a dramatic introduction. Ellington discards Van Loan's opening and replaces it with a series of rising chromatic seventh chords in the brass, a device he learned from Will Vodery. Ellington also alters the harmonies and rhythm of the fourth bar of the introduction. He later inserts two "hot" solos before the final ensemble and tag brings the work to an end. Other than that, he sticks fairly close to the score. The verse and the final chorus with reed countermelody and the tag are a literal reading of the work.

"Li'l Farina," on the other hand, was an Ellington arrangement (and maybe his composition). The title was derived from the name of the black child in the "Our Gang" comedies, a series of two-reel silent films produced by the Hal Roach studios beginning in 1922.

The actor Allen Hoskins, who played the part in the films, was managed by the music publisher and songwriter Harrison Smith, who claimed authorship of the tune. But my guess is that Ellington sold the work to Smith's publishing house. The composition is a bouncing, cheerful tune with a set of simple chord changes, which allowed for comfortable soloing by the musicians. This work, too, began with a flashy introduction. Tucker observed that Ellington paid homage to his teacher Will Marion Cook by quoting the tune "Bon Bon Buddy" that Cooke wrote for the 1909 Williams and Walker show, *In Bandanna Land*. The line of the song he quoted, "Bon Bon Buddy the chocolate drop," was a pun on "Li'l Farina." It is punctuated on the record by Greer's military drum rolls. A downward sweep of notes by the reeds, reminiscent of Don Redman's writing for Fletcher Henderson, leads into Nanton's solo. Although played with a lack of precision, this introduction is a superb theatrical opening for the solo that follows.

Later, during the transition to the verse, there is another dramatic touch. Here the scene changes from Miley's excellent solo to a sweet interlude for the reeds, which quotes from another song about a small boy, Ethelbert Nevin's "Mighty Lak a Rose" (1901). In the interlude, scored for three reeds and a trombone, one can hear the trace of the lush "symphonic" style that Ellington might have picked up by listening to Paul Whiteman. It is interesting how he makes the four instruments sound like a much larger group. The final chorus features the reeds improvising against a harmonized tune for brass in a New Orleans-style finale, a remnant of Sidney Bechet's stay with the band. Both Nanton and Miley use the "growl" on their solos, which, by the time of their next recording session five months later, would be a bedrock of the band's musical style.

During this Gennett studio session, there were musical acknowledgments to Cook, Vodery, Don Redman, Paul Whiteman, the
Broadway theater, and Sidney Bechet; and this is when the Nanton-
Miley duo was formed. These were some of the major elements that
emerged from Ellington's musical consciousness. They would evolve
into a coherent whole over the course of the summer tour.

The tour began at Nuttings-on-the-Charles Ballroom in Waltham,
Massachusetts, a Boston suburb. By then, Nanton had become quite
uncomfortable with his situation in the band. Ellington used him on
the recording date, but during the entire two weeks at the Plantation,
never asked him to solo. Following the first set, Hardwick forcibly
brought this issue to Duke's attention. "For Christ's sake, Dumpy," he
said. "How long you gonna let this man sit here without taking a
Boston?" ("Taking a Boston" was the 1920s term for a solo.) Greer said,
"Duke nodded at him, he stuck that mute and plunger in his bell, started to play, and I've never heard anything like it since."

Nanton's trombone became the next unique voice in Ellington's
orchestral palette. Nanton's playing differed from that of virtually all
other trombonists. He did not have the technique of Tommy Dorsey or
Lawrence Brown, nor the range of Count Basie's Dickie Wells or James
"Trummy" Young with the Jimmy Lunceford orchestra. But his sound
and sense of nuance were unique to the instrument. Rex Stewart, his
close friend who later joined him in the band, gave the best description
of Nanton's style: "What a variety of sounds he evoked from the instrument! From the wail of a new-born baby to the raucous hoot of a[n]
owl, from the blood-curdling scream of a tiger to the eerie cooing of a
mourning dove."

Mercer Ellington remembered Nanton placing a soda bottle in the
bell of his horn, creating a sound not unlike the tearing of a piece of
paper. After Nanton played his first solo with the band, Hardwick gave
him the nickname "Tricky Sam."

Miley was thrilled to have Nanton in the band. Harry Carney
remembered, "He and Tricky Sam got great pleasure from playing
something together in harmony that came off well. They were always
blowing for each other and getting ideas together for what they were
going to play. It was wonderful watching the two of them working and

hearing the sound they got from those plungers. What they created stayed with us as a major part of Ellington's music."

After the one-night engagement in Waltham, the band moved to Salem, on the shore north of Boston. Their base of operations was the Charleshurst Ballroom at the Salem Willows, on Salem Neck. The area was a summer resort that featured an amusement park, complete with bowling alley, pool hall, shooting gallery, carousel, and other rides.

Shribman arranged for the band to stay at the New Brunswick Hotel. Unlike Boston, which was sixteen miles away, there were few blacks in Salem, yet the band got on famously with the townspeople, especially Ellington with one particular woman. Greer said, "That Duke, he had something going on with a wealthy white woman. She was divorced. I'll never forget that chick. She drove a maroon Packard roadster, it had a ramble seat and a place in back of the front seat for golf clubs. She followed us all over New England. They were discreet, they'd never leave the club together. Duke would take a cab for a few blocks, get out, she'd come by and pick him up.

"The last night we were there she threw a party for just Duke and the band at her house. Man, you should have seen that place; it was on the water in Beverly or one of those towns up there. Other than our trip to England and France in '33, those weeks in Salem were the closest thing I ever had to a real summer vacation. We made a lot of friends up there."

One of these friends was a Lieutenant Bates on the police force (he would later become mayor of Salem and a congressman), whose help Ellington and the band members enlisted in a practical joke. One night, a note was passed to Percy Glascoe on the bandstand. It appeared to have been written by a young lady. She gave him directions to her house for dinner and a possible romantic encounter. Glascoe arrived laden with groceries and wine but found there was no woman. Instead he was greeted by an angry man waving a pistol, who accused him of attempting to seduce his wife. The musician dropped everything and fled for his life, hurried along by gunshots fired by members of the police department, who were in on the prank. Glascoe didn't take the joke well, and quit the band in a huff.

Ellington needed a replacement in a hurry. He knew an excellent young musician named Johnny Hodges who had been living in Boston;

but when Ellington finally tracked him down, Hodges was in New York City working at the Capitol Palace with Lloyd Scott's band. Hodges turned the job down, but suggested his friend Harry Carney, a sixteen-year-old Boston boy. Carney was hired for the rest of the summer.

The band played the Charleshurst every Tuesday night, and during the rest of the week they could be found at other dance halls in New England: the Highland Park in Brockton, Lincoln Park in Fall River; Cresent Gardens in Revere; Fieldston in Marshfield; Wilbur's in Somerset; the Miami Ballroom in Woonsocket, Rhode Island; and Old Orchard Pier in Maine.

For those jobs, the band was not the only featured group. Shribman advertised each engagement as a "Battle of Bands." The bands would play alternate sets, which would keep the music going nonstop. On any given night, Ellington would find himself sharing the bill with Mal Hallett, Felix Ferdinando and his Havana Orchestra, Speed Young, or the Crescent Garden's Orchestra. One night at Revere Beach, Shribman had four bands going: Ellington, Hallett, Speed Young, and the Crescent Gardens Orchestra.

Shribman also booked the bands of Fletcher Henderson, Vincent Lopez, Paul Spect, and Ross Gorman. According to Greer, the bands never shared the bill with them, but Ellington made it a point to hear them on his nights off because he was usually booked to follow them. "When we'd leave, Duke was always thinking of a way for our band to open up the following night that would really contrast with the band that had played the night before," said Greer.

After the band finished the tour on August 13, 1926, at Moseley's-on-the-Charles, they began a tour of Pennsylvania and West Virginia organized by the Spizzi Syndicate, a booking agency. They played the Liberty and Schenley Theaters in Pittsburgh for two weeks before continuing on to North Kensington and Homestead. West Virginia, the next stop, was the band's first taste of the segregated South. Miley promptly left, and the rest of the band followed him home.

The band returned to the Kentucky Club on September 24, 1926, where it was featured along with Bert Lewis accompanied by Jack Carroll at the piano, who was now a fixture at the club. The remainder of the show, now billed as the "Hospitality Gang," was the usual night-club fare, including a torch singer, comedian, dancer, and chorus line.

Ellington and his men were now in their fourth year at the club, and the owners, Frank Gary and Leo Bernstein, would also recommend them for outside engagements. The band was the featured attraction at several charity balls. The famous Broadway producers, the Shuberts, booked them for several Sunday evening concerts at the Winter Garden. Many nights, the musicians would arrive at the Kentucky Club for an eleven o'clock show after working elsewhere from seven to ten.

The last show at the Kentucky Club ended at 4 A.M., and on weekends, the evening continued for Ellington and Greer. They would take a small upright piano and "work the house," going from table to table with Ellington playing and Greer singing requests. According to Ellington, the repertoire included "pop songs, jazz songs, dirty songs, torch songs, Jewish songs." The customers were expected to tip the musicians. Greer said that occasionally Bernstein would get drunk and request the song "My Buddy." "We'd do it, he'd hug us and cry and leave two fifty-dollar bills on the piano."

On payday, the musicians would assemble in Bernstein's office after the club had closed for the night. He would give them their salary in cash. Duke got $100 and the rest of the musicians got $75 a week. With the night's receipts on the desk, Bernstein would get his dice out of his pocket and roll them on the floor, saying, "I'm in for five dollars."

Greer, a gambler par excellence, told me, "As soon as those dice hit the floor, I'd say, 'I gotcha.'" With the exception of Freddie Guy, who never gambled, all the musicians would play. Sometimes Bernstein lost a great deal of money, but because he had so much to begin with, over time he would win it all back, including the musicians' pay. This meant that on occasion they had to ask him for an advance on the following week's wages. He then had a band that didn't cost him anything for the week.

"He was a hell of guy to work for," the drummer observed. "He'd give you the shirt off his back." In fact, on one occasion, Bernstein did just that. One morning he noticed the musicians hurriedly packing their instruments after the show. Two taxis were waiting to take them uptown to a 4:30 "breakfast dance."

Before they could get out the door, the manager summoned them to his office and had them line up. He walked back and forth in front of them, "like a drill sergeant," Greer stated. He dusted off their tuxedos with a whisk broom and adjusted their bow ties. Taking the diamond pinky ring off his left hand, he placed it on Greer's, and told him to wear it and bring it back when he returned to work that night. Noticing Hardwick's dirty shirt, he told him to take it off and gave him his own. He looked them over, then dismissed the musicians with a wave of his hand, saying, "Now you look like you work for me."

At least once or twice a month on a Sunday morning, after they had closed at the club, Ellington, Guy, and Greer were dispatched to entertain customers at Polly Adler's brothel on West 54th Street. "We'd show around five o'clock," Greer said. "Polly would see we got breakfast, and we'd work until around nine in the morning. It was nothing to leave there with fifty or sixty dollars in tips. One of the girls took such a liking to Duke, she started seeing him on the side."

Besides working outside jobs, Ellington was keeping busy on another front. "Most people don't know this," Greer said. "Duke was always one hell of an accompanist. Even in those early days when we were at the [Kentucky] club, he used to pick up a good bit of change just accompanying singers for auditions or recordings."

One was Alberta Jones, who brought Ellington and Greer to the Gennett studios on October 10, 1926. Listed on the label as the "Ellington Twins," they recorded two songs with Jones, "Lucky Number Blues" and "I'm Gonna Put You Right In Jail." Three weeks later the two of them, along with Hardwick, were back in those studios, this time with Zaidee Jackson as she recorded "They Call Me Lulu" and "I'm Tired of Being a Fool over You."

With outside engagements, tips, and recordings, the musicians were making very good money. "I loved that little band, and working at the club," Greer said. "We played such quiet, tasty music, but it all changed that night [Irving] Mills walked in."

8

IN MID-NOVEMBER 1926, Irving Mills came to the Kentucky Club, accompanied by Sime Silverman, the editor of *Variety*. As he walked in, the band was playing "St. Louis Blues." It appears that Mills was so struck by their unique sound that he didn't recognize the tune and finally had to ask Ellington what it was. When told, he recollected, "I immediately thought of the quick change that I could make between him and Fletcher Henderson, who had been working for me to do the background music for my vocal artists that I had on my labels, black labels."

Three years earlier, Mills offered Fletcher Henderson employment as music director of Down South Music, Inc. However, as it turned out, the job was short-lived because the company had been created partly as a lure. The demise of the Black Swan Recording Company meant that Henderson—the talented, hardworking director of recordings—was available, and Mills desperately wanted him. In October 1923, *Phonograph and Talking Machine Weekly* wrote that Henderson was one of the best informed among contemporary blues specialists.

In 1920, following his graduation from Atlanta University, Henderson arrived in New York, expecting to study graduate chemistry at Columbia University. His father was the principal of the county training school for blacks in Cuthbert, Georgia. His mother, a pianist and music teacher, taught him classical piano. Henderson's knowledge of jazz and blues was limited to hearing Bessie Smith and Ma Rainey when they appeared at the "81" Theater while he was in college. He sometimes played piano at school dances.

Underestimating the cost of living in New York City, Henderson found that his savings ran out before school began. To earn money, he took a job as accompanist, copyist, and general helper at Pace & Handy Music Company and soon forgot graduate school entirely. He became a member of the Harlem Symphony and occasionally would accompany singers at recitals. When Pace left Handy to start Black Swan Music, he recommended to William Grant Still (Black Swan's music director) that he bring along Henderson as director of recordings. Henderson held this position until the company was sold.

The job at Down South was part-time and mainly involved accompanying contract singers at recording sessions. Henderson was either playing the piano or leading a small band for singers, including Sara Martin, Daisy Martin, Lena Wilson, and Alberta Hunter, just as he had done at Black Swan. Coleman Hawkins felt that one of the main reasons Mills had offered Henderson the directorship of Down South Music was to induce him to sign a management contract with his agency. Hawkins said that this was common knowledge among members of the Henderson orchestra in the 1920s. "He didn't need Mills, Mills needed him," Hawkins said.

The evidence bears Hawkins out. During his tenure at Black Swan, Henderson had made a name for himself as a recording director. From the beginning of 1921 through mid-1923, he was responsible for, and played in, at least 100 recording sessions. When Tin Pan Alley became involved in recording black music, Henderson's was the first name mentioned to be an accompanist. With the exception of Mamie Smith, he accompanied every well-known black singer of the day, including Bessie and Clara Smith (separately and together), Alberta Hunter, Ida Cox, Ma Rainey, Trixie Smith, Josie Miles, Violet McCoy, and Tudie Wells. He also led the band that accompanied Ethel Waters on her first tour of the South. From August 1923 through 1924, he was in the recording studio at least 175 times.

In January 1924, Henderson fell into a job as a bandleader. His recording band had just finished a session for Columbia, and as the band members were leaving the building, they were told that the owners of the new Club Alabam, located one block away on 44th Street, were looking for a band. The group auditioned and was hired. The musicians suggested that because of his height, bearing, color, and education, Henderson should be the leader.

Besides working at the club, the band began to play weekend dances throughout the city and suburbs, as well as recording sessions with Columbia, Paramount, and Vocalion. Henderson was one of the busiest musicians in town, black or white. He created the jazz dance band from an amalgam of black music and white orchestral traditions during his six-year engagement at the Roseland Ballroom, beginning in the spring of 1924.

Following in the footsteps of the white bands that preceded it, Henderson's band played the familiar tangos, waltzes, and fox trots. Henderson and his chief arranger, Don Redman, soon moved beyond imitation to experimentation. They organized the brass and reeds into legitimate orchestral sections to provide a harmonic background for the soloists, beginning with Louis Armstrong in 1924. Written arrangements integrated the band into a unified musical statement. By drawing on the African-American call-and-response technique, Redman and Henderson set the brass and reed sections against each other. Riffs were traded back and forth to build interest and excitement.

The Redman-Henderson innovations took place mainly on race recordings aimed at the black audience, where improvisation was prized. Nonetheless, their style spread rapidly, and by 1930 it had become the standard for both black and white bands, with the use of three brass instruments, three reeds, four rhythm instruments, and hot soloists linked by complex written, syncopated arrangements requiring musically literate sidemen and arrangers.

In 1925, Henderson organized a second unit, the Fletcher Henderson Rainbow Orchestra, led by Ellsworth Reynolds. This band toured Pennsylvania and the Midwest, playing college dates, dances, and any other engagement Henderson was unable to keep with the "Roseland" orchestra. This second unit played stock arrangements of his better-known scores, such as "Henderson Stomp," "Stampede," "Sugarfoot Stomp," and "Copenhagen."

Given Henderson's remarkable productivity, it is understandable that Mills courted him. Mills hoped the music directorship would lead to a management contract, allowing his agency to reap the benefits (10 percent of the gross) of any engagement that would flow from that relationship. But more importantly, he expected that his company would have publication rights to Henderson's blues compositions, where the real money was. (Mills was still looking for another "Crazy Blues," but that too failed to materialize.)

In October, Down South arranged to record Henderson's band for the Ajax label. One of the numbers was a re-recording of his "Dicty Blues." At the end of the session Henderson noticed that the copyright was assigned to Down South Music. That meant he would receive no royalties. He solved the problem by making certain that any future compositions done for the company were under the pseudonym "George Brooks," and he listed his address as c/o Fletcher Henderson, 205 West 138th Street. However, Down South Music ceased operations at the end of 1924, and there is no evidence of any material copyrighted after that time. A few years later, Mills reorganized the company as Melrose Music, Inc.

Irving Mills gave up his pursuit of Henderson in late 1925. Years later, when asked about his relationship with the bandleader, Mills said he found him unreliable in the recording studio: The music was never ready, and Henderson's musicians were either late or showed up drunk, and one never made a session at all. Mills said that when he first heard Duke Ellington's bands he was struck by the unique sound, and that their music identified them as a black band. Henderson's music, however, was too "white" for Mills' taste.

This sounds like sour grapes on Mills's part. If what Mills said was true, the recording companies would have quickly found someone to replace Henderson. Coleman Hawkins dismissed Mills's derogatory story by pointing out that during those years the band's music was arranged by Don Redman—not Henderson. Redman's work was strongly influenced by Paul Whiteman, who had also commissioned several scores from him. Further, Hawkins said, when they got into the studio, it was all business.

"Remember," Hawkins said, "besides Don and me, that band had in it at one time or another Cootie, Louis [Armstrong], Jerome Pasquall, Joe Smith, Buster Bailey, Charlie Green and Russell Smith. We were professionals. We took what we did seriously. Discipline was no problem until he [Henderson] had that car wreck in '28. By then Mills was recording Duke!"

When Mills made the statement about the quality of Henderson's music, the band was working at Roseland. The customers were white and went there to dance. This placed limits on the type of music Henderson could play, mostly stock versions of his and Redman's arrangements of popular tunes, in addition to waltzes, fox trots, and polkas. By contrast, Ellington, working at the Kentucky Club, had no constraints on the music he could play. The customers went there to hear a black band play black music, and that was what they got.

Mills was interviewed by the Yale Oral History Project in 1981, at the age of 87. He said the first time he heard about Ellington was from the owners of the Kentucky Club, who told him "they had just hired a band from Washington." It is indeed surprising that there is no mention during this interview that Mills had heard the band before the night he walked into the club.

Irving Mills was in the music business up to his ears. He was a well-known figure on Broadway, up in Harlem, and in the nightclubs, dance halls, and recording studios. Ellington and Mills had known each other since the summer of 1923, and two years later, Ellington accompanied him on the piano when Mills made a test recording of "Everything Is Hotsy Totsy Now." The Ellington orchestra had been on Broadway for the previous three years, and the Kentucky Club was known as a place where show people, entertainers, and musicians congregated. There is no way Mills could not have heard them before that night.

What I suspect happened was that the seminal ideas that were emerging during the June 21, 1926, recording session crystallized during the summer tours. The band that left the Kentucky Club in May returned in the fall with something new, namely, "the Ellington sound." This was now Duke Ellington's band playing Duke Ellington's music. Mills had not heard *that* before.

Mills himself said it was the sound of the Ellington band that impressed him that night at the Kentucky Club. I'm sure it did, but I also think something else was going on. We shall see that Mills, by playing his cards right, would have in his agency a black musician over whom he had total control, the very thing Mills was unable to do with Fletcher Henderson. Ellington didn't know it then, but after that night, his life would never be the same.

9

"HE [MILLS] USED to come to the Kentucky Club often," Ellington recollected in his autobiography. "Then one night he said he didn't know what we were doing with our music, but he liked it and would like to record some of it with our band."

For Ellington, this must have been a dream come true. Sam Coslow, one of the co-writers of "Animal Crackers" and a Mills employee, had previously approached Ellington about the possibility of recording the band for one of the many labels Mills was involved with. Ellington was enthusiastic about the idea. "That's what I want to do more than anything in the world," he nearly shouted. "How do I get on records?" Coslow said he would mention their conversation to Mills. As he left, he noticed that Ellington had a hopeful look in his eyes, "sort of like a prayer." However, it is unclear when Coslow and Ellington had the conversation. It could have been anytime during the previous two years.

When Mills came into the club in November 1926, Ellington had already been in recording studios nine times, usually accompanying singers performing other composers' songs. The only recording for which he had full composing credit was "Parlor Social Stomp." He shared credits on "Choo-Choo" and "Rainy Nights." "Li'l Farina" was likely his composition, or at least his arrangement, but he sold that outright to Harrison Smith. None of the recordings were for major companies, and Ellington did not have the wherewithal to get a contract with any of them.

Within a week of their meeting, Mills had taken care of that. He contacted the Brunswick-Balke-Collender Recording Company, which had been issuing recordings by black performers on its Vocalion popular series since 1923. In March 1926, the company began a special "race" series of recordings, the Vocalion 1000's, and were looking for black artists. Mills offered them Ellington. A contract was drawn up calling for three recording dates, on November 29 and December 29, 1926, and

February 3, 1927, with an option for one more if the company liked what it heard.

Mills made two stipulations: that only Ellington compositions would be recorded and that the company had to use the new "electric" system of recording invented by Western Electric the previous year. Mills had been making recordings since 1921, and he knew that the acoustic system of recording was not adequate to capture the band's unique sound. Most recordings of that type had a distant, closed-in sound. The new system used carbon-filled microphones and an amplifier to convert the sound to electrical impulses that would be etched on the wax matrix. It gave musical recordings a bright, crisp, more realistic sound.

On the first date on November 29, 1926, the band billed as "Duke Ellington and his Kentucky Club Orchestra" recorded "East St. Louis Toodle-Oo," "Birmingham Breakdown," "A Night in Harlem," and "Who Is She?" The first two compositions were issued, but the others never were. "Toodle-Oo" was the record company's misspelling of "Toadlo." "Toadlo" is a broken walking step. "East St. Louis Toodle-Oo" became the band's radio signature theme for the next fifteen years.

The recording date marked the debut of Louis Metcalf on second trumpet, replacing Harry Cooper. Cooper had left following the summer tour for a trip to England with the violinist Leon Abbey.

Metcalf's straightforward style of playing was in direct contrast to that of Miley. His open horn had a warm, burnished sound and, until he joined Ellington, he rarely used a mute. In an interview, he said that Ellington made his learning the growl a condition of employment, just as the bandleader had done with Harry Cooper.

Trumpeter Louis Metcalf was born in St. Louis. He moved to Chicago, and came to New York in 1923 with Jimmy Cooper's revue. The following year found him with Willie "the Lion" Smith's band at the Rhythm Club. Early in 1925, Metcalf joined Andrew Preer's Missourians at the Cotton Club. He also worked with Johnny Hudgins' variety show, Elmer Snowden, and Charlie Johnson before joining the Ellington band.

The first Vocalion recording session served a special purpose for Mills. It enabled him to get Ellington under contract, something he was unable to do with Fletcher Henderson. A corporate partnership was formed that lasted thirteen years, with Ellington as president and Mills treasurer. Each man owned 45 percent of Ellington, Inc., and attorney Sam Buzzell owned the remaining 10 percent. Mills Music, Inc., had exclusive publication rights to all of Ellington's music.

There were many, including Ellington's family, who questioned the equity of the partnership, especially when they noticed that Ellington allowed Irving Mills to claim coauthorship on several of his instrumental compositions. "The Mooche" (1929), "Stevedore Stomp" (1929), "Rockin' in Rhythm" (1931), and "Old Man Blues" (1930) had no lyrics for the company to "touch up," which would eliminate its opportunity to "cut in," a questionable practice at best. As a partner in Ellington, Inc., Irving Mills would now share the profits the band would net at the end of the year. Mills was already participating in the proceeds that Mills Music, Inc., made from publishing Ellington's music and booking his band. In essence, he was double-dipping, collecting as officer/owner of both Ellington Music and the parent corporation.

Ellington had his own agenda. In the three-and-a-half years he had been in New York, both the political economy and the racism of the music publishing business had become clear to him. The business was controlled by whites, and Ellington had no entree into the system. Now that he had a publisher, he would begin to receive royalties on his compositions and would no longer be selling them outright as he had done with most of his compositions, including the music for *Chocolate Kiddies*.

Ellington knew Irving Mills's reputation, and he respected and valued the publisher's musical judgment. Ellington wrote of Mills, "He could feel a song. He'd take a good lyricist, tell him 'Now this song needs something right there,' and the cat would go over it, and it would come out perfect."

Ellington also knew that Mills's stature in the business and his aggressive personality could be the perfect interface between Ellington and the musical establishment, leaving him free to do what he did best: write music. Mills would take care of everything else.

"He'd show up at work, usually just before we'd start," Greer said. "He'd tell Duke to have some music ready for a recording session the next day, give us the address of the studio, the time, and that was it. We never knew in advance where we'd be recording. It was something we never had to think about. He took care of the details. All Duke had to do was show up with the music."

According to Ellington, the procedure was always the same. "Have four numbers ready for recording at 9 A.M. tomorrow," he'd say. "We'd do that, and he liked what we did, and interest grew. . . . He had the contacts, and I liked to write music and play it too. The rather short time alloted didn't bother me. But because I loved doing it, I just went ahead and did it."

Louie Metcalf felt that Ellington gave away too much to his manager. "Duke knew what he wanted, and I guess to get what you want, you have to compromise." But the arrangement paid off; Ellington's assessment of Irving Mills was right on the mark. Once the contract was signed, no manager would work as hard for his client, or work his client as hard as Mills did. The ink was scarcely dry on the contract when Irving Mills began to take steps to increase his client's visibility.

Mills contacted the owners of radio station WHN, who had featured the band on the air at the Hollywood Cafe. Since the band's last broadcast in 1924, radio technology had improved to the point where the band no longer had to go to the studio to broadcast. The station would place a "wire" in the club and the bands would be on the air in what was now known as a "remote" [broadcast]. By that time, remotes were originating regularly from all the Broadway night spots: the Club Alabam, Strand Roof, Club Wigwam, Palais Royale, Club Richman, and the Roseland Ballroom. At Mills's suggestion, a wire was placed in the Kentucky Club. The band went on the air at 2 A.M. A young announcer named Ted Husing was hired to introduce the band and host the show.

The band had done two recording sessions for Victor in 1923, but nothing had come of them because the company had been slow to capitalize on the blues craze. In January 1920, Victor heard and rejected Mamie Smith. The following October, it turned down Lucille Hegamin's singing of "Dallas Blues," which later became a big hit on the Paramount label. Seven years later, when Victor announced that it was contemplating the V38500 series of "race" recordings, Mills quickly arranged an audition. On January 10, 1927, Ellington's band was in the studio, not on its own, but to accompany the black actress and singer Evelyn Preer.

Preer had made a name for herself as a serious actress a few years earlier in a production of Oscar Wilde's *Salome*. In January 1927, she was in rehearsal at the Belasco Theater on Broadway for the forthcoming production of Charles MacArthur's controversial play *Lulu Belle*. Preer had been under contract and recorded by Victor for the previous year. In her most recent session the previous October, she was accompanied by an all-white band that included Red Nichols on trumpet, Miff Mole on trombone, and Rube Bloom on piano.

It appears that the company was planning to move Preer to its "race" series of recordings. She was accompanied by a sextet that included Ellington on piano, Miley on trumpet, Hardwick on alto sax, Edgar Sampson on saxophone and violin, Prince Robinson on clarinet and tenor sax, and Greer on drums. Preer recorded two songs, "Make Me Love You" and "If You Can't Hold the Man You Love," but only the latter was issued. While Preer was an excellent actress, her singing was mediocre at best. Still, the band held its own; Miley soloed brilliantly and Sampson played some excellent jazz violin.

A longstanding problem for Irving Mills was that he had no direct access to a major recording studio. In late 1926, Brunswick-Balke-Collender announced the formation of another recording company, the Brunswick label. It, too, planned a "race" series, the Brunswick 7000s, and Mills Music, Inc., quietly invested money in the project. With that leverage, and with Vocalion undecided about picking up the band's option for a fourth session, Irving Mills signed Ellington for four recording dates with Brunswick in 1927: February 28, March 14, and April 7 and 30.

But Mills didn't stop there. The band's radio broadcasts had begun in early January, and within weeks, Columbia Recording Company contacted Mills with an eye to recording Ellington's band on its 14000-D "race" series. This posed a naming problem. Vocalion's contract called the band "Duke Ellington and his Kentucky Club Orchestra," but Brunswick listed him as "Duke Ellington and his Orchestra." To avoid further confusion and possible contractual difficulties, Columbia recorded the band as the Washingtonians, a pseudonym Mills used for the next date with Brunswick as well.

The Washingtonians was the first of many pseudonyms under which the band would record. Over the years Mills recorded the group on Vocalion, Victor, Columbia, Brunswick, OKeh, Cameo, and Harmony as "The Whoopee Makers," "The Six Jolly Jesters," "The Harlem Footwarmers," "Sonny Greer and his Memphis Men," "Joe Turner and his Memphis Men," "The Philadelphia Melodians," "The Harlem Hot Shots," "Earl Jackson and his Musical Champions," "Mills' Ten Blackberries," "The Harlem Hot Chocolates," "The Jungle Band," and the "Memphis Hot Shots." This was not an unusual practice for the time; the use of multiple names allowed musicians to sign "exclusive" contracts with several different labels.

When the band finished its fourth recording date for Brunswick at the end of April, it had been in recording studios eight times in six months. These early recordings give us the first good look at the band and their method of making music. Unlike the great majority of Ellington's previous recording dates, where he played stock arrangements usually with little or no rehearsal, these compositions were his own, and the band had been playing them for some time.

The band had recorded "East St. Louis Toodle-Oo" and "Birmingham Breakdown" at its first session for Vocalion on November 29, 1926, and played both pieces again at its first session for Brunswick on February 28, 1927. However, Mills was not satisfied with the Brunswick session, and his five years of recording experience, plus his financial interest in the company, made him a force to be reckoned with.

Greer said, "In those early days he knew the recording business better than anyone else. If he didn't like the way a number came out, he would have us back in the studio doing it again, and he wouldn't let those companies release it until he felt it was right. He insisted on nothing but the best for Duke." Mills had the band back in the studio on March 14, 1927, and the entire date was spent re-recording "East St. Louis Toodle-Oo."

The work is essentially a Miley creation. A moaning, sustained passage for the saxophones and tuba (orchestrated by Ellington) introduces the song. Then Miley states the main theme (thirty-two bars) over this background, and solos by Nanton and Hardwick follow. An orchestral interlude precedes Miley's final recapitulation of the main theme.

As Gunther Schuller pointed out in *Early Jazz*, this work—in its faltering way—is a true composition. It was not a collection of thirty-two-bar "take your turn" solos, nor was it a totally improvised piece. It had an introduction, a two-part (A and B themes) form, and individual solos, all indicating that once the "improvisations" were set, they remained unchanged and became a permanent part of the composition. "Hearing that piece changed my life," said a sixteen-year-old trumpet player named Sy Oliver. Oliver would later achieve fame as an arranger, writing first-class scores that would be recorded by Jimmie Lunceford and Tommy Dorsey.

"Birmingham Breakdown," on the other hand, is foremost a study of rhythm. The main theme is a sprightly, twenty-bar phrase that is broken down into a succession of two- and four-bar subsegments, as Schuller noted. Interestingly enough, the band switches to twelve-bar blues for the last two (collectively improvised) choruses, reflecting Miley's debt to the King Oliver orchestra.

While the composition is nominally Ellington's, the trumpet player's contributions carry the day, especially the dual improvisation by Miley and Metcalf (in Oliver-Armstrong style) in the final chorus.

While the Oliver influence is clearly evident in the last two choruses of "Birmingham Breakdown," the work, as Schuller wrote, ultimately broke the ice for the five-bar phrases of "Creole Rhapsody" (1930) or the ten- and fourteen-bar lines of "Reminiscing in Tempo" (1935). These, in turn, led to the large, asymmetrical formations of *Black, Brown and Beige* (1945).

The second Vocalion date on December 29, 1927, produced "The Creeper" and "Immigration Blues." "The Creeper" joined "Birmingham Breakdown" in looking backward toward King Oliver, as well as forward in the band's development. It features freewheeling solos by Miley, Hardwick, Nanton, and Robinson and builds to a spirited New Orleans-style ensemble, culminating in a four-bar break in the brass section, lifted from Oliver's recording of "Snake Rag." The work is based loosely on the chords of "Tiger Rag," a progression that Ellington would expand on in "Hot and Bothered" (1928), "High Life" (1929), and "Slippery Horn" (1932). He developed it further in three extremely complex works, "Whispering Tiger" (1932), "Daybreak Express" (1933), and "Braggin' in Brass" (1938), and then again in 1951 with "Before My Time." Luis Russell said, "No musician has ever done more with the chords of 'Tiger Rag' than Duke."

"Immigration Blues" is the first example of the band's excellent orchestral work built around the framework of the twelve-bar blues. Following an organ-like introduction, the theme is stated by Prince Robinson on tenor saxophone. Miley follows with the first of his many great blues solos on an Ellington recording. Schuller noted "his highly imaginative simultaneous use of the growl and plunger, [and his] playing his chorus with a penetrating nasty tone that almost creates the illusion of speech." Nanton's and Edwards's solos, which follow, compare favorably with Miley's. Overall, this work set the standard for the great blues compositions of the next decade, including "Blues with a Feeling" (1929), "Awful Sad" (1929), "Misty Mornin'" (1929), "Baby, When You Ain't There" (1932), "Bundle of Blues" (1933), and "Blue Feeling" (1934).

The third Vocalion date, on February 3, 1927 produced "New Orleans Lowdown" and "Song of the Cottonfield." The former is an uncomplicated blues played at a medium tempo. Metcalf has the opening statement, followed by Miley, Hardwick, and Miley again. Nanton solos over what would become an Ellington trademark: rich, lush scoring involving the three reeds and Edwards's tuba. An Ellington solo, followed by Miley's short coda, brings the work to a close. "Song of the Cottonfield," written by Porter Grainger, by contrast is a sprightly 32-bar chorus. It contains some deft mute and plunger work by Miley, followed by Robinson on clarinet and Hardwick on baritone saxophone.

For the Washingtonians' first Columbia session on March 22, 1927, the band began with "East St. Louis Toodle-Oo," followed by two Ellington-Hardwick compositions, "Hop Head" and "Down in Our Alley Blues." It would become standard practice for the band to record "East St. Louis Toodle-Oo" as its first work with each new company.

The third session for Brunswick, on April 7, 1927, produced the next Miley-Ellington masterpiece, "Black & Tan Fantasy." It was Miley's creation and reflected his family roots in the deep South. Although raised in New York City, he was brought up in a household whose roots were in the deep South. Making use of this rich musical background, Miley adapted the anthem ("Jerusalem, Jerusalem") from F. Steven Adams's spiritual "The Holy City" as the main theme, in a minor key. He and Nanton play it in harmony, both of them using mutes and plungers. Edwards's tuba and Guy's rock-steady banjo provide a pungent underpinning.

In response to the tension of the duo, Hardwick responds with an elegant contrasting theme, and Miley follows with one of his most striking performances. He begins quietly on a four-bar-long high B flat that suddenly erupts—as if unable to contain itself—into what Schuller rightly called a "magnificently structured creation."

The solo with growl, mute, and plunger, embellished by a series of strategically placed "blue" notes, makes it one of Miley's great works. His playing clearly inspires Ellington, who responds with his best piano work to date. Nanton responds to Miley's challenge with a wrenching, primeval twelve-bar solo complete with a "whinny." Miley returns, playing a series of breaks answered by Edwards, and he ends the work, playing the coda based on the Funeral March from the Chopin piano sonata in B minor.

Recording the work posed serious technical problems for Ellington and Mills. The combination of the two instruments playing in close harmony with mutes and plungers produced a buzz in the carbon-filled microphones.

After much trial and error, Mills found that by moving the musicians specific distances from the microphone, the buzz was eliminated. It would be another three years before Ellington would learn to use the microphone sound as a positive advantage in his work.

On April 30, 1927, the band was back in the Brunswick studios, and for the first time since he had been under contract to Mills, Ellington did not write the arrangements. This time the band played "Soliloquy," a vaguely impressionistic work written by the songwriter and pianist Rube Bloom, who was under contract to Mills.

The band plays the work straight, probably at Mills's suggestion. The recording is dull and lifeless and the band is almost unrecognizable as the Ellington orchestra. This may be due in part to the manager's trying to make "Soliloquy" appeal to white audiences.

On this date, June Clark, who was currently leading the band at the Sugar Cane Club, filled in for Miley. This was one of many sessions Miley would miss as a result of his drinking. Ellington had to put up with Miley's behavior because he was the band's prime source of musical inspiration. Even more important, Miley put Ellington in touch with his own feelings for the blues. This sensitivity would become part of Ellington's musical soul.

Miley had an exquisite feeling for the idiom. At the heart of his solos was a sense of sadness that he would embellish with the use of the growl and plunger. That device was as much a part of his instrument as the bow to a violin. Listening to a Miley solo was like listening to a first-rate blues singer at work.

As Greer said to me, "Bubber didn't *play* the blues on his horn, he sang them." He also had a great accompanist. "When I get off [on a solo] Duke is always there," Miley told an interviewer. Freddie Guy observed, "Most people never noticed Bubber and Duke could play off each other too. All they ever heard was Bubber and Tricky."

Most of the early works published under Ellington's name were really coauthored with Miley and, occasionally, Hardwick. There were often significant contributions by Nanton, who had developed into the perfect foil for Miley.

Ellington was dependent on his musicians, and they knew it. Musical composition was usually a synthesis of ideas contributed by band members. It was a group process and would remain so in one way or another throughout Ellington's musical career. Hardwick described it like this:

> In those early days, how we enjoyed what we did. We were privi-
> leged to make suggestions. If he liked it, or he didn't, he'd go along
> with it anyway. Every man had freedom of expression. . . . And then it
> was more or less like family. . . . We shared in everything, like some of
> those numbers we wrote where two or three contributed a part."

The allusion to family seems quite accurate. Ellington was doing just that. He was assembling a musical family that would become the famous Duke Ellington orchestra of the 1930s.

10

BEFORE THE BAND'S second New England tour, it saw a number of personnel changes. In May 1927, Robinson and Edwards gave notice to join Leon Abbey's band, and Rudy Jackson and Wellman Braud came on board.

Rudy Jackson was born in Fort Wayne, Indiana, in 1901 to musician parents and grew up in Chicago. When he turned seventeen, he began playing in local bands, and in 1920, Carrol Dickerson hired him. From late 1923 through the summer of 1924, Jackson worked with King Oliver. This was followed by a series of jobs in traveling revues until Billy Butler's band brought him to New York in 1925. Next, he toured with Jim Vaughn's pit band in the *Lucky Sambo* revue.

Returning to Chicago in 1927, Jackson rejoined King Oliver. When the band was booked for an engagement at Harlem's Savoy Ballroom, Jackson decided not to make the trip because there were not enough nights of work. He signed on again with *Lucky Sambo*, which was booked to play a full schedule at the Columbia Theater. When *Lucky Sambo* closed in May, he was invited to join the Ellington band.

Wellman Braud, Ellington's new bass player, was born in New Orleans in 1891 and began playing violin when he was seven. His first job was playing violin and bass in a string trio at Tom Anderson's cabaret. He later worked with the John H. Wickliffe Band and then with the Original Creole Orchestra in Chicago, where Lil Hardin was the pianist. The band's rigorous schedule had it at the Dreamland Ballroom until one in the morning, and then at Al Capone's Pekin Club from two to six.

Braud left them to join the Charlie Elgar orchestra. From March to May 1923, he was in London working with the *Plantation Review*, under the baton of Will Vodery. When Braud returned home, he put in tours of duty with Wilbur Sweatman, the *7-11 Burlesque Show*, and the *Lucky Sambo* revue before joining the Ellington orchestra.

Braud's strength as a bassist was his ability to set a strong, compelling beat, and he quickly became the heart of the rhythm section. Greer said:

> When Braud came into the band in '27, that's when things changed. We really got tight in the rhythm section. I'm not taking anything away from Edwards. He could play the hell out of that tuba, but it was going out of style. With ol' Braud on bass, Duke's piano, Freddie's banjo, and me on drums, we were tight man, real tight. We played together for the next eight years.

Braud's presence in the rhythm section did pull things together, but the permanent addition of Harry Carney created further changes in the band's character. Carney had played with the band during the previous summer, and Ellington, clearly taken with him, brought him to New York for several of the band's recording dates.

Harry Carney was born on April 10, 1910. His father frequented the opera and would sing arias and spirituals around the house, but neither he nor Carney's mother played an instrument. At age six, Carney was given lessons, which allowed him to develop his sight reading and basic chord knowledge, and gave him a more-than-passing acquaintance with the classics.

The Carneys lived on Connaught Street in Boston's South End and belonged to the Union Methodist Church. It was at the church youth club that Carney met Buster Tolliver, a composer, pianist, and clarinetist. Tolliver played in a small band, and when Carney saw how this glamorous activity served as a magnet for girls, he decided to take up the clarinet. At Tolliver's suggestion, Carney, now thirteen, joined the Knights of Pythias band. The bandmaster gave Carney lessons, and the band sent him a clarinet. He practiced diligently, learning the Albert (French) fingering system. But later, when he heard his idol Buster Bailey in person, he switched to the more common Boehm (German) system.

After studying for about a year, Carney decided to add the saxophone to his repertoire and began lessons with Jerome Pasquall, a young black man studying at the New England Conservatory of Music. There,

Carney was introduced to another of Pasquall's pupils, Johnny Hodges, who lived four blocks away from Carney on Hammond Street. By the time Hodges, who was three years older than Carney, was seventeen, he was traveling to New York City, working a few weeks, and returning home. He would share with Carney and Charlie Holmes, another pupil of Pasquall's, what he had learned. The previous summer he had recommended Carney to Ellington for the job in Salem.

By the spring of 1927, Hodges was in New York permanently, working with Chick Webb's band at the Savoy. He had been encouraging Carney and Holmes to come to the city. Carney persuaded his mother to let him go to New York over spring vacation, and the two musicians left for the city. Within days of their arrival, Hodges found them work with one of the relief bands at the Savoy, led by Fess Williams.

Banjoist Henri Saparo was organizing a band for an engagement at the Bamboo Inn, on Seventh Avenue and 139th Street, and he offered them a job, beginning on April 1. Before agreeing, Carney suggested that Saparo contact his mother and explain the situation, because she was expecting him back in Boston. The following day, Mrs. Carney came to New York to see what was going on. Saparo convinced her that her son was in good hands, and she agreed to let him stay, with the proviso that he return to Boston to finish school in the fall.

The Bamboo Inn was a Chinese-American restaurant frequented by Ellington and his wife, and Ellington would make a point of stopping by the bandstand to offer encouragement to the young Carney. But the Bamboo Inn burned down in June, and Carney and Holmes found themselves out of work. Holmes was promptly hired by Luis Russell at the Nest Club. The following Sunday, while strolling down Seventh Avenue, Carney ran into Ellington, who was making plans for his summer tour of New England. Elllington suggested that Carney join them. It would give him a free trip home, and—because their base of operations would again be Salem—Carney could spend time with his family on his days off.

With the addition of Carney, Ellington was now able to do something he had been thinking about since 1923, when he began listening to Paul Whiteman's band at the Palais Royale.

There were two things about Whiteman's band that impressed Ellington. The first was its ability to play good danceable music with an impressive, full sound. The second, and most important from Ellington's standpoint, was that Whiteman's three-man saxophone section doubled on other instruments. This allowed Whiteman's arrangers—including Bill Challis, Lennie Hayton, William Grant Still, and Don Redman—multiple combinations of reed instruments to work with. They would mix these instrumental textures with great skill to achieve the lush, rich orchestrations that were the hallmark of Whiteman's band.

When Hardwick joined the Washingtonians, his main instruments were the alto and C melody saxophones. Within three years, he became proficient on the clarinet and the soprano, baritone, and bass saxophone. Jackson played clarinet and tenor saxophone. Carney played alto saxophone and clarinet and began to play baritone sax a few months later. In 1940, he even learned the bass clarinet. With this combination of reeds available to them, Ellington and Miley began their next great collaboration.

Jackson got the process started. According to Ellington, while they were staying at the New Brunswick Hotel, Jackson brought him a tune that he had written and suggested that Ellington orchestrate it. With an expanded reed section now available to him, Ellington scored the tune, a blues melody, for three clarinets in harmony. Four months later, as he was about to record the work, Ellington named it "Creole Love Call." Jackson provided a soaring New Orleans-style line as the contrasting theme. And as he had done on "Black & Tan Fantasy," Miley provided a classic solo that became an integral part of the work. When it was re-recorded in 1930, 1949, and 1954, Miley's replacements—Cootie Williams, Ray Nance, and Willie Cook—were expected to play his solo almost note for note.

The second New England tour was almost a repeat of the first one. But this time, Ellington had company; he brought his wife and son along. Mercer remembered meeting the band members at this time, as well as the local firemen, who let him play with their Dalmatian, slide down the station's brass pole, and sit on the hook-and-ladder truck.

On opening night, June 20, 1927, the band was paired with its old adversary, Mal Hallett, for the traditional battle of the bands. Later that summer, the band jousted musically with McMullin's Orchestra, Phil Napoleon's "Victor Record Band," Dick Voynow's Wolverines, a band called the Gauchos, and Roane's Sensational Pennsylvanians. The *Salem Evening News* wrote that the two bands "put up a real good fight, and some lively jazz was the result, with continuous music throughout the evening."

But Ellington's band didn't battle every night. The *Salem Evening News* reported that the band played a dance for the Young Men's Catholic Total Abstinence Society on June 22nd at the Charleshurst, and that it provided music for a "Miss America" dance in the same hall on August 9th. Even though there were few blacks in Salem (and the newspaper announced on August 11th that "A colored dance night . . . undoubtedly will be one of the big nights of the season"), 800 people turned out to hear Ellington the next day.

The press began to notice the band. On July 2nd, in a preview article, a *Fall River Herald News* writer wrote, "This prince of melody and his band scored a tremendous hit, graciously responding to repeated calls for encores." He ended his review saying, "The inimitable presentation of the Southland's crooning melodies, masterfully blended with modern day jazz, will completely captivate everyone."

Also captivated was Robert Donaldson Darrell, editor of *Phonograph Monthly Review*, a small Boston magazine that had begun publishing the previous year with a focus on classical music. Darrell was a Harvard graduate who had done graduate work at the New England Conservatory of Music. He knew very little about jazz or popular recordings, but chose to reviewed them in order to provide his readers with comprehensive coverage. One of the recordings that came across his desk was the Vocalion issue of "East St. Louis Toodle-Oo," by Duke Ellington and his Kentucky Club Orchestra. Darrell called it a "real winner."

The following month he reviewed a copy of the Brunswick recording of "Black & Tan Fantasy" by the "Washingtonians," not realizing that both groups were one and the same. He said the music deserved first prize among the dance records for the month. Untutored in jazz, he said that Miley and Nanton were performing "stunts," but wrote, " . . . [E]xceptionally original and striking, they are performed musically, even artistically. A piece no one should miss! The snatch of the 'Chopin Funeral March' at the end deserves special attention as a stroke of genius."

Darrell later contacted the recording company and learned that the "Washingtonians" were, in fact, the Duke Ellington orchestra. He paid special attention to them in successive recordings, describing the Brunswick recordings of "East St. Louis Toodle-Oo" and "Birmingham Breakdown" as "two of the finest jazz couplings perhaps ever released."

On August 7th, 1927, Ellington was the subject of a major article in the *New York Tribune* by a staff writer known as W. E. B. The writer was particularly impressed by what was to become the band's forte, its ability to create moody slow numbers and exciting fast ones. "When you waltz you wander off in a dream, the music is so soothing. Their slow fox trot, à la Southern style, brings out that soft, weird, entrancing effect that sends you sort of creeping over the floor, and when they play a fast one for contrast, they simply sweep you off your feet," he wrote.

W. E. B. extended his account to describe the band's working habits. He said that the band devoted its afternoons to rehearsals and and its evenings to performances, and that afterwards, Ellington would often "sit up till the wee hours of the morning writing new arrangements or thinking of something different to please the dancers." In the three years since Ellington had become a serious bandleader, he had already developed the work habits that would sustain him over the rest of his career. He would use the time following the dances, when the sounds of his musicians were still in his head, to compose new music.

The season ended at the Charleshurst on August 30, 1927, with the band battling Phil Napoleon's orchestra. Over Labor Day weekend, the band traveled to Old Orchard Beach, Maine, for a dance featuring a personal appearance by Miss Universe. Then it was back home to New York by way of one-night stands in Gardner and Fitchburg, both in Massachusetts.

After leaving Fitchburg, the group stopped in Boston for some unfinished business. At a meal she prepared for the band, Mrs. Carney brought up the issue of her son's finishing high school. Ellington convinced her that her son would be better off working for him. And for the next forty-seven years, Carney's instrumental voice would anchor the band. In 1960, Carney told an interviewer, "My mother will tell me if I joined the Army, I would be retired by now!"

11

WHEN THE BAND returned to the city in the fall of 1927, for the first time in four years, it was not playing at the Kentucky Club. The room had undergone major renovations and was now the Monteray Club. Once again, Leonard Harper staged the revue, featuring blues singer Victoria Spivey, and June Clark's Ragtime Cats supplied the music. Some of the tunes for the show were written by the songwriter Mack Gordon, with lyrics by Irving Mills.

This venture didn't mean that Mills had forgotten his prime client. In fact, he had been quite busy on Ellington's behalf. He had the orchestra booked for a three-week engagement as part of the Club Ciro revue and in Clarence Robinson's revue *Jazz Mania*. His third announcement was the most important: The recording session for Victor the previous January had paid off. Mills had signed them to a recording contract beginning on October 6 and 26.

Victor was the world's leading recording company. One of its major clients was the Philadelphia Orchestra, under the direction of Leopold Stokowski. Stokowski was the first conductor to make it his business to understand recording technology. While Victor had the best technicians and engineers in the industry, Stokowski knew that engineers were not musicians. But with his knowledge of both music and recording technique, he was able to convey to them his conception of the correct balance and sound of his orchestra.

Mills, whose knowledge of the recording studio was unsurpassed, was fully aware of Victor's technology and expertise. He knew that the engineers, having recorded the niney-six-piece Philadelphia Orchestra, would consider the ten-piece Ellington band a snap. As he had done at Brunswick, Mills demanded and got the same deference from the engineers for the Ellington orchestra that Stokowski got for his. During the eight years Ellington was under contract to Victor, his recordings were always far superior technically to the other labels for which he recorded.

On the first recording date, the entire session was devoted to three takes of "Black & Tan Fantasy" and "Washington Wobble." The former work required correct placement of the musicians at the microphone before a satisfactory take could be achieved. On "Washington Wobble," Ellington was pushing forward the boundaries of orchestral recording.

"Black & Tan Fantasy" was essentially the same version as the one the band had recorded on April 7, 1927, with one major exception. Instead of Edwards's pungent tuba underpinning the composition, the work is propelled this time by Guy's hypnotic banjo playing and Braud's bowed bass. Miley and the rest of the musicians' solos are essentially the same.

"Washington Wobble" was another Ellington-Hardwick collaboration. This composition, like "Birmingham Breakdown" and "The Creeper," had one foot in the past with its rousing New Orleans finale, and one foot in the future, with Ellington's expert handling of the microphone in the recording studio.

The work begins with an introduction by the saxophones and a statement of the theme by Miley. Jackson solos; at this point, Ellington and Mills put the microphone to work. They had one placed at Braud's bass, and Braud is recorded in the foreground as he backs up the solo playing four beats to the bar.

In this recording, the bass player is no longer just a timekeeper; he has become another color in the orchestral palette. The pulsations of his instrument give the recording a sense of presence that no band had ever achieved in the studio before. Braud's talent is given extra prominence when he takes a solo four-bar break. During Braud's eight-year tenure with the band, his instrument could be heard in the foreground of all of the band's recordings, especially in the exuberant "Hot and Bothered" (1928) and "Merry-Go-Round" (1933). Besides Braud and Jackson, there are also contributions by Ellington, Miley, Nanton, and Hardwick.

Jazz Mania arrived at Harlem's Lafayette Theater on October 10, 1927, with the Ellington band in a featured spot. The critic of the *Amsterdam News* had high praise for the band, writing, "With the possible exception of Fletcher Henderson's band, Duke Ellington seems to head the greatest aggregation of colored musicians. Their work makes *Jazz Mania* one of the finest shows seen here in months."

When the band went back for its second Victor recording session, they began with "Creole Love Call." The band had played the work all summer, but Ellington felt ambivalent about it. Greer recollected, "Duke liked it all right, but every now and then he'd say, 'It needs something else but I don't know what it is.' I thought it was great just the way it was. But as it turned out Duke was right as usual."

The "something else" was unwittingly provided by vocalist Adelaide Hall (who was now an international star, as a result of her performance in *Chocolate Kiddies*). Ellington heard it, and promptly put it in place: a wordless obbligato answering the three clarinets in harmony. As Hardwick said, in Ellington's world, "Everyone had freedom of expression." Throughout Ellington's musical life, if a musician played a phrase that Ellington thought would enhance a composition, he would literally add it on the spot. He did just that with the obbligato that Hall provided. Fifty-six years later, she told an interviewer from the *New York Times* how it happened.

She was listening from the wings one day while the band was rehearsing for *Jazz Mania*. She remembered, "He started to play 'Creole Love Call,' which I had never heard before. As I listened, I started to hum a counter-melody to the tune. Somehow Duke heard it. He edged over to the side of the stage and whispered, 'Addie, keep that going. That's what I'm looking for. I'm going to record it.'

"'But I don't know what I did,' I said.

"So Duke stopped the orchestra and started again, and I started again, and found out what I had been doing."

Hall's other contribution was as vocalist on the reverse side of the recording, providing another wordless, Miley-inspired, growling vocal on his song "The Blues I Love to Sing." As it was on "Washington Wobble," Braud's bass is prominent.

On November 3, the band recorded "What Can a Poor Fellow Do" and "Black & Tan Fantasy" for OKeh. The latter piece turned out to be the more important of the two. On first hearing, the work sounds similar to the version recorded on October 8. Once again, however, Miley was missing. He was replaced by Cladys (Jabbo) Smith, one of the major trumpet talents to emerge in the wake of Louis Armstrong, and another master of the growl technique.

Smith's debut on this Ellington recording may have been a tryout, but it produced more than just an audition's worth of stress for him. Recalling the event, he said, "The night before I recorded with Duke, somebody stole my horn. I had to go to a music store to get a replacement, and the mouthpiece was too big. I had a hell of a time hitting that opening high C in my solo, but I made the session."

Playing with a new, unfamiliar instrument and mouthpiece is usually difficult for all brass players. Nevertheless, Smith recorded a superb solo, and when the recording was issued, most musicians assumed that the soloist was Miley. But before long Smith's prowess was common knowledge.

Fifty years later Smith compared his solo on "Black & Tan" with the band's recording of the composition a month earlier. "The one with me sold," he observed. "Everyone gave me praise for it." He never even owned a copy of the recording, and on hearing it again, he listened to his horn with delight. "It's still in there," he said.

When the recording was made, Harlem was in the throes of grief. The young, talented, internationally known singer Florence Mills had died two days earlier. Her funeral was a massive outpouring of public grief as she was mourned by blacks and whites alike. Beginning with famed opera star Enrico Caruso, Mills Music, Inc., had made a habit of making a celebrity's death the vehicle for a song. When Rudolph Valentino had died the previous year, Mills published "There's a New Star in Heaven Tonight." With the death of Florence Mills, "You Will Always Live in our Memory" and "She's Gone to Join the Songbirds in Heaven" were offered to the public. In mid-November, Ellington, Hardwick, Greer, and Braud accompanied Margaret Lee as she recorded the songs for Vocalion. Although the recording was never issued, Ellington immortalized Florence Mills the following year in his composition "Black Beauty."

The success of *Jazz Mania* prompted producer Clarence Robinson to stage a more lavish revue a few weeks later. A new show, *Dance Mania*, went into rehearsal in mid-November and was booked for New York, Philadelphia, Baltimore, and Washington. Ellington and Johnny

Vigal were brought in from the previous show, and Adelaide Hall was one of the featured performers. In addition, there was a line of twelve chorus girls, the comedians Joyner and Foster, and Wells and Mordecai, along with the dancers Crawford Jackson and Go-Get-'em Rogers. The glowing review of the band in *Jazz Mania* was not lost on Robinson; he gave the band members featured billing over the rest of the cast. It marked the first time in Ellington's career that his band was headlining a show.

1927 was coming to a close. Ellington had every reason to be satisfied with his relationship with Mills. He had fulfilled his hopes more than he could have possibly imagined. It took only twelve months for his music to be published and broadcast over the airwaves. There had been a second successful summer tour of New England. Mills had the band in the recording studios on an average of once a month and under contract to several major recording companies. Vocalion had issued "Black & Tan Fantasy" and "Birmingham Breakdown" in April, and "Song of the Cottonfield" and "New Orleans Lowdown" followed in October.

Mills had also begun an extensive public relations campaign on Ellington's behalf. In January 1927, a large ad appeared in *Orchestra World* magazine:

> Duke Ellington and his Washingtonians
> Extend New Years Greetings to all our friends
> Now in their fifth year at the Club Kentucky, New York City
> Brunswick recording artists

The previous month, the magazine had stressed the need for bands to have publicity, noting, "It keeps the leader and his orchestra in the limelight." As *Orchestra World* was the major trade publication for the band business, it does not require too much of a stretch to assume that Mills picked up on this obvious hint to place an ad for his band.

The same issue of *Orchestra World* ran its first article on Ellington. The language reads as if it were written by Mills or one of his associates, and was standard press-agent puffery: "So much of the charm of Duke Ellington lies in the grace of his musical translation that is difficult to describe in cold, prosaic words. The lucently rippling style of his

Washingtonians always scores heavily because it has a thrilling thread woven through it." The band recorded only "Duke's own compositions, published by Jack Mills, Inc.," the writer made sure to mention.

When the recordings of "Black & Tan Fantasy" and "Birmingham Breakdown" were released during the first week of April, 1927, Mills began a publicity campaign in the black press. The following headline appeared in the April 23 and May 7 issues of the *Pittsburgh Courier*: "Duke Ellington, Brunswick Artist, Holds Unique Place in Broadway Spotlight." This time, it appears that Mills and the Brunswick press people (Vocalion was Brunswick's subsidiary) put their heads together to publicize Ellington's first record from the company. The item was repeated in the Chicago *Defender*.

The article talked about the band's beginnings in the District of Columbia and noted its start at the Oriental Gardens and subsequent move to the Kentucky Club.

It also made reference to Ellington's age and schooling in Washington, D.C., and gave credit to Henry Grant, his harmony teacher at Armstrong High School. The remainder focused on Mills's work on Duke's behalf. "[I]n accounting for his success, Ellington insists that all his remarkable rhythms and harmonies would not be known to the public, were it not for Irving Mills of Jack Mills, Inc."

The article concluded, by stating that "Duke Ellington, until recently was a 'comer.' Today he has 'arrived.' Watch his dust from now on." In fact, Ellington had not yet arrived, but he was well on his way. With his manager's financial support, he moved his musical family uptown. Sunday night, December 4, 1927, became a landmark in his career when he began his historic engagement at the Cotton Club in Harlem.

12

"HARLEM WAS LIKE a great magnet for the Negro," the poet Langston Hughes wrote," . . . where jazz is drained to Broadway, whence a Josephine Baker goes to Paris, Paul Robeson to London . . . and Duke Ellington to fame and fortune."

When Ellington first arrived in Harlem in 1923, the community began at 125th Street, with Fifth Avenue marking the boundary to the east. Lenox Avenue, the first block west, was lined with pool halls and dives, along with a few restaurants, theaters, and the Cotton Club. The Savoy Ballroom was built three years later.

Seventh Avenue served as Harlem's Champs-Elysées, sleek and spacious, especially from 125th to 135th streets. In 1925, the fledgling *New Yorker* magazine wrote that it was "the real thing in promenades." Flanked on both sides by churches, theaters, business establishments, and shops, it was thriving, well-groomed, and active all day. And beginning at five in the afternoon, it was brilliant, glamorous, and exciting as well. As Bruce Kellner wrote, "This was the Harlem [that] thrill seekers and celebrities came to know when the twenties really began to roar." Writing in *Black Manhattan*, James Weldon Johnson observed, "It is known as being exotic, colorful and sensuous, a place where life wakes up at night."

To New York's celebrities, the area had become a local Montmartre. The nightspots that reverberated to the sound of jazz and blues made Harlem the place to be after dark. One cabaret, the "Happy" Rhones establishment at 143rd Street and Lenox Avenue, had become the private watering hole of John and Ethel Barrymore, Charlie Chaplin, and Jeanne Eagles, among others. Along with Wilkins's Club Barron, it was Harlem's earliest "black and tan" club. Both its decor and clientele were black and white. The composer W. C. Handy, Ethel Waters, Paul Robeson, and black football star Fritz Pollard from Brown University could be found rubbing elbows with white celebrities. There were also assorted well-to-do doctors, lawyers, and businessmen. Happy Rhones was the first establishment to offer floor shows and to hire waitresses. Vocalist and bandleader Noble Sissle often served as an impromptu master of ceremonies there. Happy Rhones was so successful that it soon became the model for the other Harlem night spots.

Connie's Inn, at Seventh Avenue and 131st Street, was known for its elaborate floor shows. The club was segregated, catering to white audiences, but the floor show was all black. Fats Waller, the club's former delivery boy, was one of the few blacks allowed to mingle with the guests. Although he wasn't allowed to sit at a table, the bar was open to him, as was the piano if he wished to play it.

The segregated policy of Connie's Inn had Harlem's two newspapers lining up on opposite sides. The *Amsterdam News* congratulated owner Connie Immerman for bringing "downtown," meaning "white," class and style to Harlem with this enterprise. The paper felt that the sixty black workers Immerman employed outweighed the fact the club was for whites only.

On the other hand, the *New York Age* felt the club attracted an unsavory class of clientele. "As to Mr. Immerman personally," the editor wrote, "the organization has nothing against him, but we do claim that owing to his past and present business connections with the delicatessen business, which in Harlem seems to draw an unwelcome element of people, weak in mind, loose in morals, dangerous to the community. . . ."

In late October 1925, Ed Smalls, a black businessman, opened the 1,500-seat Paradise on Seventh Avenue between 134th and 135th Streets. In less than a year, the Paradise's floor shows equaled those at Connie's Inn, and the ten-piece band led by the pianist Charlie Johnson, was one of Harlem's best. While dancing the Charleston and spinning their serving trays, waiters served the customers' drinks with courtly precision.

Unlike Connie's Inn, the Paradise was not segregated, although a large majority of the customers were white. A high entrance fee was imposed to "keep out the riff-raff." Black doctors, lawyers, businessmen, and entertainers were welcome. Luis Russell said, "They had two doorkeepers who knew everyone in Harlem. If they didn't know you, you didn't get in. If you were new in town and someone they knew spoke up for you, then it was OK."

Blacks unwilling to pay the high tariff at the Paradise, or unable to get in, would venture to Jungle Alley on 133rd Street, between Fifth and Seventh Avenues. On the block between Lenox and Seventh Avenue was a notable cluster of nightspots. Mexico's bore the nickname of its owner, George James, who was reputed to have fought in the Mexican War against Pancho Villa. It was a musicians' hangout, considered by Ellington as the "hottest gin mill on 133rd Street." Practically every night of the week there was a jam session, one night for trumpets, and others for trombones, tubas, and clarinets. Luis Russell said, "If you played an instrument, 'Mexico' had a night for a cutting contest."

On the same block was Harry Hansberry's Clam House. There, Gladys Bentley—clad in a man's tuxedo—sang truly raunchy songs that would make the most jaded sophisticates blush. Hansberry's tasty bacon and eggs had customers, black and white, lined up outside waiting to get in. Those who didn't care to wait could step next door to Tillie's Inn, also known as the Chicken Shack. At midnight, the torch singer Elmira, accompanying herself at the piano, would regale the customers with risqué versions of "Stop It Joe," "Frankie and Johnnie," and "St. James Infirmary." Besides offering bacon and eggs, Tillie's was reported to have the best fried chicken and sweet potato pie in Manhattan. Better yet, at Tillie's, a party of four could eat what would be nine dollars' worth of food downtown for around two dollars.

Eight doors west of the Chicken Shack was the Catagonia Club. Inside this dimly lit room were twenty-five tables with red and white tablecloths. At the far end of the room was a piano that had seen better days. Whenever he was out of work, Willie "the Lion" Smith would be put on the payroll by the owners, Charles Holingsworth and Jeremiah Preston. Smith would play solo piano. His presence would guarantee a plethora of musicians, both black and white, sitting in on his sessions.

Holingsworth, an exuberant, back-slapping chap, would greet everyone at the door and call him "Pod-ner." Preston, a gambler, was known downtown as "West Indian Jerry." As a result, the club was known as "Pod's and Jerry's," or simply "P&J's." The owners made a point of seating their black and white patrons indiscriminately. Walter Johnson said that "Whenever whites objected, 'Pod' would courteously escort them to the door, call a cab, and tell the driver to take them to Connie's Inn, two blocks away."

The club had the usual collection of local blacks, as well as show people like Helen Morgan, Joan Crawford, Beatrice Lillie, George Abbott, and Tallulah Bankhead and her then current black escort. Songwriters Hoagy Carmichael, Howard Dietz, and Arthur Schwartz were often in residence, and Mayor Jimmie Walker would often drop by. The heavyweight boxing titlists Jack Dempsey and Gene Tunney were also frequent guests.

A few days after their second heavyweight title fight, both Dempsey and Tunney ended up at the club. Dempsey was angry; he had lost a second fight to Tunney and felt he had been cheated out of a knockout by the famous "long count." As Dempsey entered the club, he spied the champion celebrating with his friends, and challenged him to come outside and resume the fight "man to man." The owners defused the situation by ordering drinks on the house for everyone and insisting they both shake hands.

Everything at Pod's and Jerry's cost a dollar, including the Harlem specialty, a "top and bottom." This was a mixture of gin and wine that came with a precursor of what today would be called "soul food": an order of either pig's feet, roast chicken, red beans and rice, or just plain ham and eggs.

Across the street, in the basement of 169 West 133rd Street, was the opulently decorated Nest Club. The Nest opened a few months after Connie's Inn, featuring a revue staged by Leonard Harper and Sam Wooding's band. Customers usually brought their own alcoholic beverages unless they were on good terms with the owners, Mal Frazier and Johnny Carey, or were celebrities like habitues Mae West, Otto Kahn, or Paul Whiteman. In that case, they would be served some "chicken cock," a prepared bootleg concoction packaged with a tin cover over the bottle, which was very popular in Harlem.

Pianist Luis Russell said that during the year he worked there, the Nest was never raided by the police. "A cat would come running into the place yelling about a raid going on. Carey didn't bat an eye; he'd tell us to keep playing, and not to worry about it."

The owners were local boys, born in Harlem and known to be generous to the police. "There wasn't a night in the week when you didn't see one of the officers from the 135th Street station there, eating dinner, having a few drinks, and picking up some cash if he needed it." Russell said.

Clearly, the advent of Prohibition had little effect on Harlem's cabarets. In fact, new ones had opened up and were flourishing. Cabaret owners saw the occasional police raids as a cost of doing business, at best, or the result of not paying the police off, at the worst. Along Lenox Avenue, liquor could be bought anywhere: at shoeshine stands, delicatessens, soda fountains, newspaper stands, and drug stores.

When the Yorkshire-born bootlegger Owen Vincent "Owney" Madden, "Duke of the West Side," returned to the city in 1921 after serving seven-and-a-half years in Sing Sing for manslaughter, he chose Harlem as the next place to market his wares. He moved to a penthouse in Chelsea near his Phoenix Cereal Beverage Company, which produced hundreds of gallons of "Madden's No. 1" beer daily.

Madden had ascended to the top of organized crime in New York City by sheer ruthlessness. Raised in Hell's Kitchen, as a youth he was described as "a bantam rooster out of hell." He emerged from prison, a slim, soft-spoken, dapper parolee "with the gentle smile of a cherub." Madden made a classy appearance, wearing a gray fedora pulled low over one eye, a black shirt, white tie, and (because of his horror of germs and fingerprints) white gloves. Sonny Greer described him as "a skinny, little guy with a hawk-like face, who spoke with a lisp, wore English suits, spats, and drove around town in a bullet-proof Duesenberg."

There was no doubt that Madden had power, wealth, and a quietly menacing air. Such was his influence that, in 1937, while retired in Hot Springs, Arkansas, he ordered the syndicate to let Joe Louis fight Jim Braddock, instead of Slapsy Maxie Rosenbloom, for the world heavyweight championship. Single-handedly, Madden abolished a taboo that, for more than twenty years, had denied black fighters the right to compete for the world heavyweight championship.

Madden relished the company of prizefighters and entertainers, finding he had much in common with show people. They were "for real," as his biographer, Graham Nown, explained. "They were open and genuine. Like him, they followed a precarious calling, and they seemed to understand each other." Greer claimed to have Madden's private telephone number, as did the dancer Bessie Dudley, who was one of Madden's favorites. She would dance at his private parties when not working at one of his nightclubs.

One night, as Dudley was preparing to leave work, she was stopped by one of Madden's henchmen, who demanded that she sit at his table and have a drink. She explained that it was very late, and that her mother was expecting her. However, she said would be happy to have a drink with him the following evening. He responded with a racial slur and indicated he would have her fired.

Dudley recalled:

> I was very upset and in tears when I called Mr. Madden's house. When I told him what happened, he told me to stop crying, I still had a job working for him until *he said so,* and not to worry, he would speak to the young man. The following night in my dressing room was a dozen roses. Around each stem was wrapped a twenty dollar bill. There was no card. That happened every night for a week. Then there was a note from the young man asking my forgiveness. We became very good friends.

Although he was a stylish dresser and man about town, Madden prized his anonymity to the point of paying columnists to keep his name *out* of the newspapers. He was the silent partner in several of the city's better known nocturnal establishments, the El Fey Club on West 45th Street, the Silver Slipper on Broadway, and the Stork Club. In league with the nominal queen of New York's nightlife, Texas Guinan, he operated a series of speakeasies throughout the city.

In 1923, Madden found the uptown place he had been searching for. Five years earlier, the Douglas Casino was built at 644 Lenox Avenue at the corner of 142nd Street. It was modeled on the very successful Renaissance Casino ten blocks south. The two-story building housed the Douglas Theater on the ground floor, which featured films and occasional vaudeville acts. To its right were a series of storefronts, which would later be a part of the Golden Gate Ballroom, built several years later. On the second floor was a large room intended to be a dance hall.

Two years earlier, Madden's close friend, the former heavyweight boxing champion Jack Johnson, became the nominal owner of the space and converted it into the Club Deluxe, a four-hundred-seat supper club that featured a small band. Johnson, an amateur bass player, would often sit in with them. But even with the combination of good food, music, and a former heavyweight champion on the premises, the club never did well. Black Harlem, as well as white New York, was offended by Johnson's predilection for marrying white women. The current Mrs. Johnson was often on the premises, and many felt that her presence was the main reason for the club's poor business.

By mid-1922, Johnson and his partners were casting about for a buyer. They were in luck; the room and its site were just what Madden was looking for. In January 1923, he bought out Johnson and his associates and engaged Florenz Ziegfeld's brilliant set and costume designer Joseph Urban to redo the room. The result was a seven-hundred-seat horseshoe-shaped supper club named the Cotton Club. One writer described the decor as "a brazen riot of African Jungle motifs, Southern stereotypology, and lurid eroticism." Cab Calloway provided the following description of the room:

> The bandstand was a replica of a southern mansion, with large white columns and a backdrop painted with weeping willows and slave quarters. The band played on the veranda of the mansion, and in front of the veranda, down a few steps, was the dance floor, which was also used for the shows. The waiters wore red tuxedos, like butlers in a southern mansion.

To ensure the staff's loyalty, the syndicate went outside the city for most of the employees. Busboys, waiters, and cooks were all imported from Chicago. Local bands, such as those of Armand J. Piron and Happy Rhones, were hired to provide the music. However, as a result of Madden's ownership, the club was closed by the federal government in 1925 for a violation of the Prohibition laws. Madden was indicted on a charge of parole violation, but was later acquitted.

Preparations for reopening brought an important change in management. The syndicate instructed Harry Block, the nominal owner, to hire Herman Stark as general manager and license holder. Stark was a Madden associate, and a former machine-gunner during World War I. Stark and his assistant, "Frenchy" DeMange, were no neophytes to the business. Stark knew just the man to execute the concept he had for entertainment at the club. When the club reopened in 1926, he hired Dan Healy and allowed him a generous budget to "conceive and produce" the floor shows.

Director and producer Dan Healy began his career as a performer in vaudeville, but soon was appearing in musicals. By 1930, he had been in the *Ziegfeld Follies of 1927*, Rodgers and Hart's *Betsy*, and Kalmar and Ruby's *Good Boy*. He went on to stage Jack "Legs" Diamond's *Frolics* at the Chateau Madrid, as well as shows in Atlantic City and Philadelphia. Earlier in the year that he came to the Cotton Club, he staged a production at Madden's Silver Slipper Club, featuring the young dancer Ruby Keeler.

Healy's Cotton Club productions were elaborate for a nightclub, with miniature sets, dramatic lighting, and spectacular costumes. For music, Andrew Preer's eleven-piece orchestra, the Missourians, was imported from Chicago.

The chief ingredient was "pace, pace, pace!" Healy said. The show was generally built around types—the band, an eccentric dancer, a comedian, and a star—and ran between an hour-and-a-half and two hours. There would always be a good singer, such as Aida Ward, Leitha Hill, or Ethel Waters. One or twice a year, Healy—aided by the songwriting team of Dorothy Fields and Jimmy McHugh—would stage revues called the *Cotton Club Parade*. These productions earned the institution the title "Aristocrat of Harlem," conferred on it by Lady Edwina Mountbatten when she visited the club with her friend, singer Sophie Tucker, two years later.

Despite an accolade by the wife of a future British war hero and diplomat, the Cotton Club shows were not as good as those at Connie's Inn or the Paradise. At one time or another, Walter Johnson worked at all three. "Remember this," Johnson told me, "those great shows at Connie's Inn had music by Fats [Waller], lyrics by [Andy] Razaf, and [Leonard] Harper's dance routines. Any girl he trained could outdance the line at the Cotton Club."

The shows at Connie's Inn and the Paradise were conceived and executed by black entertainers for white or mixed audiences. Those at the Cotton Club were written and choreographed by whites for white audiences and executed by blacks. By the time of Lady Mountbatten's visit, both *Billboard* and *Variety* were comparing the Cotton Club's shows unfavorably with the productions at the other two establishments.

When Andrew Preer died suddenly in May 1927, the club's management began looking for another band. While the Missourians were a good group, they had not developed a following. Their main task had been to accompany the entertainers and play danceable tunes for the customers. Preer, a violinist, led the band and directed the music for the shows. They had recorded as early as 1925 for Columbia Records as "The Cotton Club Orchestra," but Preer was content to be listed as violinist-leader, along with the rest of the personnel. It was not until three months before his death, when the band recorded for Gennett, that it was first billed as "Andy Preer and the Cotton Club Orchestra." That date produced a version of "I've Found a New Baby," which had not yet been issued by the time of Preer's death.

In keeping with the club's hiring policy, the management wanted to find a name band from out of New York to head the fall 1927 show. The Cotton Club was in luck. Just one block away, Joe "King" Oliver's Dixie Syncopators had arrived in town to begin a two-week engagement at the Savoy Ballroom.

When the Cotton Club approached Oliver about heading the fall show, he was noncommittal. His band had been booked for an extensive tour of the South, and he said he would discuss the matter in the fall when he returned to the city. However, the band was stranded in Baltimore a few weeks later when its booking agent disappeared with the receipts from one of its engagements. Oliver brought his men back to New York, but with no work in sight, the group disbanded. Pianist Luis Russell took what remained of the band to play at the Nest Club.

But the loss of his band wasn't Oliver's only problem. Earlier that year, he had developed a serious gum infection, making it almost impossible for him to play his horn. When he returned to New York, he had all his teeth removed and was fitted for dental plates. By the fall, he was practicing his horn again and rebuilding his embouchure, but he had no band. Luis Russell said that as soon as Oliver was comfortable, he began to drop in at the Nest Club once or twice a week. Oliver hinted that he had a good job lined up and suggested that the band get back together. But Oliver would never come out and say where the job was, and the musicians would never ask. Russell said, "We were making so much money in tips, the owners had to chase us down to give us our week's pay!"

The Cotton Club knew about Oliver's physical problems when they contacted him in September 1927, but he was still their first choice to headline the show. As Oliver had neither a band nor the energy to build one on short notice, the club offered to bring back the Missourians, suggesting that Oliver lead them. They would be billed as "King Oliver and his Orchestra," but he refused. To save face, he began to negotiate with management for a larger fee. Finally, Oliver turned down the job, saying that the money was not enough. This was at a time when the Cotton Club had the reputation for paying performers higher salaries than the other clubs. In desperation, Stark wired Sam Wooding, offering him $1,100 a week to bring his band into the club. Wooding, then on a lucrative vaudeville tour, asked his musicians to make the decision, knowing that they would refuse.

"It was a joke," he said. "Which would you rather do . . . go into the Cotton Club or go to Europe?" On the Continent, he and his musicians were paid handsomely. Wooding's salary was three times as much as those of his sidemen. He considered the $1,100-a-week offer insulting. Having played in Europe for royalty, he felt it would be a step down to return to Harlem.

While awaiting Wooding's decision, Stark quietly sent an emissary to Smalls's Paradise to find out if Charlie Johnson was interested. Benny Carter was in the band at the time. He told me that Johnson was uninterested in the offer for several reasons. For one thing, the musicians felt they had one of the best jobs in town. If Johnson was going to make a move, the only other job he might be interested in was the one Fletcher Henderson had downtown at Roseland.

Smalls treated the musicians as if they were members of his family. He paid them handsomely. For example, the seventeen-year-old Jabbo Smith alone was getting $125 a week. In another demonstration of Smalls's generosity, he lent two or three members of the band money to buy cars. Carter felt that even if Stark could match what Smalls was paying them, there was another reason the band members would not leave: The rigid segregation at the Cotton Club would make it impossible for black musicians to come to hear the band play. Although the general public came in droves to the Paradise for the dazzling floor shows and uptown ambience, the band drew the musicians in the audience. Jabbo Smith remembered, "One night Chick Webb's entire band showed up . . . not booked to play there, mind you, but simply coming in and getting up to play, in an attempt to cut Johnson's band."

"Every musician in town black or white, wanted to sit in and take a shot at us," Benny Carter said. "You couldn't do that at the Cotton Club, even if you were Bix Beiderbecke, Benny Goodman, [or] Tommy or Jimmy Dorsey."

The refusal of Oliver, Wooding, and Johnson to take the Cotton Club job placed the management in a bind. These failed negotiations had forced the club to postpone the show's opening to December 4, 1927. That date was drawing near, and the Cotton Club still had no band. Jimmy McHugh then suggested that if the club's management was going to audition bands, they should listen to Duke Ellington's. He had heard the band many times at the Kentucky Club, and felt it would be ideal for the show. However, McHugh's interest was more than artistic. Jack Mills, Inc., was also his publisher and, in addition, McHugh was a stockholder and the office manager of the company. From this vantage point, he was well aware of Irving Mills's prodigious effort to champion Ellington and his music. If the band got the job, McHugh would profit, too. With the blessings of the Cotton Club management, he brought the matter to Mills's attention.

Stark suggested that all concerned parties meet after he and Healy had heard the band, then playing at the Lafayette Theater. It was the last day of the New York run of *Dance Mania.* Greer said that before one of the shows, Mills came backstage and told the band that the owners of the Cotton Club were in the audience. He told Ellington to make sure Miley was there and able to play, as this was their "big chance." After the show, Healy, Stark, Ellington, Guy, and Mills went next door to a tavern. Healy told Stark he wanted the band in the show, and Stark had no objection. Stark told Mills to meet him at the club the following day to work out the details of the contract.

Mills arrived in Philadelphia with the contract a few days later. Ellington was perturbed, however, when he noticed that it called for a 10-piece band. He had gone on tour with just eight men, leaving Carney and Metcalf behind because he couldn't afford them. Mills, aware of this, and not wanting to see a great opportunity for his client

Duke the Man

Duke Ellington as a child in Washington, D.C., c. 1906.
Courtesy Frank Driggs Collection

Duke and Fred Guy
in New York, c. 1925.
Courtesy Frank Driggs Collection

Arthur Whetsol,
Fredi Washington, and
Duke, c. 1929.
Courtesy Frank Driggs Collection

Duke flips some hit records.
Corbis/Bettmann

The famous "Top Hat" shot of Ellington made right before his first European tour, 1933.
Corbis/Bettmann

Duke in Hollywood, c. 1934.
Courtesy Frank Driggs Collection

Irving Mills, Percy Grainger,
Duke, at New York's
New School, 1935.
Courtesy Frank Driggs
Collection

Edward K. Ellington, Sr.
(top) and Duke on the
Ellington train, 1936.
Courtesy Frank Driggs
Collection

Duke composing, c. 1930s.
Corbis/Bettmann

W. C. Handy and Duke on Randall's Island, New York, 1938.
Courtesy Frank Driggs Collection

Harry Carney,
Sonny Greer,
Ivie Anderson,
and Duke on the
Ellington Express,
1940.
Courtesy Frank
Driggs Collection

Sy Oliver, Duke, and Billy Strayhorn at an award dinner for
the "Foremost Arranger/Composers," 1946.
Courtesy Frank Driggs Collection

Duke and Evie Ellis
celebrating a birthday,
c. 1960s.
Courtesy Frank Driggs
Collection

Duke during the
benediction service for
the *First Sacred Concert,*
New York, January 19, 1968.
Corbis/Bettmann

Duke and Mercer, c. 1960s.

Receiving an honorary degree in music from
Columbia University, May 16, 1973.
Corbis/Bettmann

The Bands

Sonny Greer, Duke, and Sterling Conaway performing at the Louis Thomas Cabaret, Washington, D.C., 1920.
Courtesy Frank Driggs Collection

The Washingtonians, New York, 1925. Left to right: Sonny Greer, Charlie Irvis, Bubber Miley, Elmer Snowden, Otto Hardwicke, Duke.

The Washingtonians at Orchard Beach, New York, August 1926. Left to right:
Sonny Greer, Rudy Jackson (or: Max Shaw), Percy Glascoe, Edgar Sampson, Fred
Guy, Tricky Sam Nanton, Otto Hardwicke, Duke, Bubber Miley.
Courtesy Frank Driggs Collection

Performing at the Cotton Club, 1929.
Courtesy Frank Driggs Collection

Exterior of the downtown Cotton Club, c. late 1930s.
Corbis/Bettmann

Duke's last appearance at the (downtown) Cotton Club in 1938, with the Step Brothers in the background.
Courtesy Frank Driggs Collection

The band in characteristic jungle setting.
Corbis/Bettmann

The full orchestra, September 3, 1931.
Corbis/Bettmann

Johnny Hodges,
Tricky Sam Nanton,
Duke, Harry Carney,
and Wallace Jones in
Amsterdam, 1939.
Courtesy Frank Driggs
Collection

In rehearsal, c. 1944–45. Left to right: Duke, Ben Webster,
Jimmy Hamilton, Johnny Hodges, Harry Carney.
Corbis/Bettmann

Film still from *Cabin in the Sky,* January 15, 1943.
Corbis/Bettmann

Film still from *Reveille with Beverly,* January 23, 1945.
Corbis/Bettmann

get lost over the issue of two men, agreed to pay them out of his own pocket.

But one problem still remained: Ellington was under contract to Clarence Robinson for the remainder of the *Dance Mania* tour. Robinson refused to release him, and made it plain he would sue for damages if he left.

Dance Mania had finished its New York run on November 20 and reopened in Philadelphia the next day. The Ellington band was also scheduled to go head-to-head with Fletcher Henderson at the Philadelphia Academy of Music four days later and had an engagement to play the dance following the annual Thanksgiving Day football game between Howard and Lincoln universities. (This dance would turn out to be the band's first connection with a future Ellington collaborator. According to an advertisement for the dance in the *Baltimore Afro-American*, a Lincoln student named Langston Hughes was the dance's treasurer.)

Mills put the matter of Ellington's contract to the Cotton Club's management, which contacted Owney Madden. Madden had one of his associates in Philadelphia, a gangster named "Boo Boo" Hoff, drop by the theater to warn Robinson that if he valued his health, he would release Ellington from his contract forthwith. Being a prudent man, Robinson agreed. And as a compromise, Hoff allowed the band to finish the second week in Philadelphia, giving Robinson time to find a replacement.

Later that week, Mills came back to Philadelphia with Carney and Metcalf and some of the music from the forthcoming Cotton Club production. Ellington and his men spent most of their spare time rehearsing the score. After the band's last Philadelphia show ended at 11 P.M., Saturday night, December 3, 1927, the band caught the midnight train to New York, an inauspicious start to an unimagined rise to fame.

13

THE BAND ARRIVED in New York on the morning of December 4, 1927. At noon, the group was at the club to rehearse the score with the cast. Greer said he felt opening night was anything but a success. During the first show, cues were missed, the band played raggedly, and things didn't seem to mesh.

The problem was that Ellington had to both direct the band and cue the acts, something he had not done before. That was usually Ellsworth Reynolds's task, but he was in Washington rehearsing the Wilbur DeParis orchestra, the band's replacement in *Dance Mania*. This meant that Ellington was forced to conduct the music for the show from his keyboard. Although he missed a few cues during the first show, things went well enough during the second show for the band to receive a good review in *Variety*.

Variety devoted most of a column to its review of the show. The reviewer described the chorus as "almost Caucasian high yaller gals." In addition to Ellington's band, the show featured the singer Aida Ward, the Berry Brothers dance team, Edith Wilson, the adagio dance team of Henri and LaPerl, and the singer May Alix. The dancer Jimmy Ferguson (later known as Baron Lee) was master of ceremonies. The reviewer singled out the band, writing, "In Duke Ellington's dance band, Harlem has reclaimed its own after Times Square accepted them for several seasons at the Club Kentucky. The Ellington jazzique is just too bad."

A few days later, Reynolds returned and things quickly fell apart. The band members had close professional and emotional ties to Ellington and had always considered Reynolds an outsider. When Reynolds returned, the band continued to look to Ellington for musical cues. But the dancers and entertainers looked to Reynolds. Healy and Mills realized that the situation was becoming intolerable, and Reynolds was quietly dismissed. Ellington went back to directing the show from the keyboard, and soon everything ran like clockwork.

The "Ellington sound" was a more serious difficulty. Preer's Missourians had been at the club for two years and the management was used to their music, usually stock arrangements of popular songs of the day, or their own, tailored to keep the customers dancing and the management happy. But listening to a composition like Ellington's "Birmingham Breakdown," Stark, Healy, and McHugh found the lack of discernible thematic material perplexing. That and the jangling dissonance of Miley's poignant, rough-hewn, expressive growling and Nanton's primeval utterances made Stark, Healy, and especially McHugh wonder if they had made a serious mistake. At one point in the evening, after the band had played "Birmingham Breakdown," McHugh went over to Ellington at the piano and said "Play 'Mother Machree,' or I'm a goner."

Harlem musicians were similarly critical of the band. They remembered with relish the Ellington debacle at the Cameo Club. Part of their criticism sprang from jealousy, because they had expected the Cotton Club job to go to one of their own after Oliver, Wooding, and especially Johnson had turned it down. Because Ellington had been working downtown for four years, some uptown musicians didn't even consider his group a Harlem band. Luis Russell reported that, when Ellington's band first went to the Cotton Club, most musicians still thought of the group as the Washingtonians.

Beyond that, the band's musicianship itself was suspect. "I used to go by the Rhythm Club to hear their broadcast before going to work at the Nest [Club]," said Russell. "When 'Tricky Sam' or Bubber would solo, some of the older musicians would laugh!"

The band was now playing on radio station WHN three times a week, Mondays from 11:30 P.M. to midnight and Wednesday and Friday evenings from 7:00 to 7:30. Ted Husing, who had hosted the broadcasts from the Kentucky Club, was now doing the honors uptown.

Harry Carney said that after the early broadcast, they would go down to the Rhythm Club to get the musicians' reactions. "In the beginning, a lot of them made us feel like crying, they were so critical," he noted.

Duke's main cheerleaders uptown were his mentors Will Marion Cook and a musician known as "Mexico," aka George James, who also owned an uptown club. "This man had a tremendous effect on

Ellington," Mercer wrote. "He never scolded Ellington or told him when he was wrong. He'd simply say 'A wise man would do so and so....'" Mexico had great faith in Ellington, so much so that he made a bet of $100 and a hat that the band would make the grade. Cook also was very vocal about his feeling that the band would succeed.

Ellington did get a good deal of support from white musicians. Paul Whiteman and his arrangers, Bill Challis, Ferde Grofé, and Lennie Hayton, came to the club often, as did his star trumpet player, Bix Beiderbecke. Another group—composers George Gershwin and Vincent Youmans and the bandleaders Roger Wolfe Kahn, Eddie Duchin, and Leo Reisman—also appeared at the club and spoke highly of Ellington's music. They all went out of their way to congratulate the club's managers on their foresight in hiring him.

Reisman hired Miley as guest soloist with his orchestra the following August. In 1929, Youmans wanted to use the Ellington band in his ill-fated Broadway show *Great Day*, but Mills vetoed the idea. However, during the same year, Mills allowed Gershwin to use the band in the musical *Show Girl*. Four years later, Paul Whiteman played an Ellington composition at a concert in Carnegie Hall and, in 1938, another work before an audience of 18,000 at Lewisohn Stadium in New York. Nine years later, Whiteman commissioned Ellington to write an orchestral work, "Blue Belles of Harlem." A member of the Cotton Club staff remembered seeing Peter Duchin literally "clutching his sides and rolling on the floor in ecstasy" the first time he heard the Ellington brass section execute a very intricate "break" during its race-horse version of "Tiger Rag."

The first week in January 1929, OKeh issued "Black & Tan Fantasy" coupled with "What Can a Poor Fellow Do?" A more important event followed two weeks later, when Victor issued the band's sumptuously evocative recording of "Black & Tan Fantasy" and the eerie, haunting "Creole Love Call." Will Marion Cook took the lead in using these six minutes of music to forcefully argue the merits of Ellington's music. Luis Russell said that when that recording came out, the musicians who had been laughing at Ellington's music stopped, because they knew he was doing something unique.

Robert Donaldson Darrell wrote in that month's *Phonograph Monthly Review* that "A new performance of 'Black and Tan Fantasy' by

Duke Ellington eclipses even the startling Brunswick record of this remarkable piece." He went on to note that "There can't be too many disks of a work as original and inspired as this one."

Paradoxically, Ellington's unorthodox scoring was enthusiastically accepted by the management when it became clear that customers interpreted the sound of the band (including Miley's and Nanton's growling) as "jungle music." Sophisticated whites had been coming up to Harlem for years. Now average New Yorkers were venturing uptown, their curiosity piqued by two events: a stage production and a novel.

In February 1927, the producer David Belasco staged Charles MacArthur and Edward Shelton's controversial play *Lulu Belle* on Broadway. The play starred the white actress Lenore Ulric in the role of a light-skinned black woman, and Evelyn Preer was one of the costars. The play's first act was set in New York City's San Juan Hill, the city's first large black community, where Bubber Miley had grown up. The second act was set in a Harlem rooming house, and the pivotal third act was placed in the "Elite Grotto," a Harlem nightclub not unlike the Cotton Club, where white "slummers" went to be entertained by black performers. The play had a successful run on Broadway and went on tour in the fall.

A second major influence on the growth of Harlem as a white nightspot was the novel *Nigger Heaven*. It was written by a white, Carl Van Vechten, and quickly became a best-seller. It chronicled the lives of Harlem residents and led to increased attendance by whites at uptown nightspots. *Variety* noticed this trend and credited the book for having stimulated trade. "It is having tremendous sales, especially in New York, as it deals with the night life phase of that part of town that lies north of 125th Street."

Returning to the city from his native Washington, D.C., the physician and novelist Rudolph Fischer noticed the influx of whites to Harlem. He published his observations, "The Caucasian Storms Harlem," in the *American Mercury*. The magazine *Vanity Fair* reported that "Harlem's cabarets were more popular than ever." This phenomenon caused the black sociologist Charles S. Johnson to wonder aloud "if Harlem was becoming the white man's house of assignation."

By early 1928, when Claude McKay's best-selling novel *Home to Harlem* and Rudolph Fischer's *The Walls of Jerico* were published, whites

no longer had to experience Harlem through books, periodicals, or theater. They were coming uptown in droves to experience the real thing.
Harlem now represented the apotheosis of slumming.

Nathan Huggins wrote, "Into its vortex white ladies and gentlemen
were pulled, to dance the jungle dance . . . bodies thrust, clenched eyes
and teeth, staccato breath, sweat-bodies writhing and rolling with a
drum and a beat as they might never with a woman or man."

"You go sort of primitive up there," the entertainer Jimmy Durante
observed. Lena Horne, who danced in the Cotton Club's chorus line in
the early 1930s, recalled, "The shows had a primitive, naked quality
that was supposed to make a civilized audience lose its inhibitions."
The primitive quality of the entertainment was clearly sexual, as
Huggins and others noted. The Cotton Club was a place where curious
whites could travel uptown and, for the price of dinner and a few
drinks, could have a vicarious sexual experience. For those repressed
souls who were unwilling or unable to experience it at home, black
dancers, singers, and musicians would act out their own sexuality,
accompanied by music Ellington described in his autobiography as
"stark, wild and tense."

Marshall Stearns, jazz critic, Chaucer scholar, and professor of
English at Cornell University, visited the club many times while an
undergraduate at Yale. His is still one of the best descriptions of what
the shows were like. "I recall one," he wrote:

> where a light-skinned and magnificently muscled Negro burst
> through a papier-mâché jungle onto the dance floor clad in an avia-
> tor's helmet, goggles, and shorts. He had been forced down in darkest
> Africa, and in the center of the floor he came upon a "white" goddess
> clad in long, blonde tresses and being worshiped by a circle of cring-
> ing "blacks." Producing a bullwhip from heaven knows where, he res-
> cued the blonde and they did an erotic dance. In the background,
> Bubber Miley, Tricky Sam Nanton and members of the Ellington
> band growled, wheezed and snorted obscenely.

Scenarios like this one must have had a powerful effect on many of
the customers arriving from downtown. Most had driven through
Central Park by cab and exited uptown onto dimly lit Lenox Avenue.

Observing the mainly black faces, some whites must have felt as if they had journeyed from civilization into some unknown, exciting venue.

Always on the lookout for a vehicle with which to market his client, Mills seized on the "jungle" theme. He ordered the announcer of the radio broadcasts to introduce the show as "featuring the jungle music of Duke Ellington and his orchestra." That statement came as a surprise to Ellington's own family members the first time they heard the band on the air. Ruth Ellington said, "It was quite a shock. Here we were, my mother and I sitting in this very respectable, Victorian living room in Washington . . . and the announcer from New York telling us we are listening to Duke Ellington and his Jungle Music!"

Mills extended his marketing to the recording studio. He instructed Brunswick to issue all future recordings of the band under the pseudonym "The Jungle Band." Ellington responded with a series of new compositions: "Jungle Nights in Harlem," "Echoes of the Jungle," "Jungle Blues," and "Jungle Jamboree." He also introduced tangential works like "Doin' the Voom Voom" and "The Mooche" (which became a best-seller).

There were two shows every night at the Cotton Club: the first at midnight, the second at 2 A.M.. The Cotton Club had become known as the place where show people would go to relax after their own performances. Those in the know made it a point to catch the last show, especially on Sunday night when other performers had the night off, because they never knew what unexpected entertainment dividend might turn up. For the Ellington orchestra it began on a Sunday night in January 1928, when it was announced that Fred Astaire was in the house. He was then starring downtown with his sister Adele in George Gershwin's *Funny Face*.

Astaire leaped onto the stage and started to dance. According to Greer, "I picked up the tempo a bit, he followed. Bubber and Tricky got into it. The next thing I knew, he was dancing his ass off, the band was wailing, and the place was going crazy! Stark came out of his office to see what in hell was going on. When it was over, he [Astaire] applauded us!"

Other Sunday nights might find the band backing the dancer Marilyn Miller doing an exquisite soft-shoe routine, or the singing of Al Jolson, Helen Morgan, Ruth Etting, Eddie Cantor, Harry Richman,

Gilda Gray, or Sophie Tucker. One night the Marx Brothers came onstage and convulsed the audience with their inspired mayhem.

These were scintillating times. The "jungle music" and the ambience of the club were a powerful lure for New Yorkers. Besides entertainers, Owney Madden's close friend, Mayor Jimmy Walker, could be found there regularly, accompanied by his friend actress Betty Compton. Financier Otto Kahn became fascinated by the place after his son Rodger brought him one night to hear the band. He returned regularly, often bringing many of his wealthy friends.

On any given night, Carl Van Vechten, who had become "white America's tour guide to Harlem," would show up with the likes of Sir Osbert Sitwell, H. L. Mencken, F. Scott Fitzgerald, or William Faulkner in tow. The *Daily News* listed the roll of guests from the Blue Book of Broadway and the Social Register. The dancer Ann Pennington came on several occasions, as did Gertrude Vanderbilt. The newspaper observed that "Bobby Coverdale and Sailing Baruch Jr. have often played hooky from Park Avenue to bask in the atmosphere."

Hanging around backstage was a young man known to have gangster connections. A close friend and protégé of Owney Madden, he traveled with a .38-caliber revolver and drove the convoy car for Madden's fleet of beer trucks. He was a superb dancer and was known to describe himself as "the best dancer in New York when Fred Astaire's out of town."

The young man had been in several Broadway productions. When not on stage, he used Madden's El Fey Club as his base of operations. On the three or four nights a week he would show up at the Cotton Club, women would tip the headwaiter to get him to dance with them. One of his extracurricular assignments was to drive down to Broadway and pick up Madden's profits from *Diamond Lil*, a play he had financed starring his former lover, Mae West. The young man caught Mae West's eye and *they* became lovers. Five years later, this young man was starring in films, and in the process he changed the pronunciation and spelling of his name from George Ranft to George Raft.

One night when the band reported for work, Ellington was summoned to Stark's office. The manager informed him that the gangster Jack "Legs" Diamond, his close friend, was expected that evening. Diamond had been discharged from Bellevue Hospital the previous week, having survived the second attempt on his life, and this was his first night on the town. Duke was given a direct order to play whatever music Diamond requested.

Diamond arrived with his girlfriend, Kiki Roberts, and promptly asked for "St. Louis Blues." The couple danced in front of the bandstand all night. The gangster repeated his request several times, and Ellington always obliged. At closing time, Diamond walked up to the bandstand and stuffed a thousand-dollar bill into Ellington's breast pocket. "Thanks, kid," he said, "buy yourself a cigar." Diamond went into Stark's office, and later, as he was leaving, he walked past the band's dressing room. Seeing Ellington again, Diamond gave him another thousand-dollar bill. Then, with his arm around his girlfriend's waist, he strolled out the door into the morning.

From the time of Ellington's arrival, the Cotton Club had been doing excellent business. With the place packed every night, whatever doubts Stark had about the music no longer mattered. Stark told Mills he planned to keep the club open all summer, and he wound up taking the option to renew the band's contract for the full three years.

14

FOLLOWING THE BAND'S Cotton Club debut, Mills had not been idle. While the band was building up its reputation at the club every night, Mills kept the group in the recording studios by day. The three big production numbers in the Cotton Club show—"Harlem River Quiver," "Red Hot Band," and "Doin' the Frog"—were written by Dorothy Fields and Jimmy McHugh, and Jack Mills, Inc., had exclusive publication rights for all of their music. On December 19, 1927, the band was at the Victor studios recording "Harlem River Quiver" and two Ellington compositions, "East St. Louis Toodle-Oo" and "Blue Bubbles" (both Ellington-Miley collaborations).

At the band's first session for Vocalion a year earlier, its radio theme "East St. Louis Toodle-Oo" was the first composition it recorded. According to Greer, both Duke and Mills considered the work a good-luck charm. Following the Vocalion session, the band recorded it at their first Brunswick and Columbia sessions as well.

For the Vocalion session ten days after the Victor recording, the band recorded the other two numbers from the show. On "Doin' the Frog," Hardwick plays bass saxophone. The number was used in the show to feature the dancer Cora La Redd and was subsequently recorded by white jazz bandleader Frankie Trumbauer as "Raisin' the Roof."

On January 9, 1928, Mills had Ellington back in the studio recording for the Harmony label. It was clear that he wanted the band recorded no matter what the circumstances, and in this case the band recorded as the Washingtonians. The recordings were neither Ellington compositions nor music owned by his company, and—most surprisingly—Mills allowed the band to be recorded acoustically. The musicians recorded "Sweet Mama (Papa's Gettin' Mad)," "Stack O' Lee Blues," and "Bugle Call Rag." The last number served to introduce a new member of the band to the public: clarinetist Albany (Barney) Bigard.

Ten days later, they were in the OKeh studio. They recorded their first two numbers, an Ellington-Miley collaboration "Take It Easy," and

"Jubilee Stomp," as Duke Ellington and his Orchestra. For the third work of the session, the banjo and guitar player Lonnie (Lonzo) Johnson joined them. Three years earlier, while living in St. Louis, Johnson had won a blues singing contest whose prize included an OKeh contract for a series of "race" recordings. His fine single-string guitar work was also prominently featured on several sides by Louis Armstrong's Hot Five. Billed as "Lonnie Johnson's Harlem Footwarmers," he and the band recorded "Harlem Twist," which was simply another version of "East St. Louis Toodle-Oo."

That work was recorded again in the first week of March, along with "Take It Easy" and "Jubilee Stomp" during a session for the Pathé Recording Company. This recording had an interesting sequel. In August of the following year, the Plaza, Cameo, and Pathé recording companies merged to become the American Recording Company (ARC). These "dimestore" labels issued inexpensive records using a plethora of different labels. The Plaza Music company had issued recordings under the Jewel, Banner, Domino, Oriole, and Regal labels, the Cameo Record Corporation had Cameo, Romeo, Variety, and Lincoln under its banner, and Pathé Phonograph and Radio Corporation had Pathé, Actuelle, and Perfect.

The new American Recording Company took the master discs and issued the three recordings by the "Washingtonians" on Cameo and those by the "Whoopee Makers" on Pathé. These were subsequently issued on Perfect, the Pathé subsidiary, and Lincoln, the Cameo subsidiary. In October, "The Ten Blackberries" recorded "East St. Louis Toodle-Oo" again for Velvetone, and it was simultaneously issued on the Diva label. This meant that by 1930, there were recordings of "East St. Louis Toodle-Oo" on eleven different labels.

During a March 21, 1928, Brunswick session, the band was again recording as the Washingtonians. Trumpeter Arthur Whetsol had returned earlier in the month and was subbing for Bubber Miley on this session. Ellington celebrated his return by orchestrating "Firewater," a piano solo he had been playing at the club as the band returned to the stage after intermission. "Firewater" was tailored for Whetsol's pristine, wistful style of playing.

Using a mute, Whetsol played the lead four bars followed by Metcalf, also with mute, playing the second four as they traded four-bar solos for the first sixteen and the last eight bars of the piece. But after Ellington heard the first test pressing, it was clear to him that the title didn't capture the quality of the work. He renamed it "Black Beauty" and dedicated it to the late Florence Mills. This became the first of Ellington's many musical portraits.

Arthur Whetsol had returned to the band at Ellington's request. Whetsol had not gone back to Howard University as planned, because his mother had become ill. He went back to work as a musician, and Ellington soon asked him to come back to New York. Clearly, Ellington had never grown comfortable with Miley's unreliability.

Five days after the Brunswick session, the band was in the Victor studios re-recording the same three works, plus "Got Everything But You." On this occasion, the group was billed as Duke Ellington and his Orchestra. By now, a recording pattern had begun to emerge. Mills was using the band's early sessions on other, smaller labels as a workshop. Mills hoped that the definitive versions of the Ellington compositions would be realized at Victor. He had begun this practice with "Black & Tan Fantasy" and "East St. Louis Toodle-Oo," and continued it on this date with "Jubilee Stomp," "Take It Easy," and "Black Beauty."

For this Victor session, Miley was back. This time, Whetsol played the entire sixteen-bar lead in "Black Beauty," and Metcalf was out. Problems with Metcalf had begun to surface. When he joined the band 1926, Ellington had made learning the growl a condition of his employment, to compensate for Miley's unreliability. By this time, Miley's unreliability had become worse and Mills was pressuring Ellington to fire him. But, at the same time, Whetsol's return caused Metcalf to doubt whether he would be the featured soloist with the band, and he began looking for another job.

Metcalf was also the only one of the band members to question Mills's complete control over them. He felt that the band should incorporate, as the Casa Loma Orchestra did, but that idea fell on deaf ears. Metcalf was probably unaware of Ellington's contract with their manager. Even if he was, Greer, Hardwick, Miley, and Guy—the original Washingtonians—had fully accepted the fact that Mills had become a powerful force in their musical lives. Because of him, they had one of the best jobs in town, and no other band around, black or white, was recording as often as they were.

Metcalf left the band a few days after the Victor date to join Jelly Roll Morton, before forming his own band. Thirty-five years later, when he was interviewed by *Jazz Journal,* he showed no rancor towards Ellington; in fact, he said the time he spent in the band was a great learning experience.

The second version of the *Cotton Club Parade* opened on Sunday, April 1, 1928. Other than changes in one of the supporting acts, the major principals remained the same. The musicians were back in the studios on June 25 for Brunswick to record "What a Life!" (which was never issued), Spencer Williams's "Tishomingo Blues," and W. C. Handy's "Yellow Dog Blues." This session introduced (Cornelius John) Johnny Hodges, Ellington's next great soloist, to the public.

Hodges soloed on soprano sax on "Yellow Dog Blues" and on alto sax on "Tishomingo Blues," revealing a sparkling new talent on both instruments. His sound fit in perfectly with the growling of Nanton and Miley. The band was continuing to develop a distinct style, partly because Ellington was now actively writing music for the band as a whole, as opposed to dictating parts to individual members or doctoring up stock arrangements.

For the introduction to "Yellow Dog Blues," Ellington uses a high reed trio, as he had done in "Creole Love Call." He features Bigard's and Carney's clarinets, along with Hodges's soprano, in the introduction and finale and uses a Latin rhythm to underpin Nanton's solo. Hodges's contribution is a frothy solo that clearly shows his debt to his mentor, Sidney Bechet. Schuller takes note of the introduction to "Tishomingo Blues," writing that the voicing of the reeds in the introduction was a precursor to "that unusual, rich, slightly dark, and at times melancholy flavor to Ellington's saxophone writing."

The introduction split between Hodges and Bigard continues with an excellent first chorus shared by Nanton and Bigard. Miley solos, and Hodges follows with a stunning outburst on the alto. This was an auspicious beginning to a solo career that would span more than thirty-five years with the band.

Whetsol was back full-time, just in time for an interesting recording date on July 10, 1928. Two months earlier, the Lew Leslie production *Blackbirds of 1928* had opened on Broadway at the Liberty Theater. It was a huge success. Before departing its berth during the summer of

1929 to begin a long tour on the road, the show had racked up a total of 518 performances, becoming the longest-running black show in theatrical history.

The show featured Adelaide Hall and dancer Bill Robinson performing songs by Dorothy Fields and Jimmy McHugh. In addition to "Bandanna Babies" and "I Must Have that Man," there were three show-stopping numbers: "Diga Diga Do," "Doin' The New Lowdown," and "I Can't Give You Anything but Love." They had quickly become a staple in the repertoire of practically every singer and dance band, all of whom rushed to the recording studios to get their versions out to the public. It was clear to the Mills brothers that their company (as well as Fields and McHugh) would soon be awash in royalties from the sale of the sheet music and recordings.

As he had done before, Irving Mills arranged a recording session of music from *Blackbirds*, this time at OKeh. This session featured Mills on vocals (under the pseudonym Goody Goodwin) backed by the Harlem Footwarmers. He sang "Digga Digga Do" and "Doin' the New Lowdown" in what would be the first of several recordings Mills would make as vocalist with the Ellington band.

On previous dates for the company, the band's recordings had been issued under the "race" category. Mills arranged for this one to be issued in the company's "popular" series, which meant that it was geared primarily towards a white audience. (Many years later, this practice would be known in the music business as a "crossover.") In the 1920s, music companies treated "race" or black music as a distinct minority taste and marketed it specifically to that population. The idea behind a crossover was that a song could gain popularity in a black format and then cross over to a white audience, attracting additional sales along the way.

On July 27, 1928, Mills carried this concept one step further, this time in the Brunswick studios, recording the same two tunes with an all-white band. He put the group, billed as the "Hotsy Totsy Gang," together strictly for recording dates. At one time or another, it included Benny Goodman on clarinet, Jimmy McPartland on cornet, Jimmy Dorsey on alto sax and clarinet, Tommy Dorsey and Miff Mole on trombones, and Manny Klein and Phil Napoleon on trumpets.

During the seven months in which the Ellington band had been at the Cotton Club, Mills had firmly consolidated his position as a music broker. He now had an arrangement with Stark to book the club's acts. Jack Mills, Inc., had publication and recording rights to all the music from the shows. These activities now made Irving Mills the dominant member of the music firm, and a change in the name of the corporation was made. In August, *Variety* reported that the firm would now be called Mills Music, Inc.

The staff of *Variety* had become captivated by Ellington's music. On Monday nights, during preparation for publication on the following day, the late-night broadcast from the Cotton Club made the work much easier to bear. In the March 21 issue, the editor wrote, "One of the hottest bands on the air is Duke Ellington's from the Cotton Club Monday midnights. One torrid trumpet brays and blares in a lowdown style that quite defies passiveness on hearing it. The coon shouter's version of 'One Sweet Letter From You' was also quite heated."

A June 28 report on what clearly was "Black Beauty" read, "That sizzling futuristic fox trot which Ellington and his colored jazzists from the Cotton Club in Harlem have been broadcasting, is now being published by Jack Mills as a novelty piano solo."

Soon, *Variety* took it upon itself to offer suggestions in print about the kind of music Ellington should play. While on the air, he had allowed May Alix to sing one or two of the numbers from the Cotton Club show. *Variety* suggested that he avoid the "white man's music" and play his own. They chided him for omitting his most recent composition, "Black Beauty," from the broadcast. Writing that the "Indigo Foxtrot was a 'scorcher,'" the reviewer felt it was that work that brought the band to his attention.

Someone, presumably Mills, mentioned the article to Ellington, and two weeks later, under the headline "Ellington Treats," the paper reported his response. The WHN radio announcer said that "these numbers are rendered at the persistent request of *Variety*."

Two weeks later, another short article in *Variety* appeared. This time there were raves about the band's playing of "Tishomingo Blues," "San," and "St. Louis Blues." The W. C. Handy classic was a special favorite. "What a bear of a record it would make," *Variety* wrote. The writer suggested that Victor, Columbia, or Brunswick should "get the Harlem Duke of Jazz to 'can' his arrangement of 'St. Louis Blues,' and not only release it as a race record, but also on the general schedule, and it will top anything preceding it in sales. It is jazz rhapsody that inspires the jazz epicures to superlative raves."

That arrangement of "St. Louis Blues" was what caught Irving Mills' very astute ears—yet it was never recorded. Years later when I asked Carney and Greer about it, the drummer, as good as his recollection of events were, could not recall that specific piece of music. Carney remembered playing it, but thought that the other blues that they recorded that day were just better pieces of music. He was surprised when I informed him of the *Variety* quotes and Mills's response on first hearing the work at the Kentucky Club. Inasmuch as he was arranging all the recording dates, I wondered why the manager never chose "St. Louis Blues." "Maybe it's because he didn't own the copyright," said Carney, with a sly grin on his face.

Later in the fall of 1928, *Variety* reported that Ellington had a different format for the dinnertime broadcast than he did for the midnight show. Under the headline "Ellington Subdued" the paper wrote that, "his heated jazzopators from the Cotton Club in Harlem are not as 'dirty' as they are of midnights such as Monday when broadcasting during the dinner sessions. They lean more to the 'sweet' type of syncopation but can't refrain from slipping in a real wicked ditty off and on."

Clearly, Ellington was adapting to a different audience during those early evening broadcasts in an attempt to widen his appeal. The radio broadcasts, along with *Variety*'s great reviews, brought Ellington a following throughout the New York metropolitan area. A significant number of people visiting the club for the first time said they were there because they heard the band on the air. For sophisticated New Yorkers, going to hear Duke Ellington at the Cotton Club now brought with it a certain cachet.

After Labor Day 1928, Stark closed down the club until the first week in October. Everyone had a well-earned vacation while Healy organized the fall show.

15

BEGINNING IN MAY 1927, Ellington had begun expanding the size of his musical family and refining his orchestral palette. Less than two weeks after opening night at the Cotton Club, he undertook another series of additions to the band that culminated in the great Ellington orchestra of the 1930s. The process began when he replaced Rudy Jackson with Albany "Barney" Bigard.

Bigard was born in New Orleans in 1906 and began playing clarinet at the age of seven. His teacher was his uncle, Lorenzo Tio, Jr., and one of his fellow students was Jimmy Noone, who established a well-deserved reputation in Chicago in the 1930s. Besides Tio, Bigard's great-grandfather and grandfather, his brothers Emile and Alec, and one of his nephews all played the instrument. Bigard's playing was strongly influenced by his Creole background. He was taught the Albert (French) fingering system of clarinet playing, which tends to produce a woody sound rather than the reedy timbre of the Boehm (German) system.

Bigard's first job was with the band of Oliver (Oak) Gaspard in his hometown, followed by a stint with Albert Nicholas's band at Tom Anderson's Cafe. During Christmas week of 1924, Joe "King" Oliver brought him to Chicago to play in his band. Bigard remained with him for three years, going east with the band for its engagement at New York's Savoy Ballroom in May 1927. When the band fell apart, Bigard was unemployed until he joined Charlie Elgar's band in Milwaukee. But within weeks, he was back in New York, having been summoned by Luis Russell to join his band at the Nest Club. It was while playing with Russell that he connected with the Ellington orchestra.

A fellow Louisianan, Wellman Braud, came to see him, and over a drink, Braud got right to the point. He told Bigard that Ellington was looking for a clarinetist to replace Rudy Jackson. It appeared that the tune for "Creole Love Call," which Jackson claimed to have written, had been stolen from Oliver's "Camp Meetin' Blues." Oliver was now suing Ellington and Mills, and Ellington had become fed up with the whole situation. (Oliver wound up losing the suit because of a flawed copyright.) As he left, Braud told Bigard that Ellington would stop by one night to hear him play.

Bigard said he knew Ellington by sight, but had never met him. He had seen him at Mexico's and, in fact, had jammed there one night. Under the prodding of Luis Russell, he played "High Society" and impressed everyone. "Duke must have heard that, I guess," Bigard said. "He would come in and go out without much fanfare. . . . It was the same deal when he came over to the Nest. I didn't know he was there, or [when he] left, for that matter." The night after Ellington stopped by, Braud came back to tell Bigard that Ellington wanted to see him at his apartment the next day.

As soon as Bigard arrived, Ellington put a drink in his hand and began outlining his plans for the band. Ellington's personality and his superb self-confidence were the main reasons that Bigard took the job, because he was actually making more money at the Nest Club. "I was much more impressed when Joe Oliver offered me a job than when Duke did," he recalled, "because Joe's band was much better known. And yet Duke Ellington made you feel so much more at ease. Just like he was going to turn the music business upside-down and you would be a part of it. . . . I started that Friday and ended fourteen years later."

The clarinetist brought his Southern Creole style of playing to the band: delicate, supple, fluid, and velvety, yet spicily warm and virile. His distinctive style would become a part of such compositions as "Mood Indigo," "Saturday Night Function," "Ducky Wucky," "Clarinet Lament," and "Barney Goin' Easy."

Toby Hardwick left the band five months later. His drinking, absenteeism, and off-stage behavior were causing problems. Bigard said, "One night I decided I'd go with him after we got off, just to see where he went all that time. . . . All that man did was go from apartment to apartment, friends to more friends, girls to more girls. . . . Oh boy, I was dead for about a week with a bad hangover."

Sonny Greer concurred. "Bubber, Toby, and me were all heavy drinkers. After work we'd carouse all over town. Once Toby didn't show up for three days; it turned out he'd been in a car wreck. That's when we got Johnny Hodges."

Johnny Hodges remembered that Toby "had an accident, went through the windshield of a taxicab. Had his face all cut up so I had to go to work for him." Hodges could thank Bigard, in part, for his job with Ellington. The band leader was seriously thinking about adding Buster Bailey, the reigning clarinet virtuoso, to the band. Bigard, as well as Carney, foresaw a lot of undesirable competition for clarinet solos. Bigard advised Ellington to "get that little ol' young boy from Boston!" and was strongly seconded by Carney.

Hodges was two months short of his twenty-first birthday when he joined the band in May. Born on Putnam Avenue in Cambridge, Massachusetts, on July 25, 1907, Hodges was his parents' second child and only son. His parents were born in Virginia, married there, and moved to Cambridge before the turn of the century. The family lived there until shortly after Johnny was born and then moved to an apartment on Hammond Street in Boston's South End.

Like most middle-class black families, the Hodges family had an upright piano. His mother and sister played the instrument, and he learned it well enough to start playing at "house hops" (dances at private homes that paid him eight dollars a night), a practice he continued until his mid-teens. But young Johnny's heart was set on learning the soprano saxophone. "I thought it was so pretty," he said. His father was against it, but with his mother's intercession, a curved version of the instrument was bought for him sometime in 1919.

Within months, Hodges began to make a name for himself around town. Tom Whaley, a local musician and arranger (who in later years became Ellington's copyist), worked at the Avery Hotel in Boston in 1920 when Hodges came in through the back door one night and asked if he could play. Fifty years later, Whaley remembered, "He started playing, the same then as now, sweet, singing, a gifted man, another genius."

Pianist Nappy Howard recalled first meeting Hodges on July 4, 1922, when Howard was playing in York, Maine. During intermission, he heard that there was another band in town and went to hear it when his job was over. He said:

That band was jumping and at that moment a little short guy was playing a gold soprano sax, and he had all the folks cheering him on.

When the dance was over I went up and introduced myself. He appeared to be quite young, and he had knickers [on] instead of long pants, and when he told me his age I understood why. He was just sixteen. His name was Johnny Hodges.

Hodges's close friend Charlie Holmes recalled:

My older brother told me about him. I was about twelve years old. A couple of nights later I heard him playing at a dance on Tremont Street. I'd never heard anything like it. I mean he was a kid, no more than fifteen or sixteen. He was playing that saxophone then as well as he played it all down through the years. I've never known any musician except maybe Louis [Armstrong] to pick up an instrument and play it the way he did. I mean he was playing it, not playing with it. I thought he was the greatest musician I had ever heard.

Sidney Bechet had made his recording debut with "Wild Cat Blues" and "Kansas City Man Blues" in 1921. Besides bringing his music to thousands of enthralled listeners, he inspired many young musicians, including Hodges. Bigard said he developed his own style based on that recording. "I heard Sidney Bechet's records while I was in New Orleans, and I used to copy him note for note. Everybody had that record. That was all you could hear. Every time you passed someone's house that had the doors or windows open they would be playing that on their Victrola." Out in California, young Lionel Hampton spent many hours listening to the recording. Forty years later, he could remember every detail of "Wild Cat Blues." "Bechet was one of my idols as a kid," he recalled.

Holmes told me that he first heard the recording at Hodges's home one afternoon with Carney. "All of us, especially Johnny, [were] bowled over by what we heard Bechet doing. We must have worn that record out playing it again and again. After a while Johnny started sounding a lot like him. Sidney was his idol."

Hodges got a chance to meet Bechet in 1924 when Bechet came to Boston with Jimmy Cooper's *Black and White Revue*. Hodges's sister knew Bechet and brought her brother backstage to meet him. Hodges was carrying his instrument wrapped in a bag made from an old coat sleeve, and Bechet asked him to play something. Hodges responded with "My Honey's Loving Arms," and Bechet took an immediate liking to the young musician. He began giving Hodges lessons, and when Bechet returned to New York, he recommended Hodges to Willie "the Lion" Smith. Later that year, Smith brought Hodges to New York City to play in his quartet.

When the job was over, Hodges returned to Boston. At this point in his life, New York was a place to visit and learn music, not to live. "I would run back to Boston and show them what I learned," he said. "So they would all meet in my house, and we'd compare notes on what's ahead in New York and what's behind in Boston."

By the following year, Hodges was in New York on a more-or-less permanent basis, playing in jazz clubs uptown and downtown. He was now playing alto saxophone in preference to the soprano and had also learned the clarinet. He recalled, "I was playing in a little old cabaret on 135th Street. I think I got twenty-five dollars a week and made about twenty-five or thirty dollars a night in tips."

This was good money at the time; yet when Bechet opened his own joint, Club Basha (pronounced, Ba-SHAY) like his name, at 145th Street and Seventh Avenue, and offered him a job, Hodges jumped at the chance. The night before he started, Bechet presented him with a brand new, straight soprano saxophone, like the one he played, and began coaching Hodges in duets. One saxophone would carry the melody, while the other embellished or improvised against it. Having heard all of Bechet's recordings, Hodges quickly mastered his style and soon could play well enough to take over whenever his teacher was late for work—which was often.

On Fridays the Lafayette Theater had a midnight show, and most of the Harlem clubs would send their bands to play a set. It was a form of advertising. Hodges said, "Bechet and I did this duet. I think it was 'Everybody Loves My Baby' or 'I've Found a New Baby.' I'm not sure which, but this was one of the things he taught me." Their duet caused a mild sensation. Forty years later, Hodges still spoke highly of his mentor: "Sidney Bechet is tops in my book. He was my favorite! He schooled me a whole lot, and I'll say, if it hadn't been for him, I'd be playing for a hobby."

According to Greer, Ellington first heard Hodges play during their trip to New England in 1925, and offered him a job. He repeated the offer during the summer of 1926 but had to settle for Carney. Hodges declined both offers because he had found work with Lloyd Scott's band at the Capitol Palace and did not want to leave New York. Ellington finally got Hodges into the band for a few nights that fall when he substituted for Hardwick, who had returned to Washington to attend a family funeral.

At the tender age of twenty, Hodges had created quite a stir among the Harlem musicians. He and his contemporary Benny Carter ruled the roost at Mexico's "cutting contests" for alto saxophonists. Benny Waters recalled that:

> one night Jimmy Dorsey came uptown. That boy had a fabulous technique, and he "cut" Johnny on "Tiger Rag." Johnny was very upset, but Benny Carter told him not to worry, he'd get him the next time he showed up. Sure enough, when Dorsey came back the next week, Benny took him on. They did "Tiger Rag" and Benny suggested they do four choruses, taking it through the keys. When they got to B major [five sharps], Jimmy got his ass kicked. Benny always used to tell us a good musician should be able to improvise on a song in any key. Coleman Hawkins used to do it all the time.

Hodges joined Chick Webb's band in 1927 at the Black Bottom Club and moved with it to the Savoy Ballroom, where the band worked off and on until March 1928, when bookings became slim. Finally, two of Webb's best musicians decided to seek greener pastures. With Webb's blessing, trumpeter Bobby Stark joined Fletcher Henderson's band and Hodges joined Ellington's.

Hodges brought a warm, mellow tone to the Ellington orchestra and played his instruments with a frothy style that showed his debt to Bechet. In contrast, Toby Hardwick played the alto sax with a hard, clear tone. Hardwick, who played violin and clarinet as well as the soprano, alto, baritone, and bass saxophones, was the closest thing to a classically trained musician in the group.

Hodges could also growl when he played, something else he had learned from Bechet. "I always did like it," he told an interviewer.

"Bechet used to call it 'Goola.' He had a dog by that name, and it would always be somewhere around. 'I'm going to call Goola,' he'd say. That was his way of calling the dog."

Next to Bubber Miley, Hodges was the best soloist in the band. His solos had an architectural symmetry and a logic that seemed inevitable, so much so that Ellington would convert many of his ideas into full-fledged compositions. Hodges was coauthor of "The Duke Steps Out" (1929), "Beggars Blues" (1929), "Cotton Club Stomp" (1930), "Rent Party Blues" (1930), and "Harmony in Harlem" (1937), all staples in the Ellington repertoire during the 1930s.

By the mid-1930s, Hodges's style had evolved into a smooth-flowing, sensual sound that Ellington featured in such compositions as "Finesse" (1938), "Day Dream" (1939), "Warm Valley" (1940), and "Passion Flower" (1941).

While he remained Ellington's major soloist until his death in 1970, Hodges had a problem that plagued him all his life: He had trouble reading music. The band would help out whenever a new score appeared, and either Carney or Hardwick would play Hodges's part for him. He was a quick study and had to hear a song only once or twice to get it down pat.

In the late 1960s, John Bunce, Tony Bennett's music director, began to rehearse his arrangements with the Ellington band. On one occasion, they were halfway through the first number when Hodges put down his instrument and walked out of the room. The band took a five-minute break and Russell Procope explained to Bunce that it was nothing personal, that Hodges was angry at himself for not being able to read the parts. Procope played the music for him, and by the end of the second show, Hodges had his part committed to memory.

Charlie Holmes told me that he knew that Hodges, in fact, could read music. Along with Carney, Holmes and Hodges were both taught by Jerome Pasquall. Holmes maintained that Hodges could always read music when the two of them played together, but that he panicked when he was on the bandstand with his peers.

Nevertheless, Hodges was considered one of the premiere alto sax players. Luis Russell said that during the mid-1930s, one could always get a lively argument going at the Rhythm Club by asking who was the best alto sax player in jazz, Willie Smith with the Jimmie Lunceford orchestra, Benny Carter, or Johnny Hodges. In the late 1940s, this out-standing triumvirate was joined by a young man from Kansas City, Charlie Parker.

In 1961, another eminent saxophone player, John Coltrane, who had worked with Hodges a few years earlier, told an interviewer that Hodges was his favorite musician. He called him, "Johnny Hodges, the world's greatest saxophone player."

While Ellington was assembling his musical family, however, his own family was falling apart. In the summer of 1928, he and Edna sep-arated. His feelings about women had made him at best a reluctant hus-band, and soon he was acting out his ambivalent feelings in a series of affairs. "We weren't on Broadway two weeks when he began seeing a woman on the side," Greer recalled. "During the time we were at the Kentucky Club, there was always someone, plus the girl that worked for Polly Adler. One night as I was about to enter the Cotton Club, I saw a maroon Packard roadster with Massachusetts license plates parked out front. I knew that chick from Salem was back in town."

"Those white women from downtown couldn't keep their hands off Duke," a former Cotton Club chorus girl told me:

> I remember one girl from a wealthy Park Avenue family, she was so crazy about him. Her family got upset, they complained to Mr. Stark. He spoke to Duke about it. It got so bad they wouldn't let her in the club anymore. I think her family sent her to Europe so she could get over it. That Duke was something. I was surprised his wife put up with it as long as she did.

Edna had suspicions about his behavior for quite awhile. On one occasion, suspecting he had been with another woman, she actually threatened him with a gun. Freddie Guy recalled, "He told me he got in bed, and no sooner than he had got comfortable, he heard the click of a pistol, and Edna said to him, 'Motherfucker, you've been with some bitch. I can smell her all over you.'" Only by some fast talking was Ellington able to defuse the situation. "He told her a woman at the club accidentally spilled her bottle of perfume as he was giving her his auto-graph. From then on, if he was with a woman, he'd go to the Luxor Baths before he went home."

Finally, Duke's luck ran out when one relationship heated up and Edna didn't see him for a few days. She exploded, raging that she would "spoil those pretty looks," and slashed the left side of Ellington's face with a razor. The crescent-shaped scar ran from just below his ear, barely missing his acoustic nerve, to a few centimeters from his lip.

"I had just fell asleep and heard my doorbell ringing," Guy recalled. "When I opened the door Duke was standing there with blood on his shirt and holding a towel to his face. He was crying. The first thing out of his mouth was 'Edna cut me.'" The assault on his body and the concurrent blow to his narcissism were more than he could bear. Ellington moved out of the house, leaving everything behind, including his clothes, effectively ending the marriage on the spot. He supported Edna amply until her death in 1966, but never mentioned her again. More than one interviewer found himself out the door when the subject of Ellington's marriage was brought up.

In 1959, *Ebony* magazine published an interview with Edna, complete with pictures. Outside of his immediate family and members of the band, most people who met Ellington had assumed she was dead. Ellington was furious about the revelation, yet he paradoxically gave a keepsake copy to a close friend in England.

Recalling the assault some years later, Greer said, "As soon as I heard what happened I went to see him. He was staying with Freddie. Duke was very concerned about the scar and how he would look. Freddie told him to stop worrying about it and look at the bright side. We were on vacation from the club and didn't have to be back there until the first week of October. By then the cut would have healed."

The cut did heal, but Ellington carried the scar to his grave. His spiritual healing, however, was greatly assisted by the arrival of his mother. Leaving her husband and Ruth in Washington, Daisy rushed to the city as soon as she heard about his condition. Mother and son promptly went looking for a new place for them to live, and quickly settled on a seven-room apartment at 381 St. Nicholas Avenue in Harlem.

An interesting postscript concerns Daisy's asthma, which had first flared up after Ellington left home in 1923. On reuniting with her son in New York City, Daisy found that her condition had immediately subsided.

16

MILLS HAD THE band back in the OKeh recording studios on October 1, 1928. The piano transcription of "Black Beauty" had just been published, and Mills suggested that Ellington make a solo recording of the work. On this record, for the first time in his career, Ellington plays unaccompanied. On the reverse side, Ellington plays an original composition at his ragtime best, "Swampy River." The influence of James P. Johnson is unmistakable.

With that recording out of the way, the band got down to business. OKeh had Lonnie Johnson back in the studio, and Johnson, the singer Baby Cox, and the band teamed up to create "Hot and Bothered." They recorded "The Mooche" on the flip side.

Speaking of "Hot and Bothered," the British composer and conductor Constant Lambert said, "I know of nothing in Ravel so dexterous in treatment as in the varied solos in the middle . . . and nothing in Stravinsky more dynamic than the final section. The combination of themes at this moment is one of the most ingenious pieces of writing in modern music."

"The Mooche" was a prime example of Ellington's jungle style music, designed to evoke exotic African images for the Cotton Club audiences. As he did in his arrangement of "Tishomingo Blues," Ellington wrote for a high reed trio, playing one of the most eerie and haunting themes he had created up to that time. The theme, a sixteen-bar blues with interpolations by Miley, is followed by an eight-bar orchestral tutti, and then segues to a low register solo by Bigard. A Johnson solo is followed by a Miley-inspired scat vocal by Baby Cox, who had been featured in the Fats Waller revue *Hot Chocolates*. Ellington highlighted Cox as he had Adelaide Hall. Cox's voice assumes an instrumental role, and she is involved in marvelous dialogue with Bubber Miley. "Move Over" was the final work of the session.

Several days later, "The Washingtonians" (without Baby Cox and Johnson) repeated most of the October 1 session for Pathé-Actuelle.

On October 17, Duke Ellington and his Cotton Club Orchestra recorded "The Mooche" for Brunswick, this time with Johnny Hodges replacing Cox in the duet. In this recording, Miley's trenchant plunger work is answered by Hodges's regally relaxed and sinuous sound. It is one of my favorites and has all the aspects of a one-act play.

Thirteen days later, on Victor, the two protagonists were at it again. On the Victor recording, they solo brilliantly, but the work is undercut by Braud's plodding brass bass in one of the rare instances in which the Victor version is unable to hold its own with its predecessors. The other two works recorded at that session were "I Can't Give You Anything but Love," with Mills doing the vocal, and "No Papa No," with Baby Cox.

The band went back to club work on October 7. Healy's *Cotton Club Parade*, subtitled "Hot Chocolate," featured another score by Fields and McHugh. Ellington was singled out for praise in *Variety*. "On the dance end, Duke Ellington socks out that mean music as ever before, but for the rest. . . . " Once again, the critic compared the rest of the show unfavorably with the revues at Connie's Inn and Smalls.

Seated in the trumpet section on opening night was Ellington's latest addition to the band, Freddie Jenkins. Three days later, he would celebrate his twenty-second birthday. Jenkins was born in New York City and he was already playing the trumpet when he joined the 369th Regiment Cadet Band, led by the legendary Lt. Eugene Mikell, Jr. Surprisingly, Mikell, a first-rate musician and teacher and stickler for visual presentation, allowed Jenkins to continue playing his instrument with his left hand, as he had learned it. When Jenkins finished high school, he was admitted into the music program at Ohio's Wilberforce University, along with another New York musician, Benny Carter.

At Wilberforce, Jenkins joined Edgar Hayes's band, the Blue Grass Buddies. He was with them less than a year when, in 1924, at Carter's urging, Horace Henderson, Fletcher's younger brother, offered Jenkins a chair in his band, the Collegians. He remained with them until joining Ellington.

Jenkins was an unabashed devotee of Louis Armstrong, whose playing and singing he emulated. Like his hero, he had great range and power on the instrument. Always smiling on the bandstand, snapping his fingers and rolling his eyes, he radiated personality. When Hardwick returned to the band three years later, he took one look at Jenkin's antics and nicknamed him "Posey."

The addition of Jenkins did not solve Ellington's major problem in the trumpet section: Miley. Freddie Guy told me, "[Duke and I] both lived in the same building, so we'd take a taxi to work. After Metcalf left, on the drive to the club, every night Duke would always be worrying if Bubber was going to show up and, if he did, would he be sober. When we were at the Kentucky Club, we lost out on a couple of jobs because Bubber didn't show, or if he did, he was too drunk to play."

According to Greer, both the management of the club and Mills were pressuring Ellington to fire Miley. "I was in his dressing room one night when Duke told Mills straight out, Bubber had been with us from the beginning. If it weren't for him, we probably wouldn't be here at all."

Five years earlier, Miley had been dragooned into a quintet playing quiet, understated jazz in a Broadway cellar. By the sheer force of his musical personality, he had helped the group evolve into a ten-piece band, holding down one of the best jobs in town for black musicians. In so doing, he was hoisted by his own petard. The larger band and the structured floor shows greatly limited Miley's ability to solo and express himself musically. He was getting more frustrated by the day.

"You could see it on the bandstand," Greer said. "Even if he was sober, he looked like he was somewhere else. He'd play the notes all right, no mistakes. But it was like he was on automatic pilot. But when it was time to solo he was right there."

Miley was not the only one of the band members who was upset about the change in their musical lives. Greer was not too happy, either. "I hated it. I had my hustle downtown, me, Duke, and Freddie going from table to table on the weekends at the Kentucky Club. And we missed going over to Polly Adler's on Sunday mornings. It was nothing for us to take a taxi back to Harlem with over a hundred dollars in our pockets from those two gigs. I used to make more money on the weekends than I did working for a week at the Cotton Club."

By the end of January 1929, Miley was out, with an assist from Mills. "Mills buttered him up," said Greer. "He told Bubber he should be a star in his own right, just like Duke, told him he'd become his booking agent and was going to get him work. Everybody was happy the way it turned out."

Mills promised to build a show around Miley and help him organize a band, which he subsequently did. While waiting for that to happen, Miley and the clarinetist Buster Bailey accepted Noble Sissle's offer to join his band for a trip to Paris and to work at a nightclub. His replacement in the band was 19-year-old Charles Melvin "Cootie" Williams.

Williams was born in Mobile, Alabama, and raised by an aunt after his mother, a pianist, died when he was eight. He played in the school band and learned the trombone, tuba, and drums. He subsequently learned the trumpet and began working around town with Holman's Jazz Band and Johnny Pope's Band. When he was fourteen, he did a summer tour with the Young Family Band (with Lester and his brother Lee). Williams then moved to Pensacola, Florida, and joined the band of Eagle Eye Shields. His musicianship caught the ear of Alonzo Ross, and in 1927 he joined the Deluxe Syncopators on a tour that would eventually bring him to New York City in the spring of 1928. After two weeks' work, the Syncopators disbanded.

Featured in the band on soprano sax and clarinet was Edmond Hall. "I was seventeen years old," Williams recalled. "Hall sort of took me under his wing and got the two of us some work with 'Happy' Ford's band. Then one night I was in a cutting session at the BandBox; Chick Webb heard me and offered me a job. They weren't working that much, but it was a damn good band."

Williams made such an impression on Webb that, at the drummer's insistence, Williams left his rented room in Brooklyn and moved into Webb's apartment in Harlem. Each vowed never to work without the other. But other than three weeks at the Savoy Ballroom, the pickings were slim.

In January 1929, Fletcher Henderson took his band on a short road trip, and he needed a lead trumpet to fill Russell Smith's shoes. Williams was offered the job and at first turned it down, noting his loyalty to Webb. But Webb insisted that Williams take Henderson's offer. Besides, the tour schedule was not long.

The first date was in Baltimore, and the band arrived three hours late when its train, the Congressional Limited crashed near Aberdeen, Maryland. The engineer and fireman ware scalded to death, and two other railroad employees were killed. The *New York Times* reported, "Scores of passengers were shaken up, including the violinist Fritz Kreisler." After a delay of two hours, passengers reached Baltimore on a relief train.

"I was scared when the train tipped over," Williams told me:

> But that was nothing compared to what I felt when I got on the stand to play the first number. Nobody said a word to me. Chick had warned me Fletcher wrote in one key at the beginning of the piece and would modulate to another at the last chorus, and to watch out. I don't remember the piece except it was in D flat and, sure enough, he took it out in D major! . . . Fletcher's band played in all the hard keys which you don't do now. Fletcher was very conscious of sound, and he'd think about the brilliancy of certain things being geared to certain keys. He played no favorites. It seemed like ABC then, and I remember Coleman Hawkins saying, "Ain't that kid somethin'?"

When the orchestra returned to New York in mid-February, Williams took off and went back to Chick Webb's apartment, unaware that they were to fill in for a matinee performance at the Roseland Ballroom.

Williams ended up staying with the Roseland band for a few more weeks. "Then one morning the phone rang. When I answered, it was Duke. I'm pretty sure he heard about me from Chick, who told everyone he met what a good musician I was. He asked me to come to the Cotton Club, sit in with the band, and see how I liked it. Chick had all their recordings, it was quite a different sound in music. I laughed out loud the first time I heard the weird jungle sounds Bubber and Tricky were making."

Ellington's hiring of Williams came as a surprise to the local musicians. "We figured it might be one of the Smith boys [Jabbo, Russell, or Joe] or Bobby Stark," Walter Johnson said. "Cootie was a young boy, but Duke always knew what he wanted in his musicians. His orchestra was always the sum of its parts. That's why none of the guys who left him could make it on their own."

The first few nights on the bandstand were difficult for Williams. "When I heard Tricky do the growl, I had to fight to keep from laughing. Duke didn't say one word. Then it dawned on me: The man hired me to take Bubber's place, and he did the growl!"

Under Nanton's tutelage, Williams raised that form of musical expression to virtuoso level. "For me it wasn't hard learning the plunger," he said. "I'd never in my life thought to play like that so it seemed funny at first. After I'd been doing it a while, though, it became *me*. Or I became it, although I always played open horn as well."

Frank Galbreath said, "Both Bubber and Cootie played the growl with intensity. The difference was, Cootie played it with power and drive. I think that's the way Louis [Armstrong] would have sounded if he did the growl. He was Cootie's idol."

Like Armstrong, Williams had a clarion sound to his open horn that would power the brass section for the next ten years. Comparing his style with his predecessor's, Williams said, "Both expressed the truth. My plunger style was not like Bubber's. His soul wasn't my soul and vice versa. The difference wasn't in technique, it was in range and color, I think. He only liked to play one way."

Williams would not be heard using the growl on a recording sessions until seven months later. Benny Goodman told me, "Of all the lead trumpets to play for me, he was the best ever."

The Cotton Club's spring revue opened on Sunday night, March 31, 1929. Like *Cotton Club Parade, Springbirds* had music by Fields and McHugh. Featured in the show were Leitha Hill, the Berry Brothers, the adagio team of Mildred Dixon and Henri Wessels, Josephine Hall, the comedy team of Mason and Becket, and the precision dancing of the Five Blazers.

Once the band was firmly ensconced at the club, Mills began booking the members to play at theaters during the day. They headlined the show at the RKO 58th Street Theater in the second week in April and did a matinee on April 21 at the Palace Theater on Broadway. Greer and Williams both had hazy recollections of the event, but they both recalled that the band included its version of "Tiger Rag" to coincide with the song's release on Brunswick Records.

Writing in its typical shorthand, *Variety* exclaimed that "this colored cafe band from the Cotton, and one of the hottest in town was not fully prepared for vaude." The reviewer's main criticism was directed at the band's inability to play with the poise and polish of a vaudeville stage band: "When it's not torrid, it's not good." The critic was very impressed with the soloists, however, and devoted a paragraph to the brass section's plunger work. Describing it as "trick playing," he wrote that "what they can do to the bell of a trumpet or trombone makes anybody's feet move." A *Billboard* review of the same show concurred with *Variety's* assessment.

A group of Princeton undergraduates who had heard the band at the Cotton Club wanted to book it for a house party weekend on May 3 and 4. Undergrads spared no expense to bring name bands to the campus that weekend: The list of headliners included Fletcher Henderson, Miff Mole's band featuring Jimmy Dorsey, Charlie Johnson, Hal Kemp, and McKinney's Cotton Pickers.

The members of the Campus and Cannon clubs wanted Ellington, and Mills promptly signed a contract. When he later informed Stark that the band would be out of town that weekend, the manager had no objection but reminded him that, according to the contract, the salary for the relief band was to be paid out of Ellington's pocket. In his haste to get the band into the Cotton Club, Mills had overlooked that detail.

"That's how I got to play the Cotton Club for a weekend," Luis Russell recalled:

> Duke called me and asked if I could help him out. My band wasn't working so we took the gig and played the show. . . . Until that time, Mills could do no wrong in Duke's eyes. After that weekend, I think some of the bloom began to come off the rose.

Very much aware that Ellington was his meal ticket, Mills always treated him with some deference. But many members of the orchestra found Mills arrogant and condescending. "I never liked the man," Greer recollected, "We were grown men, and he'd talk to us like we were kids. He couldn't stand Freddie [Guy] and Freddie couldn't stand him."

Guy observed:

> He wanted Duke to be the star, not the band. The men were just the rank and file. But I could see through him, and the man, he hated me for it. He knew Duke and I lived in the same apartment house and

would always take a cab to work. I know he thought I was a bad influence on him. Mills could have done a lot more for the band than he did, but he never learned that if you sacrifice something now, you might pick up a million dollars later on. He wanted everybody's right arm.

Mills's arrogance cost him dearly. Four months later the band returned to Broadway. Duke Ellington and his Cotton Club Orchestra would be featured in Florenz Ziegfeld's *Show Girl*. George Gershwin did the score, with additional music by Vincent Youmans, and lyrics by Ira Gershwin and Gus Kahn. But Mills had no part in any of it. Guy recalled the event:

> I heard the rumor over my old Stromberg-Carlson radio that the Cotton Club Orchestra was to be featured with Ruby Keeler in a new Ziegfeld show, which was like the Palace Theater on Broadway. It was the top place to work in the business. When I asked Duke about it on the way to work that night, he didn't know anything; neither did the men in the band. The next day Duke told Irving what I'd said. Mills told him that I was crazy, that they weren't going to have any Negro band in the Follies. He didn't want to hear anything more about it and walked away.

The manager's attitude made Guy angry, and so did Ellington's, for that matter, because Guy thought Ellington listened to Mills too much. The next afternoon Guy went to Ellington's apartment and told him how he saw things. "Listen," he recalled telling Ellington with some annoyance, "did it ever dawn on you that this band is my living as well as yours? Have I ever sent you on a wild goose chase in my life? It won't cost you a thing to walk into Stanley Sharp's office (Ziegfeld's office manager) and say, 'How are you, Mr. Sharp?'"

Ellington was persuaded, and they took a cab to Sharp's office on Seventh Avenue. According to Guy, what happened was as follows: "Well, gee, Duke how have you been?" Sharp said. "We've been thinking about you lately."

At the behest of Will Vodery, Ziegfeld had seen and heard the band at the Cotton Club on many occasions. For some time, he had been looking for a suitable vehicle in which to present the group, as he had done with the Paul Whiteman orchestra in his 1921 edition of the Follies. *Show Girl* fit the bill. Sharp reached into the top drawer of his desk, pulled out a preliminary contract, and pushed it across to Ellington with a pen. He was in the Ziegfeld show.

"But what really broke Mills's heart about it," Guy chuckled, "was [that] when the show opened, the billing was 'Florenz Ziegfeld Presents Duke Ellington and his Cotton Club Orchestra,' not 'Irving Mills Presents. . . . 'When we saw him during a rehearsal at the club, mind you, he was crying real tears. Duke had gone over his head and got a job on Broadway!"

I am certain that some of Mills's tears had more to do with the fact that he would not see any part of the $1,200 the band earned weekly during rehearsals, or their $1,500 a week during the run of the show. Ellington signed the contract on his own; therefore, Mills was not entitled to his 10 percent as the band's booking agent.

The band began rehearsing the show on May 15, with a new addition: Juan Tizol playing valve trombone. Tizol was born in San Juan, Puerto Rico, and learned the instrument from his uncle Manuel. During his late teens he began playing with the Municipal Band of San Juan, and in 1920, Marie Lucas brought him to Washington, D.C., to join the stellar group that she had assembled for the pit band at the Howard Theater. It was there that he first met Ellington.

Tizol arrived in New York in 1928 and renewed the friendship. "Duke would always say to me, 'One of these days I'm going to send for you.' He did the following summer." While he was playing with Cliff Jackson in New Jersey, Tizol would sit in with the Ellington band on some of the radio broadcasts, as did a fellow Washingtonian, Harry White.

The classically trained Tizol had a pure sound on his instrument. Luckily for Ellington, he also happened to be a skilled copyist. Ellington would write in concert (the notes off the piano) and give Tizol the score, and Tizol would transcribe the parts.

"When he sent for me, the only other trombone was Tricky Sam," Tizol recalled. There was a big contrast in the way we played, of course, but the advantage to Duke was that I could play fast work with the saxophone section or with the trumpets. I played the second, third, or fourth part—just the notes."

On June 25, the show moved to Boston's Colonial Theater for its tryouts. Heading the cast were Clayton, Jackson, and [Jimmy] Durante, with other roles going to Ruby Keeler (Mrs. Al Jolson), Harriet Hoctor (who, along with the Albertina Rasch dancers, would dance to Gershwin's "An American in Paris"), the comedian Frank McHugh, eccentric dancer Eddie Foy, Jr., and Nick Lucas, "The Singing Troubadour." Joseph Urban provided them all with lavish settings. *Show Girl* received "rave notices," according to *Variety*. With top tickets selling for $5.50, the revue played five nights and two matinees. Chick Webb's orchestra replaced Ellington at the club for that week. While initially resistant to paying Webb out of his own pocket, Stark ultimately relented. Having "Duke Ellington and his Cotton Club Orchestra" on the marquee of the Ziegfeld Theater on Broadway was priceless advertising for the club.

Unfortunately, the show was doomed from the start. The problem was that virtually the entire cast was made up of specialty acts who were known for their own routines and couldn't do full justice to the Gershwin score.

Ira Gershwin recalled that Lucas, like the other featured performers, sang one of his current popular numbers that was not a Gershwin song, and Clayton, Jackson, and Durante performed their acts and songs throughout *Show Girl* as if they had nothing to do with the plot. Then too, there was the virtually complete "American in Paris" ballet. While its theme of homesickness was beautifully rendered, it had little connection with the surrounding show. After looking over William Anthony McGuire's libretto, Ira Gershwin observed that he "wouldn't be surprised if *Show Girl* set a record for sparseness of dialogue in a musical."

The performance of the pit orchestra under the Gershwins' favorite conductor, William Daly, was lambasted by the critics, who wrote that the Ellington orchestra "did much better on the stage."

Ziegfeld was particularly incensed with the negative review in the *Telegram*. He took out a three-column ad in the newspaper to answer the critics. Of Ellington, he wrote:

It was probably foolish of me, after spending so much money on a large orchestra, to include a complete band in addition, but the Cotton Club Orchestra under Duke Ellington that plays in the cabaret scene is the finest exponent of syncopated music in existence. Irving Berlin went mad about them, and some of the best exponents of modern music almost jumped out of their seats with excitement over their extraordinary harmonies and rhythms.

The band's scene took place in the mythical Club Caprice and featured Clayton, Jackson, and Durante. Four songs were performed by the Ellington orchestra: "Black and White" (with dancers); "African Daisies" (with the Albertina Rasch Girls); "Jimmie the Well Dressed Man" (with Clayton, Jackson, and Durante); and "Harlem Serenade" (with Ruby Keeler). "African Daisies" was not by the Gershwins and was thought to be an Ellington original, but there is no evidence to bear that out.

Ellington was impressed with George Gershwin's professionalism. As he wrote in his autobiography:

[W]hen cuts and adjustments were to be made . . . he was not the kind of guy who would be in Row A ready to take a bow on opening night. In fact, when several of his shows opened, he could be dressed like a stagehand. . . . If you didn't know him you would never guess that he was the great George Gershwin. He once told Oscar Levant that he wished he had written the bridge to "Sophisticated Lady," and that made me very proud.

Show Girl was forced to close after 111 performances on October 5, 1929. The Gershwins had to sue Ziegfeld for their money, but never collected because the impresario went bankrupt when the stock market crashed.

One person who did profit greatly from the show, however, was drummer Sonny Greer. "A few days before we left for Boston," he told me:

I went downtown to a music store to get a new set of drumsticks. One of the salesmen knew me and came running over with this guy from the Leedy Manufacturing Company. They knew I was going to be in a Broadway show with Duke and the band, and offered me a deal. In the store window was this fabulous drum set. Bass drum, snare drum, several cymbals, two tympani, tom toms, woodblocks, a xylophone, two Chinese gongs, and a set of chimes. It cost over three thousand dollars. If I agreed to pose for some pictures of me with the set of drums, I could use them for the run of the show.

After the show had closed and the band was back at the Cotton Club, Stark asked Greer what happened to the drum set he and Madden had seen him using during the production. According to Greer:

> I told him it was just a loan from the drum company, and thought no more about it. A few days later one of the waiters from the club came by my apartment and told me Stark wanted to see me, and to wear my band uniform. When I got there the guy from Leedy was there with the whole set of drums. I figured they wanted some more publicity shots. They did, and when they were all finished the guy pointed to the drums and said to me, "They're all yours, Sonny."
>
> I knew he could tell from the look on my face I didn't believe him. He said, "Your boss just bought them for you." I got scared man, real scared. I figured Stark expected me to pay him back for the drums. Just then he came in the room. I explained to him, my wife just got out of the hospital, and I couldn't afford to pay for no drums. He told me to come to his office. When we got there he asked how much money did I have on me. I had ten or fifteen dollars. He said, "Give me five" and wrote out a bill of sale. I had it framed. Later Duke told me it was Madden who insisted Stark get the drums for me.
>
> Guys would see the set, come up to me, and say "Sonny, where'd you get those drums, man? You must be rich!" I'd just smile.

The band stayed with *Show Girl* until it closed, making for an extremely busy four months for Ellington and his men. Besides appearing in the show during the evenings as well as Thursday and Saturday matinees, they were at the Cotton Club at night. Their spot in the show was just before the end of the first act, allowing them plenty of time to get uptown. "Mills always had taxicabs at the stage door waiting for us," Greer recalled.

The manager also had them in the recording studios every chance he got. Between the Victor session of October 1928 when they recorded "The Mooche" and the September 16, 1929, session, three weeks before *Show Girl* closed, he had them in the studio more than twenty times.

As I noted earlier, Mills's music publishing house had the rights to the songs from the Fields and McHugh score of *Blackberries of 1928*, including "I Can't Give You Anything but Love" and "I Must Have That Man." Mills had recorded "I Can't Give You Anything but Love" with the band at the Victor session of October 30, and he re-recorded it with the band under the pseudonym "Goody Goodwin" for the same label on November 10.

Five days later, in the same studios, the band accompanied Ozie Ware singing "Bandanna Babies" and Goody Goodwin singing "Digga Do." The band recorded "I Must Have That Man," and then, under the pseudonym "Joe Turner and his Memphis Men," the group recorded it again on April 4, 1929. By continuing to issue new recordings of the same score, Mills was attempting to spur sales of the sheet music his company published. And as a partner in Ellington, Inc., Mills also shared in the royalties from the recordings.

The band was in the OKeh studios on November 20, 1928, to record "The Blues with a Feeling." Lonnie Johnson joined the group on "Goin' to Town." Two days later, they were back in the same studio, recording "Hottentot" and the Ellington classic, "Misty Mornin'." "The Whoopee Makers" re-recorded the work in late December for Pathé-Actuelle, and the work was recorded a third time at the Victor studios on May 3, 1929.

The majority of the works during this time were recorded under the name "Duke Ellington and his Orchestra" or "Duke Ellington and his Cotton Club Orchestra." However, the use of the pseudonyms continued unabated. The "Harlem Footwarmers," for example, recorded "Jungle Jamboree," "Six or Seven Times," and "Snake Hip Dance" for OKeh, while "The Jungle Band" recorded "Rent Party Blues," "Paducah," and "Harlem Flat Blues" for Brunswick.

With all this activity, Mills still found time to pull off an extraordinary coup. During the dog days of August, he had arranged for Ellington and the band to appear in the movie short, *Black and Tan*.

17

DUDLEY MURPHY, THE director of Ellington's first film, was an American expatriate who had lived in Paris during the 1920s. He was well known on the Left Bank and boasted friendships with avant-garde artists such as Jean Cocteau, Pablo Picasso, and Ferdinand Leger. On returning to the United States in 1928, he was appointed story editor and assistant chief of production for RKO Pictures. The company planned to enter the growing market for two-reel films.

Murphy found his way to Harlem shortly after returning to New York. He was impressed with the music, nighttime glitter, and vitality that pervaded the community. He approached RKO with the idea of making short sound films around well-known compositions by black composers.

He sought out Carl Van Vechten, who gave him entree to black performers. That contact led to his first film, *St. Louis Blues*, starring the immortal Bessie Smith. Besides Smith, the W. C. Handy classic featured the dancer-comedian Jimmie Mordecai, Isabel Washington, and an orchestra conducted by James P. Johnson. J. Rosamund Johnson's choral works were sung by the Hall Johnson Choir. Van Vechten was not directly credited on either *St. Louis Blues* or *Black and Tan*, but he was certainly involved. A production still from the set of the latter film shows him with Murphy, Ellington, and members of the cast.

St. Louis Blues was filmed in the RCA studios at 145 East 24th Street. The company had recently developed state-of-the-art recording equipment that was unavailable elsewhere. This new system was capable of recording sound-on-disc and sound-on-film or either of the two alone, allowing the company to market sound-track discs of its films. The quality of the sound-on-disc was necessarily lower than that coming from film because the discs were a secondary product. The transfer to disc took place after the picture was recorded and edited on film. The RCA soundstage, the most up-to-date of its time, was in use practically seven days a week, twenty-four hours a day.

While filming *St. Louis Blues*, Murphy and Van Vechten were anxiously scouring Harlem for their next production, tentatively called *Jazz*. It is a matter of conjecture how Mills, Murphy, and Van Vechten got in touch. But both Greer and Guy remember Mills stopping at the Cotton Club after the Boston tryout of *Show Girl* to announce that the band was going to be in a movie.

Black and Tan, as it was now called, was produced by the same team that made *St. Louis Blues*. It used the same sets and also featured the Hall Johnson Choir. In the film, Ellington portrays a struggling young bandleader. He and his friend, played by trumpeter Arthur Whetsol, are rehearsing "Black & Tan Fantasy" in Ellington's flat when they are interrupted by two movers (played by Alec Lovejoy and Edgar Connor) who have been sent to repossess Ellington's piano because he has fallen behind on the payments.

Freddie, played by Fredi Washington, is a young dancer and Duke's love interest (both onstage and off during this period). She arrives with the good news that she has found a nightclub to hire Ellington and his orchestra. However, the manager stipulates that she must dance there, which she insists on doing despite a grave heart condition. She bribes the movers with a bottle of gin so that Ellington and Whetsol can play their new composition for her.

The camera comes to rest on Ellington's hands, then pulls back to reveal the full orchestra on stage at the club playing "The Duke Steps Out." On the dance floor, five tuxedo-clad men of ascending heights (the Five Blazers) perform a precision dance on the mirror-like floor.

As Washington watches from the wings, her faintness causes her to see double. We see the action through her eyes, the dancers and orchestra splitting into a revolving kaleidoscope. Washington makes her entrance and, despite her condition, goes into a wild, shimmying dance to Ellington's "Cotton Club Stomp." A sudden shot of her gyrations from below increases the eerie tension of the film. At the end of the number, Washington collapses and is carried off the stage.

The club's manager insists that the show must go on. The orchestra continues to play, as the chorus line (the Cotton Club Girls) is brought on and dances to Ellington's "Flaming Youth." In the middle of the number, Ellington stops the band in disgust, and the band members join Washington in her dressing room.

The scene jumps to Freddie's deathbed, where Ellington and the mourners (the Hall Johnson Choir) are crowded around her. Ellington is at the piano, with Guy, Braud, and Tizol in the foreground; Whetsol, Bigard, and Nanton stand at the back of the room, their figures silhouetted with chiaroscuro lighting.

At Washington's dying request, the group goes into a "full dress" version of the "Black & Tan Fantasy," the complete composition with solos by trumpet, trombone, and clarinet, as opposed to the spare, growling rendition with which the film began.

The scene is again shot from Freddie's point of view: The camera focuses on Ellington's face, which gradually blurs into darkness as the young woman dies. The band and singers end the work with the famous musical quotation from Chopin's "Marche Funebre."

Ironically, *Black and Tan* provided Ellington with the most substantial acting part of his small movie career. In most subsequent appearances, he would be confined to his customary role as bandleader and pianist. He did play a cameo part as a bandleader in the 1959 film *Anatomy of a Murder* and provided his voice for the George Pal puppetoon, *Date with Duke* in 1946. Ellington later wrote that of all the things Mills ever did, getting him and the band into the movie *Black and Tan* meant the most to him.

When reviewing the film retrospectively in the 1970s, the British Film Institute's *Film Bulletin* found it dated and awkward. Yet the reviewer admitted that this brief film, from the very onset of the sound era, managed to fuse two different categories rarely produced by Hollywood: a dramatic film that used jazz organically, and a jazz film that featured music dramatically.

When I first saw *Black and Tan* forty years after its creation, I was struck by its daring, poetic synthesis of music and images, and the total integration of the two new art forms of the twentieth century: jazz and motion pictures.

18

THE FALL PRODUCTION of *It's the Blackberries* opened at the Cotton Club on September 29, 1929. As usual, Dan Healy staged the revue, and Fields and McHugh wrote the lyrics and music. Along with the Ellington orchestra, the show featured the dance trio Mordecai, Wells & Taylor; singer Leitha Hill; Madeline Belt; Cora LaRedd; the Washboard Serenaders; and dancer Henri Wessell, who did a duet with Mildred Dixon.

Dixon had been dating Ellington and had recently moved into his apartment on Nicholas Avenue, joining his mother, his father, and Ruth, who were now living there, too.

When Ellington's son, Mercer, arrived for a visit, he was surprised at how the household was organized. Ellington and his mistress Mildred Dixon shared the master bedroom, while Mercer and his grandfather slept in a separate room. Ellington's mother (Daisy)—now permanently out of his father's bed—shared a room with Ruth. Ruth said that Daisy was overjoyed to be back caring for her son again, waiting each day for him to come through the door and shout, "Mother, I'm home to dine!"

Shortly after Daisy had arrived in New York, Ellington bought a sixteen-cylinder Pierce Arrow sedan and hired a chauffeur to drive it. "That car was something," my cousin, who happened to live in Harlem at that time, recalled. "She [Daisy] used to sit in the back like she was the queen of England. In the summer, people used to run up to the car when it stopped at a red light and ask her how Duke was. She [would] always smile and give a polite answer."

Ellington and his father were soon familiar customers at the better Fifth Avenue stores, where Ellington would purchase expensive clothing and jewelry for his mother. He would ask J. E. to go with him, explaining, "My father would insist [that] the best be examined carefully to make certain it was good enough for my mother." Although Daisy often protested Ellington's extravagance, he would quiet her by saying, "Mother, if you don't take these things, I won't work."

Daisy thoroughly enjoyed participating in her son's success. "After a couple of thousand people had stopped applauding," Ruth said, "she was still applauding." Ellington remembered her standing and waving her handkerchief at him when he came out to take his bow at the end of *Show Girl*.

J. E., however, was not completely happy about the move to New York. He was a man who had worked practically every day of his life and had left a good job in Washington, working for the government as a blueprint maker. Now he was being supported by his son. The country was in the middle of the Great Depression, and there was no work for him in New York City. What his son had done, in effect, was to force him to retire at the age of forty-nine.

J. E. often complained about having nothing to do. Ellington's response was to make him a sort of chairman of the Ellington fan club. Mills's office was being flooded with requests for autographed photos of Duke and information about him, and J. E.'s job was to process the requests. For a short time, he also served as the band's road manager. It was at this time that Ellington's father began to drink heavily.

Following the breakup of his own marriage, Ellington had recreated the family that was closer to his heart's desire. In a blatant realization of Oedipal wishes, he essentially emasculated his father (however benignly and generously), removing him from his mother's bed and elevating her to the role of de facto consort. It would cost him dearly five years hence.

Blackberries of 1930, Healy's new Cotton Club production, opened on March 2. The cast was essentially the same as the October 1929 production, but Mordecai, Wells & Taylor, Madeline Belt, and the Washboard Serenaders were out, replaced by the Berry Brothers dance team, the Three Ebony Steppers, and Celeste Coles. Also, there was a major change in the production team. Fields and McHugh had left the club to go to Hollywood. Mills and Ellington volunteered to write the music for the show, and the management accepted. However, none of their three production numbers, "Bumpty Bump," "Doin' the Crazy Walk," and "Swanee River Rhapsody," proved memorable. Ellington recycled "Swanee River Rhapsody" as "Lazy Rhapsody" in 1932.

After suffering a series of negative reviews about the choreography, Healy had finally delegated that task to Clarence Robinson. "He had those girls dancing their asses off!" Greer recalled.

Later that month, the band was back on Broadway. Charles Dillingham, Maurice Chevalier's manager, had decided to present Chevalier on Broadway at the Fulton Theater for two weeks, beginning March 30. With two successful Paramount films to his credit, *The Love Parade* and *Innocents of Paris*, the French singer was riding a wave of popularity in America.

In a great coup for Mills, he got his star attraction a Broadway engagement. With a top ticket price of $4.40, Chevalier, the Ellington orchestra, and dancers Henri Wessels and Ananias Berry from the Cotton Club played to capacity houses every night. However, this gig presented a new challenge for Ellington. Whereas there was a master of ceremonies at the Cotton Club to keep things moving, on Broadway Ellington had to announce from the stage.

"I didn't know the first thing about how to emcee," Duke later admitted, "and the thought of it had me scared half to death. Then, there we were on stage and I opened my mouth and nothing came out." But Ellington quickly got over his stage fright, and before the evening was over, he was beginning to enjoy his new task. For the rest of his life, this engagement remained indelibly imprinted in Ellington's memory as a major evolutionary step in his creation of his stage persona.

The band occupied the Fulton stage alone, playing steadily for fifty minutes, before moving to the pit when Chevalier came on for the second half of the concert. "We finished up playing 'Tiger Rag,'" Greer recalled. "Tore the place up, folks were standing in the aisles, cheering, whistling, and stamping their feet as we came offstage. Chevalier had never heard nothin' like that, and came out of his dressing room to check out what was goin' on. He was all dressed except he didn't have no pants on, man, no pants. We had a laugh about it when we saw him in Paris."

Reviewing the show in *The New York Times*, Brooks Atkinson was not happy with Ellington's music, referring to him as the "Djinn of Din." He complained that Nanton's and Williams's use of mutes and plungers distorted popular songs beyond recognition. However, his was a distinctly minority view. Robert Benchley, in the *New Yorker*, wrote that Duke Ellington's orchestra could "lift you out of your seats." "What a band!" chimed the *Daily News*. "The last note in jazz," observed Charles Darnton in the *Evening World*. In the *Daily Mirror*, Walter Winchell wrote, "Duke Ellington's band . . . last night offered a series of barbaric tempoed tunes that won approval. Mr Ellington's piano solos clicked, and the drummer is better described as the ace of cymbal dusters."

The band was back on Broadway at the Palace Theater the week of May 16, 1930. *Variety* reported that the group was on stage for thirty-five minutes and were "the hit of the show." Ellington's "colored band act" was extensively reviewed. His "standing among the colored race in modern music today" was described as "relative to that of the late Jim Europe," the famous bandleader of the World War I era. Once again, Ellington emceed. The *Variety* critic did not notice anything awkward, describing Ellington's efforts as "smooth and pleasant." The band, supported by Cora LaRedd and other acts from the Cotton Club, was held over for a second week.

Ellington's successes on Broadway did not go unnoticed by Stark and DeMange. He was now their star attraction, keeping the club filled every night, and they were proud of him. Two years earlier, the announcer Ted Husing had been sent to Stark by William Paley to request that the club switch its broadcast to the radio network Paley was putting together, which subsequently became known as CBS.

Paley's vision of a coast-to-coast radio network was rapidly coming to fruition. The broadcasts from the glamorous Cotton Club were heard mainly on the East Coast. Paley thought it would be a great coup if the band's management would agree to the switch. His major concern was that Madden, Stark, and DeMange would extract an outrageous fee for the privilege.

The manager's response surprised Paley. Their only demand was that the band receive the proper amount of exposure befitting its stature. All they expected was a first-class air check. (An air check is a live radio broadcast.) No mention of money was made. As they shook hands on the deal, Stark was reported to have said to Husing, "There's no money in it for me; it will do some good for you. However, it'll probably do some good for Duke too, so go ahead and we'll see what happens."

Ellington and Husing did become famous (the latter as a sports announcer), and William Paley's network of stations soon spread from coast to coast. "We'd play a set, people would come up to the bandstand and tell us they heard us on the air, in Walla Walla, Washington; Elko, Nevada; Boise, Idaho; Austin, Texas; and places like that," Carney noted. "After a while I got a little book and began writing in it the names of the towns people said they were from."

A visit to the Cotton Club had become a must for well-heeled out-of-towners. Stark had not foreseen that when he made the deal. Paley himself later became a regular customer at the club. His first wife, Dorothy, was an ardent Ellington fan and insisted on ending their evenings there two or three times a week.

A warm friendship had developed between the management and Ellington. Every night after the show closed, Ellington, Mildred Dixon, DeMange, and Stark would retire to the back office and play cards until daybreak. The kitchen would make breakfast and everyone would then go home.

Ellington would use the card games to make minor requests of the management. "Anything you want Duke, it's yours" was the inevitable rejoinder. One night he brought up a topic that had been troubling him for some time. He was the club's star attraction. His Cotton Club Orchestra had appeared on Broadway on three separate occasions, bringing untold free advertising for the club. His mother had seen him every time he was on Broadway, yet she was unable to see him at the institution he had helped put on the map. Stark said nothing, but quietly passed the word that "respectable Negroes" would henceforth be welcome at the club. The following Sunday evening he personally escorted Daisy, J. E., Ruth, and Mercer to their table. "We got there early, as soon as they opened," Mercer recalled. "We had dinner, heard the band, and went home."

Several nights later, Ellington made another request to management, this one more serious. Mills had been informally negotiating with Paramount for the band to appear in a film, *Check and Double Check*, to be shot in Hollywood. They were due on the lot August 15 and probably would not return to New York until mid-September, a few weeks after the club would have reopened for the fall.

Over cards, Ellington brought it up, and the managers gave him their blessing. Duke Ellington and his Cotton Club Orchestra would now be seen in a major film, shown throughout the land. The publicity would be immeasurable. Stark left it to Ellington and Mills to work out who would replace him.

The replacement proved to be one of the Cotton Club's most famous and popular acts: the Cab Calloway Orchestra. Calloway recalled:

> I was working downtown at a place they called the Crazy Cat at the corner of Broadway and 48th Street. . . . We were there a couple of weeks, though, when a peculiar thing happened. One night after our last show, the headwaiter came over to me and said, "Cab, there's some guy's here who want to talk to you." . . . I could tell from the look of them they were from the mob. Wide brimmed hats, long coats, one of them had shades. They were all white guys. I tried to look cool.

The men informed Calloway he was to be at the Cotton Club the next day, because there were people there who wanted to speak with him about a job. At this point in his career, Calloway was fronting the Missourians, Andrew Preer's old band. Since leaving the Cotton Club, they had managed to eke out a living playing mostly one-night stands. They had been forcefully brought to Ellington's and Mills's attention when they bested the Ellington orchestra in a "Battle of Bands" at the Savoy Ballroom earlier that month. "They kicked our ass that night," Greer recalled.

On arriving at the club, Calloway was met by Ellington and Mills, who layed out a business proposition for him: Calloway and the Missourians would become Cab Calloway and His Orchestra. They would replace the Ellington orchestra at the Cotton Club or for any other date it was unable to make. As he had done with Ellington, Mills formed a corporation with Calloway. Mills had a 45 percent stake in the Calloway band and was their booking agent. Mills's lawyer held 10 percent, Calloway had 35 percent, and Ellington had 10 percent.

That matter settled, the Ellington band was off to California.

19

THE FILM *Check and Double Check* brought Ellington together with one of the most popular duos on radio, Amos 'n' Andy. In Hollywood terms, it was a perfect match. Ellington broadcast nightly from the Cotton Club in the heart of Harlem and was heard from coast to coast. *Amos 'n' Andy* also aired nationally and was set in Harlem. Combining Harlem's musical beat, as exemplified by the Ellington orchestra, with Harlem's premier comics made great sense to producers out in Hollywood.

It is hard today to imagine just how popular and beloved *Amos 'n' Andy* was back in the 1930s. When George Bernard Shaw visited America, he said three things impressed him most: the Grand Canyon, Niagara Falls, and the radio show *Amos 'n' Andy*. Throughout the 1930s, the fifteen-minute, five-night-a-week radio broadcast was a seven o'clock ritual in most American homes, both black and white.

The show was the creation of two white men, Freeman F. Gosden (Amos) and Charles F. Correll (Andy). They started out in 1919 as a vaudeville team doing blackface comedy and brought their act, "Sam 'n' Henry," to radio in 1926 in Chicago. The program was slow in catching on, but when its name was changed to *Amos 'n' Andy* in 1928, it became a sudden hit. Pepsodent toothpaste offered the show its corporate sponsorship and gave it national exposure over the NBC radio network.

The show provided listeners with a fanciful window on the life and times of two southern black men who came north to make their fortune in New York City. The creators' skill was such that among the tens of millions of listeners who avidly tuned into the show from 1926 on, both blacks and whites were convinced Gosden and Correll were black.

Gosden played the part of Amos, a solid, hardworking, churchgoing black man who played life straight and believed in the basic goodness of his fellow man. Correll had the role of Andy, a deep-voiced, roly-poly, gullible character who wore a derby hat and smoked cigars. Gosden also had the role of two minor characters in the show: George

Stevens, who was known as the Kingfish of the Mystic Knights of the Sea Lodge; and Lightnin', a shuffling character with a high-pitched drawl, who would exit the room whining, "Ow wah! Ow wah!"

Whites as well as blacks began using their minstrel-like words—such as "regusted" for disgusted, "detates" for dictates, and "sumpin'" for something—in ordinary conversation. ("Sump'n 'bout Rhythm" was the name of a 1935 Ellington composition.)

Still, no other show so bedeviled the nation it entertained. The columnist Heywood Hale Broun confessed he was a fan, and no less a personality than Eleanor Roosevelt used her own radio program to speak of her devotion to *Amos 'n' Andy*. But a black St. Louis woman named Theresa Smith wrote an angry letter to the *Post-Dispatch* complaining that all *Amos 'n' Andy* ever did was to teach black children and "the world at large . . . that the Negro in every walk of life is a failure, a deadbeat and above all shiftless and ignorant." A future civil rights leader, Clarence Mitchell, wrote to the *Baltimore Afro-American,* suggesting that black fans who liked the show were about as sensible as a "jackass." Another black newspaper, the *Pittsburgh Courier,* aimed to collect a million signatures in 1931 demanding that the Federal Radio Commission banish *Amos 'n' Andy* from the airwaves.

With the issue of Ellington's replacement settled, Mills drew up the contracts with RKO and arranged to get the band out to California. He had the group booked for a tour of New England in June, followed by a two-day engagement at the Savoy Ballroom in Chicago before sending the musicians off to California. The contract that Mills had negotiated stipulated that Mills's own expenses were to be paid by RKO. "He left Chicago a day ahead of us, first-class," said Guy.

The following day, the band departed from Union Station in two private railroad cars. A baggage car carried the stage equipment and the music. Guy said, "I'll say this for Mills. He insisted we travel first-class. Everyone had a lower berth and Duke had his own compartment. No segregated hotels for us." In the South, where there were no decent hotels for blacks, the train company would put the band's cars on a railroad siding and hook up the electricity; this would serve as their southern hotel. Guy remembered that "going out to California that first time, we spent the three days sleeping, eating, drinking, and playing cards."

For the next eleven years, the trains would be Ellington's sanctuary. He had a love of and fascination for them. The train was a place where he could achieve some degree of privacy. He said that once aboard, peace descended and the sound of the train's metallic wheels soothed him. He also loved to hear the sound of the train whistle, particularly at night. "Specially in the South," he wrote, "there the firemen play the blues on the engine whistle[,] big, smeary things like a goddamn woman singing in the night."

Ellington set the railroad experience to music beginning with "Choo-Choo" in 1924. The remarkable "Daybreak Express" (1934), the insouciant "Happy Go Lucky Local" (1947), and the elegant "Track 360" (1958) were also railroad songs.

Frances Bellerby wrote, "The ever present rhythms of the wheels, the screams of the engine and the close contact with noisy humanity have inevitably contributed much to the . . . personal character of Ellington's music."

Aboard the train, Ellington had his own private compartment. "But he was never there," Guy said. "The only time he was in there was to sleep or write music. Even when he was doing that, the door was open." Unlike Glenn Miller, who treated his musicians magisterially, referring to them by their last names only, or Benny Goodman, who barely remembered their names at all, Ellington thoroughly enjoyed the cama- raderie with his men. He used the card games less for recreation than to study his musicians and get a glimpse of their musical souls. "You can't write music right," he wrote in his autobiography, "until you know how the man that's gonna play it, plays poker."

20

THE DUKE ELLINGTON Orchestra was under contract for *Check and Doublecheck* from August 4 to August 31. Ellington's fee would be $27,500, to be paid in weekly installments of $6,875.

Rehearsals for the cast began on July 28, 1930, and the first scenes were shot on July 31. The basic plot involves Amos 'n' Andy's "Fresh Air Taxicab Co. of America Incorporated" being hired to transport the Ellington orchestra to a high-society ball. They become involved with a young white couple whose desire to be married is jeopardized by the young man's inability to locate a deed to some family property. Under the rules of their lodge, "The Mystic Knights of the Sea," Amos 'n' Andy are sent to an old haunted house to keep watch for a night. While there, they stumble on the missing deed so vital to the young couple, and a happy marriage is ensured.

When the band members arrived to shoot their first scenes on August 14, Melville Brown, the director, took one look at Tizol and Bigard, both of whom were light skinned, and ordered them to wear dark makeup. The rationale for this bit of racism was that he wanted the band to have a more uniform appearance for the film. The *Baltimore Afro-American* accompanied a photo of the band with the caption: "They Must Black Up for Part in the Movies."

The orchestra's sequence starts with its arrival by taxi at the society ball where it would be playing that evening. After the band enters inside the mansion, the cab has a flat tire. Inside the house, the band is setting up and we hear the tuning up of instruments. The first piece of music played is Harry Ruby's "When I'm Blue."

The film cuts back outside, where Amos 'n' Andy are working on the flat. The dance tune is heard faintly in the background, including brief solos by Cootie Williams and Johnny Hodges. During an ensuing stretch of dialogue, Ellington's "The Mystery Song" plays in the background. This piece was written for a dance team, the Step Brothers (at the Cotton Club), and was edited to end as the dialogue does.

The Ellington band is next heard and seen in a ballroom sequence. The band plays a few bars of "East St. Louis Toodle-Oo," its radio theme, before moving into "Three Little Words," a song by Harry Ruby and Bert Kalmar. "Three Little Words" was written to be sung by Sonny Greer, but he got mike fright during the shooting.

"They tried a few takes, but I just couldn't seem to get the words to come out right," Greer remembered. "Finally I told Duke the whole damn thing was making me nervous. The next day they rewrote the script and had Cootie, Freddie, and Artie Whetsol mouthing the words. Bing Crosby and two other cats [Harry Barris and Al Rinker] sang the tune in the recording studio."

Crosby, Rinker, and Barris had recently left Paul Whiteman's band and were then appearing with Gus Arnheim's orchestra at the Coconut Grove in the Los Angeles Ambassador Hotel. According to Ellington, Crosby was initially hired to replace Greer's singing voice. But after hearing Crosby's take on the prerecording, Melville Brown insisted on using the trio instead. Ellington always felt that Crosby's version of "Three Little Words" had been heard by someone at Paramount; the company quickly signed him, and his career took off almost immediately.

The ballroom scene reaches its climax with Ellington's "Old Man Blues," originally titled "Ow wa! Ow wa! Blues," based on the vocal habit of the character Lightin' from the radio show. The sound track is edited slightly compared to the version on the Victor recording.

The camera never leaves the band during this extended number. The soloists, Carney on baritone sax, Hodges on soprano, and Jenkins on trumpet, are shown in close-up while the society folk listen appreciatively. This was a remarkable feature number for a black band in 1930.

According to Cootie Williams, Ellington thought "Old Man Blues" was the best thing he had written up to that time. Gunther Schuller called attention to "the remarkable balance between composition and improvisation."

On August 20, in the Victor Studios, the band recorded three takes each of "Old Man Blues," "Three Little Words," and an Ellington composition reportedly written for *Check and Double Check* but never used, "Ring Dem Bells." Of the "Three Little Words" takes, the final one was made with a singer named Jimmy Miller, possibly a pseudonym. The first two were with the Emmanual Hall Quartet, a male vocal group.

Clearly, Mills was dissatisfied with what he heard. Six days later, the band was back in the studios recording the same three works. The only difference was that this time Mills brought the Rhythm Boys for the three takes of "Three Little Words." When they returned to New York, the "Harlem Footwarmers" (i.e., Ellington's band) re-recorded "Old Man Blues," "Ring Dem Bells," and "Three Little Words" for OKeh.

Following a dance at the Shrine Auditorium on August 29, Ellington and his men boarded their private railroad cars for the trip back to New York. On September 6 they were back on stage at the Palace Theater for a week's engagement, sharing the bill with the popular singers Irene Bordoni, Cora LaRedd, and Frank Fay.

Brown Sugar (Sweet but Unrefined) opened at the Cotton Club on September 28, 1930. Healy had hired a new songwriting team, Ted Koehler and Harold Arlen, to supply the music and lyrics. Arlen (originally Arluck) was born in Buffalo, New York, the son of a cantor. He had arrived in New York in the spring of 1926 as pianist, arranger, and vocalist in a ten-piece band, the Buffalodians. They played an engagement at the Roseland Ballroom, which brought them to the attention of Fletcher Henderson, then in residence. He was so impressed with Arlen's arranging skills in particular that he bought Arlen's composition "Dynamite," which he soon recorded.

The bandleader used his connections to get the musicians a recording session at Columbia. On May 24, 1926, paying homage to their patron, they recorded "Deep Henderson" and "Here Comes Emaline." Two months later they were in the Banner studios, with Arlen the vocalist on "How Many Times?" and "Baby Face."

The Buffalodians soon disbanded, but Arlen—with the strong encouragement of Bix Beiderbecke—began a career as a singer. Composer Vincent Youmans hired him, accompanied by the Henderson band, for the minor role of Cokey Joe in the ill-fated musical *Great Day!* One afternoon, during the tryout in Philadelphia, Arlen filled in for the rehearsal pianist. To set up the dancers, he played a four-bar vamp. Will Marion Cook, a consultant to the show, suggested that the four bars had the makings of a pretty good tune. Youmans introduced Arlen to a budding young lyricist, Ted Koehler, and Koehler and Arlen developed their first hit, "Get Happy."

"Those shows by Arlen and Koehler," observed Cab Calloway, "were a combination of vaudeville, burlesque, and great music and dancing. Dorothy Fields wasn't really funky enough to write the kind of songs that would carry a Negro revue of that type." Taking note of Arlen's bluesy minor key tunes, Ethel Waters once described him as the "blackest white man" she ever knew.

Ellington wrote his first hit song a few weeks after the opening of *Brown Sugar*. Mills had never forgotten the sound of the septet he heard that first night at the Kentucky Club, and had been after Ellington to write something in that vein again. Finally, Mills told Ellington that he wanted the band in the OKeh Studios on October 14, 1930, with music for a septet.

On the afternoon of October 13, Ellington began putting together arrangements of "Big House Blues" and "Rocky Mountain Blues." While waiting for his mother to finish cooking dinner, he sketched a slow blues to be played by Whetsol on muted trumpet, Nanton with mute and plunger, and Bigard on clarinet. Ellington's scoring of this tune was unorthodox. The usual roles of clarinet, trumpet, and trombone were reversed. Nanton played the high voice, and Whetsol the middle, with Bigard on the bottom. Gunther Schuller observed, "The resulting tonal colors had never been heard before in all of music history."

The band played the work on the air that night, and as the Harlem Footwarmers, recorded it under the title "Dreamy Blues" the following morning. "The next day, wads of mail came in raving about the new tune," Ellington remembered, "so Irving Mills put a lyric on it, and royalties are still coming in for my evening's work forty years ago."

Mills is listed as cocomposer of the work, now titled "Mood Indigo." However, the lyrics were actually supplied by Mitchell Parrish, a staff writer for Mills Music, Inc.

Three days later, Mills had Ellington, Whetsol, Nanton, and Bigard in the Brunswick studios, where they recorded the work as "Mood Indigo." A month later, the full band recorded the work for Victor.

Check and Double Check had its premiere at the newly refurbished RKO Mayfair Theater on October 31. The owners of the Paramount

Theater on Broadway took advantage of the publicity and booked Ellington for a two-week engagement beginning that same day. His was the first black orchestra to play the Paramount. The stage show also included comedian Frank Jenks, Rice & Warner, the Four Co-eds, and the Horosco Brothers, among others. When the band closed at the Paramount, Mills booked it for two theater engagements in Harlem.

Leonard Harper produced a *Double Check Revue* on the stage of the Lafayette Theater, and two weeks later, the movie *Check and Double Check* had its Harlem premiere at the Douglas Theater. The Douglas was located downstairs from the Cotton Club and the band appeared live on the stage of the movie house. "That was the easiest gig ever," Greer said. "We'd do the stage show, go upstairs, and play some more."

On opening night, Ellington was interviewed by Janet Mabie for the *Christian Science Monitor.* She was completely charmed, and noted "his great gift for understanding and his capacity for a simple kind of friendliness. . . . People take quite appreciable pleasure when he comes in. They smile and pat their hands together and say among themselves, 'And now we shall hear something.'" She compared him with Paul Robeson, "in that both men believed [that] in the heart of Africa there lies a great secret of music."

She requested "Mood Indigo," which she had heard on the radio. "It had seemed to me, of its kind, a sort of thing just too pungently lovely to be quite sure you've actually heard it. 'It is very simple,' he said when he had finished playing it. 'It is just one of those very simple little things that you throw together. Of course, the arrangement makes it. But it really isn't anything; the melody isn't. It's funny, I threw that together, and it has caught on. I've worked desperately over things, and they haven't come out at all. Isn't it queer, not to have anything for a great deal of work, and something for no work at all?'"

He concluded the interview by saying, "I am just getting a chance to work out some of my own ideas of Negro music. I stick to that."

Check and Double Check ultimately received mostly mediocre reviews, and after an initial splash at the box office, ticket sales fell off dramatically. By the time the film reached the second-run houses, it had lost all its appeal. RKO shelved plans for a sequel, and Amos 'n' Andy would never appear in another major film.

The film's failure was due in part to the obvious burnt-cork makeup of the principals, a disillusionment to radio listeners who had imagined genuine black characters, especially because the radio voices gave a credible imitation of black speech. Also, the film's plot centered on the black characters less than the radio show did. Amos 'n' Andy's regular radio sidekicks, Lightnin' and Kingfish, were missing entirely from the film, and the action had been moved from Harlem to white suburbia.

However, the failure of the movie did not slow Ellington down. By the time of the Harlem opening, he was actively working on "Creole Rhapsody," the first of the many extended compositions he would write over his lifetime.

At this point in life, Ellington's musical creativity was constrained by the ten-inch 78-rpm recording. He was looking toward writing in a musical form longer than three minutes. On October 8, 1929, he recorded a two-sided version of "Tiger Rag" for Brunswick. While the work is six minutes long, it is, in effect, an extended jam session, with a series of excellent solos.

"Creole Rhapsody," on the other hand, stands out as Ellington's first piece of absolute music—music without words composed for close listening, rather than for dance or social entertainment. Schuller wrote that it was Ellington's 1926 "Birmingham Breakdown," with its "succession of two- and four-bar sub-segments, . . . that broke the ice for the five-bar phrases of 'Creole Rhapsody.' "

Ellington recorded the work twice in 1931, on January 20, for Brunswick and on June 11 for Victor. The January version was six minutes long. The Victor version ran for more than eight minutes, having been recorded on both sides of a twelve-inch 78-rpm disk. I agree with John Edward Hasse, who observed in *Beyond Category: The Life and Genius of Duke Ellington,* "This second performance is much better, offering—besides changing moods—numerous contrasts in tempos (indicating this was definitely a piece for listening, not dancing)."

In both versions, Ellington experimented with five-bar phrases and a trombone duet. A bold statement, not entirely integrated formally, the work is a harbinger of things to come.

There is a striking similarity between "Creole Rhapsody" and Gershwin's "Rhapsody in Blue" and "Concerto in F" as recorded by Paul

Whiteman. However, there are also significant differences. "Creole Rhapsody" is scored for five brass, three reeds, and four rhythm instruments, and there are improvisations by the piano soloist and the orchestra members. Ellington knew Gershwin and had worked with him. He himself stated that he used to listen to Paul Whiteman's recordings. "Rhapsody in Blue" was recorded in 1924, "Concerto in F" in 1928. We can assume that Ellington had heard them both.

Europeans had begun to take a great interest in Ellington's music, as he would learn within two years. Constant Lambert, who had heaped accolades on the pairing of "Hot and Bothered" and "The Mooche," wrote in *Gramaphone Notes* that all of Ellington's works up to "Creole Rhapsody" "only occupy one side of a 10 in. record, and are all the better for this limitation. A jazz record should be as terse as possible, and it would be a pity if Ellington started to produce rambling, pseudo-highbrow fantasies such as Gershwin's more ambitious essays."

In contrast, writing in *Melody Maker*, Cambridge-educated bandleader and composer Patrick Cairns "Spike" Hughes gave the work a glowing review. "It is in fact, the first classic of modern dance music," he wrote. "The individual player is for the first time subservient to the personality of the composer."

The Ellington orchestra finally left the Cotton Club on February 5, 1931, after a thirty-eight-month run. Mills had signed the group up for an eighteen-week tour, mainly for the Paramount Publix theater chain, beginning with a week's appearance at the Metropolitan Theater in Boston. It was the first appearance in this chain by any big band, black or white. The Cab Calloway orchestra would replace them at the club.

During his stay at the Cotton Club, Ellington had developed the persona of the always-debonair and sophisticated gentleman. Calloway's energetic dancing and singing and his infectious personality provided a stark contrast. He and his band were an instant success.

21

WHEN ELLINGTON ARRIVED in New York City in 1923, his major ambition was to become a songwriter. When he opened at the Cotton Club four years later, he aspired to be a composer. His first major compositions were all cooperative ventures, mainly with Miley, and occasionally with Hardwick and other band members. But by the time Ellington left the club in 1931, he had written his first major extended work, "Creole Rhapsody," and was able to compose with ease and do so on demand. What were the circumstances that made all this possible?

We can start with Ellington's run at the Cotton Club. The room provided him with thirty-eight months of steady employment, thereby freeing him from any financial worries. The combination of Mills's astute management, including many recording sessions, nightly radio broadcasts, and Broadway stage appearances, did much to enhance Ellington's self-esteem, thus helping to free up his creativity. In fact, the Cotton Club had become his atelier, where he mastered his craft and forged his unique style.

At management's request, Ellington had to produce so-called jungle music and specialty production numbers, which resulted in "The Mooche," "Doin' the Voom Voom," "Cotton Club Stomp," "Flaming Youth," "Echoes of the Jungle," "Jungle Blues," and more.

Ellington had to orchestrate a range of songs, such as "I Can't Give You Anything but Love" and "Bandanna Babies" for Fields and McHugh, Arlen and Koehler's "Stormy Weather," the current popular songs of the day, such as "I Must Have That Man" and "St. James Infirmary," or downright trash, like "Nine Little Miles from Ten Ten Tennessee." All the songs, good or bad, were given the distinctive Ellington touch.

In addition, Ellington had to provide a constant supply of original compositions designed to keep the dance floor filled and his musicians content. The early lessons from Cook and his five-year association with

Vodery gave Ellington the bedrock on which to build his mainly blues-based style in such compositions as "The Mooche," "Creole Rhapsody," "Misty Mornin'," and "Blues with a Feelin'".

"Duke could take blues chords and say more with them than any man alive," Frank Galbreath observed. The saxophonist Bob Wilber was in the studio many years later during an Ellington recording session. At its conclusion, Duke beckoned to him, suggesting he get out his horn and join Ellington in playing some blues. Mercer observed, "My father's idea of relaxation was to sit at the piano and play blues."

Ellington's next task was to get the notes on paper the way he heard them in his head. "In the beginning, he'd ask us to come to the club for an afternoon and pay us union scale for our time," Carney recalled:

> And all he'd do was voice chords. He'd take something like a C 13th, spread the notes out through the band, give a downbeat, and *bam*. The first time he did that Jenkins called it a "Christmas Chord" Then he'd move the notes around, maybe Johnny, Barney, and me would switch. Another downbeat *bam*, and maybe Artie and Cootie would switch, or Tizol and Tricky Sam, or me and Tizol or Tricky. We'd do that for two or three hours.

Many years later, Ellington's aide-de-camp Tom Whaley was given a score to copy. "The first time I was copying his music I said, 'Duke, you got an E natural up there against an E flat.' He said, 'That's all right. Put it down.' After you hear it, it sounds great."

"That man had the greatest ear for instrumental voices," Carney observed, "Like my baritone for instance. A lot of arrangers always put it on the bottom, but sometimes Duke would put me in the lead voice, the second voice or third voice according to what he had in mind. He knew our instrumental voices cold. On one of the train trips to California, Cootie picked up Tizol's trombone and started to play it. He hadn't played but a few notes, when Duke's head popped out his state room. '*What was that?*' he said. Not who, but what. Our instrumental voices were in his head all the time."

That state of affairs allowed Ellington to personalize his writing. Instead of first trombone, first trumpet, and so on, the parts would be identified by the musicians, Tricky, Artie, Johnny, Barney.

Even after the notes were on paper, Ellington would continue to revise. "Sometimes after we'd run through a new number," Cootie Williams said, "Duke would ask me or Whetsol to switch parts or Whetsol and Jenkins, or Jenkins and me, until he got the sound he had in mind."

Ellington was the only leader who was at once composer, arranger, and director of an orchestra shaped by his own hand. In that way he resembled classical composer Joseph Haydn, who had the Esterhazy orchestra at his disposal. Both men had the good fortune to hear their music played as soon as it was written, thereby spurring them on to further efforts.

Following the lead of Henderson and Redmond, Ellington wedded black musical improvisation with European orchestral scoring. Writing with his various musicians in mind, he used the entire orchestra as a jazz instrument, and stamped every facet of the music with his personality. His most important collaborator, Billy Strayhorn, summed it up when he stated, "Duke plays the piano, but his instrument is the orchestra."

Writing for particular players in the band, Ellington allowed the musicians to collaborate on the creation of a finished musical product. After playing a phrase on the piano, he would encourage the musicians to make suggestions. Cootie Williams said, "Everyone in the band would pitch in and help write songs, everything that Duke did in those days." The sections would work out the harmonies, usually on chords Ellington or someone else had provided.

Sometimes a composition would germinate and flower from within the band itself. While on tour during the 1930s, Ellington featured Bigard on the Art Hickman composition "Rose Room" while Richard Bowden Jones (Jonesy), the band boy, began to pack up.

One night as the clarinetist was playing, Hodges began backing up Bigard's solo with a five-note phrase. "The next night, I answered Johnny with a riff of my own," Lawrence Brown recalled. "Over time it developed that the full sax section would play Johnny's tune and me, Tricky, and Tizol would respond, playing my response in harmony. Other than Duke's eight-bar intro on piano, and the six-bar brass fanfare he wrote before Johnny's solo, that piece came right out of the band. When we recorded it, he named it 'In a Mellow Tone' [1940] after Johnny's tune."

Ellington's orchestra actualized the Harlem Renaissance goal of producing great art out of folk experience. From the late 1920s onward, Ellington used European scoring techniques effectively to extend and enrich the vernacular tradition.

"Significantly, while those men who promulgated the Harlem Renaissance would give credit to jazz and the dance," Nathan Huggins wrote, "it was often because they evidenced qualities in the Negro character that might be converted into the 'high art.'" Little did James Weldon Johnson and Alain Locke know that 'high art' was being created under their very noses at 644 Lenox Avenue from December 1927 to January 1931.

22

THE BROADCASTS FROM the Cotton Club and an extensive publicity campaign launched by the Publix Theater chain and Mills combined to prime Chicago for Ellington's arrival. His appearance at Balaban & Katz's Oriental Theater during the week of February 13, 1931, broke the house record. On opening day, Mills issued a press release announcing that, the night before, Ellington had finished his most recent composition, "Creole Rhapsody," and its world premiere was to be held at the Oriental. This announcement must have come as a surprise to Ellington, because he had recorded the work a month earlier!

The following week found Ellington on the South Side of Chicago at the Regal Theater. He was originally contracted to do two weeks there, but Balaban & Katz shortened it to one week and moved the band across town to their Uptown Theater for the second week. A week at the Paradise Theater was followed by another week at the Oriental, where the band broke the house record again. The musicians concluded their stay in the Windy City with a dance at the Savoy Ballroom. The *Chicago Defender* reported "an attendance of 7,200 which made dancing impossible."

Appearing with the band at the theater engagements as "featured singer" was Ivie Anderson. At age twenty-seven, she had ten years of show business behind her. She was born in Gilroy, California, and was orphaned at age nine. She spent her next eight years in St. Mary's Convent, where she received vocal training, and her first professional work was at Tait's Club in Los Angeles. Anderson subsequently toured in a Fanchon and Marco revue, on the white vaudeville circuit, in which Mamie Smith was the star.

Anderson soon earned a feature spot as a vocalist in the show, and 1925 found her in New York at the Cotton Club prior to touring with the *Shuffle Along* revue. She returned to Los Angeles and found work with Curtis Mosby's Blue Blowers, Paul Howard's Quality Serenaders, and Sonny Clay's band. Anderson became the first black singer to be featured with a white band. Anson Weeks hired her to sing with his orchestra at San Francisco's elegant Mark Hopkins Hotel. Before the 1920s were over she would sing in Australia and have her own revue produced by Fanchon and Marco.

At the time her path crossed with Ellington's, Anderson was in her twentieth week at the Grand Terrace Café, accompanied by the Earl Hines Orchestra. She had been placed on the bill at the Oriental as a special attraction by the owners of the theater circuit. At the end of the four weeks, Ellington (who had seriously been considering the idea of adding a female singer) asked Anderson to remain with the band as featured vocalist. She accepted only after repeated assurances by Hines that she was good enough.

"Actually his first choice was May Alix," said Greer. "But Freddie and me told him to grab Ivie. May was very light skinned, and could probably pass for white if you didn't know her. Ivie was brown-skinned. After what they did to Tizol and Bigard in that movie, the last thing he needed was to have to explain again and again to 'dumb, stupid crackers' that May wasn't white, she was colored."

Anderson was cast in the mold of the "sophisticated" black lady singers of the 1920s, such as Ethel Waters, Adelaide Hall, and Josephine Baker, who grew in popularity as the blues craze faded. She left Chicago with Ellington for a week's engagement at Detroit's Michigan Theater.

Richard Bowden Jones, "Jonesy," also joined the tour, as Duke's valet. Jones was a busboy at the Cotton Club when the band made its debut. "When he wasn't busing dishes, he was always hanging around backstage," Carney recalled:

> Duke would always change clothes between shows. The next thing we knew, Jonesy would be in his dressing room helping him. He did the same thing on the theater dates downtown. When we had recording dates he'd do the setups, and once Sonny got those drums, Duke knew he'd need some help with them and hired Jonesy as a combination valet-band boy. Then he took him on the road with us.

Jones was later immortalized in the Ellington composition "Stompy Jones," and he remained with the band for the next twenty years.

Mercer Ellington recalled a interactions that occasionally took place between the valet and his employer over that period of time. Jonesy would be given $100 or $200 for incidental band expenses, and periodically Ellington would call him in to account for it.

"Pop would look down the list with a very serious expression on his face, and on this occasion, one recurring item caught his eye. 'What's this, J. B.?' he asked. 'Whiskey?'

"'No,' Jonesy said sheepishly.

"'Well what is it?'

"'Jones's booty.'

"Pop managed to keep a straight face, although it was the kind of thing that amused him very much. Several months went by and several blameless swindle sheets were accepted, but then another pair of repeated initials showed up. 'J. P., J. P., J. P.,' Pop muttered. 'What that stand for?'

"'Jones's pussy,' he said, looking anywhere but at the Old Man.

"'You mean I have to buy that for you too? You better take it easy!'"

Another member of the entourage was Ned Williams, Balaban & Katz's press agent, who had spearheaded the local publicity campaign on Ellington's behalf. Mills liked Williams's work and hired him for his new venture, Mills Artists Bureau. Williams was put in charge of all Duke Ellington promotions, an assignment he would hold for the next decade.

Williams quickly earned his spurs as the group's advance man. The band left Chicago for a series of one-night stands and theater dates, beginning with a dance at the Tivoli ballroom in Waukegan, Illinois. Engagements in Wisconsin, Minnesota, Nebraska, Iowa, Missouri, Colorado, Indiana, upstate New York, Toronto, and Pennsylvania followed.

June 11, 1931, found the band at the Pearl Theater in Philadelphia. During that engagement, the group went across the river to the Victor studios in Camden, New Jersey, to record the extended version of "Creole Rhapsody." Five days later, the musicians were back at the studios to record four works that Gunther Schuller ranked "among the finest of recorded Ellingtonia." First they did "Limehouse Blues," with its lovely, liquid reed figures for the opening, and the weird, tumultuous "Echoes of the Jungle." The following day, "The Mystery Song," with its magical opening created by Ellington's ingenious use of passing tones, and the sumptuous "It's Glory" were put on wax.

The band returned to Chicago, following a circuitous route of one-night stands in western Pennsylvania, Michigan, and Ohio. A four-week gig at the Lincoln Tavern in a suburban Chicago, beginning July 12, gave everyone a chance to collect their breath.

"When we got there," Greer recalled, "Duke's parents, Mildred, Mercer, and Ruth had already arrived. The married cats all sent for their wives."

Before leaving Chicago, Mills had made an arrangement with NBC's Artists Bureau to book the Ellington and Calloway orchestras for a series of engagements at the end of the Publix Theater tour, and whenever possible, NBC would broadcast the Ellington orchestra.

While in Cleveland during the week of June 27, Mills became infuriated when he learned that Calloway had been booked by NBC at terms he considered unfavorable. Making matters worse, the booking had been made over Mills's head, by Moe Gale, owner of the Savoy Ballroom in Harlem. Mills retaliated by threatening to move the Ellington band from NBC to CBS at the end of the Lincoln Tavern engagement. However, the rift was healed and the band continued the tour as scheduled. This time the orchestra ventured as far east as Washington, D.C. (returning to Ellington's hometown for a week of performances at the Howard Theater), and as far west as St. Louis. The group finally returned to the Cotton Club on February 5, 1932, for a week, also playing at the Brooklyn Paramount Theater.

"We were on the road for a year," Cootie Williams recalled. "Other than the theater dates, half of the time we didn't know where we were at. We'd get out of the train, do the gig, and split."

With the exception of the Victor recording dates in June 1931, the band had not been in the recording studios since the tour began. Mills promptly took care of that by booking the band in the Brunswick recording studios on February 2, 4, and 11, 1932. The first number the group recorded, "It Don't Mean a Thing (If It Ain't Got That Swing)," marked Ivie Anderson's recording debut with the band. Carney said, "Bubber always used to say 'If it ain't worth singing, it ain't worth swinging, if it ain't worth swinging, it ain't worth playin'.'" The statement embodied the essence of this great musician, which Ellington put to music. "Moon over Dixie," with Greer's vocal, and the insouciant "Lazy Rhapsody" completed the session.

Two days later, "Blue Tune" and "Baby, When You Ain't There" were put on wax. At 1:20 in the morning on February 11, the band finished recording "St. Louis Blues" with its old friend Bing Crosby singing the vocal. Crosby's career had taken off, and he was currently headlining the stage show at the Paramount Theater in New York City. For the recording, a twelve-inch Brunswick, Ellington scored a four-bar introduction. Cootie Williams growls the melody and Crosby does the vocal. At the conclusion, the tempo increases and Hodges solos before trading four-bar improvs with Crosby, who does a first-rate piece of scat singing, showing his debt to his idol Louis Armstrong.

"We did that piece on stage with Bing," Greer recalled.

> I'll never forget that gig. He made Johnny come down to the mike as they traded fours. The first time they did it, I tapped the Chinese gong on the off beat and made it go woosh, woosh, woosh, woosh. They took off. When it was over he insisted Johnny take a bow with him, then looked over at me, and said "Keep that cymbal in."
>
> When we made the record we never could get the right balance. Finally Mills asked me to leave it out. Bing wasn't too happy about it.

The band did two sessions for RCA Victor on February 3 and 9. On the 3rd, it took the entire session to record a medley of "Mood Indigo," "Hot and Bothered," and "Creole Love Call." On the 9th, another medley—consisting of "East St. Louis Toodle-Oo", a piano solo called "Lots of Fingers" (also known as "Fast And Furious"), and "Black & Tan Fantasy" was recorded. These medleys were, in fact, the first stereo performances, a quarter of a century before stereo recordings became generally available.

RCA Victor and its English counterpart, HMV, began making a series of long-playing 33-1/3-rpm recordings between 1929 and 1935, many years before the LP was formally introduced by its rival, Columbia, in 1948. Some of the recordings were actually primitive stereo: Two microphones and two cutting tables produced two discs— one focused on the left side, the other on the right—that were made to be played simultaneously.

To achieve the stereo effect, these recordings had to be played using two synchronized turntables, which may explain why RCA Victor was not able to merchandise the recordings successfully. In addition, the Depression proved to be the wrong time for such expensive innovations. As it happened, because either of the pseudo-stereo recordings could be sold as regular long-playing monaural records, most of them were sold that way.

Those early LPs were made by Hoagy Carmichael, Leo Reisman, Fred Waring's Pennsylvanians, Gertrude Lawrence, Noel Coward, and the D'Oyly Carte Opera Company, in addition to Ellington. On the classical side, there were recordings by the Philadelphia Orchestra under Leopold Stowkowski, and the BBC Symphony conducted by Sir Edward Elgar.

Forty-nine years later, Ellington scholar Steven Lasker bought an Ellington disc at an auction. He thought it might be an alternate version of one of these early Ellington medleys, because the matrix and take numbers on the label differed from those on the issued recording of the performance. He brought this to the attention of Brad Kaye, a recording engineer and collector, who agreed that this might be an alternative take, and urged Lasker to find a copy of the issued medley for comparison.

When Lasker found a copy three years later, he took it to Kaye and they made visual and aural comparisons. The two performances were musically identical, but there were subtle recording differences. Lasker noticed that when Greer hit his cymbals or played orchestra bells on the issued disc, they were very loud. But on the test, they were almost inaudible.

Kaye later reported, "Suddenly I sensed the truth. Holding the two aloft, I said, 'I think what we have here are the left- and right-hand channels of a stereophonic recording!'"

When I began collecting Ellington recordings fifty years ago, I noticed that the band of the 1930s had a lean sound, compared to the lush sound it took on in its later years. That leanness often came across as a thin quality in the relatively crude monaural records of the day. On hearing the stereo recordings fifty-three years after they were made, the band comes alive with depth and color that were never fully evident on the monaural disks.

With the recordings out of the way, the band members boarded their railroad cars for a trip to the West Coast. The first stop was San Francisco for a three-week engagement at the Orpheum Theater, where Ellington received $5,000 a week. Ivie Anderson, the Four Step Brothers, and Ellington himself were singled out for praise in *Variety*'s review.

The Orpheum Theater in Los Angeles was the band's next stop. When they arrived at Union Station on the morning of March 10, 1932, the entourage (including the Four Step Brothers) was given a musical escort to the Dunbar Hotel. That night the band did a radio broadcast on station KHJ, and it opened at the theater the next morning. On March 30, Ellington was honored with a testimonial dinner at the Elks Auditorium.

By the time the band boarded the train for the trip back to New York, another musician, Lawrence Brown, had been added to the trombone section. Brown was born in Lawrence, Kansas, in 1907. In 1914 Brown's father, a minister, moved the family to Oakland, California, and later to Pasadena by way of San Francisco.

Brown's was a musical family. An older brother and his mother played piano and organ. A younger brother played violin and piano. "The leader of the choir in our church was a trombone player," Brown recalled:

> And he used to leave his horn in church all week. We lived next door and used to keep the place cleaned up. Now, I made a deduction of my own about this time. All the musical instruments were being played, but you didn't see many trombone players. This helped me decide on trombone. And I'd been taught that the trombone was the violin of the brass instruments, but I liked the cello, for its nice voice, and I thought I would try to pattern my style on the cello.

Brown received formal training on his instrument at Pasadena High School. A men's club selected him as a soloist on its radio show. While there, he was heard by the evangelist Aimee Semple McPherson, which led to his appearance before a Mother's Day crowd of 6,000 in her Los Angeles temple.

When he was nineteen, Brown left home to work professionally with Charlie Echols's seven-piece band. An engagement with Paul Howard's Quality Serenaders at Frank Sebastian's Cotton Club followed. Curtis Mosby hired Brown to work at the Club Alabam for a year, and then he was back at the Cotton Club along with Lionel Hampton and Louis Armstrong in 1932. While there, Mills heard Brown play "Trees," his featured part in the show, and insisted he meet with Ellington.

"I don't know you and I've never heard anything about you," were Duke's first words to him, "but Mr. Mills says to get you. So come on in the band." Thus began Brown's nineteen-year odyssey with the Ellington orchestra.

When I auditioned as a trombonist for the Luis Russell, Milton Larkin, and Benny Carter orchestras, I knew my success would be based on how well I *blended* with the other men in the section. Most band leaders want the timbre of the instruments to be as close as possible. Tommy Dorsey carried that one step further: He wanted all his trombone players to sound just like him!

Unlike Dorsey's, the trombone trio that Brown joined had three very distinctive voices. He brought to the section a warm burnished sound and a mobile style of playing, reflecting his love for the cello. The classically trained Tizol had a "pure" sound to his horn. That was offset by Nanton's gritty open horn, when he wasn't using the plunger. Ellington's task was to get the right blend of all three.

Ellington's addition of Brown to the trombone section caused some consternation among the jazz critics once they heard him solo on recordings several months later. Both Spike Hughes and John Hammond agreed that Brown was out of place in the band. They felt his technical prowess was not an asset, but a liability to what they saw as the essentially direct and simple music of Ellington.

While their argument might have had some merit, they completely missed the fact that Brown was another unique voice in the Ellington canon, a voice that Ellington proceeded to employ to great advantage.

"I joined the band on April 1st," Brown recalled. "When we got to New York we had a one-night stand in Harlem [at the Rockland Palace] before going downtown to the Paramount for two weeks. I noticed during the job at the Rockland Palace, Duke never called on me to solo. Later, when I asked him why, he told me I was the thirteenth member of the band. Thirteen meant bad luck. I couldn't solo until a new member was added!"

During the theater engagement, Mills did something for which Ellington never quite forgave him, causing Ellington to be publicly embarrassed and, worse, humiliating Ruth Ellington. The New York City branch of the National Association for the Advancement of Colored People had sponsored a "Miss Olympic" dance contest. Ruth Ellington had won first prize and was to be crowned at a dance at the Rockland Palace. Ellington was thrilled and offered the services of his band.

The NAACP paid for the bus to bring the musicians uptown, where a crowed of 4,000 eagerly awaited them. As the band was preparing to go on stage, Mills, after seeing the huge crowd, demanded $500 in cash before he would allow the band to play. The NAACP had agreed to pay Mills a percentage of the gate receipts taken in that night, exclusive of the money taken in advance ticket sales. The organization considered Mills' request blackmail, and refused to pay it. Mills would not allow the band to play, and the musicians packed up their instruments and left. The crowd danced to the music of the alternate band for the night, led by Ralph Cooper. Ellington and Mills were roundly criticized in the black press for their "breach of faith and betrayal of word."

"It was terrible man, terrible," Greer recalled. "Duke was bullshit at Mills. Ruth was standing there crying. If she hadn't been there, I think Duke would have punched him, that's how mad he was. Freddie Guy used to say, 'That man always wants your right arm.' He never knew when enough was enough. I know Duke saw a lawyer to see if he could get out of the contract. He and Mills were barely on speaking terms until we left for Europe a year later."

23

Lawrence Brown got his chance to solo with the band a few weeks later when Toby Hardwick rejoined the band. Hardwick had left the band in mid-1928 in order to see the world:

> I thought to myself I have no chance at all of going to Europe with this guy. The band was a hit at the Cotton Club and I guessed we'd be there for some time. So I decided, *what the hell*—give me my horn and I'll go anywhere!
> And sure enough, when I got to Paris I landed a job with Noble Sissle. We traveled all over, and later I went with Fats Waller and we landed a job at Bricktop's, and then Nekka Shaw's place. I had a ball.

After he returned home, Hardwick played briefly with Chick Webb in 1929, and then led his own band at the "Hot Feet" Club in Greenwich Village. "I kept that band for a little over three years," he said. The band members included five saxophones: Hardwick, the leader, Chu Berry starring on tenor sax, Wayman Carver playing flute and tenor sax, Garvin Bushell on the other alto, and Ted McRae on baritone. Fats Waller propelled the rhythm section. This was the first time a band had five saxophones, and Hardwick did the arrangements.

Musicians admired the band, and the club became so popular that its owner made plans to open a second location in Chicago. Unfortunately, the club owner got caught in the middle of the gang wars and was killed, thereby shortening Hardwick's career as a band-leader. Not long before folding, the band engaged the Ellingtonians in a battle of music at the Astor Hotel.

Hardwick had some doubts about taking on the Ellington band, but with Waller's strong encouragement, they made great music that night. Some time later, to Hardwick's lasting satisfaction, the Ellingtonians conceded that the honors were his. Following an engagement at Smalls's Paradise, Hardwick joined Elmer Snowden's band.

While he was with them, the band was featured in a Vitaphone movie short, *Smash Your Baggage*, filmed in New York's Grand Central Station. "When we were playing at the Paramount Theater," Greer recalled, "Toby started coming backstage and talking with Duke. We all knew it was only a matter of time before he'd be back in the band."

In the four years Hardwick had been gone, a lot had changed. The ten-piece band had grown to fourteen, and Ellington's demeanor was different. "When I rejoined the band," Hardwick recalled, "it was just like I'd never left. Except this way, maybe. It wasn't *our* thing any longer. It had become Ellington's alone. This was inevitable, I guess. Ten years ago it was '*We* do it this way,' and '*We* wrote that.' Now the *We* was royal."

Hardwick rejoined the band just in time for a series of recording dates. Mills had the band in the Brunswick studios on May 16, 17, and 18, 1932. Lawrence Brown, while a member of Paul Howard's Quality Serenaders, had been featured on a recording of "The Sheik of Araby" made in 1928. Ellington gave Brown a new arrangement of the work, and he re-recorded it with the band. "Blue Harlem" was the other work recorded that day.

"Swampy River" and "Fast and Furious," piano solos with orchestral accompaniment, were recorded the next day, along with "Best Wishes." "Fast And Furious" had been known as "Lots of Fingers" when it was recorded at Victor three months earlier.

The following day, the band recorded "Slippery Horn" (another version of "Tiger Rag") featuring the three trombones, and "Blue Ramble" and "Clouds in my Heart." "Rockin' in Rhythm" and "Harlem Romance" (also known as "Clouds in my Heart") were done on May 19 at the Banner studios.

During these recording sessions, the band members learned that their old bandmate Bubber Miley was in the hospital gravely ill. Miley had left the band in early 1929. He had become increasingly unreliable due to his heavy drinking. Now, three years later, he was near death. "He had the consumption [tuberculosis]," said Greer. "The liquor, the women, staying out all night and gettin' no sleep finally caught up with him."

Miley had been busy in his years after working with Ellington. Following a month's engagement in Paris with Noble Sissle in the winter of 1929, Miley returned to New York and took a job with the house band at the Lafayette Theater. Later that year, he joined Allie Ross's band at Connie's Inn. One of the shows featured "Snake Hips" Tucker.

On August 6, 1929, Miley began a relationship with the Boston born bandleader Leo Reisman. A first-rate musician, Reisman was a multi-instrumentalist, but led his orchestra playing the violin. Reisman began his career playing in local symphony orchestras and hotel salons.

In 1919, at the age of twenty-two, Reisman began a ten-year residency at the Brunswick Hotel in Boston. Known as the "Paul Whiteman of Boston," he had modeled his band after the "King of Jazz." Like Whiteman, he used strings, brass, and the saxophones, doubled or tripled on other reed instruments. He occasionally even included a celesta in his scores. His pianist was Eddie Duchin, who left in late 1929 to form his own band.

Reisman had a contract with the Victor Recording Company, and started bringing his band to New York City to make recordings in 1925. A regular visitor to the city, he often went uptown to the Cotton Club. He was quite taken with the Ellington orchestra, and with Miley in particular. Now that Miley was available, Reisman invited him to sit in with his band and solo when the band recorded "Can't We Be Friends?" on August 6.

Reisman was impressed with what he heard. On January 30, 1930, Miley was with them when they recorded Cole Porter's "What Is This Thing Called Love?" and Irving Berlin's "Puttin' on the Ritz." On the Porter composition, Miley's solo is subdued, and he uses his effects sparingly. Remember, this was a man skilled at backing up singers. His breaks behind the vocalist are restrained but succinct. The Berlin composition is different; with Ellington, Miley rarely soloed on a popular song. Here he eschews the catchy aspects of the tune and plays against it; a most successful performance.

Miley was tapped for five more sessions with Reisman, all at Victor between April 1930 and June 1931. They recorded "Happy Feet" on April 9, followed by sessions on May 12, which included "Rollin' Down the River," and September 13, when they recorded Johnny Green's "Body and Soul." Victor had them back in the studios on October 10, when the band re-recorded "Body and Soul," "Trees," and Ravel's "Bolero." Miley did his final session with Reisman on June 30, 1931, when they recorded "Without that Gal," "It's the Girl," "Take It from Me (I'm Talking to You)," "I Love Louisa," and "New Sun in the Sky."

Reisman was not the only one using Miley's talents. Carrol Dickerson had put together a recording band for King Oliver, with a trumpet section including himself, Miley, Oliver, and Henry "Red" Allen. They recorded "St. James Infirmary" and "When You're Smiling" for Victor. The legendary Jelly Roll Morton also used Miley, for a recording session on March 19, 1930. Miley joined a band that included Ward Pinkett on trumpet, Wilbur de Paris on trombone, Ernest Bullock on saxophone, Tommy Benford on drums, Bill Benford on tuba, and Bernard Addison on banjo to record "Little Lawrence," "Harmony Blues," "Fussy Mabel," and "Ponchartrain Blues," which featured an excellent solo by Miley.

Wilbur de Paris remembered that session. "Jelly was relaxed and the arrangements were great. We had a good time that day. Bubber liked it so much that he asked me, Pinkett, the Benford boys, and Bernard Addison to record with him." Those five musicians formed the nucleus of a recording band called "The Milage Makers" that Mills helped Miley put together for three sessions at Victor.

On May 16, 1930, the Milage Makers were in the studios accompanying the singer Frank Marvin, a Mills protégé, on "I Lost My Gal from Memphis" and "Without You Emaline." Five days later, Miley was back in the Victor studios again, this time with an all-star assembly led by Hoagy Carmichael at the piano. The group contained five future bandleaders: Benny Goodman on clarinet, Tommy Dorsey on trombone, Gene Krupa on drums, Joe Venuti on violin, and Miley on trumpet. Bix Beiderbecke held down the other chair on cornet. Other luminaries on that date were Eddie Lang on guitar; Bud Freeman on tenor saxophone, and Benny Goodman's brother, Harry, on tuba. They recorded "Barnacle Bill the Sailor" and Carmichael's "Rockin' Chair."

The Milage Makers were back in the studios on July 3, 1930, when George Bias replaced Marvin on the vocals, singing "Black Maria" and "Chattin' and Chinnin' with May." When they returned on September 11, Eva Wilson replaced Bias, vocalizing on "Loving You the Way I Do" and "The Penalty of Love." Mills, who supervised the recording session, apparently didn't like what he heard, and had everyone come back to the studio six days later to repeat it.

Miley's old friend Leo Reisman opened at the Paramount Theater on November 6, 1930, for a run that lasted early into the following year. Reisman was a superb showman and devised an act for Miley. Miley would dress as an usher and help seat the audience for the stage show. When the show started, the Reisman orchestra would ascend from the pit to stage level playing his theme song. Acknowledging the applause, the bandleader would give a downbeat and his orchestra would play an introduction. The sound of a trumpet would come from the back of the house—it would be Miley walking down the aisle, playing "St. Louis Blues." This was a showstopper.

While he was at the Paramount Theater, the jazz dancer Roger Pryor Dodge approached Miley with an idea. Dodge was about to join the cast of the Billy Rose show *Sweet and Low*. He wanted Miley onstage with him at Chanin's Theater as he danced to "East St. Louis Toodle-OO." Miley and Dodge joined the show on January 23, 1931, and remained with it for four months. In addition to accompanying Dodge, Miley played "Black & Tan Fantasy" and "Yellow Dog Blues."

Other than the Ellington musicians, Dodge's is the only contemporary account of Miley available. Dodge wrote that in addition to Miley's extraordinary musicianship, he:

> had an infectious and winning personality that was serious underneath. . . . When improvising at rehearsals he always wanted the three voices of the chord clearly stated, as it helped him a great deal. I had a little reed organ he used to like to play on while humming the blues. In spite of his quietness Bubber had a natty appearance and sported an Auburn convertible. One night when he was driving home after the Billy Rose show, his car stalled in Central Park. Bubber just got out, slammed the door and walked away.

Miley's two appearances on Broadway caused a stir, and in 1932, Mills decided to build a show—*Harlem Scandals*—around him. The revue had a cast of sixty-five, including the comedians Mantan Moreland and Tim Moore, and a chorus line. Miley fronted The Milage Makers and the revue made its debut at Philadelphia's Lincoln theater the week of January 17, 1932. Not taking any chances, Mills hired Sunny Nichols as music director.

During opening week, Miley complained of not feeling well, and a local doctor diagnosed his ailment as tuberculosis. Miley managed to complete the performances at the Lafayette Theater in the week of January 23. But when the show moved to the Harlem Opera House, the ravages of the disease caused Miley to leave the show at the end of its opening week. His condition had become acute and he spent some time at his mother's apartment on West 62nd Street before entering Metropolitan Hospital on Welfare Island, where the brilliant musician died several weeks later on May 20.

"One of his sisters called Duke," Greer recalled, "and he told us. We all went to the funeral parlor to pay our respects. There were two huge wreaths on either side of his casket. One from Duke and one from the guys in the band. It was in the Depression then. I know Duke gave his mother some money to help with the burial."

24

THE GREAT DEPRESSION was at its height during 1932. The devastating economic conditions forced many of the marginal entertainment establishments to close, particularly in Harlem. "A lot of the clubs had to stop having entertainers," Greer said. "It put a lot of cats out on the street. We all tried to help out the best we could, playing benefits and things like that. I was a damn good pool player. I'd take on guys at the Rhythm Club. The money I made playing I'd give away to my boys [friends]."

Ellington's sister Ruth remembered Duke's contribution: "On Wednesday mornings, if he was in town, musicians and artists he knew could come by for some help. Usually five or ten dollars."

Freddie Guy recalled, "The Depression didn't affect the band, though; we were working all the time. We knew it was going on. All of us had family or friends touched by it."

That summer, the band made its annual tour of New England. The group then went to the Midwest for a series of theater dates in Cincinnati and Cleveland, and then back to the scene of two earlier triumphs, the Oriental Theater and the Lincoln Tavern in Chicago, where the band was booked for four weeks, broadcasting over CBS. The musicians remained in the Midwest through mid-September, and returned to New York in time for two recording sessions at Brunswick. On September 19, they recorded "Blue Mood" and "Ducky Wucky"; then, two days later, they recorded "Lightnin'," with its bitonal introduction, and Benny Carter's composition, "Jazz Cocktail." On September 29, they went to the Capitol Theater on Broadway for a two-week engagement.

On October 25th, Ellington received an invitation from the noted Australian-born composer Percy Grainger, then chairman of the music department at New York University. The Ellington orchestra played for a class in music appreciation. Also present at the event were Basil Cameron, conductor of the Seattle Symphony, and the American composer Wallingford Reigger, a disciple of Arnold Schoenberg.

After hearing "Creole Rhapsody," Grainger casually compared Ellington's genius for melodic invention to that of Frederick Delius and Johann Sebastian Bach. After hearing Grainger's comment, Ellington quipped, "I'll have to find out about this Delius." It would be two years before Ellington would hear his first piece of impressionistic music, Frederick Delius's "On Hearing the First Cuckoo of Spring." Like Debussy and Ravel, Delius scored for full orchestra, but many times he did not use the resources of the full ensemble. Instead, he exploited the various orchestral colors provided by the instrumental choirs.

Ellington used similar ideas in his own orchestrations, even before hearing the work of Delius and others. For example, on the December recording of "Mood Indigo," Ellington had the full band in the studio, but he used reduced instrumentation to express the different moods of the piece. It is only at the very end of the composition that we hear the full orchestra.

Grainger was not the only one to appreciate "Creole Rhapsody." The work also earned Ellington an award from the New York School of Music as the "best composition" of 1932. It was chosen "because it portrayed the Negro life as no other piece had." On January 8, 1933, Ellington gratefully accepted the award presented by the mayor of New York. Paul Whiteman gave the work another hearing on January 25, at a concert he conducted in Carnegie Hall.

Meanwhile, Irving Mills had not been idle. The previous May he had formed a new agency by joining forces with another booking agent, Tom Rockwell. Mills brought with him to the new firm all of his artists, including Ellington, Calloway, and Baron Lee and the Blue Ribbon Band, a band Mills had originally created to play at the Cotton Club or for other dates when both Ellington and Calloway were unavailable. Rockwell brought to the partnership the Mills Brothers (a vocal group), (singers) Annette Hanshaw and Ruth Etting, and the Casa Loma and Don Redman's orchestras. Bing Crosby signed up with Mills and Rockwell after a salary dispute with NBC. Five months later, Mills left Mills Music, Inc., and handed full management of the publishing house to his brother Jack. This allowed Irving more time to pursue his managerial interests.

In November 1932, Irving Mills went on a much publicized trip to Europe, looking for new talent and studying the possibilities of sending over his own artists. Ellington and the Mills Brothers were reported to be in high demand in several European countries. In addition, Mills was intrigued by Hardwick's observation while in Paris that, despite the high customs duties levied on recordings, Ellington's recordings were invariably sold out.

The dawn of 1933 found Ellington in Brooklyn playing for a week at the Albee Theater, and then in Pittsburgh, Pennsylvania, for a week at the Pythian Temple. The Ellington orchestra became the first black band to play at the Avalon Club, in St. Louis, Missouri, and returned to New York after a week's run at the Stanley Theater in Pittsburgh.

In addition to performing in a series of recording dates on their own, the band members became involved in an ambitious project initiated by Jack Kapp, director of Recording for Brunswick. Kapp planned to rerecord the hit numbers from Lew Leslie's very successful *Blackbirds* revues, published by Mills Music. The recording would include a series of sessions involving members of the original 1928 *Blackbirds* cast along with other artists who appeared in the sequel *Blackbirds of 1930*, as well as some standard Brunswick recording stars.

Ellington was teamed with Ethel Waters on December 21, 1932. On the same date, Ivie Anderson recorded "Delta Bound" with the band, and it was a minor hit. The Mills Brothers joined the sessions the next day. Ellington and Waters were back in the studio on January 7, 1933.

On February 17, the band recorded an instrumental medley of hits from the show, including "I Can't Give You Anything but Love" and "Digga Digga Do." The group re-recorded "Slippery Horn" and a minor hit Ellington song, "Drop Me Off at Harlem." This last number had its genesis in a taxi. Ellington was downtown, and Broadway columnist Nick Kenny had hailed a cab and offered to share it with him. When Kenny asked, "Where to, Duke?" Ellington replied, "Drop me off at Harlem." Over the next few days, Kenny fashioned a set of lyrics based on Ellington's off-the-cuff remark, and presented them to him one night at the Cotton Club. Ellington then composed the music.

Also on that February date, Anderson recorded "I've Got the World on a String" with the band. On May 9, Mills had Anderson return to the studio to record Harold Arlen's "Happy as the Day Is Long," the riotous "Raisin' the Rent," and "Get Yourself a New Broom (and Sweep Your Troubles Away)."

Cab Calloway's orchestra was playing the show at the Cotton Club during the fall and winter of 1932–33. Mills had Calloway booked for a tour of the South beginning March 11, 1933. So, Mills lined Ellington up to fill out the remainder of the run of the Cotton Club show. Ellington would headline the spring edition of *Cotton Club Parade*, opening on April 16. Prior to that, along with the other two bands in Mills's stable—Calloway and the Blue Rhythm Band—the Ellington band would perform in a short film.

In September 1930, Paramount Pictures had inaugurated a series of "Pictoral Magazines." These were newsreel-type one-reel films, presenting entertaining information on a wide range of subjects, usually in three segments. One of the three segments would often be devoted to music and composers, and the bands led by pop singers Rudy Vallee and Vincent Lopez had already been featured. These shorts were shown before feature films at all Paramount-affiliated movie houses, guaranteeing publicity for any band. This opportunity was not lost on a promoter like Mills, who also arranged an appearance for himself onscreen when the film was made in early March 1933.

Seated behind a desk, Mills introduced the three bands—in his words, "artists representing three distinct types of modern jazz music." He said that "today each of these men stands supreme in his individual field." Baron Lee and the Blue Rhythm Band were announced as a band that could play both sweet music and "echoes of the jungle, wild and barbaric." Mills said that Calloway was one of the "most amazing personalities in the music world today."

Ellington and his men appeared between the other two bands. Mills grandly introduced Ellington with the following words:

> And now we come to one who seems to be set entirely apart from all other composers and musicians. When I first heard him he was conducting a little five-piece orchestra up in Harlem. Today he is acclaimed by the music authorities here and abroad as the creator of a new vogue of music.

In the short period of time allotted to him, approximately one minute and twenty seconds, Ellington started with a brief piano solo on his "Sophisticated Lady." The band's version of this song on Brunswick (with the Arlen-Koehler hit "Stormy Weather" on the flip side) would become a best seller following its release four months later. "Sophisticated Lady" served as a prologue to excerpts from "Creole Rhapsody," which lasted about one minute. All things considered, Ellington had the most time on the screen; Calloway and the Blue Rhythm Band had about a minute apiece.

Since the beginning of the year, composer Harold Arlen and lyricist Ted Koehler had begun working on the score for the upcoming edition of the *Cotton Club Parade*. One of the first songs written was called "Stormy Weather." The songwriters intuitively knew they had a hit. The question was: How could they get it maximum exposure? Their good friend, bandleader Leo Reisman, made a recording of it for Victor and it sold reasonably well.

Arlen thought the song would be ideal for a singer like Ethel Waters. Healy agreed, and she was approached to do the show. Waters's career had taken a downturn due to the Depression and she leaped at the opportunity to work at the Cotton Club. When it was announced that she would be headlining the show and singing "Stormy Weather," opening night was promptly sold out.

The spring 1933 edition of the *Cotton Club Parade* had "an all-star cast of 50 artists" and a "chorus of 18 girls." Seated in the audience on April 16th, opening night, were such celebrities as Sophie Tucker, Ethel Merman, Jimmy Durante, Milton Berle, Johnny Weissmuller, and Irving Berlin. The highlight of the show was Waters singing "Stormy Weather." According to *Variety*, the song became "the biggest song hit of the past ten years." Besides the Reisman recording, hit versions were made by Guy Lombardo and Ted Lewis, as well as by Ellington and Waters. Irving Berlin was so impressed with Waters that he called Mills to find out if she was available for a part in his next Broadway show. Knowing that Waters's career prior to "Stormy Weather" had been stagnant, Mills offered to become her manager. He negotiated her fee from Berlin, who cast her in his forthcoming revue, *As Thousands Cheer*, in which she sang "Suppertime" and "Heatwave."

"Stormy Weather" was such a hit that the entire show was booked downtown at the Capitol Theater for two weeks beginning May 26 to play simultaneously with the Cotton Club run. In addition to Ethel

Waters, the comedy team of Buck & Bubbles and Florence Hill were also onstage.

"Stormy Weather" was also the main feature of the nine-minute film Ellington made for Paramount, on May 23, 1933, called *Bundle of Blues*. Ivie Anderson gives a stunning performance, aided by Whetsol and Lawrence Brown. With the orchestra playing the composition, she walks onstage and sings the lyrics by a shack window as rain pours down. Sonny Greer offers pungent answers to her vocal line on vibraphone. Inspired by the film, Ellington retitled a lovely composition, originally called "Dragon's Blues," to "Bundle of Blues." It was an exquisite work, with Williams, Bigard, and Hodges playing at their best.

Anderson and the Ellington orchestra received enthusiastic response from audiences whenever they performed "Stormy Weather." Mills, protecting his interest in the Ethel Waters recording, would not permit Anderson to record the song. It was only shortly before she left the band in 1940 that Anderson belatedly recorded "Stormy Weather" for Victor.

The day after the opening of the Cotton Club revue, Mills called a press conference. He announced that Duke Ellington and his orchestra had been booked for a tour in England and on the Continent. On June 12, they would be the featured attraction at the Palladium Music Hall in London.

25

ON JUNE 2, 1933, passengers sailing to England on White Star Line's R.M.S. *Olympic* received a mild surprise. A well-dressed party of eighteen blacks, including two women, was boarding. On inquiry, they were told it was Duke Ellington and his orchestra. The white man accompanying them was his personal manager, Irving Mills, who had booked his client for a series of engagements in England and on the Continent.

Besides the Ellington orchestra and Ivie Anderson, the entourage included the dancers Bessie Dudley, Derby Wilson, and Bill Bailey (whose younger sister Pearl would become a cabaret and stage success ten years later). There was a gala sendoff party featuring music by the Mills Blue Rhythm Band, which had replaced Ellington at the Cotton Club. Families and friends of the band members were on hand to see them off. The event was duly noted in *Time* magazine, and Paramount sent a newsreel camera.

Once aboard ship, Duke was brought face-to-face with his phobia about traveling on water. It was a standing joke among his musicians that Ellington had never been to Staten Island because he could not stand the thought of taking the ferry to get there. His difficulty stemmed from hearing about the *Titanic* disaster as a youngster. (The *Titanic* tragedy occurred when Ellington was 12.) One wonders how he would have felt had he known that the *Titanic* was the sister ship of the *Olympic*, which was built six months earlier than the ill-fated vessel!

Ellington's anxiety was exacerbated when the steward informed him that the ship was steered by an automatic pilot! He asked everyone, "How can an automatic pilot see an iceberg?" He relieved his anxiety by staying up all night drinking brandy, writing music, and pacing the deck miserably until daylight, when he was certain that a real pilot, who could see an iceberg, would come on duty.

The *Olympic* was originally built as a three-class ship. In 1928 it was remodeled to accommodate only first and tourist classes. The group was booked in tourist, with Ellington and Mills having individual staterooms, and everyone else assigned two to a room. The musicians were celebrities aboard ship. Bessie Dudley and Ivie Anderson attracted the company of some of the unattached males. On the second night out, the band gave a concert in the first-class dining room, which was well received. "After that we had the run of the ship," Bigard noted.

The ocean liner was then twenty-one years old, but still retained the opulence associated with its sister ship. Years later, Greer, Guy, Carney, Williams, and Brown expressed surprise when informed of the relationship between the two ships. However, all of them were impressed with the *Olympic*'s stately grandeur. Brown remembered walking down the grand staircase that led from the first-class dining room after the concert. "It was elegance, pure elegance," he said. "I can't describe it, you had to have been there to see and experience it."

Several afternoons were spent rehearsing and fine-tuning the repertoire, including a work the band had recorded the previous year and decided to dedicate to England, titled "Best Wishes." It was not one of Ellington's better compositions, though.

Freddie Guy had brought a guitar with him. During the tour, he would occasionally switch from the four-stringed banjo to the six-stringed guitar. Ellington had been suggesting for some time that he make the switch. The metallic-percussive sound of the banjo had begun to sound and feel out of place in the rhythm section. Drummer Sonny Greer, following a suggestion by Will Vodery, began using tympani heads on his bass drum and tuning them to resonate with Braud's bass violin. The extra resonance of the guitar, with its fuller sound, was a better fit for the new rhythm section.

"I received a lot of encouragement and help from Eddie Lang," Guy said. "He was the best. Bing Crosby used him every chance he got. I picked up a book on six-string harmony for guitar in a State Street music shop in Chicago, and that's where I really learned most of the basics." Lang was one of the pioneers of jazz guitar, playing single-string melody leads as well as chords. He was a featured musician in Paul Whiteman's band and also worked with Bing Crosby as an accompanist.

Anticipating Ellington's visit, the British papers gave him substantial coverage. The *Birmingham Daily Mail* observed that some musicians regarded his arrival "with as much zest as the classical moderns view the arrival of Stravinsky or Schoenberg at the Queen's Hall." The *Daily Express* announced that "Duke Ellington, 'hot gospeller' of crazy jazz music and Harlem rhythm, arrives from America on his first visit to this country tomorrow." The music trade magazine *Melody Maker* wrote that "1933 is indeed a red-letter year for fans . . . Duke Ellington's visit is on everybody's tongue." Photographs of Ellington appeared in the *Sunday Referee, Evening Standard,* and *Daily Sketch,* to name a few. The *News-Chronicle,* in an article covering Ellington's arrival at Waterloo Station, hailed him as "the most celebrated Negro bandmaster in the world." Ellington's mentors, Will Vodery and Will Marion Cooke, had brought bands to England after the war, so Ellington was in good company. Only the more staid London *Times* would limit its comments about Ellington to a review of his show at the Palladium and a public concert.

On the negative side, there were complaints in the press and privately about the sizable $4,500 fee Mills had demanded and received from the Palladium for Ellington's appearance. After all, the country was in the throes of the Great Depression. The large amount of money being paid to a group of American musicians while many in Great Britain were unemployed was a source of irritation.

Stanley Nelson, dance band critic for the *Era,* was concerned that the British Broadcasting Company (BBC), the state-run radio station, was paying thirty pounds (approximately $150 at the time) for a broadcast of Ellington's music scheduled for the night of June 14. Nonetheless, he praised the network for arranging the event, and compared the Ellington band's playing to performances of the music of modern classical composers Paul Hindemith and Zoltán Kodály that had previously been sponsored by the radio network. The Ellington band had been heard in England the previous November, when the BBC, celebrating its birthday, arranged for the band to be heard "live" in a remote broadcast from New York.

Before leaving New York, Mills persuaded the Victor Recording Company to issue a six-record commemorative album of Ellington recordings in England. The album consisted of many of the band's best recordings made for the label between 1927 and 1930, including "Black & Tan Fantasy" (1927), "The Mooche" (1928), "Dicty Glide" (1929), and "Mood Indigo" (1930). None of these recordings had been previously issued in England. The edition, limited to 1,000 sets, was elegantly bound in orange linen.

RHYTHM, the musicians' magazine, reprinted an essay originally written for it in 1931 by Ellington, "I'll Be Seeing You." With the exception of the last paragraph, the piece, complete with musical examples, was a reflection of Ellington's thoughts on the importance of rhythm in his compositions. It also served as an introduction of the members of his band to his audience. The following month, in response to several queries, Ellington contributed an article explaining the titles of the compositions in the recently issued six-record album.

The troupe arrived at Southampton on the afternoon of June 9. A reception committee, including photographers from the magazines *Melody Maker* and *Era*, was at dockside to greet them. Included in the group was the impresario Jack Hylton, who had undertaken the financial responsibility for bringing Ellington to England. Other members were Basil Cameron, conductor of the Seattle Symphony, who had been introduced to Ellington the previous year by Percy Grainger; Henry Hall, leader of the BBC Light Orchestra; and the music critic "Spike" Hughes, who had written the glowing review of "Creole Rhapsody."

In addition to being a critic, Hughes was an accomplished musician, both a composer/bandleader and player of bass, piano, and harmonium. His band had been recording for the English Decca Company since 1930. Ellington's "The Mooche" (1928) and "Misty Mornin'" were among Hughes's band's many recordings. During a visit to New York the previous month, Hughes spent several evenings at the Cotton Club in the company of fellow jazz critic John Hammond. In his correspondence to *Melody Maker*, Hughes wrote that "Duke and his band are the only two things, apart from Toscanini, which have exceeded my wildest hopes of New York." (At that time Arturo Toscanini was the conductor of the New York Philharmonic Symphony.)

Hughes also found time to make some recordings under Mills's supervision for the British Parlophone label under the title "Spike Hughes and His Negro Orchestra." The fourteen-piece band put together by Mills and Benny Carter featured Coleman Hawkins on tenor saxophone, and included Luis Russell on one of the sessions. Russell remembered Hughes's arrangements as "stiff, but well orchestrated." Two of the recordings, "Pastorale" and "Nocturne," showed a definite Ellington influence. Shortly before Ellington arrived, the *Era* informed its readers that Hughes had orchestrated a version of "God Save the King" for the Ellington orchestra. Ellington used it as a prologue to his concerts.

London was a frenzy of social activity when the Ellington band arrived. The World Economic and Monetary Conference was beginning the following Monday; King George V presided over the opening ceremonies. One hundred sixty-eight delegates representing sixty-six nations were expected, including U.S. Secretary of State Cordell Hull and Secretary of the Treasury Henry Morgenthau. The American golfers Craig Wood, Gene Sarazen, Olin Dutra, and Walter Hagen had arrived to play in the British Open at St. Andrew's Golf Club in Scotland. They would also represent the United States in the Ryder Cup competition at Southport a week later. The Ascot races began on June 13.

Ellington's band members were not the only black performers who were making the London scene. The black singer and entertainer, Nina Mae McKinney, was a featured performer in "International Week" at the Leicester Square Theatre. Clarence Robinson's show *Dark Doings* was due the following week. Another black show, *The Cotton Club Revue*, was expected at the Palladium later that month, and blues singer Alberta Hunter was booked for King's Hall in July. Needless to say, hotel space in London was at a premium.

Mills had dispatched his secretaries, Florence Hill and Kay Hansen, to London a week before the arrival of the rest of the group. Their task was to have everything in place, including hotel rooms, when the entourage arrived. They found lodgings for the musicians and entertainers in several of the smaller hotels in the East End and Bloomsbury. Meanwhile, Mills and Ellington were quietly booked at the Dorchester Hotel on Park Lane, one of London's newer and finer establishments. For the rest of Ellington's life, this elegant Art Deco institution would be his place of residence whenever he was in London.

One of London's newspapers used Ellington's arrival as a vehicle to address the question of accommodations for blacks in the city's better hotels. The *Daily Express* headline read, "No Hotel for a Negro Band." The paper manufactured a quote from Hylton, who was alleged to have stated, "I cannot send the jazz monarch to a hostel." This issue was followed up the next day in the *Sunday Express*, where a reporter wrote:

> Is it possible for a Negro to find accommodation in first class
> hotels in London? . . . Mr. Duke Ellington, a distinguished jazz com-
> poser, has arrived in London from the United States. English musi-
> cians were eager and proud to meet him. The management of
> London's leading hotels where he sought a home took one look at his
> face and bowed him out of the premises.

The *Express*'s reporter decided to look deeper into the situation and called many of London's leading hotels, ostensibly attempting to book a room for a West African black. Among the responses were: "We are extremely sorry sir, but we have not a single room vacant"; and "Hopelessly full up . . . World Conference and Ascot, you know."

One week later, a short note appeared in the *Daily Herald* in which the management of the Dorchester denied the allegation of racism, noting that Ellington's rooms were booked *before* he arrived. "We are honored to receive him," the hotel's management said.

Once the members of the troupe were unpacked and settled, it was time to relax and rest until the following Monday. Meanwhile, Ellington had to shower, quickly change his clothes, and go to Hylton's flat on the Mayfair for a cocktail party. The house, a converted old building whose exterior was patterned in black and white bricks, was luxuriously furnished, and considered a London showplace.

In honor of Ellington's visit, the impresario assembled a cross-section of London's artistic community, including musicians, artists, writers, and newspaper columnists. Everyone was impressed with the guest of honor. The correspondent for *Melody Maker* summed up the effect of Ellington's personality on the guests, saying he had the "wonderful and rare ability of making every single person to whom he spoke feel that person was the most important person in the room."

The reporter for the *Daily Express* wrote, "The assembled musicians waiting to meet Duke Ellington discussed what 'hot' music really meant." Basil Cameron, described it as "sort of spicy music." Henry Hall, conductor of the BBC dance orchestra said that "'Hot music' was the natural result of the days when jazz conductors gave a few bars to various members of the orchestra and told them to go to it and improvise."

Ellington put the debate to rest by telling his hosts, "There is no such thing as 'hot music.' All I do is write and play Negro folk music and if the public who hear it 'pepped up' well, that is 'hot' music."

Shortly before 9:00 P.M., Ellington and Hylton left for Broadcast House, a few blocks away on Portland Street, home of the BBC. Following the impresario's introduction, they discussed Ellington's music, orchestra, and musical ambitions. In response to the question: "Do you think jazz would have a permanent place in the annals of music?" Ellington said, "It is the only music that is able to describe the present period in the history of the world . . . it would be impossible to describe [it] without jazz, as this is the jazz age."

Ellington concluded the interview by telling the audience that he would have liked to have given them a demonstration of his music, but "I am not very good without the band." Following the interview, the announcer, Christopher Stone, played Ellington recordings for the remaining fifteen minutes of the broadcast. Duke and Hylton strolled over to the Kit Kat Club, where they were serenaded by the American-born Roy Fox's band playing "Mood Indigo" in honor of the visit.

In introducing Ellington to his countrymen, Spike Hughes wrote a perceptive analysis of the band and Ellington's music in the *Daily Herald* a few days before the first performance. Calling Ellington "a prophet without honor in his own country," he wrote:

> It has remained for us to discover, at least through the medium of the gramophone, that Duke is something more than a bandleader specializing in what are vaguely called "voodoo harmonies" and "jungle rhythms." He is in fact the first genuine jazz composer. . . . Jazz is not a matter of trite, unguarded melodies wedded to semi-literate lyrics, nor is it the brainchild of Tin Pan Alley. It is the music of the Harlem gin mills, the Georgia backyards and New Orleans street corners.

Hughes's comments were quite astute. One must remember that this was 1933. With the exception of an interview in the *Christian Science Monitor* in December 1930, and an article in the New York

Herald Tribune four years earlier, a serious discussion of Ellington's music was unheard of in any newspaper until then.

The engagement at the Palladium began on Monday. There were shows at 6:30 and 9 P.M., with matinees on Wednesday and Thursday at 2:30 P.M. Ellington's appearance, as well as the extensive publicity campaign organized by Mills and Hylton, resulted in the entire two-week run's being sold out. Taking note of this, management asked on opening night if the band could be held over for a third week. But it was too late. Mills had already committed the group for a tour of the provinces and Scotland under the auspices of the Empire Theatre syndicate.

Melody Maker's correspondent recalled the opening show. "As 6:30 approached on Monday, I must confess that excitement rose to fever heat," he wrote. As the featured attraction, the band did not get onstage until after 8. The reviewer wrote that he sat through the entire show, "not to miss a thing."

As a matter of fact, he could have done so without serious loss. Except for the dancers Bessie Dudley and the duo of Bill Bailey and Derby Wilson—who were part of the Ellington entourage—the rest of the supporting acts, all local performers, could be described as nondescript at best. The one exception was Max Miller, a cockney comedian and a favorite at the house. His sly, wicked, earthy sense of humor often had him in trouble with the censors. Miller preceded Ellington on the bill. Ellington, hearing the uproarious laughter and the loud applause Miller elicited from the audience, had some anxiety as to how his band would be received. But he didn't have to worry.

"[T]he applause grew into a roar," *Melody Maker* wrote, "the pit orchestra faded out and we heard for the first time in England the magic sound of Duke Ellington and his famous orchestra. The curtain went up and there they were! Even the six brass were inaudible in the thunder of the applause."

Onstage, the band members were dressed in pearl gray dress suits. (For the matinee performances the first week, they wore brown slacks with cream jackets and white shoes. The second week, green slacks replaced the brown ones.) Ellington was downstage at the piano in the center of the band, wearing white tails. For the matinees he wore a single-breasted white suit with an orange tie.

On Ellington's left were the three trumpets. Behind them on a higher rostrum were the three trombones. Behind the saxophones on the right were the bass violin and banjo. Towering above, surrounded by his gleaming battery of percussion, was Greer.

When the applause subsided, "the band was playing 'Ring Dem Bells,' mostly as on the record. As they finished with an unexpected coda, Duke jumped down from his seat and walked to the foot-lights. It was minutes before he could make himself heard. He and the boys seemed overwhelmed by the reception," the *Melody Maker* reviewer wrote.

Everyone in the band was stunned by the audience's response, except for Hardwick. Greer remembered him turning around in his seat and whispering to Braud (who was standing behind him), "What did I tell you?" "They didn't clap politely," the drummer said, "The applause went on for a good two minutes. We couldn't believe it; we'd only played one number."

Following the applause, Ellington launched the band into "Three Little Words," the hit song from the "Amos 'n' Andy" film. The movie had recently been shown in England. Ellington and Mills were not about to miss the obvious opportunities for a commercial tie-in, which included the playing of "Ring Dem Bells" to open the show at any theater engagement. "Old Man Blues" was always the opening number in a dance hall, recreating the band's appearance in the film.

The English jazz critic Max Jones recalled:

> I was sixteen, a full time fan, a semi-pro sax player. . . . We impatiently sat through the "acts"—all twelve of them!—before the magic of the curtain rising and the band playing "Ring Dem Bells." None of us had ever heard a sound like this live before. Not to mention the spectacle of actually seeing Duke's band live before our very eyes.
>
> Remember all the guys were in the bloom of youth, Hodges twenty-six, Bigard twenty-seven, Cootie only twenty-two. Duke at thirty-four was the old man! All of that band are dead, but that week will live with me until the end of my days.

Bert Wilcox, now a jazz concert promoter, remembered:

I was a nineteen year old, and had heard that a "Harlem" band was to appear at the Palladium. I remember Max Miller finishing his act on the "front cloth" [in front of the curtain], then suddenly, it was Duke and the band in their pearl gray suits, roaring into "Ring Dem Bells." It was quite magical ... but the thing that sticks in my memory is Ivie Anderson leaning against one of the marble pillars and singing "Stormy Weather" without a microphone.

Anderson's rendition of the Harold Arlen classic brought the first ovation of the night. Clad in a demure white dress, she sang leaning against the proscenium with just a single spotlight on her and gradually walked forward to center stage, the performance gathering strength as she went. The subsequent applause reduced her to tears.

Her encore was what had become a standard part of her stage performance with the band. In her elegant voice, she sang the racy, salacious song, "Give Me a Man Like That."

After "Bugle Call Rag," Bessie Dudley followed, dancing to another Ellington classic, "Rockin' in Rhythm." Billed as "the original snake-hips girl," she appeared on stage clad in a pair of black silk tights. Accompanied by the band she did a sinuous, undulating dance, bringing cheers from the audience. Fifty-five years later, discussing the event, she told me, "I did the usual routine I had done at the Cotton Club. The English ate it up."

Bailey and Derby tap-danced to "The Mystery Song," played in stop time. The band would dramatically drop out from time to time, so the sound of the tapping feet could be heard. The show officially ended with "Whispering Tiger," one of Ellington's many variations on "Tiger Rag." In response to the sustained applause, however, Ellington beckoned to Jenkins, who danced to center stage, sang, and played the Sophie Tucker favorite "Some of These Days." Jenkins's infectious personality completely overwhelmed the audience, who brought him back for several bows. Finally, the somber strains of "Mood Indigo" quieted the audience and brought the program to a happy conclusion.

Not all of the four thousand people in the audience were enthralled by what they were hearing. Max Jones recalled, "When they played 'Black & Tan Fantasy,' during Tricky Sam's solo, somebody threw a penny on the stage ... a couple of people followed him out, and two or three more pennies fell on the stage." This was the audience's way of expressing their displeasure.

Across the board, the reviews of the opening night performance were glowing. Even the staid *Times* correspondent wrote that Ellington was "exceptionally and remarkably efficient in his own line. He does at once and with an apparently easy show of ingenuity what a jazz band commonly does with difficulty." He described Dudley's performance as "quite interesting as it is ingenious."

The correspondent of the *Daily Express* did not pretend to appreciate the full merits of the band. However, he noted, "Scores of smartly dressed young English people had come to rave over them, and did. Many hundreds of people in the hinterlands of the Palladium also raved and shouted and applauded." He concluded, "In short, [the Ellington orchestra was] a very good dance band playing ingeniously orchestrated music."

One of the "smartly dressed" was the Duke of Kent, the third son of King George V. The duke was rumored to have had an affair with the singer Florence Mills, and he was an intimate friend of the playwright Noel Coward. He was considered a London fashion plate, so much so that his good friend Ira Gershwin alluded to it in a lyrics of one of his popular songs, "I Can't Get Started." The Duke of Kent was known to own a large collection of jazz recordings, and Ellington's in particular.

The *News Chronicle* commented on the "rapturous reception" the band received, and also took note of the "small army" of autograph hunters who besieged Ellington and his musicians at the stage door. The *Daily Sketch*, while observing the band's "wildly enthusiastic welcome," noted, "A crowd of at least sixty girls and women waited at the stage door in an effort to secure Duke Ellington's autograph." The *Daily Herald* was more explicit: "There was trouble at the stage door last week. White women were waiting as usual." Some more conservative Londoners would undoubtedly have been shocked by the adulation shown to these black performers by white women.

The *Daily Herald* also put Ellington on the list of modern composers whose music created controversy on first hearing. The writer noticed that several members of the audience walked out during the performance, but observed that similar reactions had occurred to performances of classical compositions by Strauss, Schoenberg, and

Stravinsky. "Ellington," like these other modern composers, "grows on you," this critic noted.

Following the opening night concert, another convert to Ellington's magic surfaced: Stanley Nelson, the same critic who earlier had questioned the advisability of the BBC's broadcast of Ellington's music. Writing in the *Era*, he said:

> How to describe in so many words the most vital, emotional experience the vaudeville in England has ever known? . . . [T]he audience was bathed in ecstatic adoration of that tall, distinguished, gray-suited figure at the piano and the triangle of musicians building up to the back of the stage.
>
> The band was playing "Tiger Rag" [i.e., "Whispering Tiger"] with a *pianissimo* never achieved before. These half-a-dozen brass played so softly one could hear the golden whisper of those twisting, rhythmic figures. . . .
>
> What, I thought, would Wagner have made of it all? . . . I'm confident that he would have hailed this music as one of the most significant forms of modern musical art.

Nelson closed the article by publicly thanking Hylton for bringing Ellington to England. Two weeks later, Harlem, New York's *Amsterdam News* reprinted the entire article.

On the day of the radio broadcast, the Manchester *Guardian*'s columnist wrote that the band was "a remarkably efficient one of its kind, but rather given to those acrobatics known as 'putting the dirt into it.'" The rough-and-ready jazz sounds of Ellington's band were too much for this more conservative critic's ears. He was relieved to find out that there was mellower music in the band's repertoire: "a tune called 'Mood Indigo' which Ellington has written is soft, sweet and exquisitely haunting."

Duke looked forward to the BBC broadcast, because he could play his music without competing with the varied vaudeville acts with whom he shared the stage at the Palladium. Also, the British public at large would be introduced to his music. Ellington chose an interesting and varied program. After playing his radio theme, "East St Louis Toodle-Oo" (1926), the band immediately segued into "Lightnin" (1931). This was followed with "Creole Love Call" (1927), "Old Man Blues" (1930), and "Best Wishes" (1932), plus his arrangements of "Rose Room" and "Limehouse Blues." These were followed by a medley of songs orchestrated from the show *Blackbirds of 1928*, which had recently been issued in England on the Parlophone label. "Sophisticated Lady" (1932) and "It Don't Mean a Thing (If It Ain't Got That Swing)" (1932) were followed by another medley of popular tunes, "My Darling," "Down a Carolina Lane," and "I've Got the World on a String." Ivie Anderson was scheduled to sing "Stormy Weather," but time ran out and Ellington ended the show with "Mood Indigo" (1931). The poignant strains of the theme allowed the engineers to fade out and bring the program to a close.

Ellington fans who had been unable to get tickets to the Palladium, and those who couldn't get to London, were thrilled to hear the band "live" on the air. The broadcast enabled them to hear compositions live in the true sonic splendor that they had previously known only through recordings. As expected, listeners' response to the broadcast was mixed. The BBC's weekly newspaper, *Radio Times*, devoted a full column to listeners' comments:

> "It was the grandest three-quarters of an hour I have ever listened to." Rhythm Fan, Cleesthorpes, Lincolnshire.

> "I am forced to protest most strongly against our good English air being polluted by Duke Ellington and his famous orchestra." H. F. Clarke, Wanstead, E.11.

> "[S]omething that is thoroughly ugly from start to finish is fairly to be opposed." Manchester *Guardian*.

> "May I be allowed to express my very sincere appreciation of Duke Ellington's broadcast." Peter G. Clark, London, W.

> "Just a composite Babel of sound sensations, headed by a fanciful title to catch the imagination." E. C. Statham, Hornchurch.

> "Duke Ellington I suffered for fifteen minutes and then switched off. Give me Henry Hall every time." Yorkshire *Observer*.

> "May I offer my appreciation of the formidable fare provided by Duke Ellington . . . for being able to express his themes such as "Sophisticated Lady,' 'Creole Lullaby,' in tone colours of such varied hues that 'tune' becomes an unnecessary ingredient." *Amateur Musician*.

26

IN GREAT BRITAIN, a one-week engagement at a theater or variety hall ran from Monday to Saturday, because it was illegal to stage "dramatic or theatrical performances" on Sunday. However, "concerts" were legal. Therefore, the practice was established for bands to hold Sunday concerts when traveling from one theater to another. Mills took advantage of this Sunday tradition. *Melody Maker* wrote that the band was booked for a performance at the Brighton Hippodrome for Sunday night, June 18, 1933. That engagement was subsequently transferred to the Palladium, presumably because Mills could not give the hall a third week's engagement.

The Sunday concerts were a mixture of the band's performances at the Palladium and the radio broadcast, featuring "East St. Louis Toodle-Oo," "Lightnin'," "Old Man Blues," "Ring Dem Bells," "Blackbirds Medley," and "Whispering Tiger," plus Ellington's arrangement of some popular songs, such as "Down Carolina Lane." Ivie Anderson sang several songs, and Lawrence Brown was featured in his solo version of "Trees." Jenkins would sing "Some of These Days" and Cab Calloway's "Minnie The Moocher"; "Mood Indigo" would close the show. According to Lawrence Brown, these concerts would last, on average, close to two hours.

There was other work as well. As the band was usually finished at the Palladium shortly before 10 P.M., Mills booked it for a series of midnight dances within driving distance of London. These included small ballrooms in various London neighborhoods, as well as in Brighton. At most of these dates, the attendance was so great—one "dance" drew four thousand spectators—that little dancing went on—it was simply impossible. Rather, most people stood in front of the bandstand, cheering the band and soloists. At the Astoria Ballroom—despite a high admission charge of five shillings—every table was booked in advance. Many of the fans, including the Duke of Kent, followed the band from ballroom to ballroom to hear them it as often as possible.

One fan, Harry Hayes recalled, "I attended the Astoria dance, though no one danced. . . . It was a supreme joy at close quarters. I could have easily touched Johnny Hodges, so near was I to the bandstand. It was a moment of sheer magic."

The band was also booked for fancy private parties, including an affair at the very exclusive Punch's Club, where the group played for an elegant charity ball. It was Ellington's introduction to the British upper classes. The *Daily Express* wrote: "Punch's Club parties are more exclusive than the Royal Enclosure at Ascot." It went on to add, "Six hundred people got invitations to a room that usually held three hundred and they all came!" A physician to the royal family, a noted gossip columnist, and even Irving Mills were almost refused admittance. The band was late in starting, because Ellington sent his tailcoat back to the Dorchester to be properly pressed.

Sharing the bill with the band were chanteuse Lucienne Boyer, who had flown from Paris to appear at the event, and entertainer Beatrice Lillie (Lady Peel). The *Bystander* noted the attendance of some darlings of British society, including Somerset Maugham's daughter, Lisa. Other invitees included the movie stars Jeannette MacDonald and Anna May Wong. The black stage and film star Nina Mae McKinney and her escort danced to "Mood Indigo," and a maharaja was among those transfixed by "Sophisticated Lady." Members of the touring West Indies cricket team led the applause following "Old Man Blues."

The *Daily Express* took note of the profusion of colors and races at the event:

> I saw many coloured dresses and many coloured faces. There were the tired, whitefaced Mayfaries, and the hearty, pink Meltonians. Yellow was represented by Miss Anna May Wong. Then there was the coffee coloured Bessie Dudley . . . the brown-faced Maharaja of Rajpipla and of course Duke Ellington and his band.

This celebration of color did not mean that British racism had taken a day off. The *Sunday Referee* wrote that "they gave a cabaret in which a colored girl and a coon did a dance that would certainly not be allowed in any public hall in England."

On June 24, *Melody Maker*'s headline read: "ELLINGTON FEVER HEAT." The magazine was sponsoring a concert by Ellington on June 25. After its donation to the Musicians' Benevolent Fund, the remainder of the profit was to go to Hylton to reimburse him for the considerable expenses he had undertaken to bring Ellington to England. Bandleader Spike Hughes was eagerly looking forward to the event. Having heard the band in several dance halls and at the Palladium, he felt it had not done itself full justice. He wrote, "The ... concert will give an opportunity to the Duke to feature some of those quieter and more individual compositions of his which have not hitherto been played in London."

Hughes took it on himself to instruct the readers in what he thought was proper etiquette for a jazz concert:

> The applause should come at the end of each number and not in the middle in the distressing and irritating way which had marred the work of the band elsewhere. Let us show that ours is the real public, and then we shall hear something which we shall remember for many a long day.

Hughes's admonition to the audience not to applaud made sense. He was attempting to communicate that the concert was a serious event and not a repetition of a vaudeville show.

The tickets went on sale in mid-May. Because of Ellington's popularity and the extensive publicity surrounding his upcoming visit, the four thousand seats sold out within twenty-four hours. Hundreds were turned away. The *Times* noted the presence of musicians from all over Europe, as far off as Vienna, Copenhagen, and Barcelona. "Many of them with pencils and anxious eyes were making notes on their programmes," the *Times*'s critic noted. The famous American jazz singing trio the Boswell Sisters were among the many celebrities present.

As the members of the audience were being seated, Levy's Record Shoppe entertained them by playing Ellington recordings. Signs prominently displayed in the lobby and an advertisement on the back of the program informed the crowd where the records could be purchased. In the program, Ellington listed thirty-three compositions, of which he would play approximately twenty. In the complete list, twenty-six pieces were original compositions*; the non-Ellington compositions were his arrangements of Elmer Bowman's "Twelfth Street Rag," W. C. Handy's "St. Louis Blues," Elmer Schoebel's "Bugle Call Rag," Jerome Kern's "Old Man River," and "Tiger Rag" by Nick LaRocca.

In addition, the band was prepared to perform two pieces by other composers. One was "Paradise," by an Ellington favorite, Benny Carter. The song had become very popular in England as a result of Bing Crosby's recording. This was as close as Ellington would get to playing a "commercial" work on the program. The other non-Ellington composition in the possible playlist was Hughes's composition "Sirocco." Ellington included it to acknowledge Hughes's devotion to him when Hughes dedicated "A Harlem Symphony" to Ellington. Hughes had recorded "A Harlem Symphony" with his own band, having been inspired by Ellington's "Creole Rhapsody."

Overall, the concert did not go well. The publicity surrounding Ellington's music and his visit to London unfortunately elevated the concert to a social event, rather than the serious musical undertaking the sponsors were hoping for. Although there were many musicians in the audience, the great majority of people in the building had never heard the band at all. Consequently, Williams's and Nanton's "growling" with their mutes and plungers caused many in the audience to respond with laughter at what were to them strange, exotic noises.

Ellington interpreted this to mean they were bored and didn't appreciate the music. He decided that the routine from his shorter "concert" appearances might be more appropriate. So, during the second half of the program, he abandoned his original plan. Instead, Jenkins sang and danced to "Some of These Days," which was followed by "In the Shade of the Old Apple Tree"; Lawrence Brown played his solo version of "Trees"; Ivie Anderson sang "Stormy Weather" and "Minnie the Moocher"; and the band performed Ellington's "Sophisticated Lady" and "Tiger Rag." The audience shouted for

---

* "Old Man Blues" (1930), "Echoes of the Jungle" (1929), "The Duke Steps Out" (1929), "The Mooche" (1929), "Lightnin'" (1931), "Mood Indigo" (1931), "Hyde Park" (1933), "Lazy Rhapsody" (1929), "Blue Tune" (1930), "Merry-Go-Round" (1933), "Ring Dem Bells" (1930), "Creole Rhapsody" (1930), "Swing Low" (1931), "Black & Tan Fantasy" (1927), "Rockin' in Rhythm" (1931), "Black Beauty" (1927), "Blue Ramble" (1931), "Double Check Stomp" (1930), "Baby When You Ain't There" (1931), "Ducky Wucky" (1931), "Jive Stomp" (1932), "Drop Me Off At Harlem" (1932), "It Don't Mean a Thing (If It Ain't Got That Swing)" (1932), "Creole Love Call" (1927), "Cotton Club Stomp" (1929), and "The Monkey" (1930).

"Mood Indigo" but didn't get it. Finally, the whole orchestra stood up and—conducted by Duke—played Hughes's arrangement of "God Save the King." A member of the audience was overheard saying that was the first time he had heard the British national anthem applauded!

When the concert was over, Max Jones recalled, "We all stood about outside the hall at the end, you know, dazed by the whole thing and standing around as you do, reluctant to return to normality."

Ellington had the use of Hylton's Rolls Royce and his chauffeur. "When Duke came out he was, as the press said, 'mobbed,'" Jones noted. "That's not an exaggeration and people queued up around the car he got in and cheered. I see from the press report that people were still clinging to the car when they pulled away. That was the sort of reception he got."

Melody Maker had scheduled another concert three weeks later. However, a controversy was brewing among the purists, who had come to hear the "real" Ellington—not what they considered to be a vaudeville show—and the general audience. Representing the purist critics, Hughes wrote in a letter to the journal:

> Is Duke Ellington losing faith in his own music, and turning commercial through lack of appreciation? Or does he honestly underestimate the English musical public to such an extent that a concert for musicians does not include "The Mooche," "Mood Indigo," "Lazy Rhapsody," "Blue Ramble," "Rockin' in Rhythm," "Creole Love Call," "Old Man Blues," "Baby When You Ain't There" or "Black Beauty"?
>
> But last Sunday it seemed that all the courage he had acquired in London, all the determination to go his own way in music deserted him at the most inappropriate occasion. There is a saying about "giving the public what it wants" which had always struck me as being the greatest illusion from which any artist can suffer. . . . [T]he public does not know what it wants and has never known.

Hughes went on to upbraid Ellington for playing the compositions of what he called "Broadway Caucasian immigrants," including the hits "Some of These Days," "Minnie the Moocher," and "Trees."

Ellington was upset by Hughes's charges. He felt that by doing his theater routine he was responding to what the public wanted. Hylton and Mills sided with him in what had become a public debate with one of his foremost champions in Great Britain. Following that turn of events, Ellington began referring to Hughes as the "Hot Dictator."

If Duke was upset with Hughes, the review in the *Jewish Chronicle* must have lifted his spirits. The correspondent was well-versed in Ellingtonia. He wrote that during the concert he experienced "amusement, exhilaration and . . . creative inspiration." He appreciated the humor in the Ellington arrangements of "Dinah" and "The Shade of the Old Apple Tree," the displeasure of those he labeled "purists and Puritans" notwithstanding. He said that the inspiration came from "such nocturnes as 'Blue Tune' or miniature tone poems like 'Creole Rhapsody,'" and noted his preference for the shorter (original) version of the latter.

This critic rejoiced on hearing the "melancholy 'Creole Rhapsody,' the somnolently indolent 'Lazy Rhapsody,' and the melancholy sombrous 'Mood Indigo'"; he found creative inspiration in "the weird and terrible 'Echoes of the Jungle'"; and he pointed out to his readers that those works refuted the common criticism that the pungent harmonies produced by the Ellington orchestra "can have no musical point." This critic concluded that the compositions played at the concert demonstrated that "Ellington is not only a fine dance band conductor but a composer of genius."

Following the show, the Ellington band was bused back to the south coast in Sussex to play at the Regal Cinema in Hastings, then to London's Euston Station. The late train took the group to Liverpool for a week at the Empire Theatre.

On the Tuesday night of this engagement, there was a commotion in the house just before the intermission: The audience was standing and applauding the entrance of the Prince of Wales. He had been at the Royal Birkdale Golf Club in nearby Southport over the weekend, watching his good friend Walter Hagen lead the American foursome to defeat England for the Ryder Cup.

The band appeared for the second half of the show. At the end of the concert, the prince stayed in his seat and led the packed house in shouting "More! More!" The band stayed on stage for three encores, and Ellington took thirteen curtain calls. The applause remained so enthusiastic that the stagehands went to the dressing room to get the band to return to the stage. Finally, Ellington led the band in Hughes's arrangement of "God Save the King."

After the show, the prince went backstage and was introduced to Ellington. As they shook hands, he said to Ellington, "You have a very great band, one of—if not the finest—it has been my pleasure to listen to, and I do hope England welcomes you through a record stay." As he left the theater, someone asked what he thought of the event. "Wonderful! Just wonderful!" he exclaimed.

While in Liverpool, Ellington was interviewed by a Glasgow *Sunday Post* reporter. The band would soon be appearing in Scotland, and the reporter was writing an advance piece for his paper. Ellington took the occasion to address some of the criticism he had received in the press and personally. Quoting from a letter, Ellington said the writer wrote that "my music is an insult to the word . . . a program of sound effects representing the sound of a coal cart's brakes being screwed on tightly, of train smashes, and of animals in pain." Warming to the task, Ellington observed, "Some people say my music is uncouth and without form—a weird conglomeration of blatant discords which never will mean anything at all."

Looking at his interviewer with a twinkle in his eye, Ellington asked, "What, may I ask you as a Scotsman, do the same people think about bagpipe music? It is quite as weird, quite as 'tuneless.' But it is recognized as the music of a nation, a folk music." He argued that his "music was . . . a result of our transportation to the American soil, and the expression of a people's soul, just as the wild swirling of bagpipes denote[s] a heroic race that had never known the yoke of foreign dictatorship."

Ellington continued, "It is my honest belief that in Scotland I shall find an appreciation of my music not to be found south of the border." He concluded the interview by saying that his other reason for wanting to go to Scotland was not the whiskey, but rather he had promised to take back to Harlem, "at least one Haggis," the favorite food of Scotsmen. His statement caught the eye of the owners of McKean's Haggis, who supplied him with several in return for an endorsement.

En route to Glasgow, the band played a Sunday-night concert at the Blackpool Tower. Midnight dances were scheduled during the band's week-long stay in the city at the roof garden of Green's Playhouse and the Piccadilly Club, along with the full schedule at the Empire Theatre. While in the city, Ellington charmed a female reporter from the Glasgow *Daily Record* into leaving his rooms at the Adelphi Hotel and accompanying him on a shopping excursion. It was a hot day, and she interviewed him as he sought her opinion on bolts of Scottish tweed, Shetland sweaters, pullovers, and other souvenirs he was purchasing for family and friends back home.

Later, she accompanied him to the Empire Theatre for the evening performance, and observed, "Not even the film star Carl Brisson collects such a crowd at the stage door. . . . Autograph hunters particularly were out in force. Seldom have I seen so many autograph albums brandished in the air at one time."

The overwhelming response to Ellington's performances in Liverpool and Glasgow, as well as at the Palladium, was not lost on the owners of the Empire syndicate. They booked the band and the dancers for a performance in London beginning the following Monday. The 420-mile trip from Glasgow was broken up by a Sunday night concert at the newly refurbished Royal Hall in Harrogate.

The band was booked at the Holborn Empire for evening performances, and two matinees were scheduled at the Finsbury Park Empire in North London. Greer noted, "As soon as the curtain came down for the matinee, the entire band would come out front to take the bows. Meanwhile, backstage, the stagehands would be taking the music and everything else, loading it on a truck and taking it back to the other theater."

Ellington nearly missed the opening show at the Holborn. When he returned to the Dorchester from Glasgow, he requested the suite he had been given previously, next door to Mills. Due to some confusion at the front desk, he was placed across the hall, but noted that the hotel's register showed that he was supposed to be in the room he had requested. The problem was quickly corrected—but apparently no note was made to indicate the change.

Hughes arrived with a record player and a collection of Delius recordings. They sat up all night drinking, talking, and listening to music. Ellington was particularly impressed with "On Hearing the First Cuckoo in Spring."

Ellington went to bed at daybreak, expecting a wake-up call from Dick Depauw, Hylton's assistant. But when the call was made to what was thought to be Ellington's suite, there was no answer, and—to make matters worse—the key was in its box, indicating that Ellington must have left the premises. Of course, Ellington was in a different room, so this is why the key was at the desk.

As curtain time drew near, Depauw became desperate. He went to the hotel and asked the bellboys to knock on all the doors on the floor, paging Ellington. He was finally located. Depauw helped him get dressed, and they hailed a taxi and raced toward the theater. When they were in sight of the building, there was a traffic jam. Bystanders were surprised to see a six-foot-three black man clad in tails jump out of a taxi and race toward the stage door. He arrived with only seven minutes left in the show. Ivie Anderson had taken over the duties of making the introductions.

The following night, Ellington once again received acclaim from London society. Newspaper magnate Lord Beaverbrook, celebrating the end of the World Economic and Monetary Conference, threw a huge dinner party and dance at his palatial home, Stornaway House. This elegant mansion was located on Green Street, just off St. James Park. The publisher invited a distinguished list of guests, including the Prince of Wales, the Duke of Kent, and Ladies Iris Mountbatten, Diana Duff Cooper, and Bridget Poulet. The American movie stars Anna May Wong and Jeanette MacDonald also attended. The *Bystander* wrote that the event "lured Lord and Lady Warwick from their honeymoon, it was their wedding night! Winston Churchill loomed largely important . . . a Bishop was present; Lord Beaverbrook danced."

Hylton's band played soft dance music until midnight, then Ellington took over. After playing the band's radio theme "East St. Louis Toodle-Oo," he gave a downbeat. The saxophones and muted brass quietly played the introduction, as Hodges responded on soprano saxophone, followed by the trombonist Nanton soloing, and the clarinetist, Bigard, playing an obbligato behind him. A surging twelve-bar vamp led to a brass fanfare. As it sounded, those in the know recognized "Old Man Blues." The result was electrifying. The guests, moved by the visceral impact of the music, spilled out onto the dance floor. After each number, they gave the musicians loud, long, sustained applause. Lord Beaverbrook later told an aide, "They acted like a bunch of kids!"

Later that evening, Prince George asked Ellington to play his piano composition "Swampy River," a work he had recorded twice, first as a piano solo and then, four years later, with the full band. When telling the story years later, Ellington would occasionally inform the listeners that he brushed off the prince's request, saying, "I don't do solos." But Ellington's personality belies the statement. By this time, Ellington and the prince had become good friends. I am hard pressed to believe that a person with Ellington's narcissism (remember, this is a man who predicted he would bow before kings and queens) would turn down a request for one of the two piano solos he had ever recorded. He did play the work. "I was flattered, especially to have him lean over the piano as I played it" Later that evening, Ellington invited the prince to sit in at the piano, and the two of them played four-hand duets.

Meanwhile, another member of the rhythm section, Sonny Greer, was having his first encounter with royalty. As he recounted many years later, "I noticed this skinny little guy squatting near the drums and watching me, and pretty soon he asks can we play the 'Charleston.' We did and he danced like crazy. Then he asked me could he sit in on the drums, and I said 'Of course, my man.' People kept coming up and calling him 'Your Highness,' or 'Wales' but he wouldn't move. We both began to get high on whatever it was we were drinking. He was calling me 'Sonny' and I was calling him 'The Whale.'" The man was, of course, the Prince of Wales, Prince George's older brother.

As the party concluded, the Prince of Wales made a short speech, commending the host on his hospitality, and singling Ellington out for the excellence of his music. After Lord Beaverbrook's response to the prince, Ellington thanked him for his hospitality, and the audience members for their appreciation. Following Ellington's speech, the Prince shook his hand and suggested they share a drink together. Much to his surprise, Ellington found that the future king of England drank gin, a drink Ellington had always considered rather declassé. Later he told a friend, "Since that time I've always felt rather grand when I drink gin."

The fact that the band was achieving a stunning success abroad, and that Ellington was being celebrated by royalty, did not blind Mills to his first objective: promoting his client. When they returned to London, Mills told Ellington that he had set up recording dates on July 13 and 14, one for the band, and one for him alone. In March, Mills had contracted for British Columbia Records to issue Ellington's numerous Brunswick jazz sessions on the English Parlophone label for distribution in Great Britain and Europe. Mills used this connection to book a recording date for the band at the Decca studios in Chelsea. Prince George heard about it and desperately wanted to attend, but had a previously scheduled commitment. He consoled himself with the knowledge that he would see his friends two nights later at a private party.

At the Decca session, the band recorded "Hyde Park" and "Harlem Speaks," and also Ellington's arrangements of the popular songs "Chicago" and "Ain't Misbehavin'." Ellington composed "Harlem Speaks" in London. He was impressed by the documentary film *Africa Speaks*, produced by the Columbia Studios in 1930, and "Harlem Speaks" was his response to it. "Hyde Park" was originally known as "Ev'ry Tub." During the recording session, Ellington decided to change the song's name to "Park Lane" to honor the address of the Dorchester Hotel. But he had misgivings about that title also, and finally settled on the well-known London landmark, "Hyde Park."

The trip to the recording studio the following day had its roots in the *Melody Maker* concert a few weeks earlier. After seeing the advertisement for Levy's Record Shoppe in the program, Mills went to Regent Street the next day. Impressed by the number of customers requesting Ellington recordings, he approached the store's management with a suggestion. He said Ellington would make a demonstration recording for them in which he talked about his music. This single-sided record would be given free to anyone buying the recently issued six-record commemorative album.

Ellington was eager to make the recording. It was dawning on him how seriously the British public regarded his music. On the recording, called "A Souvenir of Duke Ellington," he read from a script, over his piano rendition of "Mood Indigo," discussing his music and responding to questions from *Melody Maker* editor Percy Mathison Brooks. During the discussion, Ellington indicated his surprise at the amount of technical scrutiny given to his music. Also, he mentioned how his friendship with the young English composer/conductor Constant Lambert and his wife had given him the inspiration for a new composition. It so happened that Mrs. Lambert, a Eurasian, mistakenly referred to the Ellington masterpiece as "Rude Indigo." Thus, when he returned home, Ellington composed "Rude Interlude."

As music director of the Sadler's Wells Ballet (the precursor of the Royal Ballet), Lambert had great influence on the world of English classical dance. He had already achieved fame as composer of the ballet scores "Rio Grande," "Pomona," and later "Horoscope." He was also the first English composer to see the possibilities of jazz in serious music. This stemmed from two important events in his life, both of which had connections to Ellington.

In 1922, when he was seventeen, Lambert and his close friend Angus Morrison attended a performance of *Dover Street to Dixie* conducted by Will Vodery. The show featured vocalist Florence Mills along with Johnny Dunn playing trumpet on stage and in the pit band. According to Morrison, the memory of Dunn's playing the opening flourish to "Carry Me Back to Old Virginny" remained in Lambert's musical consciousness throughout his life. The echo of this could be heard in almost all his works.

Morrison said that the overall ambience of the show was something "[Lambert] sought to recapture over and over again in his own music, 'Rio Grande,' the slow movement of the Piano Sonata, the Piano Concerto, the 'Elegiac Blues,' and even that exquisite piece written many years later, 'Aubade Heroic.'"

When Florence Mills returned to London four years later as an international star with *Blackbirds of 1926*, Lambert was a student at the Royal Conservatory of Music. Morrison said the show inspired Lambert "to narrow the gap between 'serious' music and popular music. Jazz rhythms could be adapted to invigorate . . . the jaded contemporary English music repertoire, and could combine technical skills with emotional appeal."

When Florence Mills died, Ellington memorialized her in "Black Beauty," composed in 1928. Lambert had preceded him a year earlier, with his "Elegiac Blues," a short, melancholy piece, proceeding by a wry turn of phrases to a climax that recalled the Plantation fanfare he had heard four years earlier. This could also be heard in the slow elegiac finale of Lambert's *Concerto for Piano and Nine Instruments*, composed in 1931.

Given his musical eminence, Lambert was among those invited to Hylton's cocktail party. Over several weeks, he and Duke had developed a close musical and personal friendship. One evening, Lambert and his wife, Flo, hosted a midnight dinner at their flat in Bloomsbury, with Ellington the guest of honor. At one point in the evening the two composers had a long, technical discussion regarding the manner in which Ellington had restated the theme in his composition "Swampy River."

Meanwhile, the whirlwind of socializing continued. With Prince George's help in arranging it, Ellington and Mills hosted a cocktail party for Hylton at the Dorchester to present Hylton with a check representing a percentage of the profits from the *Melody Maker* concert. In addition, Ellington and Mills gave Hylton the surprise gift of a portable bar, to thank him for the unlimited hospitality he had shown them during their stay.

The second *Melody Maker* concert was scheduled for two days later. As it approached, Spike Hughes once again attempted to teach the audience the proper etiquette for the concert. Writing under his pseudonym "Mike," he issued a plea to the audience not to laugh during the solos by Nanton and Williams while they were using their mutes and plungers.

As he had done at the first concert, Ellington listed the same thirty-three compositions from which he would draw the program. Apparently, this time the audience reaction was better. Reporting in the *Melody Maker* the following week, Hughes said he enjoyed himself

> so much last Sunday, that there is little for me to say in the way of criticism. . . . If a couple of thousand people have learned within three weeks that "Cootie" and "Tricky" are really expressing something extremely personal and moving, then there is indeed hope that these same people will realize, by the time Duke gives another concert, that applause during the performance of a piece of music is not done in the best circles.

Nonetheless, Hughes went on to scold members of the audience for their inappropriate applause:

> During the first seven numbers the audience reserved its applause for the end, but in "Echoes of the Jungle" the newly appreciated importance of Cootie proved too much and this player's solo was greeted by much tiresome handclapping. The result of this misplaced

enthusiasm was that one of the loveliest bridge passages in all Duke's music was completely inaudible and we did not hear anything until Barney Bigard started that sinister clarinet solo.

Overall, however, Hughes was pleased: "I left the theater knowing a large audience had at last a chance to hear at its best, the music of Edward Kennedy Ellington, first American composer of American music."

The musicians agreed that this was a successful show. "That last concert we gave was something," Greer said. "At the end people just stood in front of the bandstand and cheered us and cheered Duke, for a long time. I thought we'd never get out of there."

That evening, the band was on the train to Birmingham. At the last minute, Hylton and Mills had secured a week's engagement at the Hippodrome Theatre, plus a midnight dance at the Palais de Dance on June 21. The band was back in London the following Sunday afternoon. The next day, a large crowd, including Hughes, Hylton, and the Lamberts, accompanied the musicians to the Liverpool Street station and gave the band a gala send-off party. The band took the boat train to Dover and crossed the English Channel. Their next engagement would be at the Kursall Scheveningen, Holland.

Ellington felt very good about England. On a personal level, he had made friendships—beginning with the Prince of Wales—that would last a lifetime. Three years later, the prince—by then, King Edward VIII— abdicated the throne in order to marry the love of his life, a divorced American woman, Wallis Simpson. After World War II, the prince—now the Duke of Windsor—moved to New York City. He and his wife were often involved as patrons of charitable events, some of which featured the Ellington orchestra. If he was present, the one-time prince would make it a point to greet Ellington as an old friend, bring him to the head table, and introduce him, and they would share a drink.

Another friend Ellington made on the British tour was Renee Gertler, the thirteen-year-old niece of the painter Mark Gertler. She telephoned Ellington's suite at the Dorchester and was fortunate to get through. She told him that her father and uncle had difficulty getting tickets for his performances, and asked if he could help.

Embarrassed by having almost missed the first show at the Holburn, Duke offered the young woman a quid pro quo. He would provide the tickets if she would ring his room after she got out of school to make sure he was up. She did, the friendship blossomed, and they began a correspondence that continued throughout the war. By the time Ellington rturned to London fifteen years later, Renee had become Mrs. Leslie Diamond. The home she and her husband lived in, just off Park Lane, became a place to which Ellington could retreat quietly whenever he was in London.

Ellington continued to be pursued by prominent people. Following the first *Melody Maker* concert, the sculptor Jacob Epstein had made it a point to go backstage, shake Ellington's hand, and tell him how much he enjoyed the music. The young sons of the Turkish ambassador to London, Muni Ertegun, kept sneaking away from their lycée in South Kensington to hear Ellington every chance they could get. The younger child, Ahmet, recollected, "I was ten years old. It changed my life. I had never heard an American band in the flesh before. I had never seen any black people. To hear that band—[the] rows of gleaming instruments, elegant men and power. I went back three or four times." Fourteen years later, while living in New York City, Ahmet Ertegun organized the Atlantic Recording Company, which would become a leading jazz label.

Duke had become a celebrity in London. To test his fame, Hylton suggested that they walk one hundred yards through the West End to see if anyone would recognize Ellington. According to the *Daily Mirror*, they were stopped nine or ten times by people who produced scraps of paper, odd envelopes, and other pocket junk to ask for Ellington's autograph.

The previous year, the prominent African-American singer and actor Paul Robeson had been refused seating at London's tony Savoy Grill. Yet, when Ellington arrived at this famous rendezvous for dinner, the management welcomed him with open arms. But eating proved difficult; his table was stormed by scores of enthusiastic admirers, and his own dinner grew cold while he autographed menus and cards by the dozen.

On a professional level, which was more important, Ellington had presented his music to non-Americans who appreciated it and took it seriously to the point where it became a matter of public debate. Men of letters in British musical circles—Constant Lambert, the venerable critics Ernest Newman and Edgar Jackson, and the writers John Cheatle and Hannen Swaffer—discussed his work in print.

Lambert and Newman were practically at sword's point. Newman was not at all pleased with Duke or his music; in a memorable phrase, he called Ellington "a Harlem Dionysus drunk on bad bootleg liquor." But Lambert, writing in the *Sunday Referee*, took the critic—and others who questioned Ellington's musical skills—to task:

> The orchestration of nearly all the numbers shows an intensely musical instinct, and after hearing what Ellington can do with fourteen players in pieces like "Jive Stomp" and "Mood Indigo," . . . [he] is no mere bandleader and arranger, but a composer of real character to come out of America.

Lambert compared Ellington's works to those of Franz Liszt, and felt that "Ellington gave the same distinction to his genre as Strauss to the waltz or Sousa to the march."

Other British critics showed a similarly sophisticated understanding of Ellington and his musical achievements. The *Tatler's* correspondent observed, "To hear 'Mood Indigo' is to understand why what some call jazz, others regard seriously as Afro-American music."

Other critics were less sympathetic. John Cheatle gave Ellington credit for creating a mob hysteria that in later years would be replicated by Benny Goodman, Frank Sinatra, Elvis Presley, and the Beatles. In an article in *New Britain*, he described the audience: "[They] sit and clutch hands, gasp, goggle their eyes and jig their knees to the rhythm . . . [they] need to be psychoanalyzed."

However, Cheatle took issue with those who said that in America, Ellington was compared seriously to Bach and Delius. Cheatle accepted the comparison to Delius, because of the similarity in the way both Ellington and Delius used chords and chord progressions. But he totally rejected the notion that Ellington was the equal of Bach. "The only thing the two composers [Ellington and Bach] have in common is a certain rhythmic persistence. It were as sensible to compare a geranium with the Botanical Garden," Cheatle snootily stated.

Cheatle also took vehement exception to Ellington's statement at Hylton's cocktail party that the origins of his music and the melancholy of blues music in general had their roots in American black slavery. He wrote:

> The "melancholy" of the Negro Spiritual in its most primitive form, before it was ruined by concert arrangements, was a significant and moving thing. I submit that Duke Ellington's delicious Blues have no more to do with the sorrows of captivity than De Falla's Ballets with the defeat of the Spanish Armada.

Of course, Ellington's music was far more sophisticated than its blues roots; but Cheatle again exaggerated his point and failed to understand that the suffering of African-Americans hardly ended with the end of slavery.

Interviewing Ellington for the *Daily Herald* earlier, Hannen Swaffer unknowingly gave him a forum for reply. Since composing "Creole Rhapsody" two years earlier, Ellington had been thinking of a suite in five movements. He wanted to tell the story of blacks in America. "If only I can write it down as I feel it," he said:

> I have gone back to the history of my people and tried to express it in rhythm. We used to have it in Africa, a something we have lost. One day we shall get it back again. I am expressing in sound the old days in the jungle, the cruel journey across the sea, and the despair of the landing. And then the days in Harlem and the cities of the States. Then I try to go forward a thousand years, when, emancipated and transformed, the Negro takes his place, a free being, among peoples of the world.

Clearly, as far as Ellington was concerned, there was a definite correlation between being born a descendant of slaves and the music he was writing. His statement went unnoticed in the debate. However, after recording his words, Swaffer wrote: "All this was said with a quietness of dignity. I heard almost a whisper of prophesy."

Indeed, over ten years later, it was realized; the thoughts Duke set forth in the interview would be musically expressed as the suite *Black,*

Brown and Beige (1943). Billy Strayhorn told me, "I don't think it would have seen the light of day if Duke hadn't gone to England that first time. He used to tell me [that] when [he] found out his music was talked about in the press just like Stravinsky and Ravel, [and] he realized they considered him a real composer and took his music seriously, it gave him the strength to go on."

The trip to England also had an impact on the musicians. "That, we thought, was just about the greatest engagement a band could have," Harry Carney observed:

> To start with, we were greeted by so many people who knew so much about the band, that we were amazed. We couldn't understand how people in Europe, who heard us only through the medium of records, could know so much about us. They'd ask us who took which solo on this or that tune, and we had to sharpen up so that we could answer halfway intelligently. Another thing was that they knew exactly what they wanted to hear, a great and very pleasant surprise to us.

Years later, recalling the trip to England, surviving band members to a man complained about the workload. "All I remember about that trip was work, work, work. We never got a chance to do anything else," growled Lawrence Brown.

"Birmingham, Liverpool, Glasgow, I don't remember much about them; we worked every day," Cootie Williams observed. "As a matter of fact, when we went back to England in '63 and played the [Empire] theater in Liverpool, Duke and Carney had to remind me we'd played there in '33."

"We never had a day off!" Sonny Greer said. "I figured we'd have at least Sundays. The next thing we knew, Mills was booking us for concerts on those days! The nice thing about it, though, we had a pocketful of money when we got to Paris."

On the Continent, the band was originally scheduled for four concerts in the Netherlands and a one-week engagement at the Rex, an opulent movie theater in Paris. In light of the group's great success at the Palladium, Mills was now demanding $6,000 a week for Ellington's services. The management of the Rex kept stalling about the money, and finally canceled the engagement. There would now be only two performances in Holland. On July 25, the Ellington orchestra performed a concert as well as a broadcast later that day from the same stage for the Dutch Broadcasting Company.

With the Rex engagement canceled. Mills secured Paris's Salle Pleyel for three concerts on July 27 and 29, and August 1. The correspondent for the New York *Age* wrote, "The American colony, colored and white, turned out in force." Despite the high ticket price and the failing French economy, Americans abroad were most interested in seeing and hearing the band. Writing about these concerts, the African-American writer J. A. Rogers observed, "It was perhaps the most riotous scene of joy ever witnessed within the four walls of this building. The Duke Ellington concerts . . . have shown that the European public is . . . eager for properly played jazz."

Among those attending was Ada "Bricktop" Smith, who had been responsible for getting Ellington's band its first job in New York at the Club Baron. She was now the owner of Bricktop's, a successful cabaret in Montmartre. She had postponed her annual summer vacation in Biarritz to stay in Paris and keep her club open during the week Ellington was in town. She threw a party for the band after the first concert, and attended all three shows.

"After working like we did in England, we were ready to party [in France]," said Greer. "Bricktop laid out a spread for us. Food, champagne, and all kinds of cheese. What she was upset about was that had we come to town a week earlier, she would have introduced us to President Roosevelt's son [Franklin Jr.]. He used to hang out there all the time!"

That Friday night, the entire troupe was the guest of Josephine Baker at the Casino de Paris, where her show *Joy of Paris* was playing to capacity crowds. Nekka Shaw, who had hired saxohpone player Toby Hardwick to play at her club four years earlier, welcomed him and the band with open arms. She was joined by trumpet player Johnny Dunn, along with the singers Alberta Hunter and Mabel Mercer, and a collection of black expatriates currently living in Paris.

A side trip to the Casino du Deauville, the smart summer resort 150 miles south of Paris, was scheduled for Sunday night. The concert was another great success. When the band arrived in Deauville, Mills was hurriedly contacted by the owners of the casino at Monte Carlo, who were interested in hiring the band for a four-week engagement. Unfortunately, it was too late. The band was ticketed to leave France on the R.M.S. *Majestic* four days later. Mills remained behind for another week, attempting to secure bookings for Cab Calloway and the Mills Brothers.

"The last night we were there," guitarist Fred Guy recalled, "Bricktop did it again. We partied all night. Finally a huge champagne bottle was lowered from the ceiling and everyone had a drink from it." The correspondent for the *Chicago Defender* wrote, "A very large crowd of friends and admirers were at Gare St. Lazare bidding Duke and his hot jazz boys bon voyage. I am very sorry they have gone, but I know they will sleep well at sea for the coming week as they are all pretty well exhausted."

Mercer Ellington later wrote of the Paris trip, "The affection and admiration they received more than balanced whatever prejudice and surviving ignorance on racial matters that they later met." In addition, he reported another event that occurred the night before his father left Paris.

Mills, thrilled by the amount of money made on the trip and the extraordinary reception for Ellington and his music, took Ellington out to dinner, then to a brothel. After the girls were paraded before them, Mills pointed to the girls and said, "Which would you like? My treat."

"I'll take the two on the end," Pop replied.

27

ON AUGUST 3, 1933, the Ellington entourage boarded the R.M.S. *Majestic* at Cherbourg for the trip back to New York, by way of Southampton. The ship arrived in the United States on August 8. The *New York Times* took note of the distinguished passengers who had disembarked. Under "Social News," the paper listed the arrival of Sir Bede Clifford, governor of the Bahamas, and Lady Clifford. Among others were Bishop George S. Arundale of the Liberal Catholic Church of Australia, Cass Gilbert, architect, Mrs. J. L. Harriman of New York—and Duke Ellington, bandleader.

Fortune magazine had published a lengthy article on Ellington that month. As might be expected, the writer, Wilder Hobson, knew little about jazz or jazz bands. Still, the level of success Ellington and his bandmates had achieved was indicated by the fact that they were profiled in this magazine geared toward major businessmen. The piece featured full-page photographs of the band members, all dressed in white. Sadly, the captions for Johnny Hodges and Harry Carney were accidentally switched, and Carney was misidentified as "the fastest altoist in the business."

The band was back in the Brunswick studios on August 15. Ivie Anderson sang "I'm Satisfied," and the band roared through another recording of "Harlem Speaks," "Jive Stomp," and "In the Shade of the Old Apple Tree."

The *Amsterdam News* reported that the band's last remaining bachelor, Lawrence Brown, had married dancer/singer Fredi Washington. The newlyweds traveled with the band during the abbreviated summer tour of New England, then west to Chicago for an engagement at the Chicago Theater during the week of September 22.

After a year of pooling interests with Tommy Rockwell, Irving Mills had decided to dissolve this partnership. Mills also had been signed up as a combination talent scout, advisor, and record producer for what would now be known as RCA Victor records, but was allowed to keep his other business interests. His first move was to sign contracts for the three black bands that he had been recording at Brunswick: Ellington, Calloway, and the Mills Blue Rhythm Band.

On September 26, for its first session under the new contract, Ellington's band recorded the work inspired by Flo Lambert, "Rude Interlude." The work, a blues number, contained a wordless vocal by Louis Bacon. At age twenty-nine, he had come to the band having spent the previous four years with Chick Webb.

"Duke asked Louis to help out in the trumpet section." Sonny Greer said. "You see, both Freddie and Artie were getting sick. When one was well, the other wasn't. They'd both be in and out of the band for the next couple of years."

"Dallas Doings," originally known as "Blue Eagle Stomp," the other work cut at that session, was a portent of the band's upcoming tour of the South. As Lawrence Brown recalled, "I sent Fredi back to New York. Mills asked me why. He told me that when Cab played the South that spring there was no trouble, [but] I just wanted to be on the safe side."

In fact, Mills's reassurance was not true. Calloway said that when his band was delayed by a bus breakdown, the white audience in Virginia Beach, Virginia, grew angry and "somebody shouted, 'Let's take this nigger out and lynch him.' All of this was going on while I was trying to sing!"

Benny Payne, Calloway's pianist, complained to him, "They've got us coming in and leaving from the backs of theaters, dressing in toilets and eating while we sit on potato sacks in the kitchen. You know damn well they don't treat white bands like this."

When I toured the South with the Luis Russell and Milton Larkin orchestra twelve years later, nothing had changed. There were few black hotels, and in small towns we rented rooms in private homes. On arriving in town, the first thing we looked for was the local black restaurant. Fortunately, Ellington had his private railroad cars. "It was our home away from home," Fred Guy said.

"We commanded respect," Ellington recalled. "We parked those cars in each railroad station and we lived in them. We had our own water, food, electricity, and sanitary facilities. The natives would come by and they would say 'What on earth is that?' And we would say

'That's the way the President travels.'" Smiling at his interviewer, he remarked, "You do the best you can with what you've got."

The band steamed into Dallas on September 23, 1933. Mills, as usual, had mounted an extensive publicity campaign, which was reflected at the box office. The Majestic Theater grossed $22,000 in one week, breaking the previous record set by Calloway. In fact, the Ellington band broke attendance records wherever it went on that tour. Leaving Dallas, the group traveled across Texas, Oklahoma, and to New Orleans, where the musicians arrived in triumph. A huge crowd greeted them at the railway station, and two local boys who had left town and made good, clarinetist/saxophone player Barney Bigard and bassist Wellman Braud, were especially welcomed.

Then, the band went to Birmingham and on to Atlanta, in the heart of the old Confederacy. The *Atlanta Constitution* reported, "The white people who crowded the gallery were loud in their applause of the orchestra and the dancers. The dancers and concert were a decided hit, both from the white patrons' standpoint and the colored dancers."

Depending on the area and the local rules concerning segregation, blacks in some cities were permitted to hear the band if they sat in the second balcony, and usually exited via a "colored only" door. In Atlanta, the Ellington orchestra played at the city auditorium. The blacks stood on the floor of the building while the whites sat in the seats.

When the band got to Oklahoma City in October, in the audience was the young Ralph Ellison, later to become a famous author and essayist. "I was but a young boy that stood entranced around the bandstand at Slaughter's Hall," Ellison later recalled.

After eight weeks in the South, the band returned to Chicago's Regal Theater for a week-long run beginning November 30. "Man we were happy to get back up North," Sonny Greer said. "I'd never been South before. When we got off the train in Chicago I wanted to kneel down and kiss the ground."

Mills had the band go back to the Victor Studios on the night of December 4. In addition, there would be two more Chicago recording sessions, on January 9 and 10, 1934. These three sessions demonstrate Ellington and the band at the height of their powers in the mid-1930s. Within five weeks they recorded "Dear Old Southland," featuring Hodges on soprano saxophone, as well as the sorrowful "Awful Sad," and a staggering performance of "Daybreak Express." In "Daybreak Express"—based on the chords of "Tiger Rag"—Ellington musically portrays a steam engine leaving the railroad station accelerating to top speed, blowing its whistle, slowing down, and then coming to a halt— all in three minutes.

The French composer Arthur Honegger attempted a similar feat in his composition "Pacific 231." A member of the Boston Symphony who doubled as a jazz musician recalled playing the work in a student orchestra. After listening to the Ellington recording, he told me, "Duke did it better."

For the last recording session, the raucous, ebullient "Stompy Jones" was paired with the elegant "Delta Serenade," and the poignant "Solitude" was backed by "Blue Feeling."

The band members were back in their railroad cars for a series of one-week or split-week theater dates in the Midwest. From December 6, 1933, through January 4, 1934, they played in Iowa, Nebraska, and Missouri without taking even one day off. They then worked their way east via theater engagements in Michigan, Ohio, and Pennsylvania. On February 10, Ellington returned in triumph to his hometown of Washington, D.C., for a week's engagement at the Howard Theater.

Although Ellington had now hobnobbed with royalty, he had still not been officially recognized by an American leader. On his previous visit to Washington in October 1932, Ellington had called at the White House. Yet despite the fact that that meeting was publicized in the press, it never took place. Ellington biographer John Edward Hasse said that Herbert Hoover's presidential papers revealed that the meeting was stopped because the man who set it up, Charles Lucien Skinner, had a police record. Nonetheless, Ellington posed for photographers on the White House grounds without anyone from the presidential staff. The African-American press at that time fired blistering salvos at President Hoover, accusing him of being afraid to be photographed with black visitors, given the fact there would be a presidential election the following month.

On the 1934 trip, according to papers at the Franklin D. Roosevelt Library, Ellington offered to perform for Mrs. Roosevelt. He was politely rebuffed (as only the Roosevelt White House could do), with the explanation that Mrs. Roosevelt was away, and the president was busy and not planning any entertainment that week. However, the man whose friendships now included a royal prince and a future king of England would have to wait to be feted as the guest of honor at a party in that building thirty-five years later, when President Richard Nixon awarded him the Presidential Medal of Freedom.

The band members left Washington in their railway cars for a transcontinental jump to Hollywood. On February 19, they reported to the Paramount lot to work on two films simultaneously, *Murder at the Vanities* and *Belle of the Nineties*, the latter at the request of vampy actress Mae West.

Ellington was brought into *Murder at the Vanities* at the insistence of former Mills employee Sam Coslow. Now employed at Paramount as a songwriter, Coslow was doing very well, having contributed twenty songs to eight films, with at least one major hit in every one. For this production, he did it again with "Cocktail for Two" and "Live and Love Tonight." Ellington's recording of these songs for Victor would become a bestseller in the following May and June.

The band's sequence in the film was part of a symphony concert. A full symphony orchestra begins to play Liszt's "Second Hungarian Rhapsody." The orchestra is rudely interrupted twice by Ellington and his men, who suddenly pop up behind the musicians and play a few riffs. These riffs segue into Ellington's concept of the rhapsody. The symphony conductor and the orchestra leave the stage in disgust, allowing the Ellington orchestra, the dancer/singer Gertrude Michael, and a black chorus line free to present their "Ebony Rhapsody."

The symphony conductor reappears in the wings and closes the production number by mowing down the entire troupe (Ellington's orchestra and the corps de ballet) with a submachine gun, which figures in the plot. Backstage after the scene, it is found that the female star of the revue, Gertrude Micheal, has actually been shot under the cover of the noise from the machine gun.

The use of a black chorus line in *Murder at the Vanities* was a first for Hollywood. Usually, white girls in blackface were pressed into service. The black chorus line dancers were recruited from the floor show at Frank Sebastian's Cotton Club in Culver City. One of them even got married during the production. The director Mitchell Leisen recalled, "We found out one of the girls was going to get married to a boy in the company, so we decided to have the wedding right on the set. We stopped shooting for a while one day; I gave the bride away and we went back to work."

In fact the groom was not a boy in the company, but the trumpeter Buck Clayton, who would later become famous as arranger for the Count Basie and Benny Goodman orchestras, among others. The wedding was commented on in the black press, and the studio issued a picture of the bride, groom, and the minister Reverend Napoleon Greggs. Ellington is standing behind them with Clayton's trumpet at his lips.

The Ellington band had a more interesting role in *Belle of the Nineties*. Mae West's previous two films, *She Done Him Wrong* and *I'm No Angel*, were credited with saving Paramount from bankruptcy. The management had been seriously contemplating selling the studio to M-G-M. Both films broke attendance and box office records everywhere. With those successes, West was able to renegotiate her $5,000-a-week contract with Paramount. Beginning with *Belle of the Nineties*, she was to receive $300,000 per picture, plus another $100,000 for the screenplay. In addition, she had the final say on casting. Coslow and Johnson had alerted her to Ellington's availability, and she told the studio she wanted him signed.

The studio brass initially balked. They had their own orchestra under contract that played for all their pictures, and they argued that Ellington would cost too much. West reminded them that Ellington was a recording star, and would be "just right for our New Orleans setting." The studio offered a compromise: If West insisted on using black musicians in the film, they'd hire black extras and have them sit with instruments and "fake" the music, which the studio orchestra would prerecord.

West would have none of it. "I told them . . . you can't take white people and have them play black music." She held her ground and finally Emmanuel Cohen, the studio head, intervened. Ellington was signed, and the band accompanied West on the Johnson-Coslow songs "My Old Flame," "Troubled Waters," "When a St. Louis Woman Comes to Town," "Hesitation Blues," and the W. C. Handy classic, "Memphis Blues." Duke subsequently named West his favorite actress.

West exempted herself from her belief that black music should be performed only by blacks. The songs she sings in this film and her belting delivery owe everything to the black blues, ragtime, and jazz idiom that she had drawn on since she was an adolescent and shouted the dialect song "Movin' Day" in her first Brooklyn amateur contest.

The band was featured in only one scene in *Murder at the Vanities*. In *Belle of the Nineties*, the band is integrated into the plot more than most other black bands were at that time—or indeed, since. During the 1930s, orchestras in feature films, unless placed on a ballroom or theater stage (*Check and Double Check*; *Murder at the Vanities*), would be kept practically invisible, especially if employed for the backing of featured soloists. The Ellington orchestra did indeed have the customary pit band role in one part of *Belle*. But in the "Memphis Blues" sequence, West had the cameras pick out several of the band's instrumentalists to be shown in medium close-up shots during her own stage performance, as they commented on her lyrics. Remember: This was 1934, and images of black soloists mixed in with a white actress's performance were unheard of at that time.

West also used the Ellington musicians in a scene at the bar in a gambling casino. As she sings "Hesitation Blues" and "My Old Flame," there are several fairly extended shots of her accompanists, not seated stiffly in an orchestra pit, but loosely grouped around the piano. Barney Bigard sits atop the instrument, with his legs dangling from the side. Further, in this intimate setting, the band members are "faking" to their own music, not an anonymous studio orchestra. The lyrics to "Hesitation Blues" were in part by Ellington's old collaborator on *Chocolate Kiddies*, Jo Trent, who was now a staff lyricist at Paramount.

Ellington is quoted as saying that if there was one song he wished he had written it would be "My Old Flame." When Mae West sang it in the film, sensitively backed by the Ellington orchestra, it was the first time she had ever sung a torch song in a film. Ellington recorded the work again with Ivie Anderson on May 9 for RCA Victor, in a different arrangement that underscored her talent.

"We had [a] good time on the set of *Murder at the Vanities*" said Sonny Greer. "But on *Belle of the Nineties* we had a ball. That Mae was something else," he recalled:

> Every morning she'd come on the set and say "Good morning Duke, good morning boys" and we'd say "Good morning Miss West," then

she'd look over at Carney and say "Good morning Harry." He'd look straight ahead and say "Good morning Miss West." When we finished the picture she had a party for us at her house, and gave us a tour. Damned if there wasn't a mirror on the ceiling of her bedroom! She saw me looking at it and said, "Sonny, sometimes a girl wants a view of the performance." I like to cracked up. That Mae, she was somethin' else!

Before leaving the Paramount lot, the band made an unbilled appearance in another film, *Many Happy Returns*. This time, the request for the band was made by a young man on the threshold of fame, the harmonica virtuoso Larry Adler. He was to appear in the film playing Ellington's "Sophisticated Lady," which was a fixture in his programs.

During the preproduction meeting with the director, Norman Z. McLeod, Adler was informed that he would be accompanied by Guy Lombardo and his orchestra. Filled with the hubris of youth, Adler flatly refused. The matter was referred to William LeBaron, the producer. During their meeting, Adler insisted he wanted Ellington (who he knew was on the Paramount lot) to accompany him in the film.

The producer asked Adler how much he was getting paid for the film. Adler said, "Three hundred dollars." LeBaron informed him that for the production to get Ellington, it would cost more than twenty-five times that amount! The producer also informed Adler that he could be sued for breach of contract and blacklisted by the studios. Later that evening, however, Adler received a phone call from the producer. When Adler picked up the receiver and said "Hello," the producer said, "Well, you little prick, we got Ellington for you."

On March 21, 1934, Adler and the Ellington reed section, along with trumpeter Artie Whetsol and trombonist Juan Tizol, recorded "Sophisticated Lady." The arrangement is by Jimmy Mundy, who in the future would do arrangements for Benny Goodman, Harry James, Count Basie, Earl Hines, and several other bands. Mundy's arrangement is a simple one, mostly a chordal structure that could be played by any band that Adler would meet on tour. A discerning ear can pick out the Ellington saxophone section on the soundtrack. Ellington was paid $18,249 for all the work he did on the Paramount lot, whereas Guy

Lombardo received $35,000 for a single appearance in *Many Happy Returns*.

On March 16, 1934, after recording the soundtrack for "Memphis Blues" with Mae West, the band members put on their uniforms to play at the Academy Awards banquet held at Los Angeles' Ambassador Hotel. Will Rogers was the master of ceremonies.

On March 19, the band began a playing for a series of radio broadcasts once a week on NBC, in a program titled "Demitasse Revue."

The end of March found the group at the Orpheum Theater in Los Angeles for a week, then out to Culver City for a two-week engagement at Frank Sebastian's Cotton Club. San Francisco's Orpheum Theater was the musicians' next venue, where they headlined the show during the week of April 20, then back to Hollywood for two more days of recording the soundtrack for *Belle of the Nineties*.

The band worked on *Murder at the Vanities* and *Belle of the Nineties* in two segments, from February 26 to March 26, and then on May 7 and 8. On May 9, Mills had the band in the Victor studios, where it recorded Ivie Anderson singing "Troubled Waters" and "My Old Flame."

During part of the shooting of *Belle of the Nineties*, saxophonist Toby Hardwick was out of the band. "From the first week on, during the Mae West movie, Toby kept complaining he was very, very tired," Sonny Greer recounted. "He saw the studio doctor, and [the doctor] told Duke to give him some time off. Later on, Duke did the same thing for me."

Hardwick was replaced by Marshall Royal, lead alto saxophone player with the Les Hite orchestra. Royal was raised in Los Angeles. His mother was a pianist, and his father was a music teacher and bandleader. Royal's first instrument was the violin; then he played guitar before taking up the alto saxophone. From age thirteen on, he played with local bands, joining Curtis Mosby's Blues Blowers in 1929. Two years later, Royal joined Hite. Royal also played with the Ellington band during its run at the Orpheum Theater. He would later hold down similar chairs in the Lionel Hampton and Count Basie orchestras.

Four years earlier, during the filming of *Check and Double Check*, director Melville Brown wanted Ellington to add violins to the band for the ballroom scene. Royal, who doubled on violin, and two other violin-doubling reed players from the Curtis Mosby Blue Blowers, were hired to play the prerecording session. But the material ended up on the cutting room floor.

Leaving Los Angeles, Ellington and his men made their first trip through the Pacific Northwest. Hardwick rejoined them for these dates. The band had theater dates in Portland, Oregon; Seattle, Washington; and Tacoma, Washington; then the men gradually worked their way east via one-week theater engagements in Ogden, Utah; Denver, Colorado; Canton, Ohio; and Pittsburgh, Pennsylvania. The band arrived back home to work the Capitol Theater on Broadway, on June 29.

While the band was on the road, Mills was actively planning a second European tour. There were to be ten weeks of theater and dance dates in Great Britain, slated to begin the second week of September. But the British Labor Ministry objected to the planned dance dates, permitting only stage performances. Mills attempted to negotiate, but the ministry was adamant and the tour was canceled.

28

WHILE THE ELLINGTON band was in California in April and May 1934, Ellington's mother, Daisy, was diagnosed with cancer. Her physician, Thomas Amos, prescribed radiation therapy. She agreed, under the condition that the news be kept from her son. Nonetheless, Mildred Dixon told Duke of his mother's illness. In what would become a lifetime pattern for him, on hearing distressing news, he simply refused to believe it or do anything about it.

The band returned to New York in mid-June to begin a two-week run on Broadway, at the Capitol Theater. Shortly after the group's return, Daisy decided to move back to Washington. She had a distrust of hospitals and physicians, and felt she would be more comfortable with her siblings. Also, she didn't want to be a burden to her son.

Ellington spent a good deal of time and energy denying his mother's illness. During the band's next recording session, however, his unconscious broke through. On August 12, 1934, the band was in the Brunswick recording studios. The musicians recorded two Ellington compositions, "Solitude," and "Saddest Tale," plus Ellington's arrangement of "Sump'n 'bout Rhythm," a jaunty tune written six months earlier in collaboration with Mills. They also recorded "Moonglow," a Hudson-de Lange composition inspired by Ellington's "Lazy Rhapsody." "Solitude" had been recorded nine months earlier in Chicago. Along with "Mood Indigo," it would become one of Ellington's most enduring compositions. This version of "Solitude," paired with "Moonglow," was one of Ellington's most successful releases. It won a $2,500 prize from ASCAP as the year's best song.

"Saddest Tale," on the other hand, was the most revealing of Ellington's compositions recorded that day. The work, a slow blues composition, begins with a florid clarinet obbligato, reminiscent of the opening of George Gershwin's "Rhapsody in Blue." The brass section states the theme, at which point Ellington (for the only time on record) vocalizes in a sad monotone, punctuated by a snarling brass section:

The saddest tale told on land and sea,
Was the tale they told when they told the truth on me.

Mournful, poignant solos by a muted trombone, alto saxophone, muted trumpet, and bass clarinet follow. Muted brass again intones the theme. Ellington repeats the statement and the work ends quietly. Years later he said, "A sad man has to have a sad voice, and I figured I sang sad enough to fit the character."

The theme of sadness, along with death, showed up again in Ellington's next major work. Shortly after the recording session, Ellington was commissioned by Paramount Studios to write the music and appear, along with the band, in the motion picture *Symphony in Black*. This nine-minute film was directed by Fred Waller and produced by Adolph Zukor, comprising the same team responsible for making *Bundle of Blues* the previous year.

The film opens with Ellington portraying a young composer who is commissioned to write a major jazz work to be called *Symphony in Black*, with the subtitle "A Rhapsody of Negro Life." Shots of a letter commissioning Ellington to complete his symphonic work on "Negro Life," and a sign on the door of the Ellington studio, prepare the viewer for the first scene of the composer at work.

Ellington's character finishes composing the score, and the scene shifts to the theater, where the Duke Ellington Orchestra (increased to twenty-four by members of the Mills Blue Rhythm Band and extras) premieres the first part of the work, titled "The Laborers." Images of black men shoveling coal into blast furnaces and carrying bales of cotton on a river portray hard labor. Ellington wrote original music for this sequence, barely one minute in length.

The second part, "A Triangle," tells a brief story in three musical segments of a woman (portrayed by the nineteen-year-old jazz vocalist Billie Holiday) seeing her man dance with a rival in an upstairs living room ("Dance"). These segments are accompanied by the Ellington orchestra playing his 1932 composition "Ducky Wucky."

In "Jealousy," Holiday confronts the upstairs pair, played by the dancers "Snakehips" Tucker and Bessie Dudley, as they leave the building. In what could be a scene from her real life, Holiday is rudely rejected and thrown to the ground by the man. Ellington wrote original music for this section, which was also less than one minute in length.

Holiday expresses her grief in the song "Blues," a extended version of "Saddest Tale," which Ellington had recently recorded. In his version, he simply stated two lines. The extended version features a full lyric that allows Holiday's character to comment on her own plight.

"Hymn of Sorrow" is close to two minutes long. A church service with a child's coffin barely visible at the minister's feet is the focus of the scene. A muted, solo trumpet plays a doleful theme over accompanying saxophones and occasional chimes. In this composition, Ellington said, "[He] put into the Dirge all the misery, sorrow, and undertones of the conditions that went with . . . death."

This sequence was supposed to serve as the conclusion of the work. However, the film was rearranged in the editing process, making that sequence the next-to-last one. Rather than have the film end on a sad note, the producers substituted "Harlem Rhythm," a nightclub scene in which a white audience is viewing the writhing contortions of "Snakehips" Tucker as he might have danced at the Cotton Club. Snakehips's sinuous movements are reinforced by means of multiple exposures and intercutting the chorus line with the dance team, the "Three Rhythm Kings." For this sequence, Ellington recycled his composition "Merry-Go-Round."

In *Symphony in Black* as well as in *Black and Tan*, the plot is tightly linked with the Ellington score, artfully lighted and photographed. However, *Symphony in Black* achieves a closer integration of music and screenplay than *Black and Tan* mainly because there is a more or less continuous musical score and no dialogue.

Interviewed in the magazine *New Theater*, Ellington said his original version of *Symphony in Black* as a film was quite different from what finally appeared on the screen. He was bitter about it, and wanted the film to end with the "Hymn of Sorrow," saying "It was the high spot and should have come last."

Klaus Strattemann observed, "In terms of plot and music, only one film can possibly compared to *Symphony in Black, Yamecraw*." This was a 1930 Vitaphone short based on a symphonic tone poem by Ellington's mentor, James P. Johnson. Johnson attempted to sketch the dilemma of a black man torn between life in the country and in the city, reenacting the feelings of blacks about their difficult journeys from their rural homes to new lives in the inner cities. However, *Yamekraw* is not a "black band short." No black musicians appear onscreen, and the soundtrack was played by a white studio orchestra, led by Hugo Mariani, a staff conductor for the National Broadcasting Company.

Ellington recorded the soundtrack for *Symphony in Black* in December 1934, and then went back on tour. During the previous month, he had been in Washington on two separate occasions for the-ater engagements. He and the band headlined the Fox Theater's show the week of November 9, and the Howard Theater's the week of November 30, allowing him to spend time with his mother and family.

During the second engagement, Billy Taylor joined the band on tuba. Taylor was born and raised in Washington, D.C., and began play-ing the instrument when he was fifteen. He moved to New York in 1924 and he put in tours of duty with Elmer Snowden, Charlie Johnson, McKinney's Cotton Pickers, Fats Waller, and Fletcher Henderson, having also learned the string bass along the way.

Taylor's entry into the band sparked a crisis. Mills—slowly sowing the seeds that would eventually destroy his relationship with Ellington—demanded that Wellman Braud take a salary cut from $100 to $80 a week to accommodate the new musician. When the bassist refused, Mills went over Ellington's head, putting Braud on two weeks' notice and cutting his salary anyway. "When I heard about it," Fred Guy recalled:

> I spoke to Sonny, Tricky, Toby, Harry and Artie. We were in the band before Mills signed Duke in '26. We told him if he didn't leave Braud alone and give him back his money, he had our notices too. He backed down that same day. Duke was mad when [he] heard about it, and they had words. He was spending a lot of time with his family that week, his mother wasn't all that well.

In early December, the band was back in New York for a week at the Apollo Theater. Trumpeter Freddie Jenkins had left the band and was being treated for tuberculosis. His replacement was a young man Ellington had saved from drowning when he was a teenager, Rex

Stewart. The twenty-seven-year-old Stewart brought a wealth of musical experience to the band.

Stewart's mother was a pianist and his father played violin. He began studying piano and violin himself, then switched to cornet. His first professional job was playing on the riverboats that cruised the Potomac. By the time he moved to New York permanently, Stewart was also proficient on the trombone and xylophone, and on tenor and soprano saxophones, in addition to the cornet.

His ability as a multi-instrumentalist got him work in the relief bands at Smalls's Paradise and O'Connor's Cafe. He had a brief spell with Leon Abbey, and with the Jimmy Cooper Revue, prior to joining Elmer Snowden in 1925. The following year, Stewart joined Fletcher Henderson. Over the next seven years, Stewart put in five tours of duty with Henderson, interspersed with work in McKinney's Cotton Pickers on two occasions, plus a short stint with Henderson's brother, Horace. Stewart's experience with three major black bands of the era ultimately led him to form his own, which played at the Empire Ballroom from June 1933 to the fall of 1934.

"I think I hired Rex right after Labor Day," Luis Russell recalled. "He had a pretty good band, but there was no work. He was with us a few months when Duke called me and asked about him. Jenkins was in the hospital and [Duke] needed a trumpet player. At first Rex didn't want to take the job. He didn't think he was up to it. I told him if he didn't, I was going to put him on two weeks' notice."

"Duke wanted Louis Bacon to take the chair," Harry Carney said. "At one time or another he'd been in it. Louis told him he didn't like all that traveling."

Another loss was bassist Wellman Braud, who was replaced by Hayes Alvis. Alvis was born in Chicago in 1907; his first instrument was the drums, which he played in the Chicago Defender Boys Band. He also learned the tuba, and by the time he was twenty, he was touring with pianist Jelly Roll Morton, which he did for two years. When he settled in Chicago after the tour, he began playing the string bass, and from 1928 to 1930 he played with Earl Hines.

Bandleader Jimmy Noone brought Alvis to New York in 1931. When the gig was over, Noone returned to Chicago. Alvis then joined the newly formed Mills Blue Rhythm Band, and remained with it until he joined Ellington. He was one of the musicians from the band who appeared onscreen in *Symphony in Black.*

"Braud was tired of the road and tired of Mills. He'd saved his money and wanted to open a small nightclub," Carney said. "The band was going through a lot of changes. We had picked up Charlie Allen in Chicago because Artie Whetsol got sick again."

Charles Allen was born in Mississippi and attended Wendell Philips High School, where he learned trombone. His first job was with Hugh Swift's band. After switching to trumpet, he found work with Dave Peyton and Doc Cooke. He was with Earl Hines when Ellington hired him.

The week of December 28 found the Ellington band at its old stomping grounds, Chicago's Oriental Theater. While there, the band made a trip to the Columbia recording studios on January 9, 1935. The musicians recorded "Admiration"; "Farewell Blues"; "Let's Have a Jubilee," with a vocal by Ivie Anderson; and "Porto Rican Chaos," a Latin-tinged original by Juan Tizol. This was one of many charts of this genre he would contribute to the band.

Following two days at the Regal Theater on Chicago's South Side, the band had theater dates in Ohio and Missouri before returning to the Regal for a week. The musicians then worked their way back east, and were in Brunswick's New York studios on March 5. For this session only, a fifth saxophonist, Ben Webster, was added. He would join the band on a permanent basis five years later. Tizol's "Porto Rican Chaos" was redone as "Moonlight Fiesta," along with the old standard "Margie." Stewart made his recording debut at this session in a sextet with Ellington, Hodges, Carney, Taylor and Alvis. This group recorded "Tough Truckin'" and "Indigo Echoes." In all probability, they also completed the filming of *Symphony in Black* during this time.

The band left New York on March 13 for theater dates and one-night stands that would take it as far west as Cincinnati, Ohio, then as far south as Tuskegee and Montgomery, Alabama. Back in New York on April 30, the band recorded what would be another Ellington standard, "In a Sentimental Mood," plus "Showboat Shuffle." The group also re-recorded "Merry Go Round" and "Admiration Stomp."

Sonny Greer did not make the session: "I was beat man, I was beat. I just wanted to sleep all the time. Duke told me to take some time off and come back when I felt better. I took a week off and missed a recording session. Duke sent to Chicago for Avendorph to come and play for me."

Fred Avendorph was a Chicago musician; not much is known about him or how he came to Ellington's attention. "He was a pretty good drummer and kept good time," Cootie Williams observed. "But the cat Duke wanted for the gig was Manzie Johnson. He couldn't make it. He played with us a couple times at the Cotton Club, and had Sonny down pat. You couldn't tell the difference between the two. Manzie didn't want to go on the road with us either; his wife was sick." The time out appeared to help Greer, because he subsequently left New York with the band to play dances in Columbus, Ohio, and Louisville, Kentucky.

Meanwhile, Daisy Ellington's condition continued to deteriorate. By the second week in May, it had reached the point where the family overrode her objections and called Duke on the road. Ellington was contacted during the week of May 11, when the band was playing the Palace Theater in Youngstown, Ohio.

Surviving band members attest to the fact that it was at that time that Ellington was finally forced to confront the seriousness of his mother's illness. Greer told me that Ellington spent so much time on the backstage telephone that the manager of the theater offered him the use of the one in his private office.

Finally, Ellington convinced his mother to let one of her sisters bring her to Detroit, Michigan. The band was booked for a one-week engagement at the Eastwood Gardens, a suburban Detroit dance hall. He arranged for a private room on the train, and met them at the station when they arrived the morning of May 17. Daisy was to be treated at the Provident Hospital. On admission, she was already a dying woman. There was not much the hospital staff could do.

According to Greer, as soon as the band finished its last set at the dance hall, Ellington would take a quick bow and leave the stage. A waiting taxi would take him to the hospital. Most of his time was spent holding his mother's hand, and praying. Jonesy would bring him a change of clothes in the morning. He would leave in the evening, go to work, and the cycle would be repeated the next day.

But the end was near. "All the family was sent for . . . except me, who was left in New York," Mercer remembered. "When she looked around to see her family, she wanted to know where I was and why Pop hadn't sent for me. He called me immediately then, and I got there in time to talk with her. She looked up and saw me; two hours later she died."

May 27, 1935, was the saddest day of Ellington's life; his first and only true love had died. He asked Irving Mills for a loan of $5,000 to give his mother a lavish funeral. Surprisingly, Mills refused, another event that would contribute to his and Ellington's eventual breakup. Finally, Ellington's mother was buried in a bronze casket in Washington in the family plot. Ellington was left bereft and distraught.

Mercer observed:

> [T]he days after her death were the saddest and most morbid of his life . . . he just sat around the house and wept for days. Eventually his suffering was reduced to the time of the year she passed away. Then you could be sure he was drinking. He would be on a drunk for two or three weeks then come off it. . . . [E]ven this annual outbreak was gradually controlled until he got to the point where [he] hardly drank at all.

Ellington was literally paralyzed with grief. He felt a part of his life was over. He described his grieving poignantly: "Dangling out there somewhere in the wilderness of the unknown, with no desire for adventure, where things and creatures that I neither saw nor heard were moving around. . . . My ambition was dribbling away. Soon there would be nothing, I was not sure where I was. After my mother passed my sparkling parade was probably at an end."

The "sparkling parade" accurately reflected part of his relationship with her. Having his mother available to see, hear, and reap the fruits of his success was deeply gratifying for both of them. Writing about her death thirty-eight years later, Duke alluded to the fact that he was never quite the same after her death. Mercer said, "He never wore brown again, because he had been wearing it the day she died. He now detested the color green, he said it reminded him of cemeteries." For the rest of his life, Duke would remain a depressed man.

Daisy's illness and death notwithstanding, Mills kept the band working. Ellington remained in Detroit but the band went back on the road. The pianist Don Kirkpatrick (Johnny Hodges's brother-in-law) was summoned from New York to replace him. They had been informed of Daisy's death while in Pittsburgh, Pennsylvania. Ellington rejoined them at Shea's Theater in Toronto, Canada, the week of June 7. Nine days later, Sonny Greer, who had not shaken his fatigue, asked Ellington for a leave of absence and went back to New York.

"When we got to Chicago, man my ass was draggin', so Duke called Avendorph back. I didn't see the guys again until they got back to New York and we did a recording session," Greer said.

In late June, Ellington and his men boarded their private railroad cars for a series of one-night stands that took them through the Midwest and deep South. Before his mother's death, when he traveled by train, the door to Ellington's stateroom was always open, except when he was sleeping. But that changed. "After the job, he'd go in his room, shut the door and we wouldn't see him again until it was time to go to work," trombonist Lawrence Brown said.

Cootie Williams felt that, on many nights, Ellington was just going through the motions of leading the band. "He seemed to be in a world all [his] own." Fred Guy remembered hearing Ellington crying himself to sleep many nights in his compartment.

Ellington's love and fascination for the railroad proved to be a great help during these times, as he struggled to put his feelings about his mother's death in perspective. The train had always been his sanctuary. While isolated in his room, Ellington began to reconstitute himself psychologically. He wrote:

> I would sit and gaze into space, pat my foot, and say to myself, "Now Edward, you know she would not want you to disintegrate, to collapse into the past, into your loss, into lengthy negation or destruction. She did not spend all the first part of your life preparing you for this negative attitude." I believed I could hear the words, her words, and slowly but never completely I really did straighten up.

Seven weeks after his mother's death, Ellington began composing again. According to Lawrence Brown, they were in New Orleans, Louisiana. "As I walked by his stateroom, I noticed the door was open and he was writing music. It turned out to be 'Reminiscing in Tempo.'"

"The memory of things gone by is important to a jazz musician," Ellington once said. "I remember I once wrote a 64-bar piece about a memory of when I was a little boy in bed and heard a man whistling on the street outside, his footsteps echoing away. Things like that may be more important than technique."

The memories of his mother and his loss of her were foremost in Ellington's consciousness as the band worked their way north. The motion and rhythm of the train roaring through the countryside allowed him the privacy, solace, and comfort he needed to write the music and continue his grieving. "Every page of that particular manuscript was dotted with smears and unshapely marks caused by tears that had fallen," he said.

"Reminiscing in Tempo" was recorded in the Brunswick studios on the morning of September 12. The band was back at full strength, with Sonny Greer and Artie Whetsol in their old chairs. Drummer Fred Avendorph remained in Duke's employ as his social secretary, and also assisted Ned Williams with the publicity.

Throughout his life, Ellington was known for making revisions of his works up to the very last minute—more often than not, finally completing them in the recording studio. According to trumpeter Cootie Williams, this was one of the few recording dates that he could remember when everything was ready when he arrived at the studio: "The parts were on the [music] stands. Duke didn't change a thing. Once we got tuned, he gave the downbeat, and that was it."

"Reminiscing in Tempo" was an extended work, lasting about twelve minutes. Because of its length, it filled two entire 78-rpm discs, or four sides. It was a quiet, poignant piece of music, accurately reflecting Ellington's sadness as well as happy memories of his mother. The work, he said, "was written in a soliloquizing mood."

"Reminiscing in Tempo" was Ellington's most personal composition. Except for this piece, in all of Ellington's thousands of works, there was always solo space left for his musicians to improvise and expand on the piece. In this one, however, Ellington had written out the solo passages, and, according to Brown, he allowed no deviation from what was on the page.

Within the composition, Ellington expresses alternating feelings by use of the piano, saxophones, muted trumpet, and trombone. There is a wrenching plaintiveness in a muted trumpet solo on the second side. The third theme, the most elegant in the work, is followed by a brilliantly chorded piano solo. The plaintive trumpet tune comes back in statements by full orchestra and clarinet, ending the third side. The final side is a brilliantly written recapitulation of the previous three, with solo trumpet and orchestra carrying the themes. The melancholia of the earlier portions of the work gives way to an ending that, while not melancholy, is closer to sadness and resignation. "I had written my statement," Ellington said.

Mills was left with the formidable task of convincing Brunswick Recording Company to issue all four parts. Six weeks later it was sent out to the record stores; parts I and II were on one recording, and a month later, parts III and IV were issued.

Ellington's first thoughts after the recording were to wonder what the English would think about it. "I wrote it just for them," he said, "that's partly the idea of the title." Nonetheless, Spike Hughes, who gave "Creole Rhapsody" a glowing review, abhorred "Reminiscing in Tempo." He described the piece in *Melody Maker* as "A rambling monstrosity that is dull as it is pretentious and meaningless." He never reviewed another Ellington recording.

Other critics took the work more seriously. Leonard Hibbs scrutinized the work section by section, analyzing the music and demonstrating how its themes were stated, restated, and finally resolved. Hibbs's discussion made "Reminiscing in Tempo" the first work in the jazz idiom—"Rhapsody in Blue" notwithstanding—to receive such critical analysis. Hibbs concluded his review by saying, "Very briefly, I believe that Duke has allowed us to 'tune in' on his mind at work."

Horace Van Norman saw the work as highlighting Ellington's capacity to write music with challenging harmonies and rhythms: "There are . . . passages which are plainly more eloquent than anything he has written. ['Reminiscing in Tempo' is a] work of incalculable importance, and not to be judged on one or two hearings."

The singer Mel Torme, a public performer since he was seven, remembered hearing the work for the first time. "To me, that piece of music said it all," Torme recalled. "It was every back stair in Chicago, all the frustration and misery and beauty of the black friends I'd had in my youth. It was eight years before its time."

Five decades after its composition, Gunther Schuller put the debate to rest:

> For all its compositional craft and structural unity, it is the loveliness of its themes, its contemplative reminiscing mood, the sensuous, insinuating harmonies, the gentle warmth of its instrumental colors, that make "Reminiscing in Tempo" a memorable musical experience. . . . It is one of Ellington's greatest master strokes.
>
> It must be seen against the background of the gigantic forward strides that the composition, performance, and recording of this work represented, not only in jazz but in the history of black music in America.

Indeed, Schuller devoted ten pages and forty musical examples to a discussion and analysis of the work Ellington described in his autobiography as "a detailed account of my loneliness after losing my mother."

Perhaps the toughest critique came from an important and influential voice, the jazz critic John Hammond. Hammond dismissed "Reminiscing in Tempo," considering it "arty and pretentious." Hammond was a very important figure on the jazz scene as producer, general promoter, and cheerleader for bands and musicians that he loved. He had originally been supportive of Ellington, so his new tack was quite disturbing. In another article, titled "The Tragedy of Duke Ellington," Hammond accused Ellington of losing touch with his roots, saying, "[Ellington] had kept his eyes averted from the troubles of his people and mankind in general . . . his newer stuff bears superficial resemblance to Debussy and Delius without the particular vitality that used to pervade his work."

Hammond, a wealthy, young, white man with an ear for talent, also contributed heavily to liberal causes: the NAACP, National Urban League, and the trial of the "Scottsboro Boys," Southern black youths who were accused of raping a white woman. He often took it upon himself to suggest to bandleaders what musicians to hire or not to.

Many resented his meddling with their bands, as he did with Ellington when he criticized him for hiring Lawrence Brown.

"Part of the reason my father and John Hammond didn't get along," Mercer observed, "was an ego thing. Hammond was always trying to tell Pop what was best for the band, and what kind of music to write. You just didn't do that with him!"

"Reminiscing in Tempo" brought everything to a head. Writing in *Downbeat* that year, Hammond blamed the "complete sterility" of the work on Duke's hiring of "un-negroid musicians" and his failure to protest the racial abuses faced by him and his people. "The real trouble with Duke's music," Hammond asserted, "is the fact that he has purposely kept himself from any contact with the troubles of his people or mankind in general." Among other things, Hammond asserted that Ellington "keeps himself from thinking about such problems as those of the southern sharecroppers, the Scottsboro boys etc. . . . He has never shown any desire of aligning himself with forces that are seeking to remove the causes of these disgraceful conditions." As a result, Hammond maintained, Ellington's music "has become vapid and without the slightest semblance of guts."

In fact, since its debut at the Cotton Club, the Ellington orchestra had played at many charity events in Harlem, Brooklyn, and downtown New York, as well as in Ellington's hometown, the District of Columbia. Ellington responded to Hammond's criticism with a series of articles that derided jazz critics in general, and Hammond in particular. Mercer remembered hearing his father lash out one night at the "jazz critics," referring to them as "a group of motherfuckin' cocksuckers, none of whom ever played a goddamn instrument, yet because they were white, could sit in judgment on his music." In Ellington's eyes, Hammond was one of the worst offenders on this score. He had done much for musicians, but he also "perhaps stirred up the most resentment."

Ellington blamed Hammond's ardent political beliefs for warping his musical understanding, calling him "a propagandist and champion of 'lost causes'" who identified himself with "the interests of the minorities, the Negro people and the underdog. . . . The fever of battle," Ellington wrote, "has rendered his enthusiasm and prejudices a little bit unwieldy."

One senses an even deeper resentment on Ellington's part. He must have wondered what gave the grandson of the wealthy, white Vanderbilt and Sloane families the right to tell the grandson of two slaves that his music wasn't "black" enough.

I doubt if Ellington was aware of the full extent of the controversy his composition had inspired in the arena of jazz criticism. For him, the work was now put to the use for which it was unconsciously designed: helping him to continue working through his period of mourning. Given his response to his mother's death, I feel that a powerful argument could be made that the performances of the work served as the final phase of his mourning.

The composition, replete with both sad and happy memories of his mother, allowed Ellington to get back in touch with her and come to terms with the loss. His musicians validated this idea. Lawrence Brown observed, "After we recorded it, we went on tour and played [it] practically every night for maybe five or six weeks. Then we began to play it less and less. Finally we stopped playing it altogether."

Sonny Greer said, "We played that piece every night for a couple of weeks, sometimes twice. I never liked it, it was too slow and too long. Then after a while we didn't play it anymore."

"I liked playing it," Cootie Williams recounted. "We played it every night for a while, sometimes twice. One of the last times I remember playing it was in Chicago, New Years' eve, and Duke was crying. When I left the band in '41, the part was still in the book, but I don't think we'd played it in five years."

Willie Cook observed that, when he joined the band in 1951, one of the original trumpet parts was in his book. Over the next twenty years he was in and out of the band. Whenever he returned, there was always new music for him to learn. The part for "Reminiscing in Tempo" was still there. "I never played it, and I know the band never played it," he said, "but Duke never took it out of the book, either."

It appears that Ellington played the composition for approximately five or six months. The work then remained in the orchestral book as a memorial to his mother until Ellington died in 1974.

His mother's passing took a toll on Ellington's musical output; "Reminiscing in Tempo" was his only significant work of 1935, from a man who ordinarily turned out five or six noteworthy jazz compositions a year. Instead of Ellington's band's recording original compositions following his mother's death, the band and Ivie Anderson filled recording dates with a series of popular tunes of the day.

By February 1936, the pall had lifted. Ellington made the final revisions to a miniature concerto written for Cootie Williams. Reworking the main theme of "Blue Tune," he produced a masterpiece, not surprisingly a blues, titled "Echoes of Harlem."

29

FOLLOWING THE NEW Year's Eve dance at the Hotel Sherman in Chicago at the end of 1935, Ellington took some time off. He canceled some engagements in order to see heavyweight boxer Joe Louis in a prizefight. He had first met Louis a year before, at a Harlem party following Louis's knockout of Primo Carnera, and they had become good friends. Among other things, both shared a passion for ice cream. "Between the two of them they could put away a few quarts at one sitting," Harry Carney recalled. Ellington had never seen Louis in the ring professionally before.

Ellington and Cab Calloway had visited Louis's training camp in Lakewood, New Jersey, the previous September, when Louis was preparing for his forthcoming bout with Max Baer at Yankee Stadium. The two bandleaders were subsequently guests at Louis's wedding to Marva Trotter in an apartment at 381 Edgecombe Avenue on September 24, the afternoon of the fight.

"Marva was staying with Mr. and Mrs. Porter, who lived in the building. They were friends of Joe's," Mercer said. "That was where I first met him. Pop took me, Mildred, and my grandfather down to their apartment and introduced us." Ellington finally got to see his good friend fight on the night of January 18, 1936. He was also present in Chicago Stadium when Louis defeated Andy Retzlaff in a first-round knockout.

With Ellington's having seen his friend fight, he could get back to his own business, and the band played in Oklahoma, Missouri, and Kansas. The band was back in New York to work at Harlem's Apollo Theater during the week of February 8, and in the Brunswick studios on February 27 and 28. The Brunswick recordings made on those dates reveal that Ellington's depression had lifted in a burst of creativity.

As noted earlier, after Ellington wrote "Reminiscing in Tempo," he created "Echoes of Harlem," subtitled "Cootie's Concerto." After completing it, Ellington was inspired to write a series of other pieces to highlight individual members of the band. He wrote "Clarinet Lament" for Barney Bigard, "Yearning for Love" for Lawrence Brown, and "Trumpet in Spades," another version of "Tiger Rag," for Rex Stewart. The last two compositions were recorded on July 17, 1936, again for Brunswick. Twelve days later, the band cut more instrumentals, including "In a Jam," "Exposition Swing," and "Uptown Downbeat."

In addition, at the February and July Brunswick sessions, Ellington crafted a series of elegant arrangements for Ivie Anderson to sing. She is at her best on these recordings, singing such songs as "Isn't Love the Strangest Thing," "Love is Like a Cigarette," "Kissin' My Baby Goodnight," and "Oh Babe, Maybe Someday."

On June 19, Harlem was rocked by prizefighter Joe Louis's loss to Max Schmeling in the twelfth round of a bout at Yankee Stadium. "I was at that fight," Walter Johnson recalled. "Joe was a heavy favorite. When Schmeling knocked him out we couldn't believe it. Going back to Harlem that night was like going to a wake."

Ellington was at Yankee Stadium the night his friend was defeated. Inspired by the event, he composed "It Was a Sad Night in Harlem," which the band recorded on July 17. It is possible that Irving Mills suggested the idea to Ellington; Mills Music had successfully exploited headline events in the past (usually the deaths of famous celebrities) by quickly publishing topical songs.

Nonetheless, 1936 was a difficult year for the Ellington band. The economic depression following the stock market crash in 1929 had a negative effect on the entertainment business. The crash had nearly destroyed the record industry, which was faced with competition from William Paley's and David Sarnoff's radio networks, which allowed listeners to hear music for free. In addition, the arrival of sound film meant that thousands of musicians who had been playing in theaters for silent films were thrown out of work. Many cabarets, dependent on an affluent clientele, were forced to close. The Cotton Club was an exception, but it moved downtown on Broadway in 1936 following an explosive riot in Harlem.

In white America, desperate entrepreneurs felt that the American people no longer wanted jazz music, preferring dreamy, escapist music to help them forget their troubles. Such music was featured, for example, in the elegant, suave, sophisticated films starring Fred Astaire and Ginger Rogers. The repeal of prohibition in 1933 allowed clubs and dance halls to sell liquor legally once again, so that clubs catering to illegal drinking (and sinful jazz) were no longer as popular.

The generation that had come of age in 1936 wanted a different kind of music. They preferred relatively simple, strongly rhythmic music to which they could dance as well as listen. The Goodman band—ironically powered by the arrangements of three blacks, Fletcher Henderson, his brother Horace, and Jimmy Mundy—filled the bill, playing what white America called "swing." For whites, the swing era had arrived.

In 1932, Ellington had recorded "It Don't Mean a Thing (If It Ain't Got That Swing)," and the song carried the expression into people's everyday speech. The following year, Ellington said that his "and a few other orchestras have exploited a [jazz] style characterized by 'swing' which is Harlem for rhythm."

Some critics and musicians believe that swing had its beginnings in 1925, the day Louis Armstrong joined the Fletcher Henderson orchestra. Out from the shadow of his mentor, King Oliver, Armstrong was now his own person.

"He was only with us a short time, but he completely changed the character of the band," saxophonist Coleman Hawkins observed. "If you listen to our recordings before he joined the band, and the ones we made after he left, you can tell the difference. He had an impact on all of us. He taught us how to swing. You can see it in the way Redman's and Smack's [Henderson] arrangements changed."

John Hasse wrote, "Louis Armstrong's rhythmic innovations loosened up the beat of jazz, provided a greater variety of rhythms, and made the momentum more flowing . . . the rhythm of jazz was transformed . . . musicians learned to elasticize the beat."

Frank Galbreath played in the Armstrong band in the 1930s. He said:

> When I joined the band, we went right on the road and did fourteen one-night stands in a row. When we got to the Greystone Ballroom in Detroit, we were running late and had to change clothes

in the bus to get started on time. We were beat, really beat. Louis stomped off "Savoy Blues," [and] by the time we got to the last chorus, the band was roaring and he was blowing, pulling us right along with him, as tired as we were, and the place jumped all night. Nobody could swing like he did.

The Armstrong legacy could be heard wherever black bands were playing. In addition to Armstrong's own band, the orchestras of Chick Webb, Benny Carter, Willie Bryant, Teddy Hill, Don Redman, Cab Calloway, and Charlie Johnson in Harlem played with a rhythmic, swinging beat. In Chicago, Earl Hines's orchestra did the same thing at the Grand Terrace nightclub, as did the Bennie Moten—later to become the Count Basie—orchestra, in Kansas City, Missouri. The Moten/Basie orchestra was not the only band in the region playing in that style. The Alphonso Trent orchestra in Texas could hold their own with many better-known groups.

All in all, however, there was one black band that could hold its own with the successful white bands in securing the same kind of steady employment. In the spring of 1934, the Cotton Club booked a black band that had been broadcasting out of the Club Harlem in Buffalo, New York: The Jimmie Lunceford orchestra came to the city and took the town by storm. Dubbed "The Harlem Express," the Lunceford orchestra was noted less for its soloists than for its ensemble work, particularly its distinctive two-beat swing played at medium tempo. That and its practiced showmanship were widely imitated by other bands, but these other bands seldom achieved the polish and good humor of the Lunceford performances.

"They were a great show band that played with precision and sophistication," Frank Galbreath observed. "Their loping two-beat swing was ideal for white hotels and ballrooms; they played more white college proms than any black band of the '30s or '40s."

Meanwhile, Mills was still involved peripherally in the Cotton Club bookings. He was connected to Lunceford via his relationship with Tommy Rockwell, who was responsible for the booking. Mills arranged for Lunceford's band to have a recording date at Decca on September 4, 1934. Arranger Sy Oliver recalled:

As part of the deal, for the first session, we were to record three pieces by Duke and one of our own. Mills brought in sheet music of nine or ten of Duke's compositions and told us to take our pick. We were so eager to get on records, we'd have recorded the entire Mills catalogue! Willie [Smith] had just joined the band and wanted to arrange "Mood Indigo" and "Sophisticated Lady." Jimmie told him to go ahead, I did "Black & Tan Fantasy."

When Decca issued the recordings some months later, it was not the first time Ellington heard his compositions played by a black band other than his own. Spike Hughes had recorded "Misty Mornin'" in 1931, and the Mills Blue Rhythm Band subsequently recorded "Black & Tan Fantasy," "Drop Me Off at Harlem," "Cotton," and "Merry-Go-Round."

Lunceford had paid his debt to Mills at the first recording session, yet he chose to record three more Ellington compositions: "Solitude" on November 7, 1934, and "Rhapsody Jr." and "Bird of Paradise" on May 29, 1935, both arranged by Eddie Durham and Ed Wilcox, the Lunceford band's pianist. Interestingly enough, "Bird of Paradise" was never recorded by the Ellington orchestra.

The Ellington band, working steadily during these times, did an engagement at Loew's State Theater on Broadway in the week of July 10, 1936, and then went on the road as far north as Montreal, Canada, and as far west as Cincinnati, Ohio.

The recording of "Echoes of Harlem," backed by "Clarinet Lament," provided Ellington with his first instrumental hit recording since "Mood Indigo" had been issued in early 1931. Ivie Anderson's rendition of Ellington's "Oh Babe, Maybe Someday" landed a top spot in *Variety*'s May "Music Survey." As Stratemann observed, "That was no small achievement in view of the fact that most vocal hit records of the day were songs popularized in Hollywood films."

Ellington and the band returned to New York for a week at the Apollo Theater in Harlem, followed by a week at the Royale Theater in Baltimore, and then to his hometown for an engagement at Washington, D.C's, Howard Theater the week of October 2. Leaving town in their railroad cars, they played at venues in West Virginia,

North Carolina, South Carolina, and Tennessee, finally ending up in Fort Worth, Texas, October 5.

Three days later, the band had a three-day engagement at the Texas State Fair in Dallas. For two nights the group played at a place called the "Streets of All Nations." On the second day, the location was opened to blacks, during a day of special events termed "Negro Day." (It was common in Southern states to set aside a day for blacks at state fairs.) The high point of "Negro Day" at the Texas State Fair was the coronation ceremony for several beauty queens, an event presided over by Ellington.

October 31 found the band in the Paseo Ballroom in Kansas City. There was a large crowd on hand, some to hear Ellington and the rest to say goodbye to the resident band, the Count Basie Orchestra, which was leaving town the next day to follow the Earl Hines Orchestra at Chicago's Grand Terrace, and after that to perform in New York City. "It was their last night in town," baritone saxophonist Harry Carney recalled. "They had the crowd on their side. We had to scuffle to keep up with them."

On November 10, Ellington began a week's run at Chez Maurice in Dallas, Texas. His was the first band ever, black or white, to play more than one night at this establishment. Engagements at the all-white University of Texas, and at Texas A&M, followed. The band worked its way out to the West Coast via engagements in New Mexico, Colorado, and Utah. On December 11 the band opened at the Paramount Theater in Los Angeles, its first performance at that site in three years.

Mills had been in Los Angeles since mid-November, and greeted the band members when they arrived in town. Ellington's contract with the American Recording Company (ARC), the parent company of the Brunswick-Vocalion-Columbia labels, was to expire on December 31. Mills arranged for the band to record on the December 21, when Duke Ellington did a solo piano recording of four of his hit songs, "Mood Indigo," "Solitude," "Sophisticated Lady," and "In a Sentimental Mood." The full band recorded "Scattin' at the Cotton Club" and "Black Butterfly."

By this time, Artie Whetsol's illness had reached the point at which he was in and out of the band. Ellington decided to add a fourth trumpet to cover for him. Wallace Jones, Chick Webb's cousin, was in the trumpet section for the December 21 recording session. Like Webb, Jones was born in Baltimore, on November 16, 1906. Jones's first professional work was in his hometown with Ike Dixon's Harmony Birds, and by 1930 he was a member of Percy Glascoe's Kit Kat Orchestra. Webb summoned Jones to New York late that year to play in his orchestra. Jones was a member of Willie Bryant's orchestra when the call came from Ellington.

"He was the perfect cover for Whetsol," Frank Galbreath observed. "They both had the same kind of sound, you know. Had you heard him play the high D in the trumpet part in "Mood Indigo" you'd know what I mean."

Mills was on the West Coast partly to firm up a business deal. He was preparing to have Ellington and all the artists in his agency record for a company of his own, Master Records, Inc. The recordings would be done in both the Brunswick studios and Master Records's own New York studios, set to open in March.

Master Records's sold for seventy-five cents each, making it a premium-priced label; to serve the lower-end market, the company also planned to launch a budget, thirty-five-cent affiliate, Variety. Both labels were to go on the market on April 1, 1937. Mills had projected a starting catalogue of 150 to 200 recordings. To do this, he planned to tap all the artists in his agency, plus others contracted elsewhere. By December it was clear to him that many of his contractees were still awaiting the expiration of their existing contracts with other recording companies. Needing to meet his projected April release quota for Master Records, Mills began looking for new groups. He didn't have to look very far. Sitting in the Ellington orchestra were musicians he could record in small groups of six to nine. Ellington found the idea of the small groups appealing; it was a way to earn more money and keep his star soloists happy.

"We were at the Paramount Theater in L.A.," Harry Carney recalled. "Mills told us it was to be Rex's date, and brought into the studio besides him, me, Johnny, Lawrence Brown, Duke, and Billy Taylor."

On January 16, "Rex Stewart and His 52nd Street Stompers" recorded "Rexatious" and "Lazy Man's Shuffle." Three days later, "Barney Bigard and his Jazzopaters"—with Cootie Williams, Juan Tizol, Harry Carney, Ellington, Greer, and Taylor—recorded "Clouds in My Heart," "Frolic Sam," "Caravan," and "Stompy Jones." This was the beginning of a series of some 140 small-group recordings that band members made during Ellington's contract with Variety.

On December 23, the band returned for three weeks of performances at Frank Sebastian's Cotton Club in Culver City, California. While there, Ivie Anderson was tapped to sing "All God's Chillun Got Rhythm" in the Marx Brothers' M-G-M film *A Day at the Races*. In what was termed a modern version of the story of the Pied Piper of Hamelin, Anderson and a flute-playing Harpo Marx lead a crowd of blacks from shack to shack in the black quarters behind a racetrack and horse barns, singing and dancing. The crowd begins growing and also picking up tempo, continuously, as more and more stablehands emerge from their cabins to join in the frolic.

Both black and white newspapers wrote that the Ellington band was in the film. Greer, Carney, and Williams all said they were not. "A couple of us went out to the studio to give Ivie encouragement," the drummer noted. "That was about it."

Anderson's work at M-G-M concluded on January 25, 1937. She rejoined the band in Oakland, California, on January 30 for an engagement at the Hotel Oakland, where the band played "The President's Birthday Ball." The African-American newspaper the *Chicago Defender* proudly wrote, "Over 8,000 of the elite of white society from the bay cities packed into the elaborate ballroom, and many thousands more listened to the music broadcast from the band shell." One-night stands at Sweets Ballroom and the McFadden Ballroom followed on January 31 and February 1.

In early February 1937, the band members boarded their private railroad cars in San Jose, California, for a trip to the Pacific Northwest. A heavy rain and snowstorm in Northern California forced the train to stop in Dunsmuir. Several performance dates had to be canceled, but on February 9, the band was on stage at the Palomar Theater in Seattle, Washington, for four days. The musicians played a prom at the University of Oregon as they worked their way south to Los Angeles to appear in the film *The Hit Parade* produced by Republic Studios, a second-string filmmaker.

Republic was attempting to follow in the footsteps of Paramount's very successful *Big Broadcast* films. Paramount's first two productions had featured such prominent entertainers as the Mills Brothers, Cab Calloway with his orchestra, and Bing Crosby. Later, Paramount would employ George Burns and Gracie Allen, Bill Robinson, Ina Ray Hutton, and the Ray Noble orchestras, and the dance team of the Nicholas Brothers.

Republic, however, did not have the financial wherewithal to mount a production featuring entertainers of that caliber. But the recording studio was able to hire the orchestras of Eddie Duchin and Ellington, and the singers Phil Reagan and Frances Langford, who played the male and female leads.

As Stratemann has noted, the band was given top billing in most black newspapers, but in fact, its role in the film was secondary at best. The band appears very early in the film, seated on a stage. It also provides the musical entertainment in a party sequence, reminiscent of their appearance in *Check and Double Check*. Ellington's music serves as background to socialite chatter; the band is offscreen. Its soloists and singers are on view only briefly; however, they are given an introduction that sets them apart as a special attraction. On being told whose band is going to play at the party, a young woman in the film voices her approval succinctly, "Duke Ellington? Hot diggety!"

"I've Got to Be a Rugcutter," the first of the four numbers the band plays, was an original composition conceived by Ellington just for this film, and shows the band to good effect. Ivie Anderson sings the vocal backed by a trio of Harry Carney, Rex Stewart, and Hayes Alvis. (They repeated this performance on the band's first Master Records date in New York on March 5, 1937.)

The rest of Ellington's music in the early *Hit Parade* sequence is mainly relegated to the background, with one notable exception. Although the first instrumental part of "It Don't Mean a Thing (If It Ain't Got That Swing)" (the second Ellington number) is overshadowed by dialogue, when Ivie Anderson enters with her vocal, she is picked up by the camera and shown in an excellent shot leaning over Ellington's piano. She delivers the song's lyrics with the same clear enunciation that she did in her 1932 recording debut with the band.

Ellington's third number, "Along Came Pete," co-composed by Sam Stept and the lyricist Ned Washington, is a satiric ditty about one of the female characters in the film who would not have made it "if it wasn't for Pete." Ellington's final number in the sequence is the well-known "Sophisticated Lady."

Just before the closing title music, Ellington leads the band in a brief rendition of "Love Is Good for Anything That Ails You." There are brief close-ups, showing the two bass players—Hayes Alvis and Billy Taylor—along with clarinetist Barney Bigard and Ellington at the piano. Clearly, the studio could have made better use of Ellington's talents, but then no black band fared well at the hands of Hollywood producers during the swing era. It would be five years before Ellington would appear in another Hollywood film.

30

ELLINGTON RETURNED TO the Cotton Club on March 17, 1937. The club was now downtown at 200 West 48th Street and Broadway, one block south of the old Kentucky Club. The original club in Harlem had closed on February 16, 1936. The March 1935 Harlem riot had caused a serious dropoff in business. White patrons were naturally less inclined to visit Harlem after the incident.

The Cotton Club Parade, Second Edition followed a very successful Bill Robinson-Cab Calloway production that had opened in the fall of 1936. The current show had a huge cast, featuring singers Ethel Waters and George Dewey Washington. Ellington and Waters got top billing, followed by the famous acrobatic tap dancers, the Nicholas Brothers. Waters stopped the show with her rendition of "Where Is the Sun" and the double-entendred "Give It Back to Him." Bessie Dudley once again danced to "Rockin' in Rhythm," the exotic dancer Kaolah undulated to "Black & Tan Fantasy," and the Nicholas Brothers, Mae Diggs, and the chorus all danced to "Peckin'."

The Cotton Club engagement was a triumphal return to Broadway for Ellington and the orchestra. Ellington received such rave notices from the critics that Mills had them reprinted in a full-page ad in *Variety*, headlined: "Broadway is ROCKIN' IN RHYTHM to the Musical Magic of DUKE ELLINGTON and His Famous Orchestra."

The show was visually memorable, as Rex Stewart remembered:

> The governor, as Duke was called by the guys in the band, had outdone himself in outfitting the band for this one. When we appeared on stage, the audience gasped and applauded. We wore white mess jackets, boiled tuxedo shirts with wing collars, white bow ties above crimson trousers and crimson shoes. . . . And of course the Duke personified elegance and contrasts in his somber midnight tails.

Besides its appearance on Broadway, the band was on the air twice a week via the Mutual Radio network and radio station WOR. Needless to say, the recordings also continued unabated. On March 5, 1937, the band had its first session for Master Records. Ellington was now in the tenth year of his association with the Cotton Club. During this session, he rerecorded two of the numbers he had played at his debut in 1927, "The New Birmingham Breakdown" and "The New East St. Louis Toodle-Oo." "Scattin' at the Kit Kat" and "I've Got To Be a Rug Cutter" from the film *Hit Parade* filled out the rest of the recording date.

The night of April 10, there was a slight commotion in the club when the management escorted a tall, elegant, imperious man, with a shock of white hair, to a table at the head of the stage. Leopold Stokowski, conductor of the Philadelphia Orchestra, was in town to give a concert at Carnegie Hall. During intermission, he invited Ellington to his table, they shared a drink, and discussed his music. As he was leaving, Stokowski gave Ellington two box seat tickets to hear his orchestra the following night. The incident was widely reported in the black press. According to Freddie Guy, after the maestro left, one of the busboys asked the waitstaff who the distinguished guest was. He was informed, "That's the white man's Duke Ellington."

On April 15, three months before *A Day at the Races* was scheduled to be released, Mills brought Ivie Anderson into the studio after her success on the recording, "Oh Babe, Maybe Someday." She sang Ellington's arrangements of "There's a Love in My Life," "It's Swell of You," and "You Can't Run Away from Love Tonight." According to Sonny Greer, Mills had been after Ellington for quite some time to do an arrangement of "All God's Chillun Got Rhythm." (The version Anderson sang in the film had been produced by M-G-M Studios.) "Duke started on it several times, but something was always getting in the way." On June 8, the band finally recorded the work, paired with "Alabamy Home."

Juan Tizol, who had been contributing arrangements to the band since his arrival in 1930, hit the jackpot on the recording date of May 14. His composition "Caravan" was probably his greatest contribution to the Ellington book. Soloing flawlessly on his valve trombone, he was able to create an exotic Latin mood with his very personal tone. "What Tchaikovsky's 'Arab Dance from the Nutcracker Ballet' is to classical music," jazz critic Gunther Schuller wrote, "Tizol and Ellington's 'Caravan' is to jazz. It is tragic, in view of Ellington's lifelong ambition to write large extended works, that no one ever asked him to compose a substantial ballet like Tchaikovsky's ballets.

The work—backed by Tizol's other composition, the lyrical "Azure"—was, like "Mood Indigo," scored for trumpet, trombone, and clarinet in low register. Mills issued a sheet music version of "Caravan" that enjoyed a brisk sale when it appeared in the music stores. "Caravan" also won ASCAP's quarterly award.

The Cotton Club closed for the summer after the June 13, 1937, show, and the week of June 18 found the band onstage at the Apollo Theater. Later that month, as they had done in 1933, the band members appeared in a Paramount *Pictorial,* No. 889. In the 1933 *Pictorial,* Ellington had shared the musical segment with the Calloway and Mills Blue Rhythm bands. This time, he had the entire segment all to himself.

The film begins with a 78-rpm disc spinning on a turntable as the Ellington band plays "Oh Babe, Maybe Someday." The film then segues into a rehearsal fragment of "Daybreak Express," as the narrator proposes that we "look in on the noted band leader Duke Ellington as he prepares for a recording." The scene switches to a recording studio, with the group playing the same number. Ellington cuts the band off, admonishing, "this is an express train, not a freight train," and demanding to hear "that express train effect that whistles in the saxophones." After another run-through, he is content. "That's more like it," he says, and then, "This time from the top." The performance fades out under the narration.

With the rehearsal satisfactorily concluded, the film continues with a demonstration of the actual recording process, as Ellington starts "Oh Babe, Maybe Someday" again. During Johnny Hodges's saxophone solo, the announcer cuts in to further explain steps in record production. As the finished disc is seen spinning on the turntable, we hear the Ellington orchestra playing the song just prior to Anderson's entry into the vocal chorus. The image of Anderson standing in front of a microphone by Ellington's piano is at first superimposed on that of the spinning disc, until the latter disappears altogether. Although the clip is brief, it affords us a chance to watch Ivie Anderson in action.

The band was back on Broadway on July 1, 1937, three blocks away from the Cotton Club, on stage at the Loew's State Theater. *Variety* had accolades for Ivie Anderson's "Oh Babe, Maybe Someday." Then the band was back on the road for a series of theater dates and one-night stands through Pennsylvania, New Jersey, Ohio, North Carolina, Illinois, Iowa, and Wisconsin. Returning to New York, the group had a significant recording date on the September 20.

Six numbers were recorded: Tizol's "Jubilesta," Hodges's "Harmony in Harlem," and Ellington's "Chatterbox," "Dusk in the Desert," and the two-part "Diminuendo and Crescendo in Blue." "Diminuendo and Crescendo in Blue" was another ambitious creation. Like "Reminiscing in Tempo," it was an extended-form composition. While based on blues chords, it was, as Schuller observed, "a full-fledged *written* composition, with virtually no improvisation." Despite giving Ellington kudos for "risk taking," Schuller found the work flawed, and wrote that "both critics and audiences were confounded and reacted either apathetically or negatively." Not so for the man who would later become the dean of American composers, Aaron Copland, who praised the piece in a 1938 article on jazz recordings in general for *Musical America*.

During his stay at the Cotton Club, Ellington was introduced to a Harlem physician, Arthur C. Logan. A close, constant, and enduring relationship evolved that ended only at Logan's death in 1974. In the words of Logan's widow, Logan was "Edward's closest friend and his physician for thirty-seven years. They had a unique, incredible, unexplainable friendship."

Shortly after they met, Ellington consulted Logan, not about himself, but about his father. "J. E. was drinking a lot, not eating and losing weight," Fred Guy recalled. "Dr. Logan sent him to a sanitarium in the Catskills."

That appeared not to work, because the physician subsequently had the elder Ellington admitted to Columbia-Presbyterian Hospital in mid-July 1937, when it was discovered that he was seriously ill with pleurisy. Ellington was on the road, but kept in constant touch with Logan. "He'd call him almost every day," Guy observed. "When we got back to New York, Duke confided in me, he didn't think his father would ever come out of the hospital alive." Ellington wrote "Reminiscing in Tempo" in *response* to his mother's death. One wonders if "Diminuendo and Crescendo in Blue" was written in *anticipation* of his father's death.

Duke Ellington had gone on the road after his engagement at the Apollo Theater, the week of September 24. Theater dates and one-night stands in Washington D.C., Massachusetts, and Ohio followed. When the band got to the Greystone Ballroom in Detroit on October 25, "there was a telegram from Dr. Logan telling Duke to get back to New York as soon as he could," Greer said. "J. E. didn't have much longer to live."

Ellington was at his father's bedside when he died on Thursday, October 28, 1937. The band played the Detroit engagement without him, and returned to New York the next day. There was a funeral service on October 30. "Everybody was there," Mercer recalled. "Stark, Mills, the band, Harlem musicians, waiters and dancers from the Cotton Club, as well as most of the entertainers who were in town."

Ellington, Mercer, and Ruth accompanied the body to Washington, D.C. On November 2, J. E. was laid to rest at the Harmony Cemetery, next to his wife. (The cemetery was subsequently closed, and Ellington had the caskets transferred to Bronx, New York, where they were reinterred at the Woodlawn Cemetery.)

"Pop wasn't as upset, like he was when my grandmother died," Mercer remembered. "He cried a bit at the funeral parlor and the gravesite, and that was it. I know he was very worried about money." Ellington had accrued sizable medical bills; his father had been in the hospital for three months, and he was still paying off some of the expenses of his mother's death and funeral. He took a personal loan from Mills (secured by his song royalties) to keep the band going. The three railroad cars—though necessary—were also expensive. If the band played in one town for a week, the cars just sat on a siding.

"One day we were on the train going somewhere, and Lawrence Brown was complaining about all the one-night stands," Sonny Greer recalled. "Duke pointed at the ceiling and said, 'As long as this car is rolling, I'm not losing any money.'"

The band was on the road to Ohio the day after J. E.'s funeral. On November 3, it was at Memorial Hall in Columbus, Ohio. By the time the musicians arrived at the Orpheum Theater in Memphis, Tennessee, on December 2 for a five-day engagement, they had played fifteen one-night stands: three in Ohio, one in Kentucky, one in Georgia, two in Tennessee, one in North Carolina, five in Florida, one in New Orleans, and one in Birmingham, Alabama.

December 12 found them in Springfield, Illinois. Following engagements in Missouri and Iowa, they worked their way east and were back in New York the day after New Year's Day. As 1937 ended, Ellington was given numerous accolades on the occasion of the tenth anniversary of his initial run at the Cotton Club on December 4, 1927. Mills had full-page ads placed in *Variety* and *Billboard*, proclaiming "The DUKE is Still King," a claim he backed up with reprints of congratulatory letters from show-business personalities. *Life* magazine named Ellington "one of the Twenty Most Prominent Negroes in the United States."

Ellington's tenth anniversary coincided with the formation of the Negro Actors Guild. The bandleader Noble Sissle was named president; dancer Bill "Bojangles" Robinson, his deputy; and Lawrence Brown's wife, actress Fredi Washington, the guild's first executive secretary. Ellington was made an officer, mainly an honorary function with no specified duties.

"All of us felt we needed Duke in the organization," Fredi Washington recalled. "He was the most glamorous, elegant man in Harlem. Everyone in show business looked up to him."

31

IN LATE OCTOBER 1937, Mills's venture with the Master and Variety labels came to an end as a result of bad luck and poor management. A new recording company requires a substantial amount of upfront capital. And it also needs an aggressive sales force, in addition to well-known artists who would appeal to the retail and jukebox trades.

Mills was forced to depend on the sales organization of the American-Brunswick-Columbia combination for marketing. But they were having difficulty selling their own competing Brunswick and Vocalion recordings in a field already populated by RCA Victor and Decca. With the exception of the Raymond Scott band, Mills introduced no new bands with sufficient originality to appeal to record buyers. Of Mills's own artists, Ellington's band was the only one that had a following, but the Ellington band was so expensive to record, Mills was lucky to break even recording it.

When he was unable to find an outlet in Europe for the recordings, Mills finally abandoned the project in 1939. The Variety and Master labels were withdrawn from the market. From then on, all Variety recordings of the Ellington small units were issued on the Vocalion label in the United States. Mills had begun recording Cootie Williams's small groups on March 8, 1938, and Johnny Hodges's on May 20.

Both small-group leaders were encouraged to record their own original compositions—up to a point. As part of the quid pro quo, part of each session had to include numbers from either Mills's publishing house, or a cover of a previously recorded Ellington composition. Over time, Cootie would record everything from "Echoes of Harlem" to a stunning version of "Black Beauty." From the Mills catalogue, he recorded the inevitable "Digga Digga Do" through "Ain't Misbehavin'" in May 1941.

Hodges's first session consisted completely of numbers from the Mills catalogue: "Foolin' Myself," "A Sailboat in the Moonlight," "You'll Never Go to Heaven," and "Peckin'" from the Cotton Club show.

"Jeep's Blues," recorded a year later, was the first of many best sellers Ellington's small groups released.

Ellington was to headline the *Cotton Club Parade, Fourth Edition* opening on March 10, 1938. This edition of the show was the first to have a score entirely written by Ellington. Several lyricists were engaged to collaborate with him, the most prominent being Henry Nemo. The three-month engagement, including a nightly radio broadcast, was an excellent platform for Ellington to launch some hit songs that would increase his record sales. Mercer said, "Pop put in a lot of work for that show. He was hoping for a couple of hits that would bail him out financially."

Trumpeter Artie Whetsol was now out of the band permanently. Guy said, "Artie began to act strangely. The next thing we heard he was in the mental ward at the Bellevue Hospital. It later turned out he had a brain tumor." It was at this point that Harold "Shorty" Baker made the first of several appearances with the band. Baker was born in St. Louis, Missouri, and celebrated his twenty-fourth birthday around the time he first played with the band.

As a boy, Shorty's first instrument was the drums, but he switched to trumpet in the late 1920s at the urging of his older brother, Winfield, a trombonist who led a local band. By the 1930s, Baker was working on a Mississippi steamboat with Fate Marable's band. He played briefly with Erskine Tate's orchestra before coming to New York to join Don Redmond's orchestra in 1936. "With his phenomenal phrasing and tone control he was an immense asset," Ellington said.

"Steppin' into Swing Society," the first piece Baker recorded with Ellington, was also his solo and recording debut. In "Steppin'," one notices a change in the orchestra. Baker's trumpet seems to give the musicians a lift, and the ensemble work is played with an insouciant swagger. The grief and mourning one hears in "Diminuendo and Crescendo in Blue" and in "Reminiscing in Tempo" is replaced by a renewed energy. As Gunther Schuller wrote, "The struggle, torment and anguish . . . seemed to give way to a new clarity and economy, a new creative thrust."

On January 16, 1938, an event occurred that further strained Ellington's relation with his long-time manager, Irving Mills: Benny Goodman gave his famous Carnegie Hall concert. Ellington had told his manager a year earlier that he wanted to give a concert there, but Mills had scoffed at the idea. Ellington did not attend Goodman's concert, but allowed Johnny Hodges, Harry Carney, and Cootie Williams to participate in the show in a small band segment with Goodman.

The night of the Goodman concert, Ellington and Ivie Anderson were uptown at the Savoy Ballroom observing a battle of the bands between the Chick Webb orchestra, featuring Ella Fitzgerald, and the Count Basie orchestra, with Billie Holiday doing vocals. At some point during the evening, Ellington was persuaded to play the piano. The correspondent from *Downbeat* wrote that Ellington "sounded so good that the Basie band picked it up and swung right along with him." It was the "highlight of the evening."

The week of January 21, 1938, found the band at the Apollo Theater. The railroad cars then carried them to Toronto, Canada, for a prom at the University of Toronto. The group was back in the Brunswick studios on February 2, recording another Tizol composition, "Lost in Meditation." In addition, Hodges at his insouciant best was featured in "The Gal from Joe's." "Ridin' on a Blue Note" filled out the session.

On February 24, the band was back in the studios again. For this session, Ivie Anderson was featured in two of the songs that would be in the forthcoming Cotton Club show: "If You Were in My Place" and "Skrontch." "Skrontch" would be the *Cotton Club Parade*'s big dance finale. Ivie Anderson exhorted every one to learn this new dance, as they had learned "Peckin'" and "Truckin'." However, it never caught on.

The band then cut an instrumental work, an orchestral tour de force, the spectacular "Braggin' in Brass," that would be the featured number in the Cotton Club show. Like "Hot and Bothered," "Daybreak Express," and "Trumpet in Spades," Ellington used the chords of "Tiger Rag" as the basis for this composition. The work features the three trombones playing "hocket style." Basically, it is a polyphonic concept of performing, in which the theme is created out of single interlocking notes played one at a time by each instrument. In "Braggin' in Brass," played at breakneck speed, Tizol, Nanton, and Brown played individual eighth notes, in a descending pattern, with no break between them, to create a melody. As Schuller wrote, "One's initial reaction is, in fact, disbelief."

"Of all the pieces Duke wrote during those years, personally I found that one ['Braggin' in Brass'] the most interesting," Lawrence Brown recalled. "It was a true test of our musicianship; even Juan [Tizol], as good as he was, caught hell the first couple of times we rehearsed it."

The group also recorded "I Let a Song Go Out of My Heart," which was planned for the show but then dropped from the production at Mills's insistence. It was a stunning vehicle for Hodges, who said, "People picked up on it when we played it on the air, then next thing we knew we had a hit on our hands. Benny's [Goodman's] recording didn't hurt either." Many individuals believe that song, along with "Mood Indigo," was one of Ellington's best-selling records ever.

"You could hear it on every juke box in Harlem, as well as downtown," said Greer. It was the first time the band recorded a fadeout ending, which Glenn Miller would later copy in his hit recording, "In the Mood."

The Cotton Club show opened on March 10, 1938. "Swingtime in Honolulu," featuring the three Peters Sisters in their New York debut, had been substituted for "I Let a Song Go Out of My Heart." The one-legged dancer Peg Leg Bates performed "I'm Slappin' Seventh Avenue (with the Sole of My Shoe)." May Johnson, the singer and dancer, was featured in "A Lesson in C," and the band's featured spot was the showy "Braggin' in Brass." The band also played "Carnival in Caroline" and "If You Were in My Place." The Ellington band eventually recorded every song featured in the review.

The 1938 cast included "adagio dancers" Ainsy and Aland, the Four Step Brothers, the Chocolateers, Ada Ward, and Bill Maples. Ellington was reunited with his former teacher, Will Vodery, whose singing group, the "Jubileers," was also a part of the show. Despite the huge number of performers, the Cotton Club was able to turn a profit. *Billboard* reported that the club "proved the surprise of the season, averaging $30,000 to $35,000 per week, with expenses of $20,000."

On April 11, Ellington completed his recording of the Cotton Club score by putting to wax "Swingtime in Honolulu," "I'm Slappin' Seventh Avenue (with the Sole of My Shoe)," and "Dinah's in a Jam."

While at the club, Ellington found time to play at a number of outside events, all for charity. At that time, Fredi Washington's sister,

Isabel, was married to Adam Clayton Powell, Jr., the pastor of the Abyssinian Baptist Church, the largest in Harlem. When the church sponsored a benefit for a local home for the aged, Fredi agreed to be mistress of ceremonies and recruited the Nicholas Brothers and Ellington to headline the show on April 10, 1938. Ellington played piano versions of "Sophisticated Lady," "Azure," and "If You Were in My Place." The Nicholas Brothers danced, and a number of lesser-known performers presented a program of gospel songs, spirituals, and jazz.

On May 8, along with a galaxy of black performers, the band played at the Brooklyn Academy of Music at a benefit for the Urban League. Three days later, the band was at Madison Square Garden, playing for the Greater New York Fund. On May 19, Ellington and the band participated in the "Carnival of Swing" on Randalls Island. The event—organized by the disc jockey Martin Block of radio station WNEW—was to be a benefit for the unemployed musicians of New York's Local 802. The audience of 25,000 was there to hear more than twenty orchestras. "We came on late," drummer Sonny Greer recalled. "We played 'Diminuendo and Crescendo in Blue' and tore up the place. We had to play a couple of encores before they'd let us get off the stage."

Around this time, showgirl Beatrice (Evie) Ellis entered Ellington's life. They met while she was working at the Cotton Club. "She was gorgeous, absolutely gorgeous," Greer recalled. "She wasn't a singer or dancer. Her job was just to stand around and look beautiful. We used to call them 'showgirls.' Duke had his eye on her from the first time he saw her. One night I saw them leave in a cab together, and that was the end of it for poor Mildred."

Ellington moved into Evie's apartment on St. Nicholas Place, and never went back to 381 St. Nicholas Avenue, once again leaving behind everything, including his clothes. "After he and Mil had come to a parting of the ways," Mercer recalled, "we realized that if we didn't change our residence he would never come back to live with us and visit us, because he didn't want to come back and face Mil. So we left the apartment and moved."

Not surprisingly, the relationship between Duke and Evie was a stormy one. From the beginning, she pressed him to divorce Edna and marry her. His response was always the same: If he did, Edna would get a sizable portion of his assets. Evie should be happy with what they had together.

For quite some time, Ellington had been troubled by a hernia located in his lower abdomen. Dr. Logan had been suggesting off and on that Ellington have it repaired. The situation had become chronic, and Ellington was in a good deal of discomfort. The physician had arranged for surgery on more than one occasion, only to have his patient overrule him. Ellington's current excuse was that he had tickets for the second Louis-Schmeling fight, and had promised his friend he would be there. Louis won the fight by a knockout in the first round.

"Duke got free tickets for Evie, Fred Guy, me, and our wives," Greer stated:

> The fight didn't last more than a minute. The white cat seated in front of us was really salty with his date when it was all over. As soon as the bell rang for the first round, everybody stood up. She dropped her pocketbook and everything in it spilled out on the ground. By the time she got everything picked up the fight was over. She didn't see any of it! I know those tickets must have cost him fifty dollars apiece!

Fifty dollars was a great deal of money back then, more than many people's weekly salaries.

After the fight, Ellington had no excuses left for avoiding surgery. He entered New York's Wickersham Hospital and was operated on on July 1, 1938. The surgery went well and he was discharged on July 15. He recovered in time to be master of ceremonies for the annual benefit for the Jenkins Orphanage held at Smalls's Paradise. The Charleston, South Carolina, institution had a very good music school and would provide many top-notch musicians for Harlem bands. Jabbo Smith, who had recorded with Ellington in 1927, was a prominent alumnus, as was Cat Anderson, who would join the band several years later.

The band was back in the recording studio on August 4 and 9. Bass player Hayes Alvis had left the group, and Ellington saw fit not to replace him.

The engagement at Pittsburgh's Stanley Theater during the week of December 2, 1938, was the fourth time Ellington had worked at that venue, and, more importantly, the most significant. It was there that he met twenty-three-year-old Billy Strayhorn, a local musician. The young man had come backstage and played Ellington songs that he had written. The older man was completely taken by what he heard, and told him, "Why, young man, I'm going to bring you to New York, and you will be my lyric writer."

Meanwhile, Ellington's music continued to be championed by other musicians. Paul Whiteman had played Ellington's "Mood Indigo" before an audience of 18,000 at Lewisohn Stadium five years earlier. Now, he was planning another concert to be titled "Experiment in Modern Music" at Carnegie Hall on Christmas Eve. Among those billed to perform, as guests with the Whiteman orchestra, were Artie Shaw and Raymond Scott, both leading small groups; pianists Rosa Linder and Frank Signorelli; and Louis Armstrong and the Lynn Murray singers.

Whiteman commissioned six composers to contribute to a forty-minute musical anthology, which he titled "Those Bells." The prologue was Bert Shefter's "The Farmer Leaves the Hay" (the title subject was represented by church bells). The second part was Ellington's "Blue Belles of Harlem," and works by ragtime banjo player Fred Van Epps, classical composer Morton Gould, Walter Gross, and ragtime pianist Roy Bargy filled out the rest of the suite. Ellington would subsequently rearrange his composition and make it a permanent part of the band's repertoire in 1943.

Four nights after the Whiteman concert, Ellington was at the Pennsylvania Athletic Club in Philadelphia. He was booked to play an open high-school fraternity dance. It would be the first time he and the Jimmie Lunceford orchestra would meet in a fabled "Battle of the Bands," before an audience of 3,000. "Everyone in Harlem was talking about Lunceford," Fred Guy remembered. "Lunceford could do this, Lunceford could do that. When we got off the train that afternoon, we knew what we had to do."

"We played the first set," Sy Oliver of the Lunceford band recalled:

and we figured we'd put them away early, playing some of our best stuff. I think we ended the set with "Blue Blazes." We were feeling pretty good until Sonny Greer walked by, pointed over his shoulder and said, "You all better start playing somethin', Duke's here." After that it was all downhill for us. They just took us apart. I'll never forget their first set, I think it was. "Jazz Potpourri," "Old King Dooji," and "Diminuendo and Crescendo in Blue."

Lunceford's band's musical loss was exacerbated by a financial one. According to Barney Bigard, later that night—when everyone one was back at the hotel—"Ivie Anderson won all their money in a crap game!"

ELLINGTON WELCOMED IN 1939 by playing a New Year's Eve dance at the Montreal Forum. Theater dates in Schenectady, New York; Newark, New Jersey; and Hartford, Connecticut, took up most of January. While the band was in Newark, Billy Strayhorn showed up and was immediately made a member of the Ellington entourage. Also joining the group for theater dates at the time was the singer Jean Eldridge. Born in Pittsburgh, she was a superb ballad singer. Ellington envisioned her as a supplement to Ivie Anderson.

"She was a fine singer," Frank Galbreath remembered. "No one could do Strayhorn's 'Something to Live For' or Duke's 'Prelude to a Kiss' the way she did." Contemporary reviews listed her specialties as "Don't You Know I Care," "I'm in the Mood for Love," "Stardust," and Cole Porter's "Get Out of Town." Anderson remained with the band for the rest of the year, until she left to join Teddy Wilson's superb, but short-lived, dance band.

At a studio session on March 21, 1939, Jean Eldridge recorded "Something to Live For." For that number only Ellington ceded the piano stool to Billy Strayhorn. During the rest of the session, Ellington was at the piano. The band also recorded Ellington's "Portrait of a Lion," a musical portrait of Ellington's mentor, the pianist Willie "The Lion" Smith, and "That Solid Old Man."

On February 10, the Ellington and Lunceford bands were both hired to play at Cornell University's junior prom. "This time they went on first," Lunceford's arranger Sy Oliver recalled. "When they finished, we threw up our hands. Jimmie was not too happy with us that night."

About this time there was a fire in Evie Ellis's apartment building, so Duke and Evie moved to an apartment at 935 St. Nicholas Avenue. Mercer said Mills had taught his father how to "handle situations of every kind." Ellington had learned the value of good public relations, and knew how to get into the press as well as stay out of it. He took out expensive ads in the trade press to protect himself from bad publicity, knowing the publications would refrain from saying anything bad about him for fear of losing a good client. Ellington also paid individuals to keep his name *out* of the press. In that way, the public never learned of his separation from his wife and all his other relationships with women.

Mills sailed to Europe on March 11. He had two tasks in mind: to try to sell the Master and Variety recordings for distribution in England and on the Continent (which failed), and to set up Ellington's forthcoming European tour. While Mills was out of the country, Ellington went down to Mills's office and asked to take a look at the books. He studied them for a while and left without saying a word. Something had caught his eye, and whatever it was caused him to make the decision to finally sever his relationship with his manager.

Ellington had been wanting to end the relationship with Mills for quite some time. He had several reasons for his unhappiness with Mills. His manager was becoming less and less available to him. On more than one occasion, Mills's widening business interests had caused him to give Ellington short shrift. Ellington had also been criticized by the black press because of his relationship with Mills, specifically because of the way Mills had cavalierly assumed coauthorship of Ellington compositions that he had no part in creating. Harlem's Reverend Adam Clayton Powell, railed from his pulpit that "Duke Ellington was a musical sharecropper." Ellington's use of white librettists caused the *Pittsburgh Courier* to observe, "No Negro writer has written the lyrics for any of Duke Ellington's melodies since he has been under the Mills banner. What's the matter, Duke? Home rules?"

Benny Carter—who was under Mills's management for a time— believed that "Mills got rich off of Ellington. He made a lot more money than he should have." Mercer felt that his father left because he had learned all he needed. "He could now handle his own affairs," Mercer believed. But Ellington defended Mills, even after the breakup: "He always preserved the dignity of my name," Ellington wrote, "and that's the most anybody can do for anybody."

On March 23, 1939, the band (minus Jean Eldridge and Billy Strayhorn) sailed for Europe aboard the liner *Champlain*. Hitler's incursion into countries bordering on Germany to regain territory lost after World War I had Europe on edge. The threat of war hung heavily in the air. In addition, Mills had already made trouble in England by raising a controversial issue. Before sailing from New York on March 11, the impresario had enlisted several British bandleaders and many well-known musicians to petition the British Musicians Union to lift its ban against American musicians and grant Ellington a limited vaudeville permit. The union—citing a similar ban against British musicians' performing on American soil—refused. Despite their great success in England six years earlier, Ellington and his band would not play there again on this tour.

The Ellington entourage arrived in Le Havre, France, on April 1, to a tumultuous welcome. Trumpeter Cootie Williams remembered, "I was standing at the rail next to [trombonist Toby] Hardwick. He pointed to a crowd just below us and said 'Look at that.' They were carrying signs written [in] French welcoming us to France."

"Hundreds of jitterbugs stomped and shouted at the dock," Rex Stewart said:

> There were a lot of people from all over France and Europe there to welcome us: members of the various "Hot Clubs"—both fans and musicians—who all greeted us with such absolute adoration and genuine joy that, for the first time in my life, I had the feeling of being accepted as an artist, a gentleman, and a member of the human race.

Drummer Sonny Greer recalled, "As we came down the gangplank people were reaching out just to touch us. I couldn't believe it."

Later that afternoon, the band held a press conference in Paris and then took the train to Brussels, Belgium, for a matinee and an evening concert at the Palais des Beaux Arts. Both Brussels events were sold out. The band went back to Paris the following day for two concerts at the Theatre National. This recently built bomb-proof auditorium, located underneath the Palais Chaillot, seated 2,800.

Ellington had no interest in vaudeville engagements. On this tour, he would only perform concerts. Performing with other acts—including comedians and dancers—diluted the impact of his music, he felt. He also wanted his music listened to seriously, just as classical performers expected. As he had done at in England and Paris six years earlier, he listed approximately thirty compositions on the program, from which he would draw about fifteen to twenty to make up the concert.*

When Ellington left New York for the Continent, it was still unclear whether he would be allowed to perform in Great Britain. Many of his British fans, not taking any chances, had bought tickets by mail, crossed the English Channel, and filled Paris's Theatre National to capacity on both nights.

The French critics praised the shows. "By what orchestral imagination does one arrive at strange, fluted sound effects, atmospheric with powerful humor!" *Le Figaro* enthused. Ellington and his musicians "wowed the Parisians," *Variety*'s man in Paris wrote.

"We were accorded an uproarious reception, and were forced to play numerous encores," Ellington recalled.

"I thought I would never see another reception like the one we got the first time were in Paris," Harry Carney said. "That one was quite something, yet when we went back in '39, it overwhelming. They just stood and cheered and cheered and cheered."

Fred Guy recalled that, when they were backstage before the first concert in Brussels, Tizol asked Ellington to schedule "Caravan" late in the concert:

> He told Duke he had the "jitters" and needed some time to get settled in. Wouldn't you know it, after we played our theme "East St. Louis Toodle-Oo," Duke called "Caravan." Juan did a hell of a job, and when he walked back to his seat he saluted Duke. Later when I asked Duke why he did that, he said he wanted Juan to play tense. It added something to the piece.

Leaving Paris on the morning of April 6, the band embarked on a concert tour. Over the next twenty-four days, the musicians played twenty-nine concerts. "It was just like our first trip, work, work, work," trombonist Lawrence Brown complained.

---

* The concert at Copenhagen on the April 13 was typical for the tour. The band played "East St. Louis Toodle-Oo," "I Let a Song Go Out of My Heart," "Black & Tan Fantasy," "Echoes of Harlem," "Merry-Go-Round," "Stompy Jones," "Stardust," "Mood Indigo," "Rockin' in Rhythm," "Trumpet in Spades," "Pyramid," "Caravan," "St. Louis Blues," and "Prelude in C Sharp Minor."

In the Netherlands, under the sponsorship of the Dutch magazine *De Jazzwereld*, there were concerts at the Hague, Utrecht, and Amsterdam. It was there that the impending world war was apparent to all. Barney Bigard observed, "As we were heading across Holland, we could see out of the train windows that they were putting machine gun posts in all the haystacks and the ditches. It was kind of scary, I can tell you."

The band was transported across Holland to Hamburg, Germany; from there, they were to take the ferry to Malmö, Sweden. Arriving at Hamburg, the musicians found that there was a six-hour wait for the ferry. "There were German soldiers all over the place," said Sonny Greer. "Not only that, we were hungry, and figured being in Hamburg, we'd find some good hamburger joints. When we tried to order one, they looked at us like we were crazy!"

Following their arrival in Sweden, Ellington and his band gave a series of concerts in fifteen cities throughout the country. For many citizens it was their first time hearing an American jazz group, to say nothing of the fact that it was the first time they had seen black people in person. Nonetheless, the Swedish jazz aficionado Benny Aasland said that Ellington was "really accepted throughout the whole country."

The band arrived in Stockholm the morning of April 16, having taken the night train from Jonkobing. "The platforms of the railway stations all along the route were filled with people hoping to get a glimpse of the Duke," reported one newspaper.

"There was a huge crowd at the station," recalled Sonny Greer, "[and] when we got off the train, they began applauding, and people began asking for our autographs." Reviewing the concert, a Stockholm newspaper observed, "The enthusiasm of Duke's listeners knew no bounds. Following the program they stamped, whistled, [and] shouted so lustily, the very walls and foundation of the Concert Hall quaked."

"We had brought along several changes of uniform," Greer said. "People who saw more than one or two concerts—and there were many of them—commented on how well-dressed we were."

A columnist observed, "Their refined appearance made a deep impression and was a decided contrast to those slovenly, indifferent, clowning orchestras, which belong in the cheap cabarets, and never have anything of musical quality to offer."

For Ellington himself, "the most exciting event of the trip" happened in Stockholm on April 29, when he celebrated his fortieth birthday: "I was awakened in my hotel by a sixteen-piece jazz band, which entered the suite of rooms serenading us with the Swedish equivalent of 'Happy Birthday.'" Ellington's room was inundated with flowers, which continued to arrive all day. The festivities continued during that evening's concert, when several local celebrities made speeches praising Ellington and his music. The audience spontaneously arose and sang "Happy Birthday" to him again, as did "ten little girls dressed in white," as Ellington recalled, who serenaded him in English. One of these girls was fifteen-year-old Alice Babs; thirty years later, she sang the soprano part in one of Ellington's sacred concerts. The concert was broadcast live by the Swedish state-owned radio station, another unusual honor. Genuinely moved by this outpouring of affection, Ellington wrote "Serenade to Sweden" to thank his fans in that country.

On May 2, 1939, the band members sailed from Goteborg, Sweden to Dover, England. The boat train took them to London. Since their last visit, the city had changed. "The war was coming on; you could feel it," Carney said. "It wasn't the same as it was the last time we were there."

Mills had arrived a week earlier, and continued his vain attempts to get the Musicians Union to rescind its ban on American musicians. However, nothing had changed. Mills then appealed to the Ministry of Labour, which affirmed the ban. When the band members arrived, Mills gave them the news. "We were all disappointed about not being able to play in England again," Sonny Greer recalled.

"I was looking forward to it," Carney said. "To this day, I have never met fans who knew so much about our music." With mixed feelings, the musicians boarded the *Ile de France* for the trip home.

As they were boarding, it was apparent that two musicians were missing. "Sonny [Greer] and Toby [Hardwick] were nowhere to be found, and we left the dock without them," Carney recalled. "When we got outside the channel, the packet boat came out with several of the passengers who had missed the boat. When we looked over the side, sure enough, there they were, the two of them, getting on board, drunk as lords, wearing bowler hats, and with a bottle of champagne in each hand."

"Toby and I ran into some musicians who remembered us being there in '33," Greer reminisced:

> They were upset about not being able to hear us, and took us to a pub. They insisted on buying us champagne and toasting Duke. As were were leaving, they gave us bottles to take with us. Our cab got caught in traffic and we missed the train. When we got to the pier at Southampton, we could see the boat sailing away, out in the channel. The guys at the customs took one look at us, laughed and directed us to the packet boat. It turned out we weren't the only cats who didn't get there on time.

The *Ile de France* was filled to capacity. Besides its usual quota of passengers, there were refugees fleeing Hitler, and American expatriates returning home. Aboard ship, the possibility of war was the major topic of conversation. "'Tricky Sam' [Nanton] was always reading books and magazines about everything," Lawrence Brown stated, "[and] he kept mentioning to anyone who'd listen that Hitler could not be trusted and there was going to be a war. It turned out he was right. It started at the end of that summer."

The entourage arrived in New York on May 10. "I was never so glad to see that old Statue of Liberty," said Barney Bigard. "Everyone was glad to be back home," Lawrence Brown observed. "There was a huge crowd of people on the pier to welcome us, including our wives, Evie, Ruth, Mercer, Strayhorn, and Joe Louis."

Looking back on the trip, the band members, to a man, all had very positive feelings about the trip. "At the stage door, especially in Sweden, we were mobbed," Sonny Greer recalled. "People would be standing there waving scraps of paper or autograph books for us to sign. Those Swedish chicks were unbelievably beautiful. I know a couple of them wanted more than just my autograph!"

"It's hard to explain what it was like for me," Guy said:

> I remember at one of the concerts in Paris, we were playing "Diminuendo and Crescendo in Blue." There was absolute silence in the hall as we were playing. It felt as though we and the audience were

as one. When the piece was over there was a moment's silence, then the place exploded, and I felt a tremendous sense of relief.

"For me," Harry Carney recalled:

> it was like it was in '33. I was so impressed that they knew so much about our music. During an intermission in Paris, two men came up to me. One spoke English and was translating for the other. They had a bet on. The man that spoke French was insisting I took the clarinet solo on "Rockin' in Rhythm," the other fellow thought it was Bigard. I had to set them straight.

"It was interesting," Cootie Williams said. "With the exception of Paris, the audiences were practically 100 percent white. Yet we knew they were accepting us for just who we were, an orchestra of great musicians. That was a great feeling."

The formal concert settings, printed programs, and positive press reviews reinforced Ellington's perception of himself as a composer. Lawrence Brown observed, "The audiences acted as though they were at a symphony concert and Duke was like [conductors Arturo] Toscanini or Leonard Bernstein."

"Duke told me after that second trip to Europe in '39, he now knew he could write anything," Billy Strayhorn said. "It was then he began to think about *Black, Brown and Beige*. Not write it, but think about it. It would be three years before he would put pen to paper."

The trip was also personally liberating for Ellington, who told an interviewer, "When you've eaten hot dogs all your life and you're suddenly offered caviar it's hard to believe it's true."

The European trip also helped Ellington finally break off his relationship with his manager. The night before they landed in New York, he informed Mills it was over between the two of them. Fred Guy recalled, "They had a drink, shook hands and that was it. All that was left was the paperwork."

33

AFTER BREAKING HIS long-standing relationship with Mills, Ellington signed with the William Morris Agency. Morris had begun booking bands in December 1938, in a direct challenge to the Music Corporation of America (MCA), the dominant band booking agency in the country. To mount its assault on MCA, Morris had hired away from it the talented agent Willard Alexander, as well as Ned Williams from Mills Music. Williams probably played some part in the signing of Ellington. Alexander turned over the day-to-day handling of Ellington to young man named Cress Courtney. "That boy was on us like white on rice," Fred Guy recalled, "He took care of everything, just like Mills used to do, only he wasn't so goddamned arrogant."

Ellington had further distanced himself from Mills by signing a three-year contract with his old friend, the music publisher Jack Robbins. Fourteen years earlier, Robbins had purchased from Ellington and Jo Trent the score for *Chocolate Kiddies*. In return for Ellington's having given up his shares in the Cab Calloway orchestra, Mills Music, and its subsidiary Gotham Music, had given up all publishing rights to Ellington's music.

There would also be a change in Ellington's recording contract. The previous January, John Hammond had taken over as director of popular music recording for Columbia-Brunswick-Vocalion. When news of this reached Ellington—who had remained at odds with Hammond since the "Reminiscing in Tempo" controversy—he expressed his displeasure in a series of articles published in the April and May issues of *Downbeat*. Ellington charged Hammond with having a conflict of interest, because he continued to write jazz criticism while producing records. Columbia had inherited Duke's contract with Mills's Master and Variety labels, and the contract was up for renewal early the following year. Alexander was instructed to begin looking for another recording company.

Ellington and his men went back to work the week of May 25, 1939. He was back on Broadway, headlining the show at Loew's State Theater. A week's engagement at the Flatbush Theater in Brooklyn followed. The band was back in the Brunswick recording studios on June 6. At this session, Duke continued to recycle compositions he had recorded earlier, including "Doin' the Voom Voom" and "Cotton Club Stomp." Also recorded that day were a slow blues, "Way Low," and "Serenade to Sweden." The latter work was totally scored; there is no improvisation. The work glows with the mutual warmth that Ellington and the Swedes must have felt for each other.

Alexander had scheduled the band to begin a four-week engagement at the Grand Terrace Ballroom in Chicago on June 15. On June 10, however, the ballroom closed for the summer, citing poor business as the reason. Plans were made for a September reopening. The agency quickly put together a series of one-night stands and split-week theater engagements following the band's appearance at the New York World's Fair on June 2. Charlie Shribman hired the band for a series New England engagements, and by the middle of July, the group had worked their way west as far as Sioux City, Iowa. Ellington returned to New England by way of Missouri, Indiana, Ohio, and upstate New York to begin an engagement during the week of July 24, 1939, on the roof of Boston's elegant Ritz-Carlton Hotel. The Benny Goodman and Count Basie orchestras had preceded him on that bandstand.

The outdoor setting at the Ritz-Carlton, while very elegant, did not sit well with Ellington. The cool breeze off the Charles River reawakened Ellington's hypochondriacal fear of diseases. He became concerned about his health, and instructed Billy Strayhorn to take over the piano for the rest of the engagement, while he conducted standing in front of the band. "The guys in the band had never heard me play," Strayhorn recalled, and he proceeded to perform all of Ellington's parts as well as several solo pieces each night. "They were sort of like, 'Oooh!' I was very flattered."

While Ellington was in Europe, Strayhorn began exploring the musical scene in Harlem and getting to know other musicians and bandleaders. The Erskine Hawkins orchestra read through several of his scores. Also, at the insistence of Mercer and Ruth, he had moved in

with them. When not out on the town, he had been spending practically every day at their apartment anyway. "What the hell are we paying all
that rent for?" Mercer declared. "Go get your shit and move it here."

Strayhorn began a systematic study of the Ellington scores that
were around the apartment. "He cracked the code," Mercer recalled.
"He had enough training in composition to be able to appreciate Pop's
work, and it was just a matter of having the instrumentation shown to
him for him to grasp the general principles. To this day I don't know
how he did it, but he was able to capture the Ellington sound."

On June 10, Strayhorn had his sound recorded. That Brunswick
session featured Ivie Anderson singing four songs. Three of the songs
were arranged by Ellington, and the fourth was by Strayhorn, "I'm
Checkin' Out—Goo'm Bye." The work is in fact an orchestration, with
new lyrics, of "Barney Goin' Easy," composed by clarinetist Barney
Bigard for a small group session recorded two days earlier. Strayhorn's
next recording with the band, "Grievin'," an instrumental composition,
was recorded on August 20, but was rejected for release. Ellington's
"Bouncing Buoyancy" and "The Sergeant Was Shy" were also put on
wax during that session. The latter, an effervescent reworking of the
"Bugle Call Rag," is fondly remembered by the author, who played the
stock arrangement of it in high school.

Following one-night stands in Pennsylvania and upstate New York,
the band did a week at Harlem's Apollo Theater in the week of
September 15, 1939. Then they boarded the railroad cars for work that
would take them as far west as Lincoln, Nebraska. They then returned
to Chicago's Drake Hotel, to be the first black band to play the Junior
League Ball, on October 15.

The day before, October 14, 1939, they were in the recording studios. Strayhorn's "Grievin'" was re-recorded and issued, along with
"Tootin' Through the Roof," a trumpet duel featuring Cootie Williams
and Rex Stewart. Ivie Anderson sang "I Never Felt This Way Before,"
and Ellington introduced the first of many musical portraits that he
would compose over the next two years, "Weely" (a musical portrait of
Billy Strayhorn).

Two days later, the band was back in the studios again. Strayhorn and Ivie Anderson did a duet on "Killin' Myself," and the band

recorded a sorrowful blues, "Country Gal." They then hit the road to St. Louis for an engagement at the Club Caprice in the Coronado Hotel beginning on October 20.

"The second or third night there, [Johnny] Hodges came on the bandstand and raved to Duke about this bass player he had heard while he was jamming at an after-hours club," Sonny Greer recalled. "Johnny seldom raved about anybody, so Duke went to hear him the next night." The bass player was twenty-one-year-old Jimmie Blanton.

Born in Chattanooga, Tennessee, Blanton had played in local groups, and attended Tennessee State College for a brief period of time. By the time Ellington heard him, Blanton had put in a tour of duty with Fate Marable's riverboat bands, and was, at the time, working with the St. Louis-based Jeter-Pillars Orchestra. On hearing the musician, Ellington "flipped like everyone else. . . . We talked him into coming down to the hotel the next night to play a few things with us. He was a sensation, and that settled it. We had to have him, and he joined the band, although our bass man was Billy Taylor . . . so there I was with two basses!"

"The first night he sat in with us," guitarist Fred Guy recalled, "I couldn't believe the sound he got out of that bass. I told Duke, when we leave town, let's bring that boy with us!"

The arrival of Blanton had an extraordinary impact not only on the Ellington rhythm section, but also on jazz bass playing in general. Critic Gunther Schuller noted, "His tone was astonishingly full, a bigness caused not by sheer amplitude, but by purity of timbre and an uncanny ability to center each tone. No one had ever produced such a firm clean-edged sound, at once tensile and supple, powerful and graceful."

"Braud had a rock steady beat, and that was great," trumpeter Cootie Williams said. "But Jimmie had momentum, he gave us one hell of a lift!"

"His amazing talent sparked the entire band," Rex Stewart stated.

Blanton, an avid student of his instrument, practiced every chance he got. "He got really excited when I told him we were playing in my hometown, Boston, in January," saxophonist Harry Carney said. "He was looking forward to taking some lessons with the Boston Symphony bass players."

When they arrived in Chicago, Ellington, totally captivated by Blanton's musicianship, brought him into the Brunswick studios on November 22, 1939, for an historic recording session. He and Ellington recorded the first of a series of bass and piano duets, "The Blues" and "Plucked Again." Schuller observed, "Blanton's full firm tone, fleet pizzicato technique . . . certainly combine to produce an impressive debut for a young man of twenty-one, playing an instrument which had not yet achieved status as an improvising solo voice."

After touring the Midwest and the deep South, Ellington once again ended the year playing at the Sherman Hotel in Chicago. Nineteen thirty-nine had been a banner year for him, both psychologically and professionally. He had taken a major step in his personal growth, by firing Mills. It terminated a thirteen-year relationship with a man who originally found Ellington leading a six-piece band on Broadway, signed a business contract with him, guided his career, made Ellington famous, and made himself a wealthy man. Now, for the first time, he was solely in charge of his band and his destiny.

"You could see the change when we went on the road after coming back from Europe," Fred Guy recalled. "Duke was calling the shots. For the first time he was really in charge."

The triumphant tour of Europe also did a lot to enhance Ellington's sense of self-esteem. "He'd always say, while he had a great time in England and France in '33, " Harry Carney noted, "the trip in '39 meant more to him."

While in Chicago, Ellington made another addition to the band. Ben Webster joined the saxophone section, increasing their number to five. "I've always had a yen for Ben," Ellington remarked. Webster had recorded with Ellington on two occasions in 1935 and 1936, and desperately wanted to work with him. When Ellington made the decision to make an addition to the saxophone section, Webster was working with Cab Calloway. Ellington was uncomfortable hiring a musician out of someone else's band, even more so from Calloway, in whose band he once had a financial interest. He told Ben, "I would love to have you in the band, but Cab's my brother band and I can't take anybody out of his band. But, if you didn't have a job, I'd have to give you one." Six months later, the Calloway band was in Cleveland, Ohio. Ellington was booked for an engagement in Chicago. Webster put in his notice with

Calloway, and went to Chicago. He tracked Ellington down, and said, "Well, I'm unemployed."

Duke hired him full-time as featured tenor saxophonist. Born in Kansas City, Missouri, in 1909, Webster attended Wilberforce University and studied piano. He did not take up the saxophone until he was twenty-one. Despite this late start, he was soon a leading figure on the instrument, working in the Southwest. He held down a chair in Benny Moten's band during 1930–31, and Andy Kirk used him intermittently during the early 1930s. Webster moved to New York in 1934 and was immediately hired by Fletcher Henderson.

Toby Hardwick's return to the band in 1932 had brought the reed section to four members, with Hardwick, Hodges, Carney, and Bigard, who usually doubled on tenor saxophone. With the addition of a fifth reed, Ellington could keep Bigard on clarinet and still have a rich saxophone choir consisting of baritone, tenor, and two altos, or alto and soprano. All the saxophone parts had been scored for four voices. Webster had the daunting task of finding the fifth note in the chord. The other four saxophones jealously guarded their parts, and in the beginning, more often than not, Webster would hear, "Hey, you've got my note," forcing him to find another that would work. This occasionally resulted in some rich, biting, pungent, dissonant chords.

"Ben's interpretations were inspiring to Duke," Harry Carney recalled, "and he brought new life to a section that had been together for a long time. Ben was inspired and he inspired us, so that we worked together and tried to improve the section. We used to rehearse all alone, just the sax section."

Webster's Coleman Hawkins-inspired sonority gave Ellington another unique voice for his orchestral pallete. His striking, slightly unfocused tone, rhythmic momentum, and distinctive rasping timbre at moments of tension would play a key role in many of Ellington's masterpieces created over the next three years.

Also added to the band at this time was the singer Herb Jeffries. Born in Detroit, Michigan, in 1909, Jeffries had worked with Erskine Tate in the early 1930s and Earl Hines from 1931–34. He was biracial, and, after moving to Hollywood, his striking good looks won him roles in a series of cheaply produced black Westerns. One of these films had the colorful title of *The Bronze Buckaroo*, which became Jeffries's stage billing.

"Herb was a great mimic," Fred Guy recalled. "When we were on the train, he'd entertain us by doing imitations. He had [pop singer's] Russ Colombo's high tenor down pat." Ellington stated, "One day he was doing his imitation of Bing Crosby, when Strayhorn and I both said in unison, 'That's it! Don't go any further. Just stay on Bing.'"

"Duke thought Bing was one of the greatest baritones of all time," Jeffries stated:

> When I first went with Duke's band I was sort of a tenor, up in that range. But Ellington used to talk about that mellow, rich, baritone of Crosby and I began to lower my range. Then I started listening to his recordings and he sort of became my guru. One day Ellington heard me doing an impersonation on "Where the Blue of the Night," and he said that's the voice I want you to record with!

The addition of the three musicians, along with Ellington's burgeoning relationship with Billy Strayhorn, "whose musical conception was totally in accord with his own vision," Schuller noted, set the stage for what was known as the Webster-Blanton band of the early 1940s. Some think that it was the greatest Ellington band ever.

34

THE WEBSTER-BLANTON band made its debut at the Savoy Ballroom the night of January 7, 1940. The following day, the band began a two-week engagement at Boston's Southland Cafe. While there, Billy Taylor left the band. "At the end of a set he just picked up his bass and left," Sonny Greer said. "He told Duke he couldn't take being embarrassed by all that bass Blanton was playing!"

Leaving Boston, the band worked its way to Chicago for a week's engagement at the State Lake Theater beginning February 2, then to the Regal Theater on the South Side for a week. While at the theater, Ellington made his final recordings for the Columbia-Brunswick organization. Ivie Anderson sang "Solitude," "Stormy Weather," and "Mood Indigo"; "Sophisticated Lady" was the only instrumental cut that day. The break with Mills was complete, and Ellington extended his contract with William Morris for two more years.

In March, the agency had signed Ellington to record with RCA Victor. Morris drove a hard bargain. The contract stipulated that RCA would not record any other black band besides Ellington's for release on the Victor label. Three other black bandleaders under contract to RCA—Fats Waller, Erskine Hawkins, and Earl Hines—were then recording for the company's budget label, Bluebird. To be signed as an artist to the full-priced Victor line was another feather in Ellington's cap. He was treated as an equal with other white popular musicians—rather than being delegated to the dimestore division, like many other black artists.

Lionel Hampton had been recording small-group sessions for Victor, using various pickup groups, several of them including Ellington sidemen. When he formed his big band later that year, he was informed that he would be restricted to small-group recordings because of the terms in the Ellington contract. He was not able to record his full band until he switched to the Decca label in late 1941.

Ellington's contract with RCA Victor gave him free rein in the recording studio. "For the first time in his career, he could record anything he wanted." Harry Carney recalled. "He no longer had Mills looking over his shoulder, and trying to get him to record stuff from his publishing house."

Ellington remained in the Midwest for the rest of March 1940, playing theater dates and one-night stands. On March 6 he was back in Chicago at the Victor Studios for the first recording session of the Webster-Blanton band. The band that Ellington brought into the RCA Victor studios to record that day was remarkable for, among other things, its longevity. Sonny Greer had been with Ellington for almost seventeen years; Fred Guy had put in fifteen; "Tricky Sam" Nanton and Harry Carney, fourteen; Johnny Hodges and Barney Bigard, thirteen; Toby Hardwick, all in all totaled thirteen; Cootie Williams, eleven; Juan Tizol, ten; Lawrence Brown, eight; Rex Stewart, five; and Wallace Jones, approximately two years and five months.

Consequently, the addition of Webster and Blanton to the orchestra could be compared to adding superchargers to a well-oiled Rolls Royce engine. Fred Guy recalled, "You have no idea what it was like sitting next to Blanton on the bandstand every night. That boy got an incredible sound on his bass that filled the entire room. I'd sit there enveloped in sound, the chords on my guitar resounding with his incredible bass line. And Ben! Oh that Ben! You could feel the tension rise the moment he began to solo."

Ellington's band was unique because it had lasted so long, with basically stable personnel, and with very little turbulence. Two of Ellington's musical contemporaries, Don Redman and Fletcher Henderson, were no longer leading bands. Redman was working in New York City as a freelance arranger, and Henderson was currently staff arranger for Benny Goodman. He would break up his six-year-old band within three months because of illness, and form another one later that year. Ellington's other contemporary, Paul Whiteman, had a studio orchestra that he used strictly for radio broadcasts. The two bands closest to Ellington's in longevity were the Casa Loma and Andy Kirk orchestras, both ten years old.

The recording session of March 6, 1940, documented what many critics—including myself—feel was the Ellington band at another plateau. "With few exceptions every recording date produced an Ellington classic, if not two or three," jazz critic Gary Giddins observed. For that session, five pieces were recorded: "You You Darlin'," "Jack the Bear," "Ko-Ko," "Morning Glory," and "So Far, So Good."

"You You Darlin'" was Ellington's arrangement of a popular song from the Warner Brothers movie *Tear Gas Squad*, sung on the screen by the baritone Dennis Morgan. Ellington used the recording to introduce his baritone, Herb Jeffries, to the general public. Jeffries' suave, sophisticated, smooth phrasing was another welcome addition to Ellington's orchestral pallette.

"Jack the Bear" served to introduce the next new voice in the Ellington armamentarium, Jimmie Blanton. Ellington previously had written a piece he called "Take It Away." He was not happy with it and cast it aside. "Duke originally wrote the thing as an experiment," Billy Strayhorn said. "It didn't work out, and the piece was dropped. Then Jimmie Blanton came into the band, and Duke wanted to feature him as a solo man. We needed some material quickly, so I reworked 'Take It Away' as a showpiece for Blanton's bass." Thus, "Jack the Bear" was born, another testimony to the power of the Ellington-Strayhorn collaboration.

"Ko-Ko" was an updating of the early "jungle style" that Ellington had used to great effect in the Cotton Club productions. He claimed that the work was part of the score of an opera he was composing based on the history of the American Negro. Gunther Schuller described the work as "a triumph of form and content," and considered it Ellington's "Concerto for Orchestra." He was particularly impressed by the last chorus, saying," perhaps only Stravinsky has matched it in works like the 'Symphonies for Wind Instruments' and the 'Symphony of Psalms.'"

"Morning Glory" featured Stewart's lyrical cornet. Ellington recalled while sailing to Europe on the ocean liner *Champlain*, Stewart came up with "an idea for a new tune" after an all-night poker game. "I liked the idea, and we developed it, and it turned out to be a very good number." "So Far So Good" served as a vehicle for Ivie Anderson. It was released on the other side of "You You Darlin'."

Two days later the band began a week's engagement at Chicago's Colonial Theater. On March 15, the musicians were back in the studios recording "Conga Brava," "Concerto for Cootie," and "Me and You."

"Conga Brava" was another Latin-tinged composition by Juan Tizol. The stage was set in the beginning by Greer's use of the tom-toms and by Blanton's syncopated bass line. "Conga Brava" did not gain the popularity of some of Tizol's earlier works, such as "Caravan" and "Lost In Meditation," but as Schuller observed, "'Conga Brava' is most fascinating and uniquely peculiar to jazz and its African rhythmic antecedents."

Ellington had emerged from the severe depression following his mother's death in 1935 with the composition "Echoes of Harlem," a piece written to showcase Cootie Williams. That work emphasized Williams' command of the growl. On "Concerto for Cootie," the growl, while there, takes a back seat to Cootie's warm, open musical personality. The melody was Williams's own creation. "One of the biggest things that I did there was 'Concerto For Cootie'," Williams recalled. "I stood there on the steps of the bus from Boston to New York begging [Duke] to buy the song for twenty five dollars. . . . By the time we got to New York he said, 'Well, OK, I'll buy it.'"

Appraising the work, Ellington scholar Mark Tucker noted, "[A]lthough Williams may be the main speaker, his trumpet message would not so compelling without the participation of Brown, Nanton and Tizol. In the opening sections they sing 'amens,' and in the middle they lend support with sweet, organlike chords of consolation."

"Me and You" served as another vehicle for Ivie Anderson's dulcet vocal. This is one of the few recordings on which one can hear, in several places, the rock-steady strum of Fred Guy's guitar to great effect.

The following day the band left Chicago for a trip to the West, via theater engagements in Salt Lake City, Utah and Denver, Colorado. April 1 found the group fulfilling a two-week engagement at the Show Box in Seattle, Washington. The Vancouver musicians' union, Local 145, had a standing ban against non-Canadian bands. The union lifted it for Ellington, and his was the first American band to play in that city in more than ten years. *Downbeat* reported that the engagement proved a "gold-mine," and the band drew more than four thousand paid admissions.

That mission accomplished, Ellington and his men worked their way south via Portland, Oregon, playing a spring prom at Stanford University, and Sweet's Ballroom in Oakland, California. On April 24,

1940, they began a week's engagement at the Orpheum theater in Los Angeles. At the end of the engagement, the band received the news that Artie Whetsol had finally died of the brain tumor that had plagued him for the past few years.

"Duke, Toby, and Sonny were very upset at first; they went back together a long time," Fred Guy stated. "Then I pointed out to them, at last he was at peace; they all agreed with me."

In the first three days of May, the band did one-night stands in San Diego, Los Angeles, and Glendale, California, prior to a recording date on May 4, 1940. Surprisingly, only two numbers were recorded, the legendary "Cotton Tail" and "Never No Lament." In contrast to many of the pieces recorded at the preceding RCA Victor sessions, "Cotton Tail" is a straight-ahead frolic, based on the chords of Gershwin's "I Got Rhythm." As Schuller observed, "Ellington flaunts all convention by eliminating any introduction and plunging right into the theme." Greer, Guy, Ellington, and Blanton drive Ben Webster's celebrated solo. Webster also wrote the last chorus for the reed section, a harmonization of what sounds like a saxophone solo, its roots in the tradition of Henderson and Redmond.

"Never No Lament" was originally written by Ellington and recorded as an instrumental vehicle for Johnny Hodges. In 1941, the lyricist Bob Russell turned it into the hit song "Don't Get Around Much Anymore."

Leaving California, and vocalist Herb Jeffries, behind, the band worked its way back to Chicago via one-night stands through Missouri, Kansas, Nebraska, Texas, and Iowa for another RCA Victor recording session. On May 28, "Dusk," "Bojangles" (a portrait of Bill Robinson), "A Portrait of Bert Williams," and "Blue Goose" were recorded. The portraits were dedicated to two of Harlem's most beloved entertainers, the fabled tap dancer Bill Robinson, nicknamed "Bojangles," and the famous vaudeville comedian, Bert Williams.

Ellington scored "Dusk" as he had done with "Mood Indigo" and "Azure," with the clarinet in low register, and muted trombone and trumpet on top. The work, in the same key as "Mood Indigo," projects a profound sense of melancholy, underscored by an interlude written for the trombone trio.

"Bojangles" begins with an Ellington-Blanton duet reminiscent of "Jack the Bear." The work was a tribute to the art of tap dancing, a percussive, rhythmic language executed by the dancer's feet. In this arrangement the sharp, staccato phrases of the brass and reeds create that effect, carried along by an infectious beat.

The comedian W. C. Fields once described Bert Williams as "the funniest man I ever saw, and the saddest man I ever knew." In "A Portrait of Bert Williams," Ellington manages to capture the great man's essence. "[T]he dignity under the comic veneer, his famous stuttering patter are all captured by Ellington and the players (notably Stewart, Bigard and Nanton) to whom Williams was a revered figure," Schuller noted.

"Blue Goose" was in effect a song without words. It is an interesting tune that is transformed into something beyond itself by the major contributions of Johnny Hodges on soprano saxophone, along with Harry Carney, Ben Webster, and Cootie Williams.

The band left Chicago the following day, for another series of engagements in the Midwest, beginning with a dance at the University of Missouri. The railroad cars carried the musicians through engagements in Iowa, Nebraska, Oklahoma, Michigan, West Virginia, Michigan, and Washington, D.C. After a one-night stand for Charlie Shribman in Old Orchard Beach, Maine, they were back home at Harlem's Apollo Theater in the week of June 7, having spent five months on the road.

Their stay in New York was short, however; they were back in the railroad cars one week later. "We had just enough time to change our laundry," Cootie Williams recalled. Beginning with the senior prom at Cornell University, followed by one-night stands throughout the East, Northeast, and South, the band finally was back in New York at the RCA Victor studios for two sessions on July 22 and 24, 1940. Once again, Ellington celebrated his community with "Harlem Airshaft," along with "At a Dixie Roadside Diner," "All Too Soon," "Rumpus in Richmond," "My Greatest Mistake," and "Sepia Panorama."

"Harlem Airshaft" is a vivid tonal painting inspired by the ambience experienced in an uptown tenement block. An airshaft is a central area in a group of apartment buildings, which allows air to reach the upper floors of each building; this area would often become a place for communal gatherings and good times. "At a Dixie Roadside Diner" was a mediocre pop tune that had already been recorded by another band. "All Too Soon," on the other hand, was one of Ellington's great ballads of the 1940s.

Cootie Williams's clarion call to arms opens "Rumpus in Richmond. "My Greatest Mistake" demonstrated what Ellington could do with an ordinary pop tune if he set his mind to it. "Sepia Panorama" had a marvelous surging, chromatic introduction. This composition, for a time, was used as Ellington's radio signature theme.

The band was back in the railroad cars the following day, for a week's engagement at the Eastwood Garden in Detroit. A series of one-night stands followed, highlighted by playing for the opening of the Canadian National Exhibition on August 23 and 24. The tour ended in Chicago, where the band was booked for an engagement in the Panther Room of the Hotel Sherman beginning September 6. "After Harlem, Chicago was our second home," Fred Guy recalled. "I can't recall a time I didn't look forward to coming here. It was no accident I ended up living here after I left the band."

On opening night, Ellington fans received a shock. The band's radio signature theme, "East St. Louis Toodle-Oo," which had been used for the past thirteen years, had been replaced by the opening fanfare of "Sepia Panorama." "I think it was one more thing associated with Mills that he wanted to get rid of," Harry Carney recalled.

Herb Jeffries had remained in Los Angeles when the band left the West Coast in early May. He rejoined the group for the Chicago hotel engagement. The previous day, he and the band were in the recording studios, and the singer was featured on "There Shall Be No Night." Jeffries had followed Ellington and Strayhorn's suggestion to emulate Bing Crosby. On this recording, the singer was accompanied by Ellington's impressionistic piano, and utilized Crosby's smooth phrasing, clear diction, and floating falsetto to good effect.

"In A Mellow Tone" was also recorded that day, along with "Five O' Clock Whistle," featuring Ivie Anderson. On October 1, 1940, Ellington and Jimmie Blanton were back in the studios, recording another set of piano-bass duets: "Pitter Patter Panther," "Body and Soul," "Sophisticated Lady," and "Mr. J. B. Blues." On these recordings,

Ellington demonstrates what a first-rate accompanist he was. While the session was designed to feature Blanton, it is Ellington's piano that keeps things in focus especially during Blanton's bowed double-time passages.

There were two more recording sessions during the Chicago engagement. On October 17, "Warm Valley" and "The Flaming Sword" were recorded. On October 28, "Across the Track Blues," "Chloe," and "I Never Felt This Way Before" were cut. "Warm Valley" featured Hodges at his sensuous best, while "The Flaming Sword," which bears Ellington's name as composer, sounds suspiciously like a Tizol composition.

"Across the Track Blues" is a direct descendant of the many slow blues Ellington composed during his career, beginning with 1927's "Immigration Blues." Gus Kahn's 1927 hit song "Chloe" was arranged by Strayhorn, yet one could hear the hand of Ellington in it. As Mark Tucker observed, "Does the similarity mean that Strayhorn knew how to imitate his senior partner, or that there's much more of Strayhorn in arrangements credited to Ellington?" "I Never Felt This Way Before" had been recorded as an instrumental a year earlier. Ellington reset it here as a vehicle for a Jeffries vocal.

The band returned to its old stomping grounds, The Oriental Theater, the week of October 18. Following the last show on opening day, Cootie Williams put in his two weeks' notice. He had an offer to join Benny Goodman. The music world was shocked. Both Williams and Goodman received scathing letters of rebuke from the "jazz purists." The bandleader Raymond Scott acknowledged the event by writing a piece titled, "When Cootie Left the Duke."

The trumpet player recalled:

> Some people accused me of being ungrateful after all Duke had done for me. What most of them didn't know was, Duke set up the deal, and got me more money. I told him I'd be back in a year. That Goodman band, I loved it. It had a beat and there was something there that I wanted to play with. I figured it out after the first week. When the occasion demanded it, Duke's band could play with great precision. Benny did it with every number, every set, every night!

Ellington was left with the daunting task of filling Williams's chair. Frank Galbreath recalled, "I was playing with Louis [Armstrong] at the time. We all thought when Duke got back to New York, he'd give the job to Dud Bascomb [a trumpet player with the Erskine Hawkins orchestra]. I always thought he sounded more like Cootie than anyone else. Once again Duke surprised us all and hired Ray Nance."

"One morning, I'm at home," Nance recalled. "It's Strayhorn on the telephone. 'Duke wants to see you down at his hotel,' he says. I was so thrilled to think that I was even considered for the job, and that's when I joined. Just to be connected with Duke Ellington was the greatest thing that ever happened to me. I'd admired the band so long, and I used to skip school when it was at the Oriental Theater. In fact kids all over the South Side did."

A Chicago native, Ray Nance began studying piano at age six. Three years later he took up the violin, and received instruction from a friend of his mother's. His progress was so great that, five years later, his mother enrolled him in the Chicago College of Music. He continued to study violin under Max Fischel, reputed to be the best teacher at the school.

"At first," Nance recalled:

> it had been just a matter of doing what my mother said, but after a time I got to like it. I studied with Fischel for seven years, right through high school. When I graduated from Wendell Phillips at eighteen, I was playing in the school band and seriously considering becoming a professional musician. Meanwhile, I had picked up the trumpet. I practically taught myself, with the help of a great bandmaster, Major N. Clark Smith. I wanted to hear myself on a louder instrument in a way I couldn't with the violin in the orchestra. I guess it was a bit of an unusual double. Most guys double on violin and piano, or violin and guitar, or violin and saxophone.

Nance had been playing around his hometown since 1932. He worked with the Earl Hines orchestra at Chicago's Grand Terrace ballroom during 1936–37, and recorded with them. Engagements with the Fletcher Henderson and Horace Henderson orchestras followed. When the call came to join Ellington, Nance was working at Joe

Hughes's DeLuxe Club. Nance's debut with the Ellington band occurred the night of November 7 at the Crystal Ballroom in Fargo, North Dakota.

Thanks to the diligence of two young radio announcers, Jack Towers and Dick Burris, who ferried their portable recording equipment across the Red River, and with Ellington's blessing, a recording exists of this first date. Nance is heard soloing on trumpet and violin, as well as serving as vocalist on several numbers. He was also an accomplished dancer and comedian. Within days of his arrival in the band, saxophonist Toby Hardwick had given him the nickname "Floorshow."

Once again, Ellington had added another unique voice to his musical palette. The recording of the Fargo dance date was subsequently released forty years later and remains one of the great documents of the Webster-Blanton band doing an ordinary night's work.

Leaving North Dakota, the band worked its way home. On December 12, the group gave a concert in the Memorial Chapel at Colgate University, before opening at the Apollo Theater the next day. During that week, Ellington informed his son Mercer that he was to join the band as staff arranger, and would travel with the musicians out to the West Coast.

"Pop told me there was going to be a recording ban beginning the first of the year and he was going to need all the help he could get," his son recalled.

The ban was a result of the dispute between ASCAP (American Society of Composers and Publishers) and NAB (National Association of Broadcasters). ASCAP required radio networks to pay royalties on performances of music written by its members. The contract between the two organizations had expired that year, and no agreement for new terms had been reached, mainly because ASCAP was hoping to double the amount collected from the radio stations. With no agreement in sight, ASCAP banned its music from the airwaves beginning January 1, 1941.

Orchestras that previously featured ASCAP-licensed compositions had to find new, non-ASCAP pieces or revive older music now in the public domain. Ellington was a member of ASCAP; therefore, none of his music could be played on the air. Neither Billy Strayhorn, Mercer, nor Juan Tizol were members of ASCAP, and Ellington pressed them into service, providing new music for the band.

On December 28, while on their way to California, the band members stopped in RCA Victor's Chicago studios to record "The Sidewalks of New York," "Flamingo," and a work attributed to Mercer, "The Girl in My Dreams Tries to Look Like You." Mercer stated that he was surprised when his father told him he planned to record it. He said, "In part, I think it was a reward for leaving New York with him."

"The Sidewalks of New York (East Side, West Side)," a song of the Gay '90s, was arranged by Ellington. Nanton's solo with plunger adds an air of playfulness to the work. "Flamingo," arranged by Strayhorn, had a vocal by Jeffries. The Ted Grouya and Edmund Anderson ballad, when released the following summer, was a huge and enduring hit. To date, it has sold more than fourteen million copies.

35

ON JANUARY 3, 1941, Ellington and his men began their California stay with a six-week engagement at the Casa Manana in Culver City. They had worked these premises previously, when the room was known as Frank Sebastian's Cotton Club.

Back in Los Angeles, Mercer and Strayhorn shared a room, and spent their waking hours writing music. "Pop told us he had a recording date coming up, and to get stuff to him as soon as possible. We were busting our ass," Mercer said. On February 15 they were in the studios. The first number recorded was a work Strayhorn had brought with him from Pittsburgh. He had given it the title "Take the A Train."

When he and Ellington first met at Pittsburgh's Stanley Theater back in 1939, Strayhorn had inquired of Duke what was the best way to get to Harlem when he got back to New York. He was told "Take the A train," a route of the recently opened Eighth Avenue subway line. This inspired him to use this line as the title of his composition. Strayhorn had also written a set of lyrics that were (wisely) omitted from this recording.

"Take the A Train" was in the model of the many arrangements Strayhorn had been doing for local bands while living in Pittsburgh: orchestral pieces written in the manner of Fletcher Henderson. The three horn sections are arranged in a call-and-response fashion.

Ray Nance made his recording debut with a classic solo, so stunningly assured that one would think he had been sitting in the Ellington trumpet section for years. As a matter of fact, several writers assumed his muted second solo was played by Rex Stewart. When Williams, for whom the solo was originally intended, returned to the band twenty-two years later, he did little to change it, playing it almost verbatim, albeit in his own idiosyncratic style.

The band had been broadcasting over local radio stations. As a result of the recording ban, "Sepia Panorama" could no longer be used as its radio signature theme. Ellington began using "Take the A Train" on the first of the year, and continued to do so for the rest of his life.

"Take the A Train" was a hit recording and afforded Ellington an opportunity to take charge of another aspect of his musical life. While under contract to Mills Music, the publishing house held the copyright to the music, and, with creative bookkeeping, could reap a great profit. Mercer stated, "It was when Pop got a check from Victor Recording Company for $25,000 from the recording of 'Don't Get Around Much Anymore' that he realized how much money Mills made off him. When he first glanced at the check, he thought it was for $2,500. That was usually what he got from Mills!"

Taking note of the fact that fellow ASCAP member Irving Berlin owned his own music publishing firm, Ellington founded Tempo Music, Inc. The day-to-day operations were Ruth's responsibility. But the important thing was that he now had total control of all music emanating from his orchestra. "Take the A Train" was the first piece. As Mills had done with him, Ellington had signed on as co-composer of the Strayhorn masterpiece.

Tempo Music also published the other four numbers recorded that day. Three of the compositions were by Mercer: "Jumpin' Punkins," "John Hardy's Wife," and "Blue Serge." Strayhorn's "After All" concluded the day's work.

"At first, people used to think Pop wrote those three pieces and put my name on them to get around the record ban." Mercer recalled. "Don't forget, I was leading my own band and writing my own music, before he ever asked me to join him. Everyone knew, he or Strays would revoice, change harmonies, add or subtract something, before a recording. They did that to any piece, including mine. They did it all their lives!"

The band remained on the West Coast doing one- and two-night stands for the next five weeks. April 3 found the group onstage at the Paramount Theater in Los Angeles for a week's engagement. Then, the musicians were back in the railroad cars for a tour of the South and Southwest, ending up in Chicago on May 14, where Ellington went to the Victor studios to record two piano solos, "Solitude" and "Dear Old Southland."

The Musicians

Bubber Miley performing with Roger Pryor Dodge,
just after leaving the Ellington band, 1930.
Courtesy Frank Driggs Collection

Cootie Williams,
1939.
Courtesy Frank
Driggs Collection

Taft Jordan, 1944.
Photo by Duncan Butler,
courtesy Frank Driggs
Collection

Harold "Shorty" Baker.
Courtesy Frank Driggs
Collection

Ray Nance, c. 1960s.
Photo © Paul J. Hoeffler, courtesy Frank Driggs Collection

Cat Anderson, 1956.
Photo by Popsie Randolph, courtesy Frank Driggs Collection

Harry Carney, 1934.
Courtesy Frank Driggs Collection

Toby Hardwick and Harry Carney,
Hurricane Club, 1944.
Photo by Duncan Butler,
courtesy Frank Driggs Collection

Barney Bigard, c. 1941.
Courtesy Frank Driggs
Collection

Duke, Ben Webster,
and Jimmy Hamilton,
rehearsal for Carnegie
Hall Concert, 1948.
Courtesy Frank Driggs
Collection

Paul Gonsalves at the Newport Jazz
Festival, July 7, 1956.
Photo © Paul J. Hoeffler,
courtesy Frank Driggs Collection

Jimmie Blanton (with bass)
and Johnny Hodges (foreground
with saxophone), c. 1939–40.
Courtesy Frank Driggs Collection

Tricky Sam Nanton.
Courtesy Frank Driggs
Collection

Lawrence Brown, at the
Hurricane Club, 1944.
Photo by Duncan Butler,
courtesy Frank Driggs
Collection

Otto Preminger watches while
Duke and Billy Strayhorn work
on the *Anatomy of a Murder*
score, 1959.
Corbis/Bettmann

Duke with Fred Guy,
Hurricane Ballroom,
May 1943.
Photo by Gordon Parks,
courtesy Corbis

Lloyd Trottman, Duke, and Oscar Pettiford.
Courtesy Frank Driggs Collection

Jimmie Blanton (foreground) at the Savoy Ballroom, Harlem, 1940.
Courtesy Frank Driggs Collection

A famous photo of Duke and
Sonny Greer showing off the
variety of percussion instruments
in the drummer's kit.
Courtesy Frank Driggs Collection

Sam Woodyard at
Newport, c. mid-'50s.
Courtesy Frank Driggs
Collection

Ivie Anderson and Duke
in Hollywood, 1934.
Courtesy Frank
Driggs Collection

Betty Roche singing at
the Hurricane Cabaret,
New York, April 1943.
Photo Gordon Parks,
courtesy Corbis

Alice Babs, c. 1940.
Courtesy Frank Driggs Collection

Billy and Duke, 1945.
Courtesy Frank Driggs
Collection

The Music

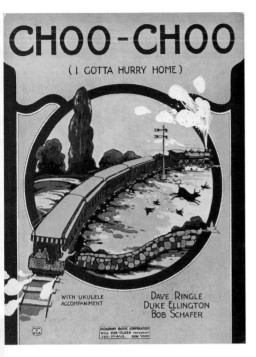

"Choo-Choo" (I Gotta Hurry Home), 1924.
One of Ellington's first published songs.
Dave Jasen

"Jig Walk Charleston" from the
play *Chocolate Kiddies*, 1925.
Dave Jasen

"Mood Indigo," instrumental version,
1931. This cover illustration was used
for many of Ellington's instrumental
compositions by Mills Music.
Dave Jasen

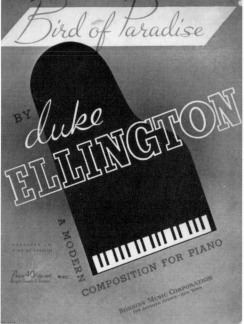

"Bird of Paradise," "A Modern
Composition for Piano," 1935.
Dave Jasen

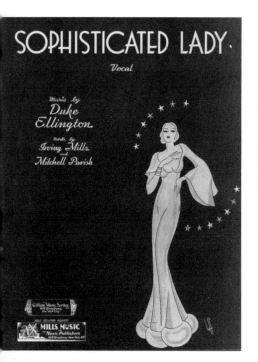

"Sophisticated Lady," 1933.
Dave Jasen

"Caravan," one of Ellington's
biggest hits, 1937.
Dave Jasen

Advertisement for Master and Variety
Records, 1937.
Dave Jasen

"Take the 'A' Train" by Billy
Strayhorn, 1941.
Dave Jasen

Johnny Hodges's composition
"Run-a-Bout," 1944.
Dave Jasen

Piano solos folio from the 1940s
containing many of Ellington's
biggest hits.
Dave Jasen

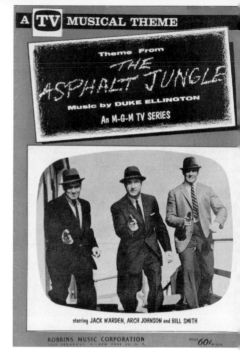

The Asphalt Jungle theme, 1961.
Dave Jasen

Reissue publication of
"Satin Doll," 1962.
Dave Jasen

After playing a dance at Wabash College, in Crawfordsville, Indiana, Ellington and his men went cross-country again, back to Los Angeles. According to this itinerary, they were due to open at Topsy's, a Southgate, California, nightclub, on May 20. When they arrived, however, they were informed the engagement had been postponed a week. Since the contract had been signed, there had been a change in policy, as well as the name. Henceforth it would be known as the Trianon Ballroom, where Ellington would hold forth through the middle of June. The room operated as a ballroom, but presented floor shows at 10 P.M. and 12:15 A.M. The band, Ivie Anderson, Herb Jeffries, and a dance team, the Four Kit Kats, were the featured attractions.

The band was back in the recording studios on June 5, 1941. For this session, Tizol contributed another Caribbean-inspired work, "Bakiff." Strayhorn's "Just a-Settin' and a-Rockin'" featured a subdued solo by saxophonist Ben Webster. Ellington's "Are You Sticking?" was another minature concerto for Barney Bigard, and "The Giddybug Gallop" was a work played at racehorse tempo, in the style of "Whispering Tiger."

With the exception of the week's engagement in Los Angeles, Ellington had been on the road for three months. His astonishing burst of creativity continued. On the night he opened at the Trianon, he was actively working on the score of his first musical, *Jump for Joy*. The show opened at the Mayan Theater in Los Angeles on the night of July 10, 1941. It had a cast headed by the well-known black actress Dorothy Dandridge, Ivie Anderson, and Herb Jeffries. Also involved were the dance team of Pot, Pan, and Skillet, Marie Bryant, Al Guster, Roy Glenn, and the comedian Wonderful Smith, in a company of sixty.

Ellington wrote a major part of the score, with assistance from Mercer, Strayhorn, and Hal Bourne. Sid Kuller and Paul Webster contributed the majority of the lyrics. Additional material was supplied by Langston Hughes, Otis Rene, Mickey Rooney, and Charles Leonard. Sid Kuller and Hal Fimberg contributed the sketches. The entire production was staged by the Hollywood choreographer Nick Castle. The reviewer from *Downbeat* complained that the show did not feature the Ellington band "as it should have," because "Duke was relegated to pit band in the revue." The decision not to have the band onstage during their specialties was an economic one. There was a union rule calling for $30 per man if the band worked both pit and the stage. Thus, the only band member to appear on stage was Rex Stewart, who was featured in "Concerto for Klinkers."

Almost close to fifty sketches and musical numbers were written, and approximately thirty were used. Some were discarded during the show's run, and others installed in their place. Clearly, the revue was a continuous work in progress. Orson Welles, after seeing one performance, dictated stage directions to revamp the show from top to bottom—"the most impressive display of mental power I've ever experienced," Ellington recalled.

The twenty-six-year-old Orson Welles, who had just completed his film masterpiece, *Citizen Kane,* was an unabashed Ellington admirer. He had seen *Jump for Joy* on more than one occasion, and was one of its most enthusiastic supporters. On August 25, he was the master of ceremonies for a CBS radio program, "Jubilee." Three excerpts from the show were presented: The Ellington orchestra did "Flamingo," with the Jeffries vocal, and Mercer's "Jumpin' Punkins"; and Wonderful Smith performed a monologue.

Welles, under contract with RKO to produce another film, commissioned Ellington to write a movie score. The film *Saga of Jazz* was never completed, but Ellington was paid $12,500 in monthly installments. As music director and composer, he began playing around with some musical ideas, many of which were left undeveloped. He would recycle some of the music in 1957 during the production of a *A Drum Is a Woman*, his musical fantasy on the origins and development of early Afro-American music presented over CBS-TV on the "U.S. Steel Hour."

According to Mercer, his father, he, and Strayhorn probably wrote "a good forty songs" for *Jump for Joy*. Eleven were used in the show. Some became standards, most notably "I Got It Bad and That Ain't Good," which featured Ivie Anderson. The singer Joe Turner left his job at New York's Café Society to join the show shortly after it opened. He performed his specialty, "Rocks in My Bed," as well as his own blues, and brought down the house. The title song was sung by the ensemble, subsequently recorded by Ellington, and was a minor hit during the 1940s, as was "The Brown-Skin Gal in the Calico Gown," sung by

Herb Jeffries; "Bli-Blip," sung by Marie Bryant; and "Chocolate Shake," sung by Ivie Anderson. "Subtle Slough," which was danced to by the trio of Pot, Pan, and Skillet, evolved into a hit song five years later. It was given a set of lyrics and retitled "Just Squeeze Me." Ray Nance sang it on the subsequent Ellington recording.

Jump for Joy was a "benchmark in American theater," as Gary Giddins has noted. It was the first all-black musical to avoid, in the words of one of its creators, the librettist and lyricist Sid Kuller, "black humor performed by blacks for white audiences from a white point of view. Our material was from the point of view of black people looking at whites."

The show's irreverence caused concern. According to Ellington, "[T]he original script had Uncle Tom on his deathbed . . . a Hollywood producer on one side of the bed and a Broadway producer on the other side, as both were trying to keep him alive by injecting adrenaline into his arms!" That scene was cut before opening night. Following threats from the Ku Klux Klan, the song "I've Got a Passport from Georgia (and I'm Sailin' for the U.S.A.)" was cut several nights after opening.

Another skit was set in the living room of the king and queen of an ancient African tribe. Both are elegantly dressed, she in the latest Parisian designer evening gown, he in a well-fitted dinner jacket. They are drinking their after-dinner brandy and coffee when they are interrupted by a telephone call. The king's courtiers inform him that an expedition is arriving from America to discover the original source of jazz.

"Oh, damn," the queen replies, in exasperation, when she is told about the call.

"Yes, my dear," the King replies, "We shall have to get out our leopard skins again."

The comedian Wonderful Smith was working as a carhop when he auditioned for one of the sketches. His telephone routine satirizing the New Deal and war preparation, from which blacks were excluded, always stopped the show. He subsequently repeated an edited version of this routine in a movie comedy called *Top Sergeant Mulligan*. According to Giddins, "The Republicans reveled in it, though a horrified Red Skelton told [the comedian], 'The communists will love you.'" President Franklin Delano Roosevelt was getting ready to launch his campaign for a third term, and Republicans hoped to use the sketch as ammunition against him.

The show had been produced on a budget of $52,000, $10,000 of which came from the actor John Garfield, who never missed a rehearsal. The show cost approximately $7,000 per week to operate but never generated enough income for its backers to send it out on the road to Broadway, as originally planned. They were further hampered by the recording ban in effect since the first of the year. That meant none of Ellington's music from the show could be played on the air, a vehicle that they hoped would generate audience interest across the country. Except for Southern California, *Jump for Joy* thus remained virtually unknown. Plans for a San Francisco performance fell through when no suitable theater could be found.

During *Jump for Joy*'s run, Ellington had the band in recording studios on several occasions. A June 26, 1941, session featured Ivie Anderson recording two numbers from the revue, "Chocolate Shake" and "I've Got It Bad and That Ain't Good." A week later, "Clementine," a Strayhorn original, and "The "Brown-Skin Gal in the Calico Gown," "Jump for Joy," and Tizol's "Moon over Cuba" were cut. On September 26, the day before the show closed, the band recorded three more tunes from the show, "Five O' Clock Drag," "Rocks in My Bed," and "Bli-Blip."

Jump for Joy, as jazz critic Barry Ulanov observed, "though it spun no narrative, told a story of Negroes in the entertainment world, what they looked like and how they acted and danced and sang and made fun. It was true to the life it depicted." Ellington wrote and helped to direct a musical comedy that portrayed blacks with dignity. The show closed on September 27, after 101 performances.

36

FOLLOWING THE CLOSING of *Jump for Joy*, the band remained on the West Coast, working theater dates in San Francisco and Los Angeles, as well as college dances and one-night stands. During the the run of the show, bassist Jimmie Blanton began to notice that he was having night sweats, shortness of breath, and felt generally run down. He had consulted a physician, and an X-ray revealed he had advanced tuberculosis.

"He had the consumption, just like Bubber," drummer Sonny Greer recalled. However, the comparison ended there. "It was really overdedication to his instrument and music that killed him," Mercer said. "He didn't have the bad habits that many men in the business have. He smoked cigarettes, but he didn't chain smoke. I don't think he ever was serious about any particular girl or even began to contemplate marriage. He had several girlfriends. . . . His love, his mistress, was the bass fiddle."

On hearing the news of Blanton's illness, Ellington sought to have the best treatment that could be found made available to him. After a series of telephone calls to physicians that he knew, he was told that the best treatment for the disease could be found at Los Angeles County General, a first-rate teaching hospital.

Ellington said:

> I made a date and took him down to the big city hospital, where there were three beautiful young, specialists. They all knew him; were fans of his, and talked about his music.
>
> "I'm getting ready to leave town," I said. "Will you take care of him?" "Yes we will," they said. "Leave him right here. He'll have to stay in the ward a couple of days or so, until we can get him a room." A room at wherever it was they sent their people for special care.

Blanton's replacement was Alvin "Junior" Raglin. Born in Omaha, Nebraska, in 1917, at age twenty-one he began a three-year tour of duty with Gene Coy's Happy Aces, a territory band working out of

Amarillo, Texas. The summer of 1941, Raglin began working in a trio at the Club Alabam in San Francisco. During the Ellington band's engagement at the Golden Gate Theater in the week of November 5, Raglin began subbing for the bass player, and joined the band full-time for the recording date of December 2, 1941.

During the December 2 session, Strayhorn's impressionistic "Chelsea Bridge" was recorded. He took his inspiration not from the bridge, which he had never seen, but from the famous Joseph Turner painting of the Battersea Bridge, which is actually located a little farther to the west on the Thames. "Raincheck," another Strayhorn original, "What Good Would It Do?" and "I Don't Know What Kind of Blues I Got," with a vocal by Jeffries, rounded out the session.

On December 6, the band members were in their railroad cars en route to a series of theater dates and one-night stands in the Pacific Northwest. On the afternoon of December 7, they arrived at Eugene, Oregon, to play a dance at the University of Oregon. "Strayhorn and I were talking about something," saxophonist Harry Carney recalled, "when I looked out the window and saw 'Tricky' [Sam Nanton] come running out of the station. He came back on the train and said, 'We're at war, the Japs bombed Pearl Harbor.' All I can remember after that, is how quiet it suddenly became; nobody said anything. I don't remember much about playing the dance that night."

The tour of the Pacific Northwest ended with a week's engagement at the Palomar Theatre in San Francisco during the week of December 15. The band then returned to Los Angeles for a rendezvous with an old friend, Sam Coslow. He had recently been named executive producer at R.C.M. Productions, a company that specialized in making "soundies," three-minute short films made for use in a coin-operated automatic viewing machine, a visual extension of the jukeboxes that played 78-rpm records.

Coslow had seen *Jump for Joy*, and the first three of the soundies that he had the band make were from the show: Ivie Anderson sang "I Got It Bad," Jeffries sang "Flamingo," and Marie Bryant and Paul White did "Bli-Blip." The band quickly churned out more short films for Coslow. "Hot Chocolate" featured four pairs of jitterbug dancers, whirling around the dance floor to "Cotton Tail." "Jam Session" was another version of Ellington's "C-Jam Blues," notable for the fact that

Greer takes a twelve-bar drum solo, the longest he had ever done, including on any Ellington recording.

The band worked its way east, and was in Chicago for a recording session on January 21, 1942. Having done "C-Jam Blues" as a soundie, Ellington then got it on record. Raglin's bass is heard to good effect, behind Rex Stewart's trumpet solo. Ellington turned to Tizol and his son for the remaining two compositions. "Perdido," written by the trombonist, evolved into a jazz standard, and is still played today. Mercer's "Moon Mist" concluded the session. The work was written by "omission," he recalled. "It had a lot more notes originally; Pop just scratched out those that were in bad taste." Gunther Schuller was very impressed with the work, and compared it to the works of Haydn and Webern.

Two days later, the band was back at its old stomping grounds, Chicago's Oriental Theatre, for a week's engagement. The musicians worked their way east via theater dates and one-nighters, arriving in New York City on February 26, having been away for thirteen months, and promptly went into the recording studio. "What Am I Here For?", an Ellington ballad, was highlighted by a Ben Webster saxophone solo. Strayhorn and Ellington combined to give Ivie Anderson a lovely background for "I Don't Mind," and "Someone," another Ellington ballad that deserved to be played more often, rounded out the session.

A day after the session, the band was playing at the Howard Theater for a week's engagement, which marked the beginning of another long tour. Mercer recalled, "Pop insisted any band member who wanted could bring his family along, and he paid for everything. That included the week in Baltimore at the Royal, and the Earle in Philly. We were on our way back to California." The band was back at Los Angeles's Trianon Ballroom on April 2, 1942, the first band to play a repeat performance there since Ellington decided to play ballrooms the previous year.

Shortly after arriving, Ellington inquired about Jimmie Blanton. He was very surprised to learn that Blanton was no longer at Los Angeles County General. While Blanton was on the ward awaiting the transfer, a well-meaning friend visited him. He was shocked to find that Ellington had left him in the ward of a city hospital and arranged for his transfer, "out somewhere near Pasadena," Ellington recalled. "When

I got back to town, there he was, on his cot. They had nothing there, no X-rays or anything. 'Well, you can't move him,' they said, and he should have been moved a month before I got there. I took one look and knew he was gone."

The band left the Trianon on May 12, to begin its usual series of theater engagements and one-night stands. Over the next six weeks the group ventured as far south as San Diego, California, and as far north as Vancouver, British Columbia. Things were very different on this trip, though. The war made it impossible for the band to travel in private Pullman cars, as the cars had been requisitioned by the U.S. Army. "We had to travel just like everybody else, sometimes in a railroad car, sometimes by bus. The trains were so packed some times we had to sit in the aisles," Harry Carney recalled. "We really missed those Pullman cars."

The band was back in Los Angeles for a recording session on June 26. Jeffries sang "My Little Brown Book," and Strayhorn contributed the hard-driving "Main Stem" (one of the author's favorite Ellington recordings of that period) and "Johnny Come Lately." The latter work was originally titled "Stomp" and was to be paired with "Dirge," of which we will hear more later.

This was clarinetist Barney Bigard's last session with the band, ending a thirteen-year relationship. While on tour, Bigard had given Ellington his two weeks' notice. He stated, "When I told him I was leaving, he just looked at me and didn't say a word. I have often wondered what he thought that night."

"Barney told me he was tired of all the traveling, and he met the woman he wanted to marry," Carney recalled. "I think he might have stayed a little longer if we still had our private railroad cars. The first time we had to take a bus, he complained during the entire trip."

To replace Bigard, Ellington looked to the east for Edmund Hall, the veteran New Orleans-style clarinetist. He was considered one of the finest jazz clarinetists around, black or white. He was Benny Goodman's favorite on that instrument. Hall was then in New York, working with Teddy Wilson at the Café Society Downtown. He was making good money and didn't want to leave town. He turned down Ellington's offer.

Ellington then recruited Chauncey Haughton. Born in Chesterton, Maryland, Haughton began studying piano at age eight, and later switched to clarinet and saxophone. He arrived in New York in 1932 with Gene Kennedy's band. He subsequently worked with Blanche Calloway, Claude Hopkins, Noble Sissle, Fletcher Henderson, Chick Webb, Benny Carter, and Ella Fitzgerald, before joining Ellington. Haughton joined the band in Denver on July 10, 1942, at the El Patio Ballroom. "He was a damn good musician," Carney recalled. "We were glad to get him."

Vocalist Herb Jeffries also chose to remain in California. He had plans to open a restaurant, and to make recordings under his own name. In my estimation, he was the best male singer Ellington ever had.

The band opened at the Panther Room of the Hotel Sherman in Chicago on July 17, 1942. There was a recording date eleven days later. This would be the band's last recording date for quite some time. James C. Petrillo, president of the American Federation of Musicians, had imposed a ban on all recordings. Petrillo, taking note of the burgeoning use of jukeboxes, realized that mechanical entertainment was putting musicians out of work. He insisted on compensation from the recording companies. When that was refused, he banned recording altogether, hoping to achieve that end. The recording ban remained in place for RCA Victor until November 1944, when the company finally came to terms with the union (other labels settled at different times).

For the final recording session, Ellington addressed the war effort. Ivie Anderson sang the infantryman's lament, "Hayfoot Strawfoot" ("three miles more, where in the heck is this mechanized war?"). Ray Nance noted, "A Slip of the Lip" ("might sink a ship"). "Sentimental Lady," an instrumental written for Hodges, became a huge hit a few years later, when lyrics were added by Bob Russell and it was retitled "I Didn't Know about You." The raucous "Sherman Shuffle" concluded the session.

Two days later, Ellington was informed of Jimmie Blanton's death. "He sent flowers from the band and paid the funeral expenses," Greer recalled. "Webster was devastated. He just sat on the bandstand and cried all night. The only person he'd let comfort him was 'Swee' Pee' [Billy Strayhorn]. Duke had a lot on his mind around that time. Ivie had put in her notice."

Anderson had been with the band for eleven years. She was a severe asthmatic, yet the illness never interfered with her singing, and she never missed a performance. She was thirty-eight years old and had been on the road for twenty years. Planning for her future, Ivie had invested her money in a restaurant, Ivie's Chicken Shack. She planned to leave for Los Angeles to oversee its operation at the close of the engagement at the Panther Room.

Once again, Chicago came to Ellington's rescue to provide a replacement for Anderson. While out one evening, Ivie and Strayhorn dropped into a nightclub on the South Side. There they heard Betty Roché, whom Ellington promptly signed to be Ivie's replacement.

Born in Wilmington, Delaware, Roché arrived in New York as a teenager. Like Ella Fitzgerald and Sarah Vaughn, she won an amateur contest at Harlem's Apollo Theater and was promptly hired by the Savoy Sultans, the house band at the Savoy Ballroom. She had also worked with Hot Lips Page and Lester Young before she arrived in Chicago.

"She was a damn good singer," Frank Galbreath said. "Duke got lucky, she could do all the stuff that Ivie used to do. The worst thing that happened to her was the recording ban."

The band members remained in the Midwest playing theater dates. Following that, they worked their way west to Hollywood. They were due at the M-G-M studios on September 26, to film *Cabin in the Sky*, and after that at Columbia studios to film *Reveille with Beverly*.

Before leaving the Midwest, Ellington added Harold Baker as fourth trumpet. Baker had worked with the band briefly in 1938. A native of St. Louis, Missouri, his first instrument was the drums. However, at the urging of his older brother Winfield, a trombonist, Harold switched to trumpet and joined his brother's band. After working with Fate Marable, he moved to Chicago and joined the Erskine Tate orchestra. He worked for a year with Teddy Wilson's band following the 1938 engagement with Ellington. In 1940, he joined the Andy Kirk orchestra and while there, married Kirk's pianist, Mary Lou Williams. They formed a sextet and were working in Chicago when Baker received the summons to join Ellington.

Cabin in the Sky was originally a Broadway stage production featuring the blues/jazz singer Ethel Waters. While it was a critical and artistic success, it did only moderately well at the box office. The backers were able to recoup their investment when the show went on tour. It was in Los Angeles for two weeks, at the Biltmore Theatre beginning July 21, 1941, playing opposite *Jump for Joy.*

On acquiring the film rights to *Cabin in the Sky,* Arthur Freed, the the head musicals' producer at M-G-M, made the decision to turn it into an all-black musical, using the finest black talent available. Besides the Ellington orchestra and Waters, the film featured Louis Armstrong, Lena Horne, the actors Kenneth Spencer and Rex Ingram, the comedians Mantan Moreland and Eddie "Rochester" Anderson, and the Hall Johnson choir, among others.

The Ellington orchestra was cast as the house band in the Paradise nightclub. The musicians' appearance in the film was confined to the sequences filmed there. They were heard in abbreviated versions of "Things Ain't What They Used to Be" and "Goin' Up." The latter was composed for a dance sequence, complete with the crowd clapping and encouraging the frenetic jitterbugging of the dancers. Solos by Ben Webster and Tricky Sam Nanton could also be heard.

Reveille with Beverly featured the dancer Ann Miller as a disc jockey who changes the format of a radio show to feature popular music. Besides Ellington, Columbia had signed Frank Sinatra, the Mills Brothers, and the orchestras of Count Basie, Bob Crosby, and Freddie Slack for appearances in the film.

Ellington's contribution to the film was "Take the A Train." The lyrics—which Strayhorn had brought with him from Pittsburgh in 1938—were sung by Betty Roché. Ellington had previously featured the song in the film *The Hit Parade* with Ivie Anderson singing, assisted by a trio from the band: saxophonist Harry Carney, trumpeter Rex Stewart, and bass player Hayes Alvis. In this new film, Carney and Stewart repeat their roles, this time assisted by Ray Nance.

The A train was a part of the New York City subway system. However, the band's sequence in the film was shot in what resembled a parlor car on the Union Pacific railroad. Stock footage of a speeding train roaring down the tracks was used for outside shots. It was certainly not the ride to Harlem that Strayhorn had originally conceived.

Leaving the West Coast, the band worked its way back east. During an engagement in the week of November 6, 1942, at the Regal Theater in Chicago, Ellington hired twenty-two-year-old Jimmy Britton to replace Jeffries. He was the first of many male singers, none of whom was able to fill the departed baritone's shoes.

Theater dates and one-night stands throughout the Midwest, Canada, and the East brought the band back to New York in mid-January 1943. Since leaving California, Ellington had been using the time between shows to write his next extended composition, *Black, Brown and Beige*. The William Morris agency had secured Carnegie Hall for its world premiere.

37

ELLINGTON HAD ARRIVED in New York City in 1923. He decided to make the premiere of *Black, Brown and Beige* the occasion to celebrate his twenty years as a bandleader. In 1940, *Downbeat* had reported that Ellington was preparing a five-part work that would present the history of the Negro from Africa to the present. It was to be called *Boola*. This was nothing new; the idea of an extended work on the black experience in America had been germinating since Ellington had returned from England in 1933.

"When I look back on it," Mercer recalled, "After he got back from England that first time, it was then he began to collect stuff on Africa and slavery. A book here and an article there." Over time, that collection grew to the point that at his death, John Edward Hasse noted, Ellington "owned 800 books on black history." In 1938, a writer for the New York *World-Telegram* noted that Ellington was collecting information about "slave ships, the civil war, cotton and John Brown."

In 1942, Ellington, now riding the crest of his enormous creativity, began putting musical ideas on paper. "He'd write a bit here, a bit there," Carney said. "He got a lot done between shows, if it was a theater date. All in all it must have taken him seven or eight months. Don't forget, he was still writing a lot of other stuff besides that."

The concert, to be held on Saturday night, January 23, 1943, and was to be a benefit for the Russian war relief. Ellington's press agents succeeded in getting that week proclaimed "National Ellington Week." This generated stories in the *New York Times*, *Newsweek*, and *Time* magazine. Invitees to the concert included Eleanor Roosevelt and Leopold Stokowski.

The band rehearsed *Black, Brown and Beige* at the Nola Studios on Broadway, which was used by many New York bands. "Duke stood before the band with the great score before him, rehearsing it piecemeal, section by section, sometimes in sequence, more often out of it," critic Barry Ulanov stated.

RCA Victor had been issuing a new recording by the band every four to six weeks. After being fed a diet of "Ko-Ko," "Jack the Bear," "Morning Glory," "Cotton Tail," and other pop numbers, musicians and critics atttending the rehearsals were perplexed by what they were hearing. Schuller noted, "Even as early as the rehearsals attended by the jazz 'intelligensia,' word began to spread that Duke's new composition was a 'disappointment,' 'a failure,' 'didn't sound like much.'"

"The only person who thought it was a great piece of music was Don Redmond," Harry Carney recalled. "A lot of the white boys couldn't figure out what was going on; they'd never heard anything like it."

"That week was a madhouse," Sonny Greer stated. "That first time we ran the work through, it didn't make any sense to me. But gradually it started to come together. Duke was still writing some of it the day of the concert!" Ellington was famous for writing up to the deadline; this time, he had no choice. At the dress rehearsal at Rye High School the night before, the finale, a gaudy, flag-waving number featuring vocalist Jimmy Britton, was deemed to be out of place.

The night of the concert, the house was packed and part of the audience was seated onstage. The concert opened with two Ellington classics, "Black & Tan Fantasy" and "Rockin' in Rhythm." These were juxtaposed with Mercer's "Moon Mist" and "Jumpin' Punkins." Three of Ellington's "portraits" followed: those of Bert Williams, "Bojangles" (dancer Bill Robinson), and Florence Mills, a reworking of 1927's "Black Beauty."

However, *Black, Brown and Beige* was the centerpiece of the concert. With the exception of Paul Whiteman's performance of the Gershwin works (the piano concerto, *Rhapsody in Blue*) and Ferde Grofé's *Grand Canyon Suite*, nothing of this magnitude had ever been attempted by a jazz band.

Ellington introduced each of the three sections. He explained to the audience that the work "was a tone parallel to the history of the American Negro." He further explained that this was a suite he had been talking about creating since the mid-1930s. Ellington believed, "It was the story of his people."

In the first part, "Black," the two major themes are the "Worksong" and the spiritual. The "Worksong," introduced by Greer's thunderous tympani strokes, creates an aura of foreboding, which leads to a magisterial theme played brass and saxophones in unison. The "Worksong" section of "Black" concludes with a second theme—this time, a mournful solo by trombonist Tricky Sam Nanton performed with plunger, which comes close to approximating human speech.

The spiritual "Come Sunday," played by saxophonist Johnny Hodges, was described by Gunther Schuller as "Ellington's most sinuously beautiful and original. It is pure Ellington, no other composer of the time could have written it." Without a doubt, it was one of the highlights of the concert.

The second part, "Brown," was an attempt by Ellington to show the contributions of blacks to the country, made with their own blood. During the American Revolution, "when things were darkest for the states there came the warriors from the West Indies," Ellington said. A harshly discordant, well-orchestrated "West Indian Dance," played with a Latin beat, pays tribute to the black soldiers from the Dominican Republic, who fought during the battle of Savannah.

Quotations from "Yankee Doodle" and "Swanee River" formed Ellington's attempt to evoke the Civil War, calling the Union and Confederate armies to arms. "Emanicpation Celebration" denoted the end of the war; this theme was stated by Rex Stewart's half-valved trumpet and Nanton's plunger trombone. That device worked so well that Ellington critic/biographer James Lincoln Collier noted, "when Ellington played a concert at the end of the year, he used them as a sample of the entire tone poem."

The third section, described by Ellington at the concert as "Mauve," was to depict the gradual urbanization of blacks during the twentieth century. It was symbolized by "The Blues." For a text, Ellington employed an elegant metrical structure based on the principles of expansion and contraction.

Betty Roche's dark, rich contralto voice soulfully intoned the work.

"Beige," written in haste, was the least satisfactory of the three parts. Gunther Schuller noted, "Its formal uncertainty reveals signs of hasty patching together of materials." However, the work did have an elegant theme, which became known as "Sugar Hill Penthouse" (Sugar Hill is a fancy neighborhood in Harlem). The work concluded with Ellington's reminding the mostly white audience that "The Black, Brown, and Beige are Red, White, and Blue." It was his statement that the blacks' struggle to participate in a democracy and contribute to the war effort must be noticed.

At intermission, Ellington was presented with a plaque signed by thirty-two eminent musicians. It was an interracial group, including Aaron Copland, Walter Damrosch, Benny Goodman, Roy Harris, Jerome Kern, Fritz Reiner, Arthur Rodzinski, Leopold Stokowski, and Paul Whiteman, as well as Marian Anderson, Count Basie, Cab Calloway, Dean Dixon, Earl Hines, Paul Robeson, and William Grant Still.

After the presentation, the crowd was jolted with the searing sounds of "Ko-Ko." Then Duke presented Billy Strayhorn. Strayhorn's "Dirge," "Nocturne," and "Stomp" were listed in the program, but only the first and last were played. "Stomp" was in fact "Johnny Come Lately," which had been recorded earlier. The "Dirge" was a new composition, and for some reason was never played again.

The Ellington concertos followed. Chauncey Haughton did Bigard's "Are You Stickin'." Tizol and Nance were featured in the trombonist's "Bakiff." Raglin did a creditable job on "Jack the Bear." Strayhorn revised "Blue Belles of Harlem," the work Ellington had written for Paul Whiteman, to highlight Ellington on the keyboard. Ellington announced that the work "featured the pianist in the band."

Strayhorn's "Day Dream," written for Johnny Hodges; "Rose of the Rio Grande," featuring Lawrence Brown; and "Boy Meets Horn," Rex Stewart's half-valve concerto, ended that section. The concert concluded with three final pieces: Ellington's "Don't Get Around Much Anymore," which had become a hit pop tune; "Goin' Up," from the movie *Cabin in the Sky*; and, finally, the somber strains of "Mood Indigo."

The concert was a financial success, grossing $7,000 and netting $2,000 for the Russian war relief. Ellington, however, got no relief. The critics reacted to *Black, Brown and Beige* mainly negatively. The classical critics complained about Ellington's lack of formal writing. Paul Bowles, at the time music critic of the New York *Herald Tribune*, the one critic most sympathetic to jazz, noted, "Between the dance numbers there were 'symphonic' bridges played out of tempo. . . . If there is no regular beat there can be no syncopation, and thus no tension, no jazz."

He felt that the work was nothing "but a gaudy potpourri of tutti dance passages and solo virtuoso work."

John Briggs of the New York *Post* dismissed the work curtly: "Mr. Ellington had set for himself a lofty goal, and with the best intentions did not achieve it." Douglas Watt in the *Daily News* snidely observed, "Such a form of composition is entirely out of Mr. Ellington's ken." A more positive opinion came from Robert Bagar, writing in the *World-Telegram*: "If you ask me, Mr. Ellington can make some two dozen brief air-tight compositions out of 'Black Brown and Beige.'"

More typical was the review by Henry Simon in *PM*. He felt that the first movement "all but falls apart in so many separate pieces." However, Simon, of all the critics, came closest to understanding what Ellington was attempting to do. He thought that the work "showed better than any of the shorter pieces, how well and how far Mr. Ellington has emancipated himself from the straightjacket of jazz formulas. He has taken a serious theme and treated it with dignity, feeling and good humor." There was no attempt by the critics to take into consideration that Ellington was venturing into new and uncharted territory. The judgment of *Black, Brown and Beige* was made after only one hearing.

The jazz critics' complaints about *Black, Brown and Beige* focused on its perceived lack of "real jazz." Forty-five years later, Gunther Schuller addressed that issue. He noted the failure of the jazz critics to recognize Ellington's attempt to go beyond the confines of "jazz" as it was commonly defined. He stated it "was the same [lack of understanding] that greeted Scott Joplin's 'Treemonisha' for not being a ragtime opera. . . . Neither Ellington nor Joplin was content to be restricted in their creative visions and imaginations by critical and popular tastes."

Schuller observed that the jazz critics' disappointment because *Black, Brown and Beige* was not written in a swing style "tells us more about *their* limitiations than those ascribed to Ellington." He then noted that the jazz critic Leonard Feather's response to *Black, Brown and Beige* was the best. Feather described the work as "the elevation of jazz to an orchestral art."

The negative reviews of *Black, Brown and Beige* had a great effect on Ellington. Ruth Ellington observed that he "sort of withdrew and was very quiet." Mercer felt that the critical response to *Black, Brown and Beige* caused his father to abandon large-scale works (as opposed to the many suites he would continue to write over his lifetime): "He said 'he'd been down that road once, and didn't plan to go there again.'" Gunther Schuller stated, "I believe its nonacceptance discouraged Duke from trying similar extended compositional challenges—at least for a while. In crucial ways it interupted the flow of his creative momentum" (which at that point in his life was awesome).

Ellington played *Black, Brown and Beige* five nights later in Boston's Symphony Hall, and a month later in Cleveland. The complete work was never commercially recorded. The following year, Ellington recorded excerpts from it: "Worksong," "Come Sunday," "The Blues," and an orchestral interlude featuring the trombones, developed and recorded as "Carnegie Blues."

Black, Brown and Beige is awash with gorgeous music. It should be made a staple of repertory orchestras. It is valuable historically and shows an Ellington who had arrived at a new position by discarding an old self. He was diving into the future, a future he produced himself, but was then afraid to follow.

The night of January 23, 1943, proved to be another landmark in Ellington's musical career. There would be others in the future, but they would be achieved with a different collection of musicians.

38

ON APRIL 1, 1943, Ellington and his men began an engagement at the Hurricane Restaurant on Broadway. It was their first job on location in New York City in five years. "It was so good to be home," Sonny Greer recalled. "We were there five or six months."

Besides playing for dancing, the band was part of the floor show. During this segment, Ellington made a spectacular entrance. He was lowered to the floor level from the ceiling, playing an upright piano on a satin-draped elevated platform as he came into view.

During this time, a series of changes began within the band. Clarinetist Chauncey Haughton was drafted into the Army in March; Ellington replaced him with Jimmy Hamilton. Hamilton had served apprenticeships with the bands of Teddy Wilson and Benny Carter. He possessed a flawless technique, like his idol, Benny Goodman. He was far removed from the New Orleans tradition of Barney Bigard, and would remain with the band for the next twenty-five years.

Trumpeter Rex Stewart left in May. He planned to move back to his home in California, to try his hand again as a bandleader. In his place, Ellington hired Taft Jordan, a veteran of the Chick Webb orchestra. Since the dissolution of that band a few years earlier, Jordan had been leading an eight-piece band off and on at the Savoy Ballroom. Stewart rejoined the band in October.

Trombonist Lawrence Brown, awaiting a draft call, moved back to California. He was replaced by another Chick Webb alumnus, Sandy Williams. Vocalist Jimmy Britton, who should have never been hired in the first place, was replaced by the blind Al Hibbler.

The most significant and painful departure at that time was that of saxophone player Ben Webster. Gruff, bellicose, with a need to dominate, Webster kept most of the band members on edge. "After he had a drink or two, he'd change," Harry Carney noted. "The kind, gentle guy, who cried like a baby the night Jimmie Blanton died, would turn into another person." Bigard felt Ellington was afraid of Webster. "He'd do a lot of things that we wouldn't dare do."

Ellington, with his need to be in control, found Webster's behavior exasperating. According to Mercer, they could not be in the same room without a disturbance erupting: "There was a sort of conflict, a matter of chemistry, where the two of them would get into arguments." Ellington, who thoroughly disliked confrontation of any kind, found Webster's personality hard to bear, and finally asked him to leave. "It was sad," Mercer said, "because nobody wanted to be in the band more than Ben." It was sad for Ellington too, because he would miss Webster's passion, drive, and devil-may-care musicmaking. Webster's final act on leaving the band was to slash one of Ellington's sports jackets with a razor.

Webster was replaced by Elber "Skippy" Williams. Williams had started out as a dancer, in a team with his brother, who also played saxophone. Prior to joining Ellington, Williams had held down chairs in the bands of Lucky Millinder, Jimmy Mundy, and Count Basie. However, he would barely last a year with the band.

Financially, Ellington was doing very well. His royalty check from RCA Victor for the first half of the year totalled $50,000. Robbins Music paid him royalties of $12,000 for the first quarter of 1943 for such compositions as "Don't Get Around Much Anymore" and "Do Nothin' Till You Hear from Me." "It only confirmed his suspicion that Mills had stolen a lot of money from him," Mercer observed.

Ellington, still reeling from the negative reviews of *Black, Brown and Beige*, decided that his next Carnegie Hall concert would feature a smaller-scaled work. Like *Black, Brown and Beige*, it too would be based on the theme of race pride. Ellington had been quite taken with the black writer Roi Ottley's book, *New World A-Comin'*, detailing the black man's past in America and his hope for a better future. The bandleader said, "I visualized this new world as a place in the distant future where there would be no war, no greed, no categorization, no non-believers, where love was unconditional and no pronoun was good enough for God."

New World A-Comin' had its premiere at Carnegie Hall on the night of December 11, 1943. The venerable hall was sold out for the occasion. Unlike *Black, Brown and Beige*, *New World A-Comin'* was a work for piano and orchestra. Mercer stated, "He was always happy to tell people that even a virtuoso like Don Shirley found one riff hard to play; but Don always countered by saying what Pop *played* and what was in the score were not the same."

The work was given a second performance the following night at Boston's Symphony Hall. The recording ban was still on at the time. Consequently, the work was never heard in the Carnegie Hall version, written for a seventeen-piece band. Ellington rescored the work for a symphony orchestra and subsequently appeared as the soloist with the NBC Symphony, New Haven Symphony, Buffalo Philharmonic, and the Cincinnati Symphony. That last performance was recorded on May 28, 1970. When awarded an honorary degree from the University of Wisconsin on June 17, 1970, Ellington performed an unaccompanied version of the work.

The defections from the band continued. Betty Roché, angered by the addition of the singer Wini Johnson, a protegée of Fats Waller, left the band in February 1944. Johnson was a very attractive young woman; however, her voice was no match for her looks. "Betty could sing all of Ivie's stuff," drummer Sonny Greer stated. "I don't know what Duke was thinking when he brought that girl [Wini Johnson] on. God! Was she beautiful, though."

Trumpeter Wallace Jones left at the same time to become a funeral director. "He said the reason he was no longer staying in show business was very simple: 'Mood Indigo,'" Mercer stated. As the lead trumpet, Jones was required to play a high D and sustain it over eight bars. The part was considered difficult for many trumpet players. "He had nightmares and cold sweats about it," Mercer recalled. Jones's replacement was Shelton "Scad" Hemphill. Frank Galbreath, a great lead trumpet player himself, while a member of Louis Armstrong's band heard Armstrong praise Hemphill as "the finest lead trumpet player of our race."

Valve trombonist Juan Tizol, weary of the road after fourteen years, left Ellington to join the band of Harry James. James was then working on the West Coast exclusively. "Juan had made the decision to live in California while we were in *Jump for Joy*," Harry Carney said. "He just wanted to spend more time with his family." Claude Jones, who had put in tours of duty with Fletcher Henderson, Cab Calloway, and Chick Webb, replaced him.

Departing with Tizol was Webster's replacement, "Skippy" Williams, who, in turn, who be replaced by Al Sears. A veteran of the Chick Webb, Zack White, and Andy Kirk bands, Sears, like Webster, had a flamboyant, emotionally direct style of playing. He would remain with the band for four years.

In September, Ellington decided to once again expand the trumpet section to five players. He hired high-note specialist William Alonzo "Cat" Anderson. Orphaned at age four, Anderson was raised in the Jenkins Orphanage in Charleston, South Carolina. He was a member of one of its famous student bands. His excellent training led to work with the bands of Claude Hopkins and Lionel Hampton.

Ellington also beefed up the vocal department of his band. Joya Sherrill, a seventeen-year-old from Detroit, had sung with the band during the summer of 1942. She was in high school at the time. Having graduated in June, Ellington brought her into the band to replace Wini Johnson. In addition, he brought on Kay Davis, a classically trained singer. Davis had studied singing and piano at Northwestern University, then taught and gave recitals for several years. Ellington would use her soprano voice as another instrument in the band, singing concert pieces or wordless vocals, in the style of Adelaide Hall.

Ellington stated:

> When I wrote "On a Turquoise Cloud" I had Kay Davis' voice in mind. She's a great musician and she could read at sight. The first time we did "Turquoise Cloud" was at Carnegie Hall [in 1947] and we had a very short rehearsal that afternoon just to run through it once. At the concert that night she put the music on the stand with the other musicians and read it right on down like we did.

The recording ban finally had been lifted in November 1944, and Ellington brought both women into the studio on December 1, 1944. Al Hibbler soloed on "Don't You Know I Care," and joined Davis on "I Ain't Got Nothin' but the Blues." Sherrill recorded "I Didn't Know about You" and "I'm Beginning to See the Light." The latter turned out to be a major hit when it was issued in 1945, and for several months was among the top ten songs. Ten days later, the musicians were back in the studios again to record four excerpts from *Black, Brown and Beige*: "Worksong," "Come Sunday," "The Blues," and "Three Dances."

The third Carnegie Hall concert was on the night of December 19, 1944. Ellington had written two new extended compositions for the event: *Blutopia* and *Perfume Suite*, written with Strayhorn. The four excerpts from *Black, Brown and Beige* were played, along with numbers from the orchestra book, notably Kay Davis recreating Adelaide Hall's famous vocalise on "Creole Love Call."

The band was back in the studios again on January 4, 1945. "Carnegie Blues," "Blue Cellophane," "Mood to Be Wooed," and "My Heart Sings" (featuring Sherrill on vocals) were recorded. "Carnegie Blues" was originally an orchestral interlude for the trombones in *Black, Brown and Beige*, which Ellington developed into a full-scale work for the orchestra.

Mid-January found the musicians on the West Coast. Besides one-night stands, they did their usual theater dates at the Golden Gate in San Francisco and the Orpheum in Los Angeles and Oakland. While at the Orpheum in Los Angeles, Greer had an accident. The band sat on a moveble stage that rolled forward as the curtain opened. "We were rehearsing the show that morning, when the stage did a sudden jerk forward," Sonny said. "I was adjusting one of the gongs and fell backward off the stage and hurt my back."

The great drummer Sidney Catlett filled in for Greer for three weeks. "That was an interesting time," guitarist Fred Guy recalled:

> Catlett was known to drive a band. I had heard him with Louis's [Armstrong's] band. We didn't know what to expect the first night. He was a big man, yet he played with very a light touch. He sat in on Sonny's drums and when Duke kicked off "A Train," he had us in a "groove" that felt like we were floating on air. I looked over at Duke, he was smiling and so was I. It was a great three weeks.

On February 16, the band was booked into Ciro's in Los Angeles. It would be the first time a high-priced, big-name black band would play at this posh nightclub. Ellington played to capacity audiences during the two weeks he was there, but the engagement was not without some unpleasantness. According to Harry Carney, on opening night, the actor John Garfield, who had helped finance *Jump for Joy*, arrived with friends. Ellington joined them for a drink; later, he was informed by the management that "the help was not allowed to socialize with the guests."

The following night, an old friend from the Cotton Club days, George Raft, arrived with a party of sixteen. The band played "Sweet Georgia Brown," which was Raft's favorite piece of music, as well as being the work he used to dance to. "We tore it up for him," Greer recalled. "So all right, we're finished, we go down, me and Duke. Here comes the maitre d' [and he said] 'I'm sorry, Mr. Ellington, but the help don't sit at the table with the guests.'"

Raft, then a reigning star in Hollywood, decided to pull rank. Greer recalled that Raft angrily replied, "'These are my friends, they can't sit down?' he said. 'I tell you what to do pal. Let's take the whole table and put it in the alley there and set everything up there and we won't disturb your guests and Sonny and Duke are going to have a sip.' They brought the whole table out in the alley. We cabareted up a storm. And George told this character, 'Listen here, fellow, any time I come in this place, and somebody's a friend of mine, don't you ever try to insult them, because I'll see that nobody comes in here. You'll have to wait on the other waiters.'"

April 4, 1945, found the band back in New York City at another swank restaurant, the 400, located at Fifth Avenue and 43rd Street. Ellington would be paid $3,500 weekly, identical to what Tommy Dorsey, who had preceded him, had been paid. He had finally reached parity with white bands. The band did coast-to-coast broadcasts nightly. In addition, beginning on April 7, the band began a series of half-hour broadcasts every Saturday over the ABC network, titled, "Your Saturday Date with the Duke." These broadcasts, unprecedented for their time, were underwritten by the U.S. Treasury to spur the sale of war bonds.

The broadcast of April 14 had to be cancelled: President Roosevelt had died two days earlier. Ellington, who had been rebuffed in trying to play for the president during his lifetime, got the opportunity to play for his funeral. Solemn classical music dominated the airwaves that day. Ellington's contribution was a program of blues and spirituals. *Variety* noted that "no other dance band could have filled the spot without arousing criticism," and the critics stated that it "provided a more moving tribute than any of the symphony works of the old masters that pervaded the networks."

Ellington opened the program with the somber strains of "Moon Mist," followed by excerpts from *New World A-Comin'*, played by him unaccompanied at the piano. Al Hibbler sang the spiritual "Nobody Knows the Trouble I've Seen," followed by the band playing "Mood Indigo," then another blues written especially for the occasion, "Chant for F. D. Roosevelt." Johnny Hodges's gorgeous alto was heard on "Come Sunday." Kay Davis sang "City Called Heaven" and supplied the vocal obbligato on "Creole Love Call." "Moon Mist" was heard as the band faded out over the air.

Mercer was in the Army at the time, stationed at Camp Shanks on Long Island. He recalled, "When I saw Pop the next day, I told him everybody thought what he did was great. Years later when we were talking about that day, he told me he felt that was one of the highlights of his career. His was the only non-symphonic music played on the air that day and he would carry the memory of that day to his grave."

I was with Luis Russell's orchestra, working at the Club Riviera in St. Louis, Missouri, that day. I was putting on my band uniform, preparing to go to work, when the phone rang. It was Russell, who said, "Come down to Abernathy's [the owner of the hotel's] suite. Duke's playing for the president's funeral." As "Moon Mist" was fading out over the air, Frank Galbreath shook his head and said, "Nobody but Duke could have pulled that off."

The band left the 400 Club on the first of May, and went on the road for three months. There were the usual theater dates and one-night stands. The Treasury broadcasts continued. Because the Treasury broadcasts were advertising merchandise (war bonds), a special permit was required from the Musicians Union to allow the band to play. Normally, the union required extra pay for musicians when they were promoting a product. However, because these broadcasts were benefiting the war effort, Ellington was given a blanket permission by James C. Petrillo, president of the union, to continue the broadcasts while on the road. Petrillo and the AFM were dutifully given credit on the subsequent forty-plus radio appearances.

The band came off the road and was back on Broadway in September at the Club Zanzibar (formerly the Hurricane) for a three-month stay. On opening night, there were complications. Louis Jordan and his Tympani Five were also featured. Ellington's contract stipulated that he was to get top billing—as did Jordan's. Concerned about possible lawsuits, the club management became creative and advertised the show without using names at all. Newspaper ads were created to give the show a mysterious aura, such as the following:

> This space was reserved to announce the cast of the new show opening at the Club Zanzibar tomorrow. However, as a gesture of cooperation with the police department, we are witholding this atomic array of explosive entertainment to avoid a near riot that would follow if everybody knew who was going to open at the Zanzibar. . . . While we may be speechless right now, this show will be the talk of the town. Not only the greatest cast of names ever assembled in a café, but the most unusual combination of potent names ever to be booked will appear together on one stage. It is so sensational, you wouldn't believe it even if we told you.

The billing feud was settled amicably three days after the show opened, when Jordan agreed to be billed as an "Extra Added Attraction," allowing Ellington to get top billing.

Trumpeter Ray Nance was not with the band on opening night. He had left to form a small group of his own, and took Alvin Raglin, the bass player, with him. Ellington did not replace Nance, but found Lloyd Trotman as a temporary replacement for Raglin. Trotman held down the chair until the week of November 19 when Oscar Pettiford arrived from the West Coast.

Pettiford, born into a large, musical family, was a multi-instrumentalist. He played in his father's touring band, which was based in Minneapolis, Minnesota. At age twenty-one, he was playing in the Charlie Barnet orchestra. Engagements with small groups led by Roy Eldridge and Dizzy Gillespie followed. "Pettiford patterned [his playing] after Blanton in his soloing," Lawrence Brown said. "See a bass didn't solo too much before Blanton. . . . And Pettiford went a step further, he did on a cello what Blanton did on bass."

"He [Pettiford] was a good bass player," Freddie Guy stated. "But nobody could fill a room like Blanton. He came in the band around the time 'Tricky' had the stroke." Trombonist "Tricky Sam" Nanton had a stroke on November 18, and was hospitalized at Harlem Hospital. Ellington immediately sent for Wilbur DeParis to replace him.

At age forty-seven, Wilbur DeParis—whose band was hired to replace Ellington so he could fulfill his Cotton Club engagement back in 1927—joined the Ellington orchestra. "He and I were in Louis's [Armstrong's] band together," Frank Galbreath recalled. "He took his work seriously, was always on time, and a great section man."

"I had just walked in the door of the Rhythm Club in Harlem, when one of the musicians told me Duke had called and was looking for me," DeParis said. "When I spoke to him on the phone he told me Nanton had had a stroke and he needed me to play the 'growl.'"

The band closed at the Zanzibar on December 4, 1945. It was then booked for engagements in the Midwest and Canada. Cornetist Rex Stewart had put in his two weeks' notice, and planned to leave when the group got to Chicago. The band continued to lose its original members. "We were at the Howard [Theater in April 1946]," Harry Carney noted. "The show was about to hit for an evening performance. Before the curtain opened, [sax player] Toby [Hardwick] and Duke got into an argument. It was over a woman, and Toby walked off the bandstand and never played with us again."

Russell Procope, a veteran of the John Kirby sextet, was recruited to replace Hardwick. "Duke asked me to come with him," Procope recalled:

Hardwick had wandered off and got lost and Duke didn't know where to find him. When I joined, it was just on a temporary basis for a broadcast he had to make in Worcester, Massachusetts. He asked me to take the train up and I had no idea I would be with him one week or even a month later. After the broadcast he said, "You might as well stay for a dance we have tonight in Providence." One night led to a week, a week led to a month, a month led to a year, and I wound up staying twenty-eight years!

Ellington observed, "Russell was a good combination, he's a good first man and he played that good New Orleans clarinet which was a complete contrast to Jimmy Hamilton, who was strictly Boehm, and Russell who was Albert." The Boehm fingering system for the clarinet was the more modern and generally accepted one for the instrument; however, older New Orleans musicians preferred the Albert system, which enabled them to achieve more dramatic slides and other effects.

"Tricky Sam" Nanton never completely recovered from his stroke. "He was back with us after about a month," Harry Carney recalled, "but Duke kept DeParis in the section to give him a rest. Then when we were in California, one morning we were all on the bus getting ready to go [and] there was no Tricky. They sent someone to his room and found him dead."

With Tizol gone, Lawrence Brown was the only remaining member of what had been considered one of the greatest trombone sections in all of jazz. "We had a one-night stand that night," Greer stated. "Duke asked DeParis to bring Tricky's horn, set it up, and leave the chair vacant. All night long, he just kept staring at that chair. Then to make matters worse, a few weeks later he heard Jonesy had died." Richard Bowdoin Jones, Ellington's valet and chief factotum since the Cotton Club days in 1927, died after a long illness on August 6, 1946.

The band then returned to New York for another Broadway engagement, in residence at the Aquarium Restaurant. While there, Ellington and Strayhorn were kept busy writing music for a Broadway show.

"One of the things Pop always wanted to do was a Broadway show," Mercer recalled. Ellington was commissioned to write the music for *Beggar's Holiday*, an updated version of John Gay's *The Beggar's Opera*. John LaTouche, who, along with Vernon Duke, had written the stage version of *Cabin in The Sky*, was the lyricist. The project had begun in early February, and Greer recalled LaTouche and Ellington, and occasionally Strayhorn, working on the score off and on through the summer. LaTouche, in fact, joined Ellington on tour for a period of time.

The plot of *Beggar's Holiday* revolved around the exploits of a suave New York mobster, his three women, and their various trials and tribulations with the law, ending with a trick electric chair sequence and a happy ending for all.

The eminent director John Houseman had been imported from Hollywood, and rehearsals began on October 21, 1946. The cast of thirty-five was headed by the singer Libby Holman and included Alfred Drake, who had made a name for himself in *Oklahoma!*, as well as Zero Mostel, who would later gain fame in *A Funny Thing Happened on the Way to the Forum* and *Fiddler on the Roof.*

The cast was interracial, which was unusual for the time, to say the least. Also, the casting worked against stereotypes: The white actor Alfred Drake was cast as Macheath (a mobster) and Rollin Smith was cast as a black chief of police. Holman left the show before opening night and was replaced by Bernice Parks. Avon Long and Marie Bryant also had featured parts. Chorus dancers and the production team of Perry Watkins and John R. Sheppard were racially mixed as well.

"Most people don't know this, but Strayhorn wrote a lot of the music for that show," Sonny Greer said. The out-of-town tryouts did not go well, and when the show returned to New York, John Houseman was replaced by George Abbott as the director. Abbott stated, "I was brought on board as [director], and it was evident to me a great many changes had to be made including some new songs and other changes in the music. I never saw Duke Ellington, never worked with him. Billy [Strayhorn] took care of whatever I asked for. He sat down and wrote it right there when it was needed."

Beggar's Holiday opened officially on December 26, 1946. It was one of the most expensive productions ever to have opened on Broadway at the time. The costs were estimated as between $300,000 and $350,000. It needed to gross at least $27,000 a week to survive. It was unable to do that, partly because it was facing competition from some of the previous season's long-running musicals, including *Annie Get Your Gun, Carousel,* and *Oklahoma!* During the run of *Beggar's Holiday,* two more musicals opened on Broadway, *Finian's Rainbow* in January 1947, and *Brigadoon* in March.

In addition, the critical response ranged from enthusiastic—"Most interesting musical since 'Porgy and Bess'," John Chapman, *Daily News*; "A brilliant musical," John Baggar, *World-Telegram*; "A score and lyrics we can be proud of," Brooks Atkinson, *New York Times*—to a stern thumbs down: "Ellington score biggest disappointment," Walter Winchell; "Evening Dosen't Come Off," Richard Watts, *New York Post*; "Evening left us cold," Coleman, *Daily Mirror.*

Although *Beggar's Holiday* was not the success its creators had envisioned, Ellington had some consolation. He had swept the tenth annual *Downbeat* band poll in unprecedented fashion, rating first in both the "Swing Band" and "Sweet Band" categories. He had previously won the "Swing Band" award in 1940, 1943, and 1945.

39

1947 BEGAN WHAT could best be described as Ellington's "wilderness years," which would last until his performance at the Newport Jazz Festival in 1956. Big bands were going out of style. Both Woody Herman and Count Basie disbanded their groups, as did Charlie Barnet. Jimmie Lunceford had dropped dead in a record store. Indeed, when Ellington won a *Downbeat* poll in 1949, the magazine noted that his was the sole winning band from the voting lists that was still working!

Solo singers, such as Peggy Lee, Patti Page, Mel Torme, Perry Como, and Dick Haymes, had broken free of the bands and now stood as performers in their own right. The small "jump" bands—such as Louis Jordan and his Tympani Five or Joe Liggins and his Honeydrippers—were all the rage and cheaper for the promoters to hire. The ballrooms and movie houses were no longer feasible places of employment. The ballrooms were closing, as people began to stay home and pursue other leisure activities. Television had begun to bring entertainment into America's living rooms. Many cinema houses were adapting their stages to take advantage of the technical advances in moviemaking, including Cinerama or Cinemascope. This often lead to eliminating or greatly reducing the performing space available. And, with a blockbuster movie on the screen, there was no need for stage acts to fill out the bill.

The younger musicians no longer modeled themselves on Benny Goodman, Benny Carter, Johnny Hodges, Roy Eldridge, or Coleman Hawkins. There were new models to emulate—Dizzy Gillespie, Miles Davis, Clifford Brown, Serge Chaloff, Thelonius Monk, and Charlie Parker—who were in the vanguard of the bebop revolution that was replacing swing. Their groups used from five to seven musicians, but still provided the excitement of a much larger group. Club owners, looking to make more money, could pay these groups less.

Ellington—who had won the *Downbeat* poll in 1946—found himself being taken to task by the magazine three years later. "Isn't it about time the Ellington orchestra was disbanded before what's left of a great reputation is completely dragged in the muck?" asked the writer Mike Levin. He felt that the group had become "a sloppy disinterested band" and wondered whether Ellington himself was "dispirited, wondering if he was written out." He concluded that "Ellington has made no good records in the past three years." Levin's point was buttressed by a review of Ellington's latest recording, of "Singin' in the Rain," in the same issue. A reviewer noted that it was "one of the worst records Ellington has made in recent years."

Both Sonny Greer and Harry Carney attested to the fact that, by the end of 1945, Ellington had become dissatisfied with RCA Victor. "He had a big fight with them over recording the pieces from *Black, Brown and Beige*," the drummer said. Not only that, according to Carney, but Ellington was also dissatisfied with the level of promotion that Victor was giving his records. "All he wanted was the same kind of publicity they gave Tommy Dorsey's records," Carney recalled. "He never felt he got that."

In May 1946, Ellington signed a contract with Musicraft Records. This company was one of the new, postwar independents, striving for recognition. It had already signed Artie Shaw, Teddy Wilson, and the singers Kitty Kallen and Sarah Vaughn, among others. The label's president, Oliver Sabin, eager to sign Ellington, offered him a contract for three years. Guaranteed was a return of $75,000 for thirty-four sides, plus a separate arrangement for the production of two albums annually. For these albums he was to draw a separate royalty at the rate of 6 percent of the purchase price, which was estimated to bring his income from the contract to the neighborhood of $100,000.

By June of 1947, however, Ellington had severed his contract with Musicraft. The company had begun to have financial problems shortly after he joined them. A new management team was brought on, and the finances improved. Ellington could have thrown a monkey wrench into the reorganization by insisting on the full terms of his contract. He had received $45,000 from the firm already, and could lay claim to $80,000 by simply declaring himself ready to make more recordings. Instead, he chose to take a $25,000 buyout, freeing himself to look elsewhere.

"Duke was smart," Harry Carney said. "Basie had told him not to tell anyone that both he and John Hammond were leaving Columbia Records." Ellington would never have signed with Columbia if Hammond were still there, and certainly wouldn't have wanted to compete with the Basie band for the label's attention. Once the announcement was made, William Morris arranged a recording contract for Ellington with Columbia, although the financial arrangement was not as good as the one he had with Musicraft. But the ink was barely dry on the contract when James C. Petrillo, president of the American Federation of Musicians, announced another ban on recordings by members of his union; this ban would last until December 15, 1948.

This led to a rush by all the recording companies to pile up backlog masters as fast as their artists could record them. On Christmas Eve, 1947, Ellington was in the Columbia studios recording his major composition of 1947, *Liberian Suite*, commissioned by the government of Liberia to celebrate the nation's centennial. The band also recorded some other outstanding Ellington compositions. Johnny Hodges was featured on "Lady of the Lavender Mist." In "On a Turquoise Cloud," Kay Davis's voice blends with the reeds and trombones to great effect. Jimmy Hamilton demonstrated his virtuosity on the clarinet with "Air Conditioned Jungle." For Lawrence Brown, Ellington had written "Golden Cress," and a newcomer in the trombone section, Tyree Glenn, was featured on "Sultry Serenade."

By 1952, Ellington had become disenchanted with Columbia. "Pop had the same complaint with Columbia that he had with RCA," Mercer observed. "The records would come out and they were never adequately promoted." Ellington asked for his release from the Columbia contract, and it was given. He promptly signed a recording contract with Capitol Records. This firm, founded in the early 1940s by the songwriter Johnny Mercer, had the reputation for aggressively pursuing major entertainers and just as aggressively promoting them.

In the summer of 1948, Ellington set sail for England on the R.M.S. *Media*. He had a return date at the Palladium Theatre beginning July 21 for two weeks. Because of the English ban on American musicians, the band did not accompany him. Ellington went as a solo act, bringing Kay Davis and Ray Nance with him. The show also featured the famed dancers, the Nicholas Brothers, and the singer Pearl Bailey, whose brother Bill had appeared in this house with Ellington fifteen years earlier.

Duke thoroughly enjoyed his stay in London. He "spent his time happily in a Curzon Street apartment, indulging himself at shops like Turnbull and Asser, where he bought shirts by the dozen down the years that followed in keeping with his reputation as a dandy dresser."

He found time to spend with Renee Gertler and her husband, Leslie Diamond. "Once breakfasting with them, he began dancing to his 1933 tune, 'Merry Go Round' which was on the Gramophone. Suddenly he stopped and shook his head. 'Kids, did I ever play *that* good?'"

Ellington, Nance, and Davis played a series of dates throughout England and Scotland, then traveled across the English Channel for a date in Paris, two in Brussels, and performances in Antwerp, Zurich, and Geneva. The troupe boarded the *Queen Elizabeth* in Cherbourg, bound for Southampton and New York City, on July 30.

For the rest of the Ellington band, the trip to England constituted a vacation. Johnny Hodges led many of the remaining members, including Jimmy Hamilton, trombonist Tyree Glenn, Strayhorn, Raglin, and Greer, in a band at the Apollo Cafe on 125th Street. They gave Ellington a welcome home party when he arrived back in New York.

"The first thing Pop did when he got back home was to go hear them," Mercer recalled. "While in Europe he had heard they were tearing it up at the Apollo Cafe and the management wanted to keep them as the house band. Johnny told him they were just waiting for him, so they could go back to work."

"We had a great time [during] those three weeks." Sonny Greer recalled. "Johnny was blowing his ass off. Man we had that place jumping. A lot of people from downtown kept coming by and wanting to sign us up. Johnny said no, he felt he had an obligation to Duke."

While Hodges chose to stay, another member of the Cotton Club band decided to leave. The year 1949 began with guitarist Freddie Guy putting in his two weeks' notice. "I'd been on the road twenty-five years," Guy said. "I had made some connections in Chicago and left the band after the concert in the Civic Opera House." Ellington never replaced him. "You grow and grow and grow and it gets more expensive. Getting rid of the guitar was a useful economy," Ellington said.

"I missed Freddie," Sonny Greer said. "He had a right arm like a metronome, and you could hear every note of those chords."

Mercer felt that around this time his father began to develop a pronounced form of paranoia. "He blamed different things on different sets of people," Mercer said:

> In world events, he believed prominent men were often influenced to act wrongly or indulge in reprisals by women somewhere in the background. He'd take headlines and check back to prove his theory. When something bad happened on the international level, he often saw the handiwork of people in powerful positions, communists, financiers, or both.

What Mercer did not know was that, beginning in 1938, the FBI had been monitoring his father's activities, and his file ran through 1963. It was clear that the agency considered him a communist sympathizer.

With the music business at a low ebb in the United States, Ellington, still savoring the memories of the past European tour, booked the band for another. England was out, but beginning on April 6, 1950, the band would play concerts in France, Belgium, the Netherlands, Switzerland, Italy, Germany, Denmark, and Sweden.

Besides Ellington, only Lawrence Brown, Carney, Hodges, and Greer were left from the band that had taken Europe by storm in 1939. Al Killian, Ernie Royal, Ray Nance, Harold Baker, and Nelson Williams made up the trumpet section. Brown was joined by Claude Jones and Ted Kelly in the trombone section, replacing Tyree Glenn. Glenn's wife flatly refused to let him go to Europe: She had learned that, while Glenn was in Paris with Don Redman's band, he had had an affair with a Frenchwoman.

Tenor saxophonists Don Byas and Jimmy Forrest joined Hamilton, Procope, Hodges, and Carney in what was now a six-man reed section. Jimmy Blanton's cousin, Wendell Marshall, was on bass. Sonny Greer was not all that well, so Duke brought along Butch Ballad as a relief drummer. In addition, Evie joined Duke when they sailed from New York on the *Ile de France* on March 29.

"She told me that was the happiest time of her life," Mercer recalled. "She had never been to Europe before, and Pop gave her money every day to go out shopping."

While in Paris, the band was visited by Ellington's London friends, the Diamonds. Leslie Diamond took Duke to task over the band's general appearance and work habits. "At the Palladium in 1933, they were all in tails," Diamond recalled. "Now they come on in crumpled suits, stained and shabby. . . . And this habit you've slipped into of letting the musicians drift on one by one. Why?"

"There was an old belief that the man who rushed to take his seat first was the one most afraid of losing his job," Mercer recalled.

"Duke would sit at the piano and 'comp' until everyone was on the stand, then he'd give a signal and the band would hit," Frank Galbreath said. "You see, once they were on the stand, he expected them to bust their ass for him. And if they didn't, they'd hear about it."

The programs Duke played in Europe consisted mainly of the old favorites. "We didn't play any of the new stuff," Sonny Greer said. "And every night we did the medley." Mercer stated, "He evolved a medley [of his hits] where he bunched them all up, and he got them all over in about ten minutes. 'I'm Beginning to See the Light,' 'Mood Indigo,' . . . And it served another purpose because when it comes to ASCAP, you get so much for the numbers you perform. He had enough in there for them to be counted as performances, and so in ten minutes he had twenty tunes he had performed that he would get dough for as far as ASCAP was concerned!" The medley was, in part, a way of financing the tour.

The band returned to the United States on June 30, 1950, having played seventy-four concerts in seventy-seven days. On the return trip, Ellington spent a good part of the time in his cabin aboard the *Ile de France*. He had begun to write his *Harlem Suite*, commissioned by Arturo Toscanini's NBC Symphony.

After a two-week rest, the band was back on the road. Ellington, who had been having trouble with the tenor saxophone chair, finally stabilized it for the next two decades with the addition of Paul Gonsalves in December 1950. He easily filled the gap that followed Webster's departure. Gonsalves had a breathy, rich tone that identified him as a Coleman Hawkins disciple, and had put in tours of duty with Count Basie and Dizzy Gillespie.

"When he came in the band, he knew every Webster solo by heart," Harry Carney said. Gonsalves once stated, "If I die tomorrow, I'll consider I've been successful, because when I began to study it was with the idea of being with that band."

In January 1951, trumpeter Cat Anderson rejoined the band. After his departure four years earlier, he had led a big band of his own for two years, then played around the Boston area with the bands of Jimmy Tyler and Sabby Lewis. He rejoined Ellington just in time to play in the premiere performance of the *Harlem Suite*. The Metropolitan Opera House had been rented by the NAACP for a benefit concert. The correspondent from *Downbeat* felt that this new extended piece was among the evening's "most successful works." In addition, the audience heard "Ring Dem Bells" and "The Mooche," and Kay Davis thrilled the crowd singing "Coloratura" from the *Perfume Suite.*

In the *Harlem Suite,* Ellington takes the listener on a Sunday stroll through the area he loved best. There are a series of elegant themes that follow the opening trumpet statement.

In this work, even though it was not played in strict tempo, Ellington manages to keep the feeling of jazz at all times. And he was able to negotiate the changes in tempo with ease. There is a stunning contrapuntal hymn using clarinet, trombone, trumpet, and occasionally the rest of the band. There are several interesting passages for the trombones, and a Carney clarinet solo. Ellington was able to keep the listeners' interest all the time.

Cat Anderson's return was offset by three devastating departures at the end of February. Johnny Hodges, Lawrence Brown, and Sonny Greer (Greer was the last of the original "Washingtonians") left the band. Sonny recalled, "Now and then Johnny and I would talk about the summer of '48 when we had such a ball playing at the Apollo Cafe. We were talking about it one night on the road, when he told me he was going to leave the band and go with Norman Grantz, and asked me if I wanted to come."

Joining Hodges, Brown, and Greer were Al Sears, tenor sax; Emmett Berry, trumpet; Joe Benjamin, bass; and Leroy Lovett, piano. "Sure I pulled Johnny and the others out of the band," the jazz producer/promoter Norman Grantz admitted. "I'd been very close to him ever since 1941, when *Jump for Joy* was in Los Angeles. . . . I felt [Hodges] was kept down in the band. I wanted to record him outside of the Ellington context, and that's why he and the others came out. . . . Johnny's band had one big hit: 'Castle Rock.'"

As we know, Ellington liked things to go smoothly, and preferred to avoid confrontation at any cost. Grantz recalled, "It disturbed him equally if the room service didn't work somewhere, or if Johnny Hodges quit the band. Both upset his life, and he hated it. So he was really piqued when I took Johnny away."

Ellington's musical life was at stake, and he responded ruthlessly. From the band of Harry James, Duke enticed away Willie Smith to replace Hodges, Juan Tizol to take his old friend Brown's chair, and Louis Bellson to play drums. The incident was known as the "Great James Robbery." "He had to pay top dollar to get them," Mercer recalled.

Harry Carney said, "Willie told me that Tizol asked him to tell Harry that the three of them were leaving. He and Harry were tight. When Willie told him, he didn't say anything for a while, then smiled and said, 'Can I come too?'"

For Ellington there was no such thing as losing. A friend once induced him to spend an afternoon at the racetrack. The man considered himself a good handicapper of horses. After each race he was astonished to see Ellington go up to the parimutuel betting window and cash in a winning ticket. It was some time later that he learned Ellington always held a winning ticket by simple expedient of betting on every horse in every race!

1951 came to a close with several new musicians being added to the band. Two excellent trumpet players, Clark Terry and Willie Cook, joined them, along with Britt Woodman, who replaced Quentin Jackson in the trombone section.

40

THE CONTRACT WITH Capitol expired in 1955. Ellington was unhappy with the label; his records were not selling and the band was in a slump. However, no other label seemed eager to sign him. As a stopgap measure, he signed with Bethlehem, a small Chicago-based recording company, for two sessions on February 7 and 8, 1956.

The return of Johnny Hodges on saxophone and the additions of Sam Woodyard in the percussion chair and Jimmy Woode on bass had, in fact, stabilized the band. The Bethlehem sessions were almost a retrospective of Ellington's career. The band cut "East St. Louis Toodle-Oo" and "Creole Love Call" from the 1920s; "Stompy Jones" and "Jeep Is Jumpin'" from the 1930s; "Ko-Ko," "Jack the Bear," "In a Mellow Tone," "Midriff," and "Cotton Tail" from the 1940s; and "Upper Manhattan Medical Group" (after Dr. Logan's medical practice) and "Unbooted Character" representing the 1950s. In addition, there were Strayhorn-Ellington collaborations on a series of standards: "Laura," "Indian Summer," "Summertime," "Deep Purple," and "I Can't Get Started."

"Those recordings sounded very good. I liked them," Mercer recalled:

> I spoke to Pop while they were working at the Flamingo Hotel in Las Vegas, during the month of May, he felt the band was starting to come together. He later called me from San Francisco to tell me how much better they sounded. He was in good spirits when he got back home. He was looking forward to doing "Night Creatures" with the New Haven Symphony. Then Newport happened.

The 1956 Newport Jazz Festival was to be a turning point in Ellington's career. The band was playing better than it had for years; the jazz world was emerging from its preoccupation with bebop and was ready to hear something new. Ellington's performance at Newport reignited his career and made him relevant—and popular—once more.

On July 7, I drove down from Boston to Newport, Rhode Island, specifically to hear Ellington, who was to open and close the show. In between, the singer Anita O'Day, the pianist Friedrich Gulda, and groups led by Bud Shank, Teddy Wilson, Jimmy Guiffre, and Chico Hamilton performed.

Hamilton did not get onstage until 11:15 and his set ended at 11:45. I wondered how much Ellington I would get to hear at that hour, inasmuch as I figured the concert would end at midnight. The band opened with the "Newport Jazz Festival Suite," which had been commissioned for the occasion, and it was met with respectful applause.

The band played a few more numbers, including "Jeep's Blues" featuring Hodges, as I, along with the rest of the crowd, were slowly moving toward the exits. Then Ellington announced "Diminuendo and Crescendo in Blue," with an interlude on saxophone by Paul Gonsalves. I found a chair and sat down to listen to the work.

Following the "Diminuendo" section, Ellington did a modulation. Gonsalves came to the microphone, and began to tear off smoothly running passages. Somewhere around the sixth or seventh chorus, someone close to me said, "Are you hearing what I'm hearing?"

"Paul or the crowd?" another person responded.

"Something's happening here," I said to him.

Gonsalves's playing electrified the members of the crowd, bringing them to their feet. Reviewing the concert for *Downbeat*, Leonard Feather wrote:

> Here and there in the reduced, but still multitudinous crowd, a couple got up and started jitterbugging. Within minutes, the whole of Freebody Park was transformed as if struck by a thunderbolt. Photographers rushed madly to the scene of each gathering knot of onlookers, while Gonsalves, Duke and the whole band, inspired by the reaction they had started, put their all into the work. He kept on rolling for twenty-seven choruses. Hundreds of spectators climbed up on their chairs to see the action.

As the band struck the final chord of "Crescendo in Blue," the crowd exploded. "I never heard anything like it; it was awesome!" my neighbor exclaimed. Ellington played four more encores to cool off the crowd, and it was after one in the morning when the audience finally left.

Reviewing the concert, Leonard Feather noted: "Within an hour, reporters and critics were buzzing about it. By the next morning it was conceded to have been one of the most exciting performances any of them ever heard."

Earlier in his life, when Ellington was asked about his success at the Cotton Club, he remarked, "I was the right guy, in the right place, at the right time, doing the right thing." In Newport, he had done it again.

While in San Francisco, Ellington was informed that *Time* magazine was planning to feature him on its cover. Following Newport, the August 20 edition of the magazine appeared, with Ellington on the cover. The seven-page story inside recounted the triumphant performance at Newport, as well as his earlier career.

I still get chills listening to the live recording made at Newport that night. It sold hundreds of thousands of copies and became one of Ellington's biggest sellers. My son, while in the Southwest Pacific serving in the Peace Corps, asked me for a tape of the recording of "Diminuendo and Crescendo in Blue." He told me later that he had made seven copies of it for his friends and coworkers. Mercer felt the work was a testament to the underrated power of the blues: "Just recall what 'Every Day' meant to Count Basie, or 'Jelly Jelly' to Earl Hines, or 'After Hours' to Erskine Hawkins, all blues."

Three days after the Newport concert, Ellington and the New Haven Symphony played a concert at the Yale Bowl. "Night Creatures" and *New World A-Comin'* were among the works played. "It went well," Mercer recalled. "They were still on a high from Newport. Pop was in great shape."

Ellington would often say, "I was born in 1956 at the Newport Jazz Festival." Actually, he was reborn on the morning of the concert. Earlier that year, he had been signed by Columbia Records. At the festival, he met the man assigned by Columbia to be his executive producer, Irving Townsend. In return for paying the performance fees for all its recording artists appearing at the festival, Columbia had obtained exclusive rights to live recordings, including use of the Newport Jazz Festival name. When they met that morning, Ellington made two things plain: He wanted money up front to meet his payroll; and his first album for

the label was to be a new extended work, *A Drum Is a Woman.*
Townsend delivered on both.

When asked in 1966 which music gave the most satisfaction,
Ellington told the interviewer, "Of the big things, *A Drum Is a Woman,*
and some of my early songs. They're not big pop successes, you know,
but in all of them you feel the weight of joy."

In *A Drum Is a Woman*, Ellington attempted to trace the history of
jazz from its African origins through all stages of evolution to New
York's 52d Street, and finally to the moon. *A Drum Is a Woman* was first
shown on CBS-TV's "The United States Steel Hour" on May 8, 1957.
Ellington narrated a series of scenes, which were performed by the well-
known African-American dancers Carmen de Lavallade and Talley
Beatty. Musical selections were sung by Ozzie Bailey, Joya Sherrill, and
Margaret Tynes.

Downbeat observed:

> Music history and television history were made on the night of
> the 8th of May when, thanks chiefly to the superhuman efforts of
> Columbia Records' Irving Townsend, who brought Duke Ellington
> and U.S. Steel together, the first television jazz spectacular was per-
> formed. Here at last was an answer to the complaints that jazz and
> television are incompatible, for the show was a sumptuous wedding of
> visual and aural delights.

The plan to tell the story of jazz using Ellington's music dates back
to *Jump for Joy*. Orson Welles put Ellington on salary to prepare such a
work. The project was set aside, however, after little more than an outline had been prepared. This outline was dug out and completely
revamped by Ellington and Strayhorn. It served as the starting point for
three months of intense writing and rewriting. "He wrote lyrics, I wrote
lyrics, he wrote music, I wrote music," Strayhorn recalled.

Ellington and Strayhorn wrote the work during a series of one-
nighters and theater dates in the South and the West. According to
Mercer, at a date in Camden, New Jersey, Ellington completely baffled
a large dancing audience by asking the band to play sixteen measures of
what later became the music in the "Congo Square" sequence. When he

heard it, he turned to the bewildered audience and explained, "I just wanted to hear how it sounded."

Clark Terry recalled Ellington preparing him to play his part:

> He said to me, "Sweetie, you're going to portray the role of Buddy Bolden." I said, "Maestro, I don't know anything about Buddy Bolden. Not too many people know much about Buddy Bolden." He said, "Oh sure. Buddy Bolden was suave, he was debonair, and he was a marvelous person, he loved beautiful ladies around him, he had a big sound, he tuned up New Orleans and across the river in Algiers he would break glasses, he was so powerful. He loved diminishes. You know all these things." He says: "You *are* Buddy Bolden! Play me some diminishes and bent notes!" So I started playing and he said, "That's it, that's it!" And that's exactly what came off on the record of *A Drum Is a Woman*. So he could masterfully psych you into doing exactly what he wanted you to do!

Irving Townsend noted, "Until the end of his life he thought *A Drum Is a Woman* was one of his supreme achievements."

Ellington had followed his triumph at Yale Bowl the previous year with two concerts at the Festival Hall in Stratford, Ontario. The annual Shakespeare Festival was holding a jazz season in tandem with its regular presentation of Shakespeare plays. After the concerts, Ellington and Strayhorn decided to write a series of musical vignettes based on Shakespearean characters "in miniature and caricature," commonly known as "Such Sweet Thunder" after the first piece. "He and Billy Strayhorn really read up on the Bard for this one," Mercer said. Among those included were Puck, Julius Caesar, Henry V, Romeo and Juliet, Lady Macbeth, and Hamlet. In these recordings, Ellington and Strayhorn manage to capture the essence of Shakespeare's thick-textured verse. The portraits are full of wit and lush beauty.

Ellington, the master orchestrator, used a quartet consisting of Harry Carney's baritone saxophone and the trombones of Britt Woodman, John Sanders, and Quentin Jackson (who were known as The Telecasters) to represent Iago and Macbeth's witches. Johnny Hodges and Paul Gonsalves warmly evoke the passion of Romeo and

Juliet on "The Star Crossed Lovers." "Sonnet for Caesar" had Jimmy Hamilton playing his rich-toned clarinet at his imperious best. Strayhorn recalled their collaboration on the Bard's works:

> [W]e had to interpret his *words*. It took . . . about six months. We had all those books we used carry around, and all those people all over the U.S. we used to see and talk to . . . we couldn't get everything in! We didn't do *King Lear*, *Coriolanus*, or *All's Well that Ends Well* either.

Ellington noted, "I was only sorry that *Richard III* was left out—he was a good subject for the blues."

The work was first heard at New York's Town Hall on April 28, 1957. A "Music for Moderns" concert was held under the direction of the conductor of the New York Philharmonic, Dmitri Mitropoulos. He conducted a chamber orchestra of fifteen Philharmonic musicians in the first New York performance of Kurt Weill's violin concerto. But it was "the Ellington opus that stole the show," *Variety* noted.

Ellington returned to Festival Concert Hall in Stratford in summer 1958. After a performance of *A Winter's Tale*, the orchestra played a concert. The featured work was "Princess Blue," dedicated to Princess Margaret of Great Britain, who was attending the Shakespeare Festival. After the concert, the band also played before some six hundred specially invited guests at a ball in honor of the princess.

When the Ellington orchestra had last been in London in 1939, union rules had forbidden it to play. Finally, in 1958 an arrangement was made for an exchange: The Englishman Ted Heath's orchestra was allowed to tour the United States, and Ellington was granted permission to play in England. Ellington and his band arrived in Plymouth, England, aboard the *Ile de France* on October 3, 1958. Over the next forty-six days, they also gave concerts in Belgium, the Netherlands, Sweden, Denmark, Germany, Switzerland, Italy, and France.

The highlight of the tour was in England, at the Leeds Festival, where Ellington resumed his acquaintance with the British royal family. The Earl of Harewood, nephew of the former Prince of Wales and the Duke of Kent, a cousin of Queen Elizabeth and Princess Margaret, and his brother, the Honorable Gerald Lascelles, a great jazz lover, had secured Ellington's services for a concert.

The queen was not able to attend, but her husband, Prince Philip, was there. Prince Philip told Ellington he was sorry he had missed the opening number, one of his favorites, "Take the A Train." That evening, Ellington was presented to Her Majesty. She was quoted in the newspapers at the time as having told Duke, "I was so sorry I couldn't come to any of your concerts, but my husband tells me he thoroughly enjoyed himself when he listened to you this afternoon."

Ellington, of course, was in his glory. "Enormous crowds had collected outside the Civic Center for the Queen's visit. As Duke Ellington stepped out of his limousine, immaculate in white tie and tails, and onto the red carpet leading to the entrance, he received an huge ovation from the crowd. Observing that the majority of the admirers were of the fairer sex, he, in typical Ellington fashion, immediately threw them kisses, which were promptly and enthusiastically thrown back."

Seven people were presented to the queen that night. Ellington recalled:

> I was so thrilled by the whole thing. I was so impressed by Her Majesty because I noticed that she spoke differently to every person who was presented to her. She spoke French to the French, German to the German and when she spoke to me, she spoke American-English. . . . And she was very casual about it and we talked a lot. As a matter of fact I was the last person on line and she was sort of relaxed when she got to me, and we talked about her family, her father King George, her uncle Prince Edward, and the Duke of Kent, whom I had an occasion to meet. The Duke of Kent and I used to play four-hand at the piano at night, and Prince Edward was at several parties at which we played when we were there in 1933. Then one night, we had to hold the show for him in Liverpool. At another party he sat in on drums. . . . Then she told me about all the records of mine her father had. Then she asked me when was your first time in England? Oh, I said, oh my first time in England was in 1933, way before you were born. She gave me a real American look; very cool man, which I thought was too much.

Ellington promised to write some music for the queen, as he had already done for Princess Margaret. His gallantry did not go unnoticed.

At a gracious party that weekend in Buckingham Palace, by candlelight, he and Strayhorn played piano solos for their hosts. Out of that encounter came the *Queen's Suite.*

Rex Stewart recalled, "When I attended a few concerts by the band . . . I was amazed he didn't change shoes [between sets as he usually did]. Later I found out the reason. These were the pumps he had worn when he was presented to the Queen of England and despite their shabby appearance, they were now his favorites."

According to Mercer, Ellington probably set about composing the *Queen's Suite* as soon as he got to his hotel room that night, after meeting her. Two weeks later, at a party given for him by the Diamonds, he played the piano he had given them as a housewarming present. Observing that one petal had fallen from the bunch of roses on the piano, Duke produced an elegant melody, which he titled "The Single Petal of a Rose." Of that composition he wrote, "'The Single Petal of a Rose' so delicate, fragile, gentle, luminous. Only God could make one, and like love it should be admired but not analyzed." Ellington later made it a part of the *Queen's Suite.*

Some of the sections of the suite were inspired by the sounds of nature he heard while driving with Harry Carney to their next enagagement. Strayhorn assisted in composing some of these works. "Sunset and the Mocking Bird" was based on a phrase of birdsong he heard while driving from Tampa to West Palm Beach, Florida. Ellington playfully said, "We would have liked to have gone back and thanked the bird, but we were much too far down the road and we didn't know what kind of bird it was anyway. But the first phrase is the melody we heard." Similarly, "Lightining Bugs and Frogs" was a result of viewing at night "a million lightning bugs . . . weaving a spangled scrim, a design in symphonic splendor, while the frog in the orchestra pit [pond in the foreground] provided the audio accompaniment."

The work was recorded on February 25, 1959. Only one copy was pressed, and it was presented to the queen; Duke stipulated that no more would be made. After his death, the recording was issued to the general public. Irving Townsend noted, "Ellington went about the composition of the *Queen's Suite* with greater concentration than he displayed for any other music with which I was associated."

Townsend also produced the recording of Ellington's film score for the movie *Anatomy of a Murder*. Ellington had a bit part in the movie, playing four-hand piano with Jimmy Stewart, the star of the film. The music industry was full of praise for the score, awarding the Columbia soundtrack a Grammy in three different categories that year: Best Musical Composition of the Year; Best Performance by a Danceband; and Best Motion Picture Soundtrack of the Year.

"Pop was very surprised and pleased when he heard he had won it for the Best Motion Picture Soundtrack," Mercer said. Five years later, Ellington told an interviewer:

> *Anatomy of a Murder* was my first film score as such. I never thought it would earn an Academy Award [nomination] because it really hadn't an outstanding melody to hang on to. Yet it was a thing that was handled properly and with respect to the music—no, that's not a good way of saying it. What I mean, it wasn't done with the intention of trying to get a tune out of it, or a movie theme that would get an award. I was trying to do background music fittingly. And that, of course, I think is important!

Variety noted that "this score . . . wins an important case for the cause of jazz. Duke Ellington's score, as written by him and played by his own orchestra is a probing exercise in moods and colors. This is one soundtrack that stands on its own feet with a minimum of dependence on the screen's story." The reviewer neglected to mention one important fact, however: This was the first film score written by a jazz composer and played by his own orchestra.

The band had another successful engagement at Newport, before sailing to Europe aboard the S.S. *United States* on September 11, 1959. The band played engagements in Holland, France, Scandinavia, Germany, and Austria, returning to the United States aboard the R.M.S. *Queen Elizabeth* on November 3.

Ellington resumed his work consisting of nightclub engagements, one-night stands, and recording sessions. He finished the year 1959 with his final engagement at the Blue Note nightclub in Chicago, ending a relationship with the owner Frank Holzfiend that began in 1949.

In March 1960, Ellington began a six-week engagement at the Starlight Lounge in the Riviera Hotel in Las Vegas; his stay was subsequently extended to twelve weeks. "I went to his birthday out in Las Vegas," Mercer said. "He was playing at the Riviera Hotel, I went to wish him a Happy Birthday, [and] he kept me there for four weeks copying music. [But] He never said he needed me!"

While in Las Vegas, Mercer assisted in a personnel change. "My contribution was Aaron Bell to the Ellington band," he said, "at a time when the rhythm section was shakier than it had ever been. The one thing that bugged him more than anything else was not to have a bass player who could really get it straight."

"Jimmy Woode was still with the band at the time," Bell recalled, "but I think he wanted to leave and go to work with his father in Stockholm. Even then, I had doubts about traveling and staying with a band, but I found I liked it too much, and I got along nicely with Duke, so I decided to stay."

The addition of Bell did help to anchor the rhythm section. "It means a lot to him to have someone he can rely on on bass," Bell said, "because a lot of the times, when he's conducting and not playing piano, we're working with a two-man rhythm section. We have a sort of affinity for each other. I wouldn't say Duke's the greatest piano player in the world, but I would say he's the most distinctive."

In May 1960, there was another personnel change; an old Cotton Club hand, Lawrence Brown, joined the band in Las Vegas to reclaim his chair in the trombone section. After Hodges's band broke up, Brown had freelanced successfully around New York, playing in various shows and on recordings. He then secured a staff position at CBS.

"There's a peculiar thing about studio musicians," Brown told an interviewer. "They're great musicians, and anyone can sit in another's chair, and it doesn't change a thing at all. My thing is too individual, and I usually played second parts."

It was during the engagement at the Riviera that there was also a major change in Ellington's life: he met Fernandae de Castro Monte. Mercer recalled, "She was a tall, strikingly handsome blonde woman who stood bold, with her boots and suede pants and suede suits with slits at the sides."

She had just concluded a singing engagement in Las Vegas when their paths crossed. Mercer stated, "A fast friendship developed and flamed very brightly during this engagement. Normally, of course, he would have detested the fact that he had to be in one place so long. The affair got to the stage where *nobody* could see [Ellington] from the time he left the stand until he came back and sat down at the piano the next evening."

At the end of the engagement, the band left by train for Los Angeles. Fernandae went down to the station to see Ellington off, "smartly dressed in a mink coat," Mercer recalled. "Just as the train was about to pull out, she opened the coat. She had nothing on under it, and she wrapped it around him to give him his goodbye kiss.... He thought it was wonderful and the whole episode stimulated his imagination no end. Several of the men and I, not to mention a couple of open-mouthed observers on the station platform, saw it happen and could hardly believe it."

Fernandae was the fifth and final woman with whom Duke became seriously involved. Beginning with Edna, the list included Fredi Washington, Mildred Dixon, and Evie Ellis. Fernandae was about forty years old when they met, and Ellington was about to turn sixty-one. She had seen a lot of the world before she came to Las Vegas, a chanteuse who had worked in Europe and lived in Algeria and Brazil.

Fernandae was also very knowledgeable in music and art. Norman Grantz recalled taking her shopping in Madrid: "She knew the city intimately. She could introduce you to art dealers ... she was certainly cognizant with art. I guess it was Johnny Hodges who first started calling her Contessa."

Don George, a lyricist and close friend of Duke, recalled, "When they arrived at an airport, he with his incredible poise and regal bearing, she with her fur coats, blonde hair and sunglasses they looked like a royal couple on the road.... Everybody knew her wherever they went. She was greeted by name, 'Bonjour Contessa'; 'Buon giorno, Fernandae.' Duke often said, 'She knows every maitre d' in the world.'"

A friend of mine, while visiting France, recalled seeing the couple at the casino in Deauville. It was the high season and tables were nonexistent, yet when they arrived, they were greeted with open arms by the management, and addressed as "Monsieur le Duke and Madame Contessa." From out of nowhere, a table appeared, and they were seated.

Many years later, Mercer defined their relationship to me:

You see, almost all the women Pop became involved with expected him to take care of *them*. Fernandae figured it out right away, he
needed a woman to take care of *him*. We'd be in some hotel lobby at
six in the morning, on our way to the airport, she'd be up, her hair in a
bandanna, wearing boots and jeans. Her bags were packed, and Pop's
bags too. She'd let him sleep up to the last minute. When the bus
came, she'd go upstairs and get him.

"Fernandae was like Duke's personal manager," Don George
recalled. "'What time is the is the car coming?' or 'What time is the
plane leaving? I'll take it from there.'" She accompanied Ellington on
every trip from then on to England, France, Italy, Germany, Austria,
Sweden, Denmark, Japan, and the Far East.

Fernandae spoke five languages, which impressed Duke greatly. On
trips to England, they always traveled to engagements in a Rolls-Royce.
George stated, "Fernandae always ordered enough at the Dorchester to
keep the ride comfortable, just in case by the time they arrived in the
next town, the restaurants were closed. . . . She had enough ingredients
in the car to keep him going: crackers, cheese, champagne, wine, steaks,
and fruit. She found grapes in places where you couldn't find grapes.
She found everything Duke liked."

Mercer recalled an incident that happened outside of the
Dorchester Hotel:

> I had just paid the bill and when I got outside, Pop was sitting in
> the car. Fernandae had forgotten something, and went back to the
> suite to get it. He called me over to remind me some old friends
> would be coming to hear us that night, and to see that they were taken
> care of, with free tickets for the party. As we were talking, one of the
> bellboys came out with the hamper. Pop called him over; he wanted to
> see what was in it before it went on the front seat. He took a look, and
> nodded to the bellboy who put it up front. Then he said quietly,
> "Sometimes that woman takes *almost* as good care of me as your
> grandmother Daisy used to do."

On another occasion, Ellington said, "She makes sure I eat all right, and
that's enough for me." This care and concern did not come without a

price. George recalled an event that happened in Ceylon. "She floated into the jewelry shop in the lobby of the hotel, picked out a ring that had a two-thousand-dollar price tag, and dickered the proprietor down to seven hundred dollars." As she was leaving the shop, she tossed her head and told her companion, "Now we have to convince Duke to pay for this."

"She did a lot for Edward," Ruth Ellington said after his death. "She interpreted for him. She did research. She was very intellectual. I certainly liked her, as I liked anyone who could make Edward happy. She left New York after he died, and even when he was alive she wasn't here *all* the time. She was always going off to the Caribbean visiting friends."

Fernandae, although she was Ellington's most expensive companion, had a very constructive effect on him. His lifestyle felt her impact: The ham and eggs and the ice cream, staples of an American diet, were replaced with escargots, and paté de foie gras. He began eating caviar, which he was convinced was good for his virility. He drank vodka because she thought it was a sophisticated drink. He began to dress more casually, as a result of Fernandae's urging him to give up some of the more flamboyant outfits he had worn.

Mercer noted, "Unlike most of the other ladies who paid him attention, she never hesitated to voice criticism when it was called for."

Fernandae could distinguish between good and bad performances by the band, as well as good and bad music. She was particularly critical of Ellington's working habits with the band. He was famed for his procrastination. Irving Townsend, his friend and producer at Columbia, was astonished when the band arrived in the studio well rehearsed to record projects like the *Nutcracker Suite*, the *Peer Gynt Suite*, and *Suite Thursday*. While there were always last-minute changes, things were much better organized than in the past.

Mercer recalled, "I was in the recording studio when they did *Peer Gynt*. Townsend was all smiles. When it was over he said to me, 'Mercer, as long as I'm making recordings with your father, I hope he keeps that girl around.'"

41

LAWRENCE BROWN ARRIVED in Las Vegas the day the band closed at the Riviera. He said, "We spent time rehearsing *The Nutcracker Suite*, because we were going to record it when we got to Los Angeles. I was pleased we were taking the train again." *The Nutcracker Suite* was Ellington and Strayhorn's update of the Tchaikovsky classic. They also made similar arrangements of the music from Edvard Grieg's *Peer Gynt Suite*.

Billy Strayhorn recalled recalled how difficult his collaboration with Ellington on these two scores was:

> It took us quite a bit of time to consider how we were going to do them. The actual writing was nothing. You could do that overnight. It was the preparation that was tremendous. In both cases, we had to consider the composers. They're not *dead*. They're alive and that's their music, and we didn't want to offend them. Arriving at the treatment we gave them was *agonizing*. The Tchaikovsky took six months. We went through them and played those pieces over and over again. We listened to them and talked about them. I flew to California and *back*. But after we decided what to use and what not to use, and how to treat it—then you could sit down and do it in a day.

The *Nutcracker* and *Peer Gynt* marked the first time Ellington devoted a full album to an arrangement of other composers' works. It was clearly done with love and humor, especially the Tchaikovsky. The titles were given the distinctive Ellington touch: "The Volga Vouty" (Russian Dance); "Sugar Rum Cherry" (Dance of the Sugar Plum Fairy); and "Arabesque Cookie" (Arabian Dance). On the last piece, Russell Procope is heard playing bamboo flute, along with contributions from Juan Tizol on tambourine and Harry Carney on bass clarinet.

Ellington celebrated Lawrence Brown's return to the band by featuring him on "Zweet Zursday" in the suite *Suite Thursday*, commissioned for performance at the 1960 Monterey Jazz Festival in California. As they did in "Such Sweet Thunder," Ellington and Strayhorn this time wrote a musical parallel to John Steinbeck's story *Sweet Thursday*, set in the novelist's favorite habitat, Monterey's Cannery Row.

The four parts of the suite—"Misfit Blues," "Schwipti," "Zweet Zursday," and "Lay-By"—comprised an Ellington-Strayhorn collaboration at its best. "It was cross country," Mercer said. "Pop began 'Misfit Blues' on a minor sixth, when they got Strayhorn's 'Lay-By,' damned if it didn't end on a minor sixth! They knew each other that well."

When the work was premiered at the festival, *Time*, *Downbeat*, and *Metronome* all panned it to varying degrees. Yet, when the recording was issued it was met with universal praise. As they did with *Black, Brown and Beige*, once again the critics were unable to judge the work at first hearing.

One wonders if part of their judgment was not colored by an elaborate spoof Ellington had performed on them. During Ray Nance's violin solo on "Lay-By," he held up a sheet of music in front of him. This made it appear that Nance needed the music in order to play the piece. "The critics all complained about Pop, once again, not having the work done on time, and the piece sounded like it needed more rehearsal," Mercer stated. "What they didn't know was, the music was held upside down, and Ray was playing with his eyes closed! Not only that, they had been playing some of the music while they were on the road."

Indeed, when I had heard the band at a dance at the Hotel Bradford in Boston two months earlier, I was very impressed with a work that featured Nance on violin. When I asked Duke for its title, I was told it was called "Strad." On first hearing the recording of *Suite Thursday*, I immediately realized that "Strad" had been renamed "Lay-By."

The Academy Award nomination for the score of *Anatomy of a Murder* led to another commission for Ellington—for the film *Paris Blues*, starring Paul Newman, Joanne Woodward, Sidney Poitier, Diahann Carroll, and Louis Armstrong.

Writing the music for this motion picture gave Ellington the opportunity to do something he ordinarily did not do: writing for musicians who were not in his band. He told an interviewer:

I have to write for specific artists—specific sounds. The visual music was to be recorded in Paris, principally by French musicians, and the underscore, which amounted to half of the music, was to be done in New York with my band. One thing I knew in advance was that there was a lot of Louis [Armstrong] in the picture so I knew I had to write Louis to sound like Louis.

Ellington had to put his talent as an orchestrator to use, writing music for the scene in which a band greets Armstrong as he arrives in Paris by train. The group included an accordion, baritone sax, clarinet, trumpet, bass, and drums.

Ellington traveled to Paris in November 1960 to oversee the recording of the score. On the night of his arrival, Paul Newman and Joanne Woodward threw a party for him. The invited guests included the actors Yves Montand, Tony Perkins, Jean Sablon, and Ingrid Bergman. The French classical composer George Auric invited Ellington for dinner, along with the flutist Claude Bolling, after which the musicians entertained the guests by playing the piano. Ellington and Fernandae went to see the singers Edith Piaf and Charles Aznavour, attended the ballet, and had dinner in some of the best restaurants in Paris. On Christmas eve, Ellington was invited to play at a Catholic midnight mass, where he moved the congregation with a performance of "Come Sunday" from *Black, Brown and Beige*.

Ellington returned to New York shortly after New Year's Day 1961, and took the band out to Las Vegas for another engagement at the Starlight Room in the Riviera Hotel.

One morning, Ray Nance, Willie Cook, Fats Ford, and Paul Gonsalves were arrested at the apartment they were sharing, taken into custody by the police, and charged with a narcotics violation. All four were released on $2,500 bail, provided by Ellington. Gonsalves and Nance were eventually brought to trial in the fall. Whereas Gonsalves was let off on probation, Nance—who had received a suspended sentence for a similar violation in New York City a few years earlier—was handed a sixty-day prison term to be served at the Las Vegas county jail.

The incident caused Ellington to be blacklisted in Las Vegas for several years. It was only after the intercession of an old friend that

Ellington was allowed to work in the casinos again. The band first played Lake Tahoe, "which was like a stepping stone to Las Vegas," Mercer recalled. "Unfortunately, the agency sold the band for the ridiculouly low figure of $8,500, and this proved a great handicap in getting the price up later."

While on the West Coast, Ellington received a commission from M-G-M to write music for the pilot of what turned out to be the TV series *Asphalt Jungle*, produced in 1961. The pilot, titled "The Lady and the Lawyer," had a full score by Ellington, but the remaining twelve episodes that ran on the ABC network from April through September of that year used only the theme Ellington had written. An assortment of studio arrangers, including Johnny Mandel and Calvin Jackson, did the scoring for the rest of the series.

"Pop told me he liked doing the music for the pilot," Mercer said. "He had never done one before, and had no interest in providing any music for the rest of the series. He wanted to move on. He was looking forward to Cootie coming back to the band."

During the spring of 1962, trumpeter Cootie Williams and pianist Teddy Wilson were working with the Benny Goodman band. "Sometimes Goodman would let you play," Williams said, "and other times he wouldn't. He has his ways as everyone knows. . . . I'd been talking with Harry Carney. 'Tell Duke . . . that I'm ready to come back.'" He rejoined the orchestra in September 1962. "He provided a sense of stability in the trumpet section," Mercer said. "There had been a lot of changes."

"We went right back on the road," Williams said. "All the way out to California and back. In January [1963] Norman Grantz took us to Europe for three months. When we got back in March, we were told we were going back in June."

While in Europe, Ellington began writing music for two separate events. Ellington had been commissioned by the Ontario Shakespeare Festival to write incidental music for its forthcoming production of *Timon of Athens*. The show opened at the Festival Theatre on July 20, 1963, to friendly reviews. Commenting on the score, *Variety* said that the "music for a ballroom ballet is catchy and otherwise unobtrusively appropriate." The show went to England the following year and played at the Chichester Festival in February 1964.

Another important work was written for the "Century of Negro Progress" exhibition, which was held in Chicago in 1963. Ellington wrote a musical/choral pageant, called *My People*, for the exhibition. The work was conceived on the basis of *Black, Brown and Beige*, with its dual theme of spirituals and blues, using some earlier music and some new material.

"I used to run out and listen to the show," Tom Whaley recalled. "*My People*, it was the education of the Negro through music. He had people coming up from the pit, they were in rags, my people, our people, our people in rags coming up and then at the end they were doctors and lawyers and everything. And he developed it and oh, it was beautiful and the last thing was 'What Is Virtue?'"

Mercer stated that "when he did *My People*, [Ellington] not only constructed the lighting and everything thing else on stage, he painted the sets. I wish I could get my hands on it—he painted the sets and drew out the whole. Everything was done exactly as he wanted it, which is why he enjoyed that show, plus it was dedicated to his main man, Martin Luther King."

Ellington and King finally got to meet when Marion Logan introduced them, standing on a windy corner on Michigan Avenue in Chicago. "Martin is sitting in his limousine and he looks up and sees Edward and jumps out of his car, and he runs over to him and they embrace like they were old friends."

The show did not do well. Its subtle racial message was out of tune with the prevailing mood of black social protest sweeping the country. The civil rights movement had brought issues to a boil with its uncompromising demands for racial equality. Reviewing the score, *Variety* noted that "while its individual components were judged excellent, the production didn't jell as a unified whole."

The demand for racial equality was heeded in one quarter, to the immediate benefit of the Ellington family. Mercedes, Ellington's twenty-four-year-old granddaughter, was hired by the June Taylor dancers, regulars on Jackie Gleason's nationally broadcast CBS television program. She was thus among the first black performers on network television, if not the first to be integrated into an otherwise all-white network TV dance troupe. Mercedes was very light-skinned, and therefore she did not stand out among the other dancers.

"Pop was thrilled and pleased when he heard the news. The night of the first show, he invited me up to his suite to watch it with him and Fernandae," Mercer said.

At end of their routine, Gleason applauded the dancers, and then announced that Duke Ellington's granddaughter had joined the troupe and had her take a bow. Mercer recalled, "When he heard 'granddaughter,' Pop stood up and said, 'What the fuck did he have to say that for!' and walked out of the room."

On September 6, 1963, the Duke Ellington Orchestra departed for its first tour of the Near and Middle East and India. Its first concert, in Damascus, Syria, drew 17,000 people. Subsequent concerts in Jordan, Pakistan, India, Ceylon, and Iraq were equally successful. In New Dehli, Ellington took ill and had Dr. Logan flown first-class to his bedside. "I found him there physically in pretty good shape," the physician recalled, "but pretty badly depressed: Edward said he had never seen such poverty."

In Ankara, Turkey, on November 22, 1963, the band was informed that the remainder of the tour had been canceled, because President Kennedy had been assassinated that day. "Edward was beside himself," Marion Logan said. "The whole tour was strange and now the President went and died on him. He had a big problem with death—not just his own, but anybody's. He couldn't deal with it."

Nevertheless, an important work came out of that tour. Johnny Hodges noted, "Duke Ellington was impressed [with that tour]; he wrote a suite about it, the *Far East Suite*." The suite was originally called *Impressions of the Far East*, and had four parts. It continued to grow during 1964, and was augmented by new movements inspired by the group's trip to Japan that fall. Ultimately the work was recorded as the *Far East Suite* in 1966.

Hodges commented on how "very little escapes [Ellington], he gets his ideas from everything he sees and hears." The same held true for Strayhorn. Both men were impressed with the vastness, the smells, the exotic beauty of the landscape, and the birds. A prime example of this influence was "Bluebird of Delhi," originally called "Mynah." Ellington introduced the work at concerts with the story that it was named after a bird that used to sing a pretty phrase (now given to Jimmy Hamilton's clarinet) in Strayhorn's room. Strayhorn talked to the bird every day, hoping to get a response from the bird, but got nowhere. One day, Strayhorn finally got a response from it when he was leaving the city: The mynah gave him a Bronx Cheer (played by the trombone in the suite) to speed him on his way.

This humorous moment was juxtaposed with an elegant solo by Johnny Hodges on "Isfahan," a city called the Pearl of Persia. "It is a place where everything is poetry," Ellington recalled. "They meet you at the airport with poetry and you go away with poetry. 'Isfahan,' a Persian poet once wrote, 'is half the world.'"

The band reached Baghdad just in time for a military coup. Jets shot up the presidential palace. Later, after Ellington arrived safely in Beirut, the local press eagerly sought his reaction to the experience. "Baghdad," he said, "It was swinging!"

The excitement of Baghdad contrasted with the serenity of Mount Harissa, located just outside Beirut, and crowned by the statue of Our Lady of Lebanon. Ellington's thoughts and feelings about it were reflected in "Mount Harissa," which featured his piano and Paul Gonsalves's tenor saxophone.

"Ad Lib on Nippon," the final piece in the suite, was written after Ellington's fall trip to Japan, and premiered in early 1965. It was inspired by a commercial work that Ellington composed in 1964 as a soundtrack for a documentary produced by American Airlines called "Cargo by Air." One of the themes from the documentary ended up being recycled for the opening of the "Nippon" movement.

In 1964, Mercer Ellington joined Cootie Williams in the trumpet section and became the band's manager. Mercer had been working as a disc jockey at radio station WLIB, and was quite successful. Al Celley, the band's road manager, had quit over the issue of back salaries owed him. Mercer, at one point, had managed Cootie Williams's band, and Williams suggested to Ellington that he offer his son the job.

The band was booked for a tour of England and Western Europe. "I'd never been to Europe," Mercer said, "so I figured I'd take the job just for the trip. Pop told me to bring my horn, just in case. The next thing I knew, I was sitting in the trumpet section." He would remain there, never take a solo, and manage the band until his father's death ten years later.

It was, in some respects, a thankless job. Mercer had to oversee men, some of whom he had known since childhood, "who had led me by the hand to the movies, who had taken me to the circus, who had bought me candy apples or gone swimming with me."

With the band's increasingly heavy schedule, Mercer had total responsibility for everything. As manager, he had to carry large sums of money with him around the world, usually in dollar bills, to pay the musicians as they traveled. Johnny Hodges insisted he be paid on a daily basis. "I don't trust myself or anyone else. . . . I'm used to getting paid at the end of every day. I want to owe nothin' to anyone and have nothin' owed to me," Hodges said.

Nevertheless, Mercer did the job well and turned out to be a very efficient manager, keeping the band to its schedule, and fighting with the promotors to provide "what I considered the proper atmosphere and convenience for Pop. I also had to fight the office that represented us in regard to bookings and the price being paid for the band. I began to make enemies and live in a world by myself. I was neither fish nor fowl."

One of Mercer's first problems was settling the issue of getting the men onto the bandstand on time. "I started beefing, hollering, and screaming, and in some cases getting into fisticuffs, in order to straighten the situation out," he said. "I almost literally had to slap the band into line. It was a real battle getting these things done."

Enforcing discipline with this collection of wayward geniuses always kept Mercer in the middle. "To show their objection to what I wanted they would go out and give a half-assed performance. Then [Pop] would get mad and blame me for the bad performance. Despite him and everything else, I would still go back and raise hell . . . the very next day to show they had got nowhere . . . and then get into another fight with [Pop] that night."

Finances were another bone of contention. Before Mercer came on board, accountant Bill Mittler demanded receipts from those persons responsible for disbursements. If he did not get them, he went directly to Ellington, and saw to it that he got them. When Mercer arrived, the books were in disarray. Some bills had not been paid, and recording sessions had been made for which musicians had not been paid. Mercer had no idea of what the overall balance was at the bank at any time. At this point in time, the band was grossing more than one million dollars a year.

"[Pop] himself didn't help matters," Mercer recalled:

> He'd get a check and just put it in his pocket, so nobody had any way of keeping track of it. Naturally this led to income tax problems. In addition there were people in New York, that he had Ruth giving money to, out of the account. It was only then that I learned that Sonny Greer was still on the payroll!

Greer had left the band in 1951.

The band flew off to Japan in June 1964 for a three-week tour. As usual, Fernandae accompanied Duke. Evie Ellis, his long-time girl-friend, had learned about the relationship very early in its development. She never mentioned it to Ellington, but complained about it bitterly to the Logans. She was aware that Fernandae was accompanying him overseas, as well as when he was on tour in the United States. When the situation became unbearable, Evie decided to force a confrontation. She flew to Tokyo unannounced, knowing her rival would be there, appeared at the hotel, and told the desk to inform Duke she was in the lobby. He came downstairs and forced her to return to New York on the next plane, telling her there was no way he would allow her to embarrass him.

On another occasion, Fernandae fared no better. In Rome, Italy, she made a suicide gesture by taking an overdose of sleeping pills. Ellington once again avoided an unpleasant situation by summoning his singer Tony Watkins. He was instructed to take her down to the grill, force her to drink coffee, and walk her around until she came to her senses. Later that evening, she and the singer were seen at a club dancing the night away.

As Ellington traveled more and more, Evie was constantly alone in the three-bedroom apartment they shared on West End Avenue. It was comfortable and spacious, and had a panoramic view of the lower city, the Hudson River, and the New Jersey Palisades. One bedroom had an upright piano and was soundproofed, so that Duke could play all night if he wanted to without disturbing anyone. On the door were their names: Ellington and Ellis.

Evie had made the apartment a haven for Ellington. "She handled everything like nobody could," Don George stated, "sent vitamins to St. Louis on such and such a date . . . called the hospital to get a prescription. . . . When I teased her about it, she laughed good-naturedly, saying, 'I've got to earn my keep.'"

All in all, Evie lived well. She had a Cadillac, a comfortable bank account, plus a lasting friendship with the Edmund Andersons, with whom she'd spend the summer in the Hamptons if Ellington was not in town. With Ellington spending more and more time on the road, she lavished attention on Davy, the miniature black poodle that had been given to her by Joe Glaser, Ellington's one-time manager.

According to Mercer, there was often hardly any place to sit in the living room because of Davy's beds, blankets, food bowls, and rubber toys. Ellington, too, enjoyed him very much and would play with him. However, because he was away for such a long periods, he took second place to Evie in the dog's affections.

For some reason, Evie and Ruth never got along. "Ruth did not allow Evie in her home," Mercer recalled. "This was one of my perennial arguments which always kept me spitting against the wind because I never wound up being on anybody's side, but I simply told [Pop] if your woman is not accepted someplace, then you are no longer confined to go there. He loved Ruth very much and he loved Evie very much. But [Evie] knew with Fernandae in his life he was not going to marry her, even after my mother died."

Meanwhile, Duke's original—and only—wife was facing a crisis of her own. Edna Ellington contracted cancer in December 1965. After numerous surgeries, she died in New York's St. Barnabas Hospital, where she had been for thirteen months, in January 1967. Ellington, then in Italy, cabled a tribute to his wife of fifty-two years: "She loved life. She was a woman of virtue and beauty. She would never lie. God bless her."

Edna and Duke had a cordial relationship after they separated. "I didn't want a divorce and neither did he," she said. "We're proud of the way we get along. He has always provided for me through the years. Whenever anything happens he'll call me or I'll call him. He'll open up when he gets angry. But Duke, and Mercer takes after him in this respect, is a lonely man."

42

IN JUNE 1965, a considerable stir was aroused in the media when it was revealed that Ellington had been denied a Pulitzer Prize. The three-man Pulitzer music jury, which recommended significant works to the fourteen-man advisory board, had decided that no music produced in 1964 was worthy of the prize. However, it recommended that Ellington receive a special citation "for the vitality and originality of his total productivity." The jury's recommendations were rarely—if ever—overturned, yet the advisory board rejected this one.

Needless to say, this decision created a good deal of controversy in the music world. Two members of the jury, Winthrop Sargent and Ronald Eyer, resigned amid widespread mutterings about racial prejudice. The advisory board gave no reason for its decision, but one can surmise that, in the board's opinion, Ellington was not a "serious" composer.

Mercer noted that his father was more upset that the matter became public than about the actual denial of the prize. "He kept saying 'Why the fuck did it have to get in the newspapers?'" When contacted by the press, however, Ellington was his usual urbane self. "I feel very lucky to have been mentioned at all for such an honor. Fate is being too kind to me. Fate doesn't want me to be too famous too young," he said.

At that point, Ellington was putting the final touches on another major composition, *The Golden Broom and the Green Apple*. The work had its premiere on July 30, 1965 at Philharmonic Hall, as part of the New York Philharmonic's French-American Festival. The festival ran from July 14 to 31 and consisted of ten concerts, along with chamber music programs by French and American artists and ensembles.

The Golden Broom and Green Apple was a three-part suite scored for symphony orchestra, jazz bass, piano, and drums. Ellington also joined the orchestra as soloist in *New World A-Comin'*, and then appeared as narrator in the Philharmonic's performance of Aaron Copland's *Preamble for a Solemn Occasion*.

Two nights earlier, Ellington, the bassist John Lamb, and drummer Louis Bellson had played at Tanglewood, the summer home of the Boston Symphony and the Boston Pops. The occasion was a benefit for the orchestra's pension fund. A crowd of 18,000 heard the Pops—under its venerable conductor Arthur Fiedler, with Ellington as soloist—play a medley of his most famous compositions. The orchestral arrangements were provided by Richard Hayman.

One week later, Duke was awarded New York City's Bronze Medal by the city's acting mayor, Paul Screvane. The medal was a "token of gratitude for outstanding contributions to New York life."

Despite these achievements and honors, the controversy surrounding the loss of the Pulitzer Prize was still painful for Ellington. It manifested itself a few months later, when the band was booked into New York's Basin Street East, along with the singer Mel Torme, an ardent Ellington admirer since his childhood. The two of them had co-composed "You Gotta Crawl Before You Walk" some twenty years earlier.

According to Mercer, when his father arrived at the club he became furious when he noticed that Torme had top billing. However, it was not unusual for the band to take second billing to a vocalist. Mercer recalled, "We took second billing behind Ella [Fitzgerald] and Tony Bennett, and a lot of other people, just to keep the band working." Nonetheless, Ellington refused to play until the billing was changed.

When Torme arrived at the club, a full-fledged row was in progress. Torme, whose respect for Ellington knew no bounds, offered to change the billing arrangement, which had been made by his manager without his consultation. But Torme's manager was adamant that the billing should remain the same. That was when Ellington's latent anger about the Pulitzer manifested itself. Mercer recalled, "Pop turned to him and said, 'Man, I almost won the motherfuckin' Pulitzer Prize!'" Nonetheless, the following year, Torme and Ellington met again in Tokyo; Ellington embraced and kissed the singer as if there had never been any incident at all.

During one of his many trips to San Francisco, Ellington met Father John S. Yaryan, an Episcopal priest, who was very interested in his music. Out of that relationship came a request from Canon C. Julian Bartlett, Dean of San Francisco's Grace Cathedral, for Ellington to play a concert of sacred music, to be part of the celebration of the building's completion and consecration to be held on September 16, 1965.

Ellington seized the opportunity. It would allow him to give praise to and celebrate his God. For his first concert in a house of worship, Ellington used his orchestra along with the Herman McCoy Choir, the Grace Cathedral Choir, the vocalists Esther Marrow and Jimmy McPhail, and tap dancer Bunny Briggs.

Ellington went back to his King James Bible for inspiration. The opening line—"In the beginning, God"—was scored for Harry Carney's majestic baritone saxophone. For the next two years, those six opening notes would reverberate through cathedrals from San Francisco, California, to Cambridge, England.

Although this was a sacred work, Ellington hoped to relate directly to a contemporary audience. For this reason, the opening language following the solemn "In the beginning . . ." quickly brings the Biblical message down to the level of the everyday. A vocalist recites a long list of common—and sometimes comical—conditions that did not yet exist "in the beginning" of time: from headaches to romantic troubles. Following Carney's declamation, Gonsalves solos over organ chords by the saxes; the choir recites the names of the books of the Old Testament; and Cat Anderson sounds a high note on the trumpet, representing man's highest aspirations. Then, Ellington accompanies the choir while it recites the names of the books of the New Testament at gathering speed. Bellson's cymbals emulate "the sounding of brass" symbolizing man's aspirations. Finally, the choir sings the main theme.

Much of the material in the body of the *Sacred Concert* was drawn from earlier works that Ellington had written based on traditional African-American spirituals. He drew from his earlier *Black, Brown and Beige* (1943), *New World A-Comin'* (1945), and *My People* (1963) for much of the music, adapting and fitting it within this new setting.

The "Come Sunday" theme from *Black, Brown and Beige* was a particular favorite of Ellington's, which he recycled three times in the first spiritual concert. "When we were in England, after a rehearsal, before one of the concerts," Mercer recalled, "for some reason or another Fernandae and I were talking about music. She thought 'Come Sunday' . . . was the single most beautiful piece of music my father ever wrote. He was sitting in a chair correcting some parts. I looked over at him, and he said, 'She's right' and kept right on with what he was doing."

For the *Sacred Concert*, Ellington used this melody for Johnny Hodges's saxophone solo, and then created a vocal arrangement for the gospel singer Esther Merrill. In addition, there was a choral arrangement sung at a brisk tempo, set to the text "David Danced before the Lord with All His Might." Ellington featured the tap dancer Bunny Briggs at the end of this section. His elegant dancing was a highlight of the performance.

When the concert was repeated over the next few years, Ellington continued to tinker with the music. However, *New World A-Comin'* always was heard at some point in the program, played beautifully as a piano solo by Ellington. It obviously held a special place for Ellington in this work.

The East Coast premiere of the [*First*] *Sacred Concert* took place at New York's Fifth Avenue Presbyterian Church, the day after Christmas. It was a slightly altered version of the San Francisco program. Brock Peters replaced Jon Hendricks, and eighteen-year-old Tony Watkins replaced Jimmy McPhail. The surprise of the evening was Lena Horne, who sang a number composed for the occasion by Billy Strayhorn, who also accompanied her at the piano.

Ellington began 1966 by putting the finishing touches to the movie score for *Assault on a Queen*. The film was to star his good friend, Frank Sinatra, who insisted on using Ellington's music for the soundtrack. Ellington was to be paid $25,000 for his work, which included travel and living expenses. Despite the lucrative fee, Ellington was not pleased with his work on the film.

When Ellington arrived in California, the shooting was over, but the film was still being edited, and cues were changed quite frequently. With the tight deadline imposed by the studio for completion of the score, Ellington was put under a great deal of pressure. He frantically worked not only in the office provided for him on the Paramount lot, but also at his Beverly Hills hotel suite, where an electric piano had been installed at his request. The portable piano subsequently became an integral part of the film score. Eventually, Ellington had a second electric piano installed on the Paramount soundstage, using it simultaneously with the concert grand during the recording sessions.

Recording this soundtrack was a new experience for Ellington and brought with it problems. For his previous film scores, he had used his own orchestra, augmented by outside men. For *Assault on a Queen*, however, the initial contract called for just the services of Ellington as composer, not for his orchestra. Contrary to his usual practice, Ellington had to write the music with no special orchestral sound or instrumental voices in mind. He finally convinced the studio to fly in the core musicians of his band—trumpeters Cat Anderson and Cootie Williams; saxophonists Jimmy Hamilton, Johnny Hodges, and Harry Carney; and the rhythm section of John Lamb and Louis Bellson—to record the music. They were augmented by West Coast studio musicians, including trombonist Murray McEachern, who had worked with Ellington on the earlier film, *Paris Blues*.

Another reason for Ellington's unhappiness with the film was that his score was not used as he composed it. Sinatra and Ellington both agreed that a really swinging piece of music should be heard under the film's climactic scene, when the pirates crack open the safe door on the *Queen Mary*. Ellington provided just that type of number and recorded it, but the director decided against it and used a simple walking bass instead. Ellington later referred to the film "as one of the bad Westerns I had seen."

Ellington returned to New York to prepare for a five-week trip to Europe. "As he got older," Mercer recalled, "he used those trips almost like a vacation." The tour began on January 24, 1966, in Lisbon, Portugal. There were engagements in the British Isles, Scandinavia, and on the Continent. On several occasions, the orchestra was joined by Ella Fitzgerald and her trio.

One of the highlights of the tour was the request for Ellington to give a *Sacred Concert* at Coventry Cathedral in England on February 22, 1966. He was clearly moved by the invitation. A friend remembered seeing him standing before the magnificent altar tapestry created by Graham Sutherland, and stating, "This music is the most important thing I've ever done or am ever likely to do. This is personal, not career. Now I can say out loud to all the world what I've been saying to myself for years on my knees."

Following a concert in Brussels, Ellington was flown to Madrid, Spain, where the American ambassador presented him with the gold medal that had been awarded to him by President Lyndon Johnson for outstanding performance and the creation of goodwill. Musically, one of the highlights of the tour was the first performance for European audiences of a piece that Ellington had written for his forthcoming trip to the African continent: *La Plus Belle Africaine.*

For Ellington himself, the tour's highlight was an invitation to inaugurate the second wing of the Castle of Goutelas, in Goutelas-en-Forêt, France. This building, dating back to the thirteenth century, had been restored as a symbolic act by French artists and artisans. It would be used thereafter for musical festivals and art exhibits.

On a bitterly cold night, Ellington arrived to find fifty children with burning torches waiting to guide him to the chateau. There, he played a solo recital on the nine-foot Steinway grand piano brought there especially for the occasion. The sound of *New World A-Comin'* reverberated throughout the room, and Ellington was rewarded with an ovation by the crowd. That inspired him to compose the *Goutelas Suite,* which he would premiere five years later. Ellington later told a friend that he had been more moved by that ovation even than the night in 1960, when ten thousand people had heard him play "Come Sunday" at a Christmas mass in Paris.

Ellington ended the year 1966 with three significant events. On December 15, he was at the White House as a guest of President Johnson for a Christmas dinner in honor of the National Council of the Arts. Two days later, he was the soloist with the Baltimore Symphony, playing *New World A-Comin'.* The next day, he was in the RCA studios, finally recording the *The Far East Suite.*

January 1967 found Ellington and the band back in Europe. They would be there until March 10, concluding the tour with a concert at the Theatre des Champs Elysees. The highlight of the tour for Ellington was the concert of sacred music given at Great St. Mary's Church in Cambridge, England.

"When we got there," Mercer recalled, "he walked off to the side, stood and stared at the building for the longest time. I think it was Tony Watkins who started to go over to him. Fernandae grabbed his arm, and said quietly, 'Leave him alone for now.'"

Mercer had been managing the band since 1964. During early 1967, one player who gave him particular trouble was drummer Sam

Woodyard, who was becoming more and more unreliable. Mercer recalled, "On the flight back [from the European tour], I mentioned to Pop the trouble we were having with [Woodyard], and maybe he should think about making a change. He agreed and we brought on Bobby Durham."

For some reason, however, Ellington kept Durham in the band only a few months before rehiring Woodyard. Mercer was puzzled by this chain of events:

> I could never figure out why he fired [Durham], one of the greatest drummers we ever had in the band. Maybe Bobby was arrogant, but he knew his work. He was clean. He was certain. He was a take-charge drummer. There was nothing about him that was not great and really right for the band. But for the first time in many years Duke Ellington arbitrarily fired someone. He just gave Bobby two weeks' notice.

"I was disgusted with Duke when he let that boy go," Cootie Williams said. "We had words about it. I told him it reminded me of when I was with Benny [Goodman]. He brought in Sidney Catlett, who could drive a band and keep good time. You want a drummer who can take charge, and Catlett did that with every band he was with, yet Benny fired him. Durham was the same way, and Duke fired him!"

Woodyard was back in the band during its engagement at Harrah's Casino in Reno, Nevada. It was there that Ellington received the news that Billy Strayhorn, his closest collaborator for the past twenty-eight years, had died after a prolonged bout with cancer, on May 31, 1967.

When he received the call from Dr. Logan that Strayhorn had died that morning, Marion Logan recalled, "Arthur said Edward just cried. He said, 'This is too much for me, Arthur,' and he just cried. Arthur said, 'Are you going to be all right?' And Edward said, 'Fuck no, I'm not going to be all right. Nothing is all right now.'"

His father was still crying when Mercer entered his room that afternoon. "It was the first time I saw him cry since Grandma Daisy died in '35," he said. "It was a big blow to the old man. He had a hard time accepting any kind of bad news, so you can imagine what it must have been like for him when Billy passed on."

The service was held in New York City at St. Peter's Church at 54th Street and Lexington Avenue. "Duke was absolutely inconsolable," Don George recalled. "There was no way to describe his incredible depression. He was a very emotional man in his love for people he cared about. And he cared tremendously about Sweetpea. . . . [He] was sitting by himself, frozen, immobile, staring straight ahead, not seeing, hearing, or recognizing anything or anybody. This was the greatest loss of his life; his brother, his right arm, at least half of himself, was lying there in that coffin being eulogized by Pastor Gensel."

Lawrence Brown said:

> [Billy Strayhorn] was a very meticulous little fellow, and he was right in 'most everything he did. Many, many times Ellington would call him up from out on the road, "Sweetpea, I want an arrangement on so and so and so."
>
> "Well, when do you need it?"
>
> "In a couple of days."
>
> And Sweetpea, "All right."
>
> And in a couple of days came the most gorgeous arrangement on that particular piece. And that was Strayhorn, and he never got the credit. Strayhorn was the genius, the power behind the throne all of those latter years. There were so many things left unfinished that Strayhorn did, many of the things you think were new, were things Strayhorn left.

Yet Mercer felt that Strayhorn's passing also inspired his father to a new burst of creativity. It was as if, seeing his own death approaching, he was motivated to write even more.

In August, Ellington brought the band into the RCA studios to record music written by his late collaborator. Many of the compositions had been recorded previously, dating back as far as 1941 for "After All" and "Raincheck" through Strayhorn's last composition, "Blood Count," premiered at Carnegie Hall in 1967.

The last number that was recorded was "Lotus Blossom." The musicians were talking and packing up their instruments. Fortunately, the microphone was still in position and the tape ready to roll when Ellington sat down at the piano. There was a hush and he began to play the piece. When he finished he said, "That was what he most liked to hear me play."

Ellington wrote an eloquent eulogy for Strayhorn on hearing of his death. The eulogy written that morning in May was in part to assuage his own grief. He had omitted from it six moving words that he felt were too overwhelming at the time—"and his mother called him Bill"—which became the name of the album.

Although he was gone, Strayhorn's voice was not forgotten. The public would hear it prominently featured in the *Second Sacred Concert* performed at the Cathedral of St. John the Divine on January 19, 1968. This was the first concert in which Ellington worked with the talented Swedish singer Alice Babs, who would become closely associated with his sacred music. Also involved were other soloists Devonne Gardner, Tony Watkins, Jimmy McPhail, and the "Les Jeune Voix" singers under the direction of Roscoe Gill, Ellington's new band singer Trish Turner, and the drummer Steve Little.

The concert of religious music ran 155 minutes and was filmed by CBS for a future special titled "Something About Believing." The concert was a benefit for Exodus House, a drug rehabilitation center.

Stanley Dance, Ellington's biographer and close friend, considered the *Second Sacred Concert* the best of the three. I agree; I was particularly impressed with Alice Babs, who sang "Heaven," accompanied by Johnny Hodges, and "Almighty God," backed by Russell Procope. Babs was also featured on "T.G.T.T." Ellington stated that the name meant "Too Good to Title", "because it violates conformity in the same way we like to think that Jesus Christ did. The phrases never end on the note you think they will. It is a piece even instrumentalists have trouble with, but Alice Babs read it at sight."

The concert ended with "Praise God and Dance." "Of all the pieces he wrote," Lawrence Brown recalled, "I thought that was the best. Duke managed to get it just right. The singing, dancing, and the music all came together. The first time we played it in the Cathedral of St. John, I wondered what my father would have thought of it. He was a minister. I don't think he would have approved. But as I played the music, I could hear a lot of Strayhorn in it."

Strayhorn's memory was further invoked on February 29, 1968, at the Grammy Awards dinner at the Hilton Hotel in New York City.

Ellington and Strayhorn's *The Far East Suite* recording was being honored with an award. He and Strayhorn were also presented with a special trustees' award for the same album.

The *Second Sacred Concert* appeared to take on a life of its own. "I thought it was the best of the three," Mercer said. "As I remember we took that one on the road with us." The following night, the *Second Sacred Concert* was performed at St. Mark's Episcopal Church in New Canaan, Connecticut, and two weeks later at the Hennepin Avenue Methodist Church in Minneapolis, Minnesota.

Grace Cathedral in San Francisco, where the [*First*] *Sacred Concert* was premiered, was the host for the *Second Sacred Concert* on April 16, 1968. Back in New York, the work was again played at Hunter College on June 2. One week later, it was performed at the North Avenue Presbyterian Church in New Rochelle, New York. The Emmanuel Baptist Church, in Brooklyn, New York, heard the work on June 16, and one week later, it was done at the Crescent Avenue Presbyterian Church in Plainfield, New Jersey.

Mercer noted, "Pop was thrilled at the requests. He was getting calls from all over the country for us to do the *Sacred Concerts*. Many times we'd be booked in a large city for a dance. Sure enough, we'd get a request from one of the churches."

One of the numbers in the *Sacred Concerts* was "Supreme Being," featuring Jimmy Hamilton's clarinet. He would play it for the last time with the band at the *Sacred Concert* held in Boyle Stadium, Stamford, Connecticut, on June 30, 1968.

"I'd been in the band twenty-five years," Hamilton said. "I thought a long time about it before I gave Duke my notice. It was after the *Sacred Concert* in Brooklyn. Duke took me aside and asked if I wanted more money. I told him no, there was just other things I wanted to explore musically. He gave me his blessing."

Hamilton's replacement, Harold Ashby, was no stranger to the Ellingtons. He had played in Mercer's band in the 1950s, and he had subbed in the band off and on since 1960. A week after Hamilton left, Ashby played Hamilton's solo in the *Second Sacred Concert* at the Festival Theater in Stratford, Ontario.

"I enjoy being with Duke," Ashby told an interviewer. "It's a different thing, a new life really. I never did get a chance to travel, and I'd never even been to Atlantic City or any of those places. Also it's a new musical experience. . . . The traveling gives you something to do, and a person's got to have something to do. When I was in South America, there was Spanish and I had a phrase book."

The band embarked on a tour of South America that fall. "South America reminded me of that trip to England in '33," Lawrence Brown said. "Work, work, work. The only time we got to see anything was on the rides back and forth to the airport."

They arrived in São Paulo, Brazil on September 2. "We were at the Municipal Theater for three days," Mercer recalled. "Then we worked every night for the next eleven days, and were back in New York on the 16th. We played some one nighters and [were] in Mexico on the 23d.

Recalling that tour, Ellington stated, "The generosity and enthusiasm of the audiences were altogether the inspiration of a lifetime, a virtual summit in my career. Everything and everyone has been so completely and warmly attuned that I am completely overwhelmed and at a loss to express my appreciation. Perhaps I can do it at a later date."

Out of that tour evolved the *Latin American Suite*. Mercer recalled, "What I remember most about Mexico and South America was when we were in São Paulo, I was in Pop's suite to check on the itinerary. He was talking about how beautiful the city was. Then looked at me and said quietly, 'I wish Billy was here to see it.'"

43

WHILE ELLINGTON WOULD mourn the loss of Strayhorn for quite some time, his grief was partly assuaged by the fact that the "establishment" was at last giving him due recognition. On June 4, 1967, the day before Strayhorn's funeral, Washington University in St. Louis conferred on Ellington an honorary doctorate of music. It was one of seventeen degrees he would receive over his lifetime.

Eight days after he received the degree from Washington University, Ellington was given a similar honor by Yale University. As a general rule, citations that accompany the awarding of an honorary degree spell out the recipient's career in a dry academic prose. Ellington's citation, however, made clever use of the titles of some of his better-known compositions:

> We are indebted to you for an important generalization: "It don't mean a thing if it ain't got that swing." Your musical compositions and performances have set our hearts singing, our spirits soaring, and our feet tapping. We hope that today your "mood is not indigo" and that your "Caravan" will continue to "Take the A Train" in the direction of more "Sentimental Moods." It might be said, "You've got it good and that ain't bad!" It is a special pleasure for Yale to confer upon you the degree Doctor of Music.

I happened to be in the audience, standing on the New Haven green that afternoon, when the honorary degrees were conferred. When Ellington's citation was read, the crowd gave him an ovation, the Yale band broke into "Mood Indigo," and he threw kisses to one and all.

As he was leaving the ceremony, I could not help overhearing a conversation between two gentlemen, both members of the Yale class of 1932, there with their wives attending their thirty-fifth reunion. They were discussing the recipients of the honorary degrees. "I don't know who any of these other characters are," the taller of the two said, "but I'm glad they did something for the Duke."

His classmate then reminded him of an incident that happened during the fall of their junior year. After a Harvard-Yale football game, they had driven to New York with their dates to hear Ellington at the Cotton Club. On the way back, they ran out of gas. "Your father wasn't too happy to come get us that morning," he said. "And the girls' parents wouldn't let them see us anymore," the taller man replied.

Both wives were astonished to learn their husbands had heard Ellington at the Cotton Club. "We've been married twenty-three years and that's the first time I've heard about *that*!" the wife of the shorter man exclaimed.

"Pop loved to get those honorary degrees," Mercer recalled:

The ones from Yale, Brown, and Columbia meant the most to him. The one from Howard didn't mean as much as I thought it would, since it was from his hometown. He told me it meant more to him to get his high school diploma from Armstrong [High School] that day. I later learned, from a member of the Howard faculty who knew my mother, that Pop was proposed for an honorary degree in the late '50s, but the President [Mordecai] Johnson said no.

He was thrilled to get one from that school in the Midwest for his sacred music. We were in the middle of recording *The River*. He took the day off, flew out there, picked up the degree and was back in the studio the next day.

On June 5, 1970, the Christian Theological Seminary in Indianapolis, Indiana, awarded Ellington a Doctor of Humane Letters degree, "for his contributions to the field of sacred music."

"The one I enjoyed the most was the one he got from the University of Wisconsin in 1971," Mercer recalled. "They had us back, the entire band for a week of master classes." Ellington, the orchestra, and assorted guests were onsite the week of July 17–21. There was a *Sacred Concert* the night of the July 19. Ellington led a master class for piano, ably assisted by his protégé, Brooks Kerr, a young pianist from New York City, who possessed an encyclopedic knowledge of Ellington's music.

The final evening featured a concert at the student union. Ellington called it a "Night of Suites." Ellington and the band did the *Goutelas Suite*, excerpts from *Togo Brava*, and the audience in the Wisconsin Union Theater heard also the premiere of the *UWIS Suite*, Ellington's "thank-you piece," as he called it, inspired by "so many nice people in Wisconsin."

In addition to the many honors from colleges and universities, foreign governments began bestowing honors on Ellington. In 1967, his head had appeared along with those of Bach, Debussy, and Beethoven on a set of four postage stamps issued by Togo to mark UNESCO's twentieth anniversary. Ellington responded with the *Togo Brava* suite, premiered at the Newport Jazz Festival in 1971.

On March 12, 1971, at a ceremony conducted at the Swedish consulate in New York City, Ellington was formally inducted into the Swedish Academy of Music. He was the first writer of nonclassical music to be made a member of that 200-year-old institution.

On July 8, 1973, Ellington was presented the Legion d'Honneur awarded by the president of France, Georges Pompidou. M. Jacques Koseiuszko-Morizet, ambassador of France, representing the president, pinned the medal on him at a ceremony in the French consulate, on Fifth Avenue. "We buried him with that one, and the Presidential Medal that Nixon gave him for his seventieth birthday," Mercer recalled.

Shortly after President Nixon's inaugural in 1969, Leonard Garment, counsel to the president, presented Nixon with the idea of giving a seventieth birthday party for Ellington. Garment, an amateur musician, played clarinet. He noted that both Ellington and Nixon played piano. That elicited an enthusiastic response from the president, and the wheels were set in motion for a gala celebration on April 29, where Ellington would be awarded the Presidential Medal of Freedom, the highest honor the country can bestow on a civilian.

Duke was no stranger to the White House. Lyndon Johnson had had him there, either to play or as a guest, on seven separate occasions. President Eisenhower, on bumping into Ellington before his inaugural ball, said "Hi, *Cab*, don't forget to play 'Mood Indigo' tonight." Despite Eisenhower's gaffe, Ellington played it four times.

For the seventieth-birthday party, Ellington was asked to submit a list of fifty people he would like to have as guests. The White House, as a gesture of respect, submitted to him its list of invitees, all of whom he approved.

"I drew up the guest list and supervised the invitations because he was so busy," Ruth said. "And we had to get it organized; we were limited in the number of people we could invite . . . but it was a wonderful occasion and a great honor."

"I must say it was a surprise to get that invitation in the mail," Freddie Guy recalled. "It was the first time I'd seen the 'Lion' [Willie 'the Lion' Smith] in twenty years."

Mercer noted that most of the family was there. "Ruth, her son Stephen, myself, my wife Evelyn, and two of our three kids, my son Edward K. and my daughter Gaye." In addition there were the Logans, Harry Carney, Tom Whaley, and Ellington's London friends Renee and Leslie Diamond, along with Stanley Dance. The musicians included Harold Arlen, Richard Rodgers, Benny Goodman, Count Basie, Cab Calloway, and Dizzy Gillespie. From the theater came Thomas Patterson, director of the Stratford (Ontario) Festival; from films, the director Otto Preminger; and other guests included assorted members of the cabinet, the Supreme Court, and Vice President Spiro Agnew. The impresario George Wein and the jazz maven Leonard Feather were also present. Absent, though, were the two most important women in Ellington's love life: Evie, alone in the apartment on West End Avenue, and Fernandae.

Ellington and Ruth changed into their evening clothes at the White House. He, the president, Ruth, and Mrs. Nixon came down the grand staircase together, stood on the receiving line, and greeted the guests. Bob Udkoff, a long-time friend of Ellington, recalled, "[He] had this thing abour four kisses, kiss you twice, that's one for each cheek, and when he said that to Nixon, Nixon got red! He drew back and laughed . . . that evening [Nixon] was charming. He had just been elected, he was ebullient."

The white-tie dinner was in the State Dining Room, where, ironically, James Ellington had once butlered a function. The guests were seated at round tables of eight for the roast beef dinner. Ruth Ellington sat with Nixon, Dizzy Gillespie, Benny Goodman, Lou Rawls, and Mahalia Jackson. Duke, seated next to Mrs. Nixon, was able to converse with Richard Rodgers, Renee Diamond, singer Billy Eckstine, and John Johnson, owner of *Ebony* magazine.

When it came time for the presentation of the medal, President Nixon said, "I've lifted my glass to emperors, kings and prime ministers, but never has a Duke been toasted. I ask you all to join me in lifting our glasses to the greatest Duke of them all."

As the medal was placed on his shoulders, Ellington was heard to say, "There is no place I'd rather be tonight except in my mother's arms."

The president drew a warm roar of laughter when, after making the medal presentation, he glanced at the citation and remarked, "I was looking at the name on this and it said, 'Edward Kennedy.' . . . "He paused before he added "Ellington." The senior senator from Massachusetts was a well-known Nixon nemesis.

In his reply to the president, Ellington said, "I am reminded of the four freedoms Billy Strayhorn created for our sacred concerts. The four moral freedoms by which he lived . . . I use those four moral freedoms by which Strayhorn lived as a measure of what we ourselves should live up to. Freedom from hate. Unconditionally. Freedom from self-pity. Freedom from the fear of possibly doing something that would benefit someone else. And freedom from the fear of being better than one's brother." He sat down to tumultuous applause.

Don George, Ellington's lyricist, recalled, "He crossed [the room] and sat down at the piano. Duke, being a consummate politician himself, had written a beautiful piano piece in the key of B major (a key he very rarely played in), a beautiful . . . wistful thing, a truly beautiful little ballad. When he finished playing, he said, 'Yes, that was something lovely, something lovely,' and he paused, then continued, 'like Pat,' and he looked through the crown and spotted Mrs. Nixon and said, 'Ah, this is her.' And they ate it up."

Bill Berry, a trumpet player, remembered the musical part of the evening. "I played for Ellington's seventieth birthday at the White House and the waiters who worked all the functions there said it was totally different from any other party they had at the White House."

It began with Nixon sitting himself at the Steinway to lead the singing of "Happy Birthday." Clark Terry joined Berry in the trumpet section of the Marine Band; Urbie Green and J. J Johnson were on the trombones; Paul Desmond and Gerry Mulligan were on the reeds. The rhythm section consisted of Hank Jones on piano, Louis Bellson on drums, Jim Hall on guitar, and Milt Hinton on bass.

Three guest pianists were also present—Earl Hines, Dave Brubeck, and Billy Taylor—as well as the singers Joe Williams and Mary Mayo. For the first time in history, television cameras were permitted to record the after-dinner entertainment, and the proceedings were broadcast over the Voice of America.

As refreshments were being served after midnight, Duke had to listen to Vice President Spiro Agnew play *his* version of Ellington songs at the piano, including "In a Sentimental Mood." Then the president announced that the East Room was being cleared for a jam session and dancing. He and Mrs. Nixon went off to bed. Duke took the dance floor with Carmen de Lavallade, the ballerina who had portrayed Madame Zajj in *A Drum Is a Woman*. The songwriter Harold Arlen was heard to observe, "Can you imagine Coolidge doing this?"

At three that morning, Ellington was back in his hotel room. He changed from his tails into traveling clothes and went to the airport. He was due that night at the Civic Center in Oklahoma City, Oklahoma, for a one-night stand.

In May 1969, Ellington gave a concert of sacred music at Washington University in St. Louis. In June, he gave another at the Roman Catholic cathedral in Kingston, Jamaica, as part of a week's tour of the West Indies. The *Sacred Concerts* also were part of Ellington's European tour that fall. The first one was at the Gustav Vasa Krykan in Stockholm, Sweden. It gave the Swedes the opportunity to hear the singer Alice Babs in person for the first time at a *Sacred Concert* performed in her hometown. She had become a vital part of every Ellington *Sacred Concert*.

The *Sacred Concert* at the church of St. Suplice in Paris was televised. The one at the Basilica de Santa Marie del Mar in Barcelona, Spain, contributed to an Ellington composition. The basilica, with its window pictures of biblical scenes, gave Ellington inspiration for the composition "Three Black Kings," a work he would not hear performed during his lifetime. Mercer recorded the work with the Warsaw Symphony several years after Duke's death.

Alto saxophonist Norris Turney had joined the band for the tour. He sat in the trombone section and played the fourth trombone part in place of Benny Green, who would not make the tour. Due to a mix-up, the booking office neglected to get Turney a visa, which would have allowed him to play with the band in East Berlin.

Turney recalled, "[W]hen we got to the border, one guy said, 'He can't go in.' So Duke got off the bus and walked very nonchalantly into the office. He had an album, gave the guy an album and they let us in. That was during the Cold War! The power of Duke Ellington."

Nineteen sixty-nine ended with the band working at Caesar's Palace in Las Vegas, through New Year's Day 1970. It was Lawrence Brown's final night with the band. "I was tired," he said. "They were going to Japan, Australia, and New Zealand. With that band I'd done enough traveling to last two lifetimes. It was time to go back to California and relax."

44

THE WINTER 1970 tour began on January 10, with the band's third trip to Japan. There were some new faces in the band: Willie Cook decided not to make the trip to Japan. Fred Stone, a Canadian musician who had worked with Ellington in Canada, was offered the chair. Julius Priester took Brown's place in the trombone section, joining Booty Wood and Chuck Cooper. Following the departure of Hamilton, the saxophone section had remained intact for the two years, consisting of Ashby, Hodges, Procope, Gonsalves, and Carney. Ellington, Joe Benjamin, and Rufus Jones formed the rhythm section.

Ellington was actively working on two commissions while on the tour. George Wein had commissioned *New Orleans Suite* for the forthcoming New Orleans Jazz and Heritage Festival in April, and the choreographer Alvin Ailey had commissioned *The River* for the American Ballet Theater.

Harry Carney said, "If, when I first joined the band, you asked me did I ever expect to be playing in Australia, I'd have looked at you like you were crazy." From Japan, the band proceeded to the west coast of Australia. The group's first visit on the continent was to the Perth Arts Festival, followed by engagements at the Centennial Hall in Adelaide, the Melbourne Festival Hall, and two concerts at the Municipal Stadium, both played to a full house of seven thousand.

"Australia, in a way, reminded me of England in '33," Harry Carney recalled. "The jazz fans and the musicians really knew their stuff. Cootie, Johnny, and I were the only ones left from the Cotton Club days. So they'd ask us to settle arguments. 'Who soloed on this record, who soloed on that?' Cootie was no help. When they asked him questions, he'd smile and say, 'Ask Carney; he knows that stuff better than I do.' Johnny's answer was always the same, He'd shake his head and say, 'That was a long, long time ago.'"

The journey ended with a concert at the Town Hall in Wellington, New Zealand, on February 9, 1970. Carney recalled, "It was a beautiful summer day down there. It was hard to remember that in two day's time, we'd be back in New York, on the road, doing one-night stands, in the middle of winter."

The usual grind of one-nighters was broken up with two concerts of sacred music at the National Presbyterian Church in Washington, D.C., on March 15-16. On April 26, another *Sacred Concert* was given at the Municipal Auditorium in New Orleans, Louisiana, as part of the New Orleans Jazz and Heritage Festival. A day earlier, Ellington premiered his *New Orleans Suite*.

"He'd been working on that off and on while we were in the Far East," Mercer said. "Originally there were just five sections when we first recorded it."

"Blues for New Orleans" featured the man who had been playing the blues with Ellington since 1928, when he first dazzled the musical world with electrifying solos on "Tishomingo" and "Yellow Dog Blues": Johnny Hodges. In addition, his old compatriot Wild Bill Davis's organ was incorporated by Ellington into the score.

Stanley Dance was in the studio when the work was recorded. He noted that Ellington was "in the studio, not the control room, conducting, routining, dancing, clapping his hands and miming his requirements as the arrangement unfolded. There occurred a last example of the complete and instant understanding the existed between him and the little giant . . . he made a quick gesture with his hand and Hodges comprehending the significance immediately stepped back from the microphone and then moved in on it confidently with a telling held note."

"Bourbon Street Jingling Jollies" introduced Norris Turney's flute, an instrument heretofore unknown in Ellington's orchestral palette. At the premiere in New Orleans, Ellington announced, "We would like to have Norris Turney come up for a solo spot. He, ladies and gentlemen, would like to give a tone parallel to the excruciating ecstasy one finds oneself suspended in when one is in the throes of the jingling jollies of Bourbon Street."

"Thanks for the Beautiful Land on the Delta" featured the tenor saxophone of Harold Ashby. In this work, Ellington used the three alto saxophones of Hodges, Procope, and Turney to play the theme.

"Second Line" was Ellington's impression of the New Orleans citizens who dance behind the brass bands. No parade would be complete without them. Booty Wood, Julius Priester, Russell Procope, and Cootie Willams contributed greatly to the merrymaking.

"Aristocracy à la Jean Lafitte" was the salute by Ellington to the pirate whose aristocratic behavior on one occasion reputedly saved the city. Fred Stone recalled, "After about three weeks in the group doing section parts, I asked him if he would give me some solos to play. He looked at me and said 'What do you want, old Clark Terry charts? . . . Wouldn't you rather I write something that suits the way you play?'" Stone has a prominent role in the work, playing fluegelhorn.

George Wein, the promoter who commissioned the suite, was enthusiastic about the work and thought it should be expanded to a full album. He had heard the first performance in New Orleans. "It gave me a chill," he said backstage. "That was Duke at his greatest." Ellington proposed to fill out the recording with a set of portraits of well-known New Orleans musicians: Wellman Braud, Louis Armstrong, Sidney Bechet, and Mahalia Jackson.

"Portrait of Wellman Braud" paid homage to the great bassist who played an important role in the band for nine years beginning in 1927. In 1928, Ellington surprised the jazz world by placing a microphone at his bass, when he recorded the ebullient "Hot and Bothered." His solid beat was a source of rhythmic strength and inspiration. Bassist Joe Benjamin, Carney, Williams, and Procope contributed greatly to the score.

"Portrait of Louis Armstrong" featured Cootie Williams, an unabashed Armstrong fan, who described him to me as "the greatest trumpet player I've ever heard." At one point, shortly after joining the band, Williams lived in Wellman Braud's apartment for a while, and got to meet his idol personally.

"Portrait of Mahalia Jackson" was the last number on the recording. Ellington held the great gospel singer in high regard. Norris Turney's elegant flute is heard. Cootie Williams preaches his solo with mute and plunger. Paul Gonsalves and Julius Priester are also heard. The work ends appropriately with a hymn.

The penultimate work, "Portrait of Sidney Bechet," was originally written with Johnny Hodges in mind. "Pop wanted him to get out his soprano sax and play it on that piece," Mercer recalled. "He knew Sidney was his idol. He asked me to talk with him about it. Johnny said, 'It will cost him.' When I told Pop, he said, 'Pay him what he wants.'"

Hodges had not played the instrument in the band for more than twenty years. "I was surprised when he told me he still had one at home," said Harry Carney. "Strangely enough, it was the one Bechet gave him. He complained that he had a hard time keeping it in tune. But then he always said that when he played it in the band."

On May 11, 1970, Ellington began recording music from *The River*, playing solo piano. When he returned home, Mercer called to tell him that Johnny Hodges had died, unexpectedly, at the age of 63. The *New Orleans Suite* was recorded without him. Ellington assigned the part to Paul Gonsalves's tenor saxophone for the recording session two days later. "Bechet is not forgotten," Stanley Dance wrote. "Gonsalves skillfully represents the lyric flow of that master, just as Johnny Hodges had done."

Hodges had been troubled with heart disease for a few years before his death. "After his health began to crack," Mercer stated, "he was lucky to be near the best possible hospital on three of the occasions when he had attacks. One occurrence was on a plane coming in from Indianapolis, when he was sitting next to an oxygen tank. There was also a doctor on board, and we rushed him to the hospital as soon as we landed. His last and fatal attack took place when he had gone to his dentist; he might have been saved then, too, but I guess his luck had run out."

In his eulogy, Ellington compared Hodges to the giants is his own musical pantheon who had passed on: Art Tatum, Sidney Bechet, Django Reinhardt, and Billy Strayhorn. He concluded by saying, "I'm glad and thankful that I had the privilege of presenting Johnny Hodges for forty years, night after night. I imagine I have been much envied, but thanks to God. May God bless the beautiful giant in his own identity." Ellington, members of the band, entertainers, and Harlem musicians who had known him all attended Hodges's funeral at the Masonic Temple on May 14.

"As we were leaving the funeral, someone asked Pop who has he going to get to take Johnny's place," Mercer recalled. "'No one,' he said, 'He's irreplaceable.'"

With the *New Orleans Suite* out of the way, Ellington was putting the final touches on *The River*. It opened in New York on June 25, 1970, to complimentary reviews. According to Mercer, the idea of *The River* had been kicking around for years. Ellington's friend and biographer, Stanley Dance, had suggested an extended work depicting the natural course of the river. He had the Mississippi in mind. Strayhorn thought it was a great idea, but nothing came of it until the American Ballet Theater made its offer.

By the time of this commission, Ellington's thoughts for most new works were spiritual in nature. *The River* is an allegory for the cycle of birth and rebirth, as Ellington noted in the opening segment: "The spring which is like a newborn baby. He is in his cradle . . . spouting, spinning, wiggling, gurgling . . . reaching for his bottle."

The ten segments that follow depict the river as it develops over time before returning to its source, the spring. Mercer noted that his father borrowed from one of his compositions in the segment called "Riba." Whitney Balliett, distinguished critic of *The New Yorker*, compared the work with early Stravinsky.

On June 28, 1970, the band arrived in the Netherlands for another tour of Europe. Over the course of five weeks, besides the Netherlands, Ellington played in France, Belgium, Switzerland, Germany, Sweden, and Yugoslavia.

"On the flight back home," Mercer recalled, "he was very animated. He felt the audience response in Europe was much different than it was in the States. He couldn't wait to get back there."

However, it would be more than a year before Ellington would return. On September 10, 1971, the band left for an extended tour of Europe. This time it included a part of the continent that the musicians had never visited before. Under the auspices of the State Department, the Duke Ellington Orchestra was booked for a tour of the Soviet Union, as a part of the cultural exchange program between the two nations.

Harry Carney recalled, "When we landed in Leningrad, we were greeted by the Red Army band marching across the airfield playing 'Take the A Train' in march tempo. Even Duke was impressed!" The opening concert was at the October Theatre. The band was there for six days. "Russia was something else," Mercer recalled. "Wherever we went, we only had to play one concert a day. Pop had a great time. Somebody dragged him off to the Hermitage Museum. He came back full of spirits and called a rehearsal the next day!"

Ellington recalled, "We did what, five weeks, and the shortest concert we did, including encores, was three hours and a half. And the longest was four hours and five minutes and at the end of this period, nobody had left the hall. Nobody had left their seats. And then after that, they normally walk down towards the stage and I'd come out and do Billy Strayhorn's 'Lotus Blossom' which is just piano, and they'd just drift away."

"He always did ['Lotus Blossom'] at the end of concerts," Mercer said, "as a sort of memorial to Billy Strayhorn." The Soviets also heard the *Togo Brava Suite* and the "medley" of Ellington favorites, along with *La Plus Belle Africaine* and *Harlem*.

The critic from *Pravda* praised the band, but was particularly struck with its "priceless sense of ease. . . . They walk on without any special ceremony, simply, one by one, as friends usually gather for a jam session."

The tour ended on October 12, after the fifth engagement in Moscow. "Moscow was great," Mercer said. "Pop played a concert with the Radio Moscow Jazz Orchestra. When he walked onto the podium for the first rehearsal, they stood and applauded for a good two minutes. He was very moved by that. When the concert was over several of the musicians had tears in their eyes."

The orchestra was directed by Maxim Shostakovich, son of the great Soviet composer Dmitri (Maxim subsequently defected to the United States). At one point, he informed Ellington that his father was a great admirer of his music, but was in the hospital, and asked, "Do you think you could possibly come by?" Ellington replied, "I'd be honored."

Ellington did visit Shostakovich, but there is no record of the conversation. But a friend observed, "He was very, very touched by that." At the American embassy, Duke was introduced to the composer Aram Khachaturian. While there, he did a *Sacred Concert* just for the employees. Between the concerts in Leningrad and Moscow, there were engagements in Minsk, Kiev, and Rostov.

While in Kiev, during one of the concerts, Ellington was alarmed to see policemen lining the halls, and asked his interpreter what was happening.

Carney said, "He got a big kick out of it, when she told him the police band, all fifty men, had come to hear his concert! He talked and laughed about that for the rest of the trip."

Duke was particularly impressed by the way the Russians treated him as an artist. He reminisced, "One hour after we arrived, we were at the Bolshoi, the next day it was the Rachmaninov opera, Shostakovitch concert, the Rimsky-Korsakov opera, you were invited to a symphony rehearsal, a radio, TV show, vaudeville show . . . nothing away from music ever."

The trip was a success beyond Ellington's wildest dreams. Duke received letters of congratulation from President Nixon and Senator Hubert Humphrey. "Then it was back to the real world," Mercer recalled. The band went back to playing one-night stands all over Europe, including Poland, Yugoslavia, Hungary, and Romania.

While in Lyons, France, Ellington received an award at the Opera House for his musical contribution to Goutelas a few years earlier. In Copenhagen, Ben Webster joined the band onstage for the concert on November 7, 1971. He had made a home in that city and was considered a jazz icon by its residents.

Eight days later, the band flew directly from Barcelona, Spain, to Rio de Janeiro, Brazil, for another tour of South America. While there, they played in Uruguay, Argentina, Peru, Chile, Ecuador, Colombia, and Venezuela.

"When we got to Caracas," Mercer said, "it dawned on me we had played sixteen concerts in fourteen days. Then we played another ten days in a row, before we flew into Chicago for a one-night stand at the Aragon Ballroom!"

During this time, Ellington and Stanley Dance were working on his autobiography, *Music Is My Mistress*. The editor at the Doubleday publishing house, Sam Vaughn, a jazz buff, had been pursuing Ellington for quite some time to write his memoirs, offering a $10,000 advance, but had always been rebuffed.

One night, during the band's annual engagement at the Rainbow Room in Rockefeller Center, Nelson Doubleday, the chairman of the board of the publishing house that bore his name, arrived with a party of friends. "At the end of the evening," Carney said, "he walked up to Duke, told him he was a genius and he must write a book.

"His response was two words, 'How much?' Without batting an eye the man said, 'Fifty thousand dollars in advance, Mr. Ellington,' and they shook hands."

"I don't know how Stanley ever got that book written," Mercer said. "He [Ellington] would have Stanley go to places like Houston and Toronto when he had long engagements, but often they would sit up all night watching dog-assed movies and not work at all. It was the same at home. Stanley would come to work, but [Ellington] would be too tired for anything but criticisms and promises. It was a miracle the book was ever finished."

By this time, Ellington was not a well man; neither were most of the veteran members of the band. The musical lifetime of working in smoke-filled nightclubs for more than forty years had caught up with Williams and Carney. Both were diagnosed with emphysema. Ellington, too, had some lung pathology that showed up on an X-ray, but the physicians were uncertain about what it was. It was later found out that he had a lymphoma, which would ultimately take his life.

Following a thorough checkup from Dr. Logan, Ellington undertook a grueling tour of the Far East, longer than anything he had done in that part of the world in the past. First, it was back to Japan again, for two weeks. "He liked going there," Mercer stated. "The Japanese promoters paid him top dollar."

The musicians had different ideas. "Everything was so damned expensive," Russell Procope complained.

The group then traveled on to the Philippines. Ellington played a concert in Manila with the National Symphony Orchestra at the Cultural Center. *Harlem* and *Night Creature* were the featured works. The conductor Rendentor Romero had memorized Ray Nance's violin solo from the second movement of *Night Creature*, and played it flawlessly. "When the movement was over," Mercer said, "Pop got up from the piano, embraced him and held up his arm with the violin, and led the applause. 'Red' [as the band members called him] was touched."

"We went to places I knew Duke would never see again. Nor me for that matter," Carney said. "Bangkok, Kuala Lampur, Djakarta, Mandalay."

While a graduate student at the Harvard Business School, the future king of Thailand would often come to hear the band. An amateur clarinetist, the king placed a garland of flowers around Duke's neck following the concert. "Wherever we went the first thing he did was to find a refrigerator for the flowers," Mercer said. "At one point he had them covered with bags of ice."

In Mandalay, as Ellington was being led from the plane to the airport building, the route was lined with music professors and musicians who presented him with twenty different bouquets. On the night of the concert, he was stunned by the total silence; no one applauded. He later learned that this was the audience's way of expressing how totally overwhelmed they were. After three hours, they were still sitting there.

The only disturbance to Ellington's equanimity was when he learned, after arriving in New Zealand, that an overambitious promoter had billed his appearance as a "Farewell Concert." "Pop was not amused," Mercer said. "If the guy was near, I think he'd have kicked him in his ass."

Music Is My Mistress, Ellington's autobiography, was finally published in 1973, when Duke was seventy-four years old. The book was mainly a collection of memories of people he had known and places he had been. When reading it, one would think he never made an enemy, suffered a slight, or experienced the painful discrimination that was part and parcel of growing up a black man in white America.

Don George was curious. He said to the editor Sam Vaughn, "Everything is moonlight and roses. Everything is great, everything is wonderful. Nobody seems quite human. Why was it written that way? Was it editorial policy?"

The editor pointed out that Ellington was an entertainer. He wanted his audience to feel good. "He wants to be loved by everyone in the audience, one by one, everyone in the audience wants to be loved, so what harm is done if he tells them he loves them."

He concluded by saying, "The value of a memoir is not whether it is accurate. It's a picture of what the man wants you to think. Memoirs are all flawed by self-service, but they still have value."

45

DUKE ELLINGTON'S LAST tour began with the premiere of his third and final *Sacred Concert* in London's Westminster Abbey on United Nations Day, October 24, 1973. Among the invited guests were H.R.H. Princess Margaret and Prime Minister Edward Heath, an excellent musician in his own right.

Ellington had played in some of the greatest churches in the world: San Francisco, New York, Coventry, Cambridge, and Barcelona. Westminster Abbey was another jewel in that crown. "He knew it was his last shot, and he wanted it to be good," Mercer said. He was surprised that his father had brought Ruth with him. In the past, she had never accompanied him overseas. It was clear that Ellington knew how gravely ill he was, but he never told his son.

Vocalist Alice Babs had flown in from Sweden the day that they arrived, and Roscoe Gill had been there most of the previous week, to rehearse the John Alldis choir. St. Margaret's Church, adjacent to the abbey, was secured for the first rehearsal. When the rehearsal began, it would be the first time Duke would look at his orchestra and only see one familiar face from the Cotton Club days: Harry Carney. Cootie Williams had remained in New York, although he was ably replaced by Barry Lee Hall. Art Baron joined the trombone section to do the plunger work. The band was familiar with most of the score, having rehearsed a good part of it during the two-week engagement at Mr. Kelly's, a nightclub in Chicago.

Alice Babs was the only person unfamiliar with the work. "That woman was something," Mercer said. "Pop accompanied her at the piano and she started to sing. Listening to her, you would have never guessed she was sight reading her part!"

The next morning, there was trouble. Paul Gonsalves suffered an epileptic seizure and was rushed to Westminster Hospital. He had to miss the concert. The night before, while out carousing with friends, he had probably had too much to drink or taken drugs. Fortunately,

Mercer had taken the precaution of bringing six saxophones on the tour, and Gonsalves's solos were allotted to Harold Ashby. Percy Marion filled Gonsalves's chair. He had been brought into the reed section one month earlier, as insurance, because Gonsalves had been becoming more and more unreliable. This additional stress only added to the strain that Ellington was under. At one point, Ellington said to his son, "I have never been so unprepared to do a performance as I am in this case."

After lunch, rehearsals were transferred to the abbey, and continued throughout the day until it was time for the audience to be admitted. "After I got on my band uniform," Mercer recalled:

> I went to look in on Pop. He was lying on the cot, barely breathing, looking like a very tired, exhausted old man. From the way he was breathing, I began to get worried. Then someone on the cathedral staff poked their head in the door, and announced that Princess Margaret would be at the west door of the abbey within a minute.
>
> He got up, and his valet Jim Lowe helped him put on his tails. It was extraordinary. It was as though the years just fell away. He stood up straight, strode briskly to the door, shook hands with the prime minister, and bowed to the princess. She took his arm and he escorted her to her seat with a broad smile on his face. You'd have never guessed it was the same person I saw a few minutes earlier lying on the cot!

Sir Colin Crowe, chairman of the United Nations Association, said a few words before the performance. He observed, "[I]f the General Assembly had their debates conducted by Duke Ellington, they might achieve better harmony." Ellington himself, dedicating his music, said: "Every man prays to God in his own language. There is not a language God does not understand."

The *Third Sacred Concert*, like its predecessors, had its strong moments. Alice Babs and Johnny Hodges performed a lovely duet on a piece called "Heaven." Ellington performed another of his "portraits," dedicated to the Reverend John G. Gensel, pastor to the jazz community. It featured trumpeter Barry Lee Hall, who had replaced Cootie

Williams, in a strong solo. Trombonist Art Baron was featured on an a capella recorder solo.

For the finale, Ellington had written "Ain't Nobody Nowhere Nothin' Without God," which was sung by Tony Watkins. As was his wont, he decided to replace that with a rousing number, "Praise God and Dance," which was sung by the entire company, when the concert was recorded. The recording featured Alice Babs, Norris Turney, Buster Cooper on trombone, Paul Gonsalves, and Cat Anderson. When this number was performed at the close of the *Sacred Concert* given at the ancient Church of Santa Maria del Mar in Barcelona, Spain, on November 10, 1973, it aroused such enthusiasm that the congregation burst into the aisles to participate.

Leaving Westminster Abbey, Ellington made a short appearance at the cocktail party being held in his honor at 10 Downing Street by the prime minister. He stayed about fifteen minutes and didn't take off his coat. The following day, he left for Malmö, Sweden, beginning a back-breaking tour of Sweden, Denmark, Germany, Austria, Portugal, Yugoslavia, Spain, France, Belgium, the Netherlands, Ethiopia, and Zambia. In Ethiopia, he was personally received by Haile Selassie, and received the Emperor's Star from the aged Lion of Judah.

Ruth had remained in London with the Diamonds. Ellington was scheduled to play a royal command performance at the Palladium, before Queen Elizabeth and Prince Philip. The band had given twenty-nine concerts in as many days, including three in Zambia and two in Ethiopia. Mercer, aware of his father's fragile health, had sent Dr. Logan a prepaid, round trip, first-class ticket to London. He was due to arrive on November 23. "He was going to meet Pop at the airport; it was a twenty-three-hour flight," Mercer recalled. "I knew that would raise [Duke's] spirits."

At that time, Logan was working with Manhattan Borough President Percy Sutton to relocate his medical group. He was looking for a new and better facility. He did not feel he could leave New York until he was certain a new a site had been secured, and kept putting off the trip to London. On Saturday night, the borough president called and informed the doctor that the city was contemplating donating a site for his clinic at 134th Street and Riverside Drive.

Logan told his wife, Marion, that he was going to the hospital to check on his patients and look at the site. Forty-five minutes later, the police called and asked her to come identify his body. He had been murdered by two itinerant blacks, who mistook him for white, mugged him, and threw the body off a viaduct, where it fell one hundred feet to the ground.

Ruth Ellington was informed by Cress Courtney of Logan's death on the afternoon of November 25; she immediately informed Mercer. Ellington was due in London the next day at six in the morning. Fearing he would cancel the command performance, Ruth and Mercer withheld from him the news of Logan's death.

Ellington completed the show, was presented to Queen Elizabeth and Prince Philip, and went back to the Audley Suite at the Dorchester Hotel, which he was sharing with Ruth and Fernandae. They were off to Edinburgh the next day, then to Glasgow and Dublin on November 29. That day, Logan was buried in New York. Mayor Robert F. Wagner addressed the two thousand who attended his rites. Governor Nelson Rockefeller issued a statement that said in part, "The death of Dr. Logan is a great tragedy and a profound loss to the city."

Some of the musicians had known of Logan's death on the day of the command performance. Ellington kept asking for the doctor; why hadn't he arrived? Feeling that he could keep it from him no longer, Mercer broke the news to him.

"It was the third time I saw him cry," Mercer said, "first Grandma Daisy, then Billy and now Dr. Logan. If ever he lost a friend, it was Arthur. Billy's death tore him up, but nothing like Arthur's."

Marion Logan recalled, "Edward called me and said, 'The worst thing has happened to me. I just don't believe that it's so. I don't know what I'm going to do. I'll never get over this. I won't last six months.'"

Sometime later, Mrs. Logan was contacted by the FBI. The two men who committed the murder had been incarcerated in Florida for an unrelated crime. While in prison, they found a copy of *Jet* magazine that contained the details of Logan's death and funeral. They were surprised, because they assumed that they had robbed a white man (Logan was light skinned enough to be mistaken for white). While discussing the incident between themselves, they were overheard by another inmate, who wrote a letter to a reporter. The reporter forwarded it to the FBI, who infiltrated the prison and verified the statements contained in the letter.

Mrs. Logan discouraged having the murderers extradited for trial. She didn't want another six months to a year of pain over that issue, or to have her child further upset. Nothing would bring her husband back, and the two criminals were already serving a ninety-year term for a similar crime in Florida.

On his return to New York, Ellington was hospitalized briefly. Then he played an engagement at the Rainbow Room at Rockefeller Center, and went back on the road. On March 22, 1974, however, he collapsed following a concert at Northern Illinois University. Ellington was seen in the outpatient department of the university hospital. Nonetheless, he went with the band to play a date in Sturgis, Michigan. Cootie Williams recalled, "That last trip he was on. He was working night by night. And I know he was sick. He was barely making it. He told Mercer don't take the bus too far away from him, that's when he left to come home."

In late March, Ellington entered the Harkness Pavilion of Columbia-Presbyterian Hospital. Ruth was very concerned about his care, and wanted a consultation from someone not connected with the hospital. She asked a family friend who knew Frank Sinatra to ask for his recommendation. The singer contacted heart specialist Dr. Michael DeBakey and had him flown to New York on his private jet plane. After consulting with Ellington's caregivers, Dr. DeBakey informed the family that Duke was getting the best care possible.

The lymphoma, which would ultimately kill him, did not extinguish Ellington's creative juices. While in the hospital, he discussed with Mercer the orchestration of *The Three Black Kings*. Mercer would conduct the first performance of this ballet when it was staged by the Alvin Ailey company at Lincoln Center two years later.

With his electric piano at his side, Ellington continued to work on his comic opera *Queenie Pie*, which was virtually completed by the time of his death. The work originally had been commissioned by the public television station WNET as a television opera, with Ellington as narrator. When the television project did not materialize, however, he decided to expand *Queenie Pie* into a full-length stage presentation. It subsequently had its world premiere at the Zellerbach Theater in

Philadelphia from September 18 to September 26, 1986. As performed then, the work contained twenty-six compositions by Ellington.

While he was in the hospital, Duke and Mercer also began editing the tapes of the *Third Sacred Concert*. At one point, he said to Mercer, "Do you know that if you took this part so far and ended it, you could splice this other part back on it?"

"From the way he said it to me," Mercer recalled, "I noticed the quality of the *you* had changed. I was pretty sure he was assigning me a task he knew he would never live to see finished. Like he was passing the mantle on. During his hospital stay, for the first time, he entrusted the judgment to me of what I should do to improve this or that, and I think that was the only time he came close to alluding to or admitting that he wouldn't be coming out of the hospital."

While Duke was in the hospital, Evie Ellis was diagnosed with lung cancer.

She had been visiting every day, "early in the morning when no one else was there," Don George said. "She brought some fancy ice cream or the strawberry cheesecake he liked, some manuscripts that he could run down on the piano he had installed."

Evie didn't want to burden Ellington with the news of her condition. The question was whether she should play the role of being well, continue to see him, and not let him know how sick she was, although she was becoming sicker and sicker. There was no way she could explain her absence for two or three weeks.

It was left to Mercer to inform his father of Evie's dilemma. "He recognized time was a factor," Mercer said. "She must go and have attention *immediately*," his father decreed. Evie was operated on at New York Hospital, was discharged, and was sent home to Ellington's West End Avenue apartment under the care of a private nurse. She and Ellington would never see each other again.

At the same time Evie was visiting Duke—and after she was diagnosed with cancer—Fernandae came every day. A wary truce existed between the women in this triangle. According to Mercer, while Evie was across town at New York Hospital, and then recovering at their home on West End Avenue, his father would give a signal, Fernandae would leave the room, and Duke would telephone Evie and speak with her at length.

Don George recalled, "Even though the intense sedation kept him alternating between periods of pain and euphoria, to the very end he called her two or three times every day to say to her, 'I love you, doll. Honest, I love you.'"

"One of the times I went to see Duke at the hospital," drummer Sonny Greer recalled, "as I was leaving, Fernandae took me aside, and made sure I'd be there for his seventy-fifth birthday party. We had a good time; she was dressed in blue, just for Duke, and she brought the cake and some caviar for him."

A friend recalled the party. "I was there ... and the hall was lined with baskets of fruit and flowers [that Frank] Sinatra sent. It must have cost $2,000-$3,000. It was a gesture, of course; they gave all that stuff away."

The friend was particularly impressed that President Nixon called. That was the day he went on television to divulge the transcripts of the Watergate case, "so he must have had a lot on his mind. This is a redeeming feature about Nixon, he took the time to call Ellington and wish him happy birthday."

Ellington's birthday was also celebrated at St. Peter's Church, which was then temporarily located in the Central Presbyterian Church at 64th Street and Park Avenue. Selections from his *Third Sacred Concert* were performed. Roscoe Gill led the orchestra and Ellington's protégé, Brooks Kerr, took his place at the piano. The concert was taped, but for some reason, Ellington never heard it.

Duke's health was failing, Mercer observed. "He walked every day, and when he got to the point where he couldn't walk in the corridors, he made sure he walked somewhere, even if it was just across the room. Just so he could say he walked somewhere that day."

"That night he was dying," Ruth recalled, "he called me in and said, 'Kisses, kisses.' I picked him up out of the bed and put him down and he said, 'More kisses.' And I picked him up and gave him more kisses, and then he looked at me as if he were taking my picture, because he was lying in bed and I was standing up and he said, 'Smile kisses.' [He] fixed me with a smile for all eternity and then as I was leaving the room he picked up the cross on the chair I had given him, kissed it twice and that night he took flight."

Mercer said, "He departed quietly that night. When the nurse said there was no longer a pulse, my mind reverted instantly to the

Third Sacred Concert, to his composition so presciently titled, 'The Majesty of God.'"

Duke Ellington died at 3:10 A.M. on May 24, 1974. It was seven months to the day since his Westminster Abbey concert, just one day earlier than the date his mother died in 1935, and a little less than the six months he had given himself to live after Arthur Logan's death.

The *New York Times* had his picture on the front page, with the caption, "Duke Ellington, Master of Music, Dies at 75." An editorial in the *Sunday Times* stated in part, "[I]n Duke Ellington, American jazz achieved its righful stature and dignity." The president of the United States, Richard Nixon, stated, "The wit, taste, intelligence and elegance that Duke Ellington brought to his music have made him, in the eyes of millions of people both here and abroad, America's foremost composer. His memory will live for generations to come in the music with which he enriched his nation."

I learned of Ellington's death while in Washington, D.C. I planned to stop off at the Walter B. Cooke funeral parlor on Third Avenue to pay my respects before continuing on the drive up to Boston. Upon arriving at the funeral parlor, I was surprised to learn that the bodies of Tyree Glenn and Paul Gonsalves were also there. Gonsalves had been playing in Holland; when the job was over he flew to Great Britain to visit friends, and was found dead in London.

More than sixty thousand people came to Cooke's to pay their last respects to Duke over that weekend. At times there were lines four abreast that spanned two city blocks. The funeral chapel remained open twenty-four hours a day. I saw Ellington's body at 2 A.M. It was in an open seamless copper coffin. On his neck was the Emperor's Star of Ethiopia; his Legion of Honor and the Presidential Medal of Freedom were also on his body.

The funeral on Monday May 27, was held in the Cathedral of St. John the Divine, where I had heard the *Second Sacred Concert*. A crowd estimated at 10,000 filled the magnificent building, and another 2,500 were standing out on Amsterdam Avenue, listening to a broadcast of the services.

The Suffragan Bishop of the New York diocese, the Right Reverend Harold Wright, presided over the service, assisted by the

Reverend Norman O'Connor and Pastor John Gensel, pastoral coun-
selor to many jazz musicians. Among those present, I recognized Count
Basie and his wife, Benny Goodman, Lena Horne, Tony Bennett, and
the singer Joe Williams. Mercer later informed me that Frank Sinatra
had sent a magnificent floral arrangement.

Performing at the service were Ruth's husband, the former opera
star McHenry Boatwright, and Ella Fitzgerald, who sang "Solitude"
and "Just a Closer Walk with Thee." There was also music from Earl
Hines, Ray Nance, Mary Lou Williams, Billy Taylor, Hank Jones, and
Pearl Bailey (representing the White House), along with her husband,
percussionist Louis Bellson.

Ellington's long-time friend and amanuensis, Stanley Dance, gave
the eulogy. The finale was a tape recording of Johnny Hodges and Alice
Babs taken from the *Second Sacred Concert* and played over the public
address system. Ellington had considered that one the best of the three
he had written. The coffin was carried by pallbearers that included the
son of Irving Mills; Edmund Anderson; George Wein; the jazz inpre-
sario, who was Ellington's last major promoter; and a visibly shaken
Harry Carney.

As soon as the service ended, I walked down to 110th Street, hailed
a taxi, and told the driver to take me to 640 Lenox Avenue. The site of
the old Cotton Club was now a housing project. Despite the cool, driz-
zly day, a large crowd of people had gathered at the spot. The majority
were people in their fifties, sixties, and seventies. We all knew why we
were there. One man had brought his great-grandaughter "to bear wit-
ness," he told me, "so she can pass on to her children and grandchildren,
she had seen the funeral of a great man."

As the cortege rolled by, everyone applauded; some of the women
had tears streaming down their faces. We stood silently for a moment
and then began to leave. As the group began to disperse, I learned that
many of the mourners were former employees of the old Cotton Club.
At least three of the women who were crying were former dancers.

Ellington was laid to rest beside his father and mother at the
Woodlawn Cemetery in the Bronx, in a section of it known as
Wildrose. A few nights later, I was talking with Sonny Greer about the
funeral. Greer said:

Man that cemetery was packed; I never seen a crowd like that
before. You knew everybody there knew Duke and loved him. Whole
lots of folks were lining up to take a rose off the casket, before it was
lowered in the ground. [Harry] Carney and I were in the limousine
together. He kept saying, "With Duke gone I have nothing to live for.
With Duke gone I have nothing to live for." I tried to cheer him up,
but nothing worked.

Carney was dead a few months later.

"Fernandae was all tore up," the drummer continued. "They had to
carry her out of the funeral parlor the last night. She kept saying to me,
'Sonny, I never loved a man the way I loved Duke, and I don't think I
ever will again. There was no one on earth like him.'"

A friend of mine was in London at the time of Duke's death. She
attended the memorial service for him at the church of St. Martin in
the Fields on June 12. The attendees included U.S. Ambassador Walter
Annenberg and his wife, Yehudi Menuhin and his wife, as well as the
Honorable Gerald Lascelles. My friend was thrilled to hear Adelaide
Hall sing her obbligato to "Creole Love Call" once again, accompanied
by John Dankworth's band. However, the most poignant moment
occurred when, after a short silence, Ellington's old friend Larry Adler,
walking slowly down the aisle, played "Mood Indigo" unaccompanied
on his harmonica. He then joined Cleo Laine and the Dankworth band
in a complete rendition of the Ellington masterpiece. At its conclusion,
my friend's teenaged daughter whispered in her ear, "Mummy, that's
soul music, isn't it?"

Evie Ellis died of cancer in April 1975, and was buried next to
Ellington. "She had been like a mother to me," Mercer recalled. "When
I was sick in the hospital, she came to see me every day, and brought me
food and things. I promised her when she passed on she'd be laid to rest
next to Pop. She was always worried about money. So I got her to move
to a smaller apartment in the building. I was at her bedside the night
she passed."

Evie's death for Mercer was "liberating," he said. "My only responsibility from there on in was the band." He had also left his wife of
thirty-five-plus years and moved to Denmark, where he subsequently
had a child with a Danish woman. On being informed of Mercer's rela-

tionship with another woman, his ex-wife told *Jet* magazine, "He would never have done that if his father were alive."

Yet Ellington's relations with women were hardly exemplary. Even as he lay dying, he maintained a relationship with two long-term mistresses, Evie Ellis and Fernandae de Castro Monte. In his shorter affairs, Ellington would often pass a woman on to a band member after he was finished with her. There were five musicians in the band who married women subsequent to their having had affairs with Ellington. "When Lawrence Brown married Fredi Washington it was no secret that she and my father had been involved, during and after the making of the film, *Black and Tan*," Mercer said. "They remained close for quite some time, until she married Lawrence when the band came back from Europe in '33."

Mercer also noted that his father rarely approved of the women that his family or band members chose as mates. Otto [Toby] Hardwick aroused Ellington's ire with his choice of a woman. Mercer said, "[Their] friendship . . . which was a long and deep one was definitely affected when he vehemently disagreed with Otto's choice of a woman. He told him he was stupid to be fooling around with her, and eventually [Otto] quit the band forever.

"He didn't agree with Ruth's choices in marriage, or me, my wife, and my son's girlfriends," Mercer said. "The only exception was Minnie, Freddie Guy's wife. Ellington thought she was a wonderful person."

There is an inherent psychological tragedy in Ellington's life. Following the breakup of his marriage, Ellington recreated the family closer to his heart's desire. Playing out his Oedipal wishes, he removed his father from his mother's bed. With such success at realizing infantile wishes, one should not be surprised, psychologically speaking, that Ellington was unable to tolerate his mother's loss when she died, nor was he ever able to commit himself fully to another woman.

There are some wishes better unattained as their accomplishment leads to unrealistic expectations and, more tragically, profound narcissism. At his death, Ellington further validated this conjecture. He left no will. Later, while clearing up his father's papers, Mercer came upon the following note: "I'm easy to please, I just want everybody in the palm of my hand."

Epilogue

DUKE ELLINGTON WAS one of the great innovators in American music. One could say that this first manifested itself in November 1926 with the recording of "East St. Louis Toodle-Oo," and then in "Black & Tan Fantasy" the following year. Both works used the mute and plunger, ably played by Bubber Miley in the former and Miley and Joe Nanton in the latter.

While "Black & Tan Fantasy" was Miley and Nanton's creation, from it came music orchestrated by Ellington to create the "Jungle Music" for the Cotton Club shows of the late 1920s and early 1930s. His capacity as an orchestrator was such that, when he recorded "Daybreak Express" in 1935, he used the saxophones to simulate the sound of the train whistle. When Mercer rerecorded the work fifty-five years later, he had to use a regular whistle. "How he did that he took to his grave," his son said.

Assessing Ellington's capacity as an orchestrator, Robert D. Darrell said, "He was the Richard Strauss of jazz orchestration." It was no accident that another composer, and no mean orchestrator himself, Igor Stravinsky, on arriving in New York for a visit in the 1930s, surprised the reception committee (on being asked what he wanted to see) that his top priority was to hear Duke Ellington play at the Cotton Club in Harlem.

In 1927, Ellington used Adelaide Hall's voice as an obbligato in "Creole Love Call." He continued to use a woman's voice as another instrument of the orchestra throughout his career; with Kay Davis in the late 1940s and early 1950s, and finally Alice Babs at the end of his life when doing the *Sacred Concerts*.

In 1928, Ellington amplified Wellman Braud's bass, heard prominently on the ebullient "Hot and Bothered" (one of his many variations on "Tiger Rag"). He moved from rhythmic propulsion to melodic invention with the addition of Jimmy Blanton's bass in 1939, recording with the young musician a series of piano-bass duets. These works have yet to be discovered by the great majority of rock bass players to this day.

In 1965, Ellington began writing his series of *Sacred Concerts*. He used this venue to give praise to and celebrate his God. Mercer recalled:

> He was quite taken with the biblical story of the "Juggler of Notre Dame." The man was a great juggler, who would sneak into the church and juggle before the altar. As the story goes, the priests found out about it and kicked him out. God intervened and told the priests to leave him alone. The man was celebrating his presence, by using the gifts that He gave him. That's how Pop felt about the *Sacred Concerts*.

On April 29, 1999, the centennial of his birth, Ellington was awarded the Special Citation by the committee for the Pulitzer Prize, the same committee that had denied him an award thirty years earlier. The citation was not for a specific piece of music, which is the norm, but for his overall contribution to, and his innovations in, American music.

Chronology

1879	January 4	Birth of Daisy Kennedy, later Duke Ellington's mother, in Washington, D.C.
	April 15	Birth of James Edward (J. E.) Ellington in Lincolnton, N.C.
1886		J. E.'s family moves to Washington, D.C.; his mother is hired as a housekeeper to the family of Dr. Middleton F. Cuthbert, a prominent Washington physician
1896		J. E. becomes coachman for Dr. Cuthbert at age seventeen; soon promoted to role of butler
1898	January 3	Marriage of J. E. and Daisy; their first child is born shortly thereafter, but either is a stillbirth or dies shortly after
1899	April 29	Edward Kennedy "Duke" Ellington born; family moves to J. E.'s parents' house shortly thereafter
1913		Duke enters Armstrong High School to study graphic arts; sneaks into the Gayety Theater, a local burlesque house, with friends
1914	Summer	While family is vacationing in Wildwood, NJ., Ellington travels to Philadelphia and hears a local pianist, Harvey Brooks. Impressed, he begins to try to teach himself piano that fall
	Fall	Ellington begins hanging out at Frank Holliday's poolroom, a gathering place for Washington's black musicians
Later 1914–early 1915		Ellington composes his first piece, "Soda Fountain Rag"
1915	Midyear	Ellington's close friend Edgar McEntree dubs him "Duke" around this time, because of Ellington's sartorial elegance and his flashy piano playing
	August	Ruth Ellington born
1916		Ellington joins with a group of high school friends to form a band

1917	Winter	Arthur Whetsol on trumpet and Otto ("Toby") Hardwick on saxophone join Duke's teenage band. They also play with local banjoist Elmer Snowden
	Spring	Duke drops out of high school; begins an affair with Edna Thompson, a neighborhood girl
1918	Early	Ellington plays his first date with the "Serenaders," as his high school group is now known
	July 2	Duke and Edna get married
1919		J. E. is promoted to role of caretaker and general handyman in the Cuthbert home; Duke forms his first professional band, and begins a booking agency and a sign-painting business (to promote the dances and events that he booked)
		In New York City, Jack and Irving Mills found the music publishing business that would bear their name
	March 11	Duke's son, Mercer Kennedy, is born
1920	Early	A second child of Duke and Edna Ellington dies at birth; Duke meets James P. Johnson when Johnson is playing in Washington, D.C., and impresses him with his rendition of Johnson's tour-de-force piano solo, "Carolina Shout"
1921	March 10	Duke makes his first trip to New York, accompanied by Sonny Greer, Toby Hardwick, Artie Whetsol, and Elmer Snowden; Duke sees James P. Johnson again, and meets Willie "The Lion" Smith
1923	Early	Clarinetist Wilbur Sweatman hires Greer and Hardwick to join his New York-based band; Ellington turns down the opportunity to move to New York, preferring to maintain his booming Washington-based band business
	Week of March 5	Ellington finally joins the Sweatman band in New York
	April	Ellington, Hardwick, and Greer return to Washington and continue to play jobs around town, often with trumpeter Whetsol and banjoist Elmer Snowden
	June	Ellington, Snowden, Hardwick, Greer, and Whetsol are hired by a vaudeville troupe to accompany their show in New York and on a subsequent tour; all except Ellington go to New York only to discover the show is canceled. Unaware of the problem, Duke comes to New York a week after the others have arrived; the five musicians begin to look for work

July	The band, under the nominal leadership of Snowden, begins working at Harlem's Exclusive Club, managed by Barron Wilkins, on the recommendation of singer Ada "Bricktop" Smith. Ellington hired as rehearsal pianist for a revue opening at Connie's Inn on the 21st; Ellington's wife, Edna, demands to come to New York and is soon hired at Connie's Inn as a show-girl
July 26	Ellington makes his first recording as part of Snowden's "Novelty Orchestra"
Late July	Whetsol leaves the band to go to Howard University in Washington; he is replaced by trumpeter James "Bubber" Miley
August	The band plays the Music Box Theater in Atlantic City; Ellington leads a group backing up blues singer Trixie Smith on his first radio broadcast
September 1	Snowden and his "Black Sox Orchestra" are hired to work at the Hollywood Club (located on Broadway and 49th Street) on a six-month contract
October 18	The Snowden band records for Victor
Late fall	Snowden breaks with the rest of the band; Ellington and Greer form new group called the Washingtonians, featuring Miley, Hardwick, and banjo player George Irvis to replace Snowden

1924	January	The band's contract is renewed at the Hollywood Club, but it is soon out of work due to a mysterious fire that closes the club
	April	Ellington's Washingtonians tour New England, the first tour sponsored by impresario Charlie Shribman
	May	The Hollywood Club reopens and the band returns to perform there; Ellington and Jo Trent sell their first song to a sheet music publisher, "Pretty Soft for You"
	June	Saxophonist Sidney Bechet sits in with the band and is hired to join it
	July	The band returns to New England for another tour
	Fall	Bechet leaves the band after failing to show up for three dates
	November	Thanks to Jo Trent, Ellington and the band have the opportunity to work as accompanists on three sessions for popular singers, including Trent himself; they also record two sides on their own

1925	January	Another fire closes the Hollywood Club
	February	The band tours New England

March	The Ellington band makes its first appearance at a Harlem theater, the Lincoln
Mid-April	The band returns to the Hollywood Club, now known as the Kentucky Club; banjoist Freddie Guy replaces George Francis
May	*Chocolate Kiddies* opens in Berlin, Germany, with a score by Ellington and Jo Trent; it features the singer Adelaide Hall
June 8	Ellington accompanies Irving Mills on a test recording of Mills's song "Everything Is Hotsy Totsy Now," with lyrics by Jimmy McHugh
Summer	Ellington meets composer/bandleader Will Marion Cook, who becomes a teacher/mentor to the young composer
Fall	Ellington begins studying music with both Cook and Cook's disciple, Will Vodery; the band leaves the Kentucky Club to go uptown and play at Harlem's Cameo Club but is fired after one night
Late November	The band returns to the Kentucky Club; Fats Waller is a featured act during the band's intermission
1926 February	The band records for Pathé, with the addition of Don Redman on saxophone
May	The Kentucky Club is closed for violating the Prohibition Act
June/July/ August	The band plays various one-nighters in New England while also working at the Plantation Club in Harlem; the band is expanded to a ten-piece unit, and "Tricky Sam" Nanton joins as a replacement for Irvis on trombone; Harry Carney joins the band during the summer tour
Mid-August –Mid-Sept.	Touring Pennsylvania and West Virginia
September 24	Returns to the Kentucky Club
October 10	Ellington and Greer (billed as the "Ellington twins") accompany singer Alberta Jones for Gennett
October 31	Ellington, Greer, and Hardwick accompany singer Zadee Jackson on a Gennett session
Mid-November	Irving Mills signs up the Ellington band; arranges for band to record for Brunswick; Mills and Ellington form Ellington, Inc., and Mills is given exclusive rights to publish Ellington's music
November 29	The first of the Mills-arranged recording dates, for the Vocalion label. The band was billed as "Duke Ellington and his Kentucky Club Orchestra" and cut its signature tune, "East St. Louis Toodle-Oo" along with three other numbers

1927	Early January	Radio station WHN begins broadcasting the Ellington band during its performance at the Kentucky Club
	February 28	The band makes its first recordings for Brunswick, under the "Washingtonians" name, so that it can continue to record as the Kentucky Club Orchestra for other labels
	March 22	The band makes its first recording for Columbia
	April 7	First recording of *Black & Tan Fantasy*, cowritten by Ellington and Miley
	May	Robinson and Edwards give notice, and are replaced by saxophonist Rudy Jackson and bass player Wellman Braud; Harry Carney joins the band
	June 20	Another summer-long tour of New England
	September	Returns to New York for a three-week engagement at the Ciro Club; Ellington signs with Victor Records
	October 10	*Jazz Mania* arrives at Harlem's Lafayette Theater with the Ellington band in a featured spot
	November	*Dance Mania*, the follow-up to *Jazz Mania*, opens in New York, again at the Lafayette, followed by a brief tour
	Late November	Band auditions for and is hired to play at the Cotton Club
	December 4	Ellington appears for the first time at the Cotton Club on the opening night of the *Revue*
1928	March	Trumpeter Arthur Whetsol rejoins the band
	April 1	Second version of *Cotton Club Parade* opens
	May	Johnny Hodges replaces Toby Hardwick on saxophone in the band
	Summer	Duke separates from his wife Edna after she cuts him with a razor blade, accusing him of having affairs with other women; Ellington's mother travels from Washington to care for (and move in with) her son
	October 1	Ellington cuts his first piano solos, "Black Beauty" backed with "Swampy River"
	October 7	The *Cotton Club Parade*, subtitled "Hot Chocolate," opens; trumpeter Freddie Jenkins joins the band
1929	January	Bubber Miley, increasingly unreliable due to drunkenness, is ousted from the band; he is replaced by Charlies "Cootie" Williams

March 31	The Cotton Club's spring revue, *Springbirds*, opens
May 15	The band begins rehearsing for its appearance in Florenz Ziegfeld's Broadway revue, *Show Girl*; valve trombone player Juan Tizol joins the band
July 2	*Show Girl* opens at the Variety Theater in New York
Summer	Ellington appears in the short film *Black and Tan*; the film also features singer Fredi Washington
September 29	The fall Cotton Club production, *It's the Blackberries*, opens; dancer Mildred Dixon, featured in the show, moves into Ellington's apartment (along with his mother and father and "sister," Ruth); Ellington's father is put in charge of answering fan mail
October 5	*Show Girl* closes after 111 performances, a victim of the Depression and lackluster reviews
1930 March 2	*Blackberries of 1930* opens at the Cotton Club for its winter season
March 30	The band appears on Broadway supporting French singing/acting star Maurice Chevalier for a two-week stint
May 16	The band appear on Broadway for a one-week run
May	Ellington moves into a larger three-bedroom apartment to house his extended family
June	Tours New England
Early July	The band plays a two-day engagement in Chicago en route to Hollywood
August 14	The band travels to Hollywood to appear in the film *Check and Double Check*
September 28	*Brown Sugar (Sweet but Unrefined)*, the fall Cotton Club show, opens
October 14	Ellington composes "Mood Indigo," one of his signature tunes. Mills takes a composition credit on the song, as well
October 31	*Check and Double Check* opens in New York; Ellington is booked at a nearby Broadway theater for a two-week stint; two weeks later, the film opens in Harlem, at a movie theater just below the Cotton Club, enabling the band to appear "live" on stage during the run of the film
1931 January 20	Ellington records his first extended work, *Creole Rhapsody*
February 5	The Ellington bands end its association with the Cotton Club, and is replaced by Cab Calloway's orchestra; it begins an eighteen-week tour

February 13   First engagement at Chicago's Oriental Theater, breaking attendance records; during the four-week run, singer Ivie Anderson appears on the bill as a special attraction; Ellington subsequently hires her for the band and she continues on the tour with them. The band tours for the balance of the year, playing dates all around the country, and returning to Chicago twice for extended runs

1932   February 2   Records "It Don't Mean a Thing (If It Ain't Got that Swing)," vocalist Ivie Anderson's recording debut

February 5   Finally returns to the Cotton Club for a week's engagement

Late February– March   Embarks on a West Coast tour, playing extended engagements in San Francisco and Los Angeles; trombonist Lawrence Brown joins the group toward the end of the tour

April   Returns to New York; Toby Hardwick rejoins the group

May 20   "Bubber" Miley dies of tuberculosis

Summer– Mid- September   Tour of New England, followed by shows in the Midwest, including a four-week return to Chicago

September 19   Back in New York

Early November   On the invitation of Percy Grainger, Ellington demonstrates jazz for a music appreciation course at NYU

November   Irving Mills travels to Europe to test the waters for Ellington's first European tour

1933   February   The Ellington band participates in recordings documenting the *Blackbirds* revues of the late '20s

March   Band appears in a Paramount "Pictorial" along with other Mills acts

April 16   Returns to the Cotton Club for its spring revue, replacing Calloway's band who are touring the South; Ethel Waters is also in the show, premiering the song "Stormy Weather"

May 23   Makes a nine-minute short film, *Bundle of Blues*, featuring "Stormy Weather" with Ivie Anderson on vocals

May 26   The entire Cotton Club revue is moved downtown for a two-week run due to its success

June 2   Sails for England, arriving a week later at Southampton

June 12   Begins European tour at London's Palladium, beginning a month-and-a-half tour of Great Britain. The band and Ellington win the respect of several important English composers, journalists, and members of the royal family

July 27	Plays Paris's Salle Pleyel and then performs several other Continental dates
August 3	Disembarks for return trip to New York; makes an abbreviated tour of New England on return
September 23	Appears in Dallas at the beginning of the band's twelve-week tour of the South; then tours the Midwest to finish off the year

1934

February 10	In Washington, D.C., for a successful week-long engagement at the Howard Theater
February 19	Arrives in Hollywood to appear in two films, *Murder at the Vanities* and *Belle of the Nineties*
March 16	Plays for the Academy Award ceremonies
March 19	Begins a new radio program, "Demitasse Revue," for the NBC network
March 26– May 7	During the break in filming, tours the West Coast playing extended engagements in Los Angeles and San Francisco; Marshall Royal replaces ailing Toby Hardwick
May 7–8	Returns to Hollywood to complete work on the films
May–June	The band makes its first tour of the Pacific Northwest
Mid–June	Returns to New York for a two-week run at the Capitol Theater; Daisy Ellington, suffering from cancer, moves back to Washington to be cared for by her sister
December	Appears for a week at the Apollo Theater; trumpeter Rex Stewart joins the band to replace Freddie Jenkins
December 28	Plays a week-long engagement at Chicago's Oriental Theater

1935

January– March	Tours
March	Films *Symphony in Black*, which also features young singer Billie Holiday
March 13– April 30	More tour dates
May 11	Ellington family contacts Duke on the road about his mother's deteriorating medical condition
May 17	Daisy meets the band in Detroit and is immediately admitted to a local hospital
May 27	Daisy dies; Ellington spends the next few months in a serious depression

Late June	Begins a series of one-nighters in the Midwest and South
September 12	Ellington records second extended work, *Reminiscing in Tempo*, his tribute to his mother
late year	Ellington takes some time off

1936

February 8	Begins a week-long engagement at the Apollo
July 10	Begins a week at Loew's Theater on Broadway, followed by further touring
July 17	Records "It Was a Sad Night in Harlem," commemorating his friend boxer Joe Louis's loss to Max Schmeling on June 19
October 2	A week at the Howard Theater in Washington, D.C.
October 18–20	Ellington band featured at the Texas State Fair as part of the exhibit "Streets of All Nations;" on the second day, the location was opened to blacks, during a day of special events termed "Negro Day"
December 11	Opens for a week-long run at Los Angeles's Paramount Theater; Whetsol leaves the band due to illness
December 23	Begins a three-week engagement at the West Coast Cotton Club

1937

February	Tours the Pacific Northwest and then returns to Los Angeles to appear in Republic Pictures' low-budget film, *The Hit Parade*
March 17	Returns to the Cotton Club, now located on Broadway, to appear in the latest version of the club's revue, along with Ethel Waters
April 1	Mills launches the Master and budget Variety labels to feature Ellington and his band members in various different small ensembles
May 14	Records "Caravan," co-composed by valve trombone player Juan Tizol, which would become his most popular number
June 13	Cotton Club closes for the season; the next week, Ellington and band play at the Apollo
Late June	Appears in a second Paramount "Pictorial" (short subject)
July 1	Back on Broadway for an engagement at Loew's State Theater
Mid-July–Mid-Sept.	On the road; Ellington's father's health begins to decline
September 20	Records Ellington's two-part work, *Diminuendo and Crescendo in Blue*
October–December	Touring

October 28 J. E. Ellington passes away

Late October Mills's Master and Variety labels fail

1938

January 16 Benny Goodman plays Carnegie Hall; Ellington doesn't attend, but allows band members Cootie Williams, Harry Carney, and Johnny Hodges to participate in the concert

March 10 Headlines the *Cotton Club Parade, Fourth Edition*, the first to feature a full score by Ellington; Artie Whetsol leaves the band, suffering from mental illness, and is replaced by Harold "Shorty" Baker

May 8 Plays a benefit for the Urban League at the Brooklyn Academy of Music; Ellington moves in with showgirl Beatrice (Evie) Ellis, leaving his family behind, although they quickly follow him to his new digs

July 1 Duke has a hernia operation; Ruth leaves for a trip to Europe with a chaperone appointed by her "brother"

December 2 Plays Pittsburgh's Stanley Theater during that week where Ellington first meets twenty-three-year-old Billy Strayhorn

1939

January–March More touring and recording; Strayhorn joins the band for some dates

March 11 Mills sails to Europe to set up another tour; Ellington and Evie move to another apartment after a fire breaks out in her place

March 23 The band sails to Europe

April 1 Arrives in Le Havre, France, band can't get permission to play in England again, due to union rules, so it focuses on dates on the Continent

April 29 Ellington celebrates his fortieth birthday in Stockholm, Sweden; young girls sing "Happy Birthday" to him onstage

May 2 Band arrives in London but still can't get permission to perform; leaves for U.S.

May 9 Ellington tells Mills he wants to end their relationship; Ellington signs with MCA for management and Robbins Music for publishing

May 10 Arrives back in New York

May 25 Headlines at Loew's State Theater on Broadway

June 2 Appears at the New York State Fair; a summer tour of one-nighters follows

June 10 Strayhorn records his first composition with the Ellington orchestra

July 24	Begins an engagement at Boston's Ritz Carlton Hotel
September 15	Week at the Apollo followed by fall tour
October 20	Arrives in St. Louis for an extended stay; bass player Jimmie Blanton joins the band
November 22	Ellington records first of series of piano-bass duets with Jimmie Blanton
December	Ellington band ends the year at the Sherman Hotel, Chicago; Ben Webster joins the band, swelling its sax ranks to five members

1940

January 7	Begins week at Boston's Southland Café
Early–Mid-February	Engagements in Chicago
March 6	First session for new label, RCA Victor, which signs Ellington to an exclusive contract
March 16	Leaves Chicago to travel West
April 24	Begins week-long engagement at Orpheum Ballroom, Los Angeles
June 7	Back in New York for a week at the Apollo
July 22	Records "Harlem Air Shaft"
September 6	Tour ends in Chicago with an engagement at the Sherman Hotel
October 18	At the Oriental Theater, Chicago; Cootie Williams leaves the band and is replaced by Ray Nance
December 13	Returns to the Apollo Theater; Duke tells Mercer that he is going to join the band as a staff arranger

1941

January 1	ASCAP bans the performance of its music on radio
January 3	Ellington and his men begin a California trip with a six-week engagement at the Casa Manana, in Culver City (previously known as the [West Coast] Cotton Club)
February 15	Records Strayhorn's "Take the A Train," which becomes their new signature tune on radio and a major hit; Ellington forms Tempo Music to publish this and other band compositions
April 3	Week at the Paramount Theater, Los Angeles
May 14	Back in Chicago to record, and then back cross-country to Los Angeles
May 27–Mid-June	Ellington performs for the first time at California's Trianon Ballroom, which becomes a regular spot for the band (and its first ballroom job)

July 10	*Jump for Joy* opens in Los Angeles, starring Dorothy Dandridge and featuring a score by Ellington; the social commentary musical is a success among California's intellectual elite, but does not make it to Broadway
September 27	*Jump for Joy* closes; Blanton begins showing symptoms of tuberculosis
December 2	Records Strayhorn's "Chelsea Bridge"
December 6	Returns to the Northwest for a tour

1942

January	Films three "soundies" for Sam Coslow
January 23	Back at Chicago's Oriental Theater
February 26	Back in New York for another session
February 27	In Washington, D.C., for a week at the Howard Theater, followed by another tour
April 2–May 12	Arrives at the Trianon Ballroom to give a repeat performance, the first band to repeat an engagement there
May 12	Begins six-week tour of West Coast
June 26	Back in Los Angeles to record; Barney Bigard and Herb Jeffries leave the band
July 17	At the Hotel Sherman, Chicago
July 30	Blanford dies; Ivie Anderson leaves the band and is replaced by Betty Roché; Howard "Shorty" Baker joins the band on trumpet
September 26	In Hollywood to film *Cabin in the Sky* and *Reveille with Beverly*
November–January 1943	Various one night stands and theater dates

1943

January 23	Carnegie Hall concert to benefit Russian war relief; premiere performance of *Black, Brown and Beige*
April 1	Begins an engagement at Broadway's Hurricane Restaurant
May	Rex Stewart leaves the band and is replaced by Taft Jordan; Ben Webster also leaves
December 11	Second Carnegie Hall concert; premiere of *New World A-Comin'*, composed for piano and orchestra

1944

| February | Betty Roché leaves the band; replaced by the good-looking, but not very talented, Wini Johnson; trumpeter Wallace Jones and trombonist/arranger Juan Tizol also leave around this time |
| December 1 | Returns to recording for the first time since the recording ban began in mid-1942 |

	December 19	Third Carnegie Hall concert, with premieres of *Bluetopia* and *Perfume Suite*
1945	Mid-January	Back on the West Coast for dates
	February 16	Booked for an engagement at the posh Ciro's nightclub in Los Angeles, the first black band to play this exclusive venue
	April 4	Back in New York, playing at the swank "400" restaurant
	April 14	Performs on coast-to-coast radio broadcast for the funeral of Franklin D. Roosevelt
	May	Begins three-month road tour
	September	Begins three-month engagement at Broadway's Club Zanzibar (formerly the Hurricane)
	November 18	"Tricky Sam" Nanton suffers a stroke and is hospitalized; replaced by Wilbur DeParis
	November 19	Bass player Oscar Pettiford joins the band
1946		
	April	Toby Hardwick leaves the band, supposedly after an argument with Ellington over a woman
	May	Signs lucrative contract with Musicraft Records; however the label folds before Ellington can collect much of the money
	late July	"Tricky Sam" Nanton dies
	August 6	"Jonesy," Ellington's valet/road manager, dies
	December 26	*Beggar's Holiday*, a multiracial reworking of *The Beggar's Opera*, with a score by Ellington, opens on Broadway
1947–56		Ellington band in decline; popularity of big bands has dropped and Ellington's work viewed as passé by jazz world, which is embracing bebop
1947	June	Leaves Musicraft; signs with Columbia in fall after John Hammond leaves the label
	December 24, 1947	Records *Liberian Suite*
1948	July 12	Ellington, Nance, and Davis travel to England to play the Palladium; play other British dates and on the continent before sailing back to the United States on July 30; the rest of the band plays as a unit in Harlem while the other three are away
1949	January	Guitarist Fred Guy leaves the band

1950	April 6	Beginning of another European tour, playing 74 shows in 77 days.
	June 30	Return to the United States
1951	January	Premiere of the *Harlem Suite* at New York's Metropolitan Opera House
	February	Johnny Hodges, Lawrence Brown, and Sonny Greer, the last of the original "Washingtonians," leave the band; Ellington raids Harry James's band to replace them
	1952–	Continued hard times
1955	March 16	Carnegie Hall concert, featuring *Night Creatures* and *New World A-Comin'*
	Summer	Works Elliot Murphy's *Aquacade*, at the amphitheater in Flushing Meadows, Long Island; Johnny Hodges rejoins band; contract with Capitol Records expires
1956	February 7–8	Records for tiny Bethlehem label
	Spring	Signs with Columbia Records
	July 7	Newport Jazz Festival appearance renews Ellington's popularity and career
	August	Appears in Stratford, Ontario, Shakespeare Festival for first time
1957	April 28	*Such Sweet Thunder* premiers at Town Hall
	May 8	*A Drum Is a Woman* is broadcast on CBS nationwide
1958	October–November	European tour, including first shows in England since 1939
1959	February 25	Records *Queen's Suite* for a custom, single album pressing given as a gift to the Queen of England
	Spring	Composes score for film, *Anatomy of a Murder*, which wins Ellington an Academy Award
	September 11	Presented Spingarn Medal by the NAACP for the "highest or noblest achievement by an American Negro"
	September 11 –November 3	European tour

1960	March	Begins 12-week engagement at the Riveriera Hotel, Las Vegas; meets Fernandae de Castro Monte, who becomes his final mistress
	May	Trombonist Lawrence Brown returns to the band
	September 24	Premiere performance of *Suite Thursday* at Monterey Jazz Festival
	Fall	Composes music for *Paris Blues;* travels to Paris to oversee recording in November
1961	January	Returns to Riviera Hotel for another engagement; several band members arrested on drug charges
	Spring	Composes music for pilot program of TV show, *The Asphalt Jungle*
1962	September	Cootie Williams rejoins band; immediately goes on tour with it
1963	January–February	Tour of Europe
	Summer	*My People*, a pageant featuring Ellington's music, is presented at Chicago's Century of Negro Progress Exposition
	July 20	*Timon of Athens* opens at Stratford, Ontario, Shakespeare Festival with score by Ellington
	September 6	Tour of Middle East and India
1964	February	Band embarks on extended European tour
	June	First visit to Tokyo
	December 17	Mercer joins band a trumpeter/road manager
1965	January–February	Tenth European tour
	Summer	Pulitzer Prize committee recommends Ellington receive its award, but is overturned by the prize's board of directors
	July 30	Premiere of *The Golden Broom and the Green Apple* at New York's Philharmonic Hall
	August 6	Acting mayor of New York gives Ellington the city's Bronze Medal for "outstanding contributions to New York life"
	September 16	[*First*] *Sacred Concert* given at San Francisco's Grace Cathedral; repeated in New York on December 26 (It would be played about 50 times all in all, including several occasions in 1966)

	December	Edna Ellington diagnosed with cancer
	Early	Resigns from RCA Victor; records *Far East Suite*; begins work on film score for *Assault on a Queen*
	January 24	Begins European tour
	February 22	Performs [*First*] *Sacred Concert* at Coventry Cathedral
1967	January	Edna dies, ending Duke's 52-year marriage; band returns to Europe
	March 10	European tour ends
	May 31	Billy Strayhorn dies of cancer
	June 4	Honorary degree awarded by Washington University of St. Louis
	June 12	Honorary degree from Yale University
1968	January 19	Premiere of *Second Sacred Concert* at Cathedral of St. John the Divine in New York; work performed many times throughout the following years
	February 29	Ellington and Strayhorn (posthumously) win Grammy awards for *Far East Suite*
	Fall	Tour of South American
1969	April 1929	Ellington honored at White House on his birthday; given the Presidential Medal of Freedom by Richard Nixon
	June	A week's tour of the West Indies
	Year-End	Plays Las Vegas; Lawrence Brown retires
1970	January–February	Third trip to Japan, along with Australia and New Zealand
	April 25	Premiere of *New Orleans Suite* at the New Orleans Jazz and Heritage Festival
	May 11	Johnny Hodges dies
	June 5	Honorary Doctor of Humane Letters degree from Christian Theological Seminary
	June 25	*The River*, with choreography by Alvin Ailey, premieres
	June 28	Begins another European tour
1971	March 12	Inducted into the Swedish Academy of Music

July–21 — Ellington band in residence at the University of Wisconsin for workshops, concerts, and awarding of an honorary degree; premieres *The UWIS Suite*

September 1 — Embarks on another European tour, including the band's first visit to the Soviet Union

November 15 — Flies directly from Europe to begin South American tour

1972 Winter — Begins tour of Far East, including Philippines

1973 July 8 — Awarded the Legion D' Honneur by the president of France

Fall — *Music Is My Mistress*, Ellington's autobiography, published

October 24 — *Third Sacred Concert* premieres at Westminster Abbey

November 24 — Dr. Arthur Logan killed in New York

November 26 — Ellington gives a command performance for the Queen of England

1974 March — Ellington collapses following a concert at Northern Illinois University; nonetheless, continues his tour of the Midwest the next day

late March — Enters Harkness Pavillion of Columbia-Presbyterian Hospital for treatment of advancing cancer

April 29 — Celebrates seventy-fifth birthday in his hospital room

May 24 — Duke Ellington dies at 3:10 A.M.

Biographies

Allen, Charles *(1908–72)*. Trumpeter with Ellington from 1934–35. Allen was born in Mississippi and learned trombone in high school. His first job was with Hugh Swift's band. After switching to trumpet, he found work with Dave Peyton and Doc Cooke. He was with Earl Hines's band in Chicago when Ellington hired him in late 1934. He remained with Ellington for about a year, and then freelanced around Chicago.

Alvis, Hayes *(1907–72)*. Bass player with Duke Ellington, 1936–38. Alvis was born in Chicago in 1907, and his first instrument was the drums. By the time he was twenty, he was touring with pianist Jelly Roll Morton, playing drums and tuba. In 1919, he settled in Chicago, where he began playing the string bass, and from 1928 to 1930, he played with Earl Hines. Bandleader Jimmy Noone brought Alvis to New York in 1931. Alvis then joined the newly formed Mills Blue Rhythm Band, and remained with that band until he joined Ellington in early 1935. He left Ellington in mid-1938, and continued to work in several bands and accompanying singers.

Anderson, Ivie *(1905–49)*. Vocalist with the Ellington orchestra, 1931–42. Born in Gilroy, California, Anderson was orphaned at age nine. She spent her next eight years in a convent, where she received vocal training. Anderson subsequently toured in revues and on the white vaudeville circuit. She arrived in New York in 1925, where she worked the Cotton Club, before returning to Los Angeles. She then traveled to Chicago, where she worked as vocalist with the Earl Hines Orchestra. Ellington first heard her when he was playing Chicago's Oriental Theater in February 1931; he hired her to join the band for the rest of the tour, and she remained with them for more than a decade. After her stint with Ellington, she opened a Chicken Shack restaurant in Los Angeles and continued to sing regularly at West Coast nightspots.

Anderson, William Alonzo "Cat" *(1916–81)*. Trumpet player with Ellington from 1945–47, 1951–58, and intermittently from 1961–71. Orphaned at age four, Anderson was raised in the Jenkins Orphanage in Charleston, South Carolina. He was a member of one of its famous student bands, and then played professionally with the bands of Claude Hopkins and Lionel Hampton. When Ellington hired him, he expanded the trumpet section to five men. After leaving Ellington in early 1947, Anderson briefly led his own band, and then rejoined the Ellington band in 1950. He formed his own band again, only to return to the Ellington fold in 1961, continuing to play with the band on an as-needed basis, while also gigging around Philadelphia. After Ellington's death, he worked in the Los Angeles area and toured Europe several times.

Babs, Alice *(1924–)*. Swedish-born vocalist who worked with Ellington on and off during the last decade of his career. She is noted for singing at the last sacred concerts on Ellington's final European tour in late 1973.

Baker, Harold "Shorty" *(1914–66)*. Trumpet player with Duke Ellington from 1942–44, 1946–51, 1957–59, and 1961–63. Baker was born in St. Louis, Missouri. Baker's first instrument was the drums, but he switched to trumpet in the late 1920s, at the urging of his older brother, Winfield, a trombonist who led a local band. By the 1930s, Baker was working on a Mississippi steamboat with Fate Marable's band. He played briefly with Erskine Tate's orchestra before coming to New York to join Don Redmond's orchestra in 1936. He replaced Artie Whetsol in the Ellington band in early 1938, although he did not permanently join the band until four years later. He worked with Ellington for most of the rest of his professional career, with several breaks to pursue other opportunities.

Bell, (Samuel) Aaron *(1922–)*. Bassist, tuba player, born in Muskogee, Oklahoma. He is best known for his stint with Ellington in the 1960s. Mercer recommended Bell to his father, and the bassist joined the band in early 1960s. After working with Ellington, Bell became a teacher and then a dean at Essex County College in Newark, New Jersey, and has performed infrequently since then.

Bellson, Louis *(1924–)*. Drummer with Ellington from 1951–53, 1954–55, and 1965. A hard-driving drummer, Bellson grew up in his father's music shop and won contests as an amateur. Influenced by Buddy Rich, he worked for Benny Goodman, Harry James, and Tommy Dorsey in the 1940s. He joined Duke Ellington from 1951–53, and then married Pearl Bailey and worked as her music director until her death. He played with various bands and often formed his own, including a big band, which he has led on and off through the 1990s.

Bigard, Albany "Barney" *(1906–80)*. Clarinet and saxophone player with the Ellington orchestra from 1928–42. Bigard was born in New Orleans and began playing clarinet at the age of seven. Born into a family of musicians, Bigard's playing was strongly influenced by his Creole background. After a few early jobs, he played with Joe "King" Oliver in Chicago from 1924–27, and then came to New York. He joined Ellington in 1928 and remained with the band for fourteen years. After working with Ellington, he did film work in California, and played with Louis Armstrong's first All-Stars band from 1947–52. He continued to work in Dixieland-style ensembles through the early 1960s in the Los Angeles area.

Blanton, Jimmie *(1918–42)*. Bass player with Ellington 1939–41. Born in Chattanooga, Tennessee, Blanton played in local, groups, and attended Tennessee State College for a brief period of time. By the time Ellington first heard him, *Blanton had put in a tour of duty with Fate Marable's riverboat bands, and was currently working with the St. Louis based Jeter-Pillars Orchestra. His* melodic bass playing wowed the members of Ellington's orchestra, and Ellington recorded several piano-bass duets with him. Blanton died of tuberculosis in 1942.

Braud, Wellman *(1891–1966).* Bass player with Ellington from May 1927–35. Born in New Orleans, Braud began playing violin when he was seven. He played with various bands and stage orchestras in his hometown, Chicago, and in London, England, before joining Ellington. His rock-steady beatkeeping was said to greatly improve the band's rhythm section. After working with Ellington, Braud formed his own trio in 1937 while continuing to gig with several bands. He retired from music-making in the mid-1950s but returned again to working in the 1960s until his death.

Brown, Lawrence *(1907–88).* Trombone player with Ellington from 1932–51 and 1960–69. Brown was born in Lawrence, Kansas, to a musical family. In 1914, Brown's father, a minister, moved the family to Oakland, California, and later to Pasadena. Brown received formal training on trombone in high school. When he was nineteen, Brown began performing professionally on the West Coast. Mills heard him in the early 1930s, and recommended him to Ellington. Brown brought to the section a warm burnished sound and a mobile style of playing, reflecting his love for the cello. He was a long-time band member, working with Johnny Hodges's small band in the early 1950s before rejoining Ellington in 1960. In 1969, he took a government job, which he held until his retirement.

Calloway, Cab *(1907–94).* Bandleader, singer, and on-stage personality, Calloway became popular for his comic songs and patter. He was hired to replace Ellington at the Cotton Club in 1931; Calloway quickly won a huge following thanks to his stage antics. Through Irving Mills, Ellington owned a small piece of the Calloway band, so he shared in this success to some extent. Calloway continued to perform on film and in live appearances until the early '90s.

Carney, Harry *(1910–74).* Baritone saxophone player with Ellington from 1927–74. Carney first played piano, then clarinet and alto sax, before switching full-time to baritone. He started playing professionally as a teen in Boston, then moved to New York. He first joined Ellington to fill his summer 1926 engagements in New England, and then became a permanent band member from 1927 until his death.

Cook, Will Marion *(1869–1944).* Black theatrical composer and musician who met Ellington in mid-1925 and gave him lessons in composition.

Cooper, Harry *(1903–1961).* Second trumpeter with the Washingtonians, from February 1925 to August 1926. Cooper was born in Lake Charles, Louisiana, and then his family moved to Kansas City, Missouri. He learned the trumpet while in high school. After working accompanying singer Virginia Liston, Cooper settled in New York in late 1924 and worked various bands. He joined Ellington's band in February 1925. He went to Europe in early 1928 and remained there for the rest of his life, working with various groups.

Cuthbert, Dr. Middleton F. Employer of J. E. Ellington; prominent Washington physician.

Davis, Kay *(1920–)*. Vocalist with the Ellington band from mid-1944. A classically trained singer, Davis studied singing and piano at Northwestern University, then taught and gave recitals for several years. Ellington would use her soprano voice as another instrument in the band, singing concert pieces or wordless vocals, in the style of Adelaide Hall.

DeParis, Wilbur *(1900–73)*. Trombone player with Ellington from 1945–47. Born in Indiana, DeParis came from a musical family (his brother, Sidney, was a trumpet player with whom Wilbur worked on occasion). After working tent shows, he settled in New Orleans in the 1920s, working with Louis Armstrong. He worked with various other bands through the 1920s and 1930s, settling in New York in the 1940s to work with Ella Fitzgerald, who was leading Chick Webb's old band. He replaced "Tricky Sam" Nanton in late 1945 in the Ellington orchestra. In 1947, he teamed with his brother to form a band that worked for the next two decades playing in a New Orleans-flavored style.

Dixon, Mildred. Dancer in the fall 1929 Cotton Club revue, who moved in with Ellington as his mistress at that time. They lived together until early 1938, when he fell in love with another Cotton Club showgirl, Beatrice "Evie" Ellis. Ellington then moved into Ellis's apartment, leaving his family (including Dixon) in his old digs.

Edwards, Henry "Bass." Tuba player with the Ellington band from mid-1925 to Spring 1926. Edwards began playing tuba in his native Atlanta at age fourteen. Moving to Philadelphia after World War I, he played in several concert orchestras, and then came to New York in the fall of 1923. When Edwards joined Ellington, he was the best-trained musician in the band. He left the band to play with light and classical orchestras.

Ellington, Daisy Kennedy *(1879–1935)*. Mother of Duke Ellington; born on January 4, 1879, eldest of nine children of James William Kennedy, a former slave of mixed ancestry. Kennedy emigrated to Washington, D.C., after the slaves were emancipated, and eventually became a member of the police force there. Daisy moved in with Duke in New York after he separated from his wife. Her death in 1935 left Ellington emotionally distraught for many months.

Ellington, James Edward *(1879–1937)*. Father of Duke Ellington; born in Lincolnton, North Carolina, on April 15, 1879 and moved with his parents to Washington, D.C., in 1886. His mother found employment as housekeeper and receptionist to Dr. Middleton F. Cuthbert, a prominent white physician. At age seventeen, J. E., as he was known, was hired as a coachman for Cuthbert, and over time he progressed to driver, butler, and, by 1919, caretaker and general handyman. Ellington moved him to New York in the early 1930s, but his father was bored, with little to do. He worked for a while handling Ellington's fan mail, but soon became an alcoholic.

Ellington, Mercer *(1919–96).* Duke's son, born in 1919. He joined his father's band in December 1940 as an arranger, remaining until 1943. He had previously had his own groups, and was brought on board by his father to supply compositions during the ASCAP strike, when Ellington could not broadcast his earlier compositions. Mercer returned to the band as trumpeter and road manager from 1965 until his father's death in 1974. Mercer continued to lead the band for a few years after Duke's death, and then settled in Sweden, where he remarried. He died of heart failure in 1996.

Ellington, William "Sonny." The son of J. E. Ellington's older brother, John; hence, Duke's cousin and his musical mentor.

Ellis, Beatrice (Evie) *(c.1905–75).* Harlem showgirl whom Ellington met in 1938. He moved in with her, leaving his family, previous mistress (Mildred Dixon), clothing, and furniture in his own apartment. They had a stormy relationship that continued even after Duke met Fernandae de Castro Monte in the early 1960s. Duke maintained both women as "mistresses," and continued to support Ellis even when he was dying of cancer. Ellis succumbed to the same disease a year after Ellington.

Gonsalves, Paul *(1920–74).* Saxophone player who joined the Ellington band in December 1950. He easily filled the gap that followed Ben Webster's departure. He had a breathy, rich tone that identified him as Coleman Hawkins disciple, and had put in tours of duty with Count Basie and Dizzy Gillespie. He remained with the band for nearly a quarter century, until his death in 1974.

Greer, William "Sonny" *(c.1895–1982).* Drummer and vocalist with the Washingtonians, and then the Duke Ellington Orchestra, from 1920–51. Born in New Jersey, Greer relocated to Washington in 1919, and then met Ellington there a year later. A flamboyant musician, Greer's onstage personality added much to the attraction of Ellington's early bands. Due to his increasing alcoholism, he was asked to leave the band in 1951; he did freelance work during the 1950s and early 1960s, and then led his own small groups through the 1970s (often playing Ellington's music).

Guy, Fred *(1897–1971).* Banjoist and guitarist with Ellington from 1925–49. He joined the Washingtonians in mid-April 1925 when they were playing at the Kentucky Club. He switched from banjo to guitar when the band made its first trip to England in 1933. He worked as a dance hall manager after leaving Ellington in 1949.

Hall, Adelaide *(1901–1993).* Noted black actress/singer who became famous appearing in numerous Broadway revues and at the Cotton Club in the 1920s and 1930s. She also recorded extensively, and contributed a wordless, vocal obbligato to Ellington's "Creole Love Call." Hall continued to perform until her death.

Hamilton, Jimmy *(1917–94).* Clarinet and saxophone player with Ellington from 1943–68. As a child in South Carolina, Hamilton showed great musical capabilities, playing several instruments. He worked in Philadelphia in the 1930s, taking up tenor sax and clarinet and working with several bands, including those of Teddy Wilson and Benny Carter. Hamilton possessed a flawless technique, like his idol, Benny Goodman. He was far removed from the New Orleans tradition of Barney Bigard, and joined the Ellington band in March 1943 to replace Chauncey Haughton, and remained with the band for twenty-five years. He retired to the Virgin Islands in 1968, continuing to teach and perform.

Hardwick, Otto "Toby" *(1904–70).* Saxophonist with the Duke Ellington orchestra from 1920–28 and again from 1932–43. A teenage friend of Ellington's, his first instrument was the violin, and he subsequently learned the bass. At Ellington's suggestion he also took up the C melody saxophone. Hardwick subsequently often played with Duke's Serenaders, and then became a charter member of the Washingtonians. He is credited as co-composer of "Sophisticated Lady." He left the Ellington band for four years between 1928–32, and then left for good in 1943 after a fight broke out between him and Duke on the bandstand, supposedly over a woman. He retired from the music world at that time.

Harper, Leonard *(1899–1943).* Dancer/choreographer who hired Ellington as a rehearsal pianist for a production he was staging at Connie's Inn in July 1923. In the 1920s, Harper became the preeminent creator of floor shows for nearly every black nightclub in New York City.

Haughton, Chauncey *(1909–).* Clarinet player with Ellington from 1942–43. Born in Chesterton, Maryland, Haughton began studying piano at age eight, and later switched to clarinet and saxophone. He arrived in New York in 1932 with Gene Kennedy's band. He worked with many leading New York bands before joining Ellington in the summer of 1942. He remained with Ellington for only about a year. He then served in the Army, returning to music briefly with Don Redman and Cab Calloway after the war, but subsequently retired from the music world.

Henderson, Fletcher *(1897–1952).* Bandleader, composer, music arranger, record company and music publishing executive, Henderson led one of the most influential New York jazz bands of the 1920s. He also produced recording sessions for many of the era's greatest blues singers.

Hibbler, Al *(1915–)*. Blind baritone vocalist/balladeer who served with the Ellington band from mid-1943 to 1951. Blind from birth, Hibbler attended the Conservatory for the Blind in his hometown of Little Rock, Arkansas, where he was trained as a singer. After working with various local bands, he joined Jay McShann in 1942. He joined Ellington in 1943, remaining with him eight years. In the 1950s, he had several hit records on his own, including his version of "Unchained Melody," which sold more than a million copies. His recording career ended in the early 1960s.

Hodges, Johnny *(1907–70)*. Saxophone player and composer with Ellington from 1928–51 and again 1955–70. Hodges was born in Cambridge, Massachusetts, to a middle-class family. Originally a pianist, he switched to saxophone as a teenager. Inspired by Sidney Bechet, he developed quickly, and had the chance to study with his idol in 1924, who brought him to New York. Hodges returned briefly to Boston, but was back in New York the next year, playing at Bechet's club and for various revues. After a stint with Chick Webb in 1927–28, he joined Ellington in May 1928. Hodges brought a warm, mellow tone to the group, but could also supply the necessary "growl" when called on. Along with Bubber Miley, he was one of the featured soloists with the band. Hodges left Ellington briefly in the early 1950s to lead his own band, but returned to working with the group until his death in May 1970.

Irvis, Charlie *(c.1899–c.1939)*. Trombonist with the Washingtonians from 1924–26. Born in Harlem, Irvis played with Lucille Hegamin's Blue Flame Syncopators and Willie "the Lion" Smith before joining the Washingtonians in the first week of January 1924. After working with Ellington, Irvis worked with various bands through the early 1930s, and also recorded with Fats Waller.

Jackson, Rudy. Saxophone player with Ellington band in 1927. Jackson was born in Fort Wayne, Indiana, in 1901 to musician parents, and grew up in Chicago. He played with various Chicago-based bands and for revues before coming to New York to join Ellington in 1927.

James, George, a/k/a "Mexico". Harlem musician and nightclub owner who was reputed to have fought in the Mexican War against Pancho Villa, which is how he earned his nickname. His club was a musician's hangout and, according to Ellington, the "hottest gin mill on 133rd Street." Mexico was an early supporter of the Ellington band when it first opened at the Cotton Club in 1927, at a time when other local musicians were critical of the out-of-towners.

Jeffries, Herb *(1916–)*. Vocalist with the Ellington band, 1939–42. Born in Detroit, Michigan, Jeffries had worked with Erskine Tate in the early 1930s and Earl Hines from 1931–34. He was biracial, and, after moving to Hollywood, his striking good looks won him roles in a series of cheaply produced black westerns. Jeffries's smooth balladeering made him an excellent addition to the Ellington band. He worked with various bands and on his own, mostly on the West Coast, after leaving Ellington; he has also appeared at Ellington reunion conventions.

Jenkins, Freddie *(1906–78)*. Trumpet player with Ellington from 1928–34 and again from 1937–38. Born in New York City, he had first-class instruction on the instrument as a military cadet, high school student, and then at Ohio's Wilberforce University, where he also began playing professionally. Hired by Fletcher Henderson's brother in 1924, he played with Henderson's Collegians until he was invited to join Ellington's orchestra in October 1928. In his playing, he emulated Louis Armstrong. He retired from music-making in 1938 due to respiratory problems, which made it impossible for him to play.

Johnson, James P. *(1894–1955)*. Pianist and composer, who met Ellington for the first time around 1920 in Washington, and later when Ellington first visited New York. Johnson was famous for composing the "Charleston" in the 1920s, and continued to write for Broadway and for the concert stage until his death.

Jones, Richard Bowden, a/k/a "Jonesy" *(?–1946)*. Cotton Club busboy who joined the Ellington band on its winter 1931 tour as an all-around factotum and assistant to Ellington, a position he would hold for the next decade and a half.

Jones, Wallace *(1906–83)*. Trumpeter with Ellington from late 1936 to 1944. Jones was the cousin of Chick Webb and, like Webb, he was born in Baltimore. Jones's first professional work was with local bands. Webb summoned him to New York in late 1930 to play in his orchestra. Jones was a member of Willie Bryant's orchestra when he was hired by Ellington.

Jordan, Taft *(1915–81)*. Trumpet player with Ellington from 1943–47. Born in South Carolina, Jordan began working professionally when he was fourteen years old; by the time he was eighteen, he was a member of the Chick Webb orchestra, remaining with it until 1941. He joined Ellington in May 1943 after briefly leading his own band, replacing Rex Stewart, and remained with Ellington for about four years. He then worked with various groups through the 1950s, as well as leading his own bands. He spent the 1960s mostly doing studio work, but returned to jazz performance in the New York area in the 1970s until his death.

Metcalf, Louis *(1905–81)*. Second trumpet with Ellington from the summer of 1926 to June 1928. Metcalf was born in St. Louis, and came to New York in 1923. He played with several New York bands before joining the Ellington band in the fall of 1926. A smoother player than Miley, he complemented the growling style that Miley introduced, although Ellington insisted that Metcalf learn the growl, too. Metcalf worked primarily in Canada in the 1930s and 1940s, but returned to New York for nightclub work in the 1950s and 1960s.

Miley, James Wesley ("Bubber") *(1903–1932)*. Trumpeter with the Washingtonians and the Duke Ellington orchestra from 1923–29. As a young child, Miley began singing in backyards for pennies, and later studied the cornet and joined the school band. In 1921, blues singer Mamie Smith signed him as a member of her band, the Jazz Hounds. After hearing the legendary cornet player Joe "King" Oliver, Miley began working with various mutes and plungers, developing his famous "growling" style. He worked as an accompanist to many blues singers through the 1920s, perfecting his style. Miley joined the Snowden/Ellington band in August 1923. His distinctive style would become a trademark of the early Ellington groups. After leaving Ellington, Miley led his own groups and did many recording sessions. He died of tuberculosis in 1932.

Mills, Florence *(1895–1927)*. Well-known Harlem actress/singer who died tragically young in 1927. Ellington composed "Black Beauty" in 1928 in her memory.

Mills, Irving. Brother of Jack Mills, co-owner of Mills Music, Inc., and its many subsidiaries. Also a recording producer and songwriter ("Lovesick Blues"), he was the "front man" for the firm while Jack managed the business. Mills met Ellington when Ellington came to him trying to sell the firm his first song, composed with Jo Trent, in the fall of 1923. Mills signed Ellington to a publishing and management contract in mid-November 1926.

Monte, Fernandae de Castro. Ellington's last mistress, whom he met in Las Vegas while he was playing at the Riviera Hotel in May 1960. Well-versed in foreign languages and possessing impeccable taste, Monte was a singer who had worked in Europe and lived in Algeria and Brazil. She went by the nickname "Contessa," although how she earned this title is unknown.

Nance, Ray *(1913–76)*. Cornet and violin player, vocalist, and singer/dancer who worked with Ellington during 1940–45, 1946–61, 1962–63, and 1965. A Chicago native, Nance began studying piano at age six. Three years later he took up the violin, and made quick progress, eventually studying at the Chicago College of Music. Turning professional in 1932, Nance worked with the Earl Hines orchestra at Chicago's Grand Terrace ballroom during 1936–37, and recorded with them. Engagements with the Fletcher Henderson and Horace Henderson orchestras followed. When the call came to join Ellington in the fall of 1940, Nance was working at Joe Hughes's DeLuxe Club. His engaging personality, vocals, and musical skills made him a valuable addition to the Ellington orchestra.

Nanton, Joe "Tricky Sam" *(1904–46)*. Trombonist with Ellington from 1926–46, noted for the range of vocal-like sounds he created. Of West Indian parentage, Nanton was raised in Harlem and began playing the local clubs in the early 1920s when he was still a teenager. He joined Ellington in the summer of 1926 and remained with the band until his death.

Perry, Oliver H. "Doc.". A professional musician trained at the Washington Conservatory, he first heard Ellington playing when he was about sixteen. Impressed with what he heard, Perry began teaching Ellington piano. He taught Ellington music theory and allowed him to sit in with his band.

Pettiford, Oscar *(1922–60)*. Bass player with Ellington, 1945–48. Born into a large, musical family, Pettiford was a multi-instrumentalist. He played in his father's touring band, which was based in Minneapolis, Minnesota. At age twenty-one, he was playing in the Charlie Barnett orchestra. Engagements with small groups lead by Roy Eldridge and Dizzy Gillespie followed. He played bass in a melodic style, like Jimmie Blanton, and joined the Ellington band in November 1945. He worked with Woody Herman from 1948–50, and then with several bands through the 1950s. In 1958, he moved to Europe, settling in Denmark where he died two years later.

Procope, Russell *(1908–1981)*. Alto saxophone and clarinet player with Ellington from 1946–74. Procope was raised in Harlem next door to Benny Carter. He worked local clubs before joining Jelly Roll Morton's band in 1928 for a year. He then worked with various bands through the 1930s, before being drafted in World War II. After the war, he replaced Toby Hardwick in the Ellington band in April 1946, remaining with the group twenty-eight years. After Ellington's death, he continued to play the master's music, appearing in the pit band of the Broadway musical, *Sophisticated Ladies*, based on Ellington's music.

Raglin, Alvin "Junior" *(1917–55)*. Bass player with the Ellington band from late 1941–44, 1945, 1946–47, and 1955. Born in Omaha, Nebraska, at age twenty-one, Raglin began a three-year tour of duty with Gene Coy's Happy Aces, a territory band working out of Amarillo, Texas. In the summer of 1941, Raglin began working in a trio at the Club Alabam in San Francisco. Raglin subbed for the ailing Jimmie Blanton beginning in November 1941, and then joined the band permanently a month later.

Redman, Don *(1900–64)*. Saxophonist and arranger, most famous for his work with Fletcher Henderson. He recorded with the Washingtonians on several sessions in early 1926.

Robbins, Jack. Music publisher who published Ellington's first song and also commissioned the composer to write the 1924 show, *Chocolate Kiddies*.

Robinson, Prince *(1907–60)*. Clarinet/saxophone player with the Ellington band from 1925–26. Virginia-born Prince Robinson was mainly a self-taught musician who had been playing since he was fourteen. In 1923, he went to

New York City to join Lionel Howard's Musical Aces before joining Ellington in the spring of 1925. After leaving Ellington, he played with McKinney's Cotton Pickers through the mid-1930s, then worked with various bands. In the mid-1940s, he joined Claude Hopkins's band, remaining with him until 1952. He then worked on his own and with trumpeter Red Allen until his death, playing in a New Orleans style.

Roché, Betty *(1920–).* Vocalist with the Ellington band from 1942–44 and 1951–53. Born in Wilmington, Delaware, Roché arrived in New York as a teenager. Like Ella Fitzgerald and Sarah Vaughn, she won an amateur contest at Harlem's Apollo Theatre and was promptly hired by the Savoy Sultans, the house band at the Savoy Ballroom. She had also worked with Hot Lips Page and Lester Young before she arrived in Chicago. She joined the Ellington band after singer Ivie Anderson left the group in late July 1942. After leaving Ellington in 1944, she worked briefly with Earl Hines, and then sporadically on her own, before returning to Ellington for another two-year stint in the early 1950s. She again went out on her own, recording a few times in the late 1950s and early 1960s before fading from the scene.

Royal, Marshal *(1912–95).* Alto saxophonist with the Duke Ellington orchestra during 1932. He was raised in Los Angeles in a musical family. Royal's first instrument was the violin; then he played guitar, before taking up the alto saxophone. From age thirteen on, he played with local bands. In 1931, he joined Les Hite's band, and then, in mid-1932, was hired by Ellington to replace Toby Hardwick, who was exhausted from constant touring. After working with Ellington, Royal was best-known for a twenty-year stint with Count Basie, from 1951–71.

Sears, Al *(1910–90).* Tenor saxophonist with the Ellington band from 1944–49. A veteran of the Chick Webb, Zack White, and Andy Kirk bands, Sears, like Ben Webster, had a flamboyant, emotionally direct style of playing. He replaced "Skippy" Williams who had lasted in the Ellington band less than a year as Webster's replacement. After leaving Ellington, he worked with Johnny Hodges's band, which scored a hit with his "Castle Rock." He became a music publisher in the 1950s, while continuing to work in a jump/R&B style under the name Big Al Sears.

Sherrill, Joya *(1927–).* Vocalist with the Ellington band from 1944–46. Born in Detroit, she had first sung with the band in 1942, while still in high school. After her graduation, Ellington hired her to replace Wini Johnson. She married in 1946, and began a solo career. She returned to the Ellington fold in 1956 to perform on the television special, *A Drum Is a Woman,* and then continued to work as a solo artist. In 1962, she toured the Soviet Union with Benny Goodman, and a year later made her last recording with Ellington. She retired from the music business shortly after.

Shribman, Charlie. Band booker and impressario who first met Ellington in early 1924. Shribman would book Ellington's bands for years of several successful tours of New England.

Smith, Cladys (Jabbo) *(1908–91)*. Trumpet player who subbed for Bubber Miley in an Ellington 1927 session, perfectly imitating Miley's style. He was an active musician during the 1920s through the mid-1930s, playing with many leading bands. Around 1935, he settled in Milwaukee and worked primarily in that city through the early 1960s, while also working full-time for a car rental company. An award ceremony in 1975 at New York's Carnegie Hall lured him out of retirement, and he continued to perform until his death.

Smith, Willie *(1910–67)*. Alto saxophone player with Ellington from 1951–52. Born in Charleston, South Carolina, Smith began playing the clarinet at age twelve, and two years later, played at local concerts accompanied by his sister on piano. He studied at Fisk University in Nashville, Tennessee, where he first met Jimmie Lunceford. Smith began playing with Lunceford in Memphis during the summer of 1929, remaining with him until 1942. After serving in the Navy in World War II, Smith left to join Billy May's orchestra. He then rejoined Harry James in the spring of 1954, remaining with James until the summer of 1963. His health began to decline at this time, and he died of cancer in 1967.

Smith, Willie "The Lion" *(1897–1973)*. Mentor for Ellington, jazz pianist who Ellington later immortalized in the piece "The Lion." Smith was one of the great stride-era pianists, second only to Fats Waller.

Snowden, Elmer *(1900–73)*. Washington, D.C.-based banjoist who became the leader of the Washingtonians. Born in Baltimore, Snowden was active on the Washington scene as a banjoist from the mid-teens. He first met Ellington around 1919, when they worked together in various loose-knit groups. Snowden became the de facto leader of the band that would be known as the Washingtonians, which traveled to New York in 1923. A dispute over payment led Snowden to leave the band in 1926, forming his own rival group. He continued to be a bandleader and musician through the early 1930s. Snowden continued to record and perform through the early 1960s, working with other early jazz-era musicians like Lonnie Johnson.

Stewart, Rex *(1907–67)*. Cornet player with Ellington from 1934–45. Born to a musical family, Stewart began studying piano and violin himself, then switched to cornet. His first professional job was playing on the riverboats that cruised the Potomac. By the time he moved to New York permanently, in addition to the cornet, Stewart was also proficient on the trombone and xylophone, and on tenor and soprano saxophones. He played with various bands and in revues before joining Elmer Snowden in 1925. The following year, Stewart joined Fletcher Henderson. Over the next seven years, Stewart put in five tours of duty with Henderson, interspersed with work in McKinney's Cotton Pickers on two occasions, plus a short stint with Henderson's brother, Horace. Stewart's experience with three major black bands of the era ultimately led him to form his own. They played at the Empire Ballroom from June 1933 to the fall of 1934. He then joined Ellington in December 1934, remaining with the group eleven years. After leaving Ellington, he led his own bands through the 1950s and also worked as a jazz broadcaster and writer.

Taylor, Billy *(1906–86)*. Tuba and bass player with the Ellington band from 1934–39. Born and raised in Washington, D.C., Taylor began playing the tuba when he was fifteen. He moved to New York in 1924 and he played with several bands, and also learned the string bass along the way. He joined Ellington to second Wellman Braud in November 1934. He is not to be confused with the jazz pianist of the same name.

Terry, Clark *(1920–)*. Trumpet and fluegelhorn player with Ellington from 1934–39. Born in St. Louis, Terry began playing trumpet at an early age. He served in the Navy in World War II, where he met Willie Smith, and then played briefly with Lionel Hampton. After working with a couple of other bands, he was hired in 1948 by Count Basie, remaining with him until the band broke up in 1950, and then played with Basie's small group. In 1951, he joined Duke Ellington. After leaving Ellington in 1959, he worked briefly with Quincy Jones before joining the "Tonight Show" band in 1960, remaining with it until the show moved to California in 1972. Since then, he has taught and played with various bands, as well as smaller ensembles for club work.

Thompson, Edna *(c.1900–67)*. Duke Ellington's first wife, whom he married in 1918. Mother of Mercer Ellington. Ellington and Edna separated when Ellington took Mildred Dixon as his mistress in early 1938; however, the couple never divorced, and Ellington continued to support Edna through his many other liaisons. They remained married for 52 years, until her death from cancer in January 1967.

Tizol, Juan *(1900–84)*. Composer and valve trombone player with Ellington from 1929–44, 1951–53, and in 1960. Tizol was born in San Juan, Puerto Rico. During his late teens he began playing with the town's Municipal Band, and in 1920, Marie Lucas brought him to Washington, D.C., to join the stellar group she had assembled for the pit band at the Howard Theater. It was there that he first met Ellington. Eight years later after working with various bands, Tizol arrived in New York, and Ellington expressed interest in hiring him. Tizol joined the band in May 1929, and quickly became valuable, not only as a musician, but also as a skilled copyist and composer. His most famous piece, which he co-composed with Ellington, was the exotic-flavored "Caravan."

Trent, Jo (1892–1954). Lyricist who worked with Ellington on his early songs, including 1924's "Pretty Soft for You," Ellington's first published song.

Vodery, Will *(1885–1951)*. Composer of popular songs and theatrical music, as well as a musician, bandleader, and arranger. He began tutoring Ellington in composition and arranging in the fall of 1925.

Waller, Fats *(1904–43)*. Jazz pianist/vocalist/personality who appeared as a special feature when the Washingtonians were playing the Kentucky Club in late November 1925; subsequently, he arranged for the show to play one night at Broadway's New Amsterdam Theater. Waller was one of the great stride pianists, as well as a talented songwriter, vocalist, and entertainer.

Webster, Ben *(1909–73)*. Tenor sax player with Ellington who worked with the band in 1935, 1936, 1940–43, and 1948–49. Born in Kansas City, Missouri, Webster attended Wilberforce University and studied piano. He did not take up the saxophone until he was twenty-one. Despite this late start, he was soon a leading figure on the instrument, working in the Southwest. He held down a chair in Benny Moten's band during 1930–31, and Andy Kirk used him intermittently during the early 1930s. Webster moved to New York in 1934 and was immediately hired by Fletcher Henderson. He then worked with Cab Calloway before Ellington hired him full-time in late 1939. After leaving Ellington, he worked for the next twenty-four years primarily as a soloist with various accompanists, finally settling in Denmark.

Whetsol, Arthur *(1905–40)*. Trumpeter with the Washingtonians and then with Duke Ellington from 1920–23 and again from 1928–38.

Whiteman, Paul *(1890–1967)*. Jazz band leader and popularizer of jazz music. Whiteman sponsored the famous Carnegie Hall concert that premiered Gershwin's *Rhapsody in Blue*. He also commissioned several pieces by Ellington. Taking the name "King of Jazz," Whiteman employed many important jazz musicians, although his orchestra's music was not very hot.

Williams, Charles "Cootie" *(1911–85)*. Trumpet player with Ellington from 1929–40 and again 1962–74. Williams was born in Mobile, Alabama. He played in the school band and learned the trombone, tuba, and drums. He subsequently learned the trumpet and began working around town. He began working professionally at age fourteen, touring the South with various acts and revues. He came to New York in the spring of 1928, and was immediately befriended by bandleader Chick Webb. After working for Webb and briefly for Fletcher Henderson, he joined Ellington in January 1929. Hired to replace Bubber Miley, he quickly mastered Miley's "growling" technique and the use of plungers for effects. Williams continued to work with Mercer until 1978, then went out on his own. He made several tours of Europe, through 1983, when illness forced him to stop performing.

Williams, Elmer "Skippy" *(1905–62)*. Saxophone player with the Ellington band from mid-1943 through 1944. Williams had started out as a dancer, in a team with his brother, who also played saxophone. Before joining Ellington, Williams had held down chairs in the bands of Lucky Millinder, Jimmy Mundy, and Count Basie. He replaced Ben Webster in Ellington's band. After leaving Ellington, he worked with various bands, including a brief stint in Milan, Italy, in the late 1950s.

Woodyard, Sam *(1925–88)*. Drummer with the Ellington orchestra from 1955–68. Born in New Jersey, Woodyard was self-taught. He had worked with Roy Eldridge and the organist Milt Buckner before joining Ellington.

Major Ellington Bands and Their Members

The following charts show the major personnel changes in the Ellington bands from 1923 until his death in 1974. The band was augmented at times for specific recordings and events, which are generally not reflected in these charts. Not all band members and changes are shown, but this gives a good representation of how the band developed and grew. Abbreviations used in the table are:

Tpt	Trumpet	Bs	Bass	Gtr	Guitar
Trb	Trombone	Sax	Saxophone	Vibes	Vibraphone
B	Baritone	Pno	Piano	Flt	Flute
A	Alto	Arr	Arrangements	Pic	Piccolo
S	Soprano	Drm	Drums	Org	Organ
T	Tenor	Bnj	Banjo		

Melody/Brass			*Rhythm*				*Vocalist*
TRUMPET	**TROMBONE**	**REEDS**	**PIANO**	**DRUMS**	**RHYTHM**	**BASS**	
The Washingtonians, 1923–Spring 1924							
Arthur Whetsol[1]	Charlie Irvis	Otto ("Toby") Hardwick	Duke Ellington	Sonny Greer	Elmer Snowden		
Tpt	*Trb*	*A/B Sax*	*Pno, Arr*	*Drm*	*Bnj*		
The Washingtonians, Summer 1924–Summer 1925							
Bubber Miley	Charlie Irvis	Otto ("Toby") Hardwick	Duke Ellington	Sonny Greer	George Francis		
Tpt	*Trb*	*A/B Sax*	*Pno, Arr*	*Drm*	*Bnj*		
The Washingtonians, Fall 1925–Summer 1926							
Bubber Miley	Charlie Irvis	Otto ("Toby") Hardwick	Duke Ellington	Sonny Greer	Fred Guy	Bass Edwards	
Tpt[2]	*Trb*	*A/B Sax*	*Pno, Arr*	*Drm*	*Bnj*	*Tuba*	
		Prince Robinson[3]					
		T Sax, Clr					

	Melody/Brass			PIANO	Rhythm			Vocalist
	TRUMPET	TROMBONE	REEDS		DRUMS	RHYTHM	BASS	

Duke Ellington and His Kentucky Club Orchestra: Fall 1926–Summer 1927

TRUMPET	TROMBONE	REEDS	PIANO	DRUMS	RHYTHM	BASS	Vocalist
Bubber Miley/ Louis Metcalf *Tpt*	"Tricky Sam" Nanton *Trb*	Otto ("Toby") Hardwick *A/B Sax* two others[4]	Duke Ellington *Pno, Arr*	Sonny Greer *Drm*	Fred Guy *Bnj*	Mack Shaw *Tuba*	

Fall 1927–Spring 1928

| Bubber Miley[5] Louis Metcalf *Tpt* | "Tricky Sam" Nanton *Trb* | Otto ("Toby") Hardwick *A/B Sax* Rudy Jackson *Clr, T Sax* Harry Carney *A/B Sax* | Duke Ellington *Pno, Arr* | Sonny Greer *Drm* | Fred Guy *Bnj* | Wellman Braud *Bs* | |

Fall 1928–Winter 1929

| Bubber Miley/ Arthur Whetsol/ Freddie Jenkins *Tpt* | "Tricky Sam" Nanton *Trb* | Johnny Hodges *A/S Sax* Barney Bigard *Clr, T Sax* Harry Carney *A/B Sax* | Duke Ellington *Pno, Arr* | Sonny Greer *Drm* | Fred Guy *Bnj* | Wellman Braud *Bs* | |

Winter 1929–Fall 1929

| Cootie Williams/ Arthur Whetsol/ Freddie Jenkins *Tpt* | "Tricky Sam" Nanton *Trb* | Johnny Hodges *A/S Sax* Barney Bigard *Clr, T Sax* | Duke Ellington *Pno, Arr* | Sonny Greer *Drm* | Fred Guy *Bnj* | Wellman Braud *Bs* | |

Fall 1929–Winter 1932

Cootie Williams/
Arthur Whestol/
Freddie Jenkins
Tpt

"Tricky Sam" Nanton/
Trb
Juan Tizol
Valve trb

Johnny Hodges
A/S Sax
Barney Bigard
Clr, T Sax
Harry Carney
A/B Sax

Harry Carney
A/B Sax

Duke Ellington
Pno, Arr

Sonny Greer
Drm

Fred Guy
Bnj

Wellman Braud
Bs

Winter 1932–Winter 1934

Cootie Williams/
Arthur Whestol/
Freddie Jenkins
Tpt

"Tricky Sam" Nanton/
Lawrence Brown
Trb
Juan Tizol
Valve Trb

Johnny Hodges
A/S Sax
Barney Bigard
Clr, T Sax
Harry Carney
A/B Sax
Otto ("Toby") Hardwick
A/Bs Sax, Clr

Duke Ellington
Pno, Arr

Sonny Greer
Drm

Fred Guy
Gtr

Wellman Braud
Bs

Ivie Anderson

Winter 1934–Late 1934

Cootie Williams/
Charlie Allen
Tpt
Rex Stewart
Crt

"Tricky Sam" Nanton/
Lawrence Brown
Trb
Juan Tizol
Valve Trb

Johnny Hodges
A/S Sax
Barney Bigard
Clr, T Sax
Harry Carney
A/B Sax
Otto ("Toby") Hardwick
A/Bs Sax, Clr

Duke Ellington
Pno, Arr

Sonny Greer
Drm

Fred Guy
Gtr

Wellman Braud
Bs

Ivie Anderson

Melody/Brass			Rhythm				Vocalist
TRUMPET	TROMBONE	REEDS	PIANO	DRUMS	RHYTHM	BASS	
Winter 1935–Fall 1936							
Cootie Williams/	"Tricky Sam" Nanton/	Johnny Hodges	Duke Ellington	Sonny Greer	Fred Guy	Wellman Braud[6]/	Ivie Anderson
Charlie Allen	Lawrence Brown	*A/S Sax*	*Pno, Arr*	*Drm*	*Gtr*	Billy Taylor	
Tpt	*Trb*	Barney Bigard				*Bs*	
Rex Stewart	Juan Tizol	*Clr, T Sax*					
Crt	*Valve Trb*	Harry Carney					
		A/B Sax					
		Otto ("Toby") Hardwick					
		A/B Sax, Clr					
Late 1936–Late 1939							
Cootie Williams/	"Tricky Sam" Nanton/	Johnny Hodges	Duke Ellington	Sonny Greer	Fred Guy	Hayes Alvis[7]/	Ivie Anderson
Wallace Jones	Lawrence Brown	*A/S Sax*	*Pno, Arr*	*Drm*	*Gtr*	Billy Taylor	
Tpt	*Trb*	Barney Bigard				*Bs*	
Rex Stewart	Juan Tizol	*Clr, T Sax*					
Crt	*Valve Trb*	Harry Carney					
		A/B Sax					
		Otto ("Toby") Hardwick					
		A/B Sax, Clr					
Late 1939–Winter 1940							
Cootie Williams/	"Tricky Sam" Nanton/	Johnny Hodges	Duke Ellington	Sonny Greer	Fred Guy	Jimmy Blanton	Ivie Anderson
Wallace Jones	Lawrence Brown	*A/S Sax*	*Pno, Arr*	*Drm*	*Gtr*	*Bs*	
Tpt	*Trb*	Barney Bigard					
Rex Stewart	Juan Tizol	*Clr, T Sax*					
Crt	*Valve Trb*						

At top (continuation):

Harry Carney
A/B Sax

Otto ("Toby") Hardwick
A/Bs Sax, Clr

Winter 1940–Fall 1940

Cootie Williams/ Wallace Jones
Tpt

Rex Stewart
Crt

"Tricky Sam" Nanton/ Lawrence Brown
Trb

Juan Tizol
Valve Trb

Johnny Hodges
A/S Sax

Barney Bigard
Clr, T Sax

Harry Carney
A/B Sax

Otto ("Toby") Hardwick
A/Bs Sax, Clr

Ben Webster
T Sax

Duke Ellington
Pno, Arr

Billy Strayhorn
Deputy pianist

Sonny Greer
Drm

Fred Guy
Gtr

Jimmy Blanton
Bs

Ivie Anderson/ Herb Jeffries

Fall 1940–Late 1942

Ray Nance
Tpt, Vln, Voc

Wallace Jones
Tpt[8]

Rex Stewart
Crt

"Tricky Sam" Nanton/ Lawrence Brown
Trb

Juan Tizol
Valve Trb

Johnny Hodges
A/S Sax

Barney Bigard[9]
Clr, T Sax

Harry Carney
A/B Sax

Ben Webster
T Sax

Otto ("Toby") Hardwick
A/Bs Sax, Clr

Duke Ellington
Pno, Arr

Billy Strayhorn
Deputy pianist

Sonny Greer
Drm

Fred Guy
Gtr

Jimmy Blanton
Bs[10]

Ivie Anderson/ Herb Jeffries

| | Melody/Brass | | | | | Rhythm | | Vocalist |
TRUMPET	TROMBONE	REEDS	PIANO	DRUMS		RHYTHM	BASS	
Early 1943–Fall 1943								
Ray Nance *Tpt, Vln, Voc*	"Tricky Sam" Nanton/ Lawrence Brown *Trb*	Johnny Hodges *A/S Sax*	Duke Ellington *Pno, Arr*	Sonny Greer *Drm*		Fred Guy *Gtr*	Alvin "Junior" Raglin *Bs*	Betty Roché/ Jimmy Britton
Harold Baker/ Wallace Jones *Tpt*	Juan Tizol *Valve Trb*	Chauncy Haughton *Clr, T Sax*	Billy Strayhorn *Deputy pianist*					
Rex Stewart *Crt*		Harry Carney *A/B Sax*						
		Ben Webster *T Sax*						
Late 1943–Late 1944								
Ray Nance *Tpt, Vln, Voc*	"Tricky Sam" Nanton/ Lawrence Brown *Trb*	Johnny Hodges *A/S Sax*	Duke Ellington *Pno, Arr*	Sonny Greer *Drm*		Fred Guy *Gtr*	Alvin "Junior" Raglin *Bs*	Betty Roché/ Al Hibbler
Harold Baker/ Wallace Jones/ Taft Jordan *Tpt*	Juan Tizol *Valve Trb*	Jimmy Hamilton *Clr*	Billy Strayhorn *Deputy pianist*					
Rex Stewart *Crt*		Harry Carney *A/B Sax*						
		Elbert "Skippy" Williams *T Sax*						
		Otto ("Toby") Hardwick *A/Bs Sax, Clr*						

1945

Ray Nance
Tpt, Vln, Voc
Shelton Hemphill/
Cat Anderson/
Taft Jordan
Tpt
Rex Stewart
Crt

"Tricky Sam" Nanton/
Lawrence Brown
Trb
Claude Jones
Valve Trb

Johnny Hodges
A/S Sax
Jimmy Hamilton
Clr
Harry Carney
A/B Sax
Al Sears
T Sax
Otto ("Toby") Hardwick
A/Bs Sax, Clr

Duke Ellington
Pno, Arr
Billy Strayhorn
Deputy pianist

Sonny Greer
Drm

Fred Guy
Gtr

Alvin "Junior" Raglin
Bs

Joya Sherrill/
Kay Davis/
Maria Ellington/
Al Hibbler

1946–late 1948

Shelton Hemphill/
Cat Anderson/
Taft Jordan/
Nelson Williams/
Bernard Flood
Tpt
Ray Nance
Tpt, Vln, Voc

Wilbur DeParis/
Lawrence Brown
Trb
Claude Jones
Valve Trb

Johnny Hodges
A/S Sax
Jimmy Hamilton
Clr
Harry Carney
A/B Sax
Al Sears
T Sax
Otto ("Toby") Hardwick
A/Bs Sax, Clr[11]

Duke Ellington
Pno, Arr
Billy Strayhorn
Deputy pianist

Sonny Greer
Drm

Fred Guy
Gtr

Oscar Pettiford
Bs

Kay Davis/
Al Hibbler

Melody/Brass				Rhythm			Vocalist
TRUMPET	TROMBONE	REEDS	PIANO	DRUMS	RHYTHM	BASS	

Late 1948–late 1950

TRUMPET	TROMBONE	REEDS	PIANO	DRUMS	RHYTHM	BASS	Vocalist
Shelton Hemphill/	Lawrence Brown	Johnny Hodges	Duke Ellington	Sonny Greer	Fred Guy	Wendell Marshall	Kay Davis/
Nelson Williams/	*Trb*	*A/S Sax*	*Pno, Arr*	*Drm*	*Gtr*	*Bs*	Al Hibbler
Harold Baker/	Tyree Glenn	Jimmy Hamilton	Billy Strayhorn				
Al Killian	*Trb, Vibes*	*Clr*	*Deputy pianist*				
Tpt	Quentin Jackson	Harry Carney					
Ray Nance	*Valve Trb*	*A/B Sax*					
Tpt, Vln, Voc		Al Sears					
		T Sax					
		Russell Procope					
		A Sax, Clr					

1951–Spring 1953

TRUMPET	TROMBONE	REEDS	PIANO	DRUMS	RHYTHM	BASS	Vocalist
Nelson Williams/	Britt Woodman/	Willie Smith	Duke Ellington	Louis Bellson		Wendell Marshall	Al Hibbler
Harold Baker/	Quentin Jackson	*A Sax, Clr*	*Pno, Arr*	*Drm*		*Bs*	
Fats Ford/	*Trb*	Paul Gonsalves	Billy Strayhorn				
Cat Anderson	Juan Tizol	*T Sax*	*Deputy pianist*				
Tpt	*Valve Trb*	Jimmy Hamilton					
Ray Nance		*Clr*					
Tpt, Vln, Voc		Harry Carney					
		A/B Sax					
		Russell Procope					
		A Sax, Clr					

Mid-1953–late 1955

| Cat Anderson/ Clark Terry/ Willie Cook *Tpt* Ray Nance *Tpt, Vln, Voc* | Britt Woodman/ Quentin Jackson *Trb* Juan Tizol *Valve Trb* | Paul Gonsalves/ Rick Henderson *T Sax* Jimmy Hamilton *Clr* Harry Carney *A/B Sax* Russell Procope *A Sax, Clr* | Duke Ellington *Pno, Arr* Billy Strayhorn *Deputy pianist* | Dave Black[12] *Drm* | Wendell Marshall *Bs* | Jimmy Grissom |

1956–Fall 1959

| Cat Anderson/ Clark Terry/ Willie Cook *Tpt* Ray Nance *Tpt, Vln, Voc* | Britt Woodman/ Quentin Jackson *Trb* John Sanders *Valve Trb* | Paul Gonsalves/ Johnny Hodges *T Sax* Jimmy Hamilton *Clr* Harry Carney *A/B Sax* Russell Procope *A Sax, Clr* | Duke Ellington *Pno, Arr* Billy Strayhorn *Deputy pianist* | Sam Woodyard *Drm* | Jimmy Woode *Bs* | Jimmy Grissom |

Late 1959–1960

| Willie Cook/ Fats Ford/ Eddie Mullins *Tpt* | Britt Woodman/ Booty Wood/ Matthew Gee *Trb* | Paul Gonsalves/ Johnny Hodges *T Sax* Jimmy Hamilton *Clr* | Duke Ellington *Pno, Arr* Billy Strayhorn *Deputy pianist* | Jimmy Johnson *Drm* | Jimmy Woode *Bs* | Ozzie Bailey, Lee Greenwood |

	Melody/Brass			Rhythm				Vocalist
TRUMPET	TROMBONE	REEDS	PIANO	DRUMS	RHYTHM	BASS		

Late 1959–1960 *(continued)*

TRUMPET	TROMBONE	REEDS	PIANO	DRUMS	BASS	Vocalist
Ray Nance *Tpt, Vln, Voc*		Harry Carney *A/B Sax* Russell Procope *A Sax, Clr*				

1961–mid-1962

TRUMPET	TROMBONE	REEDS	PIANO	DRUMS	BASS	Vocalist
Harold Baker/	Lawrence Brown/	Paul Gonsalves/	Duke Ellington *Pno, Arr*	Sam Woodyard *Drm*	Aaron Bell *Bs*	Milt Grayson
Cat Anderson/	Leon Cox *Trb*	Johnny Hodges *T Sax*	Billy Strayhorn *Deputy pianist*			
Bill Berry *Tpt*	Chuck Connors *B Trb*	Jimmy Hamilton *Clr*				
Ray Nance *Tpt, Vln, Voc*		Harry Carney *A/B Sax* Russell Procope *A Sax, Clr*				

Fall 1962–late 1964

TRUMPET	TROMBONE	REEDS	PIANO	DRUMS	BASS	Vocalist
Cootie Williams/	Lawrence Brown/	Paul Gonsalves/	Duke Ellington *Pno, Arr*	Sam Woodyard *Drm*	Ernie Shephard *Bs*	Milt Grayson
Cat Anderson/	Buster Cooper *Trb*	Johnny Hodges *T Sax*	Billy Strayhorn *Deputy pianist*			
Roy Burrows *Tpt*	Chuck Connors *B Trb*	Jimmy Hamilton *Clr*				
Ray Nance *Tpt, Vln, Voc*		Harry Carney *A/B Sax*				

Russell Procope
A Sax, Clr

1965–late 1968

Cootie Williams/	Lawrence Brown/	Paul Gonsalves/	Duke Ellington	Sam Woodyard
Cat Anderson/	Buster Cooper	Johnny Hodges	*Pno, Arr*	*Drm*
Herbie Jones/	*Trb*	*T Sax*	Billy Strayhorn[13]	
Mercer Ellington	Chuck Connors	Jimmy Hamilton	*Deputy pianist*	
Tpt	*B Trb*	*Clr*		
Ray Nance		Harry Carney		
Tpt, Vln, Voc		*A/B Sax*		
		Russell Procope		
		A Sax, Clr		

John Lamb	Tony Watkins
Bs	

Early 1969–Early 1971

Cootie Williams/	Lawrence Brown	Paul Gonsalves/	Duke Ellington	Rufus Jones
Cat Anderson/	*Trb*	Johnny Hodges	*Pno, Arr*	*Drm*
Rolf Ericson/	Chuck Connors	*T Sax*	Wild Bill Davis	
Mercer Ellington	*B Trb*	Norris Turney	*Org, Deputy*	
Tpt		*A/S Sax, Clr, flt*	*Pianist*	
Ray Nance		Harold Ashby		
Tpt, Vln, Voc		*T Sax, Clr*		
		Harry Carney		
		A/B Sax		
		Russell Procope		
		A Sax, Clr		

Victor Gaskin	Tony Watkins
Bs	

	Melody/Brass			Rhythm				Vocalist
TRUMPET	TROMBONE	REEDS	PIANO	DRUMS	RHYTHM	BASS	

1971–1972

TRUMPET	TROMBONE	REEDS	PIANO	DRUMS	BASS	Vocalist
Cootie Williams/ Money Johnson/ Eddie Preston/ Mercer Ellington *Tpt* Ray Nance *Tpt, Vln, Voc*	Booty Wood/ Malcolm Taylor *Trb* Chuck Connors *B Trb*	Paul Gonsalves *T Sax* Norris Turney *A/S Sax, Clr, flt* Harold Ashby *T Sax, Clr* Harry Carney *A/B Sax* Russell Procope *A Sax, Clr*	Duke Ellington *Pno, Arr* Wild Bill Davis *Org, deputy pianist*	Rufus Jones *Drm*	Joe Benjamin *Bs*	Neil Brookshire (aka Bobbie Gordon)/ Tony Watkins

1973–1974

TRUMPET	TROMBONE	REEDS	PIANO	DRUMS	BASS	Vocalist
Money Johnson/ Johny Coles/ Barry Lee Hall/ Willie Cook/ Mercer Ellington *Tpt* Ray Nance *Tpt, Vln, Voc*	Vince Prudente/ Art Baron *Trb* Chuck Connors *B Trb*	Percy Marion *T Sax* Harold Minerve *A/S Sax, flt, pic* Harold Ashby *T Sax, Clr* Harry Carney *A/B Sax* Russell Procope *A Sax, Clr*	Duke Ellington *Pno, Arr*	Rocky White *Drm*	Joe Benjamin *Bs*	Tony Watkins/ Alice Babs[14]

[1] He was replaced by Bubber Miley in early 1924.

[2] Miley was playing with the band during this period, but often did not make dates or recording sessions; for this reason Ellington would always have at least one trumpeter in reserve, including Pike Davis, Harry Cooper, or Leon Rutledge.

[3] Robinson was added as 2nd saxophonist/clarinet player for a 9/25 session; Don Redman replaced him on a 3/26 session. Sidney Bechet worked with the band during the summer of 1926 on clarinet.

[4] Often identified as Harry Carney (a/b sax, clr) and Rudy Jackson (clr, t sax), although recent evidence shows that they did not in fact join the band until mid-1927.

[5] Sometimes replaced by Arthur Whetsol on recordings.

[6] In spring of 1935, Braud left and was replaced by Hayes Alvis.

[7] Hayes left the band in early 1938, and Taylor carried on alone.

[8] In autumn of 1942 Ellington added another trumpet player, Harold "Shorty" Baker.

[9] Bigard left the band in mid-1942 and was replaced temporarily by Chauncey Haughton.

[10] Blanton left due to illness in the end of 1941 and was replaced by Alvin "Junior" Raglin.

[11] Russell Procope (alto sax, clarinet) replaced Hardwick by the fall of 1946.

[12] Butch Ballard preceded Dave Black in the drums chair for six months in 1953.

[13] Strayhorn died in spring 1967.

[14] Swedish singer used for special concerts and recordings.

Compositions by Duke Ellington

Compiled by Ken Bloom

All music by Duke Ellington unless indicated otherwise.

Abbreviations:
C: composer
L: lyricist

There are few facts in the world of Duke Ellington. Annotators have worked decades to develop a complete list of Ellington compositions. There are a number of factors contributing to the general confusion. First, many songs were performed by his band or recorded in one year, but published in another year; *year of copyright* is used here. Many instrumentals were given different names at different times. Ellington didn't write everything that his name is put onto; Billy Strayhorn wrote many of the compositions that are credited to Ellington. Also, Irving Mills, Ellington's manager and publisher, contributed almost nothing to the writing of songs, but has his name attached to many of them. Note under "show songs" that only songs *new to* a show are included, not older songs that were added because of their popularity. For those reasons and others, this list is necessarily incomplete.

1923
Pop songs: Blind Man's Buff (L: Trent, Jo)

1924
Instrumentals: Choo-Choo (I Gotta Hurry Home) (C: Ellington, Duke; Ringle, Dave; Schaefer, Bob)

Pop songs: Pretty Soft for You (L: Trent, Jo); Rainy Nights (C/L: Ellington, Duke; Lopez; Trent, Jo)

Show songs: *Chocolate Kiddies* (Show). Lyrics by Jo Trent: Jig Walk; Jim Dandy; With You

1926
Pop song: Parlor Social Stomp

1927
Instrumentals: Birmingham Breakdown; Black & Tan Fantasy (C: Ellington, Duke; Miley, Bubber); Black Cat Blues; Blues I Love to Sing, The (C: Ellington, Duke;

Miley, Bubber); Bouncing Buoyancy; Creeper, The; Down in Our Alley Blues (C: Ellington, Duke; Hardwick, Otto); East St. Louis Toodle-Oo (C: Ellington, Duke; Miley, Bubber); Gold Digger (C: Donaldson, Will; Ellington, Duke); Hop Head; Immigration Blues; Washington Wobble

1928

Instrumentals: Black Beauty; Blue Bubbles; Creole Love Call (aka "Creole Rhapsody"); Harlem Twist; Hot and Bothered; Jubilee Stomp; New Orleans Low Down; Swampy River; Sweet Mama; Take It Easy

1929

Instrumentals: Awful Sad; Big House Blues; Blues with a Feeling, The; Dicty Glide; Doin' the Voom Voom (C: Ellington, Duke; Miley, Bubber); Duke Steps Out, The; Flaming Youth; Goin' to Town (C: Ellington, Duke; Miley, Bubber); Harlem Flat Blues; Haunted Nights; High Life; Jazz Convulsions; Jolly Wog; Mooche, The (C: Ellington, Duke; Mills, Irving); Memphis Wail; Mississippi Moan; Misty Mornin' (C: Ellington, Duke; Whetsol, Arthur); Move Over; Oklahoma Stomp; Rent Party Blues (C: Ellington, Duke; Hodges, Johnny); Rub-a-Tub-Blues; Saturday Night Function (C: Bigard, Albany; Ellington, Duke); Sloppy Joe (C: Bigard, Barney; Ellington, Duke); Stevedore Stomp (C: Ellington, Duke; Mills, Irving); What a Life!; Who Said "It's Like That?" (C: Ellington, Duke; Mills, Irving)

Show songs: *Hot Chocolates* (Show). Lyrics by Andy Razaf: Jungle Jamboree; Snake Hip Dance

1930

Instrumentals: Blues of the Vagabond; Breakfast Dance, The; Cincinnati Daddy; Dreamy Blues[1]; Echoes of the Jungle; Jazz Lips; Jungle Blues; Jungle Nights in Harlem; Lazy Duke, The; Sweet Dreams of Love (C: Ellington, Duke; Mills, Irving); Sweet Jazz o' Mine; Shout 'Em, Aunt Tillie (C: Ellington, Duke; Mills, Irving); Sweet Mama; Syncopated Shuffle; Wall Street Wail; Zonky Blues

Pop songs: Sweet Chariot[2] (C/L: Ellington, Duke; Mills, Irving)

Show songs: *Blackberries of 1930* (Show). Lyrics by Irving Mills: Bumpty Bump; Doin' the Crazy Walk; Swanee River Rhapsody (L: Gaskill, Clarence; Mills, Irving)

Check and Double Check (Film). Lyrics by Irving Mills: Old Man Blues; Ring Dem Bells

1931

Pop songs: I'm So in Love with You (L: Mills, Irving); It's Glory; Mood Indigo (C/L: Bigard, Barney; Ellington, Duke; Mills, Irving); Rockin' in Rhythm (C/L: Carney, Harry; Ellington, Duke; Mills, Irving)

1932

Instrumentals: Baby, When You Ain't There; Blue Harlem; Blue Ramble; Blue Tune; Clouds in My Heart (C: Bigard, Barney; Ellington, Duke; Mills, Irving); Ducky

---

[1]Music later used for "Mood Indigo."
[2]Based on the hymn of the same name.

Wucky (C: Bigard, Barney; Ellington, Duke); Lazy Rhapsody; Lightnin'; Rocky Mountain Blues (C: Ellington, Duke; Mills, Irving); Slippery Horn; Swampy River; Swing Low (C: Ellington, Duke; Jenkins)

Pop songs: Best Wishes (L: Koehler, Ted); It Don't Mean a Thing (If It Ain't Got that Swing) (L: Mills, Irving); Moon Over Dixie (L: Koehler, Ted); Mystery Song, The (L: Mills, Irving)

1933
Pop songs: Drop Me Off at Harlem (L: Kenny, Nick); Sophisticated Lady (L: Mills, Irving; Parish, Mitchell)

1934
Instrumentals: Blue Feeling; Dallas Doings; Daybreak Express; Rude Interlude; Stompy Jones

Pop songs: Jungle Nights in Harlem (L: Mills, Irving); Solitude (L: DeLange, Eddie; Mills, Irving)

1935
Instrumentals: Bird of Paradise; Harlem Speaks; Hyde Park; Indigo Echoes (C: Ellington, Duke; Mills, Irving); Merry-Go-Round; Porto Rican Chaos; Reminiscing in Tempo; Rhapsody Jr.; Saddest Tale (C: Ellington, Duke; Mills, Irving); Showboat Shuffle; Tough Truckin' (C: Ellington, Duke; Mills, Irving)

Pop songs: Delta Serenade (L: Kurtz, Manny; Mills, Irving); In a Sentimental Mood (L: Kurtz, Manny; Mills, Irving); Saddest Tale (L: Mills, Irving); Sump'n 'bout Rhythm (L: Kurtz, Manny; Mills, Irving)

1936
Instrumentals: Clarinet Lament (C: Bigard, Barney; Ellington, Duke); Echoes of Harlem; Exposition Swing; In a Jam; Trumpet in Spades; Uptown Downbeat

Pop songs: I Don't Know Why I Love You So (L: Mills, Irving); Oh, Babe, Maybe Someday (L: Ellington, Duke); Yearning for Love (L: Mills, Irving; Parish, Mitchell)

1937
Instrumentals: Back Room Romp, The; Blue Reverie (C: Carney, Harry; Ellington, Duke); Demi-Tasse (C: Carney, Harry; Ellington, Duke); Downtown Uproar (C: Ellington, Duke; Williams, Cootie); Ev'ah Day (C: Carney, Harry; Ellington, Duke); Four and a Half Street (C: Ellington, Duke; Stewart, Rex); New Birmingham Breakdown; Sauce for the Goose (C: Bigard, Barney; Ellington, Duke); Sponge Cake and Spinach; Sugar Hill Shim Sham (C/L: Ellington, Duke; Stewart, Rex); Tea and Trumpets (C: Ellington, Duke; Stewart, Rex)

Pop songs: Alabamy Home (C/L: Ellington, Duke; Ringle, Dave); Azure (L: Mills, Irving); Black Butterfly (L: Carruthers, Ben; Mills, Irving); Caravan (C: Ellington, Duke; Tizol, Juan; L: Mills, Irving); Clouds in My Heart (C: Bigard, Barney; Ellington, Duke; L: Mills, Irving); Jazz a la Carte (C: Bigard, Barney; Ellington, Duke; L: Mills, Irving); Lament for Lost Love (C: Bigard, Barney; Ellington, Duke; L: Mills, Irving); Scattin' at the Cotton Club (L: Mills, Irving); Swing Baby Swing (L: Alvis, Hayes)

Show songs: *Cotton Club Parade, 2nd Edition* (Nightclub Show). Lyrics by Irving Mills: Black & Tan Fantasy (L: Miley, Bubber); Chile; Cotton Club Express; Peckin'; Rockin' in Rhythm (L: Carney, Harry; Mills, Irving); *Hit Parade, The* (Film): I've Got to Be a Rug Cutter (L: Ellington, Duke)

1938

Instrumentals: Buffet Flat; Chasin' Chippies (C: Ellington, Duke; Williams, Cootie); Crescendo in Blue; Diminuendo in Blue; Dinah's in a Jam; Drummer's Delight (C: Bigard, Barney; Ellington, Duke); Empty Ballroom Blues (C: Ellington, Duke; Williams, Cootie); Hodge Podge (C: Ellington, Duke; Hodges, Johnny); Krum Elbow Blues (C: Ellington, Duke; Hodges, Johnny); La De Doody Doo (C: Ellington, Duke; Lambert, Edward J.; Richards, Stephen); Pigeons and Peppers (C: Ellington, Duke; Ellington, Mercer); Rendezvous in Rhythm (C: Ellington, Duke; Hodges, Johnny); Rhythmoods; She's Gone (C: Ellington, Duke; Williams, Cootie); Swing Pan Alley (C: Ellington, Duke; Williams, Cootie); Swinging in the Dell (C: Ellington, Duke; Hodges, Johnny); Swingin' on the Campus; T.T. on Toast (C: Ellington, Duke; Mills, Irving); Twits and Twerps (C: Ellington, Duke; Stewart, Rex)

Pop songs: Chatterbox (C: Ellington, Duke; Stewart, Rex; L: Mills, Irving); Cotton Club (C/L: Ellington, Duke; Mills, Irving; Nemo, Henry); Dusk in the Desert (L: Mills, Irving); Gypsy without a Song (C: Ellington, Duke; Singer, Lou; L: Gordon, Irving); Harmony in Harlem (C: Ellington, Duke; Hodges, Johnny; L: Mills, Irving); I Let a Song Go Out of My Heart (L: Mills, Irving; Nemo, Henry; Redmond, John); If I Thought You Cared (C/L: Bigard, Barney; Ellington, Duke; Jackson; Mills, Irving); Jitterbug's Lullaby (Jitterbug's Holiday) (C: Ellington, Duke; Hodges, Johnny; L: Mills, Irving); Jubilesta (C: Ellington, Duke; Tizol, Juan; L: Mills, Irving); Lost in Meditation (Have a Heart) (C: Ellington, Duke; Singer, Lou; Tizol, Juan; L: Mills, Irving); Please Forgive Me (L: Gordon, Irving; Mills, Irving); Prelude to a Kiss (L: Gordon, Irving; Mills, Irving); Pyramid (C: Ellington, Duke; Tizol, Juan; L: Gordon, Irving; Mills, Irving); Ridin' on a Blue Note (L: Gordon, Irving; Mills, Irving); Steppin' into Swing Society (L: Mills, Irving; Nemo, Henry)

Show songs: *Cotton Club Parade* (Nightclub show). Lyrics by Irving Mills and Henry Nemo: Braggin' in Brass; Carnival in Caroline; Lesson in C, A

Cotton Club Parade, Fourth Edition (Nightclub show). Lyrics by Irving Mills and Henry Nemo: I'm Slappin' Seventh Avenue (with the Sole of My Shoe); If You Were in My Place; Skrontch; Swingtime in Honolulu

1939

Instrumentals: Battle of Swing; Blue Light; Blues, The; Boudoir Benny (C: Ellington, Duke; Williams, Cootie); Bouncing Buoyancy; Boys from Harlem; Buffet Flat, The; Country Gal; Delta Mood; Doin' the Voom Voom (C: Ellington, Duke; Miley, Bubber); Dooji Wooji; Exposition Swing; Fat Stuff Serenade (C: Ellington, Duke; Stewart, Rex); Gal-Avantin' (C: Ellington, Duke; Williams, Cootie); Greatful to You; Hip Chic; I'll Come Back for More (C: Ellington, Duke; Fleagle, B.; Stewart, Rex); I Never Felt This Way Before; I'm

Riding on the Moon and Dancing on the Stars (C: Ellington, Duke; Hodges, Johnny); Informal Blues; Jazz Potpourri; Just Good Fun; Lady in Blue; Lady in Doubt; Lady Macbeth; Little Posey; Lovely Coed, A; Lullaby; Mobile Blues (C: Ellington, Duke; Williams, Cootie); Old King Dooji; Portrait of A Lion; Pussy Willow; Rent Party Blues; San Juan Hill (C: Ellington, Duke; Fleagle, B.; Stewart, Rex); Savoy Strut (C: Ellington, Duke; Hodges, Johnny); Sergeant Was Shy, The; She's Gone (C: Ellington, Duke; Williams, Cootie); Slap Happy; Smorgasbord and Schnapps (C: Ellington, Duke; Fleagle, B.; Stewart, Rex); That Solid Old Man; Subtle Lament; Tootin' Through the Roof; Wanderlust (C: Ellington, Duke; Hodges, Johnny); Way Low; Weely

Pop songs: Beautiful Romance (C: Ellington, Duke; Williams, Cootie; L: Fein, Lupin); Blue Belles of Harlem; Blue Goose; Boy Meets Horn (C: Ellington, Duke; Stewart, Rex; L: Mills, Irving); Concerto for Cootie (AKA: Cootie's Concerto); Dancing on the Stars (L: Gordon, Irving; Mills, Irving); Gal from Joe's, The (L: Mills, Irving); Grievin' (C/L: Ellington, Duke; Strayhorn, Billy); I'm Checking Out—Goom Bye (C/L: Ellington, Duke; Strayhorn, Billy); I'm in Another World (C: Ellington, Duke; Hodges, Johnny; L: Gordon, Irving; Mills, Irving); Ko-Ko; Lonely Co-Ed (C/L: Ellington, Duke; Leslie, Edgar; Strayhorn, Billy); Lovely Isle of Porto Rico (AKA: Porto Rican Gal); Morning Glory; Serenade to Sweden; Something to Live For (C/L: Ellington, Duke; Strayhorn, Billy); Stevedore Stomp (L: Mills, Irving); Stevedore's Serenade (L: Edelstein, Hilly; Gordon, Irving); Watermelon Man (L: Ellington, Duke); You Gave Me the Gate and I'm Swinging (L: Farmer, J.; Gordon, Irving; McNeely, J.B.); Your Love Has Faded (C/L: Ellington, Duke; Strayhorn, Billy)

1940

Instrumentals: Across the Track Blues; Blue Goose; Bojangles; Charlie the Chulo; Concerto for Cootie; Conga Brava; Cotton Tail; Dusk; Flaming Sword, The; Girl in My Dreams Tries to Look Like You, The; Harlem Air Shaft; Jack the Bear; Junior Hop; Lick Chorus; Lull at Dawn, A; Me and You; Mobile Bay (C: Ellington, Duke; Stewart, Rex); Morning Glory (C: Ellington, Duke; Stewart, Rex); Mr. J. B. Blues C (C: Blanton, Jimmy; Ellington, Duke); My Sunday Gal; Never No Lament; Pitter Patter, Panther; Portrait of Bert Williams, A; Portrait of a Lion; Rumpus in Richmond; Sapph; Sepia Panorama; Slow Tune; Tonk (C: Ellington, Duke; Strayhorn, Billy)

Pop songs: All Too Soon (L: Sigman, Carl); Day Dream (C: Ellington, Duke; Strayhorn, Billy; L: Latouche, John); Diamond Jubilee Song (C/L: Ellington, Duke; Strayhorn, Billy); Honchi Chonch (C/L: Ellington, Duke; Strayhorn, Billy); I Never Felt This Way Before (L: Dubin, Al); In a Mellow Tone (Baby, You and Me) (L: Gabler, Milt); Lady in Blue (L: Mills, Irving); Love's in My Heart (C: Alvis, Hayes; Ellington, Duke; L: Mills, Irving); Me and You (L: Ellington, Duke)

1941

Instrumentals: Are You Sticking?; Blue Serge; Doghouse Blues; John Hardy's Wife; Lightnin'; Plucked Again; Swee' Pea (C: Ellington, Duke; Strayhorn, Billy); Swing Low

Pop songs: Baby, When You Ain't There (L: Parish, Mitchell); I'm Satisfied (L: Parish, Mitchell); Luna de Cuba[3] (C: Ellington, Duke; Tizol, Juan; L: Negrette, George); Warm Valley (L: Russell, Bob)

Show songs: *Jump for Joy* (Show). Lyrics by Paul Francis Webster: (Give Me an) Old-Fashioned Waltz (L: Kuller, Sid); Bessie—Whoa Babe; Bli-Blip (L: Ellington, Duke; Kuller, Sid); Brown-Skin Gal in the Calico Gown, The; Chocolate Shake; Flamingo; Giddybug Gallop (inst.), The; I Got It Bad and That Ain't Good; Jump for Joy (L: Kuller, Sid; Webster, Paul Francis); Just Squeeze Me (L: Ellington, Duke; Gaines, Lee); Just a-Settin' and a Rockin' (C: Ellington, Duke; Strayhorn, Billy; L: Gaines, Lee); Nostalgia; Pot, Pan and Skillet; Rocks in My Bed (L: Ellington, Duke); Sharp Easter (L: Kuller, Sid); Shhhhh! He's on the Beat! (L: Kuller, Sid); Subtle Slough (L: Ellington, Duke)

1942

Instrumentals: American Lullaby (AKA: Lullaby); Are You Sticking?; Back Room Romp (C: Ellington, Duke; Stewart, Rex); Bundle of Blues; C-Jam Blues (AKA: C Blues); Carnaval (C: Ellington, Duke; Tizol, Juan); Crescendo in Blue; Diminuendo in Blue; Dusk; Fatstuff Serenade (C: Ellington, Duke; Stewart, Rex); Good Gal Blues; Going Up; Home; I Don't Mind (C: Ellington, Duke; Strayhorn, Billy); Little Posey; Main Stem; Moon Mist; Romance Wasn't Built in a Day; San Juan Hill (C: Ellington, Duke; Stewart, Rex; Fleagle, B.); Sentimental Lady; Sherman Shuffle; So, I'll Come Back For More (C: Ellington, Duke; Stewart, Rex; Fleagle, B.); Someone; Tea and Trumpets

Pop songs: Azalea (L: Ellington, Duke); Don't Get Around Much Anymore[4] (L: Russell, Bob); Five O'Clock Drag (L: Adamson, Harold); I Don't Know What Kind of Blues I Got (L: Ellington, Duke); I Don't Mind (L: Strayhorn, Billy); Oh, Miss Jaxson (L: Ellington, Duke); What Am I Here For? (L: Laine, Frankie)

1943

Instrumentals: Across the Track Blues; Barzallai-Lou; Boy Meets Horn (C: Ellington, Duke; Stewart, Rex); Fickle Fling (AKA: Camp Grant Chant); Grace Note Blues; Graceful Awareness; Hop, Skip, Jump; Killin' Myself; Main Stem; Mobile Bay (C: Ellington, Duke; Stewart, Rex); Mood to Be Wooed (C: Ellington, Duke; Hodges, Johnny); Mr. J. B. Blues; Rockabye River; Savoy Strut (C: Ellington, Duke; Hodges, Johnny); Three Cent Stomp

Pop songs: Baby Please Stop and Think about Me (L: Gordon, Irving); Blue Ramble (L: Ellington, Duke); Chicken Feed (L: Russell, Bob); Cotton Club Stomp (C/L: Carney, Harry; Ellington, Duke; Hodges, Johnny); Do Nothin' Till You Hear from Me (L: Russell, Bob); Ring Around the Moon (L: Russell, Bob); Shout 'em Aunt Tillie (C/L: Ellington, Duke; Mills, Irving); Tonight I Shall Sleep (with a Smile on My Face) (L: Ellington, Mercer; Gordon, Irving)

---

[3]Spanish version of Lovely Isle of Porto Rico.

[4]Same music as Never No Lament.

1944

Instrumentals: Blutopia; Jazz Convulsions; Jumping Frog Jump; Main Stem (AKA: Altitude; Swing Shifters; Swing; On Becoming a Square); Mood to Be Wooed; Stomp, Look and Listen; Suddenly It Jumped; You've Got My Heart (AKA: Someone)

Pop songs: Creole Love Call (Creole Rhapsody) (L: Ellington, Duke); Don't You Know I Care or Don't You Care to Know (L: David, Mack); Hit Me with a Hot Note and Watch Me Bounce (L: George, Don); I Ain't Got Nothin' but the Blues (L: George, Don); I Can't Put My Arms Around a Memory (L: George, Don); I Didn't Know About You[5] (L: Russell, Bob); I'm Beginning to See the Light (C/L: Ellington, Duke; George, Don; Hodges, Johnny; James, Harry); I'm Just a Lucky So and So (L: David, Mack); My Lovin' Baby and Me (C/L: Calloway, Cab; Ellington, Duke; George, Don); No Smoking (L: Ellington, Duke); You Left Me Everything but You (C/L: Ellington, Duke; George, Don)

1945

Instrumentals: Air Conditioned Jungle (C: Ellington, Duke; Hamilton, Jimmy); Blue Cellophane; Bugle Breaks (C: Ellington, Duke; Ellington, Mercer; Strayhorn, Billy); Carnegie Blues; Coloratura; Downbeat Shuffle; Esquire Swank (C: Ellington, Duke; Hodges, Johnny); Everything but You (C: Ellington, Duke; George, Don; James, Harry); Fancy Dan; Franktic Fantasy (C: Ellington, Duke; Stewart, Rex); Frustration; I Love My Lovin' Lover; It's Only Account of You; Let the Zoomers Drool (C: Ellington, Duke; Hodges, Johnny); Metronome All Out (C: Ellington, Duke; Strayhorn, Billy); New World A-Comin'; Prairie Fantasy; Riff'n Drill; Subtle Slough; Translucency (C: Brown, Lawrence; Ellington, Duke); Teardrops in the Rain (C: Anderson, William; Ellington, Duke); Time's A-Wastin' (C: Ellington, Duke; Ellington, Mercer; George Don); Unbooted Character; Which Is Which Stomp; Zan; Zanzibar

Pop songs: Ev'ry Hour on the Hour I Fall in Love with You (L: George, Don); Heart of Harlem (L: Hughes, Langston); Long, Strong and Consecutive (L: David, Mack); Wonder of You, The (C: Ellington, Duke; Hodges, Johnny; L: George, Don)

Black, Brown and Beige: Blues, The; Come Sunday; Emancipation Celebration; Sugar Hill Penthouse; West Indian Dance; Worksong

Perfume Suite: Balcony Serenade (C: Strayhorn); Strange Feeling (C: Ellington, Strayhorn); Dancers in Love; Coloratura

1946

Instrumentals: Blue Abandon; Circe; Eighth Veil (C: Ellington, Duke; Strayhorn, Billy); Esquire Swank (C: Ellington, Duke; Hodges, Johnny); Fugue; Gatherin' in a Clearin', A (C: Anderson, William; Ellington, Duke); Golden Cross, The; Hey, Baby; Magenta Haze; Mellow Ditty; Rugged Romeo; Sono; Suburbanite; Sultry Sweet; Tip Toe Topic (C: Ellington, Duke; Pettiford, Oscar)

---

[5]Music same as Home.

Tonal Group: Fugueditti; Jam-a-ditty; Rhapsoditti

Pop songs: Hey, Baby; It Shouldn't Happen to a Dream (C: Ellington, Duke; Hodges, Johnny; L: George, Don); Pretty Woman (L: Ellington, Duke); Tell Me, Tell Me, Dream Face (L: George, Don); You Don't Love Me No More (L: Ellington, Duke); You Gotta Crawl Before You Walk (C/L: Ellington, Duke; Fotine, Larry; Torme, Mel; Wells, Robert)

Show songs: *Beggar's Holiday* (Show). Lyrics by John Latouche: Brown Penny; Chase, The; Chorus of Citizens; Fol-de-rol-rol; Girls want a Hero; Hunted, The; I Wanna Be Bad; I've Got Me in Between; Inbetween; Lullaby for Junior; Maybe I Should Change My Ways; Ore for a Gold Mine; Quarrel for Three; Rooster Man; Scrimmage of Life, The; TNT; Take Love Easy; Tomorrow Mountain; Tooth and Claw; Wedding Ballet; When I Walk with You; When You Go Down by Miss Jenny's; Women, Women, Women; Wrong Side of the Railroad Tracks, The

People Are Funny (Film): Every Hour on the Hour I Fall in Love with You (L: George, Don)

1947

Instrumentals: Beautiful Indians, The (Hiawatha); Beautiful Indians, The (Minnehaha); Boogie Bop Blue; Far Away Blues (C: Ellington, Duke; Hodges, Johnny); Frisky (C: Ellington, Duke; Hodges, Johnny); Golden Cress (C: Brown, Lawrence; Ellington, Duke); Golden Feather (C: Ellington, Duke; Sears, Al); Long Horn Blues (C: Ellington, Duke; Hodges, Johnny); Sultry Serenade (C: Ellington, Duke; Glenn, Tyree); Who Struck John? (AKA: Blues)

Deep South Suite: Happy Go Lucky Local; Hearsay (C: Ellington, Duke; Strayhorn, Billy); Magnolias Dripping with Honey (C: Ellington, Duke; Strayhorn, Billy); Sultry Sunset; There Was Nobody Looking (C: Ellington, Duke; Strayhorn, Billy)

Liberian Suite: I Like the Sunrise; Dance No. 1; No. 2; No. 3; No. 4; No. 5

Pop songs: He Makes Me Believe He's Mine (L: Latouche, John); I Don't Know Why I Love You So (L: Mills, Irving); Indigo Echoes (L: Mills, Irving); It's Kind of Lonesome Out Tonight (L: George, Don); Oh, Gee (L: Ellington, Duke); T.T. on Toast (L: Mills, Irving); Tough Truckin' (L: Mills, Irving); You're Just an Old Antidisestablishmentarianismist (C/L: Ellington, Duke; George, Don)

1951

Instrumentals: *Harlem Suite*

Controversial Suite: Before My Time; Later

1952

Show songs: Blues for Blanton; Personality; Rock Skippin' (C: Ellington, Duke; Strayhorn, Billy); Searsy's Blues; Smada (C: Ellington, Duke; Strayhorn, Billy)

Pop songs: Come on Home (L: Ellington, Duke)

1953

Instrumentals: Primping at the Prom

Pop songs: Ballin' the Blues (L: Ellington, Duke); Kind of Moody (L: Sigman, Carl); Merrie Mending (L: Ellington, Duke); Nothin', Nothin', Baby (Without You) (L:

Ellington, Duke); Satin Doll (L: Mercer, Johnny; Strayhorn, Billy); Silver Cobwebs (L: George, Don)

1954

Instrumentals: Alternate; B-Sharp Blues; Band Call; Chili Bowl; Janet; One-Sided Love Affair; Reflections in D; Retrospection; Serious Serenade in B-Flat Minor; Tan Your Hide (C: Ellington, Duke; Strayhorn, Billy); Who Knows

Pop songs: Blossom (C: Ellington, Duke; Strayhorn, Billy; L: Mercer, Johnny); Night Time (C: Ellington, Duke; Strayhorn, Billy; L: Julian, Doris)

1955

Instrumentals: Kinda Dukish; *Night Creatures* (Parts 1–3); My Reward; Orson (C: Ellington, Duke; Strayhorn, Billy); Reddy Eddy

Pop songs: Hand Me Down Love (L: Sigman, Carl); It's Rumor (L: Ellington, Duke); Like a Train (L: Ellington, Duke); Oo (C/L: Ellington, Duke; Strayhorn, Billy); She (L: Ellington, Duke); Twilight Time (L: Ellington, Duke); Weatherman (L: Ellington, Duke)

1956

Instrumentals: Cafe au Lait; Coolin' (C: Ellington, Duke; Terry, Clark); Cop-Out; Feetbone; Frivolous Banta (C: Ellington, Duke; Henderson, Rick); Happy One; Jumpy (C: Ellington, Duke; Stewart, Rex); Just Scratchin' the Surface; Killian's Lick; Rock 'n' Roll Rhapsody; Scenic; 610 Suite; Suburban Beauty

A Drum Is a Woman. Music by Duke Ellington and Billy Strayhorn: Ballet of the Flying Saucers; Carribee Joe; Congo Square; Drum Is a Woman, A; Finale; Hey, Buddy Bolden; Madame Zajj; Matumbe; New Orleans; Rhumbob; Rhythm Pum Te Dum; What Else Can You Do with a Drum?; Zajj's Dream

Pop songs: Sky Fell Down, The (L: Towne, Joanne)

1957

Instrumentals: Shades of Harlem; Wailing Interval; You Better Know It

Royal Ancestry (Portrait of Ella Fitzgerald). Music by Duke Ellington and Billy Strayhorn: All Heart; Beyond Category; Total Jazz

Shakespearean Suite. Music by Duke Ellington and Billy Strayhorn: Circle of Fourths; Half the Fun; Lady Mac; Madness in Great Ones; Sonnet for Caesar; Sonnet for Sister Kate; Sonnet in Search of a Moor; Sonnet to Hank Cinq; Star-Crossed Lovers, The; Such Sweet Thunder; Telecasters, The; Up and Down, Up and Down

Pop songs: Duke's Place (L: Katz, Bill; Roberts, Ruth; Thiele, Bob); Love (My Everything) (L: Ellington, Duke); Pomegranate (L: Strayhorn, Billy); Rock City Rock (L: Ellington, Duke)

1958

Instrumentals: Basement (AKA: Trombone Trio); Blues in Orbit (C: Ellington, Duke; Strayhorn, Billy); Blues in the Round; E and D Blues (C: Ellington, Duke; Sanders, John); Hi Fi Fo Fum; Jazz Festival Jazz (C: Ellington, Duke; Strayhorn, Billy); Jones (C: Ellington, Duke; Reddon, Pauline); Juniflip; Mr. Gentle and Mr.

Cool (C: Ellington, Duke; Rembert, Laura); Pauline's Blues (C: Ellington, Duke; Reddon, Pauline); Pauline's Jump (C: Ellington, Duke; Reddon, Pauline); Pleadin'; Prima Bara Dubla (C: Ellington, Duke; Strayhorn, Billy); Princess Blue; Soda Fountain Rag; Track 360 (AKA: Trains that Pass in the Night); Tune Poem

Toot Suite. Music by Duke Ellington and Billy Strayhorn: Ready-Go; Red Carpet; Red Garter; Red Shoes

Pop songs: Don't Ever Say Goodbye (C/L: Ellington, Duke; Putnam, Belinda; Putnam, Bill); Hundred Dreams from Now (Champagne Oasis), A (L: Burke, Johnny); My Heart, My Mind, My Everything (L: Ellington, Duke); Satin Doll (L: Mercer, Johnny; Strayhorn, Bill)

1959

Instrumentals: Bugs; Cop-Out Extension; Do Not Disturb; Dual Fuel (C: Ellington, Duke; Terry, Clark); Idiom '59; Launching Pad (C: Ellington, Duke; Terry, Clark); Le Sucrier Velour; Lightning Bugs and Frogs; Malletoba Spank (C: Ellington, Duke; Strayhorn, Billy); Nymph; Original; Swinger's Jump, The; Tymperturbably Blue (C: Ellington, Duke; Strayhorn, Billy)

Pop songs: But (L: Kuller, Sid); Show 'Em You Got Class (L: Kuller, Sid); Walkin' and Singin' the Blues (L: Greenwood, Lil); When I Trilly with My Filly (L: Kuller, Sid)

Show songs: *Anatomy of a Murder* (Film): Almost Cried (inst.); Flitbird (inst.); Grace Valse (inst.); Happy Anatomy (inst.); Haupe (inst.); Hero to Zero (inst.); I'm Gonna Go Fishin' (L: Lee, Peggy); Low Key Lightly (inst.); Midnight Indigo (inst.); Sunswept Sunday (inst.); Upper and Outest (inst.); Way Early Subtone (inst.)

Jump for Joy (Show). Lyrics by Sid Kuller: Concerto for Clinkers; Don't Believe Everything You Hear; Just Squeeze Me (L: Gaines, Lee; Webster, Paul Francis); Natives Are Restless Tonight, The; Nerves, Nerves, Nerves; Resigned to Living; So the Good Book Says; Strictly for Tourists; Three Shows Nightly; Within Me I Know

1960

Instrumentals: Blues in Blueprint; Idiom No. 2; Idiom No. 3; Swingers Get the Blues Too, The (C: Ellington, Duke; Gee, Matthew); Villes Ville Is the Place, Man

Nutcracker Suite: Composed by Tchaikovsky. Arranged by Duke Ellington and Billy Strayhorn: Arabesque Cookie (Arabian Dance); Chinoiserie (Chinese Dance); Dance of the Floreadores (Waltz of the Flowers); Entr'acte; Overture; Peanut Brittle Brigade (March); Sugar Rum Cherry (Dance of the Sugar Plum Cherry); Toot Toot Tootie Toot (Dance of the Reed Pipes); Volga Vouty, The (Russian Dance)

Pop songs: Like Love[6] (L: Russell, Bob)

1961

Instrumentals: Beautiful Americans, The; One More Once

---

[6]Based on an instrumental theme from *Anatomy of a Murder*.

Paris Blues: Autumnal Suite; Battle Royal; Birdie Jungle; Guitar Amour; Nite; Paris Blues; Paris Stairs; Wild Man Moore

The Girls: Introduction; Sarah; Lena; Mahalia; Dinah

Pop songs: Starting with You (I'm Through) (C/L: Ellington, Duke; Hodges, Johnny; Stewart, Pat); Without a Word of Complaint (C/L: Ellington, Duke; Hodges, Johnny; Weiss, George David)

Show songs: *Asphalt Jungle, The* (TV Show): I Want to Love You (L: Barer, Marshall)

1962

Instrumentals: B. D. B. (C: Ellington, Duke; Strayhorn, Billy); Dear (C: Ellington, Duke; Heywood, Donald); Fast and Furious (C: Ellington, Duke; Pottio, Harold); Introspection; Java Pachacha (Arranged by Ellington, Duke); Jollywog; Jump Over; Limbo Jazz; Lot O' Fingers; Night in Harlem, A; Oklahoma Stomp; *Peer Gynt Suite* (C: Grieg; Arranged by: Ellington, Duke; Strayhorn, Billy); Reconversion; Savage Rhythm; Self-Portrait of the Bean (C: Ellington, Duke; Strayhorn, Billy); Single Petal of a Rose; Slow Motion; Sponge Cake and Spinach; Sweet Dreams of Love (C: Ellington, Duke; Mills, Irving); Tell Me (C: Ellington, Duke; Gee, Jr., Matthew); What Would It Mean Without You? (C: Ellington, Duke; Mills, Irving; Brown, George); Who Said It's Tight Like This?; Wring Your Washin' Out (C: Ellington, Duke; Trent, Jo); You've Got the Love I Love (C: Ellington, Duke; Reese, Della)

Suite Thursday: Lay-By; Misfit Blues; Schwiphti; Zweet Zursday

Pop songs: And Then Some (L: Hodges, Johnny); Argentine (L: Mills, Irving; Parish, Mitchell); Blue Mood (C/L: Ellington, Duke; Hodges, Johnny); Down Home Stomp (L: Trent, Jo); Feeling of Jazz, The (L: Simon, George T.; Troup, Bobby); Framed (C: Ellington, Duke; Heywood, Donald; L: Razaf, Andy); Glamorous (L: Mills, Irving; Trent, Jo); Keep on Treating Me Sweet (L: Trent, Jo); Lazy Rhapsody (L: Parish, Mitchell); Stand By Blues (L: Hodges, Johnny); Swanee Lullaby (L: Mills, Irving; Parish, Mitchell); Sweet Dreams of Love (L: Mills, Irving); Twistin' Time (L: Bell, Aaron); What Would It Mean without You (C/L: Brown, George R.; Ellington, Duke; Mills, Irving); Who Is She? (C/L: Ellington, Duke; Mills, Irving; Schafer, Bob; Simmons, Rousseau); You've Got the Love I Love (C/L: Ellington, Duke; Reese, Della)

1963

Instrumentals: Action in Alexandria; Afro-Bossa; After Bird Jungle; Ain't But the One; Angu; Balcony Serenade; Blow by Blow; Blue Piano; Blues for Jerry (AKA: Blues to Jerry); Bonga; Caline; Coloratura; Congo; Dancers in Love; Fleurette Africaine; Fountainbleau Forest; Good Years of Jazz, The; Heritage; Hundred Dreams Ago, A; It's Bad to Be Forgotten; Jungle Triangle; Money Jungle; Moon Bow; Ninety-Nine Per Cent; *Perfume Suite*; Purple Gazelle (Angelica); Ray Charles' Place; Ricitic, The; Sempre Amore; Silk Lace; So; Strange Feeling; Take the Coltrane; Very Special; Volupte; Wig Wise; Will You Be There?; You Dirty Dog

Pop songs: Blue Piano (L: Katz, Bill; Roberts, Ruth; Thiele, Bob); Ever-Lovin' Lover (L: Ellington, Duke); Jail Blues (L: Ellington, Duke); King Fit the Battle of Alabam (L: Ellington, Duke); What Color Is Virtue? (L: Ellington, Duke)

1964

Instrumentals: It's Glory; La Scala, She Too Pretty to Be True; M.G.; Metromedia; New Tootie for Cootie; Non-Violent Integration; Rude Interlude; Springtime in Africa (C: Ellington, Duke; Bell, Aaron); Stoona; Workin' Blues

Far East Suite, The (C: Ellington, Duke; Strayhorn, Billy): Agra; Amad; Blue Bird of Delhi; Blue Pepper; Circle; Depk; Elf (Isfahan); Paki; Put-Tin; Tourist Point of View; Vict

Timon of Athens Suite: Alcibiades; Angry; Banquet; Counter Theme; Gold; Gossip; Gossippippi; Impulsive Giving; Ocean; Regal; Regal Formal; Revolutionary; Skilipop; Smoldering

Pop songs: My Man Sends Me (L: Ellington, Duke); My Mother, My Father and Love (L: Ellington, Duke); Searchin' (L: Allen, Steve); Tutti for Cootie (L: Hamilton, Jimmy)

Show songs: *Saturday Laughter* (Show). Lyrics by Herbert Martin: Big White Mountain; Bioscope Song, The; Full of Shadows; He Outfoxed the Fox; I Get Lonely for a Plaything; I Like Singing; It's Saturday; J. P. Williamson; My Arms; My Home Lies Quiet; New Shoes; Only Yesterday; They Say; This Man; You Are Lonely; You Walkin' My Dreams

1965

Instrumentals: Concerto for Oscar; Ellington '66; 58th Street Scene (C: Ellington, Duke; Strayhorn, Billy); On Account of You; Tokyo (C: Ellington, Duke; Hamilton, Jim); Warm Fire

Far East Suite, The: Ad Lib on Nippon; Fugi; Nagoya

Virgin Islands Suite (C: Ellington, Duke; Strayhorn, Billy): Barefoot Stomper; Big Fat Alice's Blues; Fade Up; Fiddle on the Diddler; Island Virgin; Jungle Kitty; Mysterious Chick; Virgin Jungle

[First] Sacred Concert: In the Beginning, God; Tell Me the Truth; The Lord's Prayer. The remaining pieces drawn from various earlier works, including *Black, Brown and Beige*, *My People*, and *New World A-Comin'*

Pop songs: Be a Man (L: Barer, Marshall); Christmas Surprise (C: Ellington, Duke; Strayhorn, Billy; L: Bartlett, Rev. D.J.); Flugel Street Rag (L: Barer, Marshall); Girl's Best Friend, A (L: Barer, Marshall); Golden Broom and the Green Apple, The (L: Barer, Marshall); Love Came (C: Strayhorn, Billy; L: Ellington, Duke); My Heart Is a Stranger (L: Barer, Marshall); Salvation (L: Barer, Marshall); Truth, The (L: Ellington, Duke); Up Your Ante (L: Barer, Marshall)

1966

Instrumentals: Imbo (Limbo Jazz); Twitch, The; Veldt-Amor; West Indian Pancake; You Are Beautiful; You Walk in My Dreams

Pop songs: House of Lords (L'Earl—Le Duke) (C/L: Ellington, Duke; Hines, Earl); Imagine My Frustration (C/L: Ellington, Duke; Strayhorn, Billy; Wilson, Gerald); Jive Stomp (L: Ellington, Duke); Mount Harissa (L: Ellington, Duke); Second Portrait of the Lion, The (L: Ellington, Duke); Song for Christmas, A (C/L: Bartlett, Dean; Ellington, Duke; Strayhorn, Billy); Spanking Brand New Doll (L: Ellington, Duke); Tell Me It's the Truth (L: Ellington, Duke)

Show songs: *Pousse-Café* (Show). Lyrics by Marshall Barer: Amazing; C'est Comme Ça; Colonel's Lady, The; Do Me a Favor; Easy to Take; Eleventh Commandment, The; Follow Me Up the Stairs; Forever; Goodbye, Charlie; Here You Are; If I Knew Now; Je N'ai Rien; Let's; Natchez Trace; Old World Charm; Rules and Regulations; Settle for Less; Someone to Care For; Spacious and Gracious; Spider and Fly, The; Sugar City; Swivel; Thank You Ma'am; These Are the Good Old Days; Wedding, The

1967

Instrumentals: Bolling; Chromatic Love Affair; Drag; Eggo; Girdle Hurdle; Lady; Lele; Malay Camp; Man Beneath, The; Man Sees Nothing; Mara-Gold; Matador, The (El Viti); My Home Lies Quiet; New Shoes; Nob Hill; Ocht O'Clock Rock; Plaything; Poco Mucho; Rock the Clock; Rondelet; Rue Bleue; Salute to Morgan State; Swamp Goo; They Say; This Man; Three; Tin Soldier; To the Better; Traffic Jam; Up Jump; Here in the World?; Workin' Blues

La Plus Belle Africaine: Canon; Cham; Circus; Come Easter; Crispy; Eliza; Fatness; Full of Shadows; I Like Singing; J. P. Williamson; Kisse; Laying on Mellow

Murder in the Cathedral: Becket; Exotique Bongos; Gold; Land; Martyr; Women's

Pop songs: Baby, You're Too Much (C/L: Ellington, Duke; George, Don)

1968

Instrumentals: Keor; Kiki; Ritz

Pop songs: Be Cool and Groovy for Me (C/L: Bennett, Tony; Ellington, Duke; Williams, Cootie); Finesse (C/L: Ellington, Duke; Hodges, Johnny); I Fell and Broke My Heart (L: George, Don); I Have Given My Love (L: Petremont, Patricia); My Lonely Love (L: Petremont, Patricia); Night Train to Memphis (C/L: Anderson, Cat; Ellington, Duke); Tokyo (C/L: Ellington, Duke; Hamilton, Jimmy); When You've Had It All (L: Petremont, Patricia); Woman (L: Ellington, Duke); You Make That Hat Look Pretty (L: Ellington, Duke); You're a Little Black Sheep (L: George, Don)

Second Sacred Concert. Lyrics by Duke Ellington: Don't Get Down on Your Knees to Pray Until You Have Forgiven Everyone; Father Forgive; Freedom (Parts 1–7); Freedom (Sweet Fat and That) (C/L: Ellington, Duke; Smith, Willie "The Lion"); Freedom (Word You Heard); God Has Those Angels; Heaven; Something 'Bout Believing; T.G.T.T.

1969

Latin American Suite: Oclupaca; The Sleeping Lady and the Giant Who Watches Over Her; Latin American Sunshine; Brasilliance

Instrumentals: Elos; Gigl; Knuf; Reva

Pop songs: Anticipation and Hesitation (L: Ellington, Duke); Just a Gentle Word from You Will Do (C/L: Ellington, Duke; Matthews, Onzy); Mexicali Brass (C/L: Ellington, Duke; Matthews, Onzy); Moon Maiden (L: Ellington, Duke); Moon Suite, The (L: Ellington, Duke)

1970

Instrumentals: Afrique; Black Swan; Fife; Fifi; 4:30 Blues; Hard; In Triplicate; Mixt; Pamp; Rapid; Rext; Soft; Spring, The; Stud; What Time Is It?

River, The (Ballet): Falls, The; Giggling Rapids, The; Lake, The; Meander; Mother, Her Majesty the Sea, The; River, The; Run, The; Village of the Virgins, The; Well; Whirlpool, The

1971

Instrumentals: Brot; Dick; Everybody Wants to Know Why I Sing the Blues; Hard Way, The; Hick; Loud; Math; Opus 69; Ray Charles' Place; Roth; Snek

Afro-Eurasian Eclipse: Acac; Buss; Dash; Dijb; Nbdy; Gong; Sche; Soso; Tego; Tenz; True; Yoyo

Goutelas Suite, The: Gigi; Gogo I; Gogo II; Goof

New Orleans Suite: Aristocracy à la Jean Lafitte; Blues for New Orleans; Bourbon Street Jingling Jollies; Portrait of Louis Armstrong; Portrait of Mahalia Jackson; Portrait of Sidney Bechet; Portrait of Wellman Braud; Second Line; Thanks for the Beautiful Land on the Delta

Pop songs: 99 Percent (L: Ellington, Duke); Blues Ain't, The (L: Ellington, Duke); Cafe (L: Ellington, Duke); Lovin' Lover (L: Ellington, Duke); Perdido Cha Cha Cha (L: Ellington, Duke); Road of the Phoebe Snow (C/L: Ellington, Duke; Strayhorn, Billy)

1972

Instrumentals: Mich

UWIS Suite, The: UWIS; Klop; Loco Madi

Pop songs: Almighty God (L: Ellington, Duke); Everyone (L: Ellington, Duke); New York, New York (L: Ellington, Duke); Tina (L: Ellington, Duke)

1973

Instrumentals: Addi; Soul Flute (Flute Ame)

Togo Brava Suite: Amour, Amour; Naturelement; Right On Togo; Soul Soothing Beach

Third Sacred Concert ("The Majesty of God"): Ain't Nobody Nowhere Nothin' Without God; Brotherhood, The; Every Man Prays in His Own Language; Hallelujah; Is God A Three Letter Word for Love?; Lord's Prayer, The; Majesty of God, The; My Love

Three Black Kings (composed, but not performed until after his death)

Pop songs: Celebration (L: Ellington, Duke); I Need a Change of Sky (L: Harburg, E.Y.); Jumping Room Only (L: Ellington, Duke); Rainy Nights (L: Ellington, Duke)

1986

Show songs: *Queenie Pie* (Opera). Lyrics by Duke Ellington and George David Weiss: All Hail the Queen; Blues for Two Young Women; Cafe Au Lait; Discovery of Queenie Pie on the Beach; Earthquake; Epilogue; Finale; Finale Act I; Hairdo Hop, The; Harlem Scat; Hawk, The; Hey, I Don't Need Nobody Now; Island Update 1; Island Update 2; It's Time for Something New; My Father's Island; Oh Gee; Queenie Pie; Rhumbop; Smile As You Go By; Soliloquy; Stix; Style; There; Truly a Queen; Two Cat Scat Fight; Woman; Won't You Come Into My Boudoir

Bibliography

Adler, Larry. *It Ain't Necessarily So.* London: Collins, 1984.

Bigard, Barney. *With Louis and the Duke.* New York: Oxford University Press, 1985.

Bushell, Garvin, and Mark Tucker. *Jazz from the Beginning.* Ann Arbor: University of Michigan Press, 1988.

Collier, James Lincoln. *Duke Ellington.* New York: Oxford University Press, 1987.

Dance, Stanley. *The World of Duke Ellington.* New York: Scribner's, 1971.

———. *The World of Swing.* New York: Da Capo Press Inc., 1970

Deffaa, Chip. *Voices of the Jazz Age.* Champaign, IL: University of Illinois Press, 1992.

Dodge, Rodger Pryor. *Hot Jazz and Hot Dance.* New York: Oxford University Press, 1995.

Driggs, Frank, and Harris Lewine. *Black Beauty, White Heat.* New York: William Morrow and Company, 1982.

Durante, Jimmy, and Jack Kofoed. *Night Clubs.* New York: Alfred Knopf, 1955.

Ellington, Duke. *Music Is My Mistress.* Garden City, NY: Doubleday & Company, Inc., 1973.

Ellington, Mercer, and Stanley Dance. *Duke Ellington in Person.* Boston: Houghton Mifflin, 1978.

Erenberg, Lewis A. *Swingin' The Dream: Big Band Jazz and the Rebirth of American Culture.* Chicago: The University of Chicago Press, 1998.

Gammond, Peter. *Duke Ellington, His Life and Music.* New York: Da Capo Press Inc., 1958.

George, Don. *Sweet Man.* New York: G. P. Putnam's Sons, 1981.

Giddens, Gary. *Visions of Jazz.* New York: Oxford University Press, 1998.

Goggins, Jacqueline. *Carter Woodson.* Baton Rouge, LA: Louisiana State University Press, 1993.

Hadju, David. *Lush Life.* New York: Farrar Straus & Giroux, 1996.

Haskins, James. *Bricktop.* New York: Athaneum, 1983.

———. *Cotton Club.* New York: Random House, 1977.

Hasse, John E. *Beyond Category: The Life and Genius of Duke Ellington.* New York: Simon & Schuster, 1995.

Hentoff, Nat, and Nat Shapiro. *Hear Me Talkin' to Ya.* New York: Rhinehart & Company, 1955.

Horne, Lena, and Richard Schickel. *Lena.* Garden City, NY: Doubleday, 1965.

Huggins, Nathan I. *Harlem Renaissance.* New York: Oxford University Press. 1971.

Hughes, Langston. *Famous Negro Music Makers.* New York: Dodd Mead, 1955.

Jewell, Derek. *Duke.* New York: W.W. Norton, 1977.

Johnson, James W. *Black Manhattan.* New York: Da Capo Press Inc., 1991.

Kellner, Bruce. *Carl Van Vecten and the Irreverant Decades.* Norman, OK: University of Oklahoma Press, 1965.

Lambert, Constant, *Music Ho!* New York: Scribners, 1934.

Leider, Emily. *Becoming Mae West.* New York: Farrar, Straus & Giroux, 1997.

Motion, Andrew. *The Lamberts, George, Constant & Kit.* New York: Farrar, Straus & Giroux, 1986.

Nicholson, Stewart. *Reminiscing in Tempo: A Portrait of Duke Ellington.* Boston, MA: Northeastern University Press, 1999.

Nown, Graham. *English Godfather.* London: Ward Lock, 1987.

Schuller, Gunther. *Early Jazz.* New York: Oxford University Press, 1968.

———. *The Swing Era.* New York: Oxford University Press, 1989.

Smith, Willie "The Lion." *Music on My Mind.* New York: Da Capo Press Inc., 1971.

Stearns, Marshall. *The Story of Jazz.* New York: Oxford University Press, 1956.

Stewart, Rex. *Jazz Masters of the 30's.* New York: Da Capo Press Inc., 1982.

———. *Boy Meets Horn.* Ann Arbor, MI: University of Michigan Press.

Stratemann, Klaus. *Duke Ellington: Day by Day & Film by Film.* Copenhagen, Denmark: Jazz Media, 1992.

Sylvester, Robert. *No Cover No Charge: A Backward Look at the Night Clubs.* New York: Dial Press, 1955.

Tucker, Mark. *Duke Ellington: The Early Years.* Champaign, IL: University of Illinois Press, 1991.

Ulanov, Barry. *Duke Ellington.* New York: Da Capo Press Inc., 1972.

Waters, Ethel. *His Eye Is on the Sparrow.* Garden City, NY: Doubleday & Company, 1951.

Sources

All quotes by Ruth Ellington Boatwright, Lawrence Brown, Harry Carney, Benny Carter, Willie Cook, Robert Donaldson Darrell, Wilbur DeParis, Bessie Dudley, Mercer Ellington, Frank Galbreath, Sonny Greer, Fred Guy, Jimmy Hamilton, Lionel Hampton, Coleman Hawkins, Johnny Hodges, Charlie Holmes, Manzie Johnson, Walter Johnson, Geraldine Lockhart, Olive Moales, Sy Oliver, Mitchell Parrish, Russell Procope, Luis Russell, Billy Strayhorn, Fredi Washington, Tom Whaley, and Cootie Williams are taken from personal interviews with the author, unless otherwise noted.

Abbreviation:
MIIM = *Music Is My Mistress*

Prelude
"I know of no other. . ." Constant Lambert, *Music Ho!,* p. 214.

1
"kneeling, sitting, standing. . ." Duke Ellington, *Music Is My Mistress,* p. 6.
"pampered and spoiled. . ." Ibid., p. 6.
"I never seen nothing like it. . ." Don George, *Sweet Man,* p. 32.
"Maybe we never had a complete genuine set. . ." Mercer Ellington with Stanley Dance, *Duke Ellington in Person,* p. 9.
"The mark is still there. . ." Ellington, MIMM, p. 9
"After all. . ." Ellington, MIMM, p. 9.
"Believing gave me that. . ." Ellington, MIMM, p. 15.
"he ran into. . ." Ellington, MIMM. p. x.

2
"Woodson's work gives. . ." Jacqueline Goggins, *Carter Woodson,* p. 31.
"They had a pride there. . ." Ellington, MIMM, p. 17.
"When I got home. . ." Ibid., p. 20.
"I learned the work. . ." Ibid.
"I had two educations. . ." John E. Hasse, *Beyond Category: The Life and Genius of Duke Ellington,* p. 254.
"You do a lot of listening. . ." Ellington, MIMM. p. 23.
"I used to spend nights listening. . ." Ibid., p. 26.
"He was intelligent. . ." Ibid.
"He was the most perfect. . ." Ibid., p. 28.
"He broke me in. . ." Ibid.

"There were a lot of people. . ." Ibid., p. 31.
"basic contempt for women. . ." Mercer Ellington, p. 128.
"It was too close to the first. . ." Stuart Nicholson, *Reminiscing in Tempo*, p. 17.

3

"From the moment I was introduced. . ." Stanley Dance, *The World of Duke Ellington*,
    p. 62.
"My first impression of the Lion. . ." Ellington, MIMM, p. 90.
"The greatest influence. . ." Ellington MIMM, p. 92.
"I took a liking. . ." Willie "The Lion" Smith, *Music on My Mind*, p. 150.
"We got to Washington. . ." Hasse, pp. 71-72.
"Guy practically owned the place. . ." Ellington, MIMM, p. 69.
"Men had to wear jackets. . ." James Haskins, *Bricktop*, pp. 77–78.
"Bon viveurs from all the strata of society. . ." Konrad Bercovici, "The Black Blocks of
    Harlem," *Harpers*, October, 1924.
"This action would go jingling. . ." Ellington, MIMM, p. 64.
"We'd got our feet on the first rung. . ." Dance, p. 57.
"Our music. . ." Stanley Dance, *The World of Swing*, p. 53.
"As I remember it. . ." Smith, p. 103.
"intelligent, a good showman. . ." Ethel Waters, *His Eye Is on the Sparrow*, p. 151.
"If a guy puts his elbows. . ." Chip Deffaa, *Voices of the Jazz Age*.
"Just a blues. . ." Ellington, MIMM, p. 73.

5

"Bubber and I. . ." Garvin Bushell and Mark Tucker, *Jazz From The Beginning*,
    p. 25.
"got Bubber stiff. . ." Nicholson, p. 48.
"at a crossroads in his life. . ." Ellington, MIMM, p. x.
"In spite of ten pianos. . ." Ellington, MIMM, p. 70.
"Jo Trent came running up to me. . ." Ellington, MIMM, p. 71.
"How was I to know. . ." Ibid.
"They were calling for encores. . ." Bushell and Tucker, p. 55.

6

"Will Marion Cook. . ." Ellington, MIMM, p. 95.
"They are pathetic, tender, passionate. . ." *New York Herald*, May 21, 1893.
"He and I would get in a taxi. . ." Ellington, MIMM, p. 95.
"You know you should go. . ." Ibid., p. 96.
"Will Vodery was a strict. . ." Ibid., p. 98.
"Sometimes he would bring. . ." Ibid.
"organized Negro music. . ." Nathan I. Huggins, *Harlem Renaissance*, p. 64.

7

"out of the whole. . ." James Lincoln Collier, *Duke Ellington*, p. 56.
"He always showed his appreciation. . ." Ellington, MIMM, p. 71.
"The first week I had to wait. . ." Tucker, p. 189.
"For Christ's sakes, Dumpy. . ." Rex Stewart, *Jazz Masters of the 30's*, p. 108.

"He and Tricky Sam..." Dance, p. 74.
"pop songs, jazz songs, dirty songs..." Ellington, MIMM, p. 72.

8

"Immediately I thought of the quick change..." Irving Mills interview, Oral History, American Music Program, Yale University.

9

"That's what I wanted to do more than any thing..." and "sort of like a prayer" Mark Tucker, *Duke Ellington*, p. 195.
"Have four numbers ready..." Ellington, MIMM, p. 73.
"Duke knew what he wanted..." Nat Hentoff and Nat Shapiro, *Hear Me Talkin' to Ya*, p. 234.
"In those early days..." Dance, p. 59.

10

"My mother will tell me..." Dance, p. 73.

11

"Everyone had freedom of expression..." Dance, p. 60
"He started to play..." Adelaide Hall interview in *The NY Times*, April 15, 1983.
"The night before I recorded with Duke..." Jabbo Smith in liner notes to *Giants of Jazz: Duke Ellington*, Time Life series of jazz recordings.

12

"Harlem was like a magnet..." Langston Hughes, *Famous Negro Music Makers*, p. 111.
"This was the Harlem..." Bruce Kellner, *Carl Van Vecten and the Irreverent Decades*, p. 18.
"It was known as exotic..." James Weldon Johnson, *Black Manhattan*, p. 160.
"hottest gin mill on 133rd Street..." Ellington, MIMM. p. 92.
"a bantam rooster..." Emily Leider, *Becoming Mae West*, p. 146.
"They were open and genuine..." Leider, p. 147.
"The bandstand was..." Hasse, p. 102.
"It was a joke..." Deffaa, p. 21.
"One night Chick Webb's whole band..." Ibid. p. 197.

13

"Mother Machree..." Gammond, p. 55.
"In the beginning a lot of them..." Dance, p. 75.
"Clutching his sides and rolling..." Nicholson, p. 122.
"Into its vortex..." Huggins, p. 89.
"You go sort of primative up there..." Jimmy Durante and Jack Kofoed, *Night Clubs*, p. 114.
"The shows had a primative, naked quality..." Lena Horne and Richard Schickel, *Lena*, p. 104.
"I recall one..." Marshall Stearns, *The Story of Jazz*, p. 183.
"It was quite a shock..." Nicholson, p. 79.
"Thanks kid..." Frank Driggs, Harris Lewine, *Black Beauty, White Heat*, p. 93.

14

"that unusual, rich, slightly dark. . ." Gunther Schuller, *Early Jazz*, p. 337.
"Duke must have heard that, I guess. . ." Barney Bigard, p. 45.
"had an accident, went through the windshield. . ." Nicholson, p. 85.
"That band was jumping. . ." Nappy Howard, *Jazz Journal*, December, 1970.
"I was playing in a little cabaret. . ."*Downbeat*, June 7, 1962.
"I always did like it. . ." Ibid.
"spoil those pretty looks. . ." Derek Jewell, *Duke*, p. 31.

16

"I know of nothing. . ." Lambert, p. 214.
"Duke would always say to me. . ." Dance, p. 114.
"wouldn't be surprised. . ." Nicholson, p. 85.
"did much better on the stage. . ." *New York Times*, July 3, 1929.

18

"My father would insist. . ." Ellington, MIMM, p. 10.
"I didn't know the first thing about how to emcee. . ." Collier, p. 98.
"There's no money in it for me. . ." Robert Sylvester, *No Cover No Charge*, p. 66.

19

"The ever present rhythms. . ." Peter Gammons, *Duke Ellington*, p. 167.

20

"Those shows by Arlen. . ." Hasse, p. 131.
"blackest white man. . ." Haskins, p. 77.
"The resulting tonal colors. . ." Hasse, p. 142
A succession of two and four bar. . ." Schuller, *Early Jazz*, p. 334.

21

"The first time I was copying. . ." Dance, p. 50.
"Significantly, while those men who. . ." Huggins, p. 188.

22

"Jonesy . . ." Mercer Ellington, p. 54.
"Suddenly I sensed the truth. . ." *Washington Post*, September 1, 1983.
"The leader of the choir. . ." Dance, p. 119.

23

"I thought to myself. . ." Dance, p. 59.
"[Miley] had an infectious and winning personality. . ." *Hot Jazz* and *Hot Dance*,
    p. 258.

24

"I'll have to find out about this Delius. . ." Hasse, p. 163.

25

"After that we had the run. . ." Bigard, p. 69.
"Is it possible for a Negro. . ." *Sunday Express*, London June 10, 1933.

"It has remained for us to discover. . ." *Daily Herald*, London, June 13, 1933.
"I was sixteen, a full time fan. . ." Smithsonian Jazz Oral History Project.
"I was nineteen years old. . ." Ibid.
"How to describe in so many words. . ." *Era*, June 16, 1933.

26

"I attended the Astoria dance. . ." Smithsonian Jazz Oral History Project.
"I saw many coloured dresses. . ." *Daily Express*, London June 28, 1933.
"The applause should come. . ." *Melody Maker*, June 24, 1933.
"We all stood outside the hall. . ." Smithsonian Jazz Oral History Project.
"Is Duke Ellington losing faith. . ." *Melody Maker*, July 1, 1933.
"While in Liverpool. . ." *Glasgow Sunday Post*, July 9, 1933.
"the mob was like a bunch of kids. . ." Derek Jewell, p. 53.
"I was flattered. . ." Ellington, MIMM. p. 84.
"Since that time. . ." Ibid., p. 84.
"[Lambert] sought to recapture. . ." Andrew Motion, *The Lamberts*, p. 135.
"so much last Sunday. . ." *Melody Maker*, July 22, 1933.
"I was 10 years old. . ." *New York*, June 20, 1988.
"The orchestration on nearly. . ." *Sunday Referee*, June 25, 1933.
"The 'melancholy' of the Negro Spiritual. . ." *New Britain*, June 28, 1933.
"If I can only write it down as. . ." *Daily Herald*, June 10, 1933.
"That we thought, was just about. . ." Dance, p. 77.
"It was perhaps the most riotous scene. . ." J. A. Rodgers, *New York Age*, August 9,
    1933.
"The affection and admiration. . ." Mercer Ellington, p. 61.
"The two on the end. . ." Ibid.

27

"somebody shouted, 'Lets take. . ." Hasse, p. 176.
"They've got us coming in and leaving. . ." Ibid.
"We commanded respect. . ." Nicholson, p. 165.
"I was but a young boy. . ." Hasse, p. 179.
"We found out one of the girls. . ." Stratemann, p. 82.
"just right for our New Orleans. . ." Leider, p. 292.
"Well you little prick, we got Ellington. . ." Adler, p. 69.

28

"put into the Dirge all the misery. . ." *New Theater*, December 1935.
"it was the high spot. . ." Ibid.
"In terms of plot. . ." Stratteman, p. 123.
"All the family was sent for. . ." Mercer Ellington, p. 68.
"I would sit and gaze into space. . ." Ellington, MIMM, p. 86.
"The memory of things gone by. . ." Gammond, p. 27.
"I wrote it. . ." Ibid, p. 89.
"Very briefly, I. . ." *Swing Music*, December, 1935.
"There are. . .passages. . ." Ibid.

"To me that piece of music. . ." Jewell, p. 157.
"For all its compositional. . ." Gunther Shuller, *Swing Era*, p. 83.
"Ellington kept his eyes averted. . ." Lewis Erenberg, *Swingin' the Dream*, p. 144.
"The real trouble. . ." Ibid.
"a propagandist and champion. . ." Ibid.

29

"his and a few other orchestras. . ." Hasse, p. 197.
"Louis Armstrong's rhythmic innovations. . ." Hasse, p. 197.

30

"The governor, as Duke was called. . ." Nicholson, p. 178.
"What Tchaikovsky's Arab Dance. . ." Schuller, p. 89.
"Edward's closest friend. . ." George, p. 240.

31

"With his phenomenal phrasing. . ." Ellington, MIMM, p. 221.
"One's initial reaction is, in fact, disbelief. . ." Schuller, p. 94.
"After he and Mil had come. . ." Mercer Ellington, p. 78.
"Why young man. . ." David Hadju, *Lush Life*, p. 57.

32

"He always preserved. . ." Ellington MIMM, p. 89.
"hundreds of jitterbugs. . ." Onah L. Spencer, "French J-Bugs in Wild Welcome for
    Ellington," *Downbeat*, May 1939.
"We were awarded an uproarious reception. . ." MIMM, p. 150.
"As we were heading across Holland. . ." Bigard, p. 75.
"really accepted throughout. . ." Hasse, p. 223.
"The platforms of the railway. . ." Ibid., p. 224.
"Their refined appearance. . ." Ibid.
"the most exciting event of the trip. . ." Ellington, MIMM, p. 152.
"When you've eaten hot dogs. . ." Barry Ulanov, *Duke Ellington*, p. 216.

33

"The guys in the band never heard me. . ." Hadju, p. 61.
"What the hell are we paying all that rent for?. . ." Hadju, p. 58.
"His tone was astonishingly full. . ." Schuller, p. 111.
"His amazing talent. . ." Rex Stewart, *Boy Meets Horn*, p. 196.
"Blanton's full firm tone. . ." Schuller, p. 112.
"One day he was doing his. . ." Nicholson. p. 210.
"When I first went with Duke's band. . ." Gary Giddens, *Visions of Jazz*, p. 237.
"whose musical conception. . ." Schuller, p. 113.

34

"With few exceptions. . ." Giddens, p. 233.
"Duke originally wrote. . ." Nicholson, p. 215.
"a triumph of form and content. . ." Schuller, p. 116.
"an idea for a new tune. . ." Ellington, MIMM, p. 150.
"Conga Brava is most. . ." Schuller, p. 119.

"although Williams may be the main speaker. . ." Mark Tucker, liner notes to "Webster-Blanton band" on RCA-Victor.
". . .dignity under. . ." Schuller, p. 121.
"Does the similarity mean. . ." Mark Tucker, liner notes to "Webster-Blanton band."
"One morning I'm at home. . ." Dance, p. 137.

35
"the original script had Uncle Tom on his death bed. . ." Giddens, p. 246.
"The Republicans reveled in it. . ." Ibid.
"though it spun no narrative. . ." Ulanov, p. 246.

36
"It was really overdedication. . ." Mercer Ellington, p. 86.
"I made a date. . ." Ellington, MIMM, p. 165.
"somewhere out near Pasadena. . ." Ellington, MIMM, p. 166.
"When I told him. . ." Bigard, p. 77.

37
"slave ships. . ." Hasse, p. 262.
"Duke stood before. . ." Ulanov, p. 251.
"Even as early. . ." Schuller, p. 141.
"was a tone parallel. . ." Ellington, MIMM, p. 181.
"Ellington's most sinuously beautiful. . ." Schuller, p. 145.
"when things were darkest for the states. . ." Hasse, p. 263.
"when Ellington played a concert. . ." James Lincoln Collier *Duke Ellington*, p. 220
"the formal uncertainty. . ." Schuller, p. 147.
"Between the dance numbers. . ." Ulanov, p. 257.
"Mr. Ellington has set for himself. . ." Ibid.
"Such a form. . ." Ibid.
"If you ask me. . ." Ibid.
"all but falls apart. . ." Ibid.
"was the same. . ." Schuller, p. 148.
"sort of withdrawn and very quiet. . ." Hasse, p. 263.

38
"He'd do a lot of things. . ." Bigard, p. 54.
"I visualized this new world. . ." Ellington, MIMM, p. 183.
"He was always happy. . ." Mercer Ellington, p. 95.
"He said the reason. . ." Ibid. p. 23.
"When I wrote 'On a Turquoise Cloud'. . ." Nicholson, p. 273.
"the help was not allowed to socialize with the guests. . ." Nicholson, p. 263.
"no other dance band. . ." Klaus Stratemann, *Duke Ellington Day by Day & Film by Film*, p. 262.
"Come down to Abernathy's. . ." Luis Russell's telephone call to the author, April 15, 1944.
"This space was reserved. . ." Stratemann, p. 263.
"Duke asked me to come with him. . ." Dance, p. 162.
"Russell was a good combination. . ." Ellington, MIMM, p. 222.

39

"Isn't it about time. . ." *Downbeat*, June 17, 1949.
"spent his time happily in Curzon Street apartment. . ." Jewell, p. 107.
"Once breakfasting with them. . ." Ibid.
"You grow and grow. . ." Nicholson, p. 276.
"He blamed different things. . ." Mercer Ellington, p. 157
"At the Palladium. . ." Jewell, p. 111.
"There was an old belief. . ." Mercer Ellington, p. 137.
"He evolved a medley. . ." Mercer Ellington, p. 167.
"If I die tomorrow. . ." Dance, p. 172.
"Sure I pulled Johnny. . ." Jewell, p. 115.
"It seemed like a stupid. . ." Nicholson, p. 301.

40

"Here and there in the reduced. . ." *Downbeat*, August 8, 1956.
"Within an hour. . ." Ibid.
"I was born in 1956. . ." Nicholson, p. 309.
"Of the big things. . ." Stratemann, p. 535.
"Music and television history. . ." *Downbeat*, June 27, 1957.
"He wrote lyrics. . ." Nicholson, p. 312.
"He said to me. . ." Nicholson, p. 312.
"Until the end of his life. . ." Ibid.
"in minature and caricature. . ." Irving Townsend, liner notes to the recording *Such Sweet Thunder*.
"He and Billy really. . ." Mercer Ellington, p. 117.
"we had to interpret his words. . ." Dance p. 32.
"I'm only sorry. . ." Ibid.
"the Ellington opus that stole the show. . ." Stratemann, p. 375.
"I was so sorry that I couldn't. . ." Jewell, p. 133.
"Enormous crowds had. . ." Stanley Dance, Press release. Ellington Archives, Smithsonian Institution of American History.
"I was so thrilled. . ." Ibid.
"When I attended a few concerts. . ." Nicholson, p. 318.
"The Single Petal of a Rose. . ." Mercer Ellington, p. 119.
"We would have liked to have. . ." Ibid.
". . . a million lightening bugs. . ." Ibid.
"Ellington went about the. . ." Collier, p. 286.
"Anatomy of a Murder. . ." Nicholson, p. 320
"this score. . .wins an important. . ." Stratemann, p. 407.
"I went to his birthday. . ." Nicholson, p. 322.
"My contribution was Aaron Bell. . ." Ibid, p. 323.
"Jimmy Woode was still. . ." Dance, p. 207.
"She was a tall. . ." Nicholson, p. 369.
"smartly dressed in a mink coat. . ." Mercer Ellington, p. 126.
"She knew the city. . ." Jewell, p. 136.
"When they arrived at an airport. . ." George, p. 142.
"Fernandae was like Duke's personal. . ." Ibid.

"Fernandae always ordered. . ." Ibid.
"She makes sure. . ." George, p. 142.
"She floated into the jewelry store. . ." Ibid. p. 143.
"She did a lot for Edward. . ." Jewell, p. 136.
"Unlike the most. . ." Mercer Ellington, p. 126.

41

"It took us quite a bit of time. . ." Dance, p. 32.
"The critics all complained. . ." Ibid.
"I have to write for specific artists. . ." Stratemann, p. 432
"It was like stepping. . ." Mercer Ellington, p. 133.
"Sometimes Goodman would. . ." Dance, p. 112.
"I used to run out. . ." Nicholson, p. 346.
"Ellington when he did *My People*. . ." Ibid., p. 348.
"Martin is sitting there. . ." Ibid.
"while its individual components. . ." Stratemann, p. 474.
"music for a ballroom ballet. . ." Ibid., p. 473.
"I found him there physically. . ." Nicholson, p. 352.
"Edward was besides himself. . ." Ibid., p. 354.
"Duke Ellington was impressed. . ." Ibid., p. 355.
"who had led me by the hand. . ." Mercer Ellington, p. 136.
"what I considered the proper. . ." Ibid., p. 137.
"I started beefing, hollering. . ." Ibid.
"To show their objection. . ." Ibid.
"She handled everything like nobody could. . ." Nicholson, p. 197.
"Ruth did not allow Evie in her home. . ." Nicholson, p. 276.
"She loved life. . ." Ibid., p. 376.
"I didn't want a divorce. . ." Ibid., p. 102.

42

"We took second billing. . ." Ibid.
"When we were in England. . ." Ibid.
"one of the bad Westerns I had seen. . ." Stratemann, p. 350.
"This music is the most important. . ." Jewell, p. 153.
"I could never figure out. . ." Mercer Ellington, p. 138.
"Arthur said Edward just cried. . ." Nicholson, p. 378.
"There was no way to describe. . ." George, p. 178.
"Strayhorn was the genius. . ." Nicholson, p. 378.
"Because it violates. . ." Duke Ellington, liner notes to *Second Sacred Concert.*
"I enjoy being with Duke. . ." Dance, p. 234.
"The generosity and enthusiasm. . ." Nicholson, p. 384.

43

"We buried him. . ." Ibid.
"I drew up the guest list. . ." Nicholson, p. 386.
"Ruth, her son. . ." Jewell, p. 190.
"He had this thing. . ." Nicholson, p. 386.
"He crossed. . ." George, p. 185.

"I played. . ." Nicholson, p. 387.
"And when we got. . ." Ibid., p. 389.

44

"In the studio. . ." Stanley Dance, liner notes to *New Orleans Suite*.
"It gave me a chill. . ." Ibid.
"Bechet is not forgotten. . ." Ibid.
"After his health. . ." Mercer Ellington, p. 110.
"On the flight back home. . ." Ibid.
"We did what, five weeks. . ." Nicholson, p. 396.
"He always did. . ." Mercer Ellington, Ibid. p. 396.
"one hour after we arrived. . ." Nicholson, p. 397.
"When we got to Caracas. . ." Ibid.
"I don't know how. . ." Mercer Ellington, p. 172.
"Everything is moonlight. . ." George, p. 237.

45

"That woman was something. . ." Ibid.
"I have never been so unprepared. . ." Ibid.
"After I got my band uniform on. . ." Ibid.
"if the General Assembly. . ." Jewell, p. 219.
"Everyman prays to God. . ." Ibid.
"It was the third time I saw him cry. . ." Ibid.
"Edward called me. . ." Jewell, p. 224.
"That last trip he was on. . ." Nicholson, p. 407.
"From the way he said. . ." Ibid.
"early in the morning. . ." Nicholson, p. 408.
"He recognized time was a factor. . ." Mercer Ellington, p. 202.
"Even though the intense sedation. . ." Nicholson, p. 408.
"I was there. . ." Nicholson, p. 406.
"The night he was dying. . ." Nicholson, p. 409.
"He departed quietly. . ." Mercer Ellington, p. 211.
"She had been like a mother. . ." Mercer Ellington, p. 205.
"When Lawrence Brown married Fredi Washington. . ." Ibid.
"Their friendship. . .which was a long. . ." Mercer Ellington, p. 127.
"I'm easy to please. . ." Mercer Ellington, p. 210.

Index

acoustic recording method, 48
Adler, Larry, 233, 399
"Ad Lib on Nippon," 360
African Americans. *See* black entertain-
    ers; black executives; black history;
    black music; black oppression
"Ain't Nobody Nowhere Nothin' with-
    out God," 393
Alix, May, 173
Allen, Charles, 241
"Along Came Pete," 259-60
Alvis, Hayes, 240-41
American Federation of Musicians, 311
American Recording Company (ARC),
    121, 299
Amos 'n' Andy (radio show), 158-59
Anatomy of a Murder (film), 349
Anderson, Ivie
    in *Bundle of Blues,* 192
    departure from Ellington band,
        311-12
    early years of, 172-73
    in *Hit Parade,* 259
    joining of Ellington band, 173
    at Palladium in London, 202
    in *Pictorial* No. 889, 263
Anderson, William Alonzo "Cat," 324,
    339
Ansermet, Ernest, 54
"Aristocracy à la Jean Lafitte," 384
Arlen, Harold, 163, 164
Armstrong, Louis, 253, 254, 355, 356,
    384

Armstrong High School, 7
ASCAP (American Society of
    Composers and Publishers), 299
Ashby, Harold, 373-74
Asphalt Jungle (television series pilot),
    357
Assault on a Queen (film), 367-68
Astaire, Fred, 117
Avendorph, Fred, 242
"Azure," 263, 271

Babs, Alice, 372, 391
Bacon, Louis, 227
Baker, Harold, 312
Baker, Harry "Shorty," 268
Bamboo Inn, 90
band battles, 91-92, 273-74
Bates, Lieutenant, 69
battle of bands, 91-92, 274
bebop music era, 333
Bechet, Sidney
    influence on Johnny Hodges, 130-
        31
    joining of Ellington band, 46
    musical style of, 46
    "Portrait of Sidney Bechet," 384-85
    praise from Ernest Ansermet, 54
    relationship with band members,
        46-47
"Before My Time," 84
Beggar's Holiday (Broadway show), 330-
    32
Bell, Aaron, 350

477

Belle of the Nineties, 231-32

Bernstein, Leo, 71-72

Bethlehem (recording company), 341

Bigard, Albany "Barney," 120,
     127-28, 310

big band era, 333-34

"Big House Blues," 164

"Birmingham Breakdown," 84
     Cotton Club response to, 112
     press review of, 93
     publicity campaign for, 99

Black and Tan (film), 149-151

"Black and Tan" clubs, 25

"Black & Tan Fantasy"
     deep south style of, 85
     issuing of, 113
     press reviews of, 92, 93, 114-15
     publicity campaign for, 99
     recording for OKeh Recording
          Company, 96-97
     recording methods for, 94

"Black Beauty," 97, 122, 125, 136

Blackberries of 1930 (show), 153

Blackbirds of 1928 (show), 123-24, 189

Blackbirds of 1930 (show), 189

Black, Brown and Beige (musical work)
     black history portrayed in, 222–23,
          315, 316-20
     criticism of, 318-20
     performance of, 316-18
     rehearsal of, 315-16
     Will Marion Cook's influence on,
          55

black entertainers
     mixing with white soloists, 232
     portrayed in *Jump for Joy,* 306
     southern treatment of, 227-28
     sudden search for, 28

black executives, operation of recording
     companies by, 29-30, 32-33

black history, portrayed in *Black, Brown
     and Beige,* 222-23, 315, 316-20

black music
     "cultural" versus popular, 29
     effect of "Crazy Blues" on, 27-29
     effect of swing on, 253-54
     internationalization of, 58
     "race" recordings, 27-28
     wedded with European orchestral
          scoring, 170, 171
     See also blues music; jazz music; race
          recordings

black oppression
     claim that Ellington's music didn't
          address, 248
     Ellington's collections on, 315
     Portrayed in *Jump for Joy,* 305

black progression, reflected in *My People,*
     358

Black Swan Recording Company, 29-30,
     73-74

Blanks, Oceola, 35

Blanton, Jimmie
     effect on Ellington band, 291
     effect on jazz, 286-87
     sickness and death of, 307, 309-10,
          311

"Blue Belles of Harlem," 114

"Bluebird of Delhi," 359-60

"Blue Bubbles," 120

"Blue Goose," 294, 295

Blue Monday (opera), 56

"blue" notes, 40

"Blues for New Orleans," 383

"Blues I Love to Sing, The," 96

blues music
     beginning of "blues fever," 27-29
     less "cultivated," more expressive
          style, 40-41
     orchestral work built around
          twelve-bar blues, 85
     See also black music; jazz music; race
          recordings

"Bojangles," 294, 295

Boola (musical work), 314-15

"Bourbon Street Jingling Jollies," 383

"Braggin' in Brass," 84, 269-70

Braud, Wellman

    departure from Ellington band, 241

    early years of, 88

    effect on Ellington band, 89

    in foreground of Ellington's music, 94

    "Portrait of Wellman Braud," 384

Bristol, Florence, 48

Britton, Jimmy, 314

broadcasting, remote, 81

Brooks, Harvey, 8

Brown, E. C., 17

Brown, Lawrence

    blending with Nanton and Tizol, 179-80

    departure from Ellington band, 339-40, 381

    joining of Ellington band, 178-79

    marriage to Fredi Washington, 401

    rejoining of Ellington band, 350

Brown Sugar (Sweet but Unrefined) (musical work), 162

Brunswick-Balke-Collender Recording Company, 78-79, 82

"Bugle Call Rag," 120

Bunce, John, 133

Bundle of Blues (film), 192

Bushell, Garvin, 23, 40

Cabin in the Sky (musical), 312-13

call-and-response technique, 64, 75

Calloway, Cab, 157, 167, 227

Cameo (recording company), 121

Cameo Club, 61

Capitol Records, 335

"Caravan," 262, 278

Carnegie Hall, 322-23

Carney, Harry

    early years of, 89-90

    instruments played by, 91

    mother of, 93

    reaction to Ellington's death, 399

"Carolina Shout," 21

Castro Monte, Fernandae de

    Ellington's affair with, 350-53, 362

    reaction to Ellington's death, 399

    visiting Ellington in hospital, 396-97

Catagonia Club, 102-03

Catlett, Sidney, 325

"Century of Negro Progress" (exhibition), 358

Charleston, the, 26

Check and Doublecheck (film)

    Amos and Andy in, 158

    screening of, 161-62

    showing of, 164-66

Chevalier, Maurice, 154

Chicken Shack (club), 102

"Chloe," 296

"Choo Choo," 48

cinemas, effect on band entertainment, 333

Ciro's (nightclub), 325-26

Clam House (club), 102

Clayton, Buck, 231

Clorindy, or the Origin of the Cakewalk (ragtime operetta), 53

Club Barron, 24-26

Club Basha, 131

Club Deluxe, 106

Club Kentucky. *See* Kentucky Club (formerly Hollywood Cafe)

clubs, in Harlem

    effect of Great Depression on, 187, 252-53

    effect of Prohibition's repeal on, 253

    See also specific names of Harlem clubs

Club Zanzibar (formerly the Hurricane), 328

Columbia Records, 28, 82, 335

"Come Sunday," 317, 366-67

Conaway, Ewell, 13

Conaway, Sterling, 16-17

Conaway Boys (band), 16-17

"Concerto for Cootie," 293

"Conga Brava," 293

Connie's Inn, 35-36, 101, 107

Cook, Will Marion
  achievements of, 52-55, 58
  early years of, 52
  Ellington's homage to in "Li'l Farina," 67
  instruction of Ellington, 55

Cook, Willie, 356

Cooper, Chuck, 382

Cooper, Harry, 63, 79

Copland, Aaron, 264

Correll, Charles F., 158-59

Coslow, Sam, 78

Cotton Club
  closure of and reopening at other location, 261
  contracting of Ellington, 110-11
  contribution to Ellington's creativity, 169
  description of, 106
  early shows at, 107-08
  Ellington band's first shows at, 112-13
  Ellington band broadcasting from, 125-26
  Famous attendees of, 117-18
  "jungle" music theme at, 115, 116, 117, 118
  management of, 106-07
  rights to music of, 124
  searching for band, 108-11
  segregation at, 109-10
  sexual atmosphere of, 116

Cotton Club Orchestra, The, 108

Cotton Club Parade, 122-23, 137, 191-92

Cotton Club Parade, Fourth Edition, 268, 270

Cotton Club Parade, Second Edition, 261

"Cottontail," 294

Courtney, Cress, 283

"Crazy Blues," 27-28, 29

"Creeper, The," 84

"Creole Love Call," 91, 96, 113

"Creole Rhapsody," 84, 165-66, 172, 188

Crosby, Bing, 161, 176, 289

Crowe, Sir Colin, 392

Cuthbert, Dr. Middleton F. (father's employer), 3

Dance Mania (show), 97-98, 111

Dancer, Earl, 24, 30

"Dardanella," 31

Darrell, Robert Donaldson, 93-94, 114-15

Davis, Kay, 324

Day at the Races, A (musical work), 258

"Daybreak Express," 84, 229, 263

"Deacon Jazz," 48, 50

DeBakey, Dr. Michael, 395

Delius, Frederick, 188

Dempsey, Jack, 103

DeParis, Wilbur, 329

Depression, The. *See* Great Depression

Diamond, Jack "Legs," 118-19

Diamond, Leslie, 219-20, 338

Dickerson, Carrol, 184

"Dicty Blues," 75-76

"Diminuendo and Crescendo in Blue," 264-65

"Dinah," 30

Dixon, Mildred, 152, 272

Dodge, Pryor, 185

"Doin' the Frog," 120

"Don't Get Around Much Anymore," 294

Dorsey, Jimmy, 132
Doubleday, Nelson, 387-89
Douglass Casino, 105-06
Douglass Theater, 105-06
"Down Home Blues," 29
Down South Music, Inc. (recording company), 32, 73, 74, 76
"Drop Me off at Harlem," 189
Drum Is a Woman, A (musical work), 304, 344-45
Du Bois, W. E. B., 29
Dudley, Bessie, 104-05, 202
Duke's Serenaders, 13
Duke Ellington and his Kentucky Club Orchestra, 79
Duke of Kent, 203
Durham, Bobby, 370
"Dusk," 294

"East St. Louis Toodle-Oo"
    press review of, 92, 93
    recording with Victor Recording Company, 120
    structure of, 83-84
    various recordings of, 79, 121
"Echoes of Harlem," 293
"Echoes of the Jungle," 117
Edwards, Henry "Bass," 59-60, 88
807th Pioneer Infantry Band, 56
Eldridge, Jean, 275
electric recording systems, 79
Ellington, Daisy (mother)
    birth of, 1
    brothers and sisters of, 3
    at Cotton Club, 156
    death of, 243
    depression of, 2-3
    living with son, 152-53
    musical abilities of, 4
    relationship with son, 4, 6, 10, 135, 153

sick with cancer, 236, 242-43
    spirituality of, 6
Ellington, Edna (wife)
    death of, 363
    marriage to Ellington, 14
    separation from Ellington, 134-35
    as showgirl, 36-37
Ellington, Edward "Duke" Kennedy
    ability to write music under pressure, 45-46, 50
    in *Anatomy of a Murder,* 349
    appeasing the press, 275-76
    Assault on a Queen, writing for, 367-68
    awards received by, 387, 404
    band-booking agency of, 13
    becoming leader of Washingtonians, 43-44
    birth of, 1
    Black, Brown and Beige, reaction to criticism of, 320
    Cab Calloway's band, stake in, 157, 167
    Capital Records, contract with, 335
    changed, independent nature, 182
    Chocolate Kiddies, writing for, 50-51
    Columbia Records, contract with, 335
    composition methods of, 169-71
    death of, 397-400
    early interests of, 7
    extramarital affairs of, 69, 134-35, 350-53, 401
    FBI investigation of, 337
    Freddie Guy relationship, 60
    Hammond, dislike of, 283
    Hardwick relationship, 18
    Henderson, music of contrasted with, 76-77

Ellington, Edward "Duke" Kennedy
   (cont.)
   Hodges, chemistry with, 383
   honorary doctorates and awards
      received by, 375-77
   in hospital, 395-97
   Hughes relationship, 210-11
   inaugurating wing of Castle of
      Goutelas, 369
   interview on BBC, 199
   introduction to music industry, 33,
      34
   at Jack Hylton's party in London,
      198-99
   jazz critics, feelings toward, 248-49
   at Kentucky Club (formerly
      Hollywood Cafe), 70-72
   leaving Mildred Dixon, 271
   Leonard Harper and, 34, 35, 36-38
   in London as solo act, 335-36
   losing, attitude toward, 340
   lymphoma of, 389
   Maceo Pinkard and, 33, 34
   major influences on life of, 8, 11-
      12, 13, 21-22, 55-58
   memory and listening abilities of,
      9, 66
   Mills relationship, 79-81, 98, 180,
      239, 243, 268-69, 276, 282
   mother of, relationship with, 6, 10,
      14, 236-37, 242-43, 244, 245,
      247, 248, 249-50
   musical education of, 4, 5, 8-9, 11-
      12, 13
   musicians of, relationship with, 87,
      160, 169, 401
   Musicraft Records, contract with,
      334
   New Dehli, reaction to poverty in,
      359
   nickname origin, 10
   optimism of, 61
   paranoia of, 337

   Paris Blues, writing for, 355-56
   Prince George, playing solo for,
      214-15
   Pulitzer Prize and, 364, 365, 404
   as rehearsal pianist for Leonard
      Harper, 36-37
   school life of, 7-8
   70th birthday party at White
      House, 377-80
   75th birthday party of, 397
   sign painting business of, 13
   son of, relationship with, 14
   spirituality of, 6, 356-66, 368, 372
   Strayhorn's death, reaction to, 370-
      73, 374
   Tempo Music Inc., founding of by,
      302
   trains, passion for, 160, 244
   water travel phobia of, 192
   wealth, early exposure to, 3-4
   Webster, conflicts with, 321-22
   without work in New York City,
      23-24
   women, feelings toward, 14-15, 337
   work habits of, 93
Ellington, James Edward (father)
   birth of, 2
   charm of, 2, 5
   living with son, 152-53
   musical abilities of, 5
   occupation of, 2, 3-4
   sickness and death of, 264-65
Ellington, Mercer (son)
   after father's death, 400
   as band's manager, 369-70
   with band after father's death,
      400
   birth of, 14
   divorce from wife, 400-01
   in Ellington band, 360, 400
   as Ellington band manager, 360-
      362
   father's passing "mantle" to, 396

recordings by, 302
relationship with father, 14
songs by, 309
"The Girl in My Dreams Tries to Look Like You," writing of, 300
visiting parents, 37, 152
working for father, 299
Ellington, Ruth
  at Duke's 70th birthday party, 378
  as Duke died, 397
  living with Duke, 152
  relationship with Duke, 10-11
Ellington, William "Sonny" (cousin), 5
Ellington band
  with *Amos and Andy*, 158-59
  in Australia, 382
  BBC broadcast of, 204-05
  in *Beggar's Holiday*, 330-32
  in *Belle of the Nineties*, 231-33
  British criticism of, 207-08, 210, 221-22
  in *Cabin in the Sky*, 313
  at Cameo Club, 61
  CBS, broadcasting on, 155-56
  changed style after Miley joined, 42
  changes to rhythm section, 89
  in *Check and Doublecheck*, 161-62, 164-66
  Chevalier, playing with, 154-55
  at Ciro's (nightclub), 325-26
  concerts, dances, and private parties in London, 206-11, 218-19
  at Cotton Club, 112, 125, 167
  in *Cotton Club Parade, Fourth Edition*, 268
  in *The Cotton Club Parade, Second Edition*, 261
  in *Dance Mania*, 97-98
  decline in popularity of, 333-34
  early sound of, 26
  efforts to contrast with other bands, 70

in England, 200-204, 211-12, 214-15, 346-48
European tours, 194-95, 196, 338
family atmosphere of, 87
Far East tour, 389-99
in France, 224-25, 277-78
in *Happy Man Returns*, 233-34
in *Hit Parade*, 258-60
at Hollywood Cafe, 37-38, 43
hotels denying rooms to, 197-98
at Howard Theater, Washington D.C., 229-30
at Hurricane Restaurant, 321
India tour, 359
Jack Robbins, contract with, 283
in *Jazz Mania*, 95-96
at Kentucky Club (formerly Hollywood Cafe), 59, 61, 70-72
leadership transferred to Ellington, 43-44
medley played by, 338
member contributions to music composition, 170
Midwest tour, 229
Mills, member's dislike of, 142-43
in *Murder at the Vanities*, 230-31
Near and Middle East tour, 359
in Netherlands, 279
New England tours, 45, 65, 91-93, 187
in *New World a-Comin'*, 322-23
on the *Olympia* (ship), 193-94
at Oriental Theater, 241
original members of, 18
Pacific Northwest tour, 235, 258
Pennsylvania-West Virginia tour, 70
Pictorial Magazine presentations, 190-91, 263
pseudonyms of, 79, 82-83, 148
in *Reveille with Beverly*, 313
Roosevelts and, 229-30, 326-27

Ellington band *(cont.)*
Show Girl, playing for, 143-47
South American tour, 374, 387
southern tour, 227-28
Soviet Union tour, 386-88
in Sweden, 279
in *Symphony in Black*, 237-39
West Coast tour, 178
William Morris Agency, signing up with, 283
without work in New York City, 23-24
work habits of, 93
Ellington Music, Inc., 80
Ellis, Beatrice "Evie"
death of, 399
Ellington's affair with, 271-72
jealousy over Fernandae, 362
lifestyle with Ellington, 363
with lung cancer, 396
visiting Ellington in hospital, 396
"Emancipation Celebration," 317
Ertegun, Ahmet, 220
"Everything is Hotsy Totsy Right Now," 60-61

Far East Suite, 359
Fifteenth Infantry, The, 28
"Firewater," 121-22
First Sacred Concert, 367
Fletcher Henderson Rainbow Orchestra, 75
Ford, Fats, 356
400 Club, 326
Francis, George, 59

Gennett Recording Company, 64, 65-66
"Georgia Grind," 64
Gershwin, George, 146
Gertler, Renee, 219-20
Girl's Suite, The, 5

"Girl in My Dreams Tries to Look Like You, The," 300
Glascoe, Percy, 69
Glenn, Tyree, 337
death of, 398
Golden Broom and Green Apple, The, 364
Gonsalves, Paul
arrest on narcotics charge, 356
death of, 398
epileptic seizure of, 391-92
joining of Ellington band, 338-39
at Newport Jazz Festival, 1956, 342
Goodman, Benny, 268-69
Gosden, Freeman F., 158-59
Goutelas Suite, 369
Grainger, Percy, 187-88
Grant, Henry, 13
Grantz, Norman, 339-40
Great Day (musical), 114, 163-64
Great Depression, 187, 252
Greer, William "Sonny"
departure from Ellington band, 339-40
discontent with Cotton Club work, 138
Ellington relationship, 18
first impression of Ellington, 16
Hardwick relationship, 18
Mills, dislike of, 142
Prince of Wales, playing with, 215
singing on "Wanna Go Back Again Blues," 64
Stark's drum gift to, 146-47
working for Wilbur Sweatman, 20
growl technique
of Hodges, 132
of Irvis, 44
London concert response to, 209
of Miley, 40-41, 85, 141
of Nanton, 68

of Oliver, Joe "King," 141
of Williams, 140-41, 140-41
Guy, Freddie
    departure from Ellington band, 336-37
    joining of Ellington band, 60
    Mills, dislike of, 142-43
    as Orient Cafe manager, 24
    switch to guitar, 194

Hall, Adelaide, 96, 98
Hamilton, Jimmy, 321, 373
Hammond, John, 247-49, 283
Happy Man Returns (film), 233-34
Happy Rhones (cabaret), 100-101
Hardwick, Otto "Toby"
    departure from Ellington band, 128, 329
    drinking problem of, 128
    early years of, 17
    Ellington's disapproval of wife of, 401
    Ellington relationship, 18
    Greer relationship, 18
    instruments played by, 91
    leading own band, 181
    musical abilities of, 26
    playing style of, 132
    rejoining Ellington band, 181, 182
    without work in New York City, 23-24
    working for Wilbur Sweatman, 20
Harlem
    Great Depression's effect on, 187
    night life of, 37, 100
    popularity with whites, 115-16
    Prohibition's effect on, 104
    See also names of specific Harlem clubs
"Harlem Airshaft," 295-96
"Harlem River Quiver," 120
Harlem Suite, 338-39

"Harlem Twist," 121
Harper, Leonard, 34-36, 37-38
Haughton, Chauncey, 310-11, 321
Healy, Dan, 107
Hemphill, Shelton "Scad," 323
Henderson, Fletcher
    as accompanist, 74
    band of, 74-75
    call-and-response technique with Redman, 75
    early years of, 73-74
    Mills relationship, 75-76
    music of, contrasted with Ellington's, 76-77
"High Life," 84
Hit Parade (film), 258-60
Hodges, Johnny, 90
    chemistry with Ellington, 383
    departure from Ellington band, 339-40
    early years of, 129
    "Harmony in Harlem," 264
    heart attacks and death of, 385
    joining of Ellington band, 123, 129, 132
    musical abilities of, 130
    pay stipulations of, 360
    playing against Jimmy Dorsey, 132
    playing style of, 132-33
    in "Portrait of Sidney Bechet," 384-85
    praise from John Coltrane, 134
    Sidney Bechet, influence by, 130-31
    trouble reading music, 133
    in "Yellow Dog Blues," 122-23
Holingsworth, Charles "Pod," 102-03
Holland, Eugene, 16
Hollywood Cafe
    Ellington band at, 37-38, 42-43, 44, 45
    renovation and change to Kentucky Club, 59

Hollywood Cafe *(cont.)*
    temporary closure of, 49
    See also Kentucky Club
Holmes, Charlie, 90, 130
horns, muting of. *See* mutes, use of
"Hot and Bothered," 84, 94, 136
Hot Chocolates (show), 36
Howard, Nappy, 129-30
Howard Theater, 17
"How Come You Do Me Like You Do," 48
Hughes, "Spike," 196-97, 199, 210-11
Hurricane Restaurant, 321
Husing, Ted, 155
Hylton, Jack, 198-99, 218
"Hymn of Sorrow," 238

"I'm Gonna Put You Right in Jail," 72
"(I'm Just Wild about) Animal Crackers," 66-67
"I'm Tired of Being a Fool over You," 72
"If You Can't Hold the Man You Love," 64, 82
"I Let a Song Go out of My Heart," 270
Immerman, Connie, 101
"Immigration Blues," 84, 85
Impressions of the Far East (musical work), 359
"In a Mellow Tone," 170
In Dahomey (show), 53
Irvis, Charles, 44, 65
"Isfahan," 360
"It's Gonna Be a Cold, Cold Winter," 47
"It's Right Here for You," 27
It's the Blackberries (show), 152
"It Don't Mean a Thing If It Ain't Got That Swing," 175, 253, 259
"It Was a Sad Night in Harlem," 252

Jack Mills, Inc., 30-31
    change to Mills Music, Inc., 124
    See also Mills Music, Inc.

Jackson, Mahalia, 384
Jackson, Rudy, 88, 91, 127-28
"Jack the Bear," 292
James, George "Mexico," 112-13
James, Harry, 340
Jazz Mania (show), 94-95
jazz music
    Ellington's comments on influence of, 199
    Great Depression's effect on, 252-53
    introduction of swing, 253
    See also black music; blues music; race recordings
Jeffries, Herb, 288-89, 311
Jenkins, Freddie, 137, 202
"Jig Walk," 50, 51
"Jim Dandy," 50, 51
Jimmie Lunceford orchestra, 254
Johnson, Charlie, 65
Johnson, Jack, 105-06
Johnson, James P., 21-22
Johnson, Lonnie "Lonzo," 121
Johnson, Manzie, 37
Johnson, Wini, 323
Jones, Alberta, 72
Jones, Claude, 323
Jones, Richard Bowden "Jonesy," 173-74, 330
Jones, Wallace, 256-57, 323
Jordan, Louis, 328
Jordan, Taft, 321
"Jubilee Stomp," 121
jump bands, 333
Jump for Joy (musical), 303-06
Jungle Alley (club), 102
"Jungle Band, The," 117
"Jungle Blues," 117
"Jungle Jamboree," 117
"jungle" music, 115, 116, 117, 118, 136
"Jungle Nights in Harlem," 117

Kennedy, Daisy. *See* Ellington, Daisy (mother)

Kennedy, James William (grandfather), 1

Kentucky Club (formerly Hollywood Cafe)

  closure of, 65

  musicians who frequented, 62

  operation of Leo Bernstein, 71-72

  remote broadcast of Ellington from, 81

  renovation and change from Hollywood Cafe, 59

  renovation and change to Monteray Club, 94

  response to Ellington band at, 61

King, Dr. Martin Luther, 358

Koehler, Ted, 163, 164

"Ko-Ko," 292

Lambert, Constant, 216-18

Lang, Eddie, 194

Latin American Suite, 374

Liberian Suite, 335

"Li'l Farina," 67

"Lightining Bugs and Frogs," 348

Loew's State Theatre, 264

Logan, Dr. Arthur C., 264, 394-95

"Lotus Blossom," 371-72, 387

Louis, Joe, 251, 252, 272

"Love Is Just a Wish (for You)," 50, 51

"Lucky Number Blues," 72

Lulu Belle (play), 115

Lunceford, Jimmie, 254-55, 273-74, 275

Madden, Owen Vincent "Owney," 104-06, 111

Maines, George H. "Captain," 62

"Make Me Love You," 82

Manhattan Casino, 28

Marion, Percy, 392

Master Records, Inc., 257, 267

McEntree, Edgar, 10

McHugh, Jimmy, 110

"Me and You," 293

"Merry-Go-Round," 94

Messin' Around (show), 65

Metcalf, Louis, 79, 122-23

Mexico's (club), 102

"Mighty Lak a Rose," 67

Miley, James Wesley "Bubber"

  in "Black & Tan Fantasy," 85-86

  chemistry with Nanton, 68-69

  conflicts with Sidney Bechet, 46-47

  departure from Ellington band, 138-39

  drinking problem of, 63, 86, 138

  early years of, 39-40

  in "East St. Louis Toodle-Oo," 83

  "growling" technique of, 141

  in *Harlem Scandals*, 185-86

  in "Immigration Blues," 85

  influence of Joe "King" Oliver on, 40

  jobs after Ellington band, 182-85

  with the Milage Makers, 184

  musical abilities, 48-49

  solos of, 87

  tuberculosis of and death of, 182, 186

  unique style of, 41, 43, 85-86

Mills, Florence, 97

Mills, Irving, 31, 33-34

  Cab Calloway, corporate partnership with, 157

  Cotton Club music, rights to and, 124

  Ellington band members dislike of, 142-43

  Ellington relationship

    breakup, 276, 282

    corporate partnership, 79-81, 98, 276, 282, 332

    initial interest, 76-77, 78

Mills, Irving, *(cont.)*
    offending of Ellington, 180,
       239, 243, 268-69, 322
    publicity campaign, 97-99
    Ethel Waters, managing of, 191
    European talent-hunting trip, 188-
       89
    Henderson relationship, 75-76
    issuing new recordings of same
       scores, 148
    Master Records, Inc., establishing
       of, 257
    Metcalf's dislike of control by, 122-
       23
    Mills Music Inc., departure from,
       188
    Pictorial Magazine presentation by,
       190-91
    RCA Victor records, working with,
       226-27
    Tom Rockwell, joining with, 188
    Victor (recording company), work-
       ing with, 94
Mills, Jack, 31
    See also Mills Music, Inc.
Mills Music, Inc.
    Cab Calloway, corporate partner-
       ship with, 157
    Ellington, corporate partnership
       with, 79-81, 80, 276, 282, 332
    Ethel Waters, managing of, 191
    issuing new recordings of same
       scores, 148
    RCA Victor, working with, 226-27
    Tom Rockwell, joining, 188
    See also Mills, Irving; Mills, Jack
Missourians (band), 108, 157
Monteray Club (formerly Kentucky
    Club), 94
    See also Kentucky Club
"Mooche, The," 80, 136, 137
"Mood Indigo," 163, 164, 399
"Moonglow," 236

"Morning Glory," 292
Morton, Jelly Roll, 184
"Mount Harissa," 360
movies, effect on band entertainment,
    333
Murder at the Vanitites (film), 230-31
Murphy, Dudley, 149-51
Music Is My Mistress (autobiography),
    387-89, 390
Musicraft Records, contract with Duke,
    334
mutes, use of
    by Charles Williams, 140-41
    by Irvis, 44
    London concert response to,
       209
    by Miley, 85
    by Nanton, 68
    by Oliver, Joe "King," 40-41
    by Williams, 140-41
"Mynah," 359-60
My People (musical/choral pageant),
    358

NAB (National Association of
    Broadcasters), 299
Nance, Ray, 298-99, 301, 356
Nanton, Joe "Tricky Sam," 65
    blending with Tizol and Brown,
       179
    chemistry with Miley, 68-69
    death of, 330
    stroke of, 329
    unique style of, 68
"Naughty Man," 49
Negro Actors Guild, 266
Negroes. *See* black entertainers; black
    executives; black history; black music;
    black oppression
Nest Club, 103-04
"Never No Lament," 294
"New Orleans Lowdown," 85
New Orleans Suite, 382, 383, 385

Newport Jazz Festival, 1956 (Rhode Island), 341-43

New World a-Comin', 322-23, 367

Nigger Heaven (novel), 115

"Night in Harlem, A," 79

"Night Life in a Negro Cafe in Harlem in New York," 50

Nixon, President Richard, 377-80, 397, 398

Nutcracker Suite, The, 354

"Oh Daddy," 29

"Oh How I Love My Darling," 48

OKeh Recording Company, 27-28

"Oklahoma Stomp," 9

"Old Man Blues," 80, 162, 163

Oliver, Joe "King"

    Cotton Club's pursuit to hire, 108-09

    influence on Miley, 40

    style reflected in "Birmingham Blues" and "The Creeper," 84

    suing of Ellington, 127-28

Oliver, Sy, 84

Olympic (ship), 192-93

"One Man Nan," 30

Oriental Theater, 172

Orient Cafe, 24, 26

P&J's (club). *See* Pod's and Jerry's (club)

Pace, Harry, 29, 30

Pace & Handy (recording company), 29

Paley, William, 155, 156

Paradise (club), 101-02, 107, 109-10

Paramount Pictures, *Pictorial Magazines* of, 190-91, 263

Paramount Records,

    "race" recordings of, 28

Paris Blues (film), 355-56

"Parlor Social Deluxe," 47

"Parlor Social Stomp," 64

Pathé Recording Company, 121

Peer Gynt Suite, 354

Perry, Oliver H. "Doc," 10-12, 13

Petrillo, James C., 311

Pettiford, Oscar, 328-29

Philadelphia Orchestra, 94, 262

Pictorial Magazines, of Paramount Pictures, 190-91, 263

Pinkard, Maceo, 26, 33, 34

Plantation Days (revue), 35

Plaza (recording company), 121

plungers, altering horn sound with. *See* mutes, use of

Pod's and Jerry's (club), 102-03

"Portrait of a Lion," 22

"Portrait of Bert Williams, A," 294, 295

"Portrait of Louis Armstrong," 384

"Portrait of Mahalia Jackson," 384

"Portrait of Sidney Bechet," 384-85

"Portrait of Wellman Braud," 384

"Praise God and Dance," 372, 393

Preer, Andrew, 108

Preer, Evelyn, 81-82

Preston, Jeremiah, 102-03

Priester, Julius, 382

Prime, Alberta, 47

Prime Minister of England, 392

Prince George, 214-15

Prince of Wales, 211-12, 215, 219

Prince Phillip, 347

Princess Margaret, 392

Procope, Russell, 329-30

Prohibition, effect on Harlem, 104, 253

Pulitzer Prize, 364, 365, 404

Queen's Suite, 348

Queen of England, 347-48

Queenie Pie (comic opera), 395-96

race recordings, 27-28, 78, 81, 82, 124

racial pride, addressed in *Black, Brown and Beige*, 315, 316-20

Raft, George, 118, 326

Raglin, Alvin "Junior," 307-08

"Rainy Nights," 48, 49

RCA Victor, 334

recording bans, 306, 311, 335

recording companies

    black-operated, 29-30, 32-33

    buying full rights to songs, 30-32

    effect of "Crazy Blues" on, 27-29

    search for black singers by, 28

    sheet music industry and, 31-32, 33, 34

recording methods

    acoustic, 48

    for "Black & Tan Fantasy" and "Washington Wobble," 94

    electric recording systems, 263

    Leopold Stokowski and, 94

    sound-on-disc and sound-on-film, 149

    stereo, 176-77

recordings, small-group, 257-58, 267-68

recording systems, electric, 79

"Red Hot Band," 120

Redman, Don, 63-64, 75

Reisman, Leo, 183-84, 185

"Reminiscing in Tempo," 84, 245-247, 248, 249

remote broadcasting, 81

Republic Studios, 258-60

Reveille with Beverly (film), 313

Reynolds, Ellsworth, 112

River, The (musical work), 382, 386

Robbins, Jack, 283

Robinson, Clarence, 23, 88

Robinson, Prince, 59

Roché, Betty, 312, 323

"Rockin' in Rhythm," 9, 80

"Rocky Mountain Blues," 164

Romero, Rendentor, 389

Roosevelt, President Theodore, 326-27

Royal, Marshall, 234-35

"Rude Interlude," 227

Sacred Concert

    in Barcelona, Paris, and Stockholm, 380

    in England, 368, 391-93

    in New Orleans and Washington, D.C., 383

    writing of, 365-66

"Saddest Tale," 236-37, 238

Saga of Jazz, 304

San Juan Hill (in New York City), 39

Saparo, Henri, 90

"Second Line," 384

Second Sacred Concert, 372, 373, 398, 399

segregation

    at Connie's Inn, 101

    at Cotton Club, 109-10

    in southern states, 227-28, 256

    of Washington, D.C., 58

"Sepia Panorama," 296

"Shame on You Suffer," 14

"She's Gone to Join the Songbirds in Heaven," 97

sheet music industry, 31-32, 33, 34

Sherrill, Joya, 324

Shostakovich, Maxim, 387

Show Girl (musical), 114, 143, 143-47

Shribman, Charlie, 45

"Single Petal of a Rose, The," 348

"Slippery Horn," 84

small-group recordings, 257-58, 267-68

Smalls, Ed, 101, 109

Smith, Ada "Bricktop," 224, 225

Smith, Bessie, 29

Smith, Cladys "Jabbo," 96-97, 272

Smith, Mamie, 27, 40

Smith, Willie "the Lion," 19-20, 22, 27, 102

Smith, Wonderful, 305

"Snake Rag," 84

Snowden, Elmer, 23-24, 26, 43

"Soda Fountain Rag," 9-10

"Soliloquy," 86

"Solitude," 236

"Song at the Cottonfield," 85

"Sophisticated Lady," 233

Southern Syncopated Orchestra, 54

Springbirds (revue), 141

St. Louis Blues (film), 149-50

"Stack O' Blues," 120

Stark, Herman, 106-07

"Steppin' into Swing Society," 268

"Stevedore Stomp," 80

Stewart, Rex, 5, 239-40, 321

Stokowski, Leopold, 94, 262

Stone, Fred, 382, 384

"Stormy Weather," 191-92

Strayhorn, Billy
    death of, 370-73
    "four freedoms" created by, 379
    meeting Ellington, 273
    moving in with Ellington, 284-85
    recording on own, 285

"Such Sweet Thunder," 345-46

Suite Thursday, 354-55

"Supreme Being," 373

Sweatman, Wilbur, 20

"Sweet Georgia Brown," 30

"Sweet Mama (Papa's Gettin' Mad)," 120

swing music, 253, 333-34

Symphony in Black (film), 237-39

"T.(oo) G.(ood) T.(oo) T.(itle)," 372

"Take it Easy," 120, 121

"Take the A Train," 301, 302

Taylor, Billy, 239, 290

television, effect on band entertainment, 333

Tempo Music, Inc. (publishing company), 302

Terry, Clark, 345

"Thanks for the Beautiful Land on the Delta," 383

"That Thing Called Love," 27

"There'll Be Some Changes Made," 29-30

"There's a New Star in Heaven Tonight," 97

"They Call Me Lulu," 72

"They Needed a Songbird in Heaven, so God Took Caruso Away," 31

Third Sacred Concert, 396, 397

Thomas, Louis, 13

Thompson, Edna. *See* Ellington, Edna (wife)

Three Black Kings, The, 380, 395

"Tiger Rag," 84

Tillie's Inn (club), 102

Timon of Athens, 357

Tin Pan Alley (in New York City), 33

"Tishomingo Blues," 123

Tizol, Juan
    blending with Nanton and Brown, 179
    "Caravan" by, 262-63
    departure from Ellington band, 323
    joining of Ellington band, 144-45

Togo Brava suite, 377

Tolliver, Buster, 89

Topsy's (nightclub), 303

Tormé, Mel, 365

Townsend, Irving, 343-44

trains
    Ellington's love for, 244
    musical imitation of, 229
    personal cars owned by Ellington
        band, 265, 310
Trent, Jo, 33, 45, 47
Trianon Ballroom, 303
Tunney, Gene, 103
Turney, Norris, 381, 383

Variety label, 267
Victor (recording company), 26, 94, 95,
    96
Vocalion 1000's (recording series), 78-79

"Wanna Go Back Blues," 64
Washington, D.C., segregation of, 58
Washington, Fredi, 150-51, 266
Washington Black Sox Orchestra, 38
Washingtonians. *See* Ellington band
"Washington Wobble," 94
Waters, Ethel, 29-30, 191
Webster, Ben, 287-88
    conflicts with Ellington, 321-22
    departure from Ellington band,
        321-22
    effect on Ellington band, 291
Wein, George, 384
Welles, Orson, 304
West, Mae, 118, 231-33
"West Indian Dance," 317
Whaley, Tom, 129
"What Can a Poor Fellow Do," 96, 113
Whetsol, Arthur
    in *Black and Tan,* 150
    brain tumor of, 268
    death of, 294

departure from Ellington band, 38
return to Ellington band, 121-22
without work in New York City,
    23-24
"Whispering Tiger," 84
Whiteman, Paul, 90-91, 273
WHN radio station, 43, 81, 112
"Who Is She?" 79
Wilkins, Barron D., 24-25
William Morris Agency (talent
    company), 283
Williams, Bert, 57-58, 294, 295
Williams, Charles Melvin "Cootie"
    "Concerto for Cootie," 293
    departure from Ellington band to
        join Goodman, 297-98
    early years of, 139-40
    "growling" technique of, 140-41
    rejoining of Ellington band, 357
Williams, Elmer "Skippy," 322, 324
Williams, Ned, 174
"With You," 50, 51
Wood, Booty, 382
Wooding, Sam, 108-09
Woodson, Carter G., 7-8
Woodyard, Sam, 370

"Yam Brown," 50
Yamecraw (film), 238-39
"Yellow Dog Blues," 123
"You Can't Keep a Good Man Down,"
    27
"You Will Always Live in Our Memory,"
    97
"You You Darlin'," 292

Ziegfeld, Florenz, 143-44

...op, Look, and Listen technique really worked for me during my recent surgery. Using the skills I have practiced and learned from *Why Worry?* allowed the higher me, the spiritual me, to win. I feel I can take on the world now. I may stumble again, but I will not fall."

—Margie C.
Imperial, Missouri

"In a world where anxiety/panic attacks are the most common emotional disorder, *Why Worry?* is a timely tool that addresses this situation with a good deal of common sense. I have found that many of the techniques worked for me and helped me through difficult times with my own disorder. I highly recommend this book for yourself or anyone you know who has to go through this devastating experience."

—Carol C.
New York, New York